International Boundary Studies Series

Borderlands Under Stress

International Boundary Studies Series

Series Editors:

Gerald Blake, Martin Pratt, Clive Schofield
International Boundaries Research Unit, University of Durham, UK

Other titles in the series:

International Boundaries and Environmental Security, G. Blake *et al* (eds)
(ISBN 90-411-0669-3)

Boundaries and Energy: Problems and Prospects, G. Blake *et al* (eds)
(ISBN 90-411-0690-1)

The Contested Maritime and Territorial Boundaries of Malaysia: An International Law Perspective, R. Haller-Trost
(ISBN 90-411-9652-8)

International Boundary Studies Series

Borderlands Under Stress

Editors

Martin Pratt and Janet Allison Brown

KLUWER LAW
INTERNATIONAL
THE HAGUE – LONDON – BOSTON

Published by
Klluwer Law International Ltd
Sterling House
66 Wilton Road
London SW1V 1DE
United Kingdom

Sold and distributed in
the USA and Canada by
Kluwer Law International
675 Massachusetts Avenue
Cambridge MA 02139
USA

Kluwer Law International incorporates
the publishing programmes of
Graham & Trotman Ltd,
Kluwer Law & Taxation Publishers
and Martinus Nijhoff Publishers

In all other countries, sold and distributed by
Kluwer Law International
P.O. Box 322
3300 AH Dordrecht
The Netherlands

ISBN 90-411-9790-7
Series ISBN 90-411-0656-1
© Kluwer Law International 2000
First published 2000

British Library Cataloguing Publication Data
A catalogue record for this book is available from the British Library

Typeset in Baskerville 10/12pt by BookEns Ltd, Royston, Herts
Printed and bound in Great Britain by Antony Rowe Ltd., Chippenham, Wiltshire.

Contents

PART I
The Evolving Meaning and Function
of International Boundaries

PART II
Borderlands Under Stress: Regional Perspectives

PART III
Islands, Sovereignty and Maritime Jurisdiction

Foreword

In 1908 Lord Curzon of Kedleston memorably described international boundaries as 'the razor's edge on which hangs suspended the modern issues of war and peace, of life and death to nations'. From the perspective of an age in which some commentators are predicting the imminent arrival of a 'borderless world', these words may seem puzzling. Yet many boundaries remain a major source of international stress. Indeed, it could be argued that the potential for problems associated with international boundaries is actually greater at the start of the twenty-first century than it was at the beginning of the twentieth.

As international political and economic relations have become increasingly complex, so have the pressures on international boundaries and the borderlands which surround them. Although there are still many examples of 'traditional' boundary problems associated with disputes between states concerning control over territory and maritime space, the papers in this volume demonstrate the vulnerability of borderlands to other forces, most notably illegal immigration and cross-border crime.

The purpose of this book is to investigate the causes and implications of borderland stress.

The first section of the book explores changing concepts of sovereignty and their impact on the meaning and functions of international boundaries. The contributions in the second and third sections offer a combination of regional appraisals and individual case studies highlighting the range of problems affecting borderlands around the world, together with an assessment of some of the initiatives that have been launched in response to those problems. Although many of the conclusions drawn are rather sobering, at the same time it is clear that in some parts of the world new and imaginative approaches to territorial organisation and management are helping to create safer, more dynamic and more prosperous borderlands. We must hope that over time these conditions will become the norm rather than the exception.

The papers in this collection represent the proceedings of the Fifth International Conference of the International Boundaries Research Unit, held at the University of Durham on 15–17 July 1998. The conference was attended by 88 participants from 37 countries.

Martin Pratt
October 1999

List of Contributors

Professor Malcolm Anderson, Director, International Social Sciences Institute, University of Edinburgh, UK

Professor Anthony I. Asiwaju, Department of History, University of Lagos, Nigeria

Dr Didier Bigo

Professor Gerald Blake, Director, International Boundaries Research Unit, University of Durham, UK

Mr Eberhard Bort

Professor Moshe Brawer, Department of Geography, Tel Aviv University, Israel

Mr Tim Daniel, Partner, D. J. Freeman Solicitors, UK

Mr Leo Dillon, Office of the Geographer and Global Issues, Department of State, USA

Dr Herbert Dittgen, Centre for European and North American Studies, Georg August Universitat Gottingen, Germany

Mr Daniel J. Dzurek, International Boundary Consultant, USA

Mr Thomas M. Edwards, Geographer, Microsoft Corporation, USA

Dr Alex G. Oude Elferink, Research Associate, Netherlands Institute for the Law of the Sea, University of Utrecht, The Netherlands

Mr Jose Z. Garcia, Director, Center for Latin American Studies, New Mexico State University, USA

Dr Richard Griggs, Head of Research, Independent Projects Trust, South Africa

Dr Peter Hocknell, International Boundaries Research Unit, University of Durham, UK

Professor Paul Huth, Institute for Social Research, University of Michigan, USA

Dr Marcelo G. Kohen, Graduate Institute of International Studies, Switzerland

Dr T. Lanusosang, Head, Department of Geography & Resource Management, Nagaland University, India

Dr Anna Matveeva, Research Fellow, Royal Institute of International Affairs, UK

Professor David Newman, Department of Politics & Government, Department of Geography, Ben-Gurion University of the Negev, Israel

Ms Liselotte Odgaard, Department of Political Science, Aarhus University, Denmark

Professor R.C. Sharma, Visiting Professor, Department of Geography & Resource Management, Nagaland University, India

Dr Richard Sigurdson, Department of Political Studies, University of Manitoba, Canada

Mr Bradford L. Thomas, International Boundary Consultant, USA

Mr Dennis Zalamans, Department of Human Geography, University of Stockholm, Sweden

PART I

The Evolving Meaning and Function of International Boundaries

1
Borderlands Under Stress: Some Global Perspectives

Gerald Blake

INTRODUCTION

The theme chosen for the 1998 International Boundaries Research Unit conference was both topical and important. There has probably never been a time when so many borderland regions worldwide have become such difficult or dangerous places in which to live. Some borderlands are in effect occupied by the military seeking to protect territory from the claims of a neighbouring state. The fundamental causes of such armed confrontations are much the same today as in yesterday's quarrels over boundaries and territories. A far larger category of causes of borderland stress, however, arises from people's basic desire to move themselves and their goods across international boundaries, and the desire of some governments to prevent them from doing so. The reasons for crossing boundaries may be legal (e.g. for trade or recreation), illegal (e.g. for smuggling) or forced (e.g. when refugees flee from political turmoil). Whatever the cause, when there is a serious contest between people determined to cross an international divide and state authorities resolved to prevent them, borderlands come under considerable stress. The effect on borderland dwellers and borderland economies can be devastating. Indeed, borderlands under stress are a powerful argument for the breaking-down of barriers between states and the progressive integration of borderland peoples.

CHARACTERISTICS OF THE STRESS-FREE BORDERLAND

Before examining some major causes of stress in borderlands, it is important to establish what a stress-free borderland might look like. Half a dozen key characteristics can be suggested. Of fundamental importance is *political goodwill*. Unless neighbouring states have the political will to maintain good relations, borderland harmony and cooperation will be impeded. What happens at the interface between two states is primarily a matter for the foreign ministry. A foreign policy which seeks constructive and practical cooperation is the bedrock of the stress-free borderland. Equally, if relations between states are poor at government level, borderlands may be used as the forum in which to demonstrate political animosity. The five other characteristics of the stress-free borderland are summarised below:

Borderlands Under Stress (M.A. Pratt and J.A. Brown (eds), ISBN 90-411-9790-7).
© Kluwer Law International, 2000.

1. Territorial questions are settled

Questions of boundary and territory no longer arise. The border, for better or worse is agreed, accepted and unambiguous. In all likelihood such a boundary will have been:

- *formally agreed*, with a boundary treaty which is well documented, and in which its alignment is properly surveyed and recorded;
- *demarcated*, unless it follows obvious physical features. There can be good demarcation practice and poor demarcation practice; ideally, the boundary markers are conspicuous and permanent;
- *maintained and managed*, since demarcation is not the end of the process, but the beginning. Boundary monuments have to be maintained and boundaries following physical features such as rivers, monitored for change. Everyday boundary-related problems have to be peacefully resolved. Such settled boundaries can become bones of contention, but the scope for disagreement or misunderstanding is minimal and there are provisions for trouble-shooting.

2. Transboundary interaction within the law is easy

Particularly where there is a dense population, borderlanders will wish to cross and re-cross the boundary for social and economic activity, with minimum delay and inconvenience. Similarly, international travellers and goods crossing the boundary can transit without major restrictions. The European Union exemplifies the ideal. But for most international boundaries, border controls remain in place, often for good reason. Some borderlands are marked by military control and restricted access. A few are scarred by de-populated villages. They have become landscapes of fear, and the boundary an intimidating and threatening feature. The stress-free ideal is clearly the border which is easily and conveniently crossed by any law-abiding person. There is no systematic censorship of newspapers, books or personal belongings.

3. The border provides a sense of security

The model border is 'permeable' for legitimate activity, but it also provides a sense of security to the citizens of the state, and especially to borderland people. Whether rightly or wrongly, the international boundary is generally linked with security in the minds of people. Such security is not easy to deliver and is most difficult along those borders which are most 'open'. Three categories of security are commonly associated with international boundaries apart from military security:

- protection from unwanted people (e.g. illegal immigrants, terrorists, criminals, refugees, bogus asylum seekers);
- protection from unwanted goods (e.g. smuggled goods, drugs, weapons, pornography);
- protection from hazards to health and the environment (e.g. diseased animals, polluted rivers, unsafe foodstuffs).

These goals are clearly very difficult to achieve.

4. Rational resource exploitation is possible

The international boundary does not have to be a deterrent to the discovery and exploitation of resources near to or straddling the boundary line. There are technical and legal mechanisms to make this feasible, although they may not always be adopted. The ideal border is one in which there are formal agreements and practical arrangements for resource management across the international divide. Sometimes a permanent committee or commission is established to manage the agreement and resolve problems as they arise. It is also important that there should be some mechanism in place to share technical knowledge about the nature and extent of the shared resource. Cooperation between technical experts on such matters can help build confidence between states in their borderlands. Several types of transboundary resource exploitation occur quite commonly in borderlands in the modern world (Blake *et al*, 1995). They include the exploitation of oil or gas reservoirs which straddle boundaries on land and offshore. The parties may agree on quotas or enter into some joint development agreement. Groundwater aquifers create similar problems between neighbouring states, but there are few effective practical or legal solutions yet in operation. Divided river basins are one of the most widespread of all transboundary resource problems, and one of the trickiest to resolve (see Figure 1). More than 200 major river basins are shared between two or more states, and several are shared by more than half a dozen states. Although there are over 2,000 bilateral agreements between states worldwide, there are many river basins with no agreements about the allocation and utilisation of scarce river water, as for example in the Tigris–Euphrates system. Straddling fish stocks and highly migratory types of fish are the subject of many bilateral and multilateral international agreements. Finally, protected areas in borderlands deserve mention. There is an increasing number of conservation areas adjacent to each other along international boundaries, in which the respective managements cooperate, for example in controlling poaching, exchanging scientific information and encouraging eco-tourism (Westing, 1993).

5. Local administration is coordinated

Efficient and effective local government should not end at the boundary, and considerable transboundary cooperation on a broad range of activities is essential to maintain a stress-free borderland. There must be coordination of road-building and major infrastructure developments, and provision for fighting crime, combating pollution, dealing with fires and responding to border incidents.

Few borders in the world could claim to exhibit all these positive characteristics, but there are some, especially in Europe, which come very close. In other words, genuinely stress-free borderlands are rare. The following sections focus on those borderlands that might be considered most under stress when viewed globally. The best that can be presented is a broad overview derived very largely from secondary sources. For the purpose of this analysis, 'borderlands' also comprise ocean space contested between rival states.

UNRESOLVED BOUNDARY AND TERRITORIAL DISPUTES

Land boundary disputes

Drawing up an inventory of unresolved land boundary disputes is not a precise science. Definitions as to what constitutes a genuine dispute vary from source to source, and lists quickly become dated. Attempts to catalogue boundary disputes around the fringes of the former Soviet Union are particularly difficult. Moreover, land boundary disputes vary in their age, scale and severity. Few boundary disputes affect the entire length of the boundary, but for convenience even a very short sector in dispute invariably results in the whole boundary being listed as disputed.

In spite of these problems, an attempt can be made to identify land boundaries under stress because of uncertainties over the location of the boundary line. Beginning with Paul Huth's excellent work *Standing Your Ground* (Huth, 1996), supplemented by listings in *Border and Territorial Disputes* (Allcock *et al*, 1992) and *The Encyclopedia of International Boundaries* (Biger, 1995), and with updates from IBRU's database, more than 50 land boundary disputes were identified in 1998 (see Figure 2). Ecuador and Peru resolved their longstanding border dispute by an agreement in October 1998. Remarkably, China and Russia can be omitted from the list following their border agreement in 1994, although several short sectors remain to be delimited and negotiations concerning these are continuing. The states of the former Soviet Union declared in December 1991 that they would respect the boundaries they have inherited, but a number of boundary and territorial disputes have nevertheless emerged; according to some analysts, there could be as many as 40 boundary and territorial conflicts to be resolved there (Kolossov *et al*, 1992).

According to the IBRU database, there are 309 land boundaries in the world. The number seems set to increase in future. With 52 land boundary and territorial disputes listed, about 17 per cent are thus actively disputed. These disputes are all declared and documented. Possibly a further 10 per cent of land boundaries could erupt into active disputes if serious delimitation or active demarcation were to begin. Given the nature and origins of most of the world's international boundaries, the percentage in dispute is surprisingly low. Approximately half the boundaries in the world were superimposed by European powers, notably Britain and France, with little regard for the underlying physical and human geographies. Their average age is well below 100 years and all over the world there are memories of earlier political maps, of suppressed nationalisms and former glories.

Disputed island sovereignty

Under the provisions of the 1982 United Nations Convention on the Law of the Sea (UNCLOS), islands can give states title to huge areas of ocean space and to the resources of the seabed and the living resources of the sea. Many islands are also strategically located near major shipping lanes and are thus equally coveted for geopolitical advantage. Not surprisingly, disputed islands can induce passionate feelings and often raise the political temperature between contestants to a dangerous level. Lives have been lost in several island quarrels in recent years. In many cases the delimitation of maritime boundaries between states has been held up because of disputed island sovereignty. For example, the Hanish Islands in the Red Sea were claimed by Eritrea and Yemen; an Arbitration Tribunal decided the sovereignty question in October 1998 largely in favour of Yemen, and will fix the maritime boundary in the light of that judgment in 1999.

Table 1 shows 33 disputed islands and groups of islands involving some 39 states. The list is based upon the authoritative work of Smith and Thomas, published by IBRU (Smith & Thomas, 1998). As with land boundary disputes, they vary greatly in scale and importance. Some islands have intrinsic value (land, people and resources) while others are valued for their location and effect on maritime jurisdiction. In future there are likely to be considerably more island disputes as more small offshore features are charted, and as more island states begin the process of maritime boundary delimitation. For example, there are no island disputes listed among the Pacific Ocean states, but it seems inconceivable that there are none. There are still some 70 dependent territories in the world, many of which comprise small groups of islands which may one day seek independence. This process might also expose some hitherto unknown island disputes.

Maritime boundary disputes

The number of potential international maritime boundaries is estimated to be around 425. To date only 160 or so – about 38 per cent – have been formally agreed. There are typically about four new agreements each year, so there is a long way to go before the offshore political map is complete.

Table 2 lists 26 overlapping claims offshore, but it excludes maritime boundary disputes related to island sovereignty disputes. A number of sources were used, including valuable work by McDorman and Chircop, Prescott, and Dzurek, updated using the IBRU database. Table 2 cannot be regarded as definitive. There are undoubtedly more maritime boundary disputes, and the more one looks the more one finds. In round terms, with 35 or so island disputes and 25 overlapping maritime claims, approximately 60 potential maritime boundaries are under stress, or 22 per cent of those 265 or so boundaries yet to be delimited. Unlike land boundaries, where a high proportion of potential trouble spots have already come to light, there may be a large number of maritime

Table 1

Disputed Island Sovereignty

Disputed islands	Contestants
Abu Musa & the Tunbs	Iran–United Arab Emirates
Corisco Bay; several islets	Equatorial Guinea–Gabon
Diego Garcia	Mauritius–United Kingdom
Falkland Islands/Islas Malvinas	Argentina–United Kingdom
South Georgia	Argentina–United Kingdom
South Sandwich Islands	Argentina–United Kingdom
Farasan Islands (southern part)	Saudi Arabia–Yemen
Hans Island	Canada–Denmark
Hawar Islands	Bahrain–Qatar
Imia/Kardak Rocks	Greece–Turkey
Juan de Nova	France–Madagascar
Bassas da India	France–Madagascar
Europa, Glorioso	France–Madagascar
Liancourt Rocks/Takeshima/Tok-do)	Japan–South Korea
Machias Seal Island/North Rock	Canada–United States
Matthew & Hunter Islands	France–Vanuatu
Mayotte	Comoros–France
Navassa Island	Haiti–United States
Northern Territories/Kuril Islands	Japan–Russia
Paracel Islands	China–Vietnam
Peñon de Alhucemas	Morocco–Spain
Peñon de Velez de la Gomera	Morocco–Spain
Isle Chafarinas	Morocco–Spain
Pulau Batu Puteh	Malaysia–Singapore
Pulau Pisang	Malaysia–Singapore
Qaruh and Umm al Maradim	Kuwait–Saudi Arabia
San Andres y Providencia	Colombia–Nicaragua
Sapodilla Cays	Belize–Guatemala–Honduras
Senkaku Islands/Diaoyu Tai	China–Japan
Sipadan and Ligitan islands	Indonesia–Malaysia
Spratly islands	Brunei–China–Malaysia–Taiwan–Philippines–Vietnam
South Talpatty Island	Bangladesh–India
Tromelin Island	France–Mauritius–Seychelles–Madagascar

Source: Smith & Thomas (1998)

Table 2

Maritime Boundary Disputes

Location	Contestants
Adriatic Sea	Albania–Greece (a: 366)
Adriatic Sea (Bay of Piran)	Croatia–Slovenia (d)
Adriatic Sea (Bay of Kotor)	Croatia–Yugoslavia (d)
Aegean Sea	Greece–Turkey (a: 371)
Baltic Sea	Latvia–Lithuania (d)
Baltic Sea	Lithuania–Russia (Kaliningrad) (d)
Barents Sea	Norway–Russia (a: 379)
Bay of Bengal	Bangladesh–India (b: 176)
Black Sea	Romania–Ukraine (d)
Caribbean Sea	Colombia–Venezuela (a: 580)
Caribbean Sea	Organisation of East Caribbean States–Venezuela (d)
Caspian Sea	Azerbaijan–Iran–Kazakhstan–Russia–Turkmenistan (d)
Gulf of Alaska (Dixon Entrance/Hecate Strait)	Canada–USA (a: 356)
Gulf of Guinea	Cameroon–Nigeria (d)
Gulf of Thailand	Cambodia–Thailand (c: 163)
Gulf of Thailand	Cambodia–Vietnam (c: 162)
Gulf of Thailand	Malaysia–Vietnam (c: 163)
Gulf of Tonkin	China–Vietnam (c: 164)
Mediterranean Sea	Spain–United Kingdom (Gibraltar) (a: 364)
North Atlantic (Faroe Bank)	Faroe Islands–United Kingdom (d)
North Atlantic (Rockall Plateau)	Denmark–Iceland–Ireland–United Kingdom (a: 382)
Persian/Arabian Gulf	Iran–Iraq (a: 375)
Red Sea	Egypt–Sudan (d)
Solomon Sea	Papua New Guinea–Solomon Islands (d)
Yellow Sea	China–North Korea (d)

Sources: a. McDorman & Chircop (1991)
  b. Prescott (1994)
  c. Dzurek (1994)
  d. IBRU database

disputes waiting to emerge. Many states have made little or no attempt to delimit maritime boundaries; when they do so, overlapping claims may be revealed.

Fortunately, maritime boundary disputes rarely give rise to armed conflict. UNCLOS and customary international law provide useful guidelines on maritime delimitation. There are also well-tried alternatives to conflict, notably the International Court of Justice and the new International Tribunal on the Law of the Sea. Alternatively, UNCLOS states are required to seek interim arrangements such as the establishment of joint development zones, 16 of which are already operating successfully at sea.

Nevertheless, maritime boundary disputes should be taken seriously. They can be expensive to police and resolve, and they can quarantine valuable resources (especially hydrocarbons) by deterring potential investors. In certain extreme cases they have poisoned the relationship between neighbouring states.

SUPPRESSED NATIONALISMS

The contemporary world political map has 192 independent political entities and some 70 dependencies – which is fewer than 270 political units dividing the world (outside Antarctica). By contrast, there are over 4,000 peoples of the 'fourth world', with their own culture, attachment to territory and common aspirations. Many of these people (but by no means all) have serious ambitions to govern themselves. They do not accept the political map of the world created relatively recently by European states. It is difficult to gauge the strength of various movements for autonomy among the peoples of the fourth world, but it is clear that some are making very serious bids for statehood, among them the Nagas, the Karens, the Tamils, the Albanians of Kosovo and the East Timorese. For a variety of reasons, more and more suppressed nationalisms seem destined to create fresh stresses in the political map of the world (Nietschmann, 1994). Better communications and political awareness are factors, and so is the fear among many fourth world people that their traditional cultures are about to be lost for ever in the face of cultural globalisation. More than 70 such groups belong to the Unrepresented Peoples Organisation (UNPO, 1997).

Worldwide, there are hundreds of peoples divided by international boundaries and some of these are among the most militant in seeking a political alternative, such as independence or autonomy. When this occurs, the borderlands come under stress as governments seek to prevent cross-border interaction and the people try to promote links with their cousins on the other side. The Kurds are a classic case of a suppressed nationalism in this predicament. Griggs and Hocknell have examined the phenomenon in IBRU's *Boundary and Security Bulletin* (Griggs and Hocknell, 1995 & 1996). One of the great challenges of the next decades will be the reconciliation of the aspirations of divided people with the wishes of the community of established states to maintain their territorial integrity. New kinds of cross-border institutions will have to be modelled, and international boundaries will need to become far more permeable in such regions if the world political map is to be prevented from disintegration.

REFUGEES

The scale of refugee movements is colossal; more than 13 million people around the world are officially classified as refugees and the United Nations High Commissioner for Refugees lists a further 9 million 'people of concern' (UNHCR, 1997a). Figure 3 is an attempt to give a bird's-eye view of some of the most important refugee movements, derived chiefly from UNHCR data. From the perspective of boundary stress, it is important to note that a high proportion of official refugees remains close to their country of origin, often in camps and settlements set up for the purpose. Refugees tend to concentrate in borderlands both because they dream of returning home, and because host countries are very cautious about allowing them to disperse. Figure 3 is too small to show the borderland areas occupied by refugees, but some are extremely extensive.

Refugees in borderlands generate stress in a number of ways. They create demand for resources such as food, water and firewood which the local area cannot provide, and their camps and settlements create serious health hazards (UNHCR, 1997b). In many cases, governments see refugees as a threat to national security and camps are targeted by security forces. Most camps are at least partially administered and sustained by international humanitarian organisations, and host governments feel uncomfortable about their lack of control in refugee-dominated regions. International boundaries in the vicinity of refugee concentrations may be virtually obliterated when refugee movements are at their height and in the immediate aftermath. When refugees remain in exile for a long period, international boundaries are managed with considerable care and attention, but the borderlands inevitably become difficult to administer. Figure 3 shows some two dozen stressed borders as a result of major movements of refugees in recent years. The great majority of these have fled from armed conflict in their own countries. Regrettably, there are likely to be more such movements in the future.

ILLEGAL MIGRATIONS

International migration in search of work or a better quality of life is an increasing phenomenon in the modern world. Discrepancies in living standards, better communications, and a growing awareness of opportunities elsewhere have all helped induce migrations for work. Non-citizens now typically make up more than five per cent of the population of industrialised countries; the figure rises to 8.5 per cent in the United States, 15 per cent in Canada and 24 per cent in Australia. In some oil-rich Arab states, non-citizens are in the majority (Weiner, 1996). However, these figures only reflect legal migrants. The number of illegal migrants worldwide must be just staggering. Some of the most notable routes for would-be migrants are shown in Figure 4, with the three most important target areas standing out, namely the United States, western Europe

9

and the Arabian peninsula. In each of these regions there are relatively low-income states such as Cuba, Morocco and Mozambique in close proximity to relatively prosperous economies.

CROSS-BORDER CRIME

International land boundaries are coming under increasing stress because of the scale and intensity of cross-border crime, much of which is associated with the activities of well-organised international gangs. Much effort is invested in attempting to break-up these criminal organisations and to intercept the criminals and their goods. International boundaries are an important focus for anti-crime activities, although the fight against international crime is also conducted in airports, along the coasts and in major cities. The international traffic in drugs is perhaps the most sensational and worrying illegal trade, but there is a whole range of other goods and illegal services being conducted across borders. Mark Galeotti has described some of the patterns of criminal activity in and around the former Soviet Union (Galeotti, 1996 & 1998) and Bertil Lintner has studied drug routes associated with the 'golden triangle', involving particularly the Burma–Thailand border (Lintner, 1991).

Thus in many borderlands of the world where the struggle to contain cross-border crime is most intense, normal life is overshadowed by fear and suspicion. Neighbouring states collaborate as best they can, but there are always allegations that the authorities on the other side of the border could do more to combat criminal activity.

CONCLUSION

Although this brief overview is inevitably flawed and incomplete, it demonstrates quite convincingly that all is not well in many of the world's borderlands. A significant number of land and maritime boundaries are troubled by disputes and there are numerous contested islands. In addition to these well documented cases, attention has been drawn to four other contemporary sources of stress whose extent and intensity may not be so well understood: the demands of divided peoples, refugees in borderland locations, illegal migrations and cross-border crime together probably affect something like one-fifth of the world's land boundaries, possibly considerably more.

This provides powerful evidence that many international boundaries cannot deliver security and stability in their adjacent borderland regions. We need to consider new ways of administering such areas, which may imply downgrading the international boundary and creating new kinds of frontier regions where states can interface with each other peacefully.

REFERENCES

Allcock, J. B. *et al* (eds.) (1992) *Border and Territorial Disputes*, 3rd Edition, Harlow: Longman.

Biger, G. (ed.) (1995) *The Encyclopedia of International Boundaries*, New York: Facts on File.

Blake, G. H., Hildesley, W. J., Pratt, M. A., Ridley, R. J., Schofield, C. H. (eds.) (1995) *The Peaceful Management of Transboundary Resources*, London: Graham & Trotman.

Dzurek, D. J. (1994) 'South East Asian offshore oil disputes', *Ocean Yearbook II*, Chicago: University of Chicago Press: 157–178.

Galeotti, M. (1996) 'Crime in Central Asia: a regional problem with global implications', *Boundary and Security Bulletin* 3(4): 68–74.

Galeotti, M. (1998) 'Russia's Far East – Russian or Eastern?', *Boundary and Security Bulletin* 6(1): 61–68.

Griggs, R. and Hocknell, P. R. (1995) 'Fourth world faultlines and the re-making of international boundaries', *Boundary and Security Bulletin* 3(3): 49–58.

Griggs, R. and Hocknell, P. R. (1996) 'The geography and geopolitics of Europe's fourth world', *Boundary and Security Bulletin* 3(4): 59–67.

Huth, P. K. (1996) *Standing Your Ground: Territorial Disputes and International Conflict*, Ann Arbor: University of Michigan Press: 197–256.

Kolossov, V. A., Glezer, O. & Petrov, N. (1992) *Ethno-Territorial Conflicts and Boundaries in the former Soviet Union*, Boundary & Territory Briefing, Durham: International Boundaries Research Unit: 1–51.

Lintner, B. (1991) *Cross-Border Drug Trade in the Golden Triangle*, Territory Briefing No. 1, Durham: International Boundaries Research Unit: 1–66.

McDorman, T. & Chircop, A. (1991) 'The resolution of maritime disputes' in Gold, E. (ed.) *Maritime Affairs: A World Handbook* (2nd edn.), Oceans Institute of Canada, Harlow: Longman: 344–386.

Nietschmann, B. (1994) 'The fourth world: Nations versus States' in Demko, G. J. & Wood, W. B. *Reordering the World: Geopolitical Perspectives on the 21st Century*, Boulder: Westview Press: 225–242.

Prescott, J. R. V. (1985) *Maritime Political Boundaries of the World*, London: Methuen.

Prescott, J. R. V. (1994). 'The Papua New Guinea–Solomon Islands maritime boundary', *Ocean Yearbook II*, Chicago: University of Chicago Press: 179–192.

Smith, R. W. & Thomas, B. L (1998) *Island Disputes and the Law of the Sea: an Examination of Sovereignty and Delimitation Disputes*, Maritime Briefing 2(4), Durham: International Boundaries Research Unit: 1–27.

UNHCR (1997a) *The State of the World's Refugees: A Humanitarian Agenda*.

UNHCR (1997b)'Crisis in the Great Lakes: anatomy of a tragedy', *Refugees*, No. 110, Winter: 1–31.

UNPO (Unrepresented Nations and Peoples Organisation) (1997) *UNPO News*, August–October: 1–43.

11

Weiner, M. (1996) 'Nations without borders', *Foreign Affairs*, March–April: 128–134. Review of Thomas Sowell (1995) *Migrations and Cultures*, Basic Books.

Westing, A. H. (ed.) (1993) *Transfrontier Parks for Peace and Nature: A Contribution to Human Security*, Nairobi: UNEP.

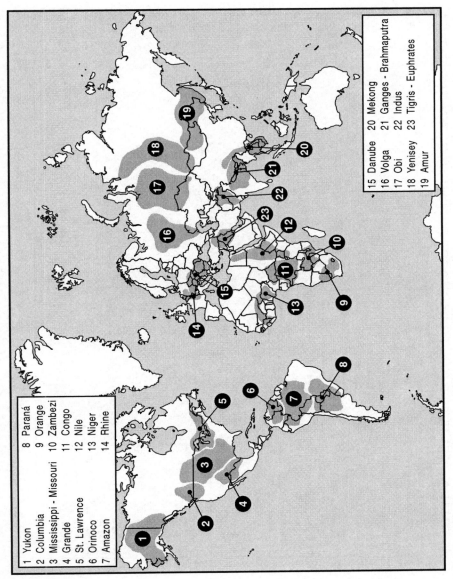

1 Yukon   8 Paraná
2 Columbia   9 Orange
3 Mississippi - Missouri   10 Zambezi
4 Grande   11 Congo
5 St. Lawrence   12 Nile
6 Orinoco   13 Niger
7 Amazon   14 Rhine

15 Danube   20 Mekong
16 Volga   21 Ganges - Brahmaputra
17 Obi   22 Indus
18 Yenisey   23 Tigris - Euphrates
19 Amur

Figure 1: Major river basins shared between states

13

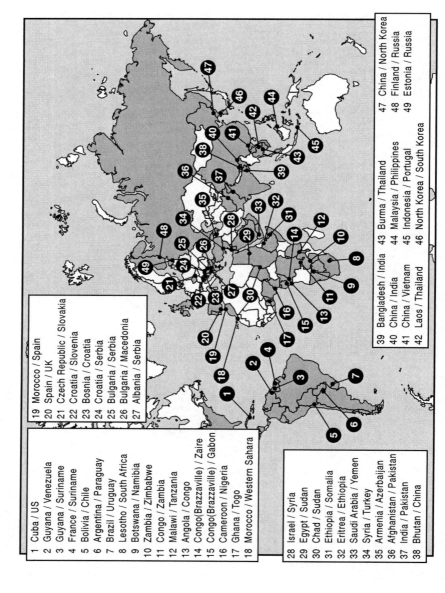

Figure 2: Unresolved land boundary disputes

1 Cuba / US
2 Guyana / Venezuela
3 Guyana / Suriname
4 France / Suriname
5 Bolivia / Chile
6 Argentina / Paraguay
7 Brazil / Uruguay
8 Lesotho / South Africa
9 Botswana / Namibia
10 Zambia / Zimbabwe
11 Congo / Zambia
12 Malawi / Tanzania
13 Angola / Congo
14 Congo(Brazzaville) / Zaire
15 Congo(Brazzaville) / Gabon
16 Cameroon / Nigeria
17 Ghana / Togo
18 Morocco / Western Sahara

19 Morocco / Spain
20 Spain / UK
21 Czech Republic / Slovakia
22 Croatia / Slovenia
23 Bosnia / Croatia
24 Croatia / Serbia
25 Bulgaria / Serbia
26 Bulgaria / Macedonia
27 Albania / Serbia

28 Israel / Syria
29 Egypt / Sudan
30 Chad / Sudan
31 Ethiopia / Somalia
32 Eritrea / Ethiopia
33 Saudi Arabia / Yemen
34 Syria / Turkey
35 Armenia / Azerbaijan
36 Afghanistan / Pakistan
37 India / Pakistan
38 Bhutan / China

39 Bangladesh / India
40 China / India
41 China / Vietnam
42 Laos / Thailand
43 Burma / Thailand
44 Malaysia / Philippines
45 Indonesia / Portugal
46 North Korea / South Korea

47 China / North Korea
48 Finland / Russia
49 Estonia / Russia

14

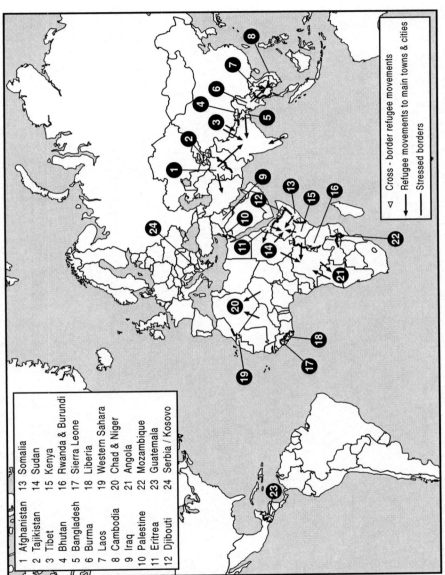

Figure 3: Refugee movements as a source of boundary stress

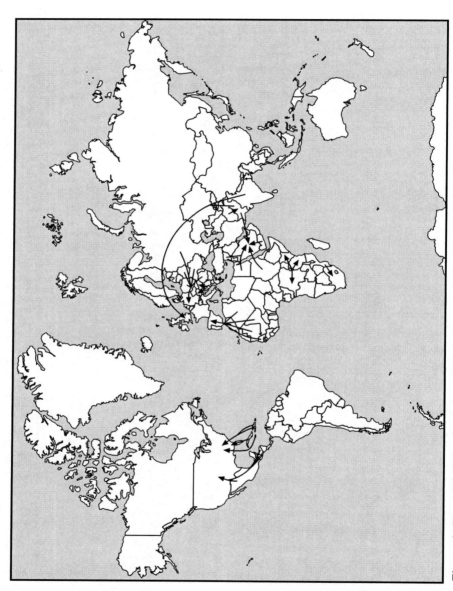

Figure 4: Examples of illegal transboundary migrations

2
Boundaries, Territory and Postmodernity: Towards Shared or Separate Spaces?[1]

David Newman

Who the hell are the Ingush? Hey, that's the Russian backyard, isn't it? Hey, listen, all this fragmentation's going too far. While we're pulling down the *economic* borders, these ethnic crazies are putting up *national* borders ... (le Carré, 1995.)

DE-TERRITORIALISATION, RE-TERRITORIALISATION AND THE WORLD POLITICAL MAP

The world around us is changing and, with it, the territorial structures and compartments which have, for the past few hundred years, formed a basic component of the state system (Agnew, 1994; Murphy, 1996). Recent discussions concerning the role of territory and boundaries in a post-Westphalian world have assumed an almost mystical disappearance of the nation-state along with its territorial compartments that make up the world political map. Notions of a 'borderless world' and political 'de-territorialisation' are seen as signalling a new world order in which the territorial component in world affairs is no longer of any importance. The impact of globalisation and the changing nature of the world political order have raised major questions concerning the role of the nation-state and the way in which territory continues to define the spatial extent of sovereignty (Johnston, 1995; Taylor, 1994; 1995). In particular, the 'end of the nation-state' thesis (Guehenno, 1995; Ohmae, 1995) questions, by definition, the role and functions of state boundaries. Some have argued that boundaries have disappeared altogether. A more cautious approach would suggest that boundaries remain an important component through which the territorial features of a state are defined and continually reconfigured, but that their roles and functions are undergoing important changes as they become more permeable and open to the transboundary movement of people, goods and information (Newman & Paasi, 1998).

This paper seeks to examine some of the territorial dimensions of *de-territorialisation*, or the 'end of the nation-state' thesis, placing the argument into a perspective which accepts the forces of change on the one hand but, on the other, attempts to locate this change within a geography of boundary differentiation, as some areas and places experience greater change than others. The paper also seeks to counter the de-territorialisation argument by focusing on

Borderlands Under Stress (M.A. Pratt and J.A. Brown (eds), ISBN 90-411-9790-7).
© Kluwer Law International, 2000.

the continued importance of territory and its physical delimiters – boundaries – in the formation of ethnic and national identities. While the flow of capital and information may be taking on an increasingly transboundary, virtual dimension, the formation and institutionalisation of national identities remain strongly tied up with the changing spatial configurations of political power (Newman, 1999a).

In particular, it will be posited that, while economic arguments lie at the heart of the 'end of the nation-state' thesis, the emerging picture is quite different when applying the test of ethno-territorial characteristics to any particular boundary case study. While some boundaries are opening up, such as in western Europe, elsewhere new boundaries are being created and new fences of separation are being erected as ethno-territorial conflicts are being fought out and/or being resolved in other parts of the world. Changing territorial dynamics must be seen in a parallel context to the formation of national and ethnic identities and the extent to which these retain an exclusive, or inclusive, territorial definition. As such, the question of shared or separate spaces becomes crucial to the way in which we understand the role of boundaries as lines which not only separate physical territories, but also continue to separate groups on the basis of their national identity. The extent to which an increase in economic or information flows helps change the way in which ethnic or national groups think about each other, is but one component in the overall boundary discourse. All told, boundaries must be examined from a multi-dimensional perspective, taking into account the diverse factors that may or may not bring about a change in their traditional functions as barriers to communication and movement.

The paper further seeks to examine the way in which the relationship between national and/or ethnic identities is reconfigured as the world political map undergoes a process of *re-territorialisation*, as some boundaries disappear and others emerge, as rigid spatial compartmentalisation and territorial fixation may be replaced with virtual spaces of identity, and as new social constructions of territory are formed through the diffusion of territorial narratives which focus on symbolic, mythical, physical and abstract homeland spaces. Re-territorialisation is not an outcome of de-territorialisation, but is itself the process through which territorial configurations of political power are changing. The relationship between national identity and territorial (re)configuration is taking on new forms in some places, while retaining some of its traditional forms in others. The impact of globalisation may weaken the link between national identity and fixed boundaries at one end of the spatial scale, while strengthening local territorial identities at the other end.

The lines that are boundaries remain strongly imprinted upon the mental images of territories and states that we carry around in our spatial imaginations. Even when these lines are becoming more permeable and transboundary movement is becoming much easier and more common, the territorial shape of the state remains a given spatial construct for most people. We tend to visualise and imagine the state as something immovable and static, rarely undergoing change. But territories are not static. Even during the 350 years of Westphalian state formations, boundaries have constantly changed as some nations and empires have expanded their territories at the expense of others while others have seen their territory undergo contraction as a result of warfare or territorial cession. The Centennia map programme, run at a fast speed, portrays 1,000 years of European history as a living organism undergoing constant change, expansion and contraction. New world territorial orders have occurred far more frequently than we acknowledge, with few states in the Westphalian order having maintained the same boundaries for any lengthy period of time.

The territorial configuration of the state with which we are most familiar is the one in which we grow up, in which we are socialised through media and classroom, and with which we identify as somehow belonging to 'us' as part of the national collective. Processes of territorial socialisation often include the demarcation of historical territories which are no longer part of the national territory, and to which the nation continues to aspire. Given contexts of conflict, aggression and territorial expansion, the state may take practical steps to gain (or regain) this territory as a process in which boundaries are re-demarcated. But at the very least, even without the adoption of such practical measures, the contemporary configuration of state territory remains strongly imprinted on the spatial imagination, with recognisable boundaries that define the outer lines of our territorial attachment. As such, the notion of a fixed territory is much easier to deal with than one which is constantly changing its shape and with which different layers of identity are tied up.

It goes without saying that if a boundary exists, something must be enclosed within it. The traditional boundary discourse in geography has been concerned with the physical lines that create separate territorial compartments (Minghi, 1963; Prescott, 1987). These lines range from the international boundaries which separate sovereign territories and states from each other, to the administrative and municipal lines which separate the diverse functional spaces within which we live and carry out our daily life patterns (Newman & Paasi, 1998; O'Loughlin & Kolossov, 1998). This discourse has changed in recent years as the multi-dimensional nature of boundaries has been discussed, both by geographers who have recognised the aspatial functionality of boundaries which 'include' and 'exclude' diverse social phenomena, and by sociologists and political scientists who have increasingly introduced notions of space and territory into their respective analyses of complex social and political processes (Newman 1999a). Boundaries, in their social sense, may still define the outer limits of group and/or national identity but, so it is argued, they are there to be crossed and traversed rather than to act as barriers. They can be viewed as much as lines of contact, where the notions of difference and group exclusiveness break down, as they have traditionally been viewed as the place of separation (Waterman, 1994; Newman & Paasi, 1998).

THE 'END OF BOUNDARY' THESIS

The post-modern thesis is, by definition, one that argues for the breaking down of paradigmal rigidity in our understanding of human society. No single model or theory of human behaviour is accepted as occupying a hegemonic position. Rather, all models and all theories are acceptable and, to put it simply, they can be mixed together in a fashion that breaks down the rigid or dogmatic notions of model building. Disciplinary boundaries are crossed as spatial, social and political theories are brought together in new forms of multi-dimensional analysis which accept the *a priori* complexity of human society to a greater extent than has traditionally been the case within the social sciences. Using the terminology that has now become the normative part of the post-modern debate, models and theories are there to be deconstructed or, in other words, broken down into the multitude of components that have gone in to making the model in the first place. In particular, the role of the scholar and his or her position in creating the model is questioned, accompanied by a quest for new and alternative narratives from scholars whose social, cultural, ethnic or economic position is different to that of the scholars/authors who occupy the position of academic hegemony and who have, consciously or subconsciously, been excluded from the process through which knowledge has been socially constructed.

The breaking down, or deconstruction, of the normative structures of social behaviour has not bypassed the territorial structures of the state (O'Loughlin & Kolossov, 1998; Albert, 1999). For some, the traditional notion of the Westphalian territorial system has been no more than a fiction (Eva, 1998), since it assumed an equality of power between states with no authority above the state system itself. But even were we to assume that this is not the case, it has become increasingly common to argue for the end of the nation-state signalling, so it would appear, the end of the Westphalian state structure, in which territorial fixation forms the basic component of sovereignty. This notion of sovereignty as an absolute form of political legitimacy that occurs within a rigidly defined state territory, determined by the course of human-made boundaries, is being called into question. State sovereignty is, so it is argued, being broken down as boundaries have become more permeable than in the past and no longer fulfil one of their basic functions – to act as physical barriers to transboundary movement.

The 'end of boundaries' thesis follows on from the notion of state de-territorialisation and the end of territorial absolutism (Taylor, 1996). The creation of virtual spaces, in which an individual is entirely removed from the place he/she may be conversing with, and the emergence of virtual communities, means that boundaries have little, if any, impact on the way in which much human interaction is now taking place. Accepting this thesis, one would argue that the process of identity formation becomes a-spatial, not linked to any specific piece of territory, that the virtual replaces the absolute, and that social and group boundaries take the place of rigidly defined territorial boundaries.

The lines that continue to appear as cartographic narrative on the face of maps, and which continue to separate national and sovereign territories are, according to this argument, no more than archaic features which, if they have not already disappeared, will do so within the next few decades as the world's territorial order takes on a new shape.

Boundary permeability has particularly taken place within the field of economic movements and the increase in global trade, often managed by a small number of multinational corporations, although Yeung (1998) argues that, even in the sphere of economic activity, national boundaries still matter in the decision-making and reach of capital. The impact of cyberspace and satellite technology has meant that boundaries are no longer effective as barriers to the dissemination of information and ideas (Brunn *et al*, 1994; Morley & Robbins, 1995; Brunn, 1998), while greater mobility has also led to the increased movement of people – both as immigrants and as migrant workers – over boundaries. Even within the field of military technology, the advent of ballistic missiles has meant that physical boundaries are no longer effective in moving the military threat away from the core areas of the country to distant boundary areas. Taken together, the mixture of economic, information and military developments has brought about an 'end of boundary' thesis, running parallel to the 'end of state' thesis, inasmuch as boundaries continue to be perceived in their role as barriers to communication and movement. It is this that has been defined as giving rise to a 'borderless' world, an argument that this paper sets out to counter.

TERRITORIAL BOUNDARIES AND NATIONAL IDENTITY

The 'de-territorialisation of the state' argument is tied up with the way in which territories overlap in the formation of national identities (Paasi, 1996a; Newman & Paasi, 1998). As globalisation takes little note of territorial boundaries, it is argued, the relationship between identity and territory becomes more complex (Shapiro & Alker, 1996; O'Loughlin & Kolossov, 1998; Paasi, 1998). National identity remains territorially focused but not territorially bound, as diaspora communities retain strong links with their national groups and with their territorial heartlands through virtual rather than physical connections. The spatial boundaries of the nation do not necessarily conform to the spatial boundaries of citizenship, resulting in multi-layered identities and, some would argue, multi-citizenships (although this remains the privilege of the few rather than the many). In reality, there are more people in the world who remain completely without citizenship, by virtue of their refugee status, than there are groups who, due to their economic status and limitless mobility, take on additional citizenships and global identities as self-defined 'citizens of the world'.

The fact that the territorial boundaries of the state do not necessarily conform to the boundaries of national identity is nothing new (Knight, 1982 & 1994). As territorial boundaries have changed constantly in the past, so too have ethnic groups been caught up in the territorial sweep of history, remaining behind as peripheral minorities in one state, or being drawn in as ethnic groups into new multi-ethnic states. The superimposition of boundaries has cut through ethnically homogeneous areas, such as those occupied by the Kurds or tribal lands in Africa, while in other cases boundaries have been artificially drawn around a multitude of tribal groups, thus creating the seeds of future ethno-territorial conflict and warfare, much of which remains with us in the contemporary period.

To suggest that spatial compartmentalisation creates national identity would, to say the least, be considered highly deterministic. But it would be equally erroneous to suggest that space does not play any role in the institutionalisation and strengthening of territorial and national identities (Knight, 1982 & 1994; Hooson, 1994). Citizenship is tied up with territory inasmuch as contemporary notions of citizenship are tied up with sovereignty (Doty, 1996; Soysal, 1996). Territory, sovereignty and citizenship form a triadic relationship which the opening of boundaries and processes of political re-territorialisation have done little to change. Processes of political, national and territorial socialisation practised through the agencies of the state continue to throw up the link between the affiliation of the individual, the individual's citizenship, and the compartmentalised territory within which this takes place.

To a certain extent, the discourse surrounding the relationship between identity boundaries and the territorial boundaries of the state is akin to one of the most traditional of boundary typologies, that suggested by Richard Hartshorne over 50 years ago (Hartshorne, 1936). His use of terms taken from fluvial geomorphology, notably 'antecedent' and 'subsequent' boundaries, can quite easily be translated into much of the contemporary discourse. 'Antecedent' boundaries were those which were created in virgin, frontier spaces and which preceded and, in Hartshorne's view, ultimately determined the spatial dispersion and formation of settlement patterns and their related ethno-territorial identities. 'Subsequent' boundaries were those which were delimited and demarcated around the existing patterns of settlement and cultural diversity, institutionalising and strengthening the territorial dimension of separate national identities which had already formed over a long period of time. While we acknowledge the fact that there is no such phenomenon as a 'natural boundary', given the fact that all boundaries are ultimately demarcated by governments based on *realpolitik* considerations, natural features which acted as barriers (such as mountains, rivers and deserts) clearly had a role to play in the formation of separate territorial identities in pre-technological periods when mobility was limited and local cultures evolved separately from neighbouring cultures. The existence of these territorial identities played, and continues to play, a major role in the way in which *subsequent* boundaries were demarcated. To put it simply, identities exist and, for as long as it is convenient to the people who determine the territorial configurations at any given time, boundaries are drawn around these existing identities – be they social, political or spatial. On the one hand, existing identities and group attachment (antecedent identities) are the forces which determine territorial and irredentist demands, be they secession from the existing state or the establishment of new independent states, while on the other it is the existing forms of territorial configuration and compartmentalisation which partially determine the way in which new identities and affiliations are formed over time.

This basic dichotomy remains relevant as the world political map undergoes its constant process of territorial reconfiguration. The break-up of the Soviet Union and the re-emergence of nation-states in central and eastern Europe (Kolossov, 1992), the emergence of the 'fourth world' nations in western Europe (Nietschmann, 1994; Griggs & Hocknell, 1995), and the transboundary national identities which have emerged through global cyberspace (Morley & Robbins, 1995; Brunn, 1998) are all located along a contemporary 'antecedent–subsequent' continuum of a world in which the relationship between territory, identity and sovereignty (particularly the latter) is geographically differentiated. Different processes affect different locations – territorial fixation and Westphalian notions of sovereignty retaining their hold in some places and loosening it in others. But even in the latter, the identity–territory relationship becomes reconfigured, but it does not disappear.

While the Hartshorne analogy may sound somewhat simplistic, perhaps even deterministic, the point to make is that the political world has always been in a state of territorial flux, and that the pre-Westphalian territorial order may not have been that much different to the new regional and intra-state territorial patterns which are emerging. Clearly, the emerging territorial order is far more stable and secure than the pre-Westphalian order, but that does not change the essential relationship between identity and territory. It simply recognises that the rigid determination of state boundaries does not necessarily parallel the complexity of national identity. Moreover, it suggests that the very notion of the 'nation-state' was, at its peak, a questionable concept inasmuch as it assumed the existence of a large number of states in the world system whose territorial configuration corresponded with some 90–100 per cent of a single national group. The desire to achieve a high level of congruence between the spatial dispersion of a national group and the territory within which this same group exercised its sovereignty was as true in post-First World War Europe as it was in the immediate aftermath of the collapse of the Soviet Union (Paasi, 1995). What has changed has been the technology that allows for greater mobility and an awareness of 'the Other', wherever that Other may be located. But the essential desire to define group/national identity by recourse to fixed territories remains as strongly rooted today as in the past.

Claims to territory are based on a combination of symbolic and concrete characteristics (Newman, 1999b). It is the symbolic and mythical dimensions of territory which are used as a means of consolidating the link between national identity and a specific space, more often than not defined as a 'homeland' in which a single national/ethnic group defines its own exclusivity. Territorial symbolism draws on historical narrative and myth as a means of emphasising unbroken links between a national/ethnic group and the events that have taken place in that territory (Paasi, 1996a). History, archaeology and religion are all used as part of the process of social construction through which the identity–territory bond is forged. This is translated into concrete claims for territorial sovereignty, claims that are justified using a combination of priority and duration arguments – 'priority' meaning that the group perceives itself as having been the first group to have settled in the region, often evidenced through archaeological evidence, and 'duration' being the argument that the group has resided in this particular space uninterrupted over a long period of time (Burghardt, 1973; Murphy, 1990).

Territorial socialisation continues to play an important role even after territorial boundaries have been demarcated and state territories have been configured. The state uses the agents of socialisation as a means of strengthening the link with the national territory, of justifying the need to defend it from aggressors and, in some cases, even to expand the territorial base at the expense of neighbouring states. Processes of territorial socialisation are particularly strong in school textbooks, notably the state narratives of history and geography, often depicted through cartographic manipulation. Field trips to sites of historical significance, the naming of landscapes on maps (Cohen & Kliot, 1981 & 1992; Nash, 1999), and the mythification of religious and/or battle sites in which the nation was victorious, are all part of the process through which territorial symbolism plays a role in the construction of national identity (Zerubavel, 1995).

Territory is also an agent of control, of spatial ordering (Taylor, 1994 & 1995; Yiftachel, 1991 & 1998). Continued territorial compartmentalisation and separation create the mechanisms of control through which identity is socially constructed and imposed upon constituents. Citizenship through consensus strengthens the attachment of an individual to the state. Enforced citizenship, especially in the case of ethnic minority groups, weakens the degree to which national identity relates to the given spatial constructs while, at the same time, strengthening alternative forms of ethnic and national identity, often with groups who share similar cultural characteristics but are located within other geographic territories. In this sense, there are two forms of political re-territorialisation taking place, each of which has different implications for the territory–sovereignty–identity triad. The first, re-territorialisation arising from economic and cyberspace globalisation, may loosen the exclusive ties between the individual and the state, but it does not – except in cases of a small elite of truly 'world citizens' – change the basic identity–citizen relationship of the individual with the state whose passport he or she continues to carry, to whom he or she pays taxes, and to whom he or she feels an affiliation (and, in many cases, an allegiance). On the other hand, re-territorialisation which arises out of the desire of ethnic and/or national minority groups to secede from the state and create new, separate, national territories, reflects the lack of national identity/affiliation with the existing state structure and a move towards new territorial configurations for the state which reflect aspirations for self-determination, autonomy and independence.

The past superimposition of boundaries through colonialism and imperialism was a major factor determining the clash between citizenship and national identity. The division of a single national territory into a number of states (such as in the case of the Kurds), or, alternatively, the inclusion of a mix of ethnic and/or national groups/tribes within a single demarcated territory, have been responsible for much of the ethnic strife which has occurred in parts of Europe, Asia and Africa during the past 70 years. But not only does this not result in a weakening of national identity, rather it often leads to the strengthening of a territorial-based identity inasmuch as dominant and subordinate groups fight for their rights to self-determination and independent government. For some it is a struggle to maintain the hegemony of the existing territorial order, while for others it is an attempt to create a new territorial order which, in their view, more closely resembles the ethno-territorial realities to which they aspire, and with which they identify. As such, these processes strengthen, rather than weaken, the basic link between territory and identity, as ethnic and national groups aspire to create new boundaries of separation, form separate ethnic spaces, and use all the symbols of statehood, such as passports, stamps, currency, flags and anthems. It is the territorial dimension and scale which changes, with global and local identity spaces being carved out of the changing world political map in addition to the existing spaces of the State system.

AN ISRAEL–PALESTINE CASE STUDY

Observers of the Israel–Palestine ethno-territorial conflict imagine a map extending from the Mediterranean Sea in the west to the Jordan River in the east, a distance of no more than 75 kilometres at its broadest, with a West Bank territory, now [at time of writing] under partial Israeli occupation and partially dissected into Palestinian autonomy exclaves, defined by the 'green line' boundary. Yet this particular version of the map came into existence for the first time in 1949, following the implementation on the ground of the Rhodes Armistice agreements between Israel and Jordan, and it changed as a result of Israeli military conquest in the Six Day War of 1967. As a complete boundary of separation, it lasted for no more than 19 years, while the period of Israeli occupation has lasted for a further 30 years. The fact that the West Bank remains a territory whose sovereignty is 'yet to be determined' ensures that this remains a clearly defined, separate territorial entity (which, in one sense, makes it much easier to handle from the perspective of international law since this status recognises the right of Palestinian self-determination without the need for secession from an existing sovereign territory), notwithstanding Israeli policies aimed at expanding settlements and road infrastructure and bringing about a situation of partial *de facto* annexation.

During a period of no more than 80 years, the Israel–Palestine territorial arena has experienced at least six major territorial changes, with boundaries being redrawn and redefined (Newman, 1999b). The Ottoman Empire was followed by division into the French and British Mandated territories, followed by the partition of Palestine and the creation of the new territorial entity of Transjordan, followed by the later partition proposals for Palestine west of the River Jordan, partition *de facto* and the establishment of the state of Israel, followed by Israeli territorial expansion during the Six Day War, and finally territorial contraction as a result of the Camp David Peace Accords between Israel and Egypt and the partial implementation of Palestinian autonomy in parts of the West Bank. Until the Camp David Peace Accords, none of Israel's boundaries were formally recognised as international lines that defined the sovereign extent of the state as accepted by both Israel and her respective neighbours. The post-1949 lines may be the lines that are set in our geopolitical imaginations, but only two of them – those with Egypt and Jordan – constitute lines of sovereign boundary demarcation. Israel's boundaries with Syria, Lebanon and a future Palestinian state remain to be determined, even though the eventual lines may not differ greatly from the existing ones.

While in the case of Syria and Lebanon the final demarcation of lines is based around traditional, tangible territorial concerns such as security areas, buffer zones and access to water resources, territorial demarcation between Israel and a Palestinian entity/state is tied up with the boundaries of identity. The redrawing of boundaries as part of the current attempts at conflict resolution is problematic not least because the discourse centres on concrete issues such as strategic sites, security and so on, while consciously ignoring the fact that the drawing of lines must enable the emergence of identity territories within the framework of the territorial state system (Falah & Newman, 1995; Newman, 1996 & 1998a). Both Israelis and Palestinians aspire to nation-states in which their respective national groups retain clear demographic superiority, if not exclusivity. Attempts to redefine the territorial lines of separation can maximise the extent to which the two types of boundary complement and reinforce each other, but cannot – without forced ethnic cleansing or 'transfer' – create maximum social and spatial separation.

In the Israeli–Palestinian context, territory has always played, and continues to play, a major role in the formation, consolidation and strengthening of separate and contested national identities. The demarcation of boundaries, past and present, has created the territorial compartments within which Israelis and Palestinians have created, or aspire to create, their modes of political affiliation through the imposition of sovereignty and the attainment of citizenship (Falah & Newman, 1995). Decades of conflict, coupled with contested histories, have negated the possibility of a bi-national entity within a single territory, despite the fact that bi-nationalism in a single shared space would best reflect contemporary notions of conflict resolution, human rights, equality and the removal of nation-dominated spaces of mutual exclusion. Each side to the conflict wants to create its own separate territory within which national identity is consolidated and citizenship remains tied in with the classic Westphalian model of state sovereignty. The territorial boundaries of the state continue to define the major parameters within which citizenship takes place, although this is not the same for the dominant and subordinate national groups. Jews residing outside the territorial compartment can take on citizenship (the Jewish diaspora) or retain their citizenship (West Bank settlers), while citizenship for Palestinian-Arabs is limited to those within the pre-1967 boundaries and, in many cases, is withheld following periods of absence from their home territory, their indigenous place of residence.

Contextually, the symbolic dimensions and attributes of the national territory are central to an understanding of the conflict (Hermann & Newman, 2000). The very notion of Zionism as a territory-oriented nationalism for a people who were geographically dispersed and disconnected from the territory in question is a classic example. The religious symbolism of the land as constituting the 'promised land' given to the Jewish people (Davies, 1982, Newman, 1998b), of the historic sites of the ancient Israelite kingdoms and their temples, of the ritual associations of the 'land of Israel' with specific religious precepts and, more recently, the emergence of contemporary myths associated with the twentieth-century settlements and their fight for survival in a hostile environment, have together provided a powerful bonding between people and land, strengthening the territorial-based national identity of the Jewish (as defined in their formal registration) citizens of contemporary Israel.

The West Bank settler movement emphasises territorial identity as the very core of its political *raison d'être*. The territory 'belongs' to them by Divine right; the West Bank region is full of ancient Biblical sites which, from their ethno-centred perspective, were central to the process of nation formation, while the religious texts and narratives of a Diaspora people, geographically disconnected from the 'national homeland', continue to occupy a central part in the contemporary theo-political discourse, emphasising the territorial dimension of national and religious identity. The semantics of space and place are central to this territorial discourse. From the settler perspective, the 1967 war was a war in which Judea and Samaria (not the West Bank) were liberated (not conquered or occupied) and through which the Jewish people have returned (not migrated) to their ancestral homeland.

Contested interpretations of archaeological evidence have resulted in conflicting claims to a single territory based on priority and duration claims. Both Israelis and Palestinians view this territory as constituting the space within which their respective national identities emerged and were formed over time. Each sees territory as being an essential component of their contemporary national identity and their right to control territory as part of their sovereignty/ self-determination. The willingness to partition territory as part of a process of conflict resolution results from *realpolitik* considerations which dictate some form of compromise for the sake of future security and/or national self-determination, not from a preparedness on either side to give up on the essential territorial component of their national identity formation. Each compares territorial partition to the amputation of a limb from the body, thus weakening the overall organism but at the same time allowing it to survive. While the concrete dimensions of the territory are divided as a means of conflict resolution, the symbolic claims to territory remain contested and are likely to continue to be contested for as long as exclusive Israeli–Jewish and Palestinian–Arab–Moslem national identities are tied up with their respective territorial focii.

DISCUSSION

The global and the local: the scale of territorial reconfiguration

The world is not experiencing de-territorialisation and an overall weakening of the link between territory and national identity. The world political map is undergoing *re*-territorialisation as boundaries become more permeable and as spatial reconfiguration takes place. In some cases the cyber diffusion of information actually broadens the extent to which national groups residing in their respective diasporas recreate and strengthen their identity link with their 'home' territory, regardless of whether the actual boundary line which delimits the territory of the state is more or less rigid in the way in which it acts as a boundary to physical movement. The link between identity and citizenship may be breaking up, but the basic link between identity formation and the spatial compartment within which such identity formation takes place remains a powerful element in the reordering and reconfiguration of both global and local politics.

This paper has focused on the relationship between territory and identity at the level of the state. As such, it focuses on national and ethnic identities and the way that this is reflected through territorial compartmentalisation of the world political map and the way in which ethnic and national groups express their sovereignty and citizenship within political spaces that are physically separate from each other. The paper does not automatically assume that these same processes operate at the level of local spaces, where the functional impact of boundaries are less rigid and where notions of sovereignty and formal affiliation (i.e. citizenship and all the accompanying documents and obligations) do not apply. But at both levels – the state and the local – the extent to which territories are more or less homogeneous in their ethnic composition is a major factor determining the nature of exclusive attachment to a given territory and the way in which processes of territorial socialisation emphasising national and territorial myths strengthen the constructed bonding between a people and their self-defined 'homeland' or 'group turf'.

Just as notions of de-territorialisation are being subsumed by alternative notions of re-territorialisation, so too notions of globalisation are becoming associated with more complex notions of *glocalisation*. As re-territorialisation takes place, it does so at both the global and the local levels, with the global becoming the new byword for economic and information communities, and the local becoming increasingly important for the strengthening of ethnic and neighbourhood identities. Local, even micro-territorial, identities are formed within urban neighbourhoods. The formal boundaries of an urban quarter do not always coincide with the perceived boundaries of turf affiliation, in much the same way as the formal boundaries of the state do not automatically coincide with the territorial dispersion of the national/ethnic group. But loyalties and affiliations to specific neighbourhoods, blocks or even streets can be very strong, and are often reflected in the struggle for scarce municipal and development resources. Neighborhood groups play up their separate identities and needs in justifying their respective demand for resources. In many cases the spatial definition of urban neighbourhoods is strongly linked to the evolution and formation of ethnic ghettos, thus strengthening the sense of spatial separation, even in societies that pride themselves on being multi-culturalist at the national level.

The 'glocalisation' thesis is particularly evident in western Europe. New forms of territorial ordering take on both macro and micro dimensions that affect the sovereign status of the state (Van der Wusten, 1994). An increasing number of decisions, economic and political, are being taken on behalf of the entire European community by a single European parliament, bringing into effect a supra-territorial entity whose impact takes little account of existing territorial boundaries. At the same time, regional, intra-state identities have come to the fore in most European countries, promoting their own economic development policies, enhancing their ethnic and linguistic differences and, in many cases, bypassing the state altogether in their dealings with the European community and other external trading partners (Newhouse, 1997).

Thus, spatial scale is an important dimension in the understanding of territorial identities. These can take on a series of overlapping spaces, ranging from the state, through the region and right down to the territorial turfs of neighbourhood groups and/or segregated ethnic ghettos. Just as the individual belongs to diverse social and economic groups, so too does the individual live and function within a number of overlapping spaces within which different identities take on a concrete expression and are demarcated by boundaries which may be more or less permeable. In this sense it is almost impossible to divorce the social and the political from the spatial and the territorial, as the latter often forms the compartment within which the former is able to express itself. At the local level too, re-territorialisation is continually taking place, mobility is enhanced and information is more diffuse. But for as long as the segregative functions of social and economic groups remain in place, they will always take place within some form of nested territorial hierarchy (Herb & Kaplan, 1999).

Towards shared or separate territories?

The discussion thus far has suggested that while the globalisation of capital and information is bringing about a de-territorialised world, territory remains important for the formation of ethnic and national identities. Boundaries continue to create the compartments – albeit more permeable than in the past – within which national groups retain an attachment to place. But even here, the de-territorialisation argument implicitly suggests that territories are increasingly becoming the domain of shared spaces rather than the exclusive domain of territorially concentrated ethnic and national groups.

This is interesting inasmuch as the Westphalian concept of fixed sovereign territories was, to a large extent, a European notion which was exported from the mother countries through imperialism and colonialism and superimposed upon territories and cultures whose notions of territory were vastly different. Nomadic populations were forced into accepting rigid notions of boundary, resulting in forced sedentarisation and much conflict between nomadic groups and state authorities (Ramutsindela, 1999). It is now the same European heartland which is promoting the post-modern discourse of state de-territorialisation as the basis for the new world order, despite the fact that ethno-territorial conflicts, many of which are themselves the outcome of previous European interventions, remain highly focused. As much of the Third World continues to struggle to come to grips with the European notions of territorial fixation, so Europe has introduced a new phase of territorial re-ordering which, largely for economic reasons, it seeks to impose upon other regions and cultures.

A brief glance at the world map shows the large number of ethno-territorial conflicts that remain to be resolved. These conflicts bear comparison to the extent that national groups continue to attempt to take control over what they see as constituting their national territory or 'homeland', and are prepared to fight and lose their lives in order to preserve hegemonic control over the 'home' territory. This includes putting into effect policies of ethnic cleansing and genocide, creating exclusive territories, both at micro- and macro-territorial levels, and creating clearly delineated fences separating the national territory from that belonging to the 'other' (Falah & Newman, 1995; Sibley, 1995; Paasi, 1996b). Try suggesting the notion of shared territories to Moslems and Serbs in Bosnia, to Greek and Turkish Cypriots in Cyprus, to warring tribes in Rwanda and Zaire, or to Jews and Arabs (Israelis and Palestinians) in a single, bi-national state of Israel–Palestine, and be prepared to be greeted with much derision. It may sound very democratic, it may be based on universal concepts of human rights and equality, of multi-culturalism and shared identities – but it is not based on the reality of protracted conflict, animosity, hatred and mistrust.

Attempts at conflict resolution continue to be characterised by a mutual determination to delineate national territories and to erect strong fences of separation between the respective groups and their spaces. It remains to be seen what will happen two generations after the cessation of violence, after the feelings of mutual mistrust begin to dissipate, when economic cooperation and an understanding of the 'other' and his or her culture results in some form of normalisation. In this respect, the western European experience may indeed prove to be a model of de-territorialisation of the state which is applicable to other regions and other cultural contexts. But, as with so many other social constructs, it remains to be tested against the experience of time.

CONCLUSION

As geographers have sought to distance themselves from what they traditionally saw as unpopular and misunderstood notions of space and place, many of the social sciences – notably sociology, economics and political science – have suddenly discovered the importance of these same concepts. But they have discovered a multi-dimensional rather than uni-dimensional space, not one that is limited to the level of fixed and concrete territorial boundaries. Space is as virtual as it is real, as symbolic as it is concrete, and boundaries are as permeable as they are iron curtains and barriers. But whatever their functional attributes, they continue to provide the territorial compartment within which identities are formed at global, national and local levels, and within which life's activities continue to be played out.

Despite the territorial reconfiguration, or re-territorialisation, of the world political map, boundaries remain important lines of demarcation, even in those areas, such as western Europe, where they have become much more permeable than in the past (Newman, 1999c & 2000). In those parts of the world faced by continuing ethno-territorial tensions and conflict, it is the spatial lines of demarcation which retain their traditional role as lines of national separation and physical barriers, albeit not to the extent that was common in the past. It is the geographic differentiation of boundaries that must be recognised, with greater permeability and an increased sharing of political spaces in some places, as contrasted with fixed lines of separation and even new fences of territorial separation in other places. The post-modern discourse focusing on the de-territorialisation of the state and the disappearance of boundaries in their traditional sense is a culture-specific, North American and western European narrative, and it remains to be seen to what extent it will become relevant to other regions as the impact of globalisation and political rapprochement themselves becomes more widespread.

NOTE

1   This chapter is a combined version of the papers presented at the IBRU Conference in July 1998 in Durham, and at an International Seminar held in Israel in January 1999 whose theme was 'Challenging the Nation State: Perspectives on Citizenship and Identity'. The paper in the latter conference was entitled, 'Boundaries, Territory and the Formation of National Identity'. I am grateful to my colleague, Prof. Oren Yiftachel, for his ongoing comments about some of the ideas developed in this paper.

BIBLIOGRAPHY

Agnew, J. (1994) 'The territorial trap: the geographical assumptions of international relations theory', *Review of International Political Economy* 1: 53–80.

Albert, M. (forthcoming 1999) 'On boundaries, territory and postmodernity: an international relations perspective', *Geopolitics*, Vol. 3 (1) (Special Issue: *Boundaries, Territory and Postmodernity*).

Brunn, S. D., Jones, J. A. & Purcell, D. (1994) 'Ethnic communities in the evolving "electronic state": cyberplaces in cyberspace' in Gallusser, W. A. (ed.) *Political Boundaries and Coexistence*, Bern: Peter Lang.

Brunn, S. D. (1998) 'A treaty of Silicon for a Treaty of Westphalia?: Territorial dimensions of modern statehood', *Geopolitics*, Vol. 3 (1) (Special Issue: *Boundaries, Territory and Postmodernity*): 106–131.

Burghardt, A. (1973) 'The bases of territorial claims', *Geographical Review*, 63: 225–245.

Cohen, S. B. & Kliot, N. (1981) 'Israel's place names as reflection of continuity and change in nation building', *Names*, 29: 227–246.

Cohen, S. B & Kliot, N. (1992) 'Place names in Israel's ideological struggle over the administered territories', *Annals of the Association of American Geographers* 82: 653–680.

Davies, W. D. (1982) *The Territorial Dimension of Judaism*, Berkeley: University of California Press.

Doty, R. L. (1996) 'Sovereignty and the nation: constructing the boundaries of national identity' in Biersteker, J. & Weber, C. (eds.) *State Sovereignty as Social Construct*, Cambridge: Cambridge University Press.

Eva, F. (1998) 'International boundaries, geopolitics and the (post) modern discourse: the functional fiction', *Geopolitics*, Vol. 3 (1) (Special Issue: *Boundaries, Territory and Postmodernity*): 32–52.

Falah, G. & Newman, D. (1995) 'The spatial manifestation of threat: Israelis and Palestinians seek a "good" border', *Political Geography* 14: 189–706.

Griggs, R. & Hocknell, P. (1995) 'The geography and geopolitics of Europe's fourth world', *Boundary and Security Bulletin*, 3 (4): 59–67.

Guehenno, J. (1995) *The End of the Nation State*, Minneapolis: University of Minnesota Press.

Hartshorne, R. (1936) 'Suggestions on the terminology of political boundaries', *Annals of the Association of American Geographers* 26 (1): 56–57.

Herb, G. & Kaplan, D. (1999) (eds.) *Nested Identities: Nationalism, Territories and Scale*. Rowman & Littlefield.

Hermann, T. & Newman, D. (2000) 'A path strewn with thorns: along the difficult road of Israeli–Palestinian peacemaking', in J. Darby & R. MacGinty (eds.), *The Management of the Peace Processes*. Macmillan Press: London, UK.

Hooson, D. (ed.) (1994) *Geography and National Identity*, Oxford: Blackwell.

Johnston, R. J. (1995) 'Territoriality and the state' in Benko, G. B. & Strohmayer, U. (eds.) *Geography, History and Social Sciences*, Dordrecht: Kluwer: 213–225.

Knight, D. (1982) 'Identity and territory: geographic perspectives on nationalism and regionalism', *Annals of the Association of American Geographers* 72: 514–531.

Knight, D. (1994) 'People together, yet apart: rethinking territory, sovereignty and identity' in Demko, G. J. & Wood, W. B. (eds.) *Reordering the World: Geopolitical Perspectives on the Twenty First Century*, Boulder, Co.: Westview Press: 71–86.

Kolossov, V. A. (1992) 'Ethno-Territorial Conflicts and Boundaries in the Former Soviet Union', *Boundary and Territory Briefing*, No. 2, Durham: International Boundaries Research Unit.

le Carré, J. (1995) *Our Game*, New York: Alfred Knopf: 286.

Minghi, J. V. (1963) 'Boundary studies in political geography', *Annals of the Association of American Geographers* 53, 407–428.

Morley, D. & Robins, K. (1995) *Spaces of Identity: Global Media, Electronic Landscapes and Cultural Boundaries*, London: Routledge.

Murphy, A. B. (1990) 'Historical justifications for territorial claims', *Annals of the Association of American Geographers* 80: 531–548.

Murphy, A. B. (1996) 'The sovereign state system as political-territorial ideal: historical and contemporary considerations' in Biersteker, T. J. & Weber, C. (eds.) *State Sovereignty as Social Construct*, Cambridge: Cambridge University Press.

Nash, C. (1999) 'Irish placenames: post-colonial locations', *Transactions of the Institute of British Geographers*, Vol. 24 (4): 457–480.

Newhouse, J. (1997) 'Europe's rising regionalism', *Foreign Affairs* 76 (1): 67–84.

Newman, D. (1996) 'Shared spaces – separate spaces: The Israel–Palestine peace process', *Geojournal* 39: 363–376.

Newman, D. (1998a) 'Creating the fences of territorial separation: the discourses of Israeli–Palestinian conflict resolution', *Geopolitics and International Boundaries*, Vol. 2 (2): 1–35.

Newman, D. (1998b) 'Concrete and metaphysical landscapes: the geopiety of homeland socialization in the Land of Israel' in Mitchell, R. W. & Brodsky, H. (eds.) *Visions of Land and Community: Geography in Jewish Studies*, Maryland: University of Maryland Press: 153–182.

Newman, D. (1999a) 'Comments on Daniel Elazar, political geography and political science', *Political Geography*, Vol. 18: 905–911.

Newman, D. (1999b) 'Real spaces – Symbolic spaces: Interrelated notions of territory in the Arab-Israel conflict' in Diehl, P. (ed.) *A Road Map to War: Territorial Dimensions of International Conflict*, Vanderbilt University Press.

Newman, D. (1999c) 'Into the millennium: the study of international boudaries in an era of global and technological change', *Boundary and Security Bulletin*, Vol. 7 (4): 63–71.

Newman, D. (2000) 'Boundaries, borders and barriers: on the territorial demarcation of lines' in Jacobson, D., Mathias, A. & Lapid, Y. (eds.) *Identity, Borders, Orders: New Directions in International Relations Theory*.

Newman, D. & Paasi, A. (1998) 'Fences and neighbours in a postmodern world: boundary narratives in political geography', *Progress in Human Geography* 22 (2).

Nietschmann, B. (1994) 'The "Fourth World": nations versus states' in Demko, G. J. & Woods, W. B. (eds.) *Reordering the World: Geopolitical Perspectives on the Twenty First Century*, Boulder, Co.: Westview Press.

O'Loughlin, J & Kolossov, V. (1998) 'New borders for new world orders: territorialities at the fin-de-siecle', *Geojournal* (in press).

Ohmae, K. (1995) *The End of the Nation State, The Rise of Regional Economies*, London: Free Press.

Paasi, A (1995) 'Constructing territories, boundaries and regional identities' in Forsberg, T. (ed.) *Contested Territory: Border Disputes at the Edge of the Former Soviet Empire*, Aldershot: Edward Elgar: 42–61.

Paasi, A (1996a) *Territories, Boundaries and Consciousness: The Changing Geographies of the Finnish-Russian Border*, Chichester: John Wiley.

Paasi, A. (1996b) 'Inclusion, exclusion and territorial identities: The meanings of boundaries in the globalizing geopolitical landscape', *Nordisk Samhallgeografisk Tidskrift* 23: 3–18.

Paasi, A. (1998) 'Boundaries as social processes: territoriality in the world of flows', *Geopolitics*, Vol. 3 (1) (Special issue: *Boundaries, Territory and Postmodernity*).

Prescott, V. (1987) *Political Frontiers and Boundaries*. Chicago: Aldine Publishing Company.

Ramutsindela, M. (1999) 'African Boundaries and their Interpreters', *Geopolitics*, Vol. 4 (2).

Shapiro, M. J. & Alker H. R. (eds.) (1996) *Challenging Boundaries: Global Flows, Territorial Identities*, Minneapolis: University of Minneapolis Press.

Sibley, D. (1995) *Geographies of Exclusion: Society and Difference in the West*, London: Routledge.

Soysal, Y. N. (1996) 'Changing citizenship in Europe: remarks on postnational membership and the national state' in Cesarani, D. & Fulbrook, M. (eds.) *Citizenship, Nationality and Migration in Europe*, London & New York: Routledge: 17–29.

Taylor, P. J. (1994) 'The state as container: territoriality in the modern world-system', *Progress in Human Geography* 18: 151–162.

Taylor, P. J. (1995) 'Beyond containers: internationality, interstateness, interterritoriality', *Progress in Human Geography* 19: 1–15.

Taylor, P. J. (1996) 'Territorial absolutism and its evasions', *Geography Research Forum* 16.

Van der Wusten, H. (1994) 'Variations of territoriality: states and borders in present day Europe' in Gallusser, W. A. (ed.) *Political Boundaries and Coexistence*, Bern: Peter Lang: 402–412.

Waterman, S. (1994) 'Boundaries and the changing world political order' in Schofield, C. H. (ed.) *World Boundaries, Vol. I: Global Boundaries*, London: Routledge: 23–35.

Yeung, H (1998) 'Capital, state and space: contesting the borderless world', *Transactions of the Institute of British Geographers*, Vol. 23 (3): 291–310.

Yiftachel, O. (1991) 'State policies, land control and an ethnic minority: the Arabs in the Galilee, Israel', *Society and Space* 9: 329–352.

Yiftachel, O. (1998) 'The internal frontier: territorial control and ethnic relations in Israel' in Yiftachel, O. & Meir, A. (eds.) *Ethnic Frontiers and Peripheries*, Boulder: Westview Press Co: 39–68.

Zerubavel, Y. (1995) *Recovered Roots: Collective Memory and the Making of an Israeli National Tradition*, Chicago: Chicago University Press.

3
Is the Notion of Territorial Sovereignty Obsolete?

Marcelo G. Kohen

GRIM PROSPECTS FOR SOVEREIGNTY?

The year 1998 marks the 350th anniversary of the Peace of Westphalia, a peace which symbolically marks the beginning of the existence of the modern sovereign state. Since 1648 the principal actors in international relations have been sovereign and equal subjects with a territorial basis. It is no coincidence that 'sovereignty' and 'territory' are inextricably linked terms: the events that led to the emergence of the modern state had as their mainstay the territorial basis of the exercise of power.

In light of this anniversary, it seems appropriate to consider the validity of the notion of 'sovereignty'. Today it suffers from a rather poor reputation. Globalisation, interdependence and integration are contemporary phenomena which supposedly render the traditional concept of sovereignty obsolete. Indeed, more and more of the powers which pertained to states not so long ago are today vested in international institutions. Moreover, sovereignty is often perceived as the last rampart to which authoritarian regimes refer in order to prevent the implementation of human rights and other contemporary values, if not to conceal atrocities and preclude judgement and condemnation. Thus, those who persist in their attachment to the notion of sovereignty are considered to be swimming against the tide of history (Henkin, 1994).

In addition, some authors have undertaken the task of 'deconstructing' the idea of sovereignty by affirming its significance on the domestic plane – that is to say, within the limits of the state – whilst marginalising its role in the realm of international relations. According to this view, 'internal' or 'national' sovereignty would still be a useful tool of political science to designate the organ having the plenitude of power. 'External' or 'international' sovereignty, on the other hand, would be an idea condemned to the shelves of history, in view of the fact that the limitations on a state's freedom of action now touch its most vital interests (Lauterpacht, 1997: 137–150). Some scholars go even further, and refer to a new notion, 'inter-sovereignty', in order to explain the relinquishment of sovereignty by states in fields of common interest, where the decisions are shared with the other members of the international community (Seara Vazquez, 1988).

There is a great misperception about sovereignty, due perhaps to the early definition given to it by the theorists who first used the term. Bodin defined sovereignty as 'la puissance absolue et perpétuelle d'une République'[1] (Bodin,

Borderlands Under Stress (M.A. Pratt and J.A. Brown (eds), ISBN 90-411-9790-7).
© Kluwer Law International, 2000.

1576), or 'summa in cives ac subditos legisbusque soluta potestats' (Bodin, 1586). This led some to consider that the power held by states, called 'sovereignty', was absolute. Yet, from the outset this was not the idea. Sovereignty has never been absolute; it has been subordinated to international law. Sovereignty simply means no dependence *on any other power*. As Vattel clearly stated in his well-known definition: 'Toute Nation qui se gouverne à elle-même, sous quelque forme que ce soit, sans dépendance d'aucun étranger, est un Etat souverain'[2] (Vattel, 1758). In a society composed of sovereign states, the law that regulates their relations is above them.[3] Needless to say, the evolution of international society, especially in the last decade, has led to the even greater interdependence of its members, having as its corollary a decrease in the number of issues which until recently fell to the domestic jurisdiction of states.

It is not the purpose of this paper to deny these important phenomena, which have changed considerably the power of states and their international relations. However, these changes, irrespective of the importance they certainly have, do not imply the disappearance of the notion of sovereignty (Virally, 1977: 179–195). What is repeatedly called the relinquishment or 'abandonment' of sovereignty should rather be perceived as an *exercise of it*: states are free to limit their jurisdiction, and to transfer part – even substantial parts – of their powers to other institutions. As the Permanent Court of International Justice stated in its first judgement:

> The Court declines to see in the conclusion of any treaty by which a state undertakes to perform or refrain from performing a particular act an abandonment of its sovereignty. No doubt any convention creating an obligation of this kind places a restriction upon the exercise of the sovereign rights of the state, in the sense that it requires them to be exercised in a certain way. But the right of entering in international engagements is an attribute of state sovereignty.[4]

Thus, the distinction must be made between the *transfer* of sovereign powers and their *relinquishment*. The clue to that distinction lies in the states' capacity to recover the sovereign powers; or, put another way, whether or not the transfer is permanent. An independent state that decides to become a member of a federal state consents to the permanent loss of part of its powers (e.g. defence, foreign affairs) in favour of the central government. It cannot recover them, unless it successfully secedes. However, an independent state that is a member of an integrated institution such as the European Union or, more generally, any international organisation, always retains the option to withdraw and, in so doing, recover the powers it has delegated.

TERRITORIAL SOVEREIGNTY

The concept of 'territorial sovereignty' has come under the same kinds of criticism as the concept of sovereignty itself. Were territorial sovereignty obsolete, this classical term of art would be no more than a purely symbolic manifestation of identity, void of its original meaning. Moreover, territorial sovereignty is traditionally confined to one particular status: the state's spatial sphere of jurisdiction. This definition does not take into account other statuses which today would be more relevant.

At the outset, the concept of territorial sovereignty must be recalled. The Arbitral Award of 7 September 1910 in the *North Atlantic Coast Fisheries Case* between Great Britain and the United States (US), dealing with the right to regulate fishing in conformity with the Anglo–American Treaty of 1818, sketched the relationship between sovereignty and territory by stating:

> Considering that the right to regulate the liberties conferred by the Treaty of 1818 is an attribute of sovereignty, and as such must be held to reside in the territorial sovereign, unless the contrary be provided; and considering that one of the essential elements of sovereignty is that it is to be exercised within territorial limits, and that, failing proof to the contrary, the territory is co-terminous with the Sovereignty.[5]

More celebrated, the Arbitral Award of 4 April 1928 in the *Island of Palmas Case* between the Netherlands and the US contains a more elaborated description of the notion of territorial sovereignty:

> ... sovereignty in relation to a portion of the surface of the globe is the legal condition necessary for the inclusion of such portion in the territory of any particular state. Sovereignty in relation to territory is in the present award called 'territorial sovereignty'.... Territorial sovereignty ... involves the exclusive right to display the activities of a state. This right has as corollary a duty: the obligation to protect within the territory the rights of other states.... Without manifesting its territorial sovereignty in a manner corresponding to circumstances, the state cannot fulfil this duty.[6]

Although these definitions serve to circumscribe the idea, they do not explain what actually characterises territorial sovereignty. It is the plenitude of state jurisdiction upon a given territory, which includes the capacity to dispose of it. To sum up, sovereignty is the highest degree of jurisdiction of a state over a given space.[7] Viewed from another perspective, territory is the only space where sovereignty can be applied. The scope of territory is often commonly understood as comprising only the emerged surfaces of the globe. Yet territory also embraces the internal waters, the territorial sea and the airspace above them.[8] Other spaces, like the exclusive economic zone (EEZ), the continental shelf, the high seas, the deep seabed and outer space, escape the possibility of being submitted to sovereignty.

The display of state power over a territory is normally the main *manifestation* of sovereignty, but it is not the main *characteristic* of sovereignty. A state can control a territory without being its sovereign. In German the term *Gebietshoheit* (and in French *suprématie territoriale*) refers to the display of state power over territory, as distinct from *territoriale Souveranität*, which is the capacity to dispose of the territory in the last resort (Verdross *et al*, 1980). This distinction is sometimes referred to as that between 'sovereignty' and the *'exercise* of sovereignty', yet the terminology can lead to confusion. Only the state that has title to the territory can dispose of it. In practice, the common situation is that in which the state that displays state power over a territory is its sovereign. The other – exceptional – hypothesis can be divided into two categories: those states that exercise power in conformity with international law, and those that exercise power illegally. An example of the former is the American and British *Gebietshoheit* over, respectively, the Canal Zone and most of Hong Kong. Panama and China transferred the display of state power to the US and Britain but retained the sovereignty. Therefore, what China recovered from Britain in 1997 was its control over the 'New Territories' of Hong Kong, not its sovereignty. Similarly, Panama will recover the administration over the Canal Zone at the end of the century.[9] An example of *Gebietshoheit* which did not conform to international law was the illegal presence of South Africa in Namibia after the termination of the mandate by the United Nations (UN).[10]

The question remains whether this theoretical construction is still valid today. To my mind, despite the very important changes that have occurred in recent years, nothing has challenged it seriously. States have probably transferred more powers to international institutions in recent decades than ever before, but in so doing they have not abandoned them and they remain, therefore, sovereign. The notion of 'international concern' has a wider scope today than before but, nevertheless, the notion of domestic jurisdiction has not disappeared. The exercise of power, whether 'national' or 'supranational', remains essentially a territorial exercise. Laws continue to be adopted in order to be applied over a given territory; the Executive continues to take decisions applicable within the limits of its territorial jurisdiction; judges are competent to deal with cases only if they have territorial jurisdiction. Even 'supranational' decisions taken by organs of the European Union are applicable only to the extent of the territorial limits designated by member states. Hence, territory continues to mark the sphere of jurisdiction of states and international institutions. A good example of the truth of this is the strong international opposition to the Helms–Burton law (Cuban Liberty and Solidarity (LIBERTAD) Act of 1996), in which the US claimed jurisdiction over the activities of foreign companies and individuals performed outside American territory. In addition, recent phenomena, united under the heading of 'globalisation', in the fields of, for example, communications, economics in general and trade in particular, and the environment are leading to a great level of interdependence. But, as Michel Virally pointed out more than 20 years ago, the opposite of independence is not interdependence, but dependence. Sovereignty and interdependence do not exclude each other (Virally, 1977: 192).

The distinction between *Gebietshoheit* and territorial sovereignty also continues to be useful. Effectiveness alone does not enable the one who actually controls the state activity of a territory to become its sovereign.[11] Indeed, recent events indicate the opposite: the more international law develops, the less mere control over a territory is decisive in the establishment of sovereignty. The judgement of the International Court of Justice in the matter of the Aouzu Strip clearly illustrates this assertion.[12]

OTHER TERRITORIAL STATUSES

Territorial sovereignty is just one of the forms that the relationship between a subject of international law and a given territory may take. It is a neglected fact that other legal statuses are possible, including administration, autonomy, condominium, trusteeship, non-self-governing territories, and special international regimes such as that applying to Antarctica.[13] The difference between the legal territorial statuses lies in the extent of the prerogatives, rights and obligations of a state or another subject of international law upon a given territory.

The question is whether territorial statuses other than sovereignty have a predominant role today. The emergence of more than 20 new independent states, and the struggle of some peoples for statehood, who thereupon acquire sovereignty over their territories, clearly show that territorial sovereignty remains essential. Furthermore, these are not 'peripheral' events. Even 'old' states remain attached to the idea of sovereignty. For instance, it is worth noting that during the negotiations for the establishment of an all-European mechanism for the settlement of disputes within the framework of the Organisation for Security and Cooperation in Europe (OSCE), the United Kingdom strongly insisted on the need to include a clause allowing states' parties to exclude from the scope of those procedures 'disputes concerning a state's territorial integrity, ... title to sovereignty over land territory, or competing claims with regard to jurisdiction over other areas'.[14]

Mandates and *trusteeships* are regimes of the past. The last trusteeship came to an end in 1994,[15] and the resurrection of this system is not foreseeable, since it was conceived in the UN Charter as a means of preparation for the future independence of the peoples concerned. At present, the case of Bosnia and Herzegovina resembles one of trusteeship, taking into account the fundamental role of international organisations and their representatives in the decision-making and supervision of the implementation of the Dayton/Paris Agreement. Sovereignty, however, has been preserved; Bosnia and Herzegovina exists as an independent state with its own authorities. Today there does not appear to be a conflict to which the system of mandates and trusteeships could be applied.

By definition, *international administration* can be nothing but an interim arrangement, put in place by the UN, until the final decision of the interested parties is reached. Subjects of international administration include Irian Jaya more than 30 years ago, whilst the future international status of the territory was being decided, and Cambodia, whilst internal conflicts were being resolved.

The so-called '*non-self-governing territories*' also constitute a remnant of the colonial past, and are therefore condemned to disappear in the near future. Realising this, the current British government has decided to transform its 'dependent territories' into 'overseas territories', as France did half a century earlier.

Other international regimes also deserve consideration – for example, the International Sea-Bed Authority set up by the UN Convention on the Law of the Sea (UNCLOS), Part XI, in order to administer the 'Area' of seabed and ocean floor beyond the limits of national jurisdiction; and the regime applicable to Antarctica, which originated in the 1959 Treaty of Washington and which has since been developed by numerous other related agreements. Part XI of UNCLOS could only be implemented through the adoption of a further agreement on 28 July 1994 – which amounted in practice to a modification of Part XI – in order to satisfy the interests of the developed countries, particularly the US. Now that the system begins to work, it must be said that it is an extraordinary development in the management of spaces and their resources. Indeed, for the first time a permanent international authority will entirely control a given space on behalf of humankind. This revolutionary regime, the 'common heritage of mankind', appears to be applicable only to what one could call 'new' spaces, such as the abovementioned 'Area' or outer space. States have agreed not to appropriate such spaces under sovereignty or even sovereign rights, as they did for other 'new' maritime spaces created in the last half of this century, such as the continental shelf or the EEZ. To establish such a regime for territory in general, and inhabited areas in particular, would earlier have required the consent of the territory's sovereign (or the parties to a dispute). It is difficult to find any reason why states would be ready to make such a concession.

The case of Antarctica is different, and, one might add, unique. As is well-known, states have differing perceptions of the legal status of Antarctica. The discussion even involves the question of whether Antarctica is a territory in the legal sense of this term, and then whether or not it is open to effective occupation as a means of appropriation. Although all parties to the Antarctic Treaty have reserved their legal position, a new international regime has been implemented since 1959. This regime is a successful one and is likely to last in the long run. The lack of permanent population, the difficulties inherent in its location and the impossibility of ensuring an adequate display of real power explain its unique character and the unlikely possibility of this regime being applied to other regions of the world.

Autonomy is a particular regime that is not self-contained – it is always connected to a higher regime, as may be seen, for example, in the cases of decentralised states, Greenland, the Aaland (Ahvenanmaa) islands and, more recently, Scotland, Wales and Northern Ireland. Autonomy is not a substitute for sovereignty; it is, in fact, subordinate to it. For this reason, disputes sometimes arise over whether a region should be given autonomy or admitted as a new sovereign state (or, indeed, granted no special regime at all) – for example, Bosnia and Herzegovina, Kosovo, and Kurdistan. The case of the Palestinian Authority is special. In this case, autonomy is a temporary regime pending the final settlement of the conflict, in accordance with the so-called Oslo Agreements.

A 'POST-SOVEREIGNTY' MEANS OF SOLVING TERRITORIAL DISPUTES?

The interest in the different regimes depicted above is due to the current temptation to solve disputes concerning sovereignty by attributing to the territory in question another legal status – for example, agreeing to a form of joint administration, 'shared sovereignty', autonomy or internationalisation, in which circumstances sovereignty would not be attributed to either of the parties. Cooperation instead of confrontation seems to be the catchword. This appears reasonable: instead of contesting what is viewed as 'nominal' sovereignty, parties to a dispute should try to solve it by dealing directly with the actual exercise of power. In short, the parties should focus upon *Gebietshoheit*, not on sovereignty. It is interesting to study whether these are effective solutions or, on the contrary, merely attempts to avoid or postpone final settlement of disputes.

Recent state practice shows that joint administration was used as an interim arrangement between Namibia and South Africa for Walvis Bay. 'Shared sovereignty', for its part, is currently invoked by the present Spanish and Argentine governments in respect of Gibraltar and the Falkland Islands (Islas Malvinas). One could also wonder whether such complicated territorial disputes as those concerning the Spratly and the Senkaku islands could not be solved by some form of joint control.

The example of Walvis Bay is significant. This former British enclave in the former German Colony of South West Africa, annexed to the Cape Colony in 1884, was claimed by Namibia as part of its territory. In 1992 South Africa and Namibia agreed to establish a Joint Administrative Authority as an interim arrangement pending a final settlement of the dispute.[16] This interim joint administration did not last very long; by the treaty of 28 February 1994 Walvis Bay was 'incorporated/integrated' into the Republic of Namibia the following day.[17] In such circumstances joint administration reveals itself as an appropriate way to prepare a final settlement. It creates a climate of confidence between the parties, facilitating the gradual transfer of powers or allowing the organisation of referendums on an impartial basis.

In contrast, 'shared sovereignty' (joint ownership, co-imperium, condominium or however otherwise termed), conceived as the permanent solution to a dispute, presents many difficulties which are not easy to avoid. Primarily, the territory does not belong to any of the co-sovereigns. It would be misleading to believe that both states could simultaneously consider it to be part of their respective territories. Consequently, the respective legislation, administration and jurisdiction of each of the co-sovereigns are not automatically applicable to the territory; nor are the international agreements applicable to the territories of the co-sovereigns extended *per se* to the 'shared' territory. In the Colonial Office Reports on the New Hebrides it is stated that:

> It is clear that ... the New Hebrides is neither British nor French and, though Britain and France each reserve sovereignty over their own nationals, there is no

territorial sovereignty (unless it can be said to be jointly exercised) and the natives bear no allegiance to either Power. Incidentally, for this reason, no multilateral convention applies to the New Hebrides unless it is applied as a result of joint agreement between the two Signatory Powers. In fact the Condominium is, *vis-à-vis* Britain and France, in effect, a foreign administration, because neither one nor the other controls or administers it.[18]

Personal jurisdiction is also problematic. Nationality – from the point of view of international law – can only be granted by a state; since the 'shared' territory is not an independent state, the possibility of a third nationality is excluded. The normal arrangement is therefore that each state has jurisdiction over its own nationals, as was the case in the New Hebrides. Not surprisingly, permanent clashes arise from this situation in which two different jurisdictions are applicable to different persons in the same territory. The situation of foreigners can also be very complicated. The example of the New Hebrides, which shows both the consequences of the existence of different personal regimes and the serious difficulties which can arise between two linguistic communities after independence, corroborates the fact that condominium is not a good permanent regime for inhabited territories.[19] In fact, the 'shared' territory is in a legal limbo: belonging to neither of the co-sovereigns, it nevertheless constitutes a sovereign territory, yet without an independent, international personality. In a true condominium, the 'holder' of the territory is the community of both states. If this is not the case, the territory is not a condominium but rather an independent state governed by an organ composed of the officials (or, in the case of Andorra, with the president of France, the Spanish Bishop of Seu d'Urgell) of two different countries.

'Shared sovereignty' cannot be envisaged as a solution to be adopted by an international tribunal dealing with a territorial dispute. As the Arbitral Award in the *Lake Lannoux Case* (France/Spain) states:

> [S]ometimes, two states exercise conjointly jurisdiction over certain territories (joint ownership, *co-imperium*, or *condominium*); likewise, in certain international arrangements, the representatives of states exercise conjointly a certain jurisdiction in the name of those states or in the name of organizations. But these cases are exceptional, and international judicial decisions are slow to recognize their existence, especially when they impair the territorial sovereignty of a state.[20]

The only possible exception concerns those parts of territory composed of water – rivers, historic bays or internal waters in general.[21]

Indeed, if one turns to international practice, the conclusion is that cases of condominia are rare and generally confined to the areas already mentioned. Other condominia applicable to land tend to be symbolic, such as the Isle of Pheasants located at the mouth of the Bidassoa River on the Franco–Spanish border; its small size and lack of population explain the continuation of this ancient regime.

Because it constitutes a third regime, to be distinguished from both of the co-sovereigns, condominium applicable to inhabited regions either amounts to the creation of an independent state or leads in the long run to the independence of the territory. Andorra, now a member of the UN – and irrespective of any discussion about its true nature as a condominium – is an example of the former, and the New Hebrides, today the independent state of Vanuatu, is an example of the latter.

There are cases in which one state party to a settlement is not willing to admit explicitly that it has relinquished its position. In such cases, use of the word 'sovereignty' is avoided. This is the case with the Treaty of the River Plate and its corresponding maritime boundary, according to which the island of Martin Garcia was placed under the 'jurisdiction' of the Argentine Republic, and was exclusively designated a natural reserve. The headquarters of the Administrative Commission of the River Plate (a bi-national entity with its own personality) is also, according to the aforesaid Treaty, located in Martin Garcia.[22] It is clear that by this treaty, and despite its wording, Uruguay recognises Argentina's sovereignty over Martin Garcia and, at the same time, Argentina consents to restrictions on the exercise of its sovereignty over the island. This solution, then, has nothing to do with so-called 'shared sovereignty'. The example is also interesting because the same treaty sets up a common zone for the River Plate, but establishes clear-cut provisions for the attribution of sovereignty to one or the other party in the event that new islands emerge.[23]

A true regime of condominium or 'shared sovereignty' must consist of a more-or-less similar distribution of functions, or the creation of organs made up of representatives of both sides. If the so-called shared sovereignty regime vests the essential powers in one of the states and grants some limited rights to the other, the case is similar to that of Martin Garcia: an implicit recognition by one of the parties of the sovereignty of the other, with some limitations on its exercise. International practice contains many examples of territories under the sovereignty of one state, in which another has certain rights – for example, military bases established in foreign territories (such as Diego Garcia), rights of passage, free zones, and utilisation of watercourses. In these cases 'shared sovereignty' is simply a way of disguising the recognition by one of the parties of the sovereignty of the other.

Sovereignty issues can also be solved by adding the element of cooperation in matters of natural resource exploitation,[24] as in the case of the Neutral Zone between Kuwait and Saudi Arabia. The agreement of 7 July 1965 is a good example of delimitation of a 'no-man's land' between two parties. It clearly states who is the sovereign of the territory, but provides for the sharing of the natural resources in the area. In fact, this treaty put an end to a situation of 'shared sovereignty' in which each party had equal rights; the treaty describes the lack of regulation over these rights as a state of affairs 'of a provisional nature which entailed serious practical difficulties'.[25] These states thus adopted a wise solution and one which sets a worthy example: instead of confusion, they delimited what needed to be delimited (i.e. the exercise of state authority over persons and territory) and shared what there was to share (i.e. natural resources).

CONCLUSION

Sovereignty still characterises the main actors in international relations. Its critics, who focus upon its use as a barrier against compliance with human rights, neglect the fact that the different endeavours to impose hegemony have been made with the idea of limiting the exercise of sovereignty. Brezhnev's 'limited sovereignty' doctrine, Johnson's 'ideological frontiers' and Reagan's 'collective self-defence' are, to this extent, paradigmatic. One cannot lose sight of the fact that it is the very notion of sovereignty which allows one to speak of equality among states, despite disparities in size, military power, economic development etc. To stress the idea of sovereignty is tantamount to affirming the equality of states from the legal point of view – equals before the law, equals in the elaboration of international legal rules.

Even those who believe that sovereignty in its external or international sense must be seen as a myth, recognise that the only exception is when the term is used to describe a state's title to territory (Lauterpacht, 1997: 149).

'Shared sovereignty', joint administration, autonomy without deciding who is the sovereign of the territory – these are, at best, only policies for temporarily dealing with territorial disputes in order to create better conditions for achieving a final settlement. In a world still essentially composed of sovereign states, where nearly the whole of the emerged surface of the earth is divided and attributed to them, the creation of such hybrid institutions is misleading. At worse, by begging the question of sovereignty, they are attempts to avoid facing the problem which is at the core of territorial disputes. Conceived as a means of final settlement, they actually create the potential basis for new, and probably even more complicated, sources of conflict. What are presented as new ways to deal with territorial problems are in fact remnants of the past, Middle Age phenomena suited to a society in which power and control over the territory was singularly dispersed. As has been stated:

> [C]ondominia appear as historical relics from the age of feudal and patrimonial states or as patently inadequate anomalies. However, even during the twentieth century, when the dogma of sovereignty gradually grew less rigorous, the condominium did not establish itself as anything greater than an emergency or temporary solution or a measure of last resort. (Schneider, 1992.)

One therefore reaches the conclusion that territorial disputes cannot avoid the crucial matter of sovereignty, on the basis that, for the time being and in the foreseeable future, the ultimate destiny of all territories (with the important exception of Antarctica) is to be submitted to sovereignty.

NOTES

1 'The absolute and eternal power of a Republic.'

2 'Any Nation which governs itself, in whatever manner, without dependence upon a foreign power, is a sovereign state.'

3 In his separate opinion appended to the advisory opinion on the *Customs Régime between Germany and Austria*, Judge Anzilotti stated that independence 'is really no more than the normal condition of states according to international law; it may also be described as *sovereignty (suprema potestas)*, or *external sovereignty*, by which is meant that the state has over it no other authority than that of international law'. *PCIJ* (1931) Series A/B, No. 41: 57.

4 S.S. 'Wimbledon' judgments. *PCIJ* (1923) Series A, No. 1: 25.

5 *UNRIAA*, Vol. XI, 180.

6 *Ibid.*, Vol. II, 838–839.

7 J. H. Verzijl defined it as 'the plenitude of exclusive competences appertaining to a state under public international law within the boundaries of a definite portion of the globe' (Verzijl, 1968). J. L. Brierly speaks of 'the fullest rights over territory known to the law' (Waldock, 1967). See also Sperdutti (1959) and Shaw (1982).

8 See *Military and Paramilitary Activities in and against Nicaragua (Nicaragua v. United States of America)*, *Merits, Judgment, ICJ Reports* (1986) 14: 111, para. 212.

9 See the Treaty between Panama and the US of 7 September 1977 and the Joint Declaration of the UK and the PRC of 19 December 1984 (texts in *International Legal Materials (ILM)* (1977) Vol. XVI: 1021–1098 and *ILM* (1984) Vol. XXIII: 1366–1387).

10 See *Legal Consequences for states of the Continued Presence of South Africa in Namibia (South West Africa) notwithstanding Security Council Resolution 276 (1970)*, Advisory Opinion, *ICJ Reports* (1971) 16: 54, para. 118.

11 On this topic, see Kohen (1997).

12 See *Territorial Dispute (Libyan Arab Jamahiriya/Chad)*, *Judgment, ICJ Reports* (1994): 6.

13 Leaving to one side military occupation, which by definition pre-supposes an interim and *de facto* situation.

14 Article 26 in the Stockholm Convention on Conciliation and Arbitration within the (then) CSCE. *ILM* (1992) Vol. 32: 564. See Caflisch (1998).

15 See UNSC Resolution 963 of 29 November 1994 on the American trusteeship of Palaos. Palaos is an independent state associated with the US and a member of the UN.

16 See the exchange of notes of 30 October and 9 November 1992 in *ILM* (1993) Vol. 32: 1154.

17 Text in *ILM* (1994) Vol. 33: 1528. The expression 'incorporation/integration' was used in this treaty in order to safeguard the positions of the parties: according to South Africa, it was a case of transfer of sovereignty ; for Namibia, on the contrary, it was the restoration of its territorial integrity.

18 Colonial Office (1955). The same can be found in previous reports.

19 On condominium in general see the reference book of Coret (1960). For a more recent study, see Sabia de Barberis (1994).

20 *International Law Reports* (1957) Vol. 24: 127.

21 As was the case of the Gulf of Fonseca, considered as a condominium among the riparian states by the Central American Court of Justice in 1917 and confirmed more

recently by a Chamber of the ICJ in the *Land, Island and Maritime Frontier Dispute (El Salvador/Honduras; Nicaragua intervening)*, *ICJ Reports* (1992): 596–602.

22 See Articles 45 and 63 of the Treaty of 19 November 1973. *ILM* (1974) Vol. 13: 251 at 259 and 261.

23 *Ibid.*, Article 44: 251.

24 On this topic, see del Castillo de Laborde (1994).

25 *ILM* (1964) Vol. 4: 1134.

BIBLIOGRAPHY

Bodin, J. (1576) *Les six livres de la République*, Bk. I, Ch. VIII.

Bodin, J. (1586) *De Republica*, Bk. I, Ch VIII.

Brierly, J.L. (1967) *The Law of Nations. An Introduction to International Law* (6th edition by Sir H. Waldock), Oxford: Clarendon Press: 162.

Caflisch, L. (1998) 'The OSCE Court of Conciliation and Arbitration: Some Facts and Issues' in Bothe M. *et al* (ed.) *The OSCE in the Maintenance of Peace and Security*, Dordrecht: Kluwer: 381–408 at 384–385.

Colonial Office (1955), *Report on New Hebrides Anglo-French Condominium for the Years 1953 & 1954*, London: HMSO: 34.

Coret, A. (1960) *Le Condominium*, Paris, LGDJ: 333.

del Castillo de Laborde, L. (1994) 'Soberanía y recursos naturales. Modo de solución de controversias referidas a recursos naturales pertencientes a más de un Estado' in *La soberanía en las relaciones internacionales*, Buenos Aires: CARI, Vol. III: 131–158.

Henkin, L. (1994) 'The Mythology of Sovereignty' in St. MacDonald, R. (ed.) *Essays in Honour of Wang Tieya*, Dordrecht: Kluwer: 351–358.

Kohen, M. G. (1997) *Possession contestée et souveraineté territoriale*, Paris, PUF: xxv and 579.

Lauterpacht, E. (1997) 'Sovereignty – Myth or Reality?', *International Affairs* 73, 1.

Sabia de Barberis, G. (1994) 'Soberanía y régimen de condominio como solución de conflictos territoriales' in *La soberanía en las relaciones internacionales*, Buenos Aires, CARI, Vol. III: 43–84.

Schneider, P. (1992) 'Condominium' in Bernhardt, R. (ed.) *Encyclopedia of Public International Law*, Vol. 1: 732–735 at 734.

Seara Vazquez, M. (1988) 'Hacia el concepto de intersoberanía', *Liber Amicorum. Colección de estudios jurídicos en homenaje al Prof. Dr. D. José Pérez Montero*, Oviedo, Universidad, Vol. III: 134–158.

Shaw, M. (1982) 'Territory in International Law', *Netherlands Yearbook of International Law*, Vol. XIII: 61–91 at 73.

Sperdutti, G. (1959) 'Sovranità territoriale, atti di disposizione di territori ed effettività in diritto internazionale', *Rivista di diritto internazionale*, Vol. XLII: 404–425 at 405.

Vattel, E. (1758) *Le droit des gens*, Bk. I, Ch. I, § 4.

Verdross, A., Simma, B. & Geiger, R. (1980) 'Territoriale Souveränität und Gebietshoheit', *Osterreichische Zeitschrift für öffentliches Recht und Völkerrecht*, Vol. 31: 223–245.

Verzijl, J. H. (1968) *International Law in Historical Perspective*. Leyden: Sijthoff, II: 12–13.

Virally, M. (1977) 'Une pierre d'angle qui résiste au temps: avatars et pérennité de l'idée de souveraineté', Institut Universitaire de Hautes Etudes Internationales (IUHEI), *Les relations internationales dans un monde en mutation*, Leyden, Sijthoff: 179–195.

4
The End of the Nation-State?
Borders in the Age of Globalisation

Herbert Dittgen

In the era of globalisation, the thesis of the 'end of the nation-state' has found widespread approval in the social sciences. This thesis claims, in a descriptive way, that the nation-state has lost control of international financial markets and transnational corporations. The market determines the fate of the citizens, whereas the state retreats and loses its authority; by the same token, the territorial borders of states lose their meaning.

In a normative sense, it is argued by Jürgen Habermas and others that the nation-state has lost its function in the light of global challenges. Therefore a new supranational or global governance is the order for a new age.

This paper tests that thesis with a new approach. It examines the functions and functional changes of borders. The assumption is that this analysis will provide a particularly vivid illustration of the changing role of the state and the changing character of 'international relations'. It is argued that borders still matter and that they even become more significant, in a political and ideological sense, under the conditions of globalisation.

The overwhelming burden of state functions can only be managed by the state's retreat to a mere coordinating function. The existence of nation-states is still necessary as a framework for responsible government and political integration. Until now, no alternative has been identified. This argument is much too easily dismissed, if at all taken into account, by those who consider the nation-state to be an anachronistic institution.

INTRODUCTION

The particularistic character of the political world, the separation of political communities into *poleis*, territorial states or nation-states, has always provoked the universalist criticism which considers the drawing of borders to be artificial and incompatible with universal humanity. Such demarcations were even suspected of being one of humankind's greatest evils. Edmund Burke, for example, wrote in *A Vindication of Natural Society* – a response to Rousseau's *Discourse on the Origin and Foundation of Inequality* – that 'this artificial division of mankind, into separate societies, is a perpetual source in itself of hatred and dissension among them' (Burke, 1993).

Borderlands Under Stress (M.A. Pratt and J.A. Brown (eds), ISBN 90-411-9790-7).
© Kluwer Law International, 2000.

In contrast to this is the traditional view which sees a system of states as a foregone conclusion and as the only possible form of international order. This order originated from traditional international law, from the writings of Vitoria, Suarez, Grotius and Pufendorf, and found its most important present-day representative in Hedley Bull. In 1979 he wrote, in an article with the programmatic title *The State's Positive Role in World Affairs*, that:

> the preservation of world order is not a matter of removing state barriers to the triumph of our own preferred values and institutions, but rather a matter of finding some *modus vivendi* as between these and the very different values and institutions in other parts of the world with which they will have to coexist.

Dreaming about a world order 'beyond the nation-state', writes Bull, would reveal a lot about 'how the policy-scientist's mind works but it is not what happens in world politics' (Bull, 1979). Without states and a system of states there would be absolutely no order.

Modern nation-states are constituted as communities of will which owe their legitimacy to the sovereignty of their people. Territory, people of the nation and exclusive authority of the state are congruent here. The ambivalent role of the nation-state has often been pointed out. The history of the nation-state is one of devastating war, massive oppression and bloody revolution. The formation of nation-states was at the same time the necessary, though not the only, condition for the development of a constitutional government. The nation-state was established in the course of European expansion as the universal principle of international order (Lepsius, 1990a).

The nation-state has, nevertheless, only rarely been seen as having a long future as a form of political order. Socialists saw it as a political order of capital – i.e. as a system of rule by the bourgeoisie. It was certain that the internationalisation of capital and the development of productive forces would eventually break its restricting borders.

It seemed that after two world wars and the experience with the barbarity of the Nazi regime that the history of the European nation-states had once again reached its end (Schulze, 1994: 239). This was the conviction of the initiators and founders of the European unification movement, who, contrary to de Gaulles' concept of a 'Europe of the Fatherlands', were interested in founding a European Federation which would eliminate all borders and all supposedly outdated restrictions of the nation-state.

Fifty years later the Iron Curtain disappeared, that border which had stood for the world's political schism during the post-war period and at the same time served as the orientation and motivation for the European unification movement. The nationalist ideology, which was thought to be declining, is now coming back with breathtaking speed in fast-spreading nationalist and particularistic movements.

Social scientists with a 'globalist' outlook do not appear to be impressed by this development.[1] On the contrary, their dominant issue is globalisation and the lifting of borders. They value the thesis that the nation-state is about to vanish, despite the revival of nationalist ambitions and the obvious attraction of the idea of national self-determination. As evidence one has only to consider the growing number of United Nations member states.

In this paper I will propose a different approach, in order to examine how conclusive the thesis of the 'end of the nation-state' really is. My reflections will centre around the concept of borders and their function, on the assumption that both the function and the functional change of borders will be especially illustrative of the changing character of the 'state' and international relations.

One of the fundamental characteristics of the modern state system is a clearly defined territory. The modern nation-state is, according to Anthony Gidden's definition, 'a bordered power container' (Giddens, 1987). The territorial state and nation-state are characterised in formal accordance with the law by a spatially restricted legal system, jurisdiction, administration and exclusive authority. This is what constitutes the formal principle of the *sovereignty* of the nation-state. Its *autonomy* must be differentiated from this. The concept of autonomy of the nation-state refers to its relationship to society both inside and outside of its territory and is dependent on both economic and social conditions, and on the international system; it designates the degree of independence the nation-state enjoys in different policy areas. Autonomy, therefore, unlike sovereignty, is a relative and informal criteria. The border as institution is an expression of the formal sovereignty of the state; the function of the border informs us about the autonomy of the state.

The following reflections on the future of the nation-state will be developed in four steps. First, I examine the three most important variations on the 'end of the nation-state' thesis. Secondly, the validity of the thesis will be tested with the help of a typology of the political and social functions of borders. Through this, it will become clear that a change in the function of borders is taking place, but it would be improper to conclude that this change signals the end of the nation-state. Thirdly, I will demonstrate that it has become apparent that the significance of ideological boundaries has not declined since the end of the east–west conflict, but that boundaries are, on the contrary, being drawn anew. Fourthly, I will deal again with the function of borders, with reference to three examples frequently advanced to prove the end of the nation-state: the European integration process, the post-national model of membership and the thesis of the loss of the nation-state's ability to integrate. Finally, I will make the point that the nation-state's loss of autonomy, as well as its preservation of sovereignty, should be judged positively, both in functional and normative respects.

THE 'END OF THE NATION-STATE' THESIS

The assertion that the nation-state is losing importance and is on the retreat, or that we are already living in a post-national age, is most commonly based on an economic perspective, which I will outline here as the first variation on the thesis of the end of the nation-state. It has by now become almost a platitude to say that we are living in a new economic and political world, in which the globalisation of trade and capital has undermined the economic autonomy of the state. Susan Strange even suspects that the consequence of this development will be the destruction of the basis of the nation-state as a focal point of political authority (Strange, 1996).

Another variation – there are naturally some large overlaps in these theses; the main point here is simply to emphasise that which is special in each case – refers to the socialisation of domestic and foreign policies. In international politics we are, accordingly, dealing more and more with transnational, non-governmental actions. International relations are being determined increasingly by international regimes and international organisations. Self-organisation is taking the place of government in domestic politics. The thesis that the world of states is being replaced by a world of societies was put forward by Ernst-Otto Czempiel:

> The relics of the world of states have been eliminated in Europe with the end of the East–West conflict. (Czempiel, 1990.)

In the societal world it is no longer a matter of merely maintaining an existence; now it is a matter of developing this existence. There are clear echoes here of the social universalism pronounced in the Communist Manifesto, which prophesied that a free association of human beings would take the place of the domination of humans over humans.

We find a third variation in the writings of Jean-Marie Guéhenno. In his book *La fin de la démocratie* he states that the age of the nation-states found its conclusion along with the end of the east–west conflict. The east–west conflict had polarised the world of nation-states like a magnet; now the magnet has disappeared and the filings have been set free to fall where they may. The territorial basis of political modernity is being undermined today by new forms of economic modernity. The case of the nation-state is replaced by a network, modelled after transnational firms, detached from territorial forms of order and representing an open system without borders. The end of the nation-state is at the same time the end of politics. Terms such as 'power' and 'legitimacy' simply lose their meaning, according to Guéhenno. The question of legitimacy becomes about as sensible as the question of the legitimacy of a computer program: 'the soft humming of the social machinery satisfies itself' (Guéhenno, 1993).

These empirical observations of the end of the nation-state are complemented by the normative argument that the nation-state is no longer suited for the job and has long served its time in view of the new global challenges. Jürgen Habermas formulated this in a concise manner:

> The nation-state once provided a convincing response to the historic challenge to provide in the process of dissolution a functional equivalent to pre-modern forms of social integration. Today we are faced with an analogous challenge. The globalisation of economic production and its financing, of technology and arms transfers, and particularly of ecological and military risks confront us with problems which cannot be solved within the framework of the nation-state or by the usual kind of agreements between sovereign states. If the signs are not

deceiving, the undermining of the nation-state's sovereignty will continue and the development and consolidation of supra-national ability to take political action is necessary. (Habermas, 1996a.)

FUNCTIONS AND FUNCTIONAL CHANGES OF BORDERS

In this section, the variations on the 'end of the nation-state' thesis will be tested by means of a typology of the political and social functions of borders.[2]

In a very general sense, one can say that there is no social or political phenomenon which is not determined by borders. Georg Simmel pointed out the spatial meaning of things and actions:

> The border is not a spatial fact with a sociological impact, but a sociological fact that shapes spatially. (Simmel, 1992.)

Niklas Luhmann holds the view that there could not be any differentiation of systems without borders (Luhmann, 1997). In this sense, borders can therefore be understood as a phenomenon of the nation-state, nationalities and social groups. They have a Janus-faced character; they include and they exclude. The drawing of social boundaries – i.e. the mechanism of inclusion and exclusion – is dependent on the respective social order. National borders are, however, based on the universal and globally recognised principle of reciprocity.

I differentiate between five different political and social functions for the borders of the nation-state:

- the traditional military function (i.e. the protective function)
- the legal function
- the economic function
- the ideological function
- the social-psychological function

The traditional military function

The original function of the border was to defend and protect; that is why it is guarded and fortified. In the course of the twentieth century the border has lost this protecting function. Advances in military technology, particularly the development of bombers and intercontinental missiles have made the border practically obsolete as a defence mechanism. The same holds true for the countries in the south, which have equipped themselves with military technology provided by the north. However, the smouldering border conflicts that can, at any moment, break out into new wars can nevertheless still be found; consider, for example, the border scuffles between Ecuador and Peru or between India and the People's Republic of China.[3]

Today one needs protection not only from the militarily strong neighbour but also from the economically weak neighbour, whose economic crisis or civil war leads to a massive movement of refugees across the border (Weiner, 1993). The countries of the south are often the helpless victims of such migrations; consider the recent history of the former Zaire and other African states. The northern countries are increasingly closing their borders against refugees and improving their policing and administrative systems in order to curb illegal immigration. This is particularly the case along the north–south borderline between the United States and Mexico and along the east–west border between Germany and Poland (Andreas, 1996). This leads to the conclusion that the defence function of these borders is being redefined. An end of state sovereignty and a loss of control over borders is, however, not becoming evident.

The legal function

Borders provide the framework for constitutional and legal systems and for administrative organisation; it is a frequently overlooked fact that this is the most important function of the border. Here, the border is not primarily in place to mark the range of the purview of law, but rather to mark the area in which these laws can be realised in the first place. Legitimate sanctioning mechanisms are only possible inside these borders. The protection of human rights, despite their universal validity and derivation from human nature, is dependent on the protection of fundamental rights by constitutional states. Civil and fundamental rights become completely effective only for citizens:

> As long as the individual is not recognised as a (partial) legal entity in international law, protection by international law can only be realised by the home state, the state of which he or she is a citizen. (Kimminich, 1997: 202.)

Stateless people and refugees find themselves, therefore, in a precarious situation. This is a topic which Hannah Arendt depicts very vividly, in the light of her experiences during the Second World War, in her book *The Origins of Totalitarianism* – a depiction which has lost none of its depressing actuality over time (Arendt, 1951). The rules set forth in international refugee law put states under an obligation to act in a certain way if a refugee has crossed a border and meets a certain definition; but the law does *not* establish the right to enter a country. It is true that refugees enjoy a certain international legal status, but this status does not provide for a subjective right to asylum. The international protection of human rights has yet to cross the threshold of sovereignty. The individual has no direct function as a legal entity at the level of international law; the state of which he or she is a citizen acts as mediary (Kimminich, 1992).

One cannot, therefore, speak of the end of the nation-state with regard to the legal function of the border. And one would not want to, either. It is true that international organisations are recognised by international law, but nation-states remain the most important institutions for enforcing these laws and for providing legal protection (Dahrendorf, 1994). This, incidentally, holds true for the democratic constitutional state as a whole; there is practically no democratic method of control and no democratic public beyond the territorial state.

The economic function

Currently the dominant topic has been the border's loss of function in the world economy. Regional free-trade zones as well as global trade and financial markets seem to make borders anachronistic institutions. The crucial factor for economic welfare is no longer the national economy, but rather competition on the world market. The nation-state has no control over the global flow of capital or the transactions of transnational corporations. This development is usually referred to by the term 'globalisation'. However, equating economic globalisation with the end of the nation-state may be a false conclusion, as I shall briefly substantiate.

With regard to politics, globalisation means, first, that the political arenas in which decisions are made are changing. The framework of the territorial state, which is organised hierarchically and in a state of relative autonomy, is being shattered. Governmental policies are becoming more and more embedded in a widely branching and denser network of transnational and inner-societal dependencies and negotiation relationships. A form of global control, as former German Minister of Economic Affairs Karl Schiller once propagated, is impossible in this multitude of intricate networks. The state as governmental entity often only plays the role of coordinator between a multitude of participating actors in this negotiation systems (Scharpf, 1991). State intervention is shifting increasingly from the macroeconomic to the micro-economic level; the key concepts here are deregulation, industrial policies and the promotion of research and development. Even classical diplomacy is falling more and more under pressure to promote trade and industry. When President Clinton or the German Chancellor visit China they are accompanied for the most part by representatives of business, and the success of their trip is measured primarily by the number of contracts they bring home for their national industries.

The border's loss of function in connection with the economy is thus insufficient cause to deduce the end of the nation-state. On the contrary, the new function of the nation-state, both in domestic and foreign affairs, becomes recognisable here. Internationally the nation-state is becoming a 'competition state' within the framework of a world market (Cerny, 1997). It is also taking on a coordination function inside the transnational negotiation system, just as in domestic politics.

However, the legitimacy of the nation-state is challenged by the fact that economic globalisation severely impairs its integrating function as welfare-state. Increasingly, citizens are going to have to do without the redistributing policy of the national welfare-state. In view of the reduced possibilities of setting autonomous policy, the state's much-vaunted claim to regulate is no longer redeemable. Citizens are supposedly experiencing the administrating state more intensively than ever; experiencing the true impotence of the state must therefore be that much more sobering for them – for example, in labour market policy (Dahrendorf, 1997).

The ideological function

One can speak of an ideological border in connection with a nationalist ideal. Territorial claims can be justified by such an ideological definition of borders. An ideological border can be a part of the political ends of a state if it defines itself as a homogeneous nation-state. Current examples of this type of ideological definition of borders exist in the demand for a Greater Serbia or in the Greek nationalist ideology which has led to conflicts with Albania, Macedonia and Turkey.

Borders separating ideological spheres of influence are an occurrence of the twentieth century. The most impressive and, at the same time, most gruesome manifestation of such an ideological border was the 'anti-fascist defence wall' dividing Germany, equipped with self-firing weapons. It was supposed to protect citizens from making a foolish mistake based on a lack of socialist awareness: the mistake of trying to flee. This ideological boundary divided not only Europe; it split almost the entire globe into the spheres of influence of the two superpowers. The movement of the non-aligned states was comparatively weak.

One might assume that with the end of the east–west conflict the last ideological conflict ended, and that the age of ideology is now over. But the opposite seems to be true. The drawing of ideological boundaries has increased since the end of the east–west conflict. This phenomenon will be dealt with below; first, I will consider the fifth type of border function in my typology.

The social-psychological function

Borders have an important social-psychological function. The individual constructs a territory for herself or himself (Goffman, 1971), and a forced entry into this space without an invitation or an agreement provokes emotional reactions of fear and hostility. Just as in the physical sense, these premises can only exist and offer orientation when there is a general idea of space. It is therefore necessary to have distinguishable units in political and social life. But the horizon for orientation doesn't necessarily have to be the borders of a nation-state and it doesn't at all have to necessitate the drawing of national borders which create a national identity through the construction of foe images. Local, regional and continental boundaries could just as well serve as an orientation. The cosmopolitan, whose horizon is an abstract idea of humanity and whose thoughts are not bound by borders, will always be an exception (Coulmas, 1990). Politics must take this human disposition or limitation into account. It has already been pointed out that nation-state borders have lost much of their value for orientation due to the disintegration of the traditional nation-state model. This leads to the increased importance of other local and regional orientations and relationships.

This correlation becomes dramatically clear in the countries of the south in which the nation-state is either weak or has totally collapsed. Civil war between different ethnic clans reigns when there is no government framework to provide order; two examples of the collapse of state authority and its results are Somalia and Liberia. This correlation should also provide a warning for those who consider the nation-state functionally to be an anachronism. If the nation-state defines itself as heterogeneous, with a foundation built on a separation of powers, pluralism and the protection of fundamental rights, then it will also be able to moderate and politically channel any minority problems, which are found everywhere in different degrees of virulence. The violent insistence upon the right to self-determination will probably be the most frequent cause of conflict in the world for years to come. It has been shown that drawing new borders and founding new nation-states in order to grant minorities their right of national self-determination is not a satisfactory solution to the problem, since these new borders inevitably bring about a new set of minority conflicts (Horowitz, 1997). This is evident in the problems connected with the implementation of the Dayton Agreement in Bosnia. Integration within a pluralist and federal nation-state still seems to be the best solution.

THE DRAWING OF NEW IDEOLOGICAL BORDERS

Borders have not forfeited their security functions, even in the European context. As I have already indicated, it is possible to say almost the same thing about ideological boundaries. With the end of the east–west conflict it was hoped that these kinds of boundaries would become meaningless and that the political integration of Europe would now include eastern Europe. However, the break-up of the Soviet Union, Czechoslovakia and Yugoslavia have brought to life a multitude of successor states which define themselves as nations. This massive reorganisation of the European political stage along national lines has created new and explosive national and minority conflicts (Brubaker, 1996). We are observing not the end of the nation-state, but rather its rebirth with a very close connection to nationalism; a symbiosis which most people in Europe were inclined to ascribe to a past epoch.

Both the rebirth of nationalism and the revival of the imperial 'barbarian-border' may be seen as the guiding metaphors for international order since the end of the east–west conflict. If we follow Jean-Christoph Rufin, we see that the end of the east–west conflict was accompanied by the institution of a new ideological border, a modern *limes*, which divides the northern world from the southern world – i.e. the new barbarian world (Rufin, 1991). The new *limes* between north and south is a continuous dividing line; the border-patrol in San Diego, the coastguard in Florida, the customs officers in Marseilles and the Russian police in Azerbaijan all patrol a *limes* along which north and south meet without necessarily being forcibly confronted with each other. We are living in an era of limited universalism. Law, democracy and social justice are universal ideals, but they are realised and applied only within the countries of the north. The countries of the south serve as a means of contrast whose purpose is to strengthen national identity and unity in the north – just as communism did in the days of the east–west conflict.

Samuel Huntington generated an international discussion with his 'clash of civilisations' thesis. He sees conflicts along the fault lines of civilisations as the dominant feature in world politics of the future. The values of western civilisation are unique and cannot be realised on a universal scale; the west is therefore inevitably heading for a conflict with other civilisations – i.e. the rest (Huntington, 1996).

These theses cannot be discussed here in detail, but it can generally be considered certain that globalisation does not lead to the elimination of cultural borders. On the contrary, terms such as 'globality' and 'locality', 'tradition' and 'modernity' can really only be understood as counter-ideas – as opposite sides of the same differentiation (Giesen, 1996). The diversity of cultures and their special characters only become evident with the globalisation of communication. This perception of diversity can lead to insecurity about one's own identity and, as a result, to a demonisation of that which is unfamiliar. The need for bonding and a collective identity becomes stronger in a world where everything is fluid and changeable. Ethnicity, origin or gender are increasingly perceived as unchangeable bonds, as boundaries which cannot be put into question in the political process.

These new boundary formations are also promoted by the fact that technological advances and globalisation tend to widen the spatial horizon. We are in immediate contact with contemporaries who are the product of a different history. This 'coincidence of non-simultaneousness' which is generated by globalisation, leads to contact between strangers who tend to disassociate themselves from one another. The framework of the nation-state is – especially in view of these new boundary formations which contain the potential for a variety of conflicts – not becoming obsolete; on the contrary, it is still essential. The nation-state is still the most important institution to ensure the rule of law in an explosive world.

THE END OF THE NATION-STATE: CASE STUDIES

European integration and the nation-state

European integration should now be looked at a little more closely on the basis of the border typology just presented, since the process of European integration is frequently equated with the end of the nation-state. The internal European borders disappear and jurisdiction in economic and social politics is transferred into the hands of European institutions and communalised. The nation-state is the offspring of the European modern age and has become the universal principle of international order during the process of European expansion. Does the European Union mark the end of the nation-state and is this development going to be trend-setting for world order?

If we look at Europe with regard to the functions of borders it becomes clear that something historically unprecedented is taking place. States are giving up national sovereignty in favour of common institutions. However, the result is again a territorially bound, political unit, just like a nation-state. Internal borders are being torn down and common external borders are being simultaneously put up. A European Union would, in fact, be unimaginable without external borders. An examination of this external border is instructive. Since the end of the east–west conflict it has once again become moveable, raising the question of which criteria should determine where the new border will lie. Who belongs to Europe? Even without being able to follow this question any further here, it is clear that the drawing of borders in the European Union depends on the outcome of the discussion about its further integration or, alternatively, expansion.

The control of immigration is increasingly becoming a central topic of discussion regarding European borders. Even though the coordination and harmonisation of the politics regarding the right to asylum and the realisation of the Schengen agreement have still not been completed, it has become evident that the European Union is developing an intensive and well-structured control within its first pillar of the Union treaty, both within its interior and on the outer border. All of these are also characteristics of an effective nation-state.

What is pioneering and new, however, is the fact that within the European Union a framework is developing for an effective, multi-level policy-making. But this new form of governance doesn't render the nation-state obsolete; rather, it will lead to a new role for the nation-state, as a coordinator within a multi-layered policy-network.

From citizenship to post-national membership?

Although they have differing perspectives, several new books agree that the institution of citizenship, in view of globalisation and the development of international law, is losing its meaning (Soysal, 1994; Jacobson, 1996; Sassen, 1996). They argue that a variety of membership forms not defined by borders are taking the place of citizenship. The thesis concerning the increasing loss of importance of citizenship is in fact another variation on the thesis of the 'end of the nation-state'. Soysal is correct in her assumption that the idea of an unbending and exclusive loyalty of a citizen to his or her nation belongs to a past epoch, that modernisation and democratisation have lead to the development of a variety of identities. Yet, as even she concedes, the rights of a citizen can be realised and secured only within the framework of a nation-state (Soysal, 1994: 165). Only within the scope of the European Convention of Human Rights was the first human-rights regime developed, which actually led to a significant restriction of national sovereignty. The convention allowed for the immediate guarantee of human rights for those individuals within its jurisdiction without reference to their nationality (Kimminich, 1997: 354). Despite this European exception with regard to the effective protection of rights, the national authorities and courts are as decisive as ever. A hearing before the European Court of Human Rights, including the necessary advance exhaustion of the national legal remedies, takes up to six years. The national institutions of justice are in practice, therefore, still critical.

Social rights, despite the opinion that they can increasingly be enjoyed independent of citizenship, are recently even more strongly bound to it. Union citizens, for example, possess further-reaching social rights than citizens of third countries. Even in the United States, according to new welfare legislation, social rights are reserved for citizens and restricted for legal immigrants (Dittgen, 1997). The nation-state and citizenship are, from the point of view of social equality, as important now as they ever have been.

The notion that admission of citizens, naturalisation and legal residence will be largely defined by an international rights regime or world economy is not convincing. Saskia Sassen, however, held this thesis, and came to the conclusion that 'state sovereignty is being partly de-centred onto non- or quasi-governmental entities for the governance of the global economy and international political order (Sassen, 1996: 98). In reference to the moving of persons across borders, the sovereignty of a nation remains largely untouched. With only a few exceptions, there are no international laws that can force entry into a country (Sohn & Buergenthal, 1992). Particularly with regard to the issue of migration, nation-states defend their sovereignty determinedly and successfully.

The most important argument against this thesis of post-national membership is not only to be found in the fact that basic political rights, such as active and passive voting rights, are bound to citizenship; citizenship is also the fundamental institution that connects the individual bearer of rights to the protective agencies of the state (Klusmeyer, 1996). The public arena within which citizens act together remains defined by borders.

Is the nation-state's ability to integrate exhausted?

The constitutional scholar Rudolf Smend defined integration as the *raison d'être* and central duty of the state:

> Because, and so long as it integrates itself, the state is created both by and from the people – this lasting process is in essence its spiritual and social realisation. (Smend, 1928.)

In modern history, this achievement of integration was made possible by the nation-state. However, the promise of participation by the nation-state goes hand in hand – and this shows the nation-state's two faces – with the willingness to employ force both internationally and domestically. As Hagen Schulze writes:

> From the beginning, it was the definition against the neighbour and the struggle with their rivals through which the European nations found themselves. (Schulze, 1994: 126.)

With the nation-states that subscribed to an ethnic-national ideology, this integration was also tied to its radical opposite, namely the elimination of 'heterogeneity' (Schmitt, 1926). The drawing of national borders had the function of constructing national identity through exclusion.

Independent of its self-understanding and constitutional order, there is at present an increasing doubt as to the nation-state's ability to integrate, which gives the impression of being a process of globalisation. Richard Münch writes:

> The social integration through the nation-state is eroding, the international, supra-national and the word societal integration is not growing at the same speed. (Münch, 1998: 17.)

What, however, does social integration mean? Here, as well, a consideration of the function of borders can offer a clearer picture.

The concern surrounding the integration potential of political communities is as old as political philosophy itself. Jürgen Habermas describes the specific modern characteristics of this theme:

> Since the end of the 18th century the modern discourse has, under continually changing titles, had the same topic: the weakening of social bindings, privatisation and disunity, in short: those deformations of a one sided rationalised everyday practice which cause the requirement of an equivalent to the uniting power of religion. (Habermas, 1998.)

Analysts of modernity such as Karl Marx and Alexis de Tocqueville used such terms as '*Entfremdung*' and 'isolation' to describe the weakening of ties among men which is the central characteristic of the modern world (Dittgen, 1986).

The alleged end of the nation-state is often greeted with open arms, because it could provide a chance to 'revive' local democracy. Richard Münch wrote:

> If anything, the nation-state was a mere caricature of the republican idea of democracy, being as it was too big, too heterogeneous, and too centrally organised. (Münch, 1998: 408.)

There can be no doubt about the importance of communal autonomy for a lively democracy. If, however, the community is played out as a place of 'real democracy', as opposed to the nation-state, it shows how foreign this opinion is to the idea and the institutions of representative democracy. The dangers that threaten the minority and plurality in small political communities through majority rule and the pressure to conform are misjudged. Rousseau's concept of direct democracy instead of the concept of the separation of powers within a constitutional state serve as a model here.

In the *Federalist Papers* James Madison demonstrated the significance of federalism for the protection of minority rights, and used this quality as his central argument in favour of a federally organised republic. If Rhode Island were to be left on its own, he argued, within this small community conflicts would result in the suppression of the minority and eventually, because of the continued conflicts, this would lead to a call for an authoritarian government. In a large federal republic such as the United States, however, among the great variety of interests, parties, and sects which it embraces, a coalition of a majority of the whole society could seldom take place on any other principles than those of justice and the general good ... the larger the society, provided it lie within a practicable sphere, the more duly capable it will be of self-government. And happily for the republican cause, the practicable sphere may be carried to a very great extent by a judicious modification and mixture of the federal principle. (Hamilton *et al*, 1961.)

Madison's argument for a large republic has not lost its validity. To champion localism and regionalism as remedies for the modern tendencies towards individualism is a deceptive and, for political freedom, even dangerous illusion.

The religious cult of ethnic nationalism as a means to bridge class cleavages and religious schisms was central to the formation of nation-states in Europe. Ethnic nationalism, 'one of the most powerful, if not the most powerful social belief system of the 19th and 20th centuries' (Elias, 1992), also offered the ideology for the process of 'nation-building' for the emerging nations of the third world (Tibi, 1987). Nationalism charged the meaning of borders with ideology. Through the construction of an 'us' and 'them', the identity of the collective was strengthened. Ethnic nationalism has lost none of its attraction. Proof of this lies with the new drawing of borders in Europe after the end of the east–west conflict, and the politicising of ethnic identity in the countries of the south.

In view of the factual cultural plurality and the pluralisation of the social environments, the fictional character of a collective national culture in modern nation-states will become all too clear, and will therefore be incapable of exercising a durable social, integrative function. In an increasingly mobile and integrated world, can *Demos* and *Ethno*s not be the same? In practice, viewing them as identical has always led to a stifling and forced assimilation of other ethnic, cultural, religious or socio-economic groups within a political association (Lepsius, 1990b). The modern nation-states are national states and are characterised by an increasing cultural pluralism. The thesis of the weakening of the ability of the nation-state to integrate identifies the nation-state with pre-political ethnic nationalism or conceptualises the state in terms of Hegel's idea of moral totality (*Sittlichkeit*).

The nation-state's ability to integrate can only be meaningfully discussed in relation to its self-understanding and its form of government. There are two main ideas of self-understanding. The *Volknation* is based on the assumption of a pre-political unity as an ethnic or cultural community. The republic, however, is not bound by such requirements, but rather trusts in the integrational strength of law – i.e. constitutional, civic and political rights. For this form of government, political integration is not assumed to pre-exist; it is a permanent responsibility. Despite the persistent virulence of ethnic nationalism – also a reaction to the globalisation process – it cannot serve as the future model of integration. The tendency of atomising, differentiation and the internationalisation of modern society as a result of global communication will remove the fundamental basis of ethnic nationalism.

The idea of the collective culture of the nation and the cosmopolitan idea of a universal republic are diametrically opposed (Oberndörfer, 1993 & 1998). The closed borders of a collective identity are not reconcilable with the pluralism and the open character of the republic, which is based upon the autonomy of the individual as a legal entity. The borders of a republic do not define membership of a pre-political collective, but of a constitutional state, which protects the rights of the individual through the legitimate use of coercion within its boundaries, and provides for political participation and governance. The citizens of a republic are not members of a *volk* but citizens of a constitutional state. A consequence is the principle of openness to immigration, because the criteria for accepting new citizens is not based upon their biology or culture, but upon whether or not they accept the constitution.[4]

The nation-state with a republican order makes political integration possible because it excludes arbitrary force and guarantees political and cultural freedom and the integrity of the different co-existing lifestyles (Oberndörfer, 1998; Habermas, 1994). Dolf Sternberger coined the term 'constitutional patriotism' to identify this relationship of the citizen to the state (Sternberger, 1990). An encompassing social integration cannot and should not succeed in a nation-state, according to a liberal understanding. The republic, as a well-ordered community, is, as John Rawls correctly claims, a union of social unions (Rawls, 1971). The constitution provides the framework for the political process and the institutions of government, and the guarantee of an ordered and non-violent area for political debate and action.

The constitutional state is not a 'cold project', as Ralf Dahrendorf writes (Dahrendorf, 1993). It is true, however, that a constitutional tradition must first be developed before it can reach the hearts of the citizens and provide the self-evident foundation for political action. As the example of the United States proves, the constitution can be the life-blood of a nation, and be honoured and celebrated. Alexis de Tocqueville correctly observed that this rational patriotism (*patriotisme réfléchi*) is distinct from the old European religious love for the fatherland (*amour instinctif de la patrie*) He writes:

> There is another species of attachment to country which is more rational. It is perhaps less generous and less ardent, but it is more fruitful and more lasting: it springs from knowledge; it is nurtured by the laws; it grows by the exercise of civil rights; and, in the end, it is confounded with the personal interests of the citizen. (de Tocqueville, 1951.)

If the citizens identify with their constitution, then political integration occurs within the borders of the constitutional state. The problem of social integration and the ethos of the citizens must, however, be seen within the context of the institutions of civil society and economic life as well. In this respect, political integration in a republic also depends on circumstances over which it has only very limited control.

With regard to the central thesis of this paper, the arguments presented here contend that political integration can only be guaranteed within the sphere of the nation-state, because all constitutions are constitutions of nation-states.

Republics do not integrate by exclusion, but rather through the guarantee of citizen rights and political and social justice. Republics, which define themselves as being universal defenders of human rights, assign their borders no ideological differentiation function, but rather emphasise the connecting function of borders. Republics work not only towards domestic integration, but towards international integration. They do not fight wars with one another, but rather promote political and economic cooperation within the community of liberal democracies (Doyle, 1992). An equally successful alternative to the political integration of the nation-state is yet to be found.

CONCLUSIONS: THE NATION-STATE'S LOSS OF AUTONOMY AND RETENTION OF SOVEREIGNTY

Globalisation is, qualitatively, not a new phenomenon. To put it simply, we are experiencing an accelerated intensification of transnational relations. This intensification of social contacts leads to losses and changes in the functions of the borders of the nation-state and also leads to new social and ideological boundary formations. A close examination of these altered functions of the border shows that we are not dealing with a general loss of function for the nation-state. However, a loss of autonomy, caused by increasing interdependence and economic integration, can be observed. When the end of the nation-state is referred to, a certain concept of 'state' usually underlies this thesis: the notion of a hierarchical, integrated state which must be able to assert itself against competing powers domestically and must maintain a power position as an equal rival internationally. This model of state is based on a clear separation of state and society. According to this premise, the loss of autonomy which I described must be seen at the same time as a loss of sovereignty.

But if one frees oneself from this concept of the state and looks at domestic and foreign policy under the real conditions of social change, it becomes apparent that a loss of autonomy for the state does not necessarily mean the same as loss of sovereignty. A transborder socialisation of domestic and foreign policy is taking place, meaning that political decisions will not be able to be autonomously executed by the government against external influences. On the contrary, today government politics are embedded in a continually branching and thickening net of transnational and domestic societal interdependencies. But this loss of autonomy does not at all mean the end of the state's sovereignty – i.e. the end of its monopoly of power or of its territoriality.

This development of loss of autonomy on the one hand and retention of sovereignty on the other appears in a positive light both from a normative and from a functional point of view:

- as far as the loss of autonomy is concerned, because governments can only live up to the increasing load of responsibilities through the coordination of different domestic and foreign policy networks

- as far as the retention of sovereignty of the nation-state is concerned, because there is no recognisable alternative setting for a democracy, understood as responsible government and political integration.

In conclusion, it could be said that the nation-state is not the end of history, but it must not be the 'soulless despotism' of a global state, as Immanuel Kant so appropriately called it. As he said, a consensus on principles and agreement upon a peace cannot be brought about and secured by means of a world government '(on the churchyard of freedom), i.e. by means of the debilitation of all forces, but rather by means of their equilibrium and their vivacious rivalry' (Kant, 1975a).

Since rational law transgresses all boundaries, cosmopolitan law is a consequence of the idea of the constitutional state. Only under the condition of cosmopolitan law will a symmetry between the legalisation of social and political relations on both sides of national borders materialise (Kant, 1975b; Habermas, 1996b). With the spread of the republic as a form of government guaranteeing cosmopolitan law, the gap between the particularistic political organisation and the universality of the law may not be completely overcome, but it might at least be made bridgeable.

NOTES

1   There is, however, also the different view held by several authors who are not suggesting a movement beyond the nation-state, but rather stress the continuing importance – or even the rebirth – of the nation-state. Amongst these are Anderson (1991), Brubaker (1996) and Smith (1995).

2   For a comprehensive analysis, see Anderson (1996). For the history of the term, see Febvre (1973). For a convincing historical typology, see Osterhammel (1995). For the issue of globalisation and the nation-state, see Smith (1995); Ruggie (1993); Brock & Albert (1995); and Beck (1997).

3   For a comprehensive survey of border conflicts, see Allcock *et al.* (1992).

4   At this point a basic problem of some of the 'communitarian' critics of liberalism becomes evident. Michael Walzer, for instance, points out the illegitimate character of the role of citizens over non-citizens. However, in his opinion this type of rule is not illegitimate because it violates citizens' inalienable rights or the fundamental principle of equality, but rather because it violates the type of community he idealises. This community is characterised by a strong commitment and broadly-shared common values. Walzer elevates the community to a level of almost religious importance, perhaps even, as he writes, 'the most important good that gets distributed'. He stresses accordingly the necessity of differentiation and the importance of controlling borders: 'Admission and exclusion are at the core of communal independence. They suggest the deepest meaning of self-determination. Without them, there could not be *communities of character*, historically stable, ongoing associations of men and women with some special commitment to one another and some special sense of their common life.' (Walzer, 1983.) This echoes the German Romantic idea, expressed in particular in the writings of Johann Gottfried Herder, that all nations have their distinctive and unalterable

character. In Walzer's world of 'communities of character' the border has the same ideological function as in ethnic nationalism. The collective will elevates its own value and differentiates itself from others. This concept of social integration is incompatible with the liberal notion concerning the autonomy of the individual.

REFERENCES

Allcock, J.B. *et al.* *(1992) Border and Territorial Disputes* (3rd edn.), Harlow: Longman Current Affairs.

Anderson, B. (1991) *Imagined Communities. Reflections on the Origin and Spread of Nationalism*, London/New York: Verso.

Anderson, M. (1996) *Frontiers. Territory and State Formation in the Modern World*, Oxford.

Andreas, P. (1996) 'U.S.–Mexico: Open Markets, Closed Borders', *Foreign Policy*, No. 103: 51–69.

Arendt, H. (1951) *The Origins of Totalitarianism*, New York: Harcourt, Brace: 266–287.

Beck, U. (1997) *Was ist Globalisierung? Irrtümer des Globalismus – Antworten auf Globalisierung*, Frankfurt.

Brock, L. & Albert, M. (1995) 'Entgrenzung der Staatenwelt. Zur Analyse weltgesellschaftlicher Entwicklungstendenzen', *Zeitschrift für Internationale Beziehungen*, Vol. 2, No. 2: 259–285.

Brubaker, R. (1996) *Nationalism Reframed. Nationhood and the National Question in the New Europe*, Cambridge: Cambridge University Press.

Bull, H. (1979) 'The State's Positive Role in World Affairs', *Daedalus*, Vol. 108, No. 4, Fall: 111–23.

Burke, E. (1993) 'A Vindication of Natural Society' in Harris, I. (ed.) *Pre-Revolutionary Writings*, Cambridge: Cambridge University Press: 28.

Cerny, P. G. (1997) 'Paradoxes of the Competition State: The Dynamics of Political Globalisation', *Government and Opposition*, Vol. 32, No. 2: 251–274.

Coulmas, P. (1990) *Weltbürger. Geschichte einer Menschheitssehnsucht*, Reinbek.

Czempiel, E-O (1990) 'Konturen einer Gesellschaftswelt. Die neue Architektur der internationalen Politik', *Merkur*, Vol. 44. No. 10/11: 850–851.

Dahrendorf, R. (1993) 'Freiheit und soziale Bindungen. Anmerkungen zur Struktur einer Argumentation' in Michalski, K. (ed.) *Die liberale Gesellschaft. Castelgandolfo–Gespräch 1992*, Stuttgart: 11.

Dahrendorf, R. (1994) 'Die Zukunft des Nationalstaates', *Merkur*, Vol. 48, No. 9/10: 751–761.

Dahrendorf, R. (1997) 'Prosperity, Civility and Liberty: Can we Square the Circle?', *After 1989. Morals, Revolution and Civil Society*, London: Macmillan: 68–79.

de Tocqueville, A. (1951) *De la Démocratie en Amérique*, Tome I, Paris: 246.

Dittgen, H. (1986) *Politik zwischen Freiheit und Despotismus. Alexis de Tocqueville und Karl Marx*, Freiburg i.Br./München: 78–83.

Dittgen, H. (1997) 'The American Debate about Immigration in the 1990s: A

New Nationalism After the End of the Cold War?', *Stanford Humanities Review*, Vol. 5, No. 2: 254–283.

Doyle, M. W. (1992) 'An International Liberal Community' in Allison, G. & Treverton, G. F. (eds.) *Rethinking America's Security. Beyond Cold War to New World Order*, New York: 307–333.

Elias, N. (1992) *Studien über die Deutschen. Machtkämpfe und Habitusentwicklung im 19. und 20. Jahrhundert*, Frankfurt: 194.

Febvre, L. (1973) 'Frontière: the word and the concept' in Burke, P. (ed.) *A new kind of History and other Essays*, New York: 208–218.

Giddens, A. (1987) *The Nation-state and Violence. Volume Two of a Contemporary Critique of Historical Materialism*, Los Angeles: 13.

Giesen, B. (1996) 'Kulturelle Vielfalt und die Einheit der Moderne', *Leviathan*, Vol. 24, No. 1: 92–108.

Goffman, E. (1971) *Relations in Public: Micro Studies of the Public Order*, London.

Guéhenno, J-M (1993) *La fin de la démocratie*, Paris.

Habermas, J. (1994) *Faktizität und Geltung. Beiträge zur Diskurstheorie des Rechts und des demokratischen Rechtsstaats*, Frankfurt: 642–643.

Habermas, J. (1996a) 'Der Europäische Nationalstaat – Zur Vergangenheit und Zukunft von Souveränität und Staatsbürgerschaft', *Die Einbeziehung des Anderen. Studien zur politischen Theorie*, Frankfurt: 129–130.

Habermas, J. (1996b) 'Kants Idee des ewigen Friedens – aus dem historischen Abstand von 200 Jahren', *Die Einbeziehung des Anderen. Studien zur politischen Theorie*, Frankfurt: 234.

Habermas, J. (1998) *Der philosophische Diskurs der Moderne. Zwölf Vorlesungen*, Frankfurt: 166.

Hamilton, A., Madison, J. & Jay, J. (1961) *The Federalist Papers*, New York: 325.

Horowitz, D. L. (1997) 'Self-Determination: Politics, Philosophy, and Law' in Shapiro, I. & Kymlicka, W. (eds.) *Ethnicity and Group Rights*, Nomos XXXIX, New York: 421–463.

Huntington, S. P. (1996) *The Clash of Civilizations and the Remaking of World Order*, New York.

Jacobson, D. (1996) *Rights across Borders. Immigration and the Decline of Citizenship*, Baltimore/London.

Kant, I. 'Zum ewigen Frieden. Ein philosophischer Entwurf', *Werke*, Vol. 9, Darmstadt (1975): 226.

Kant, I. 'Idee zu einer allgemeinen Geschichte in weltbürgerlicher Absicht', *Werke*, Vol. 9, Darmstadt (1975): 41–45.

Kimminich, O. (1992) 'Human Rights vs. Reason of State: International Law. On the History of International Institutions', *Universitas*, Vol. 34, No. 3: 164–169.

Kimminich, O. (1997) *Einführung in das Völkerrecht*, (6th edn.), Tübingen/Basel: A. Francke.

Klusmeyer, D. B. (1996) *Between Consent and Descent: Conceptions of Democratic Citizenship*, Washington, DC.

Lepsius, R. M. (1990a) 'Der Europäische Nationalstaat: Erbe und Zukunft' in

Lepsius, R. M. (ed.) *Interessen, Ideen und Institutionen*, Opladen: Westdeutscher Verlag: 256–69.

Lepsius, R. M. (1990b) ' "Ethnos" oder "Demos". Zur Anwendung zweier Kategorien von Emerich Francis auf das nationale Selbstverständnis der Bundesrepublik und auf die Europäische Einigung' in Lepsius, R. M. (ed.) *Interessen, Ideen und Institutionen*, Opladen: Westdeutscher Verlag: 249.

Luhmann, N. (1997) *Die Gesellschaft der Gesellschaft*, Frankfurt: chapter 4.

Münch, R. (1998) *Globale Dynamik, lokale Lebenswelten. Der schwierige Weg in die Weltgesellschaft*, Frankfurt: 17.

Oberndörfer, D. (1993) *Der Wahn des Nationalen. Die Alternative der offenen Republik*, Freiburg.

Oberndörfer, D. (1998) 'Integration oder Abschottung? – Auf dem Weg zur postnationalen Republik', *Zeitschrift für Ausländerrecht und Ausländerpolitik*, Vol. 18, No. 1.

Osterhammel, J. (1995) 'Kulturelle Grenzen in der Expansion Europas', *Saeculum*, Vol. 46, No. 1: 101–138.

Rawls, J. (1971) *A Theory of Justice*, Cambridge, MA: 527.

Rufin, J-C. (1991) *L'empire et les nouveaux Barbares*, Paris.

Ruggie, J. G. (1993) 'Territoriality and Beyond: Problematizing Modernity in International Relations', *International Organization*, Vol. 47, No. 1: 139–174.

Sassen, S. (1996) *Losing Control? Sovereignty in the Age of Globalisation*, New York.

Scharpf, F. W. (1991) 'Die Handlungsfähigkeit des Staates am Ende des zwanzigsten Jahrhunderts', *Politische Vierteljahresschrift*, Vol. 32: 621–634.

Schmitt, C. (1926) *Die geistesgeschichtliche Lage des heutigen Parlamentarismus*, Berlin: Duncker & Humblot.

Schulze, H. (1994) *Staat und Nation in der europäischen Geschichte*, München: Beck.

Simmel, G. (1992) 'Soziologie: Untersuchungen über die Formen der Vergesellschaftung', *Gesamtausgabe*, Vol. 11, Frankfurt: 697.

Smend, R. (1928) *Verfassung und Verfassungsrecht*, München/Leipzig: 20.

Smith, A. D. (1995) *Nations and Nationalism in a Global Era*, Oxford: Polity Press.

Sohn, L. B. & Buergenthal, T. (eds.) (1992) *The Movement of Persons Across Borders*, Washington, DC.

Soysal, Y. N. (1994) *Limits of Citizenship. Migrants and Postnational Membership in Europe*, Chicago/London.

Sternberger, D. (1990) 'Verfassungspatriotismus', *Schriften* X, Frankfurt.

Strange, S. (1996) *The Retreat of the State. The Diffusion of Power in the World Economy*, Cambridge.

Tibi, B. (1987) *Vom Gottesreich zum Nationalstaat. Islam und panarabischer Nationalismus*, Frankfurt.

Walzer, M. (1983) *Spheres of Justice: A Defense of Pluralism and Equality*, New York: Basic Books.

Weiner, M. (ed.) (1993) *International Migration and Security*, Boulder: Westview Press.

5
Corporate Nations:
A New Sovereignty Emerges

Thomas M. Edwards[1]

INTRODUCTION

This paper presents a general exploration of an observation with a rather broad scope. It addresses the meaning and function of international boundaries in the coming century in relation to transnational corporations (TNCs) and their influence upon the perception of spatial sovereignty. It does not strive to make definitive statements about the nature of 'nationhood' or the future of sovereignty, but it does attempt to point to some possible geopolitical trends on the horizon.

The geographic landscape of the past few decades has seen an upheaval and redirection that is unprecedented in relation to the decades that came before. This landscape consists of not only the basic territorial boundaries with which we are familiar, but also the cultures, economies and controlling philosophies that contribute to geographic differentiation. For over a hundred years the discipline of *geopolitics* has helped to guide discussion on how these aspects of the geographic landscape interact on a political level – i.e. how real-world geography is influenced by the presence of boundaries and their sovereign creators. Indeed, much of the recent past's geographic transitions have been focused on changes within and between sovereign national entities.

However, a clear – if not obvious – trend has emerged that reveals a strong movement of the power base away from a focus on territorial sovereignty, and towards one centred on economic control. Stated simply, this trend is 'the receding power of the state relative to the global economy in mastering space' (Tuathail, 1996: 251). Much attention in this area has been given to the TNCs that have been growing exponentially in response to robust international markets demanding their goods. While this has worked well for the TNCs, it prompts many questions as to how such corporate entities are affecting, altering and shaping the territorial entities in which they thrive. By operating on such a global scale, within and between sovereign entities, the TNCs have in turn begun to operate at a similar level to sovereign nations when it comes to protecting their interests abroad.

When coupled with the very rapid advances in telecommunications, global interpersonal connectivity, and a shifting paradigm of information use – all created and established by TNCs – these new entities challenge the very notion

Borderlands Under Stress (M.A. Pratt and J.A. Brown (eds), ISBN 90-411-9790-7).
© Kluwer Law International, 2000.

of territoriality and the presence of 'real' boundaries. The following discussion endeavours to explore the nature of this new and evolving relationship between what we know to be sovereign nations and what we believe could be emerging forms of sovereignty for new geopolitical entities.

REDEFINING GEOPOLITICS

Geopolitics has been a guiding discipline for helping to define various kinds of global political interactions, yet we need to be clear about the definition of the term as it is used in the context of this discussion. The term itself is often associated today with concepts or perceptions that do not always agree with Rudolf Kjellen's original intentions in 1899, but they do not necessarily have to conform – new times require new definitions.

The classical definitions of geopolitics deal primarily with the notion of political spheres of influence – e.g. the Eastern Bloc, the west, and other supranational aggregations. However, with the dynamic political and economic changes of recent times, the definition of geopolitics has changed. Halford MacKinder's theories were groundbreaking for their time, and quite influential, but it is clear today that

> command of a particular part of the earth's surface does not apparently give a special advantage in spite of arguments developed earlier in the century that control of East Europe and the interior of Asia would give control of the 'world island'. (Cole, 1983: 241.)

At its best, geopolitics can serve as a proactive mechanism for discerning potential problems within various geographies, by studying the factors influencing local geography. At its worst, it can be contorted and manipulated to act as a propaganda device for purely nationalistic aims (e.g. the well-studied example of Nazi Germany).

Other forms of geopolitics have evolved more recently – for example 'critical geopolitics'. This newer variety seeks to use geopolitics as a critical filter for discerning the nature of the global power structure and its various influences on political and social systems. In this way, it acts as a voice of conscience in the field, taking a step back to examine how perceptions of politics have been formed and moulded over time. Critical geopolitics is a useful aspect of broader geopolitics as it helps to draw out the *deus ex machina* behind real world events, and as it also 'deliberately attempts to avoid appearances of supporting or justifying the policies and arguments of any individual state' (O'Loughlin, 1994: 175).

Another more recent iteration that also deserves attention in geopolitical thought is Dijkink's concept of 'geopolitical visions'. Essentially, a geopolitical vision is:

> any idea concerning the relation between one's own and other places, involving feelings of (in)security or (dis)advantage (and/or) invoking ideas about a collective mission or foreign policy strategy. (Dijkink, 1996: 11.)

In line with more post-modernist thought, this definition of geopolitics incorporates a cognitive dimension but it still 'requires at least a Them-and-Us distinction and emotional attachment to a place' (Dijkink, 1996: 11). It deviates even more from the classic definitions in that it devolves itself of the strict inclusion of political structures and allows room for a broader perception of geography and place.

So geopolitics should not be viewed as a static study of social and political environments; we are no longer in the era where 'geopolitics rested on the realist theory of international relations, and on the geography of states' (Black, 1997: 110). It has become a dynamic tool – a mechanism for portraying the temporal snapshot of a particular state or region or people, as well as a mechanism for predicting large-scale changes in the short- and long-term futures. It still focuses on the political mechanisms that exist between states, but does so while realising that the world today is a much more complex system.

However, even these definitions do not adequately serve the purpose of this discussion and do not address the nature of the political-economic system that is quickly developing – that is, the information-based economy. Information technology is rapidly changing the way in which nation-states interact with one another, but they are still far from reaching the ultimate goal of having what Microsoft terms a 'digital nervous system' (DNS). Most governments are still wallowing in decades (or even centuries) of political dogma and administrative procedure that is quite difficult to overcome. A DNS, put simply, is the way in which information is managed within a homogeneous organisation on the small and large scale – whether in one's home, in a corporation or even within a country (Gates, 1997). As the notion of the DNS propagates, it is important to be aware that the DNS – like any other by-product of a particular organisation or national entity – is the DNS for a particular cultural and political context. Indeed, most information is context-dependent, both in its source and in its destination.

If one imagines the existence of many DNSs distributed globally – the DNSs not only of large TNCs but of nation-states and supranational aggregates (e.g. the UN, NATO) – it may be seen that the interaction of information between context-dependent DNSs can produce many potential problems. While the networks may be physically connected in the correct manner, and while information formats may be compatible, there are no effective means of resolving context differences in the content of the information moving through and between the DNSs. When opposing viewpoints on the same information are not compatible, we have the potential for a geopolitical crisis.

If we then view geopolitics in the context of a world interacting more and more frequently via information exchange, the DNS and other means to come, the definition of geopolitics changes significantly. Instead of focusing on territoriality and power bases, it considers the basic global interaction that is taking place in this new realm, and arrives at a definition of geopolitics that is better suited to the Information Age, a definition for *information geopolitics*: the interaction between two or more DNSs of differing geographic contexts.

However, the world is not overflowing with DNSs at this time. The existence of true DNSs is mostly in the realm of the transnational corporations which create them (and even then in incomplete stages of development); the vision of a broad 'paperless' society is far from having arrived. It is appropriate then to revise the above definition to incorporate a more generic perspective that works in the interim. When viewed on a broader, less technology-dependent scale, *information geopolitics* is: the geographic ramifications of global information interacting with local information. The terms 'global' and 'local' are used here to define the context of scale – information used and/or accepted transnationally as compared to information that remains locally significant – to a country, an organisation or any particular group of people. The *global information standard* involves a level of understanding and availability of knowledge that is beyond the grasp of local government and/or cultural control. It is the information considered generally acceptable on a global basis; it is the 'international' viewpoint or the shared opinion among nation-states and citizens. The *local information standard* contains strong references to local 'reality' that may conflict with the global viewpoint, which could include geographic facts, historical facts, the naming of people or features, the appearance of a map, etc. For example, declaring Canada as the country that contains the hydrologic feature Hudson Bay is an accepted, international fact that could pass from geographic context to geographic context without challenge. However, declaring a single country as the sole sovereign power over all of Jammu and Kashmir will undoubtedly face opposition from the local information contexts involved in the dispute.

Notice that this new definition is purposefully less specific about boundaries or nationality. The boundaries are constructs of the political systems in which they were designed and established – so we look past the boundaries themselves and towards the underlying culture that created them. The global and local context distinction emphasises that

> the clash of civilisations will dominate global politics. The fault lines between civilisations will be the battle lines of the future. (Huntington, 1998: 159.)

It is this 'real world' cultural interaction on the basis of information exchange that defines the 'geographic ramifications'. Information, while contained and transmitted virtually, has real-world geopolitical effects that must be considered on the global and local scale.

THE NOTION OF 'NATION'

> Membership in the United Nations is open to all other *peace-loving states* which accept the obligations contained in the present Charter and, in the judgment of the Organisation, are able and willing to carry out these obligations.' (United Nations Charter – Article 4, Section 1.)

As evident above, admission into the United Nations is granted on the condition that a political entity is a 'peace-loving state'. Regardless of the peace-loving portion, what does it mean to be a 'state' or a 'nation' – or a 'nation-state'? What forces define the aggregation of people into a homogeneous political body that can then declare itself 'sovereign', and perhaps even 'peace-loving'? In the previous section, the author redefined geopolitics in order to proceed with a more relevant meaning. Likewise, the concept of the nation-state needs to be considered here in the light of evidence telling us that

> the clarity of the state frontier is now fading because the exercise of sovereign authority in certain domains is becoming either very difficult or impossible. (Anderson, 1996: 178.)

There is no single clear and acceptable definition of what defines a 'nation'. In fact, the terms 'nation-state', 'nation', 'state' and 'country' are often used interchangeably. Defining what is meant by these terms is important, in that by doing so the author intends to draw out the most basic factors that contribute to the identity of a nation-like group. We also need to examine these factors as they relate to the emerging global information economy. First, consider the traditional Webster's dictionary definitions of these terms:

nation-state: A form of political organisation under which a relatively homogeneous people inhabits a sovereign state; *especially*: a state containing one as opposed to several nationalities.

nation: A community of people composed of one or more nationalities and possessing a more or less defined territory and government.

state: A politically organized body of people usually occupying a definite territory; *especially*: one that is sovereign.

country: A political state or nation or its territory.

For the sake of eliminating redundancy, the term 'country' will be considered as a synonym of 'nation-state'. If one compares the remaining definitions, there are some clear similarities. They indicate that a 'nation' exists when the following basic conditions are true:

- a homogeneous group of people exists
- the people occupy a definite geographic territory
- the people are organised under some kind of political system.

Through discussions with US State Department personnel, the author learned that the definition they employ consists of the following three factors being met:

- a group of people is organised under a government
- the government has control over a defined territory
- the government handles its own foreign affairs (i.e. it is not dependent on any other nation).

Here again is another list of criteria which, when fulfilled, define what constitutes a 'nation' (Minahan, 1996: xvi); it may be noted that the list is similar to those above:

- the display of outward trappings of national consciousness, particularly the adoption of a flag
- a national claim to a recognisable geographic area
- the formation of a specifically nationalist organisation or political grouping that reflects the nation's claim to self-determination.

When aggregated, all of these factors contribute to a generic definition of 'nation' that will be applied here. The classic 'nation' is a geopolitical entity that satisfies the existence of three major factors:

- people: a homogeneous group
- territory: a geographically defined area
- government: an organising, nationalistic body.

There are many other subfactors that could be introduced to refine the definition, such as:

> formal and real independence, recognition by other states in the international system of states; the expectation of permanence; a State apparatus; a circulation system; an organised economy. (Knight, 1994: 72.)

However, the basic definition of 'nation' as presented will suffice for the purposes of this discourse.

Within various sources there appears to be a strong distinction made between the terms 'nation' and 'nation-state'. The key issue separating the two concepts is territorial control. If we adhere strictly to our 'nation' definition above, we are left open to accepting the presence of many possible nations in today's geopolitical landscape; in fact 'estimates of the number of stateless nations in the world run as high as 9,000' (Minahan, 1996: xvi). So the distinction we make between a 'nation' and a 'nation-state' is that in the former the conditions of nationhood have been met, but in the latter the conditions of 'statehood' have been met – i.e. the nation actually controls the territory it has defined as being its own. The notion becomes clear that 'the nation is the basis of political legitimacy all assume that *the nation is bounded, that it has frontiers*' (Anderson, 1996: 42). For example, the Kurdish people generally meet the conditions of nationhood but they have not satisfied the condition of statehood – they don't control the territory they view as being their exclusive realm. The idea of territorial control incorporates some degree of political, economic and militaristic influence over the geography – it is actual control over space.

Therefore, a 'nation-state' is a nation that wholly controls its geographic space and by so doing has obtained its sovereign status. It is the attainment of sovereign status (i.e. statehood) that solidifies political control and it is this sovereignty that secures nation-states the right to self-determination. In short, 'the exercise of a state's authority over its territory implies that sovereignty is complete and exclusive' (Knight, 1994: 75). If the nation-state then wishes to act as a 'peace-loving state', it has the freedom to do so – or not. So the generic 'nation' definition above can be revised to reflect the 'nation-state', as follows:

- people: a homogeneous group that demonstrates national consciousness
- territory: a geographically defined area exclusively controlled by the governing body
- government: an organising, nationalistic body that solely represents the national interests abroad.

Why is the definition of the 'nation-state' so relevant to our focus on TNCs and the changing notion of geopolitics in an information-based society? It is important when we consider that 'in the broad sweep of history, nation-states have been a transnational form of organisation for managing economic affairs' (Ohmae, 1995: 141). The nation-state serves as the fundamental geographic unit through which international political and economic systems interact, evolve and conflict. By understanding the current perception of the nation-state we can move forward to examining how this perception – like geopolitics – is being altered by technological change.

THE STATE OF SOVEREIGNTY

How relevant are the conditions of sovereignty in today's evolving information-based economies and cultures? When considering the basis of present and future geopolitics as being the flow and interaction of information of various contexts, do these conditions hold much meaning anymore? These are not easy questions to answer and they certainly cannot fully be explored here, but an attempt should be made to make a surface evaluation of their relative importance.

People

The geopolitical process of individuals becoming a people, a people becoming a nation, and a nation becoming a nation-state starts, obviously, with human beings. The process exists by and for people and, as such, people are its most critical element. Many studies and texts have been produced on the subject of nationalism and identity and the factors involved in their evolution. It is sufficient here to note that the phenomenon of people politicising themselves into nations and nation-states is a global phenomenon; it is not regionally or temporally unique – it is human nature.

In the face of rapidly changing technology and, more significantly, the increased presence of global information amongst local societies (through mere exposure, not necessarily through extensive technological implementation), it is not human nature that is changing but rather the end result of that applied nature. Many of the present ethnic conflicts and struggles for nationalism can be argued as being remnants of failed colonialism and imperialism. Small nations such as Chechnya, East Timor, Kosovo and others are taking advantage of an opportunity they have long awaited and are continuing the process towards statehood that has been interrupted for decades. Cultural identities continue to remain strong in many regions yet, without a doubt, the processes of economic modernisation and social change throughout the world are separating people from longstanding local identities. They also weaken the nation-state as a source of identity. (Huntington, 1998: 161.)

Kenichi Ohmae's commentaries on the state of nations and the emerging global economy reveal a keen understanding of this change in the people and how the information market forces are reshaping social identities so rapidly and so profoundly. Consider the following passage:

> This late-20th-century wave of immigration [from the old economy to the new borderless economy] is being driven, on the surface, by the development of global brands and popular culture and, at a much deeper level, by the infectious spread of new information-related technologies. It is a new kind of social process, something we have never seen before, and it is leading to a new kind of social reality: a genuinely cross-border civilization, nurtured by exposure to common technologies and sources of information, in which horizontal linkages within the same generation in different parts of the world are stronger than traditional, vertical linkages between generations in particular parts of it. (Ohmae, 1995: 38.)

This powerful trend that Ohmae mentions could be a temporary one, a transitional process as technology is further introduced into many aspects of life on the small and large scale. But even if this represents a limited process, there are enormous implications for the existing concept of nation-state. A person will give allegiance to the primary force in their life that provides them with identity. When younger generations are influenced more by TNCs and their products, they will take up their identity less with the nation-state in which they were born and more with the powers that establish the information and cultural context upon which they rely. Ohmae concludes this point by mentioning that

> as more and more individuals pass through the *brutal filter* separating old-fashioned geographies from the global economy, power over economic activity will inevitably migrate from the central governments of nation-states to the borderless network of countless individual, market-based decisions. (Ohmae, 1995: 39.)

The new social phenomenon involves the rise of the individual and the small interests as potential 'players' in the global political and economic system. Commonality is still a drawing factor between individuals and their nature to aggregate will not be suppressed. But the nation-state, depending on its own will and goals, will strive to maintain some level of control over the globalisation of its people by trying to restrict information flow or technological implementation.

Consider this pertinent and recent example from Microsoft's presence in Iceland. The Windows operating system is a hegemonic piece of software technology that can be found in practically every country in the world, and Iceland is no exception. For its primary market countries, Microsoft produces a language-specific version such as British English, French, German and so forth. But in the case of Iceland, Microsoft decided not to produce an Icelandic language version of Windows 98 because of the relatively small market size compared to the production cost. This upset Icelandic officials, and with good reason. Iceland has been maintaining a strict language-preservation programme for decades, not allowing foreign terms to be introduced until they have undergone a conversion to Icelandic. But because Windows is an essential technological dependency in this computer-literate society, and because it will be released in Iceland in an English version, Icelanders face an impending flood of non-Icelandic terminology which will pollute their language barriers. In summary, they state that this

> has everything to do with the shamanistic powers computers seem to exercise over the minds of the young and with the marketing strategies of far-away Microsoft. (Walsh, 1998.)

Consider another brief example where technology is not even the primary player in the contest between cultural identities. A recent national survey in Canada revealed that many Canadians are losing key elements of their own heritage, which are being replaced by pieces from their neighbour, the United States. For example:

> when asked who said, 'The medium is the message', some said it was Bill Gates of Microsoft rather than the Canadian academic Marhsall McLuhan. (DePalma, 1998.)

Officials put the blame mainly on 'the myths put out by Hollywood and the American entertainment industry'. But the problem is also recognised globally and as a result of a conference on the subject in Canada,

> government ministers from Europe, Latin America and Africa agreed to form a working group aimed at giving cultural issues greater prominence in foreign policy, trade and investment negotiations. (DePalma, 1998.)

As long as multimedia and computing technology is produced with a global emphasis – i.e. working from a global information standard – or even if supposed global information is produced with a clear cultural bias, the information standards of local regions will continue to be threatened. When propagated for long enough, perhaps for a few generations or less, the end result is a people whose nationalistic connections are wholly diluted, if not completely severed.

Territory

The implications of a people losing interest in the goals and *raison d'être* of their nation-state are serious. But could they extend as far as a loss of concern for the 'real' territory upon which their nation's sovereignty and their own personal freedoms have been established? For most of human history, the importance of land and territorial control was absolute; in fact, it could be argued that the great majority of conflicts have been contests over geographic control. If, through exposure to more global information, individuals are conditioned over time to disregard the importance of geographic space, then the perceived need for territorial control will diminish, and thus sovereignty as we know it today will be endangered. Regardless of the future outcome, at this moment, perceptions of frontiers are changing, from one frontier to several, from line to zone, from physical to cultural, from spatial to functional, from impermeable to permeable. (Anderson, 1996: 190.)

Since people are the architects of the geopolitical system in which they thrive, it is true that 'as with all regions that pertain to human social organisation, a state's territory is a social construct' (Knight, 1994: 76). The territory does exist in the real world but, clearly, without the human imposition of ownership and value onto the land, the concept would be an empty one. Even schoolchildren ponder the lack of big, fat lines painted on the landscape to delineate state from state, wondering where those states really are if the big, obvious lines they see on maps are not there in the real world. We cannot overlook the role that cartography plays in reinforcing the concept of geographic control. In fact, 'claims to an identity between people and territory can be asserted through maps and extended back through time' (Black, 1997: 143). Maps have served for centuries as the spatial surrogates for the abstract spatial concept that we cannot see in the real world – the nation-state. We can cognitively perceive evidence of the existence of a nation-state: the homogeneity of the people, the flag flying overhead, the different language, etc. All are symptoms of statehood. We can measure the area of the nation-state and prove its existence geographically. However, in the end,

> territory is more than just a physical and measurable entity. It is also something of the mind because people impute meaning to and gain meaning from territory. (Knight, 1994: 77.)

The global proliferation of information across geographic contexts weakens the hold of nationalistic tendencies and the connection to territorial value. Nationalistic groups now seeking statehood realise the importance of territorial control and thus continue their struggles for independence from the colonial powers. Yet for those nations that have attained sovereignty, and whose populace is becoming 'wired' to the global networks and influenced by TNC marketing, territorial control is not a serious, daily issue. In this way, one might imagine a form of technological transition taking place as nations become states and as states become technologically enhanced. This relates directly to Ohmae's 'brutal filter' concept mentioned above. For the common citizen, finding a connection with the land/territory is neither as important nor as cognitively significant as finding a connection to the global scene – e.g. to other people of similar age and interests. When perception of geographic space is weakened by the introduction of a global information perspective, territorial value decreases.

In the end, the overall value of territory to the people begins to decrease in the face of globalised information. When local information contexts are slowly dissolved, often through the economic intrusion of TNCs, then some context must take its place – and that context will be the one being introduced by the TNCs and other external forces. Consider carefully that

> even if a few states can still defend their territory against an invading army none can control the flow of images and ideas that shape human tastes and values. The globalised 'presence' of Madonna, McDonald's, and Mickey Mouse make a mockery of sovereignty as exclusive territorial control. (Krieger, 1993: 853.)

Some pundits praise the kind of liberation that a global information context can bring to the people of an oppressed nation-state, while others condemn it as the worst form of cultural destruction. Whatever the case, the truth is that this process is currently underway and, as a result, 'real' geographic space is being forfeited in favour of virtual space – the space where information resides and ideas are created and disseminated. When one realises that 'the political boundaries of nation-states are too narrow and constricted to define the scope and activities of modern business' (Korten: 123), we begin to see the kind of powerful forces the nation-states face.

Government

The government aspect of sovereignty is essentially the agglomeration of the people and territorial aspects; the control of territory by a homogeneous people requires an organising body to administer the state's affairs. It is not difficult to imagine how state governments might react in the face of the broad and sweeping technological changes aforementioned. If a nation's people slowly begin to lose their national identity and in turn the importance of territorial control, then the last bastion of hope for maintaining the state's sovereignty will lie in the government originally created to protect the state's interests.

Many national governments have had to change their administrative practices and, even more, their whole perspective on what they govern in the face of rapid economic and technological advances. Regional military and economic alliances in the past few decades have even led governments to yield some degree of their sovereignty to a supranational group for the purpose of solidarity in economic and military control. However, 'sovereign states have only reluctantly surrendered parts of their sovereignty to supranational groups since the 1950s' (Cole, 1983: 233). Reluctantly, yes, but the trend is ever-increasing at the close of the twentieth century, with the advent of the European Union and other economic alliances such as GATT, NAFTA, ASEAN, OECD, ECO and so forth. One can hardly blame the governments for taking such action – the isolationism of the pre-Second World War era is gone and, in the face of regional economic powers, the need for aggregation of effort in order to remain viable in a global market is paramount. It is this strong emphasis on economy, on the flow of goods, services and information, that is significant here. Sovereign governments are beginning to work towards a level of economic cooperation and competition that is unprecedented, but they are discovering that the transnational corporations have already 'arrived' – i.e. the TNCs are already operating at a level of sophistication and market penetration that is beyond the scope and capabilities of most nation-states. The TNCs were developed and have thrived on principles of economic gain and market savvy that nation-states are only now beginning to realise.

The TNCs fully appreciate the advantages they possess in this emerging arena and, as the development of a global information infrastructure continues (e.g. the implementation of digital nervous systems worldwide), they have been politically active to protect their interests within the nation-states. This has led some analysts to conclude that 'all over the world, national, provincial, and local governments have become pawns of global corporations and the Corporate Agenda' (Brecher & Costello, 1998: 301). This might be construed as a more extreme viewpoint, but it does point out the reality that TNCs do operate on a level that is unique and apart from the nation-state governments. Some may argue, for example, that the Microsoft/US Department of Justice confrontation is not about monopolistic practices but is really about the US trying to preserve some of its sovereign economic control in the face of a formidable new economic force. TNCs enjoy an almost untouchable status in some regions as the perceived carriers of economic up-turn and prosperity for the more impoverished countries. But does this mean that the role of national government is diminishing to the point where it only serves as an unwitting tool for TNCs? Some staunchly disagree and believe that 'the role of the nation-state in creating an innovation society is absolutely critical to the well-being of its citizens in the information age' (Carnoy, 1993: 91). At the moment, the need for partnership is apparent; we are in transitional mode and any type of overly rapid upheaval to the sovereignty system would undoubtedly cause widespread social confusion. The severity of TNC infiltration into the fundamental processes of statehood has yet to be objectively evaluated. However, we can see some rudimentary signs. When governments begin to legislate or take other formal actions against TNCs at an increasing rate, the perception is that the nation-states are beginning to understand the nature of the global information economy and are taking action to secure their place within it.

The focus of the transition into the realm of information geopolitics will be on the relationship between national governments and TNCs – this is where the 'battle lines' will be drawn. Whether or not a peaceful settlement is secured will remain to be seen. At this point in time we can discern the early signs of contention between the remnants of the nation-state paradigm – the governments – and the new entities of an evolving information-state paradigm – the TNCs. What is currently clear is that

> the greater the political power of corporations and those aligned with them, the less the political power of the people, and the less meaningful democracy becomes. (Korten: 140.)

This is so because the global information economy is much less reliant upon nation-states as the primary unit of interaction. Due to advanced, progressive and relatively inexpensive information technology, the primary unit of interaction is becoming the region, the small group and even the single individual acting on its own accord, by a 'personal sovereignty'. If and when national societies reach this most intrinsic, personal level, people will begin to connect, interact, aggregate and socialise according to common factors that transcend nationalism and sovereignty – at which point the significance of the nation-state as a geographic entity will diminish even further.

TRANSNATIONAL INFORMATION

Consideration and subsequent examination of the primary components of sovereignty – the people, territory and government – in the context of an evolving global information economy, has led this discussion to a patent realisation. At the global scale, we discover the fierce competition of many powerful TNCs to position themselves not only as the primary conduits of information, but as the primary originators of information. The notion that 'multinational corporations and nation-states are key actors in shaping the direction of the information economy' (Carnoy, 1993: 8) is generally true at the present time, but the roles they play, and for what duration, remains to be seen in this transitional model. Having briefly examined the nation-state and its changing applicability, it would be prudent at this point to do the same with the TNC.

Many texts have been written on the subject of TNCs and their methods, goals and effects on the global scene. This paper will not even begin to attempt a summary of this area of study. It is sufficient to point out that many different opinions exist on how beneficial or detrimental the TNC has been to the global economy and local political systems and cultures. The author would contend that how one views the TNC depends chiefly upon where one stands in terms of gaining or losing from the imposition of broader TNC involvement. The real 'threat' exists in the fact that much of the advancement of local and global societies rests on the achievements of the various TNCs and their relatively unhindered dissemination of these advances. In short, the TNCs are creating the global information infrastructure while nation-states simply act as the top-level political system with which TNCs must negotiate; but this is typically a minor filter. The simultaneous focus of a TNC is at different levels than the nation-state: it is above, below and within the operational sphere of geopolitics (when applying the classic definition). Most TNCs realise that

> the success of an industry or region is not the function of a nation *per se*, but of the particular combination of individuals, institutions, and culture in this industry or that region. (Ohmae, 1995: 64.)

What advantage does a TNC really have over a nation-state and why will this make a difference? The answer has already been alluded to here, but clarity on this point is crucial. Information technology – including mainframe and personal computers, software, peripherals, multimedia and, most importantly, networks – is the fundamental instrument through which TNCs operate. Whether or not their intention is to put these components in place, they are absolutely necessary for success in today's dynamic economic system. The more proficient any individual, TNC or nation-state becomes at realising the potential of the technology, the more successful they are likely to be in managing information flows. There are three main advantages that can be gained from implementing information technology:

> (1) to compress time, (2) to overcome geography, and (3) to alter the structure of relationships, such as bypassing intermediaries. (Malecki, 1997: 208.)

The idea of overcoming geography by the use of high-speed telecommunications and networks goes beyond the obvious high-speed transmission of data between locations. This is the underlying power of the technology – the removal of information boundaries between states and more importantly, between individual citizens. Information, for better or worse, acts as a binding medium when shared across diverse geographic contexts. It begins to create a familiarity between cultures that hundreds of years of international relations have failed to yield. Stated even more appropriately, information is

> the raw material of the economic process, itself quite indifferent to space, because the technologies of information transmission are now supposedly approaching the point where the friction of distance is nil. (Storper, 1997: 237.)

The elimination of distance and the diminution of geographic space are key factors that characterise the global information system. It is in this realm of 'virtual space' that TNCs can be found – along with a growing host of individuals and emergent nations that are finding a home on the global networks.

The *modus operandi* of the TNC working to build its global infrastructure is not entirely noble, however. After all, the focus is on the global information economy; therefore the focus is on producing revenues wherever possible. The process of globalisation allows TNCs 'to look for ways to sell their product in as many different places as possible' (*The Economist*, 1998b). While some corporations may be operating on a more philanthropic basis, the fact is that most exist for the simple goal of expanding markets and increasing their global revenue. If they happen to raise the standard of living in some regions, or create a new infrastructure, or bring international citizenry towards a more common understanding – that is a by-product. And conversely, if they happen to disrupt local customs and practices, it is most likely not by intention but simply by virtue of their global presence interacting on a local level. Consider, for example, how McDonald's restaurants have altered some basic practices in Asia:

> children's birthdays (previously uncelebrated in many places), queuing in Hong Kong (previously a scrum; now more likely to be in a line), the way that Japanese eat their food (previously always sitting down; now more likely to be standing up), and even smiling at strangers (previously close to an insult in China). (*The Economist*, 1998a.)

The responsibility of the TNCs should be to examine their potential markets very carefully and discern how to ease themselves into a market while causing the least amount of disruption. Disruption of culture, language, mores and even sovereignty will occur; the problem is how to minimise the effects as much as possible and, to do this, some form of 'recontexting' must take place. Many TNCs do try to take great care when creating information for a locality or preparing to move in physically and establish a foothold to provide services. But because TNCs mostly operate on a global information standard, there will come a point at which the conflict between the global and local information contexts must be resolved. Typically, the TNC ends up prevailing in the contest – either because the nation-state does not have strong enough legislation or the citizens value the benefits of the TNC's presence enough that they are willing to relinquish some aspects of their cultural identity in favour of new, imported aspects.

Microsoft's example

At Microsoft, we use the term 'localisation' to refer to the process by which products are tailored for local markets. Localisation is a lengthy exercise in which language is translated from US English and content is altered as necessary to fit the local information expectations of that market. The latter is in itself a difficult and detailed task, and is usually the point at which problems arise. Microsoft strives to consider its market geography and analyse the best market approach, but problems inevitably arise. These problems usually relate to the breakdown of the appropriate 'interface' between the global information contained in the Microsoft products and the local information expected in the market. This breakdown can be caused by a number of things, not least a lack of local knowledge on the part of the information creator who is working in a different geographic context; an American in Redmond, Washington, USA is unlikely to understand the local information expectations of a Turkish person in Ankara, Turkey. So the aim of localisation is

> achieving a balance between being global, with the scale advantages associated with size and global scope, and being local within each regional or national market and network of resources. (Malecki, 1997: 202.)

The history of geopolitical errors at Microsoft may be seen as a gallery of localisation events where the crucial global–local information interface was not diligently established beforehand. Some of the mistakes can be traced to a fundamental ignorance of world geography on the part of individuals (in itself a commentary on the state of geography education in the US; but this is not the place to discuss this issue). Other mistakes were due to a pure lack of local knowledge that probably could not have been anticipated. The majority of problems Microsoft has encountered have involved the cartography in its various products, from Windows to Office to Encarta World Atlas. This is not surprising, since

> maps can serve as tools of debate, highlighting these spatial implications and thus apparently providing graphic evidence of the nature of the practice of power and of what can be seen as a need to challenge it. (Black, 1997: 120.)

We know that one of the first things customs agents in some countries will examine is the maps in the products; they load the product onto their computer, open it up, and take a look to see if Microsoft's insidious global information is acceptable to the local information market. In some specific cases, such as Turkey, India and China, the answer was a resounding no. In some countries it is true that 'unofficial maps, such as those made by or for one of the parties to a legal dispute, are sometimes admitted in court' (McEwen, 1998: 19). In Latin American countries this legal complication can include *any* cartography sold in the country, regardless of the source, which potentially makes Microsoft a contributor of evidence in a potential real-world boundary arbitration (for or against the host country!). In these situations, Microsoft is forced to make a market decision: comply with the local information needs and change the product, or bypass the local information market completely and proceed to sell in those nation-states which will accept the global standard.

Consider a few key examples of geopolitical problems that Microsoft has faced:

Product: Windows 95 (1995)
Location: India
Problem: This was probably the first major, public geopolitical issue confronted by Microsoft. The original specification for Windows 95 included a time-zone map in which users could select their country's time zone and the country would be highlighted and outlined on a small bitmap image. The outline for India was lacking the highly sensitive Jammu and Kashmir region, by only a few pixels. However, this was enough to cause the government of India to ban Windows 95 until the country outline was fixed. This was hyped up in the media and was a generally embarrassing fiasco for Microsoft.
Solution: The solution involved removing the country outlines from the map *completely* and showing a borderless world map in the time-zone feature, where only the time zones themselves were highlighted. The interesting part of this incident is that a Microsoft competitor, not the Indian government, was the one who initially raised this as an issue.

Product: Encarta World Atlas and Encarta Encyclopaedia (1996)
Location: South Korea
Problem: This was a case where the revelation of a single error in Encarta World Atlas (EWA) unleashed a public backlash and the uncovering of more errors in Encarta Encyclopaedia (EE). It started initially with a border error near Chon-ji Lake and Paektu-san Mountain on the China/North Korean border. Chon-ji is a lake in a caldera of an extinct volcano and Paektu-san is the highest peak around the caldera's rim. The location has great spiritual significance for Koreans. The EWA map

showed both features to be completely within China; this was offensive to the Koreans.

Solution: After much research, it was found that an agreement had been reached – perhaps decades ago – between China and North Korea, which established a border running through Chon-ji, giving half of the lake to North Korea and placing Paektu-san within North Korea. This fact was not reflected on our maps, which were using older data from the US government. After sufficient source material for the new border was received, the data in EWA was fixed – despite the Korean public's hostile claims that Microsoft was conspiring with Japan to undermine Korean culture. Other map issues were the always-sensitive Liancourt Rocks (Tok-do, Take-shima) and the lack of the 'East Sea' label for the Sea of Japan.

This incident gave rise to a review by the Koreans of other content in both EWA and EE. The Koreans found an error that was offensive to them in a historical passage, so this re-ignited some hostility towards Microsoft. This content was also fixed and, eventually, the Microsoft Korea subsidiary met with the South Korean Ministry of Foreign Affairs and Ministry of Information to settle the problems. A peaceful conclusion was reached and the government agencies were generally pleased – but at the cost of significant public loss-of-face for Microsoft.

Product: Encarta World Atlas (1997)
Location: Japan
Problem: Microsoft made headway into the Japanese reference product market by releasing a Japanese (Kanji) version of EWA. Besides the technical challenge of creating a Kanji-based atlas, there were also several geopolitical problems. The stance of the Japanese government is that the southern Kuril islands belong to Japan, as well as the disputed island Take-shima and the islands of Senkaku-shoto. The Microsoft Japan office wanted all of these areas shaded as Japanese territory, even though Japan does not control the southern Kurils and Take-shima.
Solution: There was a lot of negotiation between Microsoft headquarters and Microsoft Japan over these issues. In the end, market forces prevailed and the disputed areas were all shaded as Japanese territory on the map, with a label indicating that the territory is disputed. The text content in the product mentions the disputes.

The examples above and their related solutions are only brief examples of the myriad issues that Microsoft faces as a TNC attempting to penetrate new global markets. The challenge for Microsoft, unlike some TNCs, is that a mistake found in one product might affect the sales potential of other products. As an example, the problem in India with Windows 95 did not threaten only Windows 95 – it threatened the sale of all Microsoft products in that market. Like any other TNC, Microsoft would prefer to expand into new markets but if the potential risks outweighed the benefits, then Microsoft might forsake the market in favour of another one involving less risk. Some nation-states are more adamant about enforcing their sovereignty, and they do so by reinforcing their local information standard. In the end it makes only a small difference to the TNC; there are many more potential markets to enter. Reasons for choosing not to enter a market are complex but, when viewed simply, the decision is based on information geopolitics. Microsoft, as a primary producer of information-management tools as well as content, is unwilling to become embroiled in disputes over competing local information contexts. If anything, it would prefer to work around such disputes and still enter the market.

In many of the geopolitical issues facing Microsoft, the nation-state is struggling to reassert its sovereignty via the information medium. Indeed, these struggles exemplify the truth that

> our very concept of 'world', an ideological construct that is usually more philosophical than geographical in content, can be framed and articulated by cartography. (Henrikson, 1994: 50.)

Many governments are fully aware of the power of cartography and, even more so, the power of the global information venue provided by TNCs and their related information technology and products. Therefore, national governments strive to utilise the TNC as a means of elevating their local information context into the global context. Why? Because if a country is successful in promoting its local viewpoint and convinces a TNC to incorporate this local context into the broader, global information stream, then that country's local context is globally legitimised, at the expense of other neighbouring contexts that might differ. When unwary, the TNC can be used as an ignorant participant in the perpetuation of misinformation on a global scale. However, the TNC is not always unaware of what it is getting into; this is where another interesting dimension to the problem comes into play. In order to establish itself and gain access to a local market, a TNC may *consciously* favour one local information context, on the basis of market revenues. For example, if Argentina yields significantly more revenue than Chile for a certain company's product in Latin America, the company may decide to proceed with showing Argentina's viewpoint, at the expense of Chile's (if the two viewpoints are incompatible). The product may not sell in Chile and may actually yield some negative reactions there but, within the global economy as a whole, the loss to the TNC of Chile is a trifle. The TNC gets what it is really after – the larger revenues – and appeases at least one local information market in the process. In fact, clearly biasing itself towards one local context may improve the TNC's ability to thrive in that single market – more than if it had compromised between the two countries' viewpoints. So there are times when a TNC may decide to opt for the inclusion of a local information context into its global scheme.

Microsoft strives to avoid situations in which its information media are being employed as tools for local geopolitical agendas, and it attempts on every occasion to reach a compromise between differing local information contexts. The company is not always successful in avoiding these problems, mainly because of a lack of local geographic understanding. However, Microsoft is taking steps company-wide to be more attentive to these issues. Measures include the creation of the Geopolitical Product Strategy (GPS) group. The GPS mission is to help protect Microsoft's global markets against closure and in turn preserve local market trust in Microsoft's product integrity. But even with the existence of the GPS group, Microsoft will continue to face difficult decisions on a market-by-market basis. The real challenge, as dictated by information geopolitics, is to proactively discern the proper interfaces between the global and local information contexts long before the products are even produced. This is the challenge Microsoft and many other TNCs face during the process of localisation.

The nation-state, with its unique local information context, is then in the position of having to compete with other nation-states to access the global information context and to place itself within it. Because TNCs are not only the creators of this global information realm but its primary administrators, nation-states struggle to reaffirm their sovereignty in a world where real boundaries, territorial control and the notion of sovereignty are challenged by virtual markets, globalised information and technologically empowered individuals.

NEW SOVEREIGNTIES AND INFORMATION GEOPOLITICS

Consider the major trends outlined so far in this discussion and how they relate to the role of nation-states and TNCs in information geopolitics:

- the profusion of information technology on a global scale and a subsequent, unprecedented level of individual access to knowledge
- people becoming more connected with individuals in other countries than those with their own nationalistic tendencies
- geographic territory becoming less important as compared to information access and the control of the *image* of territory (e.g. cartographic information)
- national governments yielding control to intranational bodies to form economic alliances to control information flows and to protect local/ regional information contexts
- transnational corporations acting as conveyors of global information, choosing to accept/reject local contexts as part of the global information system based on market viability
- nation-states jockeying for access to the global information stream, each trying to assert its own local context as being globally significant, or else forfeiting the local context in favour of the global one.

When these trends in the developing information economy are examined *en masse*, it would appear that both nation-states and TNCs have a unique role to play. The trends above solidify the supposition that

> the past two decades have seen the most rapid and sweeping institutional transformation in human history. It is a conscious and intentional transformation in search of a new world economic order in which business has no nationality and knows no borders. (Korten: 121.)

The turnabout has been so rapid, in fact, that it is clear that individuals, groups, nation-states and even TNCs are not fully aware of the extent of the revolution. If there is any truth-value to this suggestion, and growing evidence indicates that there is, then the world may be poised for a significant geopolitical paradigm shift. But if the geopolitical landscape changes in response to information technology, then what will the next paradigm entail? This is the key question to which we now turn our attention.

At the present time it is evident that both nation-states and TNCs are acting out similar but somewhat uncoordinated roles in the global information economy. This could in part be due to the fact that the information economy is still evolving and thus there are no clear roles to play. Until now nation-states have been carrying out their individual 'manifest destinies' and exercising their right to self-determination as gained through their sovereign status. Likewise, TNCs have been operating mostly as just big businesses, not only because that's what they are but also because of their unrealised, hegemonic nature in the world scene. When positioned together in the current global system, the nation-states and TNCs carry on a mainly contentious interaction that is based on one entity trying to circumvent the other's regulations or practices; it is not necessarily a constructive relationship. This is a broad generalisation, however; not all of the interactions between these two entities are negative. When nation-states realise the advantages of the borderless TNC, they often take appropriate steps to remedy the situation and come to realise that 'technological capacity gives many states the possibility of operating beyond boundaries, including space' (Krieger, 1993: 853). So we then have both nation-states and TNCs manoeuvring for strategic economic positions, both adopting similar tactics and both relying heavily – if not exclusively – on information technology as the means to this end.

A convergence is occurring between the function of nation-states and that of TNCs within the global economic system – a convergence based in part on the existence of information technology and the advantages it provides. The author would suggest that, for the most part, both parties are currently playing out their roles unaware of the long-term implications. On the information geopolitics field of play, the contest will go on between the global information context and the local information context. On one side the nation-states are trying to maintain their sovereign perspective, while on the other the TNCs are trying to globalise geographic information and homogenise national citizens into being good transnational consumers. While TNCs have the option of catering to specific local contexts – and some do on a limited basis – it is more cost-effective and beneficial to future revenues to create a homogenous consumer base. The goal of the two players is the same: maintain the national citizens as consumers of your information. The struggle is actually over what information the citizens will be allowed to consume. What becomes quite blatant is the role of the individual and interest groups in dictating how the large, global players interact. Again, we are talking about a level of personal empowerment that has never existed before. And at this personal level, boundaries and territory are much less significant; the only boundaries that matter are those of perceived personal space and the amount of freedom one has to access information.

Corporate Nations

So what becomes of the nation-state and the TNC when citizens are better informed, less ignorant and aware of their role in the information economy? And what becomes of the citizen, the homogenous groups and stateless nations of people? This discussion now arrives at a certain level of appropriate conjecture.

In the immediate future, one can foresee a possible aggregation of the nation-state and TNC into what may be called a 'Corporate Nation'. The Corporate Nation extends the powers of both the nation-state and the TNC, creating a new geopolitical entity. A Corporate Nation is an entity less concerned with geographic territory and more concerned with connecting with individuals on a personal level. A Corporate Nation is a hegemonic entity which, through its actions, propagates a modified global information context that overrides local contexts whenever possible; the modification rests primarily in the particular goals of the Corporate Nation. Certainly not every TNC shares the same vision of a global information system and, as stated before, all information is ultimately context dependent. Therefore, Corporate Nations may have a global information context that differs from that of others in terms of how they operate and by what model, theory, etc. The Corporate Nation operates from the following perspectives on the conditions of sovereignty discussed above:

- **People:** individuals empowered by technology, able to make free consumer choices regardless of geographic contexts and limitations. An individual becomes a *de facto* citizen by using the Corporate Nation's products or services. An individual has the right to switch allegiances if the Corporate Nation fails to provide what is expected.
- **Territory:** the place where consumers exist, and where raw materials for technology manufacture are available. It is necessary for the location of resource bases and infrastructure, but otherwise not significant.
- **Government:** in nation-states, a barrier through which commerce must pass, full of regulations and tariffs although it may strive towards fairness; a necessary evil. In other Corporate Nations, it is merely an interface to another domain of information, goods and services.

The overriding goal of the Corporate Nation is not sovereignty; its sovereignty has already been declared by its existence and proven success in the global market. What remains important is the right of self-determination. A Corporate Nation will insist on the right to innovate, to expand and to continue to provide services and information on a global basis, without impediment from nation-states still self-confined to the local information standard. Sometimes self-determination is driven strictly by the desire for financial gain, but it may also be a genuine desire to improve quality of life for the local market. For a nation-state, becoming a Corporate Nation means relinquishing the right to its unique local information context and embracing a more global standard. For the TNC, becoming a Corporate Nation involves the acquisition of some state-like accountability and incorporation into an arena where its actions will have real consequences.

While a Corporate Nation might have geographic territory in its possession, the entity primarily exists in a virtual space – i.e. it exists through the information products it generates and disseminates. In this way, the real citizens of the Corporate Nation are not necessarily the end-users of the products; *they are the products themselves.* Much criticism has been levelled at TNCs in recent times for disregarding the welfare of local national citizens. If true, this would only reinforce the concept that is carried over to the Corporate Nation: the products are the citizens and it is the duty of the nation to protect its citizens. In nation-states today, the primary carriers of information and culture are people: information is exchanged through diplomats, students, businesspeople and so forth. In the information economy, the technology-reduced friction of distance allows information sent via networks or bundled in a software package to act as the surrogate carrier of culture. Over time, as more and more localities build their digital nervous systems, the precedent of accepting these 'virtual citizens' (i.e. products) will be established. Undoubtedly, just as with TNCs and nation-states today, the Corporate Nation will take any necessary action to protect its citizens and keep them viable in and between their targeted markets. It is very doubtful one will see a Corporate Nation positioning warships off the coast of a nation-state, but it is very likely that a Corporate Nation may cut off access to global networks or withdraw some vital information infrastructure services.

The Corporate Nation is not too dissimilar, then, from the existing TNC, but is a point of convergence of the TNC and the nation-state. The implication is that the current nation-state will have to evolve *more* than the current TNC in order to become a Corporate Nation. TNCs already have an advantage in the global markets because, as stated before, they are chiefly responsible for creating the infrastructure upon which the market is being built. But more than the technology itself, what is really at stake for the nation-states is their sovereignty based on their control of territory. This notion will change over time and, in the final analysis, the nation-states who make the transition into the global information economy and become Corporate Nations will simply be Corporate Nations with territory – a distinction from non-territorial Corporate Nations that may not be very substantial. It is conceivable that the price of joining the global system will be releasing some degree of territorial control (such as in the European Union).

A spectrum of new geopolitical entities

As the global information economy grows and develops further into the future, we will see unique roles ascribed to the primary players of the former geopolitics model – and more than just the Corporate Nation. The Corporate Nation is proposed here as the next plausible development for nation-states and TNCs alike but, realistically, the information economy of the future will allow for many new kinds of geopolitical interaction.

New players will enter the information geopolitics scene and new roles in the system will be possible. We will see many roles being performed by many diverse geopolitical entities, widely ranging in scale and power, and also varying in the amount of technological adaptation that has taken place. While the primary fuel of the system – information – will be more clearly defined as a commodity, the acting players and their interactions will actually become very complex. The spectrum proposed here is based on the notion of scale, starting with the single individual citizen and propagating the concept to the highest aggregation possible – the global state. The table below provides a brief summary:

Table 1

	People	Territory	Government
Individual	A citizen empowered by information technology; an information user with a distinct identity.	The virtual networks; a virtual 'home', local geography.	Adheres to the local information context while accessing the global.
Clan	A group of citizens united with a common identity; information users and distributors.	Shared virtual spaces, neighbourhoods, small regions.	Builds its own local context while accessing the global.
Nation	A homogeneous aggregation of individuals and clans, united by a common identity or purpose, connected via information technology; creates, distributes, and uses information.	Large, distributed virtual spaces, possible geographic space.	Self-determining with its own local context, with its own global access.
Info-nation or Virtual nation	A virtual nation-state, comprised of a people, virtual territory, and a governing system; maintains a unique information domain.	A nation without geographic territory; possesses a well-established, influential virtual presence. Sovereignty is based on control of information	Self-governed nation, answering to itself on a virtual basis. New local context is created or a new interface to the global context within a local one.

91

Table 1 *(cont.)*

	People	Territory	Government
TNC	A transnational business operation established for the purpose of creating, disseminating and controlling information technology.	Exists virtually, distributed across many geographic contexts. May be based in one nation-state.	Follows national government regulations as much as necessary to penetrate local markets. Thinks globally, acts locally.
Nation-state	Classic definition: a defined people, geographic territory and government body.	Exists geographically – sovereignty is based on control of territory.	Government exists to regulate and legislate, to protect national citizenry (i.e. reinforce the local context).
Corporate Nation	A unified corporate body of individuals, together for the purpose of succeeding in the global economy.	Exists virtually or geographically or both; geographic territory is secondary to control of information assets.	Self-governing, tolerates nation-state governments (local contexts) as a hindrance, interfaces better with other Corporate Nations (other global contexts).
Intra-nation	An aggregation of nations, info-nations, nation-states and/or corporate nations, based on common goals and regional information contexts.	Virtual or geographic, the space is an aggregation of individual national entities.	Control is relinquished to a higher body for decision-making, local contexts are aggregated into regional contexts for better interface to the global context.
Global-state	A fully aggregated political-economic system wherein the global information context has absorbed all local information contexts.	Exists virtually and geographically, *de facto* control over most territory – despite possible rogue nations.	Disaggregated sovereignty is gone, self-determination exists only at the highest level by a governing body.

The implications of such a system are prodigious but this is only one possible model. This is not a strict hierarchy with a simple transition from one state of existence to the next. Many of these new entities of information geopolitics will exist unto themselves with no need to evolve, while others may aggregate and expand. Obviously, the global state is the pinnacle of the hierarchy – a point at which information geopolitics is irrelevant on a global scale. This state is not being proposed here as a positive, logical end to the process, merely as a possibility. When viewing this possible system, we need to ask again about the ways in which electronic information and mapping technologies are reconfiguring the contemporary world the techniques of data exchange and representation legitimise new social practices and institutions in ways we have only begun to recognise and regulate. (Pickles, 1995: 231.)

At this point in time we can only begin to surmise what kinds of geopolitical entities may arise in response to the information paradigm shift that is underway.

CONCLUSIONS

In the course of this discussion, little emphasis has been directly placed on boundaries and territoriality. However, these being the by-products of a broader geopolitical sphere of action, the implications are clear. Undoubtedly, many questions can be raised throughout this discourse; there are many 'what ifs' and 'maybes' to be addressed, any one of which could change the direction of the current geopolitical trends. There are many barriers still in existence that can prevent the global information economy from ever reaching fruition. Some of these barriers are sadly blatant, such as the fact that

> more than 1.3 billion people live on less than a dollar a day, about 60 percent of them in South Asia and Sub-Saharan Africa. Infant mortality rates remove over 90 per thousand live births in Sub-Saharan Africa and 70 in South Asia, compared with 40 in East Asia. (The World Bank, 1997: 4.)

Equally troubling is the fact that

> in far too many countries the private sector continues to struggle under severe trade restrictions and high taxes. Poor public infrastructure acts as a drag on market efficiency by increasing costs, reducing competitiveness, and restricting access to domestic and international markets. (The World Bank, 1997: 38.)

The serious economic and political disparity that exists between nation-states today certainly cannot be overlooked. While one may find Coca-Cola in the middle of a Third World country, this is by no means an indication that the country is benefiting from the presence of a TNC, or that this nation-state is on the brink of transition into a Corporate Nation.

Currently, more negatives than positives are seen deriving from TNCs and the early form of information/media economy that is emerging. We are in a time of transition and there will be both positive and negative outcomes. But it would be prudent for individuals, nations, nation-states and TNCs to realise that

> economic globalisation is neither in the human interest nor inevitable. It is axiomatic that political power aligns with economic power. The larger the economic unit, the larger its dominant players, and the more political power becomes concentrated in the largest corporations. (Korten: 140.)

If this trend remains strong into the next century, then the field of information geopolitics will be ripe for growth and the evolution of Corporate Nations, as well as other new forms of sovereignty, will not be unlikely at all. The current global system is undoubtedly still a long way from the world of information geopolitics as outlined here; but the potential does exist.

More and more people throughout the world are realising that 'the production of information is shaping politics and, by default, establishing new rules for post-industrial society' (Barnet & Cavanagh, 1994: 334). As we focus our attention on the state of geopolitics and the future viability of nation-states and boundaries, let us consider then what the new geopolitical 'rules' might be, and who will be writing them.

NOTE

1   The ideas and opinions expressed by the author in this text do not represent any official ideas and opinions of the Microsoft Corporation.

BIBLIOGRAPHY

Anderson, M. (1996) *Frontiers: Territory and State Formation in the Modern World*, Polity Press.

Barnet, R. J. & Cavanagh, J. (1994) *Global Dreams: Imperial Corporations and the New World Order*, Simon & Schuster.

Black, J. (1997) *Maps and Politics*, University of Chicago Press.

Brecher, J. & Costello, T. (1998) 'Reversing the Race to the Bottom' in Tuathail, G., Dalby, S. & Routledge, P. (eds.) *The Geopolitics Reader*, Routledge: 299–304.

Carnoy, M. (1993) 'Multinationals in a Changing World Economy – Whither the Nation State?', *The New Global Economy in the Information Age*, Pennsylvania State University Press.

Cole, J. P. (1983) *Geography of World Affairs*, (6th edn.), Butterworths.

DePalma, A. (1998) 'Canadians aim to protect culture from Americanism', *New York Times*, 5 July, from online resources.

Dijkink, G. (1996) *National Identity & Geopolitical Visions – Maps of Pride & Pain*, Routledge.

Gates, B. (1997) 'Speech to the National Governor's Association', Microsoft Corporate Information (internal web source), 30 July.

Henrikson, A. K. (1994) 'The Power and Politics of Maps' in Demko, G. &. Wood, W. B. (eds.), *Reordering the World*, Westview Press: 49–70.

Huntington, S. P. (1998) 'The Clash of Civilisations?' in *The Geopolitics Reader*, Tuathail, G., Dalby, S. & Routledge, P. (eds.), Routledge: 159–169.

Knight, D. B. (1994) 'People Together, Yet Apart: Rethinking Territory, Sovereignty, and Identities' in Demko, G. &. Wood, W. B. (eds.), *Reordering the World*, Westview Press: 71–86.

Krieger, J. (1993) 'Sovereignty' in Krieger, J. (editor-in-chief), *Oxford Companion to Politics of the World*, Oxford University Press: 851–853.

Malecki, E. J. (1997) *Technology & Economic Development*, Addison Wesley Longman Ltd.

McEwen, A. (1998) 'Temple of Dispute – The Fine Line of Border Negotiation', *Mercator's World*, Vol. 3, No. 4, July/August: 16–19.

Minahan, J. (1996) *Nations without States*, Greenwood Press.

O'Loughlin, J. (1994) *Dictionary of Geopolitics*, Greenwood Press.

Ohmae, K. (1995) *The End of the Nation State – The Rise of Regional Economies*, Simon & Schuster, Inc.

Pickles, J. (1995) *Ground Truth – The Social Implications of Geographic Information Systems*, Guilford Press.

Storper, M. (1997) *The Regional World – Territorial Development in a Global Economy*, Guilford Press.

The Economist (1998a) 'The personal touch', 16 May, Economist Review section: 4–5.

The Economist (1998b) 'The science of alliance', 4 April: 69–70.

The World Bank (1997) *World Bank Atlas – 1997*, The World Bank.

Tuathail, G. Ó. (1996) *Critical Geopolitics*, University of Minnesota Press.

Walsh, M. W. (1998) 'Icelanders, Microsoft in War of Words', *Los Angeles Times*, 29 June, from online resources.

6
Territorial Disputes and International Conflict: Empirical Findings and Theoretical Explanations

Paul K. Huth

While territorial conflict has been a recurring feature of international politics, systematic research on the theoretical and empirical relationship between territorial disputes and interstate military conflict is still in the early stages of development. In this paper I review the existing empirical and theoretical literature in order to draw conclusions about whether territorial disputes are a central cause of interstate war, as claimed by some scholars (e.g. Vasquez 1993). I will focus my analysis around the following questions:

- Have empirical tests produced results which indicate a significant and strong correlation between the presence of a territorial dispute between states and the likelihood of militarised conflict and war?
- If there is evidence of a strong empirical correlation between territorial disputes and war, what theoretical arguments provide a basis for explaining a causal relationship between territorial disputes and international conflict?
- What would be the testable implications of theoretical arguments that explain why territorial disputes are an important cause of international conflict? What would be the different causal pathways by which territorial disputes lead to international conflict?

This study is divided into the following sections:

- a discussion of what is meant by the term 'territorial dispute' and the other types of issues that are often disputed between states
- a review of the findings from a number of recent empirical studies which indicate a consistent relationship between territorial disputes and patterns of international conflict
- an analysis of theoretical arguments that attempt to explain why territorial disputes often escalate in to armed conflict
- a proposal for an agenda for future research which focuses on developing and testing more specific hypotheses about the causal pathways by which territorial disputes escalate.

Borderlands Under Stress (M.A. Pratt and J.A. Brown (eds), ISBN 90-411-9790-7).
© Kluwer Law International, 2000.

ISSUES IN DISPUTE BETWEEN STATES

Before turning to a review of existing empirical findings, it is necessary to discuss briefly what types of issues are often disputed by governments. I will begin with the concept of a territorial dispute and then turn to other disputed issues.

A territorial dispute exists when there is a disagreement between two governments over where their homeland or colonial borders should be fixed, or when one country contests the right of another to exercise any sovereign rights over some or all of its homeland or colonial territory. In either of these two situations, both governments seek control of and sovereign rights over the same territory (Huth 1996: chapter 2). Many territorial disputes centre around conflicting claims as to exactly where a border should be located. In other cases, however, the legitimacy of a border is severely questioned when one country seeks to incorporate some or all of the territory controlled by another state. Table 1 provides a summary list of territorial disputes in the international system between 1919 and 1995 (see the Appendix for a more detailed discussion of the concept of a territorial dispute and description of the cases).

The factors that make territory valuable to governments can include its natural resource endowment, the religious and ethnic composition of its population, or its military-strategic location. There can be diverse reasons why two countries cannot agree on the exact location of a boundary or, more fundamentally, who has legitimate rights to sovereignty over territory. In many disputes the problem is rather technical and based on legalities, as governments contest the interpretation and meaning of ambiguously written treaties and historical documents which helped establish existing boundaries. In other cases, however, political conflicts stemming from deep-seated ideological and cultural differences can lead governments to seek control over territory in order to establish political dominance or to counter perceived political and security threats.

Table 1

Territorial Disputes 1919–1995

Region	Total	Time Period		
		Pre-1945	Post-1945	Across both periods
Europe	95	60	27	8
Middle & Near East	89	36	32	21
Africa	48	17	26	5
Asia & Pacific	64	14	40	10
Americas	51	30	6	15
TOTAL	347	157	131	59

In the remainder of this paper I will often make comparisons between territorial and other issues that are contested in international disputes. It is therefore necessary to identify what those non-territorial issues typically are. Drawing on the work of other scholars who have assembled datasets on international disputes, crises and wars (e.g. Holsti, 1991; Luard, 1986; Brecher & Wilkenfeld, 1997; Jones *et al*, 1996; Sherman, 1994), I would identify the following types of non-territorial issues as often producing conflict between states:

- **Political:** Attempts by one country to politically de-stabilise the regime of another and remove its existing leadership from power. In such cases conflicts have arisen due to differences in political ideology and/or the belief that a particular national leader poses a threat to the security of another country or its political leadership.
- **Economic:** Economic conflicts relating to such issues as barriers to trade and the protection of home markets, the nationalisation of foreign property and adequate levels of compensation, and compliance with bilateral and multilateral economic agreements.
- **Migration:** Problems relating to cross-border movements of populations which governments find difficult to control or manage. One important set of cases revolves around large-scale refugee movements stemming from political and economic turmoil within neighbouring states; a different set of issues arises over problems of illegal border-crossings by citizens in one country who seek to evade existing immigration laws and establish illegal residence in another country.
- **Protection:** Efforts by one government to protect the rights of its citizens abroad and ensure their security when foreign governments are suspected of pursuing discriminatory policies or are unable to ensure basic law and order.

REVIEW OF EMPIRICAL RESULTS

The results of a number of recent historical and quantitative empirical studies converge on the conclusion that there is a strong correlation between territorial disputes and various types of international conflict behaviour. Figure 1 summarises the main findings which indicate that territorial disputes are systematically related to the emergence and escalation of militarised confrontations between states. A variety of different types of dataset have been utilised to produce these consistent empirical results. I begin by summarising findings that have been generated by scholars working with these multiple datasets:

Datasets on war and issues at stake

Two comparative historical studies by Kalevi Holsti and Evan Luard are particularly important because the authors have identified the issues over which states have fought wars since the inception of the modern state system in the seventeenth century (Holsti, 1991; Luard, 1986). The data presented by Holsti supports the conclusion that territorial disputes have been the single most frequent issue related to the outbreak of war over the past four centuries. However, he also identifies a broad range of political and economic issues in addition to territorial conflicts, and argues that multiple issues can be associated with the outbreak of an individual war. For example, he lists 21 issues other than territory which have been in dispute between states in a total of 177 wars from 1648 to 1989 (Holsti, 1991: 308). Territorial issues, then, are not the only issue over which wars have been fought, but Holsti nevertheless presents strong evidence that territorial disputes, compared to other issues in dispute, are much more frequently associated with war. He calculates that across five different historical periods the percentages of wars involving territorial issues range from as high as 85 per cent to no lower than 45 per cent (Holsti, 1991: 308). Vasquez re-analyses Holsti's data and argues that he has actually understated the frequency of territorial issues (Vasquez, 1993: chapter 4); Vasquez therefore re-codes the data and concludes that territorial disputes are associated with somewhere between 80 and 90 per cent of all wars (Vasquez, 1993: 130).

Evan Laurd has also attempted to identify the issues over which states have fought wars and, like Holsti, considers a diverse set of issues such as religion, commerce and trade, national unification, ethnicity, and ideological struggles, along with territorial conflicts (Luard, 1986). It is not possible to pinpoint the frequency with which territorial disputes are related to war across historical periods, since Luard does not present data on the issues at stake for each war in his dataset. He does argue, however, that no single issue predominates across all three periods that he examines (1648–1789, 1789–1917 and 1917–1983). Nevertheless, in his discussion of cases for each historical period and from the list of cases presented in the appendix to his book, it seems that territorial claims come up again and again, even when Luard argues that other issues (ethnicity and national unification) were in dispute. Thus, while Luard does not claim that territorial issues are the single most frequent issue associated with wars, his actual data and discussion of many cases indicate otherwise. I agree with Vasquez (1993: 131–32) that Luard clearly understates the frequency of territorial conflict, and I would argue that if one were to carefully code each war identified by Luard to determine if territory was in dispute when a war was initiated, the resulting conclusions about the centrality of territorial disputes to the outbreak of war would be very similar to Holsti's.

In conclusion, when wars are classified according to the issues in dispute, Holsti and Luard's datasets point to the same conclusion: territorial disputes have consistently been an issue over which governments have been willing to go to war.

However, there is one important limitation in the research design employed in the historical studies of Holsti and Luard, and caution must therefore be exercised in drawing this conclusion from their data. In both cases the scholars select only cases of wars for analysis and, therefore, while territorial disputes are correlated with the presence of war, we do not know whether the absence of war is also correlated with a relatively low frequency of territorial disputes between countries. As a result, additional datasets that include both war and no-war outcomes must be examined before any confident conclusions can be drawn about the empirical relationship between territorial disputes and armed conflict.

The militarised interstate dispute (MID) dataset

The MID dataset contains over 2,000 cases of disputes between countries from 1816 to 1992 in which at least one state threatens or resorts to the use of military force but the actual outbreak of war is quite rare (Jones *et al*, 1996). Scholars have presented evidence from the MID dataset that military escalation is more likely when territorial issues are at stake between states. Paul Hensel has reported that MIDs from 1816 to 1992 that involve territorial disputes are three times more likely to escalate to high levels, including war, than other issue-types (Hensel, 1996a). He also notes that states that are the initial targets of militarised actions at the outset of a MID involving territory are more than three times more likely to reciprocate with a military response. Thus, when state leaders are confronted with a military threat to territorial interests, they are unlikely to back away from a military confrontation. Paul Senese reports findings very similar to those of Hensel in his study of MID escalation to war (Senese, 1997). He finds that a territorial dispute increases the baseline probability of war by more than nine times. Senese also examines patterns of fatality levels in MIDs and reports that the likelihood and severity of fatalities is positively and strongly correlated with territorial issues (Senese, 1996 & 1997).

Hensel, in his study of the evolution of enduring rivalries, finds that the frequency of MIDs is higher if a territorial dispute exists between two countries (Hensel, 1996b: chapter 4).[1] Other scholars such as Gary Goertz and Paul Diehl have, in turn, presented strong evidence that enduring rivalries since the early nineteenth century have been much more likely to lead to wars than non-enduring rivalries (Goertz & Diehl, 1992a & 1993). Vasquez has also argued that, while not all enduring rivalries escalate to war, the risks of war increase significantly if the rivals are entangled in a territorial dispute (Vasquez, 1996).

The behavioural correlations of war dataset

Russell Leng has constructed a dataset of 40 international crises from 1816 to 1980 which contains information on the diplomatic and military actions of the crisis participants (Leng, 1993). Utilising this dataset, Leng has found strong evidence linking territorial disputes to war in his work on crisis bargaining and escalation. He reports that when states have vital or very salient security interests at stake, the chances of escalation and war increase because states are more likely to adopt coercive, bullying bargaining strategies and less likely to compromise. Vital or salient security interests in turn are defined by Leng to include disputes over control of national territory.

The international crisis behaviour (ICB) dataset

Michael Brecher and Jonathan Wilkenfeld have compiled a dataset on crises from 1919 to 1994 which contains over 400 cases and includes a broad range of information on the behaviour of the states involved and the attributes of each crisis (Brecher, 1993; Brecher & Wilkenfeld, 1997). David Rousseau and co-authors utilised the ICB dataset and report that in crises from 1919 to 1988 territorial disputes are the most frequent issue at stake, comprising close to 50 per cent of the cases (Rousseau *et al*, 1996). This finding is quite consistent with the earlier reported work of Hensel on the greater likelihood of target states reciprocating the initial threat of force by challenger states in MIDs given a territorial dispute (Hensel, 1996b). In addition, the prevalence of territorial disputes in crises helps us to understand why Holsti finds that so many wars involve territorial issues (Holsti, 1991). Since most wars progress through stages of diplomatic conflict and then become crises which militarily escalate, it follows that if many crises centre on territorial issues, then we would expect to find many wars that have escalated from crises to involve such issues as well.

Brecher and Wilkenfeld do not directly test for the impact of territorial disputes on crisis behaviour, but two findings in their work do provide support for the importance of territorial disputes:

- They identify protracted conflicts between states which produce multiple crises in their dataset and these protracted conflicts are more likely to escalate and involve armed violence than are non-protracted conflicts (Brecher, 1993; Brecher & Wilkenfeld, 1997). When their list of protracted conflicts is examined it is very evident that a territorial dispute exists between states in many cases (Brecher, 1993: 72; Brecher & Wilkenfeld, 1997: 821). This finding parallels the results from the MID dataset which show that territorial disputes are highly correlated with enduring rivalries.

- When military-security issues are at stake, crises are more likely to emerge and to escalate to high levels of violence, and the presence of a territorial dispute is coded as a military-security issue in the ICB dataset (Brecher, 1993: chapter 3).[2] Once again, these findings from the ICB dataset on the correlation between territorial disputes and escalation and violence are very similar to the results generated by the MID dataset on escalation to war and levels of fatalities.

Dyad datasets

Another type of dataset used in empirical research on international conflict consists of pairs of states. Scholars examine the frequency of various forms of military conflict within these pairs of states over time. Stephen Kocs and Vasquez both argue that even after taking into account geographic proximity between states, the presence of a territorial dispute between states is strongly correlated with the outbreak of war between states in a dyad (Kocs, 1995;

Vasquez, 1995). Kocs, for example, reports that war is 40 times more likely among contiguous states if there is a territorial dispute within the dyad.

The range of consistent and convergent findings reported above indicates then that there is strong empirical evidence of a correlation between territorial disputes and the likelihood of militarised conflict and war between states. As presented in Figure 1, the presence of a territorial dispute is correlated with the escalation of MIDs, international crises and enduring rivalries or protracted conflicts to war.

SHERFACS dataset

The only possible exception to this pattern of consistent findings would be the results reported by William Dixon in his study of 688 international disputes from 1946 to 1984 (Dixon, 1996) using the SHERFACS dataset (Sherman, 1994).

Dixon reports that the presence of boundary or irredentist claims is not strongly related to higher levels of escalation across different phases of a dispute (Dixon, 1996). There are several important characteristics of the SHERFACS dataset, however, which lead me to the conclusion that it is very difficult to interpret the results of Dixon's study.

First, the coding scheme of SHERFACS does not specify what level of military force is used in a dispute. Instead, any use of force is classified as falling into a single phase or level of hostility for the dispute. As a result, no distinctions are made between minor or very limited uses of force and large-scale attacks associated with war. The findings of Hensel and Senese using the MID dataset are that escalation to war is more likely if territorial issues are in dispute (Hensel, 1996b; Senese 1997); but Senese also finds that patterns of escalation short of war involving shows of force and limited uses of force do not differ significantly between territorial disputes and other issue types (Senese, 1996). As currently constructed, then, the SHERFACS dataset does not directly address the question of whether territorial disputes are more likely to escalate to war than other issues.

Secondly, the SHERFACS dataset divides up a single dispute into one of six possible phases according to the degree of military escalation. As a result, for any given dispute that does escalate to the phase or level of military force, the phase following the cessation of military conflict will necessarily be coded as a lower level of escalation. The result is that for any dispute involving military conflict, there will always be a negative correlation between the use of force in one phase and the level of subsequent escalation for the next phase following the termination of armed hostilities. Thus, even if territorial disputes are strongly and positively related to the outbreak of armed hostilities, they will also be strongly correlated with a subsequent de-escalation phase. This pattern, then, of an upswing in escalation followed by some level of de-escalation might very well produce a weak overall correlation between territorial disputes and escalation, as Dixon reports. If this is indeed how the data is coded in the Dixon study, then all of the phases immediately following the end of armed hostilities need to be removed from the dataset before any valid tests can be conducted on the links between territorial disputes and patterns of escalation.

Thirdly, a possible problem could be that the category of boundary and irredentist claims in the SHERFACS dataset under-reports the number of actual territorial disputes. Consequently, the correlation between territorial disputes and escalation could be weakened. In particular, the concern is that Dixon reports that ethnic/religious issues in dispute are positively related to escalation, but a number of territorial disputes arise because the territory is populated by ethnic and religious groups with ties to one country. For example, in the Huth dataset of 129 territorial disputes from 1950 to 1990, 30 cases (about 23 per cent) involve conflicts in which an ethnic group is divided by existing borders and one government seeks to annex disputed territory populated by its ethnic co-nationals. In the SHERFACS dataset, however, it is not clear whether the category of ethnic/religious issues in dispute overlaps with the category of territorial disputes. If they do not overlap, then the SHERFACS dataset is probably excluding from its set of territorial disputes cases of conflicts with a high likelihood of escalation.

Conclusion

The overall conclusion that I draw is that empirical work to date has produced a strong set of results. Of course, the number of empirical studies at this point in time is not large, so the degree of confidence one can have in drawing strong conclusions should be tempered. The only missing link in Figure 1 is that no empirical studies have tested and confirmed that the presence of a territorial dispute is highly correlated with the initiation of a MID. If such a test were conducted and supportive findings produced, we would then have a set of empirical findings which would establish that, for each of the principal stages at which a dispute can escalate and eventually result in war, the presence of a territorial dispute strongly increases the risks of heightened conflict.

The final empirical finding to report is that while territorial disputes increase the risk of militarised conflict and war between states in a strong and consistent way, the fact remains that most territorial disputes do not involve militarised behaviour or large-scale armed conflict. In my own research on 129 territorial disputes between 1950 and 1990, 50 per cent of all territorial disputes did not involve any MIDs, less than one-third evolved into enduring rivalries, and war broke out in less than 20 per cent of the disputes (Huth, 1996a & 1996b). As noted, I have extended my dataset on territorial disputes to cover the period 1919 to 1995 and there are 347 disputes during that time (see the Appendix). In this larger dataset, similar patterns of armed conflict are present. Thus, about 60 per cent of the territorial disputes did not involve any MIDs and war occurred in fewer than 20 per cent of the disputes. There is further evidence in the MID dataset that most territorial disputes do not escalate. For example, Hensel reports that only about seven per cent of all MIDs involving territorial issues escalated to war (Hensel, 1996b). Finally, Goertz and Diehl in their study of over 800 territorial exchanges between states from 1816 to 1980 note that about 30 per cent of all territorial transfers involved military conflict at some point in time (Goertz & Diehl, 1992b). In conclusion, while scholars have produced strong evidence that territorial disputes are more likely to escalate to militarised conflict than other issues, it remains true that state leaders in most territorial disputes rely on diplomatic means to pursue their country's interests and recognise the genuine risks of military conflict.

THEORETICAL EXPLANATIONS

What theoretical arguments can be advanced for drawing a causal connection between the presence of a territorial dispute and the increased likelihood of MIDs, crises and war? If we refer to Figure 2, why would an international dispute over contested territory follow a trajectory that is more likely to result in outcomes such as 3a or 4a as opposed to 1a–1b, 2a–2b or 4b–4c?

The prevailing argument advanced by scholars is that contested territory as a type of issue in dispute is particularly salient or important to national leaders and they are therefore more willing to risk armed conflict in pursuit of territorial claims. Thus, foreign policy leaders are less willing to make concessions over territorial issues and more resolved to use military force to achieve territorial goals than in the case of other issues that might be contested in a dispute (Hensel, 1996a & 1996b; Vasquez, 1993). I will argue below that this line of argument by itself is insufficient and that a compelling explanation requires that additional factors be considered. Scholars are not incorrect in considering issue saliency to be important, but it is one part of a larger argument in which several features in combination make territorial disputes more likely to escalate to war.

Before exploring the logic of this argument in detail, I want to address what is often viewed as a counter-argument to the proposition that territorial disputes are a distinctly important factor in explaining war (Vasquez, 1995). The opposing argument is that geographic proximity between states is more important than territorial disputes in explaining war. It is plausible to argue that because of proximity, state leaders are more likely to believe that military options are viable and potentially effective, thus resulting in a higher rate of military force being employed by contiguous states involved in a dispute. Numerous studies (i.e. Bremer, 1992; Brecher, 1993; Brecher & Wilkenfeld, 1997; Diehl, 1985; Sense, 1996) report strong positive correlations between proximity and various measures of dispute escalation and armed violence. Nevertheless, this type of argument is unsatisfactory. Militarised conflict and war carry substantial risks, and I do not find it compelling to argue that the increased *opportunity* to use force is sufficient to explain why state leaders will resort to military means, knowing as they do the risks of such a course of action (see Siverson & Starr, 1991). Recent findings from Senese nicely illustrate this point (Senese, 1997). He reports that while proximity between states is correlated with a higher probability of escalation to war among MIDs, he also finds that the presence of a territorial dispute has a much stronger effect on the likelihood of war regardless of whether states in a MID are contiguous. The general point is that when we include in our tests variables which help to explain why state leaders might be motivated and resolved to use force, we see that the empirical results are much stronger. A focus on the kinds of issues in dispute proves very helpful, then, in understanding the reasons why state leaders might risk military conflict.

Territorial disputes are undoubtedly correlated with geographic proximity between states. In my dataset of 347 territorial disputes from 1919 to 1995, about 90 per cent involve states whose homeland or colonial borders are contiguous. Instead of viewing proximity and territorial disputes as competing variables in empirical tests, it makes more sense to view a focus on territorial disputes as helping to more fully explain the theoretical importance of proximity as a causal factor leading to war. Proximity is related to militarised conflict and war not only because of the link to military capabilities and opportunities to use force, but also because contiguous countries become involved in disputes over conflicting claims of sovereign rights to bordering territory. In this sense, then, I do not consider the variable of geographic proximity as challenging the theoretical utility of an approach which focuses on territorial disputes as a cause of war.

Why is it, then, that territorial disputes and questions of control over territory might significantly increase the risks of armed conflict and war? I would argue that there are four reasons that, when taken together, explain why territorial disputes are more likely to result in military conflicts:

1.   the high value placed on the control of disputed territory
2.   the greater capacity of foreign policy leaders to mobilise domestic support behind territorial claims
3.   the appropriateness of military force as an instrument for achieving territorial goals
4.   the propensity for leaders in authoritarian states to dispute territory.

The combined effect of these four factors is to produce higher expected utilities for disputing and escalating territorial disputes compared to expected utilities for making concessions, or accepting the status quo for challenger states (see Figure 3).

The value of territory

The first component of the argument centres on the multiple ways in which the control of contested territories would contribute to central foreign policy as well as the domestic political goals of state leaders. The multi-dimensional benefits of securing borders and controlling territory include military security, economic development and growth, and political goals such as national unification. Territorial disputes often involve questions of access to and control over human and natural resources which state leaders expect will contribute to the attainment of important internal as well as external security goals. For example, natural resource deposits within disputed territory hold the promise of generating considerable state revenues through export sales. In other cases, control of bordering territory would provide an effective defensive barrier to military attacks by ground forces from a threatening country. Finally, the incorporation of neighbouring territory could unite an ethnic group within the borders of a single state which would better protect that ethnic population from discrimination and violence by neighbouring states.

Are territorial disputes, however, distinctive in that they typically include issues at stake which are highly valued by state leaders? In contrast, are other issues – such as economic disputes over trade policy or nationalisation, attempts to overthrow neighbouring governments, or efforts to combat terrorism against citizens abroad – less salient? I think the answers to these questions are not as clear as we might think. I agree with the position that territorial issues are generally viewed as quite salient, but whether territorial disputes are consistently more salient than other issues at stake is debatable.

For state leaders who feel threatened by the political and economic ideologies of other regimes abroad, the goal of overthrowing such regimes could be very salient. The concern that regimes abroad are making attempts at, or will have the effect of, destabilising and possibly causing the removal of political leaders from power, cuts right to very core of issues which are of vital importance to state leaders. If we believe that a fundamental goal of foreign policy leaders is to remain in power, then threats to their political survival should produce a strong counter-response which could include a greater willingness to use military force. Put differently, as an issue at stake, domestic security and tenure in office should be just as salient as improving external security by the control of disputed strategic territory.

Another set of cases to consider is economic disputes, a common source of conflict between governments. One could ask the question: are economic disputes related to control of territory more prone to conflict than economic disputes unrelated to territory? In either situation I would argue that economic issues are more positive-sum in nature and thus divisible, and that in either case politically powerful economic interests could pressure governments to pursue certain economic policies. Furthermore, the economic outcomes associated with any dispute settlement could translate into important political results for leaders regardless of whether territory is at stake. Is there any reason to believe that the economic stakes in territorial disputes are consistently larger than the stakes in non-territorial-based economic conflicts? I find it difficult to answer affirmatively. Perhaps a stronger case for the higher saliency of territorial disputes can be linked to disputes involving national unification and support for ethnic co-nationals in neighbouring countries. Territorial disputes in these cases are often linked to larger goals of political self-determination – and self-determination has been a powerful political force since the nineteenth century. Other issues, by contrast, be they economic or political-ideological rivalry, don't have that connection to questions of political self-determination. Of course, it still remains problematic to argue that territorial disputes linked to national unification and self-determination are more salient to state leaders than disputes in which leaders fear that their regime is threatened by political subversion from neighbouring countries.

One possible implication would be that if the distribution of issues at stake in territorial disputes were clearly leaning towards issues of national unification, protection of ethnic nationals or control of strategic territory, that would help explain why territorial disputes were very likely to escalate. We don't have systematic data on the issues at stake in territorial disputes over an extended period of time so it is not possible to draw firm conclusions on this question. In my study of 129 territorial disputes from 1950 to 1990, however, we find that strategic territory was at stake in 25 cases, national unification in 36, and the protection of ethnic minorities in 30 (Huth, 1996: 75–81). In total, about 71 per cent of the territorial disputes (91/129) involved at least one of these three issues. There would seem to be some evidence, then, that territorial disputes tend to be over issues that are likely to have high saliency for state leaders.

Nevertheless, the weakness of the relative saliency argument centres on why territorial disputes would be more salient than disputes in which leaders sought to overthrow other regimes out of fear that those regimes were threats to their domestic political survival or their country's military security. Part of the answer may lie in the problems of measurement in existing empirical tests which compare issue-types of territorial disputes and regime change. The MID dataset contains a variable which codes whether a dispute centres on regime change (Jones *et al*, 1996). Scholars such as Hensel and Senese have used the MID dataset in their empirical analyses (Hensel, 1996a & 1996b; Senese, 1996 & 1997). A possible limitation of the MID coding scheme, however, is that, regarding one country seeking to remove the regime of another, it does not provide information on how much of a threat (internal or external security) the other regime posed to its leaders. I would suspect that if we pulled out those cases where high threats existed, the patterns of escalation for those regime-change cases and territorial dispute cases might be quite similar.

In conclusion, the logical basis for arguing that territorial issues are generally more salient to leaders than other issues is open to question and such an explanation is therefore not sufficient to explain why territorial disputes seem to stand out as being strongly correlated with war. Instead, I would argue that the high saliency of territorial disputes is a necessary part of the explanation since saliency-type arguments establish that important issues are at stake in territorial disputes. If we understand that high stakes are involved in territorial disputes, then we would expect leaders to accept higher costs to obtain highly valued ends, and also why it would be unattractive to leaders to avoid conflict by renouncing territorial claims or offering substantial concessions (see Figure 3). Thus, while the saliency of territorial disputes should be correlated with a higher utility for conflict and a lower utility for no conflict, it is possible to argue that other features of territorial disputes further bias expected utility calculations in favour of conflict and escalation.

Mobilisation of political support

One such additional factor is that political leaders can draw upon the language, themes and symbols of nationalism to mobilise support for territorial claims. Compared to non-territorial economic issues or conflicts of political ideology and regime change, I would argue that leaders can more effectively draw on popular and elite sentiments of patriotism and nationalism to justify support for territorial claims. The result is that we would expect foreign policy leaders in territorial disputes to be able to garner broader support with a unifying theme of nationalism which could enable the government to build a more durable domestic coalition in support of territorial claims. For example, by appealing to nationalism, state leaders may be able to avoid more divisive debates about whether the specific issues at stake in the territorial dispute only concern limited groups and interests in society. Similarly, by using nationalism to legitimise claims to disputed territory, leaders may be able to convince political opponents to support the government even though they dislike government policies on other domestic and foreign policy issues. From the perspective of the domestic politics of building support for foreign policy goals, territorial disputes should provide a very favourable issue around which state leaders can mobilise and maintain support.

The converse of building support behind territorial claims is the ability of state leaders to be able to fight off domestic opponents who seek to challenge a government's policy. Once again, appeals to nationalism can be used by the government to disarm political opponents by equating opposition to territorial claims with unpatriotic behaviour and by raising questions about the nationalist credentials of domestic opponents. If political opponents and aspiring leaders are generally rational and strategic, then we would expect them to criticise existing government policies when they believe the political prospects of successfully challenging the government are likely to be high and the political risks low. Opposition elites would be more cautious in challenging a government over a territorial dispute, since they risk a credible threat of being attacked as unpatriotic. Furthermore, it is likely they would find considerable political support for the regime on the issue of the territorial dispute within the population and among other political elites. Given these unfavourable prospects facing opposition elites, the strategically sensible decision would be to avoid conflict on the issue of territorial claims and focus on more controversial policies being pursued by the government.

While nationalism can be used to mobilise domestic support and undercut political opponents, it also constrains the diplomatic options of state leaders, particularly their willingness to make territorial concessions. Having invoked nationalist principles to legitimise territorial claims, leaders open themselves up to charges of hypocrisy and deceit if they subsequently make substantial concessions to settle a territorial dispute. Thus, nationalist arguments, once relied upon to build support, can also be used to discredit a government and its leadership. Put differently, the domestic political costs of accommodation in territorial disputes should be higher compared to most other foreign policy issues given that ruling elites are more likely to draw upon nationalism to justify their policy position.

In sum, we should expect state leaders involved in territorial disputes to be more willing to accept the risks of military conflict in pursuit of territorial goals. A supportive domestic political context should exist for military action and incurring financial and military costs, since appeals to nationalism can be drawn upon to convince citizens to accept such costs. If we refer to Figure 3, we find not only that territorial goals are highly valued, but that the political prospects for using force to pursue such goals are favourable as well. Furthermore, in many territorial disputes we would expect state leaders to believe that they would be very likely to incur domestic political costs for making concessions in a territorial settlement. Thus we see that by taking into account some aspects of the domestic political context of territorial disputes, the expected utility calculations of states are further biased in favour of conflict over accommodation.

Utility of military option

The effectiveness of military force is quite high for territorial issues compared to non-territorial issues. The occupation and taking of territory is what military organisations plan for and are trained to execute. As a result, the direct result of the successful use of military force in many armed conflicts is the ability to take control of territory. While the political utility of military force can be low for issues relating to the settlement of economic disputes over trade, refugee movements or terrorist attacks, it is quite appropriate for the pursuit of territorial goals. The implication is that it is more likely that the military will advise political leaders in territorial disputes that armed force can be used successfully to achieve concrete military objectives, and that the achievement of those military objectives will advance desired political-territorial goals.

This close link between military outcomes and political goals for territorial disputes is not as likely in disputes where one government seeks to overthrow another. As I argued above, overthrowing hostile regimes may be a very salient goal for state leaders – particularly for weak or unstable regimes – but the ability of armies to use military force to secure friendly neighbouring regimes can be quite elusive and costly. For example, military victories can force defeated leaders to flee from national capitals, but governments can function and still direct military forces from more remote or protected regions of the country, or even function in exile. Furthermore, when armies advance into national capitals and the interior of countries to establish new governments, they often find themselves vulnerable to guerrilla warfare as they become committed to a longer-term military presence in support of weak governments. The new political leaders, who have been selected by the foreign power, find it difficult to mobilise local support and thus the victorious army must remain in order to protect the regime from internal opposition. Conversely, if a long-term military presence is rejected by the victorious side, then existing or new leaders in the defeated country are likely to have strong domestic political incentives to oppose a conciliatory foreign policy towards their enemy. In the first case, the military finds itself acting as an occupation force in a hostile political-military environment, whereas in the second case military costs are reduced but political leverage over the policies of the defeated regime have been weakened.

While it is true that the military defeat of another country increases the chances of the defeated leaders being removed (Bueno de Mesquita *et al*, 1992; Bueno de Mesquita & Siverson, 1995), it is less clear that changes in leadership represent a change in regime ideology or basic policies. The general point is that the large-scale use of military force to try and overthrow threatening neighbouring governments and replace them with new compliant leaders is a policy which military organisations are weary of pursuing. This is because the invasion of territory and the establishment of a long-term military presence risks provoking defiance and a political backlash against groups which cooperate with a foreign military power. A preferred policy for military leaders would be to provide training, financial support and weapons to domestic opponents of a foreign regime in the hope that hostile regimes can be toppled by armed insurgencies and coups carried out by these foreign groups. This suggests that even when state leaders attach considerable importance to overthrowing regimes, we would not necessarily expect a large-scale military force involving their own armed forces to be relied upon. This may help to explain why disputes over changes of regime are not as likely to escalate to war as territorial disputes, even though the issues at stake may be highly salient to state leaders.

Authoritarian states as challengers

The final argument is that territorial disputes are more likely to escalate to wars because leaders from authoritarian governments are more likely to pursue changes in the territorial status quo than leaders from democratic states, and leaders in authoritarian systems face fewer domestic constraints and risks in resorting to the use of force. Thus in territorial disputes we typically find leaders who are more willing to gamble on the risky option of military force because they operate in a domestic political environment which makes it more difficult for political opponents to hold leaders accountable for failed or costly uses of force in pursuit of territorial claims.

The work of Bruce Bueno de Mesquita and Randolph Siverson is very useful in building the foundation for this argument (Bueno de Mesquita & Siverson, 1996). They argue that non-democratic leaders enter into interstate disputes which involve private goods more frequently than democratic leaders, who are predisposed to become involved in conflicts over issues relating to public goods. They argue that territorial disputes often involve private goods, while disputes over regime-change are focused on public goods. Thus, authoritarian states are involved in more territorial disputes while democratic states are involved in disputes over regime-change; empirical results using the MID dataset confirm this. In my dataset of 129 territorial disputes from 1950 to 1990, challenger states are largely democratic in only about 20 cases (about 16 per cent) (Huth, 1996: 136–37), which is consistent with the expectations of Bueno de Mesquita and Siverson. Furthermore, if my empirical test of territorial dispute initiation is re-analysed to include a variable which codes whether or not a challenger state is democratic, we find that democratic challengers are less likely to initiate territorial disputes.[3]

The argument that non-democratic leaders are more capable of withstanding domestic opposition following military setbacks is confirmed by other studies by Bueno de Mesquita and Siverson (Bueno de Mesquita *et al*, 1992; Bueno de Mesquita & Siverson, 1995). In their empirical analyses of regime duration and leadership survival after military defeats in war, they report that, while all regimes and leaders are more politically vulnerable after defeat in war, the probabilities of regime-change and leadership turnover are greater in democratic countries.

There are two general implications for patterns of escalation in territorial disputes if we refer to Figure 3. First, the lower domestic risks associated with the use of force are positively related to a higher net utility for pursuing territorial claims, since fewer expected domestic costs have to be subtracted from expected gains. Secondly, authoritarian leaders may be more willing than democratic leaders to initiate the use of force in situations where the military prospects of success are more uncertain, since they face fewer domestic risks following the use of force. This does not imply that authoritarian leaders consistently escalate tension in the face of an unfavourable military balance; only that they might be more risk-acceptant in situations where expected benefits are high but military options are more limited.

Problems of commitment and misrepresentation

While I have argued that several features of territorial disputes in combination bias expected utility calculations in favour of escalation, a different approach would shift the analysis to questions of strategic misrepresentation or problems of credible commitments to negotiated settlements. James Fearon in particular has argued that problems of misrepresentation and the commitment to honour agreements are two powerful general explanations for why countries cannot resolve some disputes short of armed conflict and war (Fearon, 1995).

Fearon does not focus on territorial disputes in his analysis and he was not attempting to explain why territorial disputes might be more prone to lead to war than other disputed issues. Fearon advances a general argument about why war arises and I am interested in the question of whether his basic argument can help us understand why territorial disputes are more likely to escalate in to war. If I apply the general logic of Fearon's argument to territorial disputes, I am – for several reasons – not convinced that they can help our discussion.

First, is it logical to argue that state leaders in territorial disputes would be distinctly prone to strategic misrepresentation of their interests and military capabilities in order to maximise their chances of a favourable settlement? If strategic misrepresentation were unusually common in territorial disputes, it would help to explain a higher incidence of crises and wars. A possible explanation for a very high rate of misrepresentation in territorial disputes would be that their high saliency causes leaders to use misrepresentation more frequently in order to achieve highly desired goals. Thus, the high saliency of an issue in dispute would be correlated with a high rate of strategic misrepresentation. However, I am not convinced that territorial disputes are consistently more salient than other issues that are often contested in international disputes. If several other issues are salient as well, then substantial differences in the frequency of misrepresentation would be unlikely when we compare territorial disputes to other issues. My concern with the Fearon-type argument is not that strategic misrepresentation would not hinder the peaceful settlements of territorial disputes, but that such problems are probably not significantly more prevalent in territorial disputes than in other issues.

Secondly, different pieces of empirical evidence suggest that commitment problems in territorial disputes are not distinctly acute. Put differently, do potential territorial settlement agreements often break down because the states involved have a very difficult time credibly committing to such agreements? Three sets of empirical findings raise questions about the explanatory power of such an argument:

- First, the historical record since the early nineteenth century indicates that a clear majority of territorial agreements that were signed to delimit and demarcate borders have not been broken and subsequently rejected by states. My own research indicates that 89 per cent of territorial agreements signed between 1816 and 1990 were in force in 1995, with states complying with the terms of the agreement (Huth, 1996: 92). Overall, the record of state compliance with territorial dispute settlements does not seem obviously low and may even be high compared to other types of agreements such as arms control.

- Second, Douglas Gibler reports that, of the 27 interstate alliances linked to territorial settlements formed between 1816 and 1980, in none of them did the states renege on the terms of the territorial settlement during the life of the alliance (Gibler, 1996). While the empirical evidence reported above indicates that in practice state leaders often do honour territorial settlement agreements, it could nevertheless still be true that state leaders perceive or believe that other states are unreliable in abiding by the terms of agreements. If that were true, then problems of credible commitments could still hinder the settlement of territorial disputes.

- Third, the findings of Hensel and Dixon that territorial disputes are associated with higher rates of compromise and negotiated settlements (Hensel 1996a; Dixon, 1996), however, seem contrary to this last argument. If leaders' perceptions are that other states will often renege on the terms of a territorial agreement, then we would not expect leaders in territorial disputes to conclude compromise agreements at relatively high rates compared to other types of disputed issues.

The finding that territorial disputes are more likely to result in negotiated agreements involving some degree of compromise may also not be consistent with some of the arguments I have previously discussed about the high saliency of territorial issues, or the domestic political risks of making concessions over territorial claims. Before such a conclusion is warranted, however, we need to think more carefully about what we should expect to find. It might be argued, for example, that a higher rate of more formal negotiated agreements over territorial issues would not be surprising. This may reflect the saliency of territory and the desire of state leaders to get other countries to state explicitly their willingness to make concessions and accept particular definitions of boundary lines. Such formal documents and treaty texts can also be used by one country to put another's reputation for reliability at risk if it attempts to repudiate them. In this context, formal agreements and written documents can serve as evidence to substantiate claims in the event that a dispute arises over the terms of an existing treaty. Furthermore, it may be that some form of negotiated agreement in territorial disputes is often reached only after armed conflict has occurred or in anticipation of violence. Thus, I have found that while challenger states are generally reluctant to make territorial concessions, the likelihood of making concessions increases following military defeats (Huth, 1996a: chapter 6). This suggests that it may be important to understand the pattern of conflict which preceded the signing of an agreement in a territorial dispute. For example, it may be that Hensel and Dixon are picking up on the fact that cease-fire agreements are often signed after armed hostilities occur and that the terms of cease-fire agreements are coded as constituting some form of compromise even though no actual territorial settlement is reached. Finally, the Dixon and Hensel findings do not tell us how long it takes a territorial dispute to reach a settlement in comparison with other disputed issues. Thus, while it may be true that MIDs involving territorial disputes are more likely to end in some form of a negotiated compromise agreement, it may also still be true that it generally takes longer for territorial disputes to be settled by compromise or concessions than it takes other issues. For example, in my study (Huth 1996a: 141, 144) I found that concessions were offered in only about 16 per cent of the years that challenger states were involved in territorial disputes, but that about 40 per cent of all territorial disputes were resolved by concessions or compromise. Thus, it could be that the outcome of a negotiated settlement is more frequent for territorial disputes but that the time required to reach such a settlement is longer.

FUTURE RESEARCH

This concluding section outlines an agenda for future research on territorial disputes by discussing a number of hypotheses that follow from the four central arguments presented in the previous sections. If we start with the basic logic associated with each of these arguments, what types of diplomatic and military behaviour would we expect to observe that would result in a higher likelihood of armed conflict and war? What are the causal pathways that would account for the generally strong and consistent empirical findings reported by scholars linking territorial disputes to conflict escalation? Some of the hypotheses I present will focus on comparisons between territorial disputes and other types of international disputes regarding conflict behaviour, while others are directed at explaining differences in conflict behaviour only among territorial dispute cases. The hypotheses presented are by no means exhaustive; they are examples of the kinds of hypotheses that can be derived from the general arguments outlined in the previous section. My goal is to suggest possible avenues for future theoretical and empirical work.

If territorial disputes are quite salient to state leaders, then a number of implications would seem to follow (H = hypothesis):

- H1: The period of time required before challenger states make concessions to settle a dispute should be greatest for those territorial disputes in which strategic issues are at stake, or when they centre on questions of political self-determination and national unification.
- H2: For those territorial disputes in which strategic issues are at stake, or which centre on questions of political self-determination and national unification, state leaders should be less likely to agree to various forms of third-party arbitration and adjudication.
- H3: For those territorial disputes in which strategic issues are at stake, or which centre on questions of political self-determination and national unification, strategies of issue linkage and side payments should prove less effective in reaching a negotiated settlement.
- H4: The propensity of democratic state leaders to accept compromise settlements to territorial disputes should be relatively low when strategic issues are at stake, or when they centre on questions of political self-determination and national unification.

H1 argues that the duration of territorial disputes should be a function of the salience of the issues at stake. We would expect state leaders to resist concessions on important issues for a longer period of time since they would prefer to avoid the domestic political risks of such a policy. H2 posits that the willingness of leaders to turn to more binding conflict-resolution procedures should be inversely related to the saliency of issues in dispute. H3 argues that side payments and the strategy of offering to an adversary offsetting gains on non-territorial issues in return for territorial concessions should not be highly effective. The reason is that securing gains on other issues may very well be viewed by the adversary as insufficient compensation for failing to achieve gains with regard to salient territorial goals. Given the high salience of territorial issues it should be more difficult to locate alternative issues which will be sufficiently attractive to an adversary that its leaders can be induced to trade off territorial losses with non-territorial gains. H3 argues that, while democratic institutions and norms should induce leaders to move towards negotiated settlements of disputes, we would still expect to find that democratic leaders would be least forthcoming in offering compromise solutions when salient issues are contested.

If we focus on the relatively high use of military force to achieve territorial goals, several hypotheses can be proposed:

- H5: Compared to international disputes which centre on efforts by one country to overthrow a neighbouring regime, the use of force in territorial disputes should more frequently involve regular armed forces engaging in large-scale military operations. In contrast, for cases of attempted regime change, leaders should more frequently resort to the indirect use of force by supporting armed insurgencies and rebel attacks.
- H6: Compared to other international disputes, territorial disputes should be characterised by a higher likelihood of arms races between states.
- H7: Compared to other international disputes, changes in the status quo in territorial disputes should more frequently be due to the successful use or threat of military force by challenger states.

In H5 the argument is that while military means may frequently be turned to in both types of dispute, the critical difference will be that conventional military attacks will be more appropriate to seizing disputed territory than to attempting to overthrow foreign governments. H6 is premised on the logic that if conventional military operations are best suited to seizing or defending territory, then state leaders involved in a territorial dispute should have strong incentives to build up their military capabilities and to counter threats posed by an adversary's increasing military strength. H7 posits that since military force is well-suited to seizing disputed territory, we would expect changes in the status quo to be accomplished by military actions more frequently in territorial disputes.

If territorial disputes are highly salient to state leaders and they believe that military force is particularly effective for achieving territorial goals, then we might argue as follows:

- H8: Compared to other international disputes, the pathway to compromise settlements in territorial disputes should be characterised by a high incidence of prior military conflicts and/or threats of force between states.
- H9: Compared to other international disputes, territorial disputes should be characterised by a higher likelihood of state leaders resorting to militarised behaviour in support of negotiations and diplomatic initiatives.
- H10: Compared to other international disputes, territorial disputes should be characterised by a higher likelihood of state leaders resorting to militarised behaviour following the failure of negotiations and diplomatic initiatives.

Each of these hypotheses is premised on the logic that high saliency should help convince leaders that the risks of military conflict are worth accepting, and that military threats and the use of force are often credible means by which to support diplomatic efforts.

The next set of hypotheses focus on the ability of foreign policy leaders to mobilise political support behind territorial claims:

- H11: Compared to other international disputes, domestic opposition groups and its leaders should less frequently challenge government policy in territorial disputes.
- H12: Compared to other international disputes, when domestic opposition groups and leaders do challenge government policy in territorial disputes, their policies should be more hawkish than the regime's.
- H13: Compared to other international disputes, governments should be more capable of maintaining elite and public support for territorial goals despite greater financial costs and military risks.

The common argument supporting H11 and H12 is that ruling elites can use nationalism to deter political opposition from challenging its policies in territorial disputes. As a result, if opposition groups are going to criticise the government's policies, they will most likely claim that the government's policies are too accommodating and not tough enough. H13 proposes that state leaders can effectively appeal to nationalism and patriotism to legitimise and sustain popular support for territorial claims even when the pursuit of such claims imposes greater economic burdens and results in greater loss of life due to more frequent military conflicts. In contrast, if economic and military costs are suffered for the sake of other disputes, then support for regime policy should be less stable and more difficult to sustain.

The final set of hypotheses is derived from the argument that leaders from authoritarian regimes are more likely to be involved in territorial disputes:

- H14: Among territorial dispute cases, leaders of authoritarian regimes should initiate MIDs and escalate them to large-scale armed conflicts more frequently than democratic leaders.
- H15: Among territorial disputes, the prospects of using military force are most uncertain in cases in which the sharpest differences should exist between leaders of authoritarian and leaders of democratic regimes regarding the likelihood of initiating and escalating military conflicts.
- H16: Among territorial dispute cases, leaders of authoritarian regimes should be more likely than democratic leaders to engage in major reversals of policy in which unilateral concessions are made.

These final three hypotheses draw upon the argument that since authoritarian leaders are in a better position to suppress political opposition, they are more likely to pursue military and diplomatic policies which are risky. As a result, the domestic political risks of a military or diplomatic defeat should have less of a deterrent effect on the decisions of authoritarian leaders.

Collectively, these hypotheses provide an agenda for future research, since existing empirical work has been concentrated on determining whether there is a relationship between territorial disputes and various outcomes associated with international conflict such as enduring rivalries, crisis escalation and war. Scholars, however, have not tested for the more specific causal steps and processes which produce such international outcomes. These hypotheses and their supporting logic represent potentially new and more fully developed explanations for patterns of conflict among territorial disputes and other types of international dispute. Hopefully, they will stimulate new empirical tests and encourage other scholars to refine existing arguments and develop new and more compelling theoretical explanations.

NOTES

1   Enduring rivalries are defined by Hensel to include a high frequency of MIDs over an extended period of time (1996b: chapter 1).
2   In this chapter one of the hypotheses tested by Brecher is that multiple issues in a crisis should lead to a greater risk of crisis initiation, escalation and violence. The results reported in the tables, however, do not support this hypothesis but they do support the hypothesis that military-security issues are correlated with patterns of crisis initiation and escalation.
3   Specifically, if the equation reported in Table 3 (Huth 1996: 72) is re-analysed by adding a variable which measures how democratic the challenger state is, the logit coefficient for this new variable is negative and significant ($b = -0.026$, t–ratio $= -4.92$).

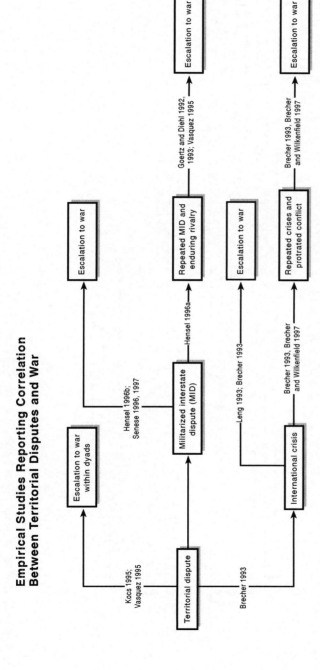

Figure 1: Empirical studies reporting correlation between territorial disputes and war

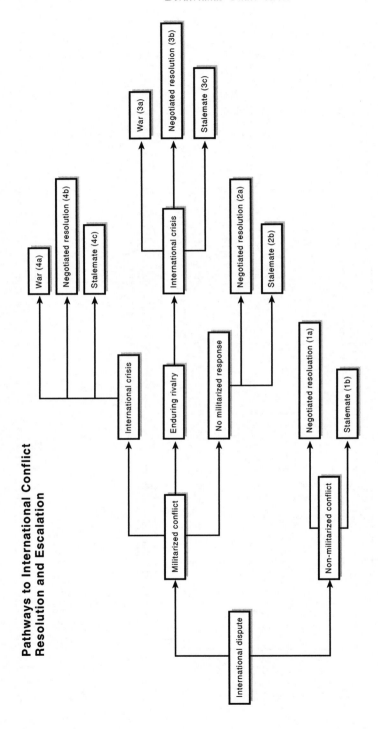

Figure 2: Pathways to international conflict resolution and escalation

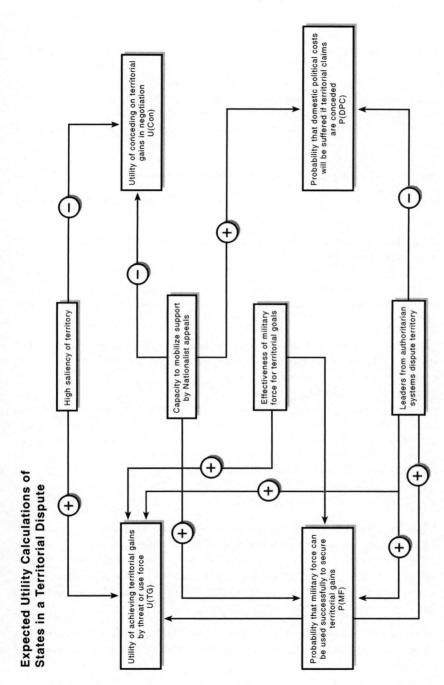

Figure 3: Expected utility calculations of states in a territorial dispute

APPENDIX

This appendix is divided into two sections. The first examines the concept of territorial disputes in international politics and discusses a range of coding issues that I have addressed in my efforts to create a dataset of territorial disputes. This discussion reflects my experience in creating an initial dataset of 129 territorial disputes from 1950 to 1990, and my subsequent efforts to expand that dataset back to 1919 and forward to 1995. I have compiled a dataset of 347 territorial disputes for the period 1919 to 1995. The second section presents, in a series of tables, a complete list of the cases in my territorial dispute dataset.

A. Territorial conflict in the international system

In the twentieth century territorial conflict has centred around six different types of dispute:

1) **Disputes between two states over competing claims to their homeland territory**
   These are largely disputes between neighbouring states over the location of land or river borders or the sovereignty of offshore islands, or whether the very sovereignty and independence of neighbours should be recognised and accepted.

2) **Disputes between two states in which competing claims are directed at the homeland territory of one state and the overseas territory of the other state**
   These are disputes which centre largely on the history of major powers establishing spheres of influence and colonial empires abroad, and result in territorial conflict with local states over the location of borders, the sovereignty of islands and rights to military bases. Examples are: China in the first half of the this century raising issues of leased territories with Britain and France; borders with the British Empire in India; Thailand's border with French Indochina; Ethiopia's borders with Italian and British colonies; and Liberia's borders with French and British colonies.

3) **Disputes between two states in which the competing claims are directed at the overseas territory of both states**
   These disputes arise when two colonial empires come into direct territorial contact and the borders and rights to offshore islands need to be established. Examples include border disputes among the European colonial empires in Africa and in the Middle East.

4) **Disputes between one state and a second, new, aspiring state which seeks to establish its independence by ceding from the homeland territory of an existing state**
   These are disputes arising from the political and military weakness of central

122

governments who are typically unable to exert effective administrative and military control of territories along the periphery of their existing borders. Examples are: the formation of a number of independent states in European Russia and Central Asia following the collapse of the Tsarist regime during the First World War; the drive by Tibet and Outer Mongolia for independence from China; and the more recent struggle by Eritrea for independence from Ethiopia.

5) **Disputes in which political units within the colonial and overseas empire of a state seek to establish and be recognised as independent states**
The history of de-colonisation across all regions of the international system is made up of such disputes, as emerging states pressured British, French, Dutch, Spanish, Portuguese, Belgian, US, and Japanese governments to relinquish control of colonial and overseas territories.

6) **Disputes between states which centre on claims to territorial rights to waters or land along the seabed**
These are disputes regarding the extension of territorial water rights off coastlines and islands, the seabeds located beneath territorial waters, and the location and extent of continental shelves.

The first five categories of territorial dispute focus on competing claims to land-based territory or islands above seas and oceans, while the sixth focuses on territorial claims which extend into and along the bottom of seas and oceans. In my research I have studied territorial disputes which fall into the first three categories. I have not analysed the break-up of existing states, typically during periods of civil war or revolution, the decolonisation of colonial empires, or the large number of maritime disputes.

One borderline dispute which may lie in either category 1 or 4 should be discussed. I would include in category one those cases in which a central government recognises the independence of a new state which has recently ceded from the homeland, but subsequently reverses that policy. Thus, I would include several post-First World War disputes which arose because the new Soviet regime recognised – by treaty and public statements – the independence of some former Russian republics and territories after the Russian civil war, and then changed its policy and integrated them into the subsequently proclaimed Soviet Union. In contrast, I would classify disputes in which the central government never recognises or accepts proclamations of self-determination and territorial independence as belonging in category 4 – e.g. Serbia and the collapse of Yugoslavia in the 1990s.

In addition, the six categories listed above do not include the initial process of state formation and the many territorial conflicts which arose as smaller political-territorial units were merged into larger units, or the process of colonisation and empire-building by states. For the territorial disputes I have studied, these historical processes have already taken place. I have focused on the resulting territorial interactions between states and their colonial possessions in the twentieth century.

A more complete history and analysis of territorial conflict in the international system would include:

1. competition between non-state territorial units which results in state formation
2. imperial expansion of states to include control of territory beyond homeland territory
3. conflict over territorial rights between state actors over homeland and/or empire territory
4. resistance of political-territorial units within colonial empires to subordinated political status and the struggle for political-territorial independence.

These four stages of territorial conflict do not progress in a sequential order but overlap and occur simultaneously in the international system across various regions. In my previous and ongoing research I have only attempted to study category three above, and even within that category I am not attempting to study all types of territorial dispute (maritime disputes are excluded).

Territorial disputes are broadly defined either as disagreements between governments over the delimitation of existing international boundaries, or as the refusal of one government to recognise another government's claim to exercise sovereignty over a territory. A more complete and specific definition is presented in my recent book (Huth, 1996: chapter 2).

A note on how cases of military occupation might be coded is required. I have included as territorial disputes cases where a state's occupation of a foreign territory is linked to an interest in annexing that territory. In other words, there needs to be evidence that the occupation is connected to territorial goals (e.g. Japanese policy in Manchuria 1931–1932, and Israeli occupation of Arab territories after the Six Day War). In contrast, I exclude all cases of occupation which are unconnected to territorial goals and are largely political in nature (e.g. US interventions in Central America in the 1920s and 1930s, and Soviet forces in Austria after the Second World War).

Coding issues

A number of coding issues have arisen in my research efforts to compile a dataset of territorial disputes. In creating a dataset I have collected the following information for each territorial dispute:

- those states seeking to change the status quo (challenger states) by gaining territory and those states seeking to preserve the status quo (target states)
- the beginning and end dates of each dispute
- the outcome of each dispute in terms of changes, if any, in the territorial status quo
- the dates of any militarised disputes initiated by challenger states in an

attempt to overturn the status quo and the outcome of such military confrontations

- the dates of any talks or negotiations held over disputed territory involving the challenger and target and the outcomes of such talks.

Some of the most important coding issues have been as follows:

- **How to code recurring instances of the same dispute**
  The issue is whether or not to merge into a single case a territorial dispute in which the challenger has claims to the same territories but there is a gap of several/many years between periods in which the claim was put forth and pursued – i.e. where the challenger ends the first period of conflict by reaching some form of a settlement or agreement, but some years later renews the claim despite the earlier resolution. I have coded these instances as multiple cases even though they involve the same challenger pressing similar territorial claims. The issues in dispute have not changed over time but, given the earlier resolution of the dispute, I think it is appropriate to code the renewal of the claim as the beginning of a dispute. We could call these renewals of the claim a second phase to the dispute. The critical factor to me is that the challenger in an earlier period had reached some agreement on the issue in dispute and thus the dispute had ended. Without such an agreement I would not code multiple cases, but would instead argue that the dispute was not actively pursued for some period and then at a later date the challenger put the dispute back on the agenda of bilateral relations. Disputes often lapse into periods where there is no diplomatic activity or pursuit of a claim, but such inactivity is different from a case where the challenger actually signed an agreement or acknowledged the resolution of the dispute at a previous point in time.

- **How to code challenger status**
  The coding of challenger status in some cases needs to be thought through carefully. In particular, there are two ways of coding cases in which the challenger occupies and attains *de facto* control over disputed territory while the target state refuses to recognise the challenger's gains. Either way is plausible and my concern is to code these types of case in a consistent fashion and not shift between the two possible approaches within a single study or analysis. The first approach (which I have adopted in the tables below) is: a challenger with *de facto* control of disputed territory should be coded as the target and the former target should be coded as the new challenger. The reason for this is that the original challenger has gained what it sought and therefore no longer seeks to overturn the status quo, but in fact seeks recognition and acceptance of the new status quo; whilst the original target is now seeking to overturn the new status quo and has therefore become the challenger. Underlying this change in labels is the notion that effective control/occupation of territory is critical to determining the status of challenger v. target. A different approach would

be to rely on more legal terms and argue that, since the target has not recognised the challenger's control of territory, the status quo is defined by the formal/legal status of the territory. Thus, without international legitimacy based on some agreement, the challenger remains the challenger. If the latter approach is adopted, then the challenger should be coded as occupying by military force the disputed territory until such time as the target reaches some agreement with the challenger.

● **How to code multiple claims against a single state**
Another issue arises over cases in which the challenger has, geographically speaking, several distinct claims against a single state. Should each claim be coded as a dispute or should they be combined into a single, multi-dimensional dispute? I have used a case-dependent approach. I have combined multiple claims in to a single dispute when the challenger and target have discussed and treated the multiple claims as a set or package of issues. By contrast, where the parties have generally separated out the claims in talks and negotiations, I have coded multiple disputes/cases. In practice, most cases of this kind have been treated as single disputes by the involved parties, and have been coded accordingly.

● **How to code 'legitimate' challenger claims**
Another issue is how to code whether the challenger had any claim to the territory it was challenging. In some cases this question was difficult to answer because there was a discrepancy either between the actions of the legislative and executive bodies, or between the executive's declaratory policy and actual operational policy. In the first case I always sided with the actions and policy of the executive body in terms of assessing whether a dispute existed or what the claims were. I have found frequent evidence of political parties, individual legislators and even legislative bodies issuing claims which the governing power did not support. However, if an agreement or treaty signed by the executive stipulates that the legislature must ratify the agreement, the rejection of the agreement by the legislature means that the dispute persists and the executive has to renew talks. In the second case I relied on official declaratory policy in order to minimise the need to infer the intentions and motives of policy-makers. In some cases the problem arose because the executive did not have full control over its foreign policy apparatus and, as a result, individual military or political officials pursued independent policies. In a smaller number of cases the issue was that the executive declared one policy but pursued another. Perhaps the best example of this is Armenia v. Azerbaijan in the 1990s; the Armenian government has on several occasions disavowed any direct territorial claims but its military support for ethnic Armenians in Nagorno–Karabakh suggests otherwise.

126

- **How to distinguish between delimitation and demarcation of a border**

  In coding the existence and duration of a territorial dispute, it has been repeatedly important to distinguish between the process of delimitation and demarcation of a border or boundary. Delimitation refers to determining the location of a border in a treaty or written document, usually with respect to an attached map; demarcation refers to the practice of actually placing on the ground physical markers to locate the boundary between two states. Demarcation presumes an agreement on delimitation in either specific or general terms. It is common, however, for a team of demarcation experts to have to interpret or make decisions on the ground about boundary markers, since treaties and maps may not be detailed enough to provide precise guidance. Thus, treaties and agreements often make allowance for the fact that the process of demarcation may lead to border adjustments. In my research I have generally excluded the demarcation process from the domain of territorial disputes. Only when problems of demarcation are so serious that they lead one or both states to reject, disavow or seek modification to an existing treaty or agreement do I consider this a territorial dispute. Furthermore, I do not code the absence of demarcation as evidence of a territorial dispute. It is not unusual for countries to agree on delimitation in a treaty and then not carry out demarcation or complete demarcation for an extended period of time. In my research I have coded disputes as ending when the treaty of delimitation has been signed, regardless of when demarcation is completed or even attempted.

- **How to code latent disputes**

  A final issue to consider is what might be labelled 'latent' disputes. The most interesting and difficult cases to code are those in which the evidence indicates that governments recognise that there is no commonly accepted definition of a border in some area, but at the same time they do not seem to press their claim or interpretation of where the border should be located. It can be difficult to tell from the sources whether the parties have made official claims but have agreed (perhaps tacitly) not to pursue them, or whether they have never actually communicated a claim but understand that a difference of opinion exists. Several of the Saudi borders fall into this grey area and I have struggled with whether or not to include certain cases as disputes; another example is the border between North Korea and China.

B. Dataset of territorial disputes

The tables below list territorial disputes between countries, arranged by region. For each dispute, the first-named party is the challenger who seeks to change the territorial status quo, and the second-named party is the defender who is the target of territorial claims and is attempting to maintain the territorial status quo. The dates provided for each case mark the beginning and end of the challenger's claim to territory.

Table 2

Territorial disputes in Europe 1919–1995

1. Albania vs. Greece 1919–21: Claims to Epiros which extend beyond borders established in 1913
2. Albania vs. Yugoslavia 1919–21: Claims to territories that extended beyond borders established in 1913
3. Austria vs. Hungary 1919: Claims to Burgenland
4. Austria vs. Italy 1945–46: Claims in South Tyrol including Bolzano and sections of Trentino
5. Belgium vs. Germany 1919: Claims to Eupen and Malmedy
6. Britain vs. France 1919–53: Claims to islands of Minquiers and Ecrehos off the French coast in the English Channel
7. Bulgaria vs. Greece 1922–23: Claims to Greek Thrace
8. Bulgaria vs. Greece 1945–47: Claims to Greek Thrace
9. Bulgaria vs. Romania 1940: Claims to Southern Dobroju
10. Croatia vs. Slovenia 1993–95: Claims to sections of newly established international border
11. Cyprus vs. Turkey 1974–95: Opposition to the Turkish partition of Cyprus and the formation of a Turkish Cypriot state
12. Czech Republic vs. Slovakia 1993–94: Claims to several small sections of newly established border
13. Czechoslovakia vs. Austria 1919: Claims to Bohemia, Moravia, Gmund, and Themenau
14. Czechoslovakia vs. Hungary 1919–20: Claims to Slovakia, Bohemia, Moravia, and Silesia
15. Czechoslovakia vs. Hungary 1946–47: Claims to small areas located in Bratislava
16. Czechoslovakia vs. Poland 1919–20: Claims to Teshen, Spiza, and Oriva
17. Denmark vs. Germany 1919–20: Claims to Schleswig
18. Denmark vs. Norway 1919–33: Claims to extend sovereign rights over Greenland along eastern coast
19. East Germany/Soviet Union/ vs. US/West Germany/France/UK 1948–71: Claims to West Berlin as part of East German territory and desire to terminate Western occupation rights
20. Estonia vs. Latvia 1919–20: Claims to Hainasion in Gulf of Riga, island of Ruhuu, and town of Valga
21. Estonia vs. Russia 1992–95: Claims to bordering territory of Petseri and eastern bank of the River Narva annexed by the Soviet Union during WWII
22. Finland vs. Soviet Union 1919–20: Claims to East Karelia
23. Finland vs. Soviet Union 1941–47: Claims to all territory gained by the Soviets in Winter War of 1939–40 as well as additional territory in eastern Karelia
24. France vs. Britain 1919–53: Claims to islands of Minquiers and Ecrehos off the French coast in the English Channel
25. France vs. Germany 1919: Claims to Alsace-Lorraine, Rhineland, and Saar
26. France vs. Italy 1945–46: Claims to small sections of territory in Po Valley
27. Germany vs. Austria 1938: Call for union with Austria
28. Germany vs. Belgium 1925–40: Claims to Eupen and Malmedy

29. Germany vs. Czechoslovakia 1938–39: Claims to Sudetenland and Silesia
30. Germany vs. France 1922–36: Desire to re-establish full sovereign control over territories of the Rhineland and Saar
31. Germany vs. Lithuania 1938–39: Claims to Memel
32. Germany vs. Poland 1938–39: Claims to revision of border and Danzig
33. Greece vs. Albania 1919–24: Claims to revise borders established in 1913
34. Greece vs. Albania 1945–1971: Claims to Northern Epirus
35. Greece vs. Bulgaria 1919: Claims to Thrace
36. Greece vs. Bulgaria 1945–47: Claims to Thrace beyond pre-WWII borders
37. Greece vs. Cyprus 1969–82: Goal of *enosis*
38. Greece vs. Italy 1919–28: Claims to the Dodecanese Islands
39. Greece vs. Turkey 1919–23: Claims to Epirus, Thrace, Dodecanese Islands, and Smyrna
40. Greece vs. Britain 1951–59: Desire to incorporate Cyprus (*enosis*) as part of Greece
41. Hungary vs. Austria 1919–21: Claims to Burgenland
42. Hungary vs. Czechoslovakia 1938–39: Claims to Subcarpathia
43. Hungary vs. Romania 1939–40: Claims to Transylvania
44. Hungary vs. Yugoslavia 1940–41: Claims to territory lost in 1920 Peace Treaty
45. Ireland vs. Britain 1922–95: Claims to Northern Ireland
46. Italy vs. Albania 1919–20: Claims to Port of Valona and Sasseno Island as well as protectorate rights
47. Italy vs. Albania 1939: Demand right to base troops on national territory and occupy islands
48. Italy vs. Austria 1919: Claims to Brenner Pass, South Tyrol, Istrian Peninsula
49. Italy vs. Greece 1940–41: Claims to Corfu and other islands along with Northern Epirus
50. Italy vs. Yugoslavia 1919–24: Claims to Istrian Peninsula, Fiume, Dalmatian Coast, and off-shore islands
51. Italy vs. Yugoslavia 1945–1975: Claims to Trieste
52. Latvia vs. Estonia 1919–20: Claims to Hainasion in Gulf of Riga, island of Ruhuu, and town of Valga
53. Latvia vs. Lithuania 1919–21: Claims along length of border
54. Latvia vs. Russia 1994–95: Claims to Abrene and adjacent territory which were annexed by Soviet Union during WWII
55. Lithuania vs. Germany 1919: Claims to Memel
56. Lithuania vs. Latvia 1919–21: Claims along length of common border
57. Lithuania vs. Poland 1919–38: Claims to Vilna
58. Netherlands vs. Belgium 1922–59: Claims to several small enclaves along border
59. Netherlands vs. West Germany 1955–60: Claims to several small sections along border
60. Poland vs. Czechoslovakia 1919–24: Claims to Teshen, Spiza, and Oriva and then small border adjustment near Jaworzina
61. Poland vs. Czechoslovakia 1938: Claims to Teshen and Silesia
62. Poland vs. Germany 1919–22: Claims to Danzig, Prussia, and Upper Silesia
63. Poland vs. Lithuania 1919–23: Claims to Vilna
64. Poland vs. Soviet Russia 1919–21: Claims to large sections of Ukraine and Belarus
65. Romania vs. Hungary 1919–20: Claims to Transylvania, Banat, and Hungarian Plain
66. Romania vs. Hungary 1945–47: Claims to all of Transylvanian territory lost to Hungary in 1939–40

67. Romania vs. Soviet Russia 1919–20: Claims to Bessarabia
68. Romania vs. Yugoslavia 1919–22: Claims to Banat and territory awarded to Yugoslavia at Versailles
69. Russia vs. Ukraine 1992–95: Russian call for exclusive naval base rights at Sevastopol
70. Slovakia vs. Czech Republic 1993–94: Claims to several small sections of newly established border
71. Slovenia vs. Croatia 1993–95: Claims to territory inland of Piran Bay as well as several small sections along length of border
72. Soviet Russia vs. Finland 1919–20: Claims to Petsamo and areas along border
73. Soviet Russia vs. Poland 1919–1921: Claims to territory along borders of Ukraine and Belarus with Poland
74. Soviet Russia/Union vs. Romania 1920–40: Claims to Bessarabia and then Bukavina and Herta
75. Soviet Union vs. Romania 1941–44: Claims to Bessarabia, Bukovina, and Herta which the Soviets had annexed in 1940 but Romania took back in June-July 1941
76. Soviet Union vs. Estonia 1939–40: Claims of right to occupy territory, establish military bases, cede border territories/islands
77. Soviet Union vs. Finland 1938–41: Claims to sovereignty/right to establish naval bases on islands in the Gulf of Finland and at Porkkala and claims to bordering territory of Petsamo, Karelia, Sallo, and Kuusamo
78. Soviet Union vs. Latvia 1939–40: Claims of right to occupy territory and establish military bases
79. Soviet Union vs. Lithuania 1939–40: Claims of right to occupy territory and establish military bases
80. Spain vs. Britain 1919–95: Claim to sovereignty over the British naval base at Gibraltar
81. Sweden vs. Finland 1920–21: Claims to sovereign rights over Aaland Islands
82. Turkey vs Britain 1955–59: Desire to annex or partition Cyprus prior to its independence
83. West Germany vs. Czechoslovakia 1955–73: Refusal to accept Czech re-incorporation of Sudetenland territory following WWII
84. West Germany vs. East Germany 1955–72: Refusal to accept sovereignty of East Germany and claim to East Germany as part of a reunified Germany
85. West Germany vs. France 1955–56: Claims to Saar region
86. West Germany vs. Poland 1955–70: Refusal to recognize post-WWII western Polish borders (the Oder-Neisse Line)
87. West Germany vs. Netherlands 1955–60: Claims to several small sections along border
88. Yugoslavia vs. Albania 1919–25: Claims along border near Lake Okhrida
89. Yugoslavia vs. Austria 1919–20: Claim to Klagenfurt Basin
90. Yugoslavia vs. Bulgaria 1919: Claims to Strumica Valley in Macedonia
91. Yugoslavia vs. Greece 1925–29: Claims to Port of Salonica
92. Yugoslavia vs. Greece 1945–46: Claims to Port of Salonica
93. Yugoslavia vs. Hungary 1919–20: Claims to Croatia-Slavonia and Banat
94. Yugoslavia vs. Italy 1919–24: Claims to Istrian Peninsula, Fiume, Dalmatian Coast, and off-shore islands
95. Yugoslavia vs. Italy 1945–75: Claims to Trieste

Table 3

Territorial disputes in the Near East, Middle East and North Africa 1919–1995

1. Armenia vs. Azerbaijan 1919–20: Claims along border in districts of Zangezur, Nakhichevan, and Karabakh
2. Armenia vs. Georgia 1919–20: Claims to Borchula district
3. Armenia/Soviet Russia vs. Turkey 1919–21: Claims to Kars, Ardahan, and Turkish territory extending to Mediterranean Sea
4. Azerbaijan vs. Armenia 1919–20: Claims along border in districts of Zangezur, Nakhichevan, and Karabakh
5. Azerbaijan vs. Georgia 1919–20: Claims to large section of territory from Daghestan to Batum
6. Chad vs. Libya 1973–94: Claim to regain Aozou Strip after Libya occupies it in 1972
7. Britain vs. France 1919–20: Claims to areas along Syrian-Jordanian border
8. Britain vs. France 1919–32: Claims to areas along Syrian-Iraqi border
9. Britain vs. France 1919–20: Claims to areas along Syrian/Lebanese-Palestine border
10. Britain vs. Iraq 1919–20: Status of Iraq as independent state
11. Britain/Iraq vs. Najd/Saudi Arabia 1922–81: Claims to border areas of Saudi Arabia (UK is challenger 1922–31, Iraq is challenger 1932–81)
12. Britain/Jordan vs Najd/Saudi Arabia 1922–65: Claims to border areas extending to Aqaba (UK is challenger 1922–45, Jordan is challenger 1946–65)
13. Britain/Kuwait vs. Saudi Arabia (Najd) 1919–95: Claims to land border areas as well as offshore islands (UK is challenger 1919–60 and Kuwait thereafter)
14. Britain/South Yemen/Yemen vs. Saudi Arabia 1935–95: Claims to ill-defined border areas (UK is challenger 1935–66, South Yemen 1967–90 and Yemen thereafter)
15. Britain/UAE vs. Saudi Arabia 1934–74: Claims to and around Buraimi Oasis as well bordering territories along what becomes the Qatari coastline (UK is challenger 1934–70 and UAE thereafter)
16. Britain vs Saudi Arabia 1949–58: Claims to islands in close proximity to Bahrain
17. Britain vs. Turkey 1922–26: Claims to Mosul region along Iraqi-Turkish border
18. Egypt vs. Britain 1922–56: Claims to Sudan as part of Egypt
19. Egypt vs. Sudan 1958–95: Claims to sections along border after Sudanese independence
20. Egypt vs. Britain 1922–54: Call for restrictions and then withdrawal of British military base rights and troops in Suez Canal Zone
21. Egypt vs. Israel 1948–88: Initial disputes over sovereign rights to territory in demilitarized zones and desire to gain territory in Negev and then later claims to territory occupied by Israel after the Six Day War
22. Eritrea vs. Yemen 1995: Claim to Hanish islands in the Red Sea
23. France vs. Britain 1919–20: Claims to areas along Syrian/Lebanese-Palestine border
24. France vs. Britain 1919–20: Claims to areas along Syrian-Jordanian border
25. France vs. Britain 1919–32: Claims to territory along Syrian-Iraqi border in the Jabel Sinjar area which forms border with Turkey
26. France vs. Spain 1919–28: Claims to Tangier
27. France vs. Syria 1919–20: Status of Syria as independent state
28. France vs. Turkey 1919–21: Claims to Cilicia and along what becomes Syrian border with Turkey
29. Georgia vs. Armenia 1919–20: Claims to Borchula district

30. Hijaz vs. Najd 1919–26: Claims to Khurma and Turba along border
31. Iran vs. Britain 1919–70: Claims to Bahrain Islands
32. Iran vs. Britain 1919–71: Claims to islands of Abu Musa and Greater and Lesser Tunb
33. Iran vs. Britain/Iraq 1920–75: Claims in Shatt-al-Arab Waterway and along several small sections of land border (UK is target 1921–31 and Iraq thereafter)
34. Iran vs. Saudi Arabia 1949–68: Claims to offshore islands of Farsi and Al-Arabiyah
35. Iran vs. Soviet Union 1919–57: Claims both east and west of the Caspian Sea as well as islands in the Caspian
36. Iran vs. Turkey 1919–32: Claims to sections along border in the Khotur region
37. Iraq vs. Britain/Kuwait 1938–94: Claims to border areas, Bubiyan and Warba islands, and recognition of Kuwait as an independent state (UK is target 1938–60 and Kuwait thereafter)
38. Iraq vs. Britain 1941: Call for greater restrictions and limits on British base and troop rights
39. Iraq vs. Britain 1947–48: Call for greater restrictions and limits on British base and troop rights
40. Iraq vs. Iran 1979–95: Claims in Shatt-al-Arab Waterway
41. Israel vs. Egypt 1949–67: Disputes over sovereign rights to territory in demilitarized zones established after 1948 war
42. Israel vs. Jordan 1949–67: Disputes over sovereign rights to territory in demilitarized zones established after 1948 war
43. Israel vs. Syria 1949–67: Disputes over sovereign rights to territory in demilitarized zones established after 1948 war
44. Italy vs. Britain/Egypt 1919–25: Claim to Jaghbub and Sallum areas along Libyan-Egyptian border
45. Italy vs. France 1919: Claims to territory along Libyan-Algerian border in areas of Ghadames, Ghat, and Tummo
46. Italy vs. France 1919–35: Claims to border rectifications following WWI along Chad-Libya border in areas of Borku and Tibesti
47. Italy vs. Turkey 1919–21: Claims to Adalia and Smyrna
48. Jordan vs. Israel 1948–94: Initial claims to territory along demilitarized zones as well as limited claims to change border in return for recognition of Israel while later disputes center on Israeli occupation of West Bank and Jerusalem after the Six Day War
49. Libya vs France/Chad 1954–72: Claim to the Aozou Strip (France is target 1954–59 and Chad thereafter)
50. Mauritania vs. Spain 1960–75: Claims to territory of Spanish Sahara
51. Morocco vs. France/Algeria 1956–72: Claims along border in south in the Tindouh area (France is target 1956–61 and Algeria thereafter)
52. Morocco vs. Spain 1956–95: Claims to Spanish enclaves and offshore islands
53. Morocco vs. Spain 1956–75: Claims to Spanish Sahara
54. Najd vs. Hijaz 1919–26: Claims to Khurma and Turba along border
55. North Yemen vs. Asir 1919–26: Claims to border areas and independence of Asir
56. North Yemen vs. Britain/South Yemen 1919–1990: Claims to border areas of Aden and all territory that becomes South Yemen (UK is target 1919–66 and South Yemen thereafter)
57. North Yemen vs. Najd-Hijaz (Saudi Arabia) 1927–34: Claims to border areas in Asir and Najran
58. Oman vs. Saudi Arabia 1971–1990: Claims to territory in Buraimi Oasis
59. Oman vs. United Arab Emirates 1971–93: Claims to Buraimi Oasis and then northern coast of Ras al-Khaimah

60. Oman vs. South Yemen/Yemen 1981–92: Claims along border in Dhofar
61. Qatar vs. Bahrain 1971–95: Claims to Hawar islands and Dibal and Jarada shoals
62. Russia vs. Azerbijain 1994–95: Russian call for military base rights
63. Russia vs. Georgia 1993–95: Russian call for military base rights
64. Saudi Arabia (Najd) vs. Britain/Iraq 1922–81: Claims to border areas of Iraq (UK is target 1922–31 and Iraq thereafter)
65. Saudi Arabia (Najd) vs. Britain/Kuwait 1919–95: Claims to land border areas of Kuwait as well as offshore islands (UK is target 1919–60 and Kuwait thereafter)
66. Saudi Arabia (Najd) vs. Britain/Jordan 1922–65: Claims to border areas of Jordan extending to Aqaba region (UK is target 1922–45 and Jordan thereafter)
67. Saudi Arabia vs. Britain/South Yemen/Yemen 1935–95: Claims to ill-defined border areas (UK is target 1935–66, South Yemen 1967–90 and Yemen thereafter)
68. Saudi Arabia (Najd-Hijaz) vs. Britain/UAE 1934–74: Claims to Buraimi Oasis, Sila and bordering territories along what becomes the Qatari coastline (UK is target 1934–70 and UAE thereafter)
69. Saudi Arabia vs. Britain/Oman 1934–1990: Claims to territory in Buraimi Oasis (UK is target 1934–70 and Oman thereafter)
70. Saudi Arabia vs. Britain 1949–58: Claims to islands in close proximity to Bahrain
71. Saudi Arabia vs. Iran 1949–68: Claims to offshore islands of Farsi and Al-Arabiyah
72. Saudi Arabia vs. Qatar 1992: Claims to small section of bordering territory along the Qatari coastline
73. Saudi Arabia (Najd-Hijaz) vs. North Yemen 1927–34: Claims to border areas in Asir and Najran
74. Soviet Russia vs. Georgia 1920–21: Border claims and then dispute over independence of Georgia
75. Soviet Union vs. Iran 1919–57: Claims both east and west of the Caspian Sea as well as islands in the Caspian
76. Soviet Union vs. Turkey 1945–53: Claims to military base rights and joint control of Straits as well as claims to Kars and Ardahan
77. Spain vs. France 1919–28: Claims to Tangier
78. South Yemen/Yemen vs. Oman 1981–92: Claims along border in Dhofar
79. Syria vs. Israel 1948–95: Initial disputes over sovereign rights to territory in demilitarized zones and desire to gain territory beyond UN designated border and then subsequent claims to Golan Heights territory occupied by Israel after the Six Day War
80. Tunisia vs. France 1956–62: Call for France to withdraw from military bases
81. Tunisia vs. France/Algeria 1959–70: Claim to Sahara region along border (France is target 1956–61 and Algeria thereafter)
82. Turkey vs. Armenia/Soviet Russia 1919–21: Claims to territory in Kars and Ardahan (Armenia is target 1919–20 and Soviet Russia in 1921)
83. Turkey vs. Britain 1922–26: Claims to Mosul region along Iraqi-Turkish border
84. Turkey vs. France 1925–29: Claims along southern border with Syria
85. Turkey vs. France 1937–39: Claims to Alexandretta
86. Turkey vs. Georgia/Soviet Russia 1919–21: Claims to Artvin, Ardahan, and Batum (Georgia is target 1919–20 and Soviet Russia in 1921)
87. in the Khotur region as well as in the north in the Little Ararat region
88. United Arab Emirates vs. Iran 1971–95: Claims to islands of Abu Musa and Greater and Lesser Tunb
89. United Arab Emirates vs. Oman 1971–93: Claims to Buraimi Oasis and several other sections of border including northern coast of Ras al-Khaimah

Table 4

Territorial disputes in Sub–Sahara Africa 1919–1995

1. Belgium vs. Portugal 1919–1935: Claims to small sections of territory along Angola-Zaire border including islands and boundary line in Congo River
2. Belgium vs. Portugal 1926–1927: Claims to territory of Matadi along Angolan-Congo border
3. Benin vs. Niger 1960–65: Claim to Lete island
4. Botswana vs. Namibia 1992–95: Claim to islands in Chobe River
5. Britain vs. Ethiopia 1945–54: Claims to Ogaden and then western section of Eritrea
6. Britain vs. France 1919: Claims to territory along Central African Republic-Sudan border
7. Britain/South Africa vs. Portugal 1919–26: Claims to territory including Rua Cana Falls along South Africa-Angola border (UK is challenger 1919 and South Africa thereafter)
8. Britain vs. Portugal 1919–27: Britain contested small section of Mozambique border with Swaziland near tripoint with South Africa
9. Britain vs. Portugal 1930–37: Claims to islands and location of boundary in Ruvuma River along Mozambique-Tanzania border
10. Comoros vs. France 1975–95: Desire to annex Mayotte
11. Ethiopia/Italy vs. Britain/Kenya 1919–43, 1945–70: Claims to Gaddaduma wells territory along border with Kenya (Ethiopia is challenger 1919–35 and Italy is challenger 1936–43, UK is target 1919–62 and Kenya thereafter)
12. Ethiopia/Italy vs. Britain/Sudan 1919–43, 1945–72: Claims to territory along border with Sudan (Ethiopia is challenger 1919–35 and Italy is challenger 1936–43, UK is target 1919–35, 1945–55 and Sudan thereafter)
13. Ethiopia vs. Italy 1919–36: Claims to bordering territory of Italian Somaliland near tripoint with British Kenya
14. Ethiopia vs. Britain 1924–36, 1945–49: Claims to ports within British Somaliland
15. Ethiopia vs. France 1924–36: Claims to port of Djibouti
16. France vs. Britain 1919: Claims to territory along Central African Republic-Sudan border
17. Gabon vs. Equatorial Guinea 1972: Claim to several small islands in Corisco Bay
18. Ghana vs. France/Ivory Coast 1959–66: Claim to Sanwi district along the southeastern section of the border (France is target 1959 and Ivory Coast thereafter)
19. Ghana vs. France/Togo 1958–66: Call for unification of Togo with Ghana (France is target 1958–59 and Togo thereafter)
20. Italy vs. Britain 1919–24: Claims to Jubaland region along border of Italian Somaliland and British Kenya
21. Italy vs. Britain 1924–30: Claims to territory along border of Italian and British Somaliland
22. Italy vs. Britain 1919–1934: Claims to Sarra Triangle territory along Libya-Sudan border
23. Italy vs. Ethiopia 1919–1936: Claims to territory along Italian Somaliland-Ethiopia border near tripoint with British Kenya
24. Italy/Somalia vs. Ethiopia 1950–95: Claims to territory along (former) Italian Somaliland-Ethiopia border and then claims for union of Somalia populated areas of Ethiopia with Somalia (Italy is challenger 1950–59 and Somalia thereafter)

25. Italy vs. France 1919–43: Claims to territory of Djibouti including Djibouti-Addis Ababa railway line
26. Italy vs. France 1938–43: Claims to Corsica and bordering territory of Libya-Tunisia
27. Lesotho vs. South Africa 1966–95: Claims to large sections of territory within Orange Free State, Natal, and eastern Cape Province
28. Liberia vs. France 1919–60: Claim to bordering territory previously annexed by France along border with Ivory Coast
29. Liberia vs. France 1919–58: Claim to bordering territory of French Guinea previously annexed by France
30. Madagascar vs. France 1973–90: Claims to islands of Glorioso, Juan de Nova, Bassas da India, and Europa
31. Malawi vs. Zambia 1981–86: Claim to small section of territory along eastern province border
32. Mali vs. Mauritania 1960–63: Claims to Eastern Hodh and territory in western sector of border
33. Mali vs. Burkino Faso 1960–87: Claims to territory along Beli River in the Dori district
34. Mauritius vs. France 1976–95: Claim to island of Tromelin
35. Mauritius vs. Britain 1980–95: Claim to Diego Garcia islands
36. Morocco vs. France/Mauritania 1957–70: Desire for unification of Mauritania with Morocco (France is target 1957–59 and Mauritania thereafter)
37. Namibia vs. South Africa 1990–94: Claims to Walvis Bay and Penguin Islands
38. Niger vs. Benin 1960–65: Claim to Lete island
39. Nigeria vs. Cameroon 1965–95: Claims to islands and territory in Bakassi peninsula
40. Portugal vs. Belgium 1919–1935: Claims to small sections of territory along Angola-Zaire border including islands and boundary line in Congo River
41. Portugal vs. Britain/South Africa 1919–26: Claims to territory including Rua Cana Falls along South Africa-Angola border (UK is target 1919 and South Africa thereafter)
42. Portugal vs. Britain 1936–37: Claims to islands and location of boundary in Ruvuma River along Mozambique-Tanzania border
43. Seychelles vs. France 1976–95: Claim to island of Tromelin
44. Somalia vs. Britain/Kenya 1960–81: Call for annexation of northeastern province of Kenya populated by ethnic Somalis (UK is target 1960–62 and Kenya thereafter)
45. Somalia vs. France 1960–77: Desire for incorporation of Djibouti as part of Somalia
46. Togo vs. Ghana 1960–95: Claim to southern bordering territory populated by Ewe tribe
47. Uganda vs. Tanzania 1974–79: Claim to Kagera Salient
48. Zaire vs. Zambia 1980–95: Claim to Kaputa district along northern border

Table 5

Territorial disputes in Central Asia, the Far East and Pacific 1919–1995

1. Afghanistan vs. British India 1919–21: Claim to border area north of the Khyber Pass
2. Afghanistan vs. Iran 1919–35: Claims along central border sector
3. Afghanistan vs. Pakistan 1947–95: Refusal to recognize Durand Line and desire for incorporation of Pathan-populated territory

4. Afghanistan vs. Soviet Union 1919–46: Claims to Pendjeh, islands in Amour and Pyandzh Rivers, and delimitation of river borders
5. Britain/India vs. France 1919–54: Initial dispute over territorial limits of French enclaves and then call by India for France to relinquish all control over enclaves of Pondechery, Mache, Kerikal, and Yaman
6. Cambodia vs. South Vietnam/Vietnam 1954–85: Claim to sections of land border at several points as well as islands in the Gulf of Thailand
7. Cambodia vs. Thailand 1954–62: Claims to territory in and around Preah Vihear
8. China vs. Afghanistan 1949–63: Claims along border in Pamir region
9. China vs. Bhutan 1979–95: Claims to small sections of border
10. China vs. Britain 1919–30: Return of leased territory of Port Weihaiwei
11. China vs. Britain 1919–84: Call for termination of British control and resumption of Chinese sovereignty over Hong Kong
12. China vs. Britain/India 1919–62: Claims to bordering territory of India along eastern and western sectors (UK is target 1919–46 and India thereafter)
13. China vs. Britain/Burma 1919–60: Claims to small sections of border in Yunnan (UK is target 1919–47 and Burma thereafter)
14. China vs. France 1919–45: Return of leased territory of Port Kwangchou-wan
15. China vs. France/South Vietnam/Vietnam 1932–95: Claims to Paracel and Spratly Islands as well as small sections of land border (France is target 1932–53 and South Vietnam 1954–75 and Vietnam thereafter)
16. China vs. Japan 1919–45: Claims to leased territories in Shantung (Kiaochaw Bay) and in Liaotung Peninsula (Port Arthur and Dairen)
17. China vs. Japan 1951–95: Claim to the Senkaku Islands
18. China vs. Nepal 1949–61: Claims to bordering territory along the border with Tibet
19. China vs. Kazakstan 1993–94: Claims along border
20. China vs. Kyrgystan 1993–95: Claims along border
21. China vs. Outer Mongolia 1946–62: Border dispute after China recognizes Outer Mongolia as independent state
22. China vs. Pakistan 1947–63: Claims along border between Kashmir and Xinjiang
23. China vs. Portugal 1919–75: Dispute over border location and then claims to sovereignty over Macau
24. China vs. Soviet Union/Russia 1919–95: Call for revision of unequal treaties defining the length of the border from Central Asia to Manchuria
25. China vs. Soviet Union 1946–55: Call for termination of Soviet base rights at Port Arthur and withdrawal of Soviet forces
26. China vs. Tajikistan 1993–95: Claims along border
27. France/South Vietnam/Vietnam vs. China 1932–95: Claim to Paracel and Spratly Islands (South Vietnam until 1975 and Vietnam thereafter)
28. France vs. Thailand 1945–46: Claims to regain territories along border with Laos and Cambodia which had been conceded to Thailand in 1941
29. India vs. China 1963–95: Seeks to restore status quo along border to pre–1962 war position
30. India vs. Pakistan/Bangladesh 1947–95: Claims to sections of border including numerous small enclaves (Pakistan 1947–71 and Bangladesh thereafter)
31. India vs. Pakistan 1947–48: Claims to Jammu and Kashmir following independence
32. India vs. Pakistan 1947–48: Claims to Junagadh
33. India vs. Pakistan 1947–68: Claims to Rann of Kutch
34. India vs. Portugal 1947–61: Call for Portugal to withdraw from Goa and other enclaves

35. Indonesia vs. Netherlands 1950–62: Claim to West Irian
36. Indonesia vs. Malaysia 1980–95: Claims to islands of Sipadan and Ligitan
37. Iran vs. Afghanistan 1919–35: Claims along central border sector
38. Japan vs. China 1932–45: Claim to Manchukuo as an independent state and desire to extend military occupation further into Manchuria
39. Japan vs. France 1939–45: Claim to Spratly Islands
40. Japan vs. France 1941: Demand right to establish military bases in southern Indo-China
41. Japan (Manchukuo) vs. Outer Mongolia 1935–40: Claims to bordering territory
42. Japan (Manchukuo) vs. Soviet Union 1935–45: Claims to bordering territory and sovereignty of islands in disputed rivers
43. Japan vs. Soviet Union 1951–95: Claims to Kurile Islands
44. Malaysia vs. China 1979–95: Claim to Spratly Islands
45. Malaysia vs. Singapore 1980–95: Claim to Pedra Branca Island
46. North Korea vs. South Korea 1948–95: Call for unification of South with North Korea
47. North Vietnam vs. South Vietnam 1954–75: Call for unification of South with North Vietnam
48. Pakistan vs. India 1947–68: Claims to Rann of Kutch
49. Pakistan vs. India 1947–95: Claims to Jammu and Kashmir following independence
50. Pakistan/Bangladesh vs. India 1947–95: Claims to enclaves along border and small sections of the border
51. Portugal vs. India 1962–74: Refusal to recognize Indian annexation of Goa and other enclaves
52. Nepal vs China 1949–61: Claims to territory along the border with Tibet
53. Papua New Guinea vs. Australia 1974–78: Claim to islands along coastline
54. Philippines vs. China 1971–95: Claim to Spratly Islands
55. Philippines vs. Malaysia 1962–95: Claim to Sabah
56. Portugal vs. Indonesia 1975–95: Refusal to recognize Indonesian annexation of East Timor
57. South Korea vs. Japan 1951–95: Claim to Takeshima Islands
58. South Vietnam/Vietnam vs. Cambodia 1954–85: Claim to small sections of land border at several points as well as islands in the Gulf of Thailand (South Vietnam until 1975 and Vietnam thereafter)
59. Thailand vs. France 1919–41: Claims to boundary line and sovereignty of islands in Mekong and then larger claims to territory of Laos and Cambodia
60. Thailand vs. France/Cambodia 1949–53: Claims territory in and around Preah Vihear (France is target 1949–52 and Cambodia thereafter)
61. Thailand vs. Laos 1984–95: Claims to territory in the north along Mekong and in Ban Rom Klao region
62. United States vs. Japan 1919–22: Dispute over Japan's mandate rights to Island of Yap
63. United States vs. Netherlands 1919–28: Claims to Palmas (Miangus) Islands
64. Vanuatu vs. France 1982–95: Claim to Matthew and Hunter Islands

Table 6

Territorial disputes in North and South America 1919–1995

1. Argentina vs. Britain 1919–95: Claim to Falkland Islands
2. Argentina vs. Chile 1919–95: Claims along Andean border in Palena and Laguno del Disierto as well as islands in the Beagle Channel
3. Argentina vs. Paraguay 1919–45: Claims to border along Pilcomayo River
4. Argentina vs. Uruguay 1919–73: Claims to islands in the Rio de la Plata River and boundary line in the river
5. Bolivia vs. Argentina 1919–25: Claims along length of border
6. Bolivia vs. Chile 1919–95: Claims to provinces of Tacna and Arica
7. Bolivia vs. Paraguay 1919–38: Claims to border in Chaco Boreal region
8. Brazil vs. Argentina 1919–27: Claims to boundary line along bordering rivers and islands
9. Brazil vs. Bolivia 1919–28: Claim to boundary line along bordering rivers and islands
10. Brazil vs. Britain 1919–26: Claims along border of British Guyana
11. Brazil vs. Colombia 1919–1928: Claims along border
12. Brazil vs. Paraguay 1919–27: Claims to boundary line along bordering Paraguay River and islands
13. Canada vs. Britain 1919–27: Claims to border with New Foundland in the Labrador Peninsula
14. Colombia vs. Brazil 1919–28: Claim to small section along southern section of border
15. Colombia vs. Nicaragua 1919–28: Claims section of Mosquito coastline and Corn Islands
16. Colombia vs. Peru 1919–34: Claims to territory in Leticia and Loreto regions
17. Colombia vs. United States 1919–28: Claim to Serrana Bank Islands
18. Colombia vs. Venezuela 1919–24: Claims along southern section of border including the La Guajira Peninsula
19. Cuba vs. United States 1959–95: Call for US withdrawal from military base at Guantanamo
20. Dominican Republic vs. Haiti 1919–35: Claims along length of border on the island of Hispaniola
21. Ecuador vs. Peru 1919–42: Claims to border in the Maranon region
22. Ecuador vs. Peru 1950–95: Claims to border in the Maranon region
23. El Salvador vs. Honduras 1919–92: Claims along border and to islands in the Gulf of Fonseca
24. Guatemala vs. Britain 1936–95: Desire to incorporate Belize as part of Guatemala and then claim to territory in order to gain outlet to sea (UK is target until 1980 and Belize thereafter)
25. Guatemala vs. Honduras 1919–33: Claims along length of border
26. Haiti vs. Dominican Republic 1919–35: Claim along length of border on the island of Hispaniola
27. Haiti vs. United States 1919–95: Claim to Navassa Island
28. Honduras vs. El Salvador 1919–92: Claims to border and islands in the Gulf of Fonseca
29. Honduras vs. Guatemala 1919–33: Claim along length of border
30. Honduras vs. United States 1921–71: Claim to Swan Islands
31. Mexico vs. United States: 1919–63: Claims to El Chamizal along Texas border
32. Mexico vs. France 1919–32: Claim to Clipperton Island

33. Nicaragua vs. Colombia 1919–28: Claim to archipelago of San Andreas and Providencia
34. Nicaragua vs. Colombia 1980–95: Claim to archipelago of San Andreas and Providencia
35. Nicaragua vs. Honduras 1919–60: Claim to territory along eastern section of the border
36. Nicaragua vs. United States 1969–70: Claim to Corn Island
37. Netherlands/Suriname vs. Britain/Guyana 1928–95: Claim to bordering territory near the New River (Netherlands is challenger 1928–74 and Suriname thereafter, UK is target 1928–65 and Guyana thereafter)
38. Netherlands/Suriname vs. France 1919–95: Claim to bordering territory of French Guiana near the Maroni River (Netherlands is challenger 1919–74 and Suriname thereafter)
39. Panama vs. Costa Rica 1919–41: Claim to border between coridilleras and Caribbean Sea
40. Panama vs. United States 1923–77: Claims to establish full sovereignty over the Canal Zone
41. Paraguay vs. Argentina 1919–45: Claims to border along Pilcomayo River
42. Paraguay vs. Brazil 1919–27: Claims to boundary line along bordering Paraguay River and islands
43. Peru vs. Chile 1919–29: Claims to Tacna and Arica
44. Peru vs. Colombia 1919–34: Claims to territory in Leticia and Loreto regions
45. Peru vs. Ecuador 1919–42: Claims to border in Maranon region
46. United States vs. Canada 1973–95: Claims to Seal Island and North Rock in the Gulf of Maine and Bay of Fundy
47. Uruguay vs. Argentina 1919–73: Claims to islands in the Rio de la Plata River and boundary line in the river
48. Uruguay vs. Brazil 1919–95: Claim to Brasilera Island and boundary line in the Arroyo de la Invernda area
49. Venezuela vs. Britain 1919–42: Claim to the island of Patos
50. Venezuela vs. Britain/Guyana 1951–95: Claims to the Essequibo region (UK is target 1951–65 and Guyana thereafter)
51. Venezuela vs. Colombia 1919–24: Claims along southern section of border including the La Guajira Peninsula

REFERENCES

Bueno de Mesquita, B., Siverson, R. & Woller, G. (1992) 'War and the Fate of Regimes', *American Political Science Review* 86, 3: 638–646.

Bueno de Mesquita, B. & Siverson, R. (1995) 'War and the Survival of Political Leaders', *American Political Science Review* 89, 4: 841–856.

Brecher, M. (1993) *Crises in World Politics*, New York: Pergamon Press.

Brecher, M. & Wilkenfeld, J. (1997) *A Study of Crisis*, Ann Arbor: University of Michigan Press.

Bremer, S. (1992) 'Dangerous Dyads', *Journal of Conflict Resolution* 36, 2: 309–41.

Fearon, J. (1995) 'Rationalist Explanations for War', *International Organisation*, 49, 3: 379–414.

Diehl, P. (1985) 'Contiguity and Escalation in Major Power Rivalries, 1816–1980', *Journal of Politics* 47, 4: 1203–1211.

Dixon, W. (1996) 'Third-Party Techniques for Preventing Conflict Escalation and Promoting Peaceful Settlement', *International Organisation* 50, 4: 653–82.

Goertz, G. & Diehl, P. (1992a) *Territorial Changes and International Conflict*, New York: Routledge.

Goertz, G. & Diehl, P. (1992b) 'The Empirical Importance of Enduring Rivalries', *International Interactions* 18, 2: 151–63.

Goertz, G. & Diehl, P. (1993) 'Enduring Rivalries', *International Studies Quarterly* 37, 2: 147–72.

Hensel, P. (1996a) *The Evolution of Interstate Rivalry*, Urbana–Champaign: PhD Dissertation, University of Illinois.

Hensel, P. (1996b) 'Charting a Course to Conflict', *Conflict Management and Peace Science* 15, 1: 43–74.

Holsti, K. (1993) *Peace and War*, New York: Cambridge University Press.

Huth, P. (1996a) *Standing Your Ground*, Ann Arbor: University of Michigan Press.

Huth, P. (1996b) 'Enduring Rivalries and Territorial Disputes, 1950–1990', *Conflict Management and Peace Science* 15, 1: 7–41.

Jones, F., Bremer, S. & Singer, J. D. (1996) 'Militarised Interstate Disputes, 1816–1992', *Conflict Management and Peace Science* 15, 2: 163–213.

Kocs, S. (1995) 'Territorial Disputes and International War, 1945–1987', *Journal of Politics* 57, 1: 159–75.

Leng, R. (1993) *Interstate Crisis Behaviour, 1816–1980*, New York: Cambridge University Press.

Luard, E. (1986) *War in International Society*, London: I. B. Tauris and Company.

Rousseau, D., Gelpi, C., Reiter, D. & Huth, P. (1996) 'Assessing the Dyadic Nature of the Democratic Peace, 1918–88', *American Political Science Review* 90, 3: 512–33.

Senese, P. (1996) 'Geographical Proximity and Issue Salience', *Conflict Management and Peace Science* 15, 2: 133–61.

Senese, P. (1997) 'Dispute to War', paper delivered at the 1997 annual meeting of the International Studies Association.

Sherman, F. (1994) 'SHERFACS: A Cross-Paradigm, Hierarchical and Contextually Sensitive Conflict Management Dataset', *International Interactions* 20, 1–2: 79–100.

Siverson, R. & Starr, H. (1991) *The Diffusion of War*, Ann Arbor: University of Michigan Press.

Siverson, R. & Bueno de Mesquita, B. (1996) 'Inside-Out: A Theory of Domestic Political Institutions and the Issues of International Conflict', paper presented at the 1996 annual meeting of the American Political Science Association.

Vasquez, J. (1993) *The War Puzzle*, New York: Cambridge University Press.

Vasquez, J. (1995) 'Why Do Neighbours Fight – Proximity, Contiguity, or Territoriality?', *Journal of Peace Research* 32: 277–93.

Vasquez, J. (1996) 'Distinguishing Rivals That Go to War from Those That Do Not', *International Studies Quarterly* 40, 4: 531–58.

7
Crossing Borders: Immigration, Citizenship and the Challenge to Nationality

Richard Sigurdson

INTRODUCTION

Our era has yet to realise the much-hyped goal of a 'borderless world'. Nevertheless, rapidly expanding cross-border migration and changing patterns of immigration provide major sources of stress in international borderlands. Large numbers of immigrants and refugees arrive each year in North American and European nation-states, bringing with them their own forms of social and cultural organisation. Moreover, patterns of immigration have shifted, the sources of immigrant minority groups have changed, transborder international minority communities have developed, and the linear pattern of migration has given way, to some degree, to multi-destinational migration practices. As a result, host nations face a variety of stresses which challenge established policies and institutions of citizenship and force a rethinking of accepted concepts of nationality and national identity. These challenges are complicated by the additional stresses related to the phenomenon of globalisation and the threats to national sovereignty posed by the internationalisation of markets and economic organisations and by the transformations in telecommunications media.

This paper seeks to analyse the impact of cross-border migration on western ideas and practices of citizenship, and on the politics of nationality. As the population of legal immigrants and undocumented transborder migrants grows within the boundaries of established western nation-states, questions about the meaning of citizenship and society's obligations to minority communities have taken centre stage. And as these nation-states struggle to come to terms with culturally alien minorities, many social scientists and popular commentators are asking how the new identities presented by immigrants will challenge the existing national identities in the host nations and how this will affect the governability of international borderlands.

This paper attempts to explore these issues by first setting out what is involved when modern nation-states are confronted by incoming immigrant groups. This is dealt with under three headings:

- immigration and the establishment of immigrant minority groups
- citizenship in theory and practice
- nationality and the challenge of cultural plurality.

Borderlands Under Stress (M.A. Pratt and J.A. Brown (eds), ISBN 90-411-9790-7).
© Kluwer Law International, 2000.

The paper then analyses the various types of institutions and policies open to western states which receive large numbers of immigrants, with the intention of examining the political philosophies and practices which have emerged in Europe and North America to deal with the relationship between dominant host countries and their immigrant minority communities. Five broad types of political regulation of cultural diversity are discussed:

- rejection or expulsion of immigrant minority groups (racism)
- restriction of immigrant citizenship (guestworker systems)
- assimilation with the protection of negative rights (political equality)
- integration through positive rights (moderate multiculturalism)
- state promotion of cultural pluralism (active multiculturalism)

The range of possibilities thus covers the racist expulsion of existing immigrants; the perpetuation of the myth that the presence of immigrants is only temporary; the denial of cultural plurality as a sphere for government action; the acceptance of certain positive state measures intended to maximise equality of opportunity and conditions for immigrants; and finally the wholesale adoption of cultural plurality in the service of a new national identity or re-invented founding myth. After rejecting the racist alternative and finding the 'guestworker' and 'political equality' models inadequate, the paper assesses the merits and difficulties associated with the available institutions of multiculturalism. Special attention is given to multiculturalism, since it provides potentially the most productive response to the challenge which new-immigrant citizenship makes on nationality and collective identity.

The problems of citizenship and nationalism are very complex and have taken on new dimensions in the light of both globalisation and increased immigration. The old idea of the nation-state based on a universalist notion of citizenship has given way to new and more challenging demands for the recognition and accommodation of differentiated citizenship. Given this new ideological attitude to difference, models of immigrant incorporation depending upon either the guestworker system or the difference-denying insistence on formal equality will fail to serve the interests of minority communities in modern, multicultural democracies. At the same time, the adoption of the value of cultural plurality in policies of multiculturalism produces problems of its own, especially in multinational countries with entrenched subnational groups and in societies where the influx of alien incomers is perceived by certain groups as a threat to the dominant majority and its national way of life. In such cases, cultural democracy and the state promotion of cultural plurality are likely to encourage new varieties of nationalist or quasi-patriotic counter-resistance projects. Such new nationalisms cannot be expected to help forge closer international unions nor to provide for the peaceful integration of national and immigrant minorities. Nevertheless, the threat of newly reinforced and reactionary resistance to multiculturalism should not be seen as outweighing the benefits of the egalitarian incorporation of ethnic groups and immigrants through government promotion of cultural plurality.

IMMIGRATION AND THE ESTABLISHMENT OF MINORITY IMMIGRANT GROUPS

The sense of a new and growing cultural plurality in western societies is the result of both changing ideological attitudes towards race and ethnicity and shifting patterns of international migration. Since the earliest European explorations of other lands, the philosophy and politics of the western world (represented, for example, by the missionaries) assumed the superiority of 'white' society over the less advanced societies of non-white, non-Christian foreigners. The opening up of the 'New World' also encouraged massive overseas migration, dwarfing the traditionally modest patterns of migration within Europe. In the nineteenth and early twentieth centuries, anywhere from 52 to 70 million Europeans emigrated, largely to North America (Moch, 1992: 147; Jacobson, 1996: 20). At the same time, the colonial adventures of Europeans had resulted in various systems of oppression and dependence, ties which would later complicate relations between migrants and host nations in the post-colonial period (Rex, 1997: 464–7).

As the system of nation-states solidified in the nineteenth century, European states created boundaries around their populations – physical borders, ideological boundaries, national policies, national languages, and obligations to the state – which tended to impede migration (Soysal, 1994: 17). By the First World War states had become highly centralised, laws had been formalised to define citizenship (usually on the basis of nationality), passports and national identity cards were issued, some ethnic minority populations were coercively relocated or expelled, and strict immigration controls became the norm. However, as labour shortages accompanied increased industrial production, especially in the post-Second World War era, European states relaxed their restrictions and began to admit large numbers of foreign nationals as guestworkers. Between 1950 and the early 1970s, Austria, Belgium, Germany, France, Luxembourg, the Netherlands, Sweden and Switzerland established guestworker systems. Most foreign workers were young men from Mediterranean countries – Italy, Spain, Portugal, Greece, Yugoslavia and Turkey – who were expected to reside in the host nations only temporarily. Hence, work and resident permits were issued for restricted periods designed to correspond with the cyclical needs of the labour market. It was assumed that foreign workers could easily be sent home at times of high unemployment. These guestworkers were not expected to play a role in the national culture, and did not enjoy the full rights and benefits accorded to indigenous workers. By the late 1960s the importation of immigrant workers had reached its peak and it was officially curtailed in most jurisdictions by the early 1970s. This was followed by a period of adjustments to account for the fact that, contrary to expectation, the foreign workers had become more or less permanent residents of their new countries. Family reunification policies were enacted, followed by the expansion of legal rights to resident aliens throughout Europe.

In addition to the guestworker phenomenon, several European countries –

including Britain, France and the Netherlands – received large numbers of migrants from their colonies or former colonies in India, Pakistan, the Caribbean, Algeria, Surinam and Indonesia. Although colonial migrants had greater legal rights and residency privileges than guestworkers, they too were expected eventually to return to their homelands, as economic independence was anticipated to be sufficient to meet the aspirations of the formerly colonial peoples. In most cases, however, this did not occur and colonial immigrants became a permanent part of the societies of the metropolitan centres. Ultimately, as the former colonies achieved political independence and new pressures mounted in the host nations, migrants from the colonies came to be defined as aliens in the host countries and found themselves subject to the general immigration rules.

Finally, most European countries have admitted waves of political refugees from Eastern Europe, Asia and Africa. Many countries in western Europe have also recently experienced significant inflows of illegal immigrants from distressed eastern European societies.

Overall, then, European nations, though increasingly restrictive in their official policies, have been unable to fully prevent new flows of migrants from abroad.

Matters are somewhat different in countries that are self-described 'immigrant nations', such as the United States (US), Canada, Australia and New Zealand. But here too, where doors were generally more open to newcomers than was the case in Europe, inflow was initially controlled and regulated according to a racially-biased strategy. From the late nineteenth century until the 1930s, when cross-border migration was at a peak, the criteria for entry involved the immigrants' perceived ability to 'fit in' to the new society and to conform to the existing social and cultural practices. The overriding assumption in these societies was (and often still remains) that all of those allowed to enter would, in due course, become permanent citizens and active participants in the politics and culture of their new nation. During the early period, large-scale immigration to North America for the purpose of permanent settlement was mainly from Europe. Immigration from Asia was highly discouraged and Chinese immigrants faced exceptional discrimination. In America the emphasis was on the rapidity of assimilation into the 'American Way of Life'. While naturalisation involved entering what was often called the 'cultural melting pot', it was taken for granted that the process of assimilation would be easier for white Christian Europeans (preferably from northwestern Europe rather than the southeastern regions). In Canada, there was a greater emphasis on fitting in to one of the two founding nations – French and English. In reality, however, the usual immigrant experience outside the French province of Quebec (and even in the English-dominated Quebecois city of Montreal) was to be educated about Canada's ties to Britain and encouraged towards an Anglo-Saxon cultural conformity. Indeed, up until 1946 Canadians were simply subjects of Britain, and preferential treatment for British applicants for citizenship remained in place until 1976 (Brown, 1996: 13).

Immigration to North America was reduced to a trickle from the Depression until after the First World War. But immigration returned to dramatically high levels in the 1950s. At that time political as well as ethnic and cultural considerations became incorporated into immigration policies. In the US, for instance, the policy in place until 1965 included a national-origins quota but also attempted to satisfy Cold War objectives by admitting political refugees from communist countries. As David Jacobson explains:

> The category 'alien' took on a primarily ideological, as opposed to an ethnic, association. Alien *beliefs*, not nationalities, were now the focus of concern. (Jacobson, 1996: 48–9.)

After 1965, US immigration policy emphasised family reunification, as well as skills and qualifications, rather than national origins. With the passage of the Immigration Act of 1990, after the Berlin Wall had been knocked down and communism defeated, ideological criteria became marginal.

Meanwhile, the new problem of illegal immigration had taken hold of the American public imagination and it became the focus of political debates about immigration policy. In Canada changes to the naturalisation rules coincided with a return to very high levels of immigration from 1950 through the 1980s. Progressively liberal entry requirements, and a commitment to sponsored immigrants, resulted in an increasingly multi-racial Canada with large and well-entrenched immigrant communities. Canadian policy was among the first to entirely eliminate considerations of race, nationality, religion and sex. However, the point system now used to assess non-family-class applicants tends to favour some groups, and certainly some classes of people, over others.

Finally, both Canada and the US continue to accept large numbers of regular immigrants – up to 750,000 a year in the US and 250,000 a year in Canada – as well as many political refugees and an undetermined number of undocumented aliens. In both countries there has also been a dramatic shift away from a primarily European to a primarily third-world source of immigrants.

At present, then, virtually all western countries are confronted with large numbers of incoming immigrants and with the need to mediate relations between minority immigrant communities and the larger population. Moreover, the rapidity of communications and the increased ease of geographical mobility have resulted in new dynamics of transnational immigrant community organisation and domestic immigrant minority community mobilisation. As John Rex points out, there are three points of reference for immigrant minority communities:

> One is to the culture, the economy and the politics of the homeland; a second is to the problems of survival and success in the land of present settlement; and a third to onward possibilities in the global economy. (Rex, 1997: 464.)

As regards the homeland, immigrants will naturally remain in contact with relatives and friends back home. They will visit and perhaps send money to those at home, and will likely remain interested in the politics and culture of the homeland. It is this continued attachment to home that leads some critics of widescale immigration to question certain immigrant groups' ability or willingness to assimilate to the new country. Others charge that some groups use their new country as a base to wage battles and incite conflicts internal to the homeland.

Of course, the connection to the homeland is real and important to immigrant communities, providing a psychological and emotional link to a society that is known and trusted and is a source of security and identity. Nevertheless, immigrant minority communities are also oriented towards their country of settlement, within which they will have to fight against being treated as inferiors because of their racial or colour characteristics and their cultural distinctiveness. Immigrant minority groups will organise for collective action and attempt to benefit as much as possible from participation in the social, economic and political institutions of their new country. This normally entails a fight against racism and a struggle for equal treatment and for equality of condition. For the most part, recognised immigrant community associations will lead the way and provide the liaison with local, regional and national governments. In many cases immigrant groups will join or cooperate with other minority groups in pursuit of joint interests. However, the longer a group is in residence in the new land, the harder it is to remain cohesive in its goals and distinctive from the cultural mainstream. Second- and third-generation members of the community are likely to develop new loyalties, assimilate into the modern nation-state, or otherwise separate themselves from their ethnic or religious community. Thus the relationship between the modern state and contemporary ethnic minority communities is far from static and unchanging; both the nations of settlement and the communities of immigrants are changing and adapting to external and internal pressures and to modernising elements.

Finally, there is the possibility of onward immigration. The modern migrant has the option of moving on to seek better economic opportunities or an improved quality of life. Such options strengthen the bargaining position of transborder migrants, especially among the entrepreneurial class of immigrants. The 1990s has seen an increase in the 'astronaut' phenomenon among certain transborder migrants, whereby immigrants maintain ties to a homeland but attach themselves to various countries, taking up residence as their interests dictate. This onward mobility reflects the variety of immigrant experience in the contemporary, 'globalised' world:

> ... when we speak of the culture of a migrant community we have to remember that we are speaking of families whose membership stretches across several nations and societies. (Rex, 1997: 466–7.)

CITIZENSHIP IN THEORY AND PRACTICE

Given these increased levels of immigration and the resulting cultural diversity in the contemporary world, it is no wonder that traditional notions of citizenship have been upset by the new pressures. Discussions of citizenship are complicated by the fact that it means different things to different people, according to context and situation. There are at least three aspects or dimensions to the contemporary understanding of citizenship. First, citizenship refers to *membership*. Who belongs to the community? This is sometimes dealt with by a strictly 'legal' definition of the citizen as someone who has been accorded the status of full political rights and a full legal capacity within the state. A second dimension of citizenship is that of *entitlement*. Here the question is: what rights does a citizen enjoy? What does one get for one's inclusion in the political community? Finally, citizenship is about *social expectations*. How, precisely, does one belong to the community? What is expected of citizens? What can a citizen expect from fellow citizens?

As far as the first aspect is concerned, legal citizenship is an exclusive status that confers on the individual specific rights and privileges within national boundaries. It is regarded as a first principle of national sovereignty that an independent state can regulate population movements and decide who is in and who is out. Not surprisingly, nation-states are immensely protective of their power to confer such status and to manipulate their memberships according to legislated entry requirements and 'alien' laws. There are a variety of means for regulating legal citizenship status, and the laws are often detailed and complex. Still, as a comparative exercise, one could canvass existing legislation and compile an empirical list of citizenship requirements for each existing nation-state. Relevant to such a survey would be factors such as the criteria for application, the formal qualifications for admission, the duration required for permanent residency, the rules for family reunification or sponsorship, etc. This would reveal telling differences of policy between the various European and North American countries mentioned so far in this paper. For instance, Germany tends towards a policy based on the principle of *jus sanguinis*, the inherited blood connections common in historic states where there was a pre-existent, 'primordial' or ethnic community. France, on the other hand, tends towards a functionally defined citizenship along the lines of the Jacobin ideal of a 'civic' rather than an 'ethnic' nation (Safran, 1997: 327). And, of course, there is a significant difference between nations which employ a guestworker system and those which do not.

Nevertheless, recent literature suggests that in spite of the different institutional rules or national attitudes towards citizenship, there is a convergence of practice which, in effect, extends equal rights, entitlements and benefits to all residents – citizens and non-citizens alike. In her study of European guestworkers, Yasemin Soysal documents the various ways in which guestworkers participate in their host societies as social, economic and political actors with a broad range of rights and privileges. She explains how the guestworker experience demonstrates that 'national citizenship is losing ground to a more universal model of membership, anchored in deterritorialised notions of persons' rights' (Soysal, 1994: 3). According to David Jacobson, too, transnational migration is steadily eroding the value of citizenship as the basis for nation-state membership (Jacobson, 1996). As rights have come to be predicated on residence and not citizenship status, the line has been blurred between citizen and alien. This devaluation of formal citizenship has resulted in the increased importance of international human rights codes, which are premised upon universal 'personhood' rather than national membership. At the same time, the inability of states to regulate illegal transborder migration further devalues formal citizenship. Social, civil, economic and even political rights and entitlements are extended to illegal immigrants on the basis of their residency in the host nation, and thus there is little incentive for transborder migrants to naturalise as citizens even when this option is made available to them.

In terms of entitlements, then, formal citizenship is not the crucial factor. However, the incorporation of non-citizen entitlements (to economic rights, social welfare benefits, and so on) certainly does diverge from place to place, in spite of this post-nationalist emphasis on universal personhood; that is, host societies still differ dramatically in their approaches towards the incorporation of immigrant minority communities into the modern nation-state. True, we should not focus solely on the extension of political rights, like the right to vote, as a measure of full citizenship. But crucially important is the question of what citizens get for their membership in the community and what sorts of treatment they can expect from their fellow citizens and from government. For immigrant minority communities, major issues include both the protection of *individual* rights – especially the right not to face racial, ethnic or sexual discrimination – and the protection of certain *collective* or group rights to preserve and promote cultural distinctiveness. Here the argument that both citizens and non-citizens are equally protected by international human rights codes takes us only so far. A fuller measure of inclusion is the extent to which the standards of universal citizenship are supplemented by various elements of what Will Kymlicka refers to as multicultural citizenship, including provisions for what he calls polyethnic rights – e.g. public funding for minority cultural practices or exemptions from laws and regulations that disadvantage certain minority ethnic groups (Kymlicka, 1995).

Of course, this is by no means an uncontroversial move in modern, multi-ethnic, liberal democracies. Generally speaking, we can distinguish between two powerfully attractive models of citizenship as social expectations. One can be called the liberal-individualist model of *universal* citizenship. Here the premium is on the individual and the formal equality of rights. This view stresses the individual, including the individual's ability to transcend group or collective identity. In this scenario, individual citizens in a liberal democracy can expect to be free to choose their identity. They will not be defined by their station in life, or by their racial or ethnic background, or by their religious affiliation. Formal equality and equality before the law are the cornerstones of this approach. Regarded as undemocratic and unfair is any type of preferential treatment based on racial or ethno-cultural heritage; such practices, the argument runs, would 'particularise' human beings, thus perpetuating exclusion and ghettoisation rather than inclusion and participation. Of course, barriers to free and equal participation by minority groups should be torn down, but in no way should this involve the privileging of minority individuals in societal competition.

Critics of this view argue that it ignores the very real problems faced by minorities in preserving their identity. And they say that it discounts the way that the so-called 'level playing-field' actually privileges the dominant groups and prevents minorities from defining and defending themselves. They therefore propose an alternative – the cultural-pluralist model of *differentiated* citizenship. According to this view, true equality requires an appreciation of the value of 'difference'. This politics of difference would replace the liberal priority of abstract equality of individual rights with some sort of institutionalised recognition of group identity. Solidarity and group cohesion must be preserved among those sharing a language, culture, heritage or a set of common characteristics. This notion does not deny the necessity of preserving the liberal commitments to universal equality, but it recognises that beyond the protection of individual rights there must be a respect for persons as members of identity-conferring groups. It is this second alternative – variously dubbed 'radical multiculturalism', 'identity politics', 'the politics of difference', 'the politics of presence' and 'the politics of recognition' – that is most often regarded as a threat to the traditional notions of universal citizenship and to the insistence upon the unique and sacred values of nationality.

NATIONALITY AND THE CHALLENGE OF CULTURAL PLURALITY

The focus on nationality in this paper assumes that there is such a meaningful concept and that it is linked in important ways to the notion of identity. Following Benedict Anderson, we can say that national communities are 'imagined communities' or that they are communities constituted by belief (Anderson, 1991). Nations exist when their members recognise one another as fellow nationals and compatriots, and believe that they share relevant characteristics (of language, culture, religion, history, and so on). Nationality is also an identity that embodies historical continuity, as nations stretch backwards into the past and forwards into the future. And national identity connects a group of people to a particular geographical place. A nation, in other words, must have a homeland. Thus a national community must always be (in aspiration if not in fact) a political community. Finally, national identity requires that people who share it should have something in common – a set of 'national characteristics' or, better, a 'common public culture' (Miller, 1995: 25). This is what John Rex refers to, more precisely, as 'the shared public political culture of the public domain' (Rex, 1996). It is important to note here that this shared public culture need not be based on race or ethnicity and need not be monolithic or displayed in equal measures by all members.

Nationality is widely considered to be under siege in the contemporary, 'post-modern' world. This decline is not happening everywhere – as is painfully obvious in current crises like the one in Kosovo – but it appears to be evident at least so far as the populations of western liberal democracies are concerned. The idea that all members of the community see each other as compatriots sharing similar characteristics is challenged by the diversity of identities and loyalties in modern, multi-ethnic states. The existence of transnational immigrant communities and the increasing irrelevance of borders challenges the political and geographical imperatives behind nationality. The rise of supra-national entities like the European Union (EU) undermines state sovereignty as does the entry of western states into international trade or investment agreements like the General Agreement on Tariffs and Trade (GATT) or the North American Free Trade Agreement (NAFTA). And, of course, the cultural diversity of the modern world, coupled with the striking homogeneity of popular culture around the globe, undermines the sense of a unique, shared public political culture within each nation-state.

As we have seen, political sociologists and other students of cross-border migration have concluded that new mobility pressures have eroded the legitimacy of the nation-state (Jacobson, 1996: 72). According to Martin Heisler, the increasing transnational ties arising in international immigrant communities cut across the vertical ties required in the nation-state, producing three principle effects that erode the legitimacy of the nation-state: first, the ability of the state to govern comes into question; secondly, societal expectations of effective government are not met; and thirdly, the fundamental relationship between state and citizen is broken (Heisler, 1986). Likewise, Rogers Brubaker argues that the model of the nation-state where membership is egalitarian, sacred, national, unique and socially consequential is an anachronism (Brubaker, 1989). And Yasemin Soysal finds that:

> the classical formal order of the nation-state and its membership is not in place. The state is no longer an autonomous and independent organisation closed over a nationally defined population. (Soysal, 1994: 163.)

An important part of this story, at least in the West, is the extent to which people today are suspicious of the assertions of nationalists and unsure about the moral and political correctness of national thinking.

> People are both less sure of what it means to be French or Swedish, and less sure about how far it is morally acceptable to acknowledge and act upon such identities. (Miller, 1995: 165.)

This is exacerbated by the fact that the older, self-confident nationalisms have been replaced, to a large extent, by diffident or aggressive nationalisms positioned as counter-resistance movements against the perceived threats of intermixing. Indeed, there is a palpable fear of cultural hybridity and the new, 'global' culture among many members of national majority populations. This is evident in America, where politicians like Pat Buchanan represent a populist 'backlash against globalisation in the name of preserving American national sovereignty' (Luke, 1997: 10), and in Australia, where Pauline Hanson's One

Nation Party has mobilised opposition to Aboriginal rights and Asian immigration. Of course, this phenomenon is even more starkly represented in Europe by the Front National in France or the Haider in Austria. Faced with this sort of xenophobia as an example of current nationalist thinking, many observers conclude that nationalism is a discredited ideology and that being on the side of progress necessarily entails opposing nationality and eschewing national thinking. This helps support the cause of those who promote an emerging global civil society, an ideal that now appears closer to reality than ever.

In fact, just as the world is witnessing renewed assertions of national identity and fierce battles over ethnicity and territory in places like the former Yugoslavia, theorists are busy predicting the demise of nationality and the creation of a new, global civil society. As one such prophet puts it, the metaphor for the international system which is now developing 'is of an egg-box containing the shells of sovereignty; but alongside it a global community omelette is cooking' (Booth, 1991: 512). Likewise, various predictions are out there for the emergence of a new 'cosmopolitan' culture (Hannerz, 1990) or the establishment of a 'unitary global culture' (Tenbuck, 1990). But while there is no doubt that identification with the nation-state as the primary source of identity has begun to break down (especially in western liberal democracies), and new forms of collective identity have come forward, it is still too early to write the obituary for nation-states and nationality. Though nation-states have been compelled to recognise that their borders are porous and their populations increasingly heterogeneous, this has not led to a global abdication of power by national governments. And this is probably for the best. As William Connolly explains, globalisation does not correspond to an appropriate site for dealing with concerns over democratic accountability, since democracy can only be institutionalised within territorial space (Connolly, 1992). Hence many theorists are calling not for the retreat of the state in the face of globalisation and cultural diversity, but for a restructuring or reconstituting of the nation-state in ways that make easier the integration of all its residents into a multi-faceted society. The nation-state, then, is not

> withdrawing from the lifeworld, nor is there a decentralisation and redistribution of power downwards to subnational localities and communities. There are, however, greater demands on the state to take on board concerns of minority groups and local contingencies, but this is not representative of some shift in the 'will to power' at the state level. (Marden, 1997: 58.)

THE RELATIONSHIP BETWEEN MODERN NATION-STATES AND IMMIGRANT MINORITIES

Faced with the reality of incoming minorities and existing minority immigrant communities within their boundaries, modern democratic nation-states must struggle to take on board new concerns and accommodate new demands without undermining their own *raison d'être*. Generally speaking, the modern nation-state may adopt one of five possible policy approaches (or some combination thereof). These can be examined as alternative political agendas for dealing with the challenges posed by cultural plurality, as expressed in different ideals and practices of citizenship and different conceptualisations of the requirements of nationality.

Rejection or expulsion of immigrant minorities (racism)

The first alternative is to try to keep out or attack immigrants. Proponents of this view deny the need for immigration, preferring the policy of a protected labour market and the ideal of an ethnically homogeneous society. This is the strategy of the extreme right-wing in Europe and North America, where it is premised upon crudely racist assumptions. Representatives of the racist right have had an influence on public discourse, especially related to immigration issues and in debates over the appropriate levels of cultural diversity within the nation-state. In Europe, parties such as Le Pen's Front National are capable of gaining sometimes significant levels of representation in parliament. What is more, the mainstream parties, recognising the perception that a high intake of immigrants reduces job prospects for indigenous workers and that many voters register significant levels of discomfort with alien minorities and their different ways of life, feel pressure to modify their own policies in an exclusionary way. As Rex sees it,

> there is a minority vote of about 10–20 per cent which makes hostility to immigrants and the demand for repatriation the centre-piece of its programme, and the mainstream parties adjust their own policies to win back those votes. (Rex, 1997: 469.)

In spite of this influence, the crass policy of rejection or relocation of immigrant minority communities is simply not an option in western European societies with large ethnic-minority populations.

In North America, where the first-past-the-post electoral system is less generous to minor parties than is the proportional representation model used in most European countries, the threat of electoral victory by radical, fringe, anti-immigration parties is slight. But the mainstream parties, especially the Republicans in the US and the Progressive Conservatives in Canada, are open to infiltration by extremists and racists, and they have on occasion succumbed to the pressure to reduce the numbers of immigrants or to try to alter the flow from certain sources. Moreover, new parties and leaders can emerge to capitalise upon widespread public concern over immigration and national identity. Such was the case in the US with Ross Perot in 1992 and Pat Buchanan in 1996, and it is very much a factor in the popularity of the new Reform Party in Canada. Indeed, there have been calls in Canada for the deportation of immigrants who commit crimes within the country, even if they were only small children when they arrived. And in the US there is a good deal of support for harsher measures against illegal immigrants, especially the millions who cross the southern US border with Mexico. But matters are complicated by phenomena such as the support for political refugees from Cuba, who cross regularly into Florida, and sympathy for those escaping repressive or otherwise hostile situations in the Caribbean basin. As Jacobson observes, drastic actions, like the mass deportation of undocumented aliens that took place in the 1950s, are now 'beyond the pale of legitimate debate' and are 'politically untenable' (Jacobson, 1996: 61). In spite of the presence of fringe elements and some anti-immigration activists, then, exclusionary or retaliatory policies are not acceptable in contemporary North American politics.

Restriction of immigrant citizenship (guestworker systems)

Of course, the restriction of formal citizenship is still a popular alternative in many western democracies, especially in western Europe where the guestworker system was in place. Economic realities encouraged these countries to accept guestworkers but political imperatives led them to deny these incoming foreigners the rights of political citizenship. As we have seen, western European nations have recently attempted to fortify their boundaries through restrictive border controls or have otherwise moved to accommodate the demands of right-wing nationalist parties. Nevertheless, they have been unable either to stem the tide of incoming migration or to reverse the trend towards extension of quasi-citizenship rights to resident aliens. But by retaining the theory of guestworker status, governments perpetuate the myth that the presence of foreign workers is temporary. This justifies a kind of 'estate system' in which immigrant workers and their families are differentially incorporated into society (Rex, 1997: 469). In spite of the social welfare and other benefits now guaranteed to alien residents, immigrant cultural minorities in many western European states are treated as second-class citizens, or what Tomas Hammar calls 'denizens' (Hammer, 1990).

Even more unjustifiable is the unofficial version of this policy that is in evidence where illegal immigration is tolerated within a society for economic reasons, but the state refuses to provide equal services for the undocumented migrants. Such a situation potentially exists in the southwestern US, where Chicano workers and their families are denied social services or even schooling for their children, as was proposed in California. The guestworker system has already proved itself untenable; and in the long run, other forms of second-class citizenship will not be able to withstand the pressures for equality and justice, as expressed for instance in international law, human rights codes and international trade and labour agreements.

Assimilation with the protection of negative rights (political equality)

An alternative strategy, and one that contrasts sharply with the first two, is the policy of assimilation. This approach rests on a philosophy of equal rights for all individuals and allows for relatively easy naturalisation of immigrants. But the expectation is that immigrant minorities will abandon their own cultures and organisations as a price for admission to the nation. The state, in this scenario, is there to ensure egalitarian conditions for individual interests within the civil society and in the political institutions set up on the citizens' behalf. But it is not there to interfere in private matters or to ensure that one's cultural practices are preserved and promoted. Thus the rights protected are largely *negative*, since they forbid representatives of the state to impede upon individual liberties or to discriminate on the basis of race, religion or ethno-cultural background. In accordance with this philosophy, as Denise Helly explains,

> all individuals have similar rights, and as a result immigrants cannot be singled out as members of separate cultural categories within the population. No special political status can be allocated to individuals or groups by reason of cultural difference. (Helly, 1993: 17.)

By the same token, this means the exclusion of minority cultural education and the discouragement of minority political activism. France is a good example of this strategy. French nationhood is politically constituted, yet it is expressed in terms of cultural unity. While outsiders are welcome, France demands assimilation into the French national identity (Jacobson, 1996: 22). For a long time the French government placed legal restrictions on migrant organisations; and even now, after the restrictions were lifted in 1981, large immigrant organisations based on ethnicity are few in France, and their relation to the state is weak or strained. In France, in fact,

> mention of ethnic categories is to a large extent absent both from state policies, which refuse to recognise collective identities, and from the ways that migrants organise and formulate their positions. (Soysal, 1994: 107.)

This insistence upon the liberal-individualist model of citizenship, whereby the rights of individual citizens are enforced uniformly and regardless of racial or ethnic criteria, excludes considerations of cultural 'difference' from the political realm. Hence policies based on this assimilationist model have come under attack as immigrant minority groups organise and mobilise themselves, often with the help of their associations in the wider, international or global arena. In the US, for example, this assimilationist model was once the cornerstone of the naturalisation policy, and was expressed in the metaphor of the 'cultural melting pot'. Today, however, 'hyphenated identities' (e.g. Japanese-American, African-American) are commonplace in the American political lexicon. This speaks for the power of organised minority communities in the contemporary world, but also for the widespread socialisation of the North American population towards a new and more egalitarian ideology of cultural difference.

In fact, the ideologies and mechanisms of assimilation have lost force throughout the western world. There are several reasons for this, according to William Safran (Safran, 1997: 328–9). First, the promotional rhetoric of assimilation is less appealing than it used to be because the national cultures of

Britain or Germany or any other industrialised nation are no longer as distinct from one another as they used to be and therefore cannot defend themselves against the powerful homogenising forces of American influence. Secondly, immigration has been so massive, and the diversity of cultural importation so great, that the assimilation machinery has simply overloaded. Thirdly, the spread of neo-liberal, market-oriented ideology, and the privatisation that comes with it, have helped remove from the state many of the primary responsibilities crucial to assimilation (e.g. schooling, culture, the mass media, welfare). Fourthly, worldwide cultural homogeneity has gone so far that the preservation of ethnic cultural particularities is one of the only means of escape from the general cultural monotony and social alienation of the age. Finally, the retention of ethno-cultural identity, and the collective organisations which express it, serve as a bulwark against the heavy centralising structures of the modern state and hence work as a defence mechanism against over-integration and over-politicisation.

Integration through positive rights (moderate multiculturalism)

Another alternative is to attempt to integrate immigrant minorities into society by means of a moderate form of multiculturalism distinguished by the extension of positive rights and the promotion of cultural democracy. In virtually every advanced democratic country the state has intervened to rectify injustices suffered by recognisable groups. This intervention asserts *positive* rights: that is, the state actively prescribes a set of actions rather than simply denying or proscribing action, as is the case with *negative* rights. Since certain immigrant minority communities are known to suffer disproportionately from poor schooling, high rates of unemployment and inadequate housing, positive government measures in these areas serve to benefit immigrants even when they do not target them specifically. And other positive intervention is directly aimed at incorporating immigrant groups into the larger society. Language classes or remedial training for immigrants is a prime example of this sort of policy.

Another key feature of moderate multiculturalism is the strategy of *affirmative action* (or 'positive discrimination'). Here the goal is to improve the level of immigrant minority participation in society. This usually involves setting aside certain positions within the workforce (usually positions in the public sector) or in educational institutions for particular ethnic groups or, more generally, for members of 'visible minorities'. Other forms of positive action are rooted in the recognition that certain groups are disadvantaged within society, and so intervention is designed to benefit them. This may include taking tough action against employers who exploit illegal immigrants; providing for both national and native (or 'heritage') languages in schools; offering targeted social services to specified ethnic communities; establishing rent controls, subsidised housing and other measures aimed at preventing the ghettoisation of immigrant minorities in lower-income areas; and promoting racial tolerance through public education campaigns or by taking other forms of positive action to counter racism.

Variations of these sorts of measures are now common in Europe and North America, where governments have realised the need to go beyond the mere protection of individual rights in order to integrate immigrants into society and to create new opportunities for fuller participation. The hallmark of the multicultural approach is the recognition and tolerance of cultural diversity. According to this view, persons belonging to an ethno-cultural minority should not be deprived of their right to have and to practice their own customs. This includes the right to use their own languages and to open schools where this is feasible. Indeed, the 1966 United Nations International Covenant on Civil and Political Rights, which entered into force in 1976, enshrines just these freedoms:

> In those States in which ethnic, religious or linguistic minorities exist persons belonging to such minorities shall not be denied the right, in community with the other members of their group, to enjoy their own culture, to profess and practise their own religion, or to use their own language.

While positive measures aimed at aiding in the transmission of the cultures and religions of immigrant minorities are still rare in many European nations, various innovative policies are in place in Australia, Canada and the US, designed to promote the distinctiveness of national minorities (such as African-Americans or Aboriginals) and also to help transmit the cultures of immigrant minorities.

State promotion of cultural pluralism (active multiculturalism)

So far, the multicultural strategies mentioned in this paper have been aimed at alleviating the economic or political disadvantage experienced by immigrants in order to integrate them more effectively into the existing society. Another alternative is to accept wholeheartedly the politicisation of cultural pluralism and the promotion of ethnic difference. This is the basis for official policies of multiculturalism which formally recognise ethnic communities and their distinct institutions and customs. These policies 'legitimize and propagate the practices of ethnic communities' and, by active state intervention, seek to 'transform existing societal relations by creating new ethnic political elites and legitimate lobby groups'. The intention here is to promote, on the one hand, 'a public recognition by the dominant group of the rights of marginalised or historically-dependent cultural populations', and on the other, 'a higher level of social and political participation by these populations'. Rather than expecting assimilation or even similarity, multicultural states defend cultural variation as part of the human heritage,

> and thus they encourage inter-ethnic contacts, promote equality amongst cultural groups, and create a working definition of the national collectivity (in light of the absence of a consensus concerning historical myths). (Helly, 1993: 23.)

In 1971 Canada became the first western country to establish multiculturalism as official state policy. That policy, as stated by the then Prime Minister, Pierre Trudeau, had four broad objectives: to help cultural groups retain and foster their identity; to assist cultural groups in overcoming barriers to their full participation in Canadian society; to promote creative exchanges and interconnections among all Canadian cultural groups; and to help immigrants acquire at least one of the official languages. In 1977 Australia adopted an official policy of multiculturalism, addressing many of the same issues as Canada. With subsequent revisions of the legislation, Canada set up an elaborate federal bureaucracy to oversee the policy and promote its goals. When Canada repatriated its Constitution in 1982 and included a new Charter of Rights and Freedoms, a key section provided that the Charter 'shall be interpreted in a manner consistent with the preservation and enhancement of the multicultural heritage of Canadians'. Meanwhile, multiculturalism expanded to the provincial and municipal arenas. By the 1980s civic governments, such as Toronto's, established multiculturalism offices and put in place measures to ensure equity in employment and special representation rights for visible minorities within their jurisdiction. Finally, in 1988 Canada proclaimed An Act for the Preservation and Enhancement of Multiculturalism in Canada, making it the first nation to 'recognise and promote' as a matter of policy 'the understanding that multiculturalism reflects the cultural and racial diversity' of society and acknowledges the freedom of all members of society to 'preserve, enhance and share their cultural heritage' (Ungerleider, 1992: 14–16).

There have been many different suggestions to account for the bold assertion of multiculturalism in Canada. Some saw it as a sop to the immigrant vote by the Liberal Party, which had traditionally benefited most from immigrant support in previous generations; others saw the policy as an attempt to thwart the rising tide of Quebec nationalism; and still others saw it as an extension of the welfare state and the Canadian principles of state intervention. Not to be ignored, however, was the government's desire to ensconce a founding myth for Canada, especially at a time when national unity was under threat from separatists in Quebec and regionalists in the westernmost provinces. An accurate characterisation comes from Denise Helly, who emphasises that the ideology underlining Canadian multiculturalism was

> to establish Canada as a land of egalitarian integration for all cultures and populations of the planet. The respect for cultures and minorities became one of the cornerstones of Canadian society in search of an identity, and one of the primordial principles for integrating multiple Canadian populations. Canada became a nation which could evolve constantly according to shifts in immigrant populations, thereby allowing for constant re-definition and reaffirmation. (Helly, 1993: 25–26.)

According to this view, it is crucial that Canada does not have a firm sense of a 'national founding' as does the US, which is regarded as the creation of a single 'people' on a given territory. The history of Canada has been shaped by politics of difference and by multiple and divided loyalties. Thus multiculturalism serves the purposes of ongoing nation-building, but provides a new, post-modern founding myth – Canada as a land of all cultures, nationalities, identities; Canada as a 'community of communities'. Such a policy of multiculturalism approximates the ideals of post-national membership by stressing universal personhood, multiple and fluid sources of identity, plural and hybrid identifications, and differentiated citizenship rights. There is a place both for longstanding internal populations – Aboriginal, English and French – and for the waves of new immigrants that must be incorporated and re-incorporated into the multicultural society. Nationality is de-linked from Canadian citizenship to the extent that the Aboriginal (First Nations), British North American and Québécois 'nations' are constituent parts of the body politic, as are the multi-ethnic immigrant settlers from generations past to present. Finally, the Canadian State is restructured and reoriented by multiculturalism to serve not a single 'national purpose' but a multinational and multicultural plurality of purposes.

When understood as an active or militant demand for uncompromising pluralism, multiculturalism speaks a language different from either assimilation or integration. Multiculturalism multiplies cultures, embracing plurality and difference. It is thus positioned against arbitrary cohesion or unity. As one commentator puts it, multiculturalism is 'suggestive of paternal confusion and maternal promiscuity' (Eisenstein, 1996: 68). In practice, of course, multiculturalism in Canada and Australia (or in Sweden, Britain and the US) is a far more prosaic matter. It usually involves the establishment of some measures designed to combat racial or ethnic discrimination, the recognition of ethnic community organisations and their representatives, and special efforts in a variety of administrative fields to recognise and accommodate cultural diversity. As long as the policy is not used by the state to manipulate and control minorities, multiculturalism can be an effective way to improve democratic participation by minorities and to advance the cause of racial and ethnic toleration. But on its own, it will be limited in its ability to redress historical and contemporary discrimination, as well as the class- and gender-based inequalities experienced by immigrants and racial minorities. In the final analysis, however, multiculturalism (in either its moderate or more active form) is preferable to alternative models for immigrant incorporation, which implicitly seek to replace it with an assimilationist or integrationist model founded upon an unrealistic liberal framework of liberal individualism.

Of course, multiculturalism is not without its critics and its implementation can cause unrest and hostile counter-resistance. For instance, there are the expected criticisms from the political right-wing, which links the policy of multiculturalism to growing immigration and refugee pressures from third-world countries and raises worries about taking on immigrants at a time of global economic decline. Backlash takes the form of support for new parties, such as the Reform Party in Canada or the One Nation Party in Australia, which make opposition to multiculturalism a main plank in their platform. However, such assaults on the policy are often thinly-veiled attacks on the legitimacy of demands for full membership by minorities. This shows up, for instance, in the discomfort with active participation in the Canadian political community shown 'by groups which diverge from white British (or in Quebec, French) standards of physical or cultural acceptability' (Abu-Laban & Stasiulis, 1992: 381). In Canada, however, reasonable criticisms of the multiculturalism policy have emerged from various other sources since the 1980s. Among the harshest critics are minority immigrant writers who have faulted the policy for not adequately redressing racial inequalities or for ghettoising minority concerns. Others have treated multiculturalism as a source of division because it does not encourage interaction between all groups and leads minority individuals to place their ethno-cultural interests ahead of their duties to Canada. Critics from Quebec have attacked the policy for its intentional undermining of Quebec nationalism. French-Canadians in general complain that their traditional status as one of the two 'founding nations' has been undermined by multiculturalism, and that the policy encourages non-Quebeckers to equate being a French-Canadian with being, say, a Ukranian-Canadian. Even more devastating is the critique from First Nations critics who fear that their special status as the original inhabitants of the land is not fully recognised if 'Native-Canadian' becomes yet another category of ethno-cultural heritage.

What these criticisms point out is that multiculturalism can be a divisive policy in a multinational state that receives subsequent waves of ethno-cultural immigrants. Special measures need to be taken to ensure some form of political and social autonomy for component nations or subnational groups. This would entail recognition of certain self-government rights as well as certain special representation rights (Kymlicka, 1995: 26–33).

CONCLUSION

This paper demonstrates that the problems of citizenship and nationalism are very complex and that they have taken on new dimensions in light of both globalisation and increased immigration. The old idea of the nation-state based on a single, uniform nationality has given way under pressure from transborder migration and successive waves of immigration in countries throughout the western world. At the same time, the universalist notion of citizenship has given way to new and more challenging demands for the recognition and accommodation of differentiated citizenship. Given this new ideological attitude to difference, models of immigrant incorporation depending upon either the guestworker system or the difference-denying insistence of formal equality will fail to serve the interests of minority communities in modern, multicultural democracies. Multiculturalism is regarded as the best available strategy for immigrant incorporation. At the same time, the adoption of the value of cultural plurality in policies of multiculturalism can produce problems of its own, especially in multinational countries with entrenched subnational groups. And attempts to accommodate the diversity represented by culturally alien incomers will be experienced by certain groups as a threat to the dominant majority and its national way of life. In such cases, cultural democracy and the state promotion of cultural plurality are likely to encourage new varieties of nationalist or quasi-patriotic counter-resistance projects. Such new nationalisms cannot be expected to help forge closer international unions nor to provide for the peaceful integration of national and immigrant minorities. Nevertheless, the threat of newly reinforced and reactionary resistance to multiculturalism should not be seen as outweighing the benefits of the egalitarian incorporation of ethnic groups and immigrants through government promotion of cultural plurality.

BIBLIOGRAPHY

Abu-Laban, Y. & Stasiulis, D. (1992) 'Ethnic pluralism under siege: popular and partisan opposition to multiculturalism', *Canadian Public Policy* 18: 365–86.

Anderson, B. (1991) *Imagined Communities* (rev. edn.), London: Verso.

Booth, K. (1991) 'Security and anarchy: utopian realism in theory and practice', *International Affairs* 67: 527–42.

Brown, R. C. (1996) 'Full partnership in the fortunes and in the future of the nation' in Laponce, J. & Safran, W. (eds.) *Ethnicity and Citizenship: The Canadian Case*, London: Frank Cass.

Brubaker, W. R. (1989) 'Membership without citizenship' in *Immigration and the Politics of Citizenship in Europe and North America*, Lanham: University Press of America.

Connolly, W. (1990) *Identity/Difference: Democratic Negotiations of Political Paradox*, Ithaca: Cornell University Press.

Eisenstein, Z. (1996) *Hatreds: racialised and sexualised conflicts in the 21st century*, New York and London: Routledge.

Hammar, T. (1990) *International Migration, Citizenship and Democracy*, Aldershot: Gower.

Hannerz, U. (1990) 'Cosmopolitans and locals in world culture', *Theory, Culture and Society* 7: 237–52.

Heisler, M. (1986) 'Transnational migration as a small window on the diminished autonomy of the modern democratic state', *Annals* (AAPSS) 485: 153–66.

Helly, D. (1993) 'The political regulation of cultural plurality: foundations and principles', *Canadian Ethnic Studies* 25: 15–35.

Jacobson, D. (1996) *Rights Across Borders: Immigration and the Decline of Citizenship*, Baltimore and London: The John Hopkins University Press.

Kymlicka, W. (1995) *Multicultural Citizenship*, Oxford: Clarendon Press.

Luke, T. (1997) 'Reconsidering nationality and sovereignty in the new world order', *Political Crossroads* 5: 3–17.

Marden, P. (1997) 'Geographies of dissent: globalisation, identity and the nation', *Political Geography* 16: 37–64.

Miller, D. (1995) *On Nationality*, Oxford: Clarendon Press.

Moch, L. (1992) *Moving Europeans: Migration in Western Europe Since 1650*, Bloomington: Indiana University Press.

Rex, J. (1996) 'National Identity in the democratic multicultural state', Paper delivered to the Joint Conference of the Association for the Study of Ethnicity and Nationalism and the Centre for Research in Ethnic Relations held at the London School of Economics, 3 May 1996 (URL http://www.bsos.umd.edu/CSS97/papers/asencre.html).

Rex, J. (1997) 'The problematic of multinational and multicultural societies', *Ethnic and Racial Studies* 20: 455–73.

Safran, W. (1997) 'Citizenship and nationality in democratic systems: approaches in defining and acquiring membership in the political community', *International Political Science Review* 18: 313–23.

Soysal, Y. N. (1994) *Limits of Citizenship: Migrants and Postnational Membership in Europe*, Chicago and London: The University of Chicago Press.

Tenbuck, F. (1990) 'The dream of a secular ecumene: the meaning and limits of politics of development', *Theory, Culture and Society* 7: 193–206.

Ungerleider, C. S. (1992) 'Immigration, multiculturalism, and citizenship: the development of the Canadian social justice infrastructure', *Canadian Ethnic Studies* 24: 7–22.

8
International Boundaries in the Twenty-First Century: Changing Roles and Depiction

Bradford L. Thomas

INTRODUCTION

Over the last few centuries the international community has gradually come to accept the concept of the sovereign state as the highest form of political authority on the globe. The concept emerged principally in seventeenth-century Europe and spread to the rest of the world initially through contact with European-based empires. It subsequently received much more widespread adoption as formerly colonial peoples achieved independence from those empires, first in the Americas and then throughout the rest of the world in the rapid decolonisation that followed the Second World War. The new states emerging from colonialism in most cases adopted as their sovereign territories the colonial administrative areas within which they had previously been governed. However, while the sovereign state concept has continued to enjoy widespread acceptance, in more recent times its utility has been called into question with increasing frequency.

Political control over territory is one of the requisite components of the sovereign state. Accordingly, the sovereign state concept carries with it the idea that the limits of that control are defined by finite lines called international boundaries. Whether or not states actually exercise political control uniformly over their defined territories, such boundaries have proved to be essential to delimiting the administration of state power vested in sovereign national governments. Traditionally, international boundaries have defined what may be termed the 'national territory'. (The word 'national' is used here in the sense of pertaining to the sovereign state, not in relation to the idea of a 'nation-state' and the issue of whether the territory of a perceived 'nation' and the territory of a sovereign state are ever coextensive.)

Political developments in more recent times have brought significant change to the characteristics of national territory, with increasing diversity in what constitutes its extent and/or the nature of its delimitation. First, it has expanded in many places into the sea – both into the territorial sea, over which the coastal states exercise 'full' sovereignty, and farther offshore into areas over which the sovereign state exercises only partial, economic sovereignty. Secondly, some sovereign states have entered into unions or alliances that sacrifice a measure of national sovereignty to a larger territorial unit, with the result that their national territorial boundaries have lost part of their economic, political or

Borderlands Under Stress (M.A. Pratt and J.A. Brown (eds), ISBN 90-411-9790-7).
© Kluwer Law International, 2000.

military control functions. One might say that this diminished function of international boundaries is part of the definition of a new and broader national territory as the boundaries of the union or alliance gradually supersede the original boundaries – when, for example, border functions that once occurred along the upper Rhine are now found essentially along the Oder, and in the future may migrate to the Bug and the Drava as the European Union expands eastwards. Finally, there seems to have emerged an increasing tendency to devolve power to segments of territory within a sovereign state, some of which themselves attain a status closely approximating sovereignty. In some cases, this has given self-identified 'nations' a politically defined national territory for the first time; in all cases it has in some measure loosened the ties between that territory and the national territory of the sovereign state in which it lies.

If international boundaries are supposed to mark the limits of national territories that have any meaning in the light of political developments, then each of these developments has profound implications for the cartographic depiction of the realities of the world's political structure.

THE 'UNIFORM' INTERNATIONAL BOUNDARY

With the spread of the international boundary concept, the international diplomatic and legal community has persistently refined the standard by which an international boundary is judged to be legitimate. It must be negotiated between the officially recognised governments of two sovereign states to their mutual satisfaction; the agreement on that negotiation must be signed by official representatives of each government; and then, before coming into effect, it must be ratified by each of those governments and the instruments of ratification exchanged between them. A more recent addition has been the very useful, sometimes even critical custom (albeit a voluntary one) of depositing the complete text of the agreement and the instruments of its ratification with the United Nations (UN) and/or other international organisations. A unitary standard for a 'full international boundary' has emerged and a great deal of time and effort has been expended, by both individual sovereign states and the international community as a whole, to ensure that this standard is properly implemented around the world wherever it is needed.

International boundaries have also tended to take on a fairly standard set of functions over time. In addition to marking the territorial extent of a sovereign state's power, they also serve to control the movement of people and goods – or even ideas – from one sovereign state to another. In these functions, international boundaries have most often served as barriers, blocking or restricting such movements, generally with the aim of preserving the security, economy or cultural integrity of the state. However, in this age of widespread travel and shipment by air, similar 'boundary' functions have to be exercised at international airports. Moreover, international electronic communication technology has pretty much destroyed any 'cultural screening' that international boundaries once performed. Nonetheless, a kind of standard of international boundary functions has developed, usually comprising a set of procedures that must be adhered to in order to cross a boundary; although this standard is considerably more variable in content and not so tightly defined as the legal one which established the boundary in the first place.

INTERNATIONAL BOUNDARIES AND MAPS

Like the sovereign state that it circumscribes, the international boundary is a social construct.[1] It is not visible on the surface of the earth either from satellites in space or on the ground itself, and thus is often described as one of the 'invisible' elements of the map. Even if demarcated with monuments at intervals, there are stretches between the monuments where no line is to be seen. Unless some notable land-use differentiation, infrastructural termination or change, or administrative structure such as a wall, fence, forest swath or fortification makes the boundary indirectly visible on the earth's surface, we cannot normally find in the terrain that which is symbolised on the map, as we can with visible natural or human-built features. It is the spatial plot of the network of international boundaries that creates the world political map, a mental spatial construct of the 'reality' of the political geography with which we live, and by which our diplomatic, political and military colleagues order most of their knowledge and actions regarding world affairs (Figure 3).

With invisible realities such as, for example, a statistical distribution or a subterranean phenomenon, the geographic structure or spatial pattern of the reality is not understandable until it is mapped. Similarly, the image of the world's political geographic reality is not known until we put boundaries and tints on our political maps (Figure 4). It is the map that essentially creates our knowledge of that reality. As Denis Wood put it,

> knowledge of the map is knowledge of the world from which it emerges. ... It [forces] us to admit that the knowledge it embodies was socially *constructed*, not tripped over and no more than ... *reproduced*. ... What is at stake is not latitude and longitude, ... but ... *ownership*: that is what is being mapped here. (Wood, 1992: 18, 21, emphases in original.)

Thus, it is of particular importance to the conduct of foreign affairs that the map's depiction of the world's political geography resemble the reality of that spatial structure as closely as possible, whether it be the framework of sovereign states or some more fluid ordering of national territories.

The idea that there is one highest level of political expression in the world – the sovereign state – and one unitary standard for the boundaries separating one sovereign state from another has logically led to the adoption of one standard cartographic symbol for representing all boundaries meeting that standard. This cartographic convention has been considerably reinforced by the standard set of functions that those boundaries have tended to perform. It has served us well as long as full sovereignty has remained the highest operative level of political/territorial organisation, and the area of its control has defined the national territory associated with it.

However, certain forces at work in our modern world transcend the sovereignty of the sovereign state, eroding its power and authority – UN interventions, other inter-governmental or non-governmental organisation activities, transnational corporations, global financial markets, global electronic communications, environmental degradation, and intercontinental ballistic missile targeting, to name just some of the more overt occurrences; not to mention illegal immigration and drug smuggling. International boundaries are either irrelevant to the functioning of such forces or ineffectual in controlling them. Added to these woes is the internal 'weakening' (to some) of the sovereign state through ethnic factionalism, secessionist movements or devolution of power to local areas.

Some writers foresee the passing of the sovereign state as 'the dominant political formation of our time'[2] – or, as Daniel Bell has put it, 'too small for the big problems of life and too big for the small problems' (*The Economist*, 1997a). Most at least catalogue its decline or the 'erosion' of its sovereignty.[3] Taylor, on the other hand, while analysing the 'difficulties states are having in coming to terms with contemporary social change', maintains that it is still premature to assume the demise of what he calls the 'state-container' (Taylor, 1994: 157, 161). In a subsequent analysis, however, he considers the world system of sovereign states in their multiplicity, or 'interstateness', and foresees the passage of this system, along with 'interterritoriality' ('the presumption that every section of occupied land across the world is the sovereign territory of some state'), in favour of trans-stateness – i.e. practices that bypass states. He conjectures that 'internationality' relations among the multiplicity of 'nations' (with or without states) can operate in a world 'freed from association with states and the need for exclusive access to territories' (Taylor, 1995). Murphy, in a similar vein, notes that 'challenges to the existing order are manifest at different scales and in overlapping spaces', and foresees 'the need for a more flexible, multi-layered approach to political territorial governance in the twenty-first century' (Murphy, 1996: 110–111). Newman, on the other hand, sees a regional differentiation between the western European and North American experience, where many of the traditional functions of boundaries are being shed, and

> parts of the world where new nation-states, or 'nation-dominant' states, have been creating their own new fences and boundaries in the first stages of renewed political independence... or as part of a process through which ethno-territorial conflicts are resolved.[4]

We are not greatly concerned here with whether the sovereign state as a form of political territoriality is threatened with demise. There are still numerous aspects of modern life which are dependent on territorial control by such political authorities. But clearly, whatever the status of the sovereign state, the territorial expression of what is considered its national territory is diversifying. With this diversification, the reality associated with the lines separating those territories has gone through some profound changes. The time seems to be fast approaching when we can no longer with any useful meaning use a single cartographic symbol to depict the lines defining national territories. The realities of political geography seem to have slipped out from under our standard methods of depicting it. If the political map is to retain its credibility, our cartographic symbolisation must diversify with the reality it is designed to depict.

There is undoubtedly a certain inertia, conscious resistance, even, to changing the symbolisation of international boundaries. But, as diversification in sovereignty status and definition of national territory become more and more characteristic of the highest levels of political organisation in the world, failure to depict these developments creates a modern example of what J. B. Harley has called 'political silences' on maps (Harley, 1988: 57). Some of these omissions from the maps may be intentional, the result of the desire to promulgate an earlier status quo cartographically in support, perhaps, of certain foreign policies. Others, probably the bulk of political map 'silences', may be 'merely a function of the slowness with which cartographers [revise] their maps to accord with the realities of the world' (Harley, 1988: 70).

Whatever the origin of the 'silences' on political maps, as the difference broadens between the world constructed in our heads by the map and the reality of the political world with which we must deal, these 'silences' actually start to cry out for representation. As Murphy puts it,

> [n]ew questions are being asked about the scale of political-territorial organisation, about the role of substate and superstate formations, and about the nature of the territorial state itself. In the process, it is becoming increasingly difficult to simply treat the world political map as an unproblematic, untransmutable given. (Murphy, 1996: 110.)

We are faced with two choices: continue as before, doggedly holding to a single symbol to depict the limits of national territories according to earlier realities; or give voice to the 'silences' of undepicted current realities and design a symbolisation that will convey them. To be sure, the variations in national territory are intricate and complex and the depictions are going to be complicated far beyond the simple single-line symbol we currently enjoy. But, to borrow from Lewis and Wigen writing in a different, though similar context, 'responsible cartography requires at least making the effort. Complexity does not excuse obliteration' (Lewis & Wigen, 1997: 133–134). Let us now turn to the kinds of complexities that characterise today's political geography.

INTERNATIONAL BOUNDARIES IN THE SEA?

One of the developments that has diluted the idea of a single, finite line bounding national territory is the delimiting of maritime zones by sovereign states intent on capturing the resources in and under the sea off their coasts. The maritime limits established under the 1982 United Nations Convention on the

Law of the Sea (LOS Convention) have essentially created a set of zones of progressively diminishing national jurisdiction moving seaward from the shore.

Although the right of states to claim maritime zones can be traced back to the seventeenth century, when the concept of the territorial sea began to emerge, claims to zones of maritime jurisdiction really took off following the 'Truman Proclamation' of 1945 concerning the US continental shelf and the 1958 Geneva conferences on the law of the sea.[5] The Third United Nations Law of the Sea Conference during the 1970s prompted an all-time high in maritime claims, many now including the more comprehensive exclusive economic zone (EEZ) concept developed by the Conference, even before the resulting UNCLOS was signed in 1982. By 1990 there were 80 EEZ claims (Smith, 1990: Table 1, Graph 1). With the entry into force of UNCLOS in 1994, there was another flurry of activity, both of maritime claims and of further ratifications.

The expansion of jurisdiction by coastal sovereign states into the sea gives new dimensions to the traditional land-based definition of national territory. The LOS Convention has set the legal nature and geographic limits of this offshore jurisdiction, but interpretations of these limits vary. As is well known, the development of the LOS Convention involved, among other disagreements, a tussle between two major interest blocs: the coastal states, which wanted maximum jurisdiction over the oceans, and the so-called maritime powers, which wanted to restrict that jurisdiction as much as possible. The result can be seen to satisfy both sides. In favour of the maritime powers, a geographic cap of 12 nautical miles (nm) was set on the territorial sea. This area constitutes the only 'maritime' zone (i.e. seaward of internal waters or archipelagic waters) over which full state sovereignty extends – although this sovereignty is not quite as complete as sovereignty over land territory since UNCLOS provides for innocent passage for foreign vessels in the territorial sea.[6] The coastal states, on the other hand, gained an extension of the geographic breadth of full state sovereignty into the seas; traditionally the limit (albeit not always honoured) had been three nautical miles.

The inclusion of sea areas as national territory is a well-established concept. As well as specifying coastal state sovereignty over the territorial sea and the airspace above it (Article 2), the LOS Convention also allocates even broader expanses of ocean to the national territory of 'archipelagic states' (those consisting of one or more 'archipelagos'). Such states are qualified to enclose the waters between their islands with archipelagic straight baselines and are accorded full sovereignty over those archipelagic waters and the airspace above them (Article 49). An archipelago is defined as:

> a group of islands, including parts of islands, *interconnecting waters* and other natural features which are so closely interrelated that such islands, *waters* and other natural features form an intrinsic geographical, economic and political entity, or which historically has been regarded as such.' (Article 46; emphasis added.)

This is certainly a description of national territory. Buchholz, writing about Fiji's straight baselines, recognises this aspect when he notes that, for the first time, the resulting archipelagic regime 'provides an areal awareness of the otherwise scattered and highly differentiated country – an effect of high significance for the political perception of the national entity' (Buchholz, 1990: 80). Figure 1 serves to illustrate his point.

As of 1997, 83 percent of the world's coastal states (including many maritime powers such as the United States) claim the maximum 12 nm territorial sea (Smith, 1997). Gradually, many countries that had previously claimed territorial seas of greater breadths have adjusted those claims to the 12 nm standard, and many whose previous territorial sea claims were smaller have extended them out to 12 nm. In the latter cases, there has been a seaward extension of national territory, in the full sovereignty sense of that concept, including national sovereign airspace, minus only the provision for innocent passage of surface vessels. Many states have also taken advantage of UNCLOS's provisions for straight baselines along deeply indented or island-fringed coasts to nudge their territorial seas even farther out to sea.

Except for some navigation charts, for the purpose of which it is obviously essential, we have not been accustomed to depicting the territorial seas of coastal states on our maps. Indeed, in most small-scale cartography, a breadth of 12 nm would not even show. At larger scales, excepting nautical charts, a number of factors have often deterred cartographers from such depictions: undetermined or contested territorial sea boundaries; natural changes in coastlines which alter the position of coastal baselines and, hence, territorial sea limits based on them; even, in some cases, the possibility of legal liability on the part of the cartographer for misleading depictions. But the reality is there. It is not much of a leap from charts which support air or sea navigation to the political perception of national territory. Is this lack of depiction not a 'silence' on our larger-scale general purpose or political maps? In Figure 1, which is still a fairly small-scale map, the territorial sea is big enough to be depicted. As its outer limit is the real boundary of full state sovereignty, it is therefore shown here with a conventional international boundary symbol.

Beyond the territorial sea, in the EEZ or continental shelf, state jurisdiction is limited to 'economic sovereignty' – i.e. control over exploration and exploitation of marine resources. In fishing zones, which have developed in state practice outside the LOS Convention, jurisdiction is limited to the resources of the water column above the seabed. From the point of view of the maritime powers, nothing has changed – the waters in these zones are, in fact, international waters, with the attendant high seas rights of navigation and overflight. On the other hand, the coastal states have gained exclusive national control over marine resources out to 200 nm and sometimes (in the case of some continental shelves) even further.[7] Although this does not represent full state sovereignty, it is an extension of state authority, both legally and territorially, over what had been the case before.

While including territorial seas and archipelagic waters as national territory is justifiable, there is some confusion about the popular perception of extended maritime zones. Fine distinctions regarding the limits of state control over these zones are almost impossible to enforce in the media and sometimes foreign ministry spokespersons take advantage of this lack of popular understanding to publicly press a policy position. The ambiguous term 'territorial waters' is used with disturbing frequency in both press and government releases in contexts where it is obvious that the reference is to an EEZ, continental shelf or fishing zone, and usually with regard to some maritime jurisdictional dispute, leading some to confuse the status of the area with the full state sovereignty of the territorial sea.

Apart from ambiguous terminology, there is a perceptible tendency to inflate the territorial significance of extended maritime zones. Surely some of this practice must stem from the choice of terms in the LOS Convention, which refers to the '*sovereign rights* of the coastal state in exploring and exploiting, conserving and managing [its] natural resources' (Article 56; emphasis added). But the perception goes beyond a simple, though qualified term. For example, in a recent statement regarding Scarborough Reef in the South China Sea, the Philippines' foreign secretary, while carefully distinguishing between areas of Philippine sovereignty and Philippine jurisdiction, did seem, with the choice of the word 'and' instead of the word 'or', to merge both kinds of area into that state's national territory:

> We maintain that the Scarborough Shoal is part of our territory. Article 1 of the Philippine Constitution states that the *national territory* comprises the Philippine archipelago, with all the islands and waters embraced therein, and all other territories over which the Philippines has *sovereignty and jurisdiction*. (Sarne, 1997; emphasis added.)

US experts are certainly not beyond such tendencies. A 1993 US Geological Survey brochure, entitled 'The Exclusive Economic Zone: An Exciting New Frontier', compares the 3.9 billion acres of the US EEZ proclaimed by President Reagan in 1983 to the 2.3 billion land acres of the US and its territories, and likens it to the Louisiana Purchase of 1803 which doubled the area of what then comprised the United States (McGregor & Offield, 1993: 2). The underlying implication is that the US has gained territory and the word 'frontier' in the title educes its historic image of expanding territorial control. Even Glassner, who is eminently knowledgeable on the Law of the Sea, apparently can't resist inserting a rather popularly appealing, embellished notion when describing the creation of the US Outer Continental Shelf in 1983: 'Few Americans realise that on 10 March 1983 the *territory* of the United States more than doubled' (Glassner, 1996: 201; emphasis added). Although he subsequently clarifies that the US does not have sovereignty over this 'land', he notes the acquisition of 'sovereign resources' (in the language of the proclamation). Are such representations ill-informed – or are they, in fact, 'telling it like it is'?

Despite popular misinterpretation or expert misrepresentation, there is a reality that emerges. The abovementioned may be merely examples of a wider trend in popular thinking but they are also, in effect, a manifestation of the political geographic 'reality' of today's state authority over extended maritime zones. In the minds of many, even those in officialdom, the national territory is no longer limited to the area under full sovereignty. Is this not another 'silence' on our maps? Were we to depict this territorial extension of state authority on our maps, it would clearly show up even at small scales. Does not Figure 5 foretell the political map of the future? A proper and careful cartographic depiction, designed to differentiate the extended maritime zones of authority from areas of full state sovereignty, could build a popular understanding of the actual nature of different marine areas of the national territory. Figure 2 shows such a depiction at slightly larger scale than Figure 5, as applied to Fiji's national territory.

No changes are envisioned to the provisions of the LOS Convention for maritime zones at this time, so the breadth of the zones of diminishing state authority extending into the sea should remain fairly stable for the foreseeable future. These zones of diminishing authority could be shown on maps either using line symbols of varying design and density or using different densities of shading (Figures 1 and 2). On colour maps the hues that distinguish one sovereign state from another could grade into the sea in diminishing percentage value. All of these should be precisely defined in map legends. Undetermined or contested boundaries (as with the hypothetical equidistance lines in Figures 1 and 2) could be handled in the same way as such problems are on land, although area tones or colours would require special handling.

From the perspective of resources, at least, there is no longer any part of the seabed that is not under some political jurisdiction. Under the LOS Convention, exploitation of the mineral resources of 'the Area' (i.e. the remaining deep ocean floor beyond the 200 nm limit or extended continental shelves of greater breadth), is to be administered for the common good of all the world's states by the International Sea-Bed Authority (ISBA). Normally, we might not be inclined to depict areas under such UN jurisdiction on our political maps, but one might nonetheless raise the question here, tentatively, for possible consideration.[8] Another map 'silence'?

INTERNATIONAL BOUNDARIES – IN NAME ONLY?

Back in 1940 the American geographer S. Whittemore Boggs opined that the functions of boundaries were

> in general negative rather than positive. To at least some degree they restrict the movement of peoples and the exchange of goods, of money, even of ideas. ... International boundaries are intended to serve protective functions of various kinds. They can not promote trade or human intercourse as is sometimes contended. (Boggs, 1940: 11.)

Today, with the globalisation of the world's economy and the disappearance of Cold War tension, many of the world's sovereign states, through bilateral trade agreements or multilateral economic integration, are eliminating many, if not all, of the functions performed by their boundaries. Most of these efforts are aimed at removing tariff or other economic barriers to free trade, as with the North American Free Trade Agreement (NAFTA) or South America's MERCOSUR (Figure 6). The most advanced effort of this kind is the gradual, painstaking movement by members of the European Union (EU) towards not only economic, but social and political integration, eliminating controls on the movement of people and labour across boundaries as well as restrictions on the movement of goods and capital (Figure 7).

Pressures from refugee flows and illegal migrants *have* led to calls for tighter immigration controls, particularly around the peripheral boundary of the sovereign states otherwise united in reducing their mutual boundary functions. Continued illegal narcotics smuggling also prompts more intensive efforts to seal borders. Nevertheless, as a result of economic and incipient political/social integration, the number of functions represented by international boundaries varies greatly around the world. The relative porosity of international boundaries is one of the realities undepicted on today's world political map – another yawning map 'silence'. Although the lines symbolised as 'full' international boundaries on the map may be of equal legal – or *de jure* – status, they may also be quite dissimilar in regard to their economic or even political functions – or *de facto* status. Does not the reality of variably porous boundaries deserve incorporation into the world political map and a more constant place in our world consciousness? Figures 6 and 7 illustrate, by variations in tones, the political realities of regional integration but not the consequences for international boundaries.

How can we make international boundaries on political maps more informative? We need to vary the prominence of the international boundary symbol in relation to the restrictiveness – i.e. impermeability – of the boundary depicted. This could be done by varying the line weight or darkness of the boundary symbol. Figure 8 shows a projected map of Europe in 2002 in which the symbol for international boundaries is varied in darkness according to a simplified two-level categorisation of boundary functions. Could this be the way ahead for political maps of the future?

Because functional variation in international boundaries has so far resulted mainly from economic integration, it raises the corollary question of what to do with hierarchical relationships – as in the case of once-sovereign states surrendering much of their sovereignty to a higher, supra-national union. The EU, for example, is an increasingly active player on various diplomatic fronts around the world. How long can cartographers continue to ignore on their maps an entity that has, or soon may have, much of the power previously reserved for sovereign states? Certainly, we should not abandon depiction of the sovereign states that comprise a united entity, but we will surely need a hierarchical symbolisation, similar to that shown on Figure 8, to show the reality of their relationship with that entity.

It should be mentioned in passing that cartographic depiction in cases of hierarchical relationships is not only a matter of line symbols or shading. Placenames play an especially significant role in the conceptualisation and identification of political territories (Paasi, 1995: 48), including even the generic terms attached to them. As well as line symbols and shading, different sizes and style of typeface can also be applied to the names of political units on the map, to reinforce messages of hierarchical political relationships.

However, the depiction of the relative porosity of borders does present a rather daunting challenge to the international boundary and cartographic community. It has been difficult enough in the past just to collect consistently accurate data on the alignment of international boundaries, especially those that are under dispute or in doubt. The proposal proffered here would require a wholly new level of data on the different functions and degree of restrictions associated with each bilateral segment of international boundary. This might impose an overwhelming burden on boundary specialists and cartographers alike. Perhaps a programme could be set up to marshal such data on boundary functions at an international central institution – for example, the International Boundaries Research Unit (IBRU) – to which experts responsible for collecting data for their respective countries could send information to be entered into a central database. Once the information is collected, different methods of depicting different types of boundary could be devised.

The challenge is there. Will we in the international boundary community rise to it? The alternative may well be increasingly unrepresentative political maps with less and less to say about the realities of the modern political world. Figure 9 shows a response: a depiction of national territories showing both the variable functions of boundaries and the extended maritime jurisdictions.

DEVOLUTION AND 'INTERNATIONAL' BOUNDARIES

With the breakdown of most communist governments and the end of the Cold War, the world experienced a surge of campaigns for independence – or, at least, increased political autonomy – by various substate groups or would-be nations whose political expression or self-determination had been suppressed by powerful central governments. Some of these campaigns, though fortunately not all, have been waged in violence. The result has been a devolution of state power and authority from the hands of sovereign state governments into the hands of various substate peoples. In most cases this devolution has, in name at least, stopped short of full independence (Figure 11).

Some observers see a relationship between this trend and the globalisation of the economy (Beetham, 1984: 219) or the global information revolution (Muir, 1997: 111), both of which tend to reinforce regional disparities within states. Others, however, see devolution as contributing to the preservation of the sovereign state, at least as regards Europe: 'If there is a turn-of-the-century message in Europe, it may be "devolve or die" ' (*The Economist*, 1997b: 53, 54). In the cases of some indigenous peoples, the trend might also be related to the increasing influence in international affairs of non-governmental and inter-governmental organisations on their behalf (e.g. Glassner, 1996: 221–223).

Yet some form or other of devolution has been around for a long time, in practice if not in name. One can think of such examples of self-government as Iceland (from 1918 to 1944), the Faroe Islands (from 1947), Puerto Rico (from 1952), the Cook Islands (from 1965), Greenland (from 1979), the Northern Mariana Islands (from 1986), and Aruba (from 1986). Some might even include the Republic of the Marshall Islands (from 1986), the Federated States of Micronesia (from 1986), and the Republic of Palau (from 1994), all of which achieved independence (from US-administered UN trusteeship) as 'freely associated states' with the US. Another kind of devolution that has been around for a while is the more decentralised, truly federal state, such as Germany or perhaps Canada.

Some may question why we should feel any pressure to represent devolved political units cartographically on any basis equivalent to that of the sovereign state. Why not continue representing them as subordinate divisions of the sovereign state in which they are located? The answer is, because the distinction is not always clear. Some units which have received devolved authority have behaved like sovereign states. The standard minimum criterion for the status of a political entity as a 'sovereign state' has always been control of its own foreign policy. For example, under 'freely associated state' status, the Marshall Islands, the Federated States of Micronesia, and Palau control their own foreign policy and are subject to the US primarily for defence reasons. The US maintains a diplomatic presence in each country and shows them on maps as independent states. On the other hand, the Cook Islands, a 'freely associated state' with New Zealand, also control their own foreign policy, maintaining their own foreign ministry, signing treaties (such as the maritime boundary agreement with the US), and belonging to UN and regional organisations. On occasion their foreign policy has even been at odds with that of New Zealand (Glassner, 1996: 137; US Department of State, 1983). Yet on maps we continue to show the Cook Islands as a New Zealand dependency. Another example of 'substate' political entities forging international ties of their own is found in the increasingly expansive 'Four Motors' agreement, encouraged by the reduced barrier functions of EU boundaries, between Catalonia, Rhône-Alpes, Baden-Württemburg and Lombardy (Murphy, 1994: 222).

What of the future? It may hold not only the increasing autonomy of devolved political entities – even to the point of full or partial control of foreign affairs – but, even more likely, the playing off of special relations with intergovernmental or non-governmental organisations against the home government (e.g. *The Economist*, 1997b: 53). Such entities would clearly be functionally more 'sovereign' than a customary 'first-order administrative division' and, in exercising virtual political as well as economic autonomy, surely have more authority over their respective territories than that of a coastal sovereign state over its EEZ. For example, how will we be depicting Scotland in future maps? It certainly will have moved beyond 'first-order administrative division'. What about Chechnya? The Turkish Republic of Northern Cyprus? East Timor? Tibet? Taiwan? What about the Croat-Muslim Federation or the Republika Srpska if, heaven forbid, Bosnian integration should stall? Are we prepared for the cartographic representation of a virtual Joseph's coat of overlapping or multi-layered 'sovereignty' situations?

DIMINISHED JURISDICTIONS ON LAND

One can find a counterpart on land to maritime zones of progressively diminishing jurisdiction: the areas currently under the Palestinian Authority. Most cartographers – and not just those representing a government's foreign policy – have abjured the depiction of the different zones of control under the interim stages of the Peace Process, often with the convenient excuse that the final settlement of the status of the occupied territories is pending. On the other hand, when depiction of the current reality is needed, cartographers do produce such maps (for example, Figure 10). With the Peace Process stalled and with Palestinians continuing, with increasing frustration, to press their claim to a sovereign state, depiction of the actual reality of Palestinian control could become an increasingly conspicuous 'silence' on the map. Conversely, if the Peace Process were to move ahead to a final status settlement, it could conceivably involve some sort of zone or zones of diminishing jurisdiction or servitudes granting access through Palestinian or Israeli territory.[9] What of our map depictions then?

Cartographic challenges for other sorts of 'anomalous' political units, to borrow Glassner's classification (Glassner, 1996: chapter 11), can be envisioned. Bi-national territories such as *condominia* of truly joint administration, or neutral zones supposedly of no administration, have largely disappeared from the land areas of the world political map. But they persist at sea in the form of joint development areas and, in the case of the Gulf of Fonseca, an International Court of Justice-ruled condominium. If we 'admit' maritime zones to the political map, as suggested above, each of these would represent a zone of diminished jurisdiction for the countries involved but, in this case, through sharing sovereignty with one or more other countries. International territories, such as various experiments at free cities, have also disappeared from the map. But there is the case of 'the Area', as noted earlier, under ISBA administration and, given the state of political unrest in the world, the possibility arises of some land area falling, even temporarily, under UN administration.

CONCLUSION

Let me conclude by casting this discourse in a somewhat broader context. We are witnessing a perhaps unprecedented era of change in the political ordering of the world. Unfortunately, we are also witnessing a pitiable degeneration of geographic awareness on the part of much of the world's population, at just the time when this same population, and especially its leaders, must be better informed of international affairs than ever before. It ill behoves us, therefore, to reinforce whatever geographic ignorance may prevail by creating maps that are increasingly less informative about political geography.

Unfortunately, the path to more informative maps is a daunting one. Depiction of the increasingly diverse political geography of the world will require fresh and imaginative classifications of the boundaries of national territories. This, in turn, will require an unparalleled data-collection effort. Not only will boundary alignments have to be pinned down with greater accuracy, but a wealth of information on the differing status and varying functions of boundaries will be needed. A central institutional collection point of international stature and repute will surely be needed. We are fortunate, at least, that one of the factors changing the political order, the global communications revolution, should help us in this task.

Regardless of the daunting nature of the challenge, the fluid nature of modern political geography dictates fluidity in the design and symbolisation of the political boundaries on future maps. The political community is busy reinventing the political world order. The cartographic community must catch up or be relegated to producing maps of little more than historical value. The 'silences' on current political maps need a voice.

NOTES

1 See, for example, Knight, 1994: 76; Biersteker & Weber, 1996: 3; Paasi, 1995: 42–43; Taylor, 1995: 8.
2 Beetham, 1984; see also excellent reviews by Taylor, 1994: 157, and Newman & Paasi, 1998: 191–193.
3 Taylor, 1994; Knight, 1994: 84; Murphy, 1994: 216–223 and 1996: 107–112; Glassner, 1996; 139–141; Muir, 1997: 98–113.
4 Newman, 1997: 2; see also Newman & Paasi, 1998: 199–200.
5 Glassner (1996) has a good overview of the development of the Law of the Sea and maritime zones, covered in chapters 31 and 32.
6 While internal waters and archipelagic waters are considered legally tantamount to land areas, the LOS Convention also prescribes innocent passage for them (in the case of internal waters, where the area was not internal waters before being enclosed by straight baselines). In archipelagic waters, the even more liberal archipelagic sealanes passage, allowing ships and aircraft high seas navigation and overflight, is permitted within specified sealanes.
7 One expert source has identified 29 places around the world (excepting Antarctica) where, on the basis of submarine topography, continental shelves legally extend beyond 200 nm under LOS Convention provisions. See Prescott, 1998.
8 Note the portions of seabed mining concessions, now under ISBA jurisdiction, that appear southeast of Hawaii in Figure 4.
9 Noteworthy in the 1994 Peace Agreement between Israel and Jordan is the access granted to Israel to work certain Israeli-developed farmlands falling under Jordanian sovereignty.

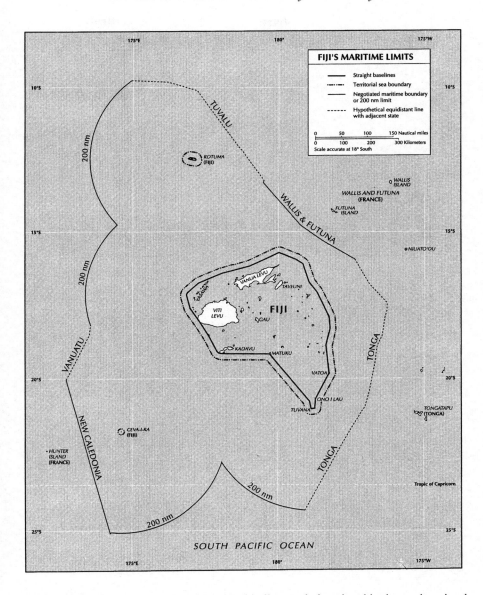

Figure 1: Fiji's national territory as depicted in line symbols ordered in decreasing visual prominence according to diminishing levels of jurisdiction. The agreed maritime boundaries and 200 nm limits are shown more prominently than the hypothetical equidistance lines with adjacent states because they are the established or agreed outer limits to Fiji's EEZ, not subject to contest or modification. The hypothetical equidistance lines with adjacent states are where maritime boundaries do not exist; they remain to be negotiated and the final boundaries might not be in those exact locations.

(Source: GeoSystems, Inc., 1998)

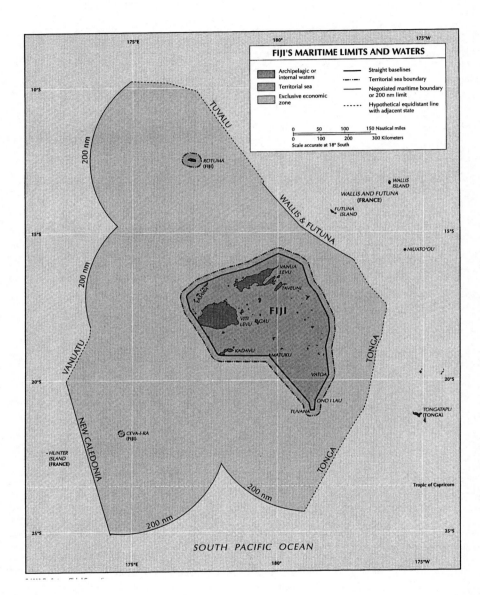

Figure 2: Fiji's national territory as depicted in area symbols; grey tones ordered in decreasing darkness according to diminishing levels of jurisdiction.

(Source: GeoSystems, Inc., 1998)

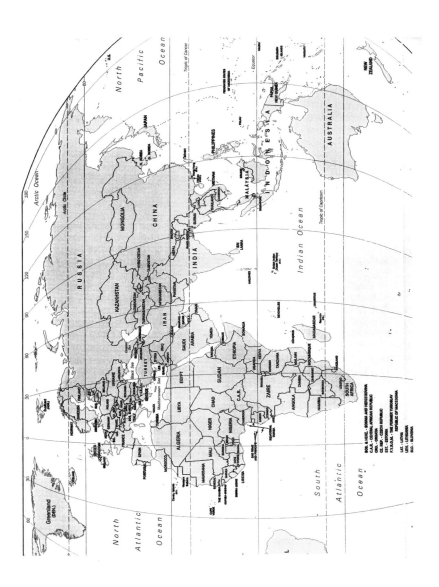

Figure 3: A portion of a standard line-symbol world political map depicting the framework of sovereign states.

(Source: US Government)

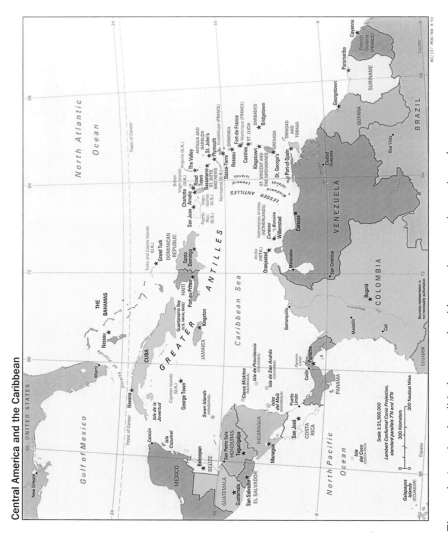

Figure 4: A regional political map made with sovereign states in varying colours.

(Source: US Government)

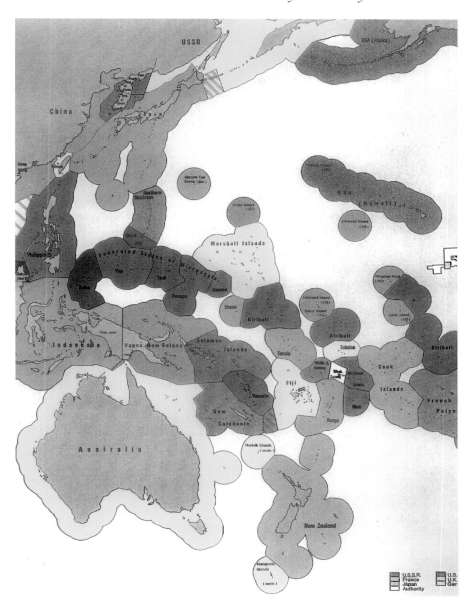

Figure 5: Western portion of a coloured map showing potential 200 nm zones in the Pacific Ocean. The political map of the future could be similar, only with the land area of each state shown in a distinctive, full colour and its extended maritime zone shown in a lighter screen of that same colour.

(Source: Buchholz, 1990)

Figure 6: A map of economic blocs in the Americas.

(Source: US Department of State)

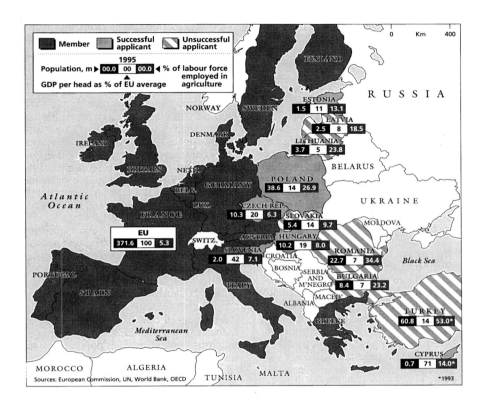

Eastward ho, they said warily

Figure 7: A map of the European Union and its projected expansion.

(Source: *The Economist*, 19 July 1997. © 1997 The Economist Newspaper Group, Inc. Reprinted with permission. Further reproduction prohibited.)

Figure 8: A possible cartographic depiction of Europe's boundaries as they may be in 2002, according to variable levels of functions.

(Source: GeoSystems, Inc., 1998)

Figure 9: A possible cartographic depiction of Europe's 2002 boundaries, with current extended maritime zones (only maritime boundaries agreed as of 1998 are shown). Hypothetical equidistance lines which would complete the national territories of some of the coastal states have been omitted. While this avoids possibly controversial depictions, it also emphasises the unfinished business of defining national territories in the current extension of jurisdiction into the seas.

(Source: GeoSystems, Inc., 1998)

Areas of Control (U)

Unclassified

Figure 10: A map of the West Bank showing zones of full and limited jurisdiction of the Palestinian Authority. Note the use of a 100 per cent red tone for the areas under Palestinian Authority control, and the diminished screen of the same hue for areas where the Authority is limited to civilian control only. Such a technique could also serve for shading maritime zones on colour political maps. (Note: This map was produced in January 1997. That same month the Israelis and the Palestinians signed an agreement providing for immediate Israeli withdrawal from most of Hebron.)

(Source: US Government Printing Office)

186

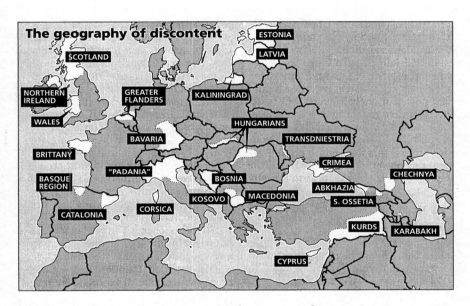

Devolution can be salvation

Figure 11: A map showing actual and potential areas of political devolution in Europe.

(Source: *The Economist*, 20 September 1997. © 1997 The Economist Newspaper Group, Inc. Reprinted with permission. Further reproduction prohibited.)

BIBLIOGRAPHY

Beetham, D. (1984) 'The Future of the Nation-State' in McLennan, G., Held, D. & Hall, S. (eds.) *The Idea of the Modern State*, Buckingham: The Open University.

Biersteker, T. J. & Weber, C. (1996) 'The Social Construction of State Sovereignty' in Biersteker, T. J. & Weber, C. (eds.) *State Sovereignty as Social Construct*, Cambridge: Cambridge University Press: 1–21.

Boggs, S. W. (1940) *International Boundaries: A Study of Boundary Functions and Problems*, New York: Columbia University Press.

Buchholz, H. (1990) 'Law of the Sea Boundaries in the South Pacific: Maritime Zones and Mining Area Claims' in Grundy-Warr, C. (ed.) *International Boundaries and Boundary Conflict Resolution; Proceedings of the 1989 IBRU Conference*, Durham: International Boundaries Research Unit.

Glassner, M. I. (1996) *Political Geography*, (2nd edn.), New York: John Wiley & Sons, Inc.

Harley, J. B. (1988) 'Silences and Secrecy: The Hidden Agenda of Cartography in Early Modern Europe', *Imago Mundi*, Vol. 40: 57–76.

Knight, D. B. (1994) 'People Together, Yet Apart: Rethinking Territory, Sovereignty, and Identities' in Demko, G. J. & Wood, W. B. (eds.) *Reordering the World: Geopolitical Perspectives on the Twenty-first Century*, Boulder, San Francisco, Oxford: Westview Press: 71–85.

Lewis, M. & Wigen, K. (1997) *The Myth of Continents: A Critique of Metageography*, Berkeley, Los Angeles, London: The University of California Press.

McGregor, B. A. & Offield, T. W. (1993) *The Exclusive Economic Zone: An Exciting New Frontier*, US Department of the Interior, US Geological Survey, Washington: US Government Printing Office.

Muir, R. (1997) *Political Geography: A New Introduction*, New York, Toronto: John Wiley & Sons, Inc.

Murphy, A. B. (1994) 'International Law and the Sovereign State: Challenges to the Status Quo' in Demko, G. J. & Wood, W. B. (eds.) *Reordering the World: Geopolitical Perspectives on the Twenty-first Century*, Boulder, San Francisco, Oxford: Westview Press: 209–224.

Murphy, A. B. (1996) 'The Sovereign State System as Political-Territorial Ideal: Historical and Contemporary Considerations' in Biersteker, T. J. & Weber, C. (eds.) *State Sovereignty as Social Construct*, Cambridge: Cambridge University Press: 81–120.

Newman, D. & Paasi, A. (1998) 'Fences and Neighbors in the Postmodern World: Boundary Narratives in Political Geography', *Progress in Human Geography*, Vol. 22, No. 2: 186–207.

Newman, D. (1997) 'Creating the Fences of Territorial Separation: The Discourses of Israeli-Palestinian Conflict Resolution' *Geopolitics and International Boundaries*, Vol. 2, No. 2, Autumn: 1–35.

Paasi, A. (1995) 'Constructing Territories, Boundaries and Regional Identities' in Forsberg, T. (ed.) *Contested Territory: Border Disputes at the Edge of the Former Soviet Empire*, Aldershot: Edward Elgar: 42–61.

Prescott, V. (1998) 'National Rights to Hydrocarbon Resources of the Continental Margin Beyond 200 Nautical Miles' in Blake, G. H. *et al* (eds.) *Boundaries and Energy: Problems and Prospects*, London: Kluwer Law International: 51-82.

Sarne, E. R. (1997) Message to int-boundaries e-mail list from Center for International Relations and Strategic Studies, Foreign Service Institute, the Philippines, 22 July, 13:04:59, quoting a 5 June 1997 statement before the Senate Foreign Relations and Defense Committees by Foreign Affairs Secretary Domingo Siazon.

Smith, R. W. (1990) 'The State Practice of National Maritime Claims and the Law of the Sea', paper presented to the conference on 'State Practice and the 1982 Law of the Sea Convention', Cascais, Portugal.

Smith, R. W. (1997) 'Summary of Maritime Claims As of May 13, 1997', US Department of State, Office of Ocean Affairs, unpublished factsheet.

Taylor, P. (1994) 'The State as Container: Territoriality in the Modern World', *Progress in Human Geography*, Vol. 18: 151–162.

Taylor, P. (1995) 'Beyond Containers: Internationality, Interstateness, Interterritoriality', *Progress in Human Geography*, Vol. 19: 1–15.

The Economist (1997a) 'Britain's Celtic choice', 26 July: 14.

The Economist (1997b) 'Devolution can be salvation', 20 September: 53–55.

US Department of State (1983) *Maritime Boundaries: United States–Cook Islands and United States–New Zealand (Tokelau)*, Limits in the Seas, No. 100, 30 December.

Wood, D. with Fels, J. (1992) *The Power of Maps*, New York, London: The Guildford Press.

9
International Boundary Classification: A Simplified Cartographic Approach

Leo Dillon[1]

INTRODUCTION

The need for accuracy in boundary depiction has become exponentially more important over the last decade. As little as 200 years ago most nation-states were separated from one another by sparsely settled frontier areas. But with the increase in world population and the resulting need to exploit all available resources, and with an increasing national consciousness of the spatial element of sovereignty, the existence of an underdeveloped zone between neighbours is no longer tenable.

These factors have been magnified greatly over the last few years, due in part to emerging technologies in the geospatial sciences that enable far greater accuracy in boundary delimitation than previously existed. But boundaries themselves, and the legal regimes that underlie them, have recently been the subject of greater scrutiny than was the case only a generation ago. Governments are becoming increasingly aware that loosely-defined boundaries can become a *casus belli*, as seen recently between Eritrea and Ethiopia in the Horn of Africa. And in the aftermath of one recent conflict the need to define boundaries more precisely became apparent: the boundary between Kuwait and Iraq, loosely and unilaterally delimited before the Gulf War, is now densely demarcated. Another legacy of that conflict has been a resolve among the neighbouring states in the Arabian Peninsula to bring legal resolution to their loosely defined or undefined boundaries (Thomas, 1994: 92).

Cartographers working at small to medium scales may tend to disregard the practice of boundary classification, preferring to use one symbol for international boundaries and basing their representation on the best sources available to them. Others will employ a myriad of boundary types and categories. Among the common terms used for boundary classification are: administrative, disputed, demarcated, delimited, defined, indefinite, intercolonial, provisional, approximate, political, *de jure*, *de facto*, armistice line, line of control, cease-fire line and zonal. These terms, some of which are obsolete, often contain contradictions and can cause confusion, especially when applied to various scales. On the other hand, oversimplification does not do justice to the complex nature of international boundaries. Therefore a need can be said to exist in small- to medium-scale mapping for a reduced but comprehensive number of categories for boundary classification.

Borderlands Under Stress (M.A. Pratt and J.A. Brown (eds), ISBN 90-411-9790-7).
© Kluwer Law International, 2000.

PROPOSED FRAMEWORK FOR INTERNATIONAL BOUNDARY CLASSIFICATION

The classification system proposed below has evolved from the need to provide US government cartographers working at small to medium scales with a simplified system for portraying international boundaries in a manner consistent with policy. It is based on previous US government policies, which have changed as necessary to fit new contingencies. It is designed for land boundaries; the subject of maritime boundaries will be discussed later. In the context of this paper, however, this system should be viewed as a model for the depiction of international boundaries in any environment.

The need to develop and implement this system is enhanced by efforts underway in the US government to create both a database and a standard for international boundaries at a large scale for use in digital geographic products. The Federal Geographic Data Committee (FGDC) recently formed a working group on international boundaries. Its main purpose is to develop a federal standard for international boundary and sovereignty data. When completed, this standard could be presented to the International Standards Organization (ISO) as a model for an international standard. The standard would be able to categorise accurately any conceivable range of boundary types and classifications.

The US National Imagery and Mapping Agency (NIMA) is in the process of developing a digital international boundary database. Its purpose is to analyse every international boundary segment, using the best available sources. Drawing from the standards developed by the FGDC subcommittee, it would contain attribute data for content, symbology, data exchange, metadata and juridical status of each boundary or boundary segment. This database will give US government cartographers working at the largest scales access to the highest resolution data for all international boundaries. Since boundary data is not uniform in precision, some data will be precise to a resolution of a metre, whereas others will necessarily be generalised depictions derived from the best known sources. In this database the widest variety of classifications can be employed for maximum precision.

But a cartographer producing a small- to medium-scale map of a politically diverse area could be hard pressed to accurately depict the many types of boundaries encountered in such an area at such a scale, particularly if that cartographer were working with such constraints as small size or black and white output. Excessive information concerning the status and nature of boundaries does not aid the map viewer when the subject being portrayed is not the boundaries. For instance, a page-sized map depicting transportation networks in the Arabian Peninsula might lose much of its intended emphasis if the thematic content had to compete with a legend explaining the several types of boundary depiction found there.

The following classifications seek to bridge the divide between oversimplification and overcomplication.

International boundary (definite)

This classification is intended to include all generally established and accepted international boundaries. Some examples of a well defined boundary are Canada–USA, with approximately 6,000 pillars demarcating less than 5,200 kilometres (km) of land boundary, and Italy–Switzerland, where approximately 400 treaties and agreements define minute sections of the 740km boundary (IBS No. 12). Conversely, the 1,561km boundary between Mauritania and Western Sahara is marked by only 39 pillars, of which 14 are concentrated on a less than 80km section around Cap Blanc (IBS No. 149).

Problems: Many boundaries that fall into this category have been delimited by treaty or agreement but have not been defined with precision. Many long-accepted boundaries owe their existence to treaty delimitations based upon imprecise criteria. One example of this is the boundary between the Democratic Republic of the Congo and Sudan, which is aligned to the Congo–Nile watershed. In other cases, such as the boundary between Côte d'Ivoire and Guinea, there is no relevant international agreement and the alignment depends upon French administrative practice during the colonial period (Brownlie, 1979: 301).

Indefinite boundary

This classification encompasses boundaries in which evidence of delimitation is unsuitable or unavailable, but some form of status quo exists between the two states. It can be broken up into two broad categories:

1. Boundaries that are not actively disputed but are vaguely delimited, such as the riverine portion of the boundary between the Republic of the Congo and the Democratic Republic of the Congo, where no division has been made of the wide river and its islands (IBS No. 127).
2. Boundaries shown by a conventional line where there is no treaty evidence but where no active dispute exists; this category encompasses most of the boundaries of many states that were formerly administrative units of a larger state, such as the USSR and Yugoslavia.

Problems: A precise definition of what distinguishes an indefinite from a definite boundary needs to be established; many boundaries that fall in the definite category have elements of the indefinite, such as the abovementioned Côte d'Ivoire–Guinea example.

Disputed boundary

This classification is for cases where an active dispute exists between the two states concerning the location of their boundary. Since minor and often unportrayable disputes exist along many if not most international boundaries, this category is intended to be limited to those disputes involving sufficient territory to depict on standard maps, and where the two states involved are seeking an alteration to the status quo.

Problems: Revanchist or belligerent states often declare a dispute unilaterally, making claims to territory despite an existing legal foundation for a boundary. An example of this is Libya's claim to the Aozou Strip. Sometimes states will make territorial claims on the basis of often complex historical criteria – for example, China's claim to most of the Indian state of Arunachal Pradesh. Also, there are instances where neither state will acknowledge the existence of a dispute despite differing interpretations of the boundary alignment. Uruguayan and Brazilian official maps, for instance, show slight variations in their common boundary.

Other lines of separation

This classification covers any known division between states which is not a legal international boundary. Categories under this classification include the following:

Military disengagement line
A division between two belligerent states, usually established during or after a period of hostilities. Examples include the demarcation line and demilitarised zone separating the two states on the Korean Peninsula, the line of control between India and Pakistan in Kashmir, and Israel's 1949 armistice lines with Lebanon and Syria.

Administrative boundary
A line defining administrative control of territory. This falls into two groups: one in which a political boundary has not been established; and one in which a political boundary exists but the administrative boundary portrays *de facto* control. An example of the former would be the line dividing Oman and United Arab Emirates administration of the Musandam Peninsula along the Strait of Hormuz. An example of the latter would be the 'Ilemi Triangle' between northwest Kenya and Sudan, where ethnic Turkana pastoralists from Kenya administer a territory beyond the known treaty line (Brownlie, 1979: 917–919).

Provisional boundary
A line dividing a disputed boundary or territory pending a final settlement, in which an agreement of convenience has been reached without prejudice to future claims. The most notable example of this is the southern half of the Ethiopia–Somalia boundary.

Military base/leased area
A line defining a military base or leased area where sovereignty is exercised by another state. Examples of this would be the US Naval Base in Guantanamo Bay, Cuba, and the two British Sovereign Base Areas in southern Cyprus.

Problems: This classification tends to be a catch-all for boundaries that do not fit neatly into the other categories, but it needs to be limited to those cases where the line is not recognised as a legal international boundary. More than the other categories, this classification requires a notation on the map, where scale permits, specifying the type of line portrayed. This classification is also transitional in nature, and needs periodic review.

No defined boundary

This classification refers to any land division between states in which no known boundary exists. The largest example of this would be the Saudi Arabia–Yemen boundary east of the Treaty of Taif line.

Problems: Policy is an important factor in determining which boundaries fall into this category. For instance, US government maps depict the frontier between Oman and the United Arab Emirates south of the Musandam Peninsula as a case of 'no defined boundary', despite the existence of (potentially contested) boundaries delineated in 1950 that define the emirates of the then Trucial Coast. The policy on official maps from the UK, however, is to depict these lines as *de facto* – possibly because they were drawn by British political agents (Schofield, 1992). Another problem with this category is how to portray the spatial element of the two states involved. For instance, when using different colours for the two states, where should the colours meet? This problem is compounded in the digital environment, where enclosed polygons are often required.

PRACTICAL PROBLEMS

This classification system seeks to provide a model for generalising international boundaries for small to medium scales. It does not and can not suppose a universal classification, but rather provides a framework for international boundary classification in any milieu. However, the system is fraught with practical problems. Boundaries are subject to political, physical and social considerations, some of which are described below.

The most difficult and resolute obstacle to a universal agreement on boundary status is *political policy*. The political nature of boundaries themselves necessitates that differences in opinion will exist, even among parties with a high degree of comity. The classification system proposed above, however, can be considered independent of such policy concerns; cartographers can adapt their clients' policy concerns into whichever category seems most fitting.

Another problem with employing this or any other classification system is *the changing nature of boundaries*. When a boundary's legal basis has been defined through physical features, valid differences in interpretation can occur. For instance, when the International Court of Justice (ICJ) issued its 1992 decision on the boundary between El Salvador and Honduras, it ruled a boundary between all but a small portion of the 420 square kilometres of disputed territory. This small portion was ruled beyond the jurisdiction of the Court because, although the two parties had agreed on a named physical feature as a boundary point, they did not agree on its location (Dillon, 1993: 1). How, then, to classify the gap in the boundary: 'disputed', 'indefinite', or 'no defined boundary'? Another example of an ongoing dispute based upon interpretation of physical features is the 'icefields' sector of the Chile–Argentina boundary.

The other problem with physical features defining boundaries is physical changes. This applies mostly to boundaries set in rivers, which shift course and often require a continuing programme of boundary maintenance and rectification. But if a river that defines a boundary changes course and the two states do not come to a timely agreement on the new alignment, does the cartographer consider this boundary, once categorised as a definite boundary, to be indefinite or in dispute? Does the existence of a treaty defining a river thalweg as an international boundary imply a definite boundary, even if a precise delineation has not been made? Botswana and Namibia, whose Linyanti River boundary was generally considered solid, have taken a dispute over river islands to the ICJ. Does this imply that the entire river boundary is indefinite?

Changes in boundary status are also caused by *discrete political changes*. Boundary agreements can be announced publicly without the attendant data necessary to portray the boundaries with accuracy. A recent example of this is the 1998 agreement between China and the Russian Federation respecting the eastern portion of their boundary. Although the federal authorities have both publicly stated that an agreement has been reached which precisely delimits all but a few segments of their 3,600km boundary, the details of the agreement – including the delineation – have not yet been made publicly available. The cartographer producing small- to medium-scale maps of the area may confidently classify the agreed portions of the boundary as definite, since the scale would not depict any noticeable change. But working at large scales, the cartographer does not have the data necessary to portray the boundary as definite.

Another example of this would be the Zambia–(formerly) Zaire boundary segment between Lake Mweru and the tripoint with Tanzania. This segment was officially regarded as an indefinite boundary on US government maps until an agreement was publicly reached between the two countries in 1989. Details of the agreed alignment were never made public, however, leaving cartographers with little choice but to portray it as a straight line segment, as was the previous practice. In the absence of documentation, however, does this remain an indefinite or a definite boundary?

MARITIME BOUNDARIES

Although this paper chooses not to delve too deeply into the subject, the classification system proposed above can be loosely applied to maritime boundaries. In their most elemental form, maritime and land boundaries share the same political characteristics. One major difference is that agreements establishing maritime boundaries sometimes contain provisions for jurisdiction of the maritime space beneath the surface. A cartographer asked to portray maritime boundaries faces similar problems of quality; substituting the terms 'indefinite' and 'in dispute' with 'hypothetical' and other terms could, with forethought and a little imagination, be achieved.

SYMBOLOGY

The symbology used for the various classifications is up to the cartographer, but clearly a hierarchy is desirable, with definite boundaries more dominantly displayed than others. Although this paper does not seek to impose a standard for symbolic treatment of boundaries, the following is offered for informational purposes. Currently, on small- to medium-scale US government maps, an informal portrayal policy exists. International boundaries are portrayed by solid lines. Indefinite boundaries are also usually portrayed by solid lines, but carry a disclaimer stating that the boundaries are not necessarily authoritative. Disputed boundaries are depicted with a line symbol distinct from and subordinate to definite boundaries, with the notation 'in dispute' where scale permits. Boundaries falling under the 'other line of separation' category are shown with a distinct and subordinate line symbol, with the type of boundary notated where scale permits. In the 'no defined boundary' category, predictably, no boundary is shown.

CONCLUSION

In conclusion, regardless of the milieu a cartographer works in – commercial, governmental, institutional – it is in the best interests of cartography as a science and an art to portray boundaries with sensitivity. Those cartographers working principally at scales exceeding 1:1,000,000 are in need of a simplified approach to classifying boundaries that takes into account the differing nature and quality of boundaries. The system should be able to handle the more specific requirements arising from large-scale mapping while keeping the number of categories limited. If employed correctly, the map viewer will achieve a general understanding of the nature of the international boundaries shown without being distracted by too much data.

NOTE

1   The author is a cartographer with the Office of the Geographer and Global Issues in the United States Department of State. The views and opinions expressed in this paper are his and do not necessarily reflect those of the US government.

BIBLIOGRAPHY

Brownlie, I. (1979) *African Boundaries: A Legal and Diplomatic Encyclopaedia*, London: C. Hurst and Co.; Berkeley, Los Angeles: University of California Press.

Dillon, L. (1993) 'El Salvador–Honduras Boundary: After the ICJ Decision', *Geographic and Global Issues Quarterly*, Vol. 3, No. 3: 1–2.

IBS No. 12 (1961) *International Boundary Study No. 12: Italy–Switzerland Boundary*, Office of the Geographer, US Department of State.

IBS No. 127 (1972) *International Boundary Study No. 127: Congo–Zaire Boundary*, Office of the Geographer, US Department of State.

IBS No. 149 (1975) *International Boundary Study No. 149: Mauritania–Spanish Sahara Boundary*, Office of the Geographer, US Department of State.

Schofield, R. (ed.) (1992) *Arabian Boundary Disputes, Vol. 19: United Arab Emirates–Oman and Saudi Arabia–Oman*, London: Redwood Press Ltd, for Archive Editions: 585–595.

Thomas, B. L. (1994) 'International Boundaries: Lines in the Sand (and the Sea)' in Demko, G. J. & Wood. W. B. (eds.) *Reordering the World: Geopolitical Perspectives on the Twenty-first Century*, Boulder, San Francisco, Oxford: Westview Press: 87–100.

PART II

Borderlands Under Stress:
Regional Perspectives

10
Fragmentation or Integration: What Future for African Boundaries?

A. I. Asiwaju

INTRODUCTION

This essay aims to draw attention to the ongoing public debate on the future of the territorial structure and boundaries of African states in the face of the endemic and ever-worsening political crises that have gripped virtually all the states in the post-colonial period. Professor Ali Mazrui, the renowned Kenyan political scientist, provided an apt summary of the main issues of the debate when he asserted that

> Over the next century, the outlines of most present-day African States will change in one of two ways. One will be ethnic self-determination which will create smaller states, comparable to the separation of Eritrea from Ethiopia. The other will be regional integration towards larger political and economic unions.... (Mazrui, 1993.)

Clearly, African state boundaries are expected to undergo a significant transformation in the twenty-first century.

This discussion casts its lot not with a future of 'ethnic self-determination which will create smaller states', but with the alternative future of regional integration which will force a re-orientation of the boundaries from their prevailing posture as irritants of conflict into a new framework of opportunity for international cooperation, on the model of the European Union.

The paper is in two parts. In the first part, the basically Afro-septic arguments for boundary revision are outlined and evaluated. The second part draws attention to the generally ignored fact of the extraordinary stability of the territorial structures and boundaries of modern African states and the ever-increasing prospects and pressures for regional integration and transborder cooperation. Especially emphasised is the evidence in support of contemporary innovations and renewal of regional and sub-regional integration projects and institutions, combined with unprecedented stimulation and some important experiments in transborder cooperation policy initiatives, notably in the Maghreb and West Africa, as well as Eastern and Southern Africa.[1] Admittedly, the processes for regional integration and transborder cooperation policy achievements have been slow and are less noticeable than the more dramatic episodes of conflicts within and between the states. However, they provide the pointers to a more enduring alternative future.

Borderlands Under Stress (M.A. Pratt and J.A. Brown (eds), ISBN 90-411-9790-7).
© Kluwer Law International, 2000.

ARGUMENTS FOR BOUNDARY REVISION

The protagonists and leading opinions

The calibre of the opinion leaders who favour boundary revision as a solution to Africa's deepening political and development crises makes it difficult to ignore their arguments. The opinions range very widely, from a repeated call for a 'Berlin II'[2] by the current head of the Tutsi-dominated government of Rwanda to the unveiled neo-imperialist advocacy of Norman Stone, until recently Professor of Modern History at Oxford, who has asserted unequivocally that 'only a programme of enlightened re-imperialism from Europe can put right the bloody mess made of its former colonies in Africa' (Stone, 1996). Darcus Howe wrote in the *New Statesman* that 'the old Africa, with its boundaries imposed by the imperialists, is on its last legs'. In his view,

> the post-colonial leaders have long abandoned the mandate bestowed on them by the independence movements to reshape their continent's boundaries ... the OAU long ago turned into its opposite, became a source for the continued legitimation of the old borders. (Howe, 1996.)

This view of the Organization of African Unity (OAU) as betrayer would appear to be powerfully corroborated by Professor Wole Soyinka. In an interview with *The Guardian*, he is quoted as follows:

> One hundred years ago at the Berlin Conference, the colonial powers that rule Africa met to divvy up their interests into states, lumping various peoples and tribes together in some places, or slicing them apart in others like some demented tailor who paid no attention to the fabric, colour or pattern of the quilt he was patching together. One of the biggest disappointments of the Organization of African Unity when it came into being more than 20 years ago was that it failed to address the issue ... [We] should sit down with square-rule and compass and re-design the boundaries of African nations. (Soyinka, 1994.)[3]

The map drawn by Makua wa Mutua and published in the *Boston Globe* of 22 September 1994 might have been influenced by Soyinka's prescription of 'sit[ting] down with square-rule and compass and redesign[ing] the boundaries of African nations' (Figure 1). The map suggests a radical restructuring of the present-day African continent of 54 national states into one of just 15, based on a highly debatable combination of what the author has referred to as

> historical factors, especially demographic contours of Africa's pre-colonial states and political formations, ethnic similarities and alliances based on cultural homogeneity and economic viability.

The obvious mismatch between Makua wa Mutua's map and the actual political map of Africa provides the clearest illustration of the kind of confusion which the founding Fathers of the Organization of African Unity tried to avoid by the decision to retain the erstwhile colonial boundaries in the interest of peace in the region.

Yet further predictions for boundary revision have come from other influential directions in consequence of the unabating African crisis, especially the current events in the Great Lakes region. One was the view of Richard Cornwell, Director of the Africa Institute in Pretoria. He has predicted that

the Great Lakes crisis is going to be Africa's Palestine. It is a sore that's going to flare up nastily and fairly regularly.[4]

In a tone clearly reminiscent of Cecil Rhodes and his British South African Company, Cornwell noted that, while 'post-Cold War Africa has become a less stable place', the status of the countries – notably Zaire (now the Democratic Republic of the Congo, or DRC), Liberia and Sierra Leone – as 'el dorados for miners of gold, diamonds and strategic minerals' is likely to lead to situations where prospecting companies will go in with their private armies and there will be a return to the days of chartered companies. There have even been media reports that in the OAU secretariat in Addis Ababa 'the border is already being talked about in corridors' and that 'like it or not, it is an idea whose time has come'.

Assessment of the pro-revision arguments

One preliminary observation is that the argument for boundary revision in Africa is not new. Similarly, the fact that the argument is supported by a combination of Africans and outsiders, politicians and intellectuals alike is not new. In the late 1950s and early 1960s, as Saadia Touval has discussed (Touval, 1964), President Kwame Nkrumah of Ghana was the most outspoken about what he called 'the danger inherent in the colonial legacies of irredentism and tribalism'.

The All-Africa Peoples Conference, held in Accra under Nkrumah's political shadow in December 1958 anticipated Wole Soyinka by close to 40 years in its denunciation of the

artificial frontiers drawn by imperialist powers to divide the peoples of Africa, particularly those which cut ethnic groups and peoples of the same stock. [5]

The conference called for 'the abolition or adjustment of such boundaries' and appealed to leaders of 'Independent States of Africa to support permanent solutions to this problem founded upon the true wishes of the people' – or what Ali Mazrui was later to call 'ethnic self-determination'. Professor R. J. Harrison Church, the pioneer British geographer of west Africa, is known to have given some support to the idea of revising boundaries when he observed in the mid-1950s that 'the unrealistic boundaries need revision ... African peoples will not tolerate much longer their division by such lines'.

The truth, of course, is that none of the early anxieties about the boundaries in Africa have ever materialised. There have been neither widespread border conflicts nor the anticipated generalised irredentism. Rather, what has remained remarkable about the African continent is the durability of its inherited colonial boundaries. The many cases of political crisis, including some spectacular and often tragic changes of regime and even the collapse of state machinery, as in Liberia and Somalia, have had surprisingly little or no adverse effects on the stability of corporate state territories and their defining boundaries. Whether by governments or by rebels – and the distinction is usually tenuous in Africa where yesterday's rebel leaders are often today's heads of state and government – the struggle is usually for control of the so-called 'inherited' state territories. Even in the case of Eritrea, recently separated from Ethiopia, the only case so far in which a new state has emerged from an existing, recognised, larger state, the struggle has been for statehood within a pre-established colonial territorial framework – that of a former Italian colonial possession.

Stability of boundaries in Africa has been guaranteed by a combination of three factors. The first is the general lack of interest on the part of most 'partitioned Africans' in boundary shifts. What they appear to want – and indeed ask for – is peace and cooperation across borders, rather than the prevailing conflict perpetrated by state actors. Secondly, there is the doctrine and practice of states in Africa to 'respect ... the sovereignty and territorial integrity of each State' and, in particular, 'to respect the borders existing on [the] achievement of national independence', as enshrined in the Charter of the OAU (Article III, paragraph 3, and Article IV) and the famous Cairo Resolution of 1964. Finally, there is the over-all supportive attitude of the international community which, within the general rules and procedures of the United Nations, cannot afford to risk the chaos that is bound to result from a systematic dissolution of Africa's post-colonial states and a continent-wide revision of state boundaries.

REGIONAL INTEGRATION AS AN ALTERNATIVE FUTURE

If the *status quo* is likely to prevail for most of Africa's state boundaries, the future must be expected to lie in the regional integration processes currently under renegotiation at the levels of both the entire continent and, more especially, its constituent sub-regions. There is an increasing adoption – or, at least, stimulation – of transborder-cooperation policy initiatives by African states engaged in several regional integration projects.

Establishment/re-establishment of regional integration projects

In the past ten years or so, there has been a remarkable renewal of efforts to strengthen, create and re-create regional integration projects. Examples include:

- the African Economic Community Treaty, opened to signature at the OAU Summit in Abuja, Nigeria in June 1991 (renewing the spirit of the Lagos Plan of Action of 1979)
- the creation in 1989 of the Arab Maghrebian Union (AMU), embracing Algeria, Libya, Mauritania, Morocco and Tunisia
- the upgrading of the Economic Community of West African States

(ECOWAS) into a supra-national organisation based on a radically revised treaty approved in Accra, Ghana, in 1993, plus the heightened image of ECOWAS brought about by the spectacularly successful, though essentially detractive peace-keeping operations of the Nigeria-led ECOWAS Monitoring Group (ECOMOG) first in Liberia and then in Sierra Leone[6]

- the re-invigoration of CILSS (Comité Permanent Inter-Etats de Lutte Contre La Secheresse dans le Sahel, or the Permanent Inter-State Commission for Campaign Against Drought and Famine in the Sahel) based in Ouagadougou, Bourkina Faso, embracing the mostly Francophone Sahelian states in west Africa that were adversely affected by the droughts of the 1970s and 1980s
- the re-articulation of the Southern African Development Coordination Conference (SADCC) as the post-Apartheid Southern African Development Community (SADC)
- the reconceptualisation of IGADD (Inter-Governmental Authority on Drought and Development), the CILSS equivalent in the Horn of Africa, as the IGAD (Inter-Governmental Authority on Development)
- the conversion of the Preferential Free Trade Area of Eastern and Southern Africa (PTA) into COMESA (Common Market of Eastern and Southern Africa).

These developments represent more than changes in name. They reflect a new re-orientation and determination on the part of the participating states to make the regional integration endeavour a greater success than has been the case in the proverbial 'lost decades' of the 1970s and 1980s.

Transborder cooperation policy initiatives

The second category of relatively recent developments, more directly relevant to the question of a future re-orientation of African boundaries, relates to policy innovations which seek to emphasise boundaries between states engaged in particular regional integration projects, as factors of international cooperation. Such policy initiatives seek to take factors such as transboundary natural and human resources and turn them into opportunities for cooperation rather than the basis for conflict and war that they have been.

The new border-focused cooperative policy initiatives are especially manifest in the AMU and ECOWAS and the inter-related areas of SADC and COMESA. Some of the details may be summarised by sub-region, as follows.

AMU

Here, transborder cooperation policy is reflected in the following instruments:

- the Algeria–Tunisia Friendship Treaty of 19 March 1988, whose primary aim is co-development of border areas
- the Libya–Tunisia Agreement of 1988 which ended the dispute over the continental shelf in and around the Mediterranean Gulf of Gabes and

established a joint venture for the development and exploitation of the transborder hydrocarbon resources

- the Algeria–Morocco Agreement of 29 May 1991 which stated that special priority should be given to the joint development of border areas.

In addition, there has been

- the achievement of regional networks of infrastructural facilities and services such as the large-scale pipeline distribution of Libyan and Algerian petroleum products and gas to Tunisia and Morocco and, through them, to southern Europe and beyond
- the construction of a Maghrebian rail-link and highway project
- the creation of Air Maghreb and a Maghrebian Shipping Line.

ECOWAS

In ECOWAS, the transborder cooperation policy initiative is reflected in the following programmes:

- Nigeria's high-profile transborder cooperation policy vis-à-vis her neighbours in the west and central African sub-regions between 1988 and 1993[7]
- the creation and operation of such vibrant institutional structures as the Nigeria–Niger Joint Commission for Cooperation and the Lake Chad Basin Commission
- the provisions in Chapter 58 of the ECOWAS Revised Treaty for the creation of 'national border administration authorities' on the model of Nigeria's National Boundary Commission, itself created in 1987 to ensure peaceful settlement of conflicts, promote cross-border cooperation and stimulate border-region development both between and within member states
- the exceptional performance of the Liptako–Gourma Integrated Development Authority (head office in Ouagadougou, Bourkina Faso) created in 1970 to reverse the double marginalisation of the overlapping border regions of west Africa's land-locked states of Bourkina Faso, Mali and Niger[8]
- the 'market-driven' approach to integration on the basis of research into cross-border trade in west Africa, sponsored by the OECD/Club du Sahel in Paris[9]
- the Gulf of Guinea Commission, proposed by Nigeria and agreed by Cameroon in 1992, which would have embraced Nigeria, Cameroon, Equatorial Guinea, Gabon, and Sao Tome and Principe, and prevented the later and current militarisation and aggressive litigation between Cameroon and Nigeria over the Bakassi Peninsula (Asiwaju, 1998).

SADC and COMESA

Transborder cooperation policy initiatives are still at a rudimentary stage in both the southern and eastern African sub-regions but they are being actively stimulated, especially in the context of the ongoing Research Project on the Development of Border Regions in Eastern and Southern Africa, vigorously pursued since 1995 under the auspices of the United Nations Center for Regional Development, Africa Office, Kenya (Asiwaju & de Leeuw, 1998).

CONCLUSION

The evidence, then, is less in support of a future of territorial fragmentation of African states; it is more in favour of the alternative future of regional integration towards larger political and economic union.

Rather than pushing towards the ultimate dissolution of state territories and boundary revisions, African crises manifest problems that question the capacity of the individual states acting in isolation. In the Great Lakes region, for example, such manifestations include cross-border spill-over of armed rebellions and the massive movement of refugees back and forth across the national boundaries of Rwanda, Burundi, Tanzania, Uganda and, perhaps most tellingly, the former Zaire. Shared environmental problems, such as drought and desertification in the Sahelian zone, similarly demand a regional rather than narrow national responses. Research results on cross-border trade and the inter-related issue of food security in west Africa, replicated in eastern and southern Africa under the auspices of USAID in Nairobi, have emphasised the existence of large-scale, cross-border exchanges and the need, therefore, to base regional integration projects on this and related grass-root realities (Igue & Soule, 1995; Ackello-Ogutu & Echessah, 1997a and 1997b).

Most struggles, whether conducted by governments or rebels, are for the exercise of control over territories that have already been defined by the so-called 'inherited' borders. The crises with which the continent is confronted are concerned less with state territories and boundaries than with modes of government, most of which currently involve a generalised inequity and widespread kleptocracy – or what Richard Joseph in his Nigerian case study has called 'prebendalism' (Joseph, 1990).

These are not issues that are effectively addressed by proposals merely for redrawing boundaries. Although boundaries, as 'shells' or 'outer-crust', are inseparable from the political entities that they define, they are effects that must not be mistaken for cause, symptoms that must not be mistaken for the disease. Thus, rather than suggesting the need for territorial revision of the state structures, what African crises call for is a whole range of policy revisions – including revisions to address issues that have hindered the equitable manage-ment of transboundary resources within and across national territories and boundaries – which transform factors of conflict into windows of opportunity for cooperation between and within states.

This re-orientation calls for an urgent action plan on the part of policy-makers and a re-dedication of support on the part of African and Africanist research communities within and outside the continent. With regard to relevant policy decisions, the OAU needs to energise its conflict-resolution machinery and expand its capacity to handle border issues, with a focus on anticipating and preventing border conflicts between and within adjacent member states. In doing so, the OAU stands to profit from the experience of Europe where, in the context of the post-1945 commitment to regional integration, border problems similar to those of post-colonial Africa are being successfully tackled. Especially recommended is the adoption of instruments with a continent-wide application, on the model of the European Outline Convention on Trans-frontier Cooperation Between Territorial Authorities or Communities which came into force in 1984. Having so wisely resolved through its Charter of 1963 and the Cairo Resolution of 1964 to legitimise the inherited colonial boundaries in the interests of the peace and stability of the continent, the OAU must not permit itself to enter the twenty-first century without taking the long-overdue next logical step of ensuring the conversion of the inherited borders from barriers into bridges.

African and Africanist researchers have a responsibility to focus on projects that explore the peaceful, cooperative and regional integration potential of the existing boundaries. African research institutions outside the continent, notably those in Europe and North America (e.g. the imaginative, border-focused Program on International Cooperation in Africa (PICA) inaugurated in 1989 at Northwestern University, Illinois, USA), must collaborate with parallel institutions within Africa (e.g. the Centre for African Regional and Border Studies currently being established at the University of Lagos, Nigeria[10]) and permanently focus on the twin questions of boundaries and regional integration in Africa.

NOTES

1   For leading studies, see Biad (1993), Igue & Soule (1995), and Asiwaju & de Leeuw (1998).

2   'Berlin II' takes its name from the 1884-85 Berlin Conference, at which the major European powers are believed to have agreed on the division of large areas of Africa.

3   See also Wole Soyinka's interview with *Woche*, a German weekly newspaper, on 22 November 1996, in which he castigated African boundaries as 'Murderous Borders' and, reflecting on the crisis in Zaire, reasserted his advocacy for redrawing the frontiers.

4   Cornwell's comment was quoted in a Reuter's report in early 1997 entitled 'Africa: continent of chaos and riches', circulated on the NAIJANET e-mail list.

5   The author's book, *Partitioned Africans*, subsequently made it clear that he included all of Africa's boundaries in this statement.

6   ECOWAS has also been boosted by an agreement for Nigeria to extend the distribution of its liquefied gas to such states as Benin, Togo and Ghana.

7   For example, the bilateral transborder cooperation workshops with Benin in 1988, Niger in 1989, Cameroon in May 1992 and Equatorial Guinea in November 1992.

8   This performance was a notable achievement in the face of the ensuing Mali–

Bourkina Faso border conflicts and the subsequent Tuareg rebellion in the area of the Authority's operations.

9   Like Nigeria's transborder cooperation policy initiatives, the 'market-driven' approach emphasises the prior integration of limitrophe national economies as first steps towards larger regional integration schemes (Egg & Igue, 1993).

10   For a more elaborate discussion, see Asiwaju (1998).

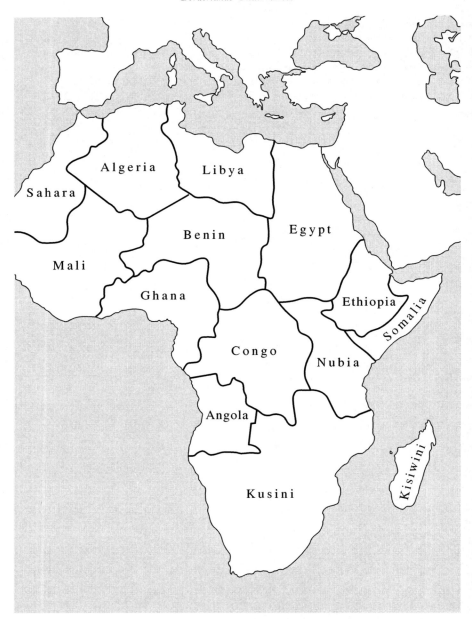

Figure 1: Makua wa Mutua's proposal for redrawing the boundaries of Africa

(Source: *Boston Globe*, 22/9/94)

REFERENCES

Ackello-Ogutu, C. & Echessah, P. N. (1997a) *Unrecorded Cross-Border Trade Between Tanzania and Her Neighbours: Implications for Food Security*, Nairobi: USAID/Technoserve.

Ackello-Ogutu, C. & Echessah, P. N. (1997b) *Unrecorded Cross-Border Trade Between Kenya and Uganda: Implications for Food Security*, Technical Report No. 59, Nairobi, USAID/Technoserve.

Asiwaju, A. I. & de Leeuw, M. (eds.) (1998) *Border Region Development in Africa: Focus on the Eastern and Southern Sub-Regions*, Nagoya: United Nations Centre for Regional Development.

Asiwaju, A. I. (1984a) *Artificial Boundaries*, Inaugural Lecture Series, Lagos: University of Lagos Press.

Asiwaju, A.I. (ed) (1984b) *Partitioned Africans: Ethnic Relations Across Africa's International Boundaries*, 1884–1984, Lagos: University of Lagos Press; London: C. Hurst and Co. Publishers; New York: St. Martin's Press

Asiwaju, A. I. (1998) 'Boundaries and Regional Integration: A Research Agenda for Africa' in *Actes du Colloque International: Etats et Frontières en Afrique Sub-Saharienne-Expériences Comparées et Chances d'Integration. Histoire et Perspectives*, Aix-en-Provence, 7–9 May.

Biad, A. (1993) 'North Africa' in UN Regional Centre for Peace and Disarmament in Africa (Lome, Togo) Workshop on the Role of Border Problems in African Peace and Security, New York: United Nations.

Egg, J. & Igue O. J. (1993) *Market-Driven Integration: The Impact of Nigeria on Its Immediate Neighbours (Benin, Niger, Chad and Cameroon)*, Paris: Club du Sahel/OECD.

Howe, D. (1996) 'The mass movement of refugees across African borders last weekend is a warning, a return to a post-colonial question never properly resolved', *The New Statesman*, 22 November.

Igue, O. J. & Soule, B. G. (1995) *L'Etat Entrepôt au Benin: Commerce Informel ou Solution à la Crise?*, Paris: Karthala.

Joseph, R. (1990) *Prebendalism and Nigerian Politics*.

Makua wa Mutua (1994) 'Redrawing the Map Along African Lines', *Boston Globe*, 22 September.

Mazrui, A. (1994) 'The Bondage of Boundaries', *150 Economist Years*.

Nugent, P. & Asiwaju, A. I. (eds.) (1996) *African Boundaries: Barriers, Conduits and Opportunities*, London: Frances Printer.

Soyinka, W. (1994) 'Blood Soaked Quilt of Africa', *The Guardian*, London, 17 May.

Stone, N. (1996) 'Why Empire Must Strike Back', *The Observer*, London, 18 August.

Touval, S. (1964) *The Boundary Politics of Independent Africa*, Cambridge: Harvard University Press.

11
African Boundaries:
New Order, Historic Tensions

Tim Daniel

The Secretary-General of the United Nations (UN), Kofi Annan, told the Security Council on 16 April 1998 that:

> For the United Nations there is no higher goal, no deeper commitment and no greater ambition than preventing armed conflict.

The context in which he spoke these words was his address on the Causes of Conflict and the Promotion of Durable Peace and Sustainable Development in Africa.

In his speech the Secretary-General recognised that conflict in Africa poses a major challenge to the UN. Since 1970, he said, more than 30 wars had been fought in Africa. In 1996 14 of the 53 countries of Africa were afflicted by armed conflict, accounting for more than half of all war-related deaths worldwide and resulting in more than 8,000,000 refugees, returnees and displaced persons. At the same time, however, the Secretary-General stated that the vast majority of those 30 wars were intra- rather than inter-state conflicts.

The message from this is that conflict in Africa has as its main aim not the settlement of border disputes by armed conflict, but the establishment of political control which leads to the destruction of civilians and entire ethnic groups. As Mr Annan says, preventing wars such as these is no longer a matter of defending states or protecting allies; it has become a matter of defending humanity itself.

The side-effects of these terrible civil wars which have raged around the continent causing huge numbers of refugees are bound to put borderlands under stress. The presence at or near a country's border of thousands or indeed millions of nationals from a neighbouring state leads to stresses which are not just territorial. They weigh most heavily on the economies of the affected countries and world aid is frequently called upon to assist in resolving the resulting burdens.

This paper does not aim to examine these tragic conflicts; the subject is too vast, the reasons behind the conflicts too diverse and the consequences too widespread throughout the world to comprehend in one short essay. Instead, the paper considers the issues of border disputes, self-determination and the resolution of boundary matters in Africa in the latter half of this century. In so doing, it touches upon the historic causes of disputes and their different means of resolution. Lastly, it considers whether any pan-African pattern emerges from

Borderlands Under Stress (M.A. Pratt and J.A. Brown (eds), ISBN 90-411-9790-7).
© Kluwer Law International, 2000.

the resolution of African boundary issues which may provide guidance to the rest of the world – the 'new order' mentioned in the title.

Any student of international boundaries – and particularly a British student – would recognise that Africa has, in this century and the last, presented a fascinating microcosm (or perhaps 'macrocosm', given the size of the continent) of boundary problems. In his illuminating book *The Scramble for Africa*, Thomas Pakenham paints this astonishing portrait:

> Suddenly, in half a generation, the scramble gave Europe virtually the whole continent ... thirty new colonies and protectorates, 10 million square miles of new territory and 110 million dazed new subjects.... Africa was sliced up like a cake, the pieces swallowed by five rival nations – Germany, Italy, Portugal, France and Britain (with Spain taking some scraps) and Britain and France were at each other's throats. At the centre, exploiting the rivalry, stood an enigmatic individual and self-styled philanthropist controlling the heart of the continent: King Leopold II, King of the Belgians.

Britain was brought to the brink of war with France and by the end of the nineteenth century was plunged into the Boer War – the costliest, bloodiest war Britain had fought since defeating Napoleon at Waterloo.

Throughout the whole of the 18th century and the majority of the 19th not a great deal was known about the interior of Africa. Names were given on a regional basis; countries did not exist as such, still less states. But by 1893 Africa was beginning to 'fill up' (see Figure 1).

Between 1926 and 1946 the picture changed dramatically. Suddenly there were countries and boundaries everywhere (Figure 2). Only three independent states remained: Liberia, Egypt and Ethiopia. Every other country in Africa was tied to a European colonial power, a situation which prevailed until after the Second World War.

Thirty years later, in 1978, the picture had again undergone a dramatic transformation: the colonial shackles had been thrown off and almost every state was independent (Figure 3). The transformation was, for the most part, bloodless. The country of this author's boyhood, Southern Rhodesia, suffered one of the most traumatic transitions, before reverting to a historic title, Zimbabwe; so old was this title that its origins were still not known for certain at the time of independence, although it is now thought to be 400 or 500 years old.

As Pakenham put it, the pieces of the colonial cake had now become, for richer or for poorer (mainly for poorer), the 47 independent nations of Africa (Figure 4).

Kofi Annan, in his speech, referred to the historical legacies of Africa as starting with the Congress of Berlin in 1885, when the colonial powers partitioned Africa into territorial units. As he said, these partitions were frequently arbitrary and in the 1960s the newly independent African states inherited these boundaries together with the problems they posed. He referred also to the deliberate colonial policy of Balkanisation, which was designed to put people at loggerheads rather than bring them together.

These problems threatened to bring an endless cycle of bloodshed and destruction to Africa through boundary wars. However, in 1964 Africa itself, acting as a single continent, took the first, decisive step to defuse all the potential issues raised by the colonial legacy. The Assembly of Heads of State and Government of the Organization of African Unity (OAU) met in Cairo and adopted a resolution (the 'Cairo Resolution') whereby all members of the OAU pledged themselves 'to respect the borders existing on their achievement of national independence'.

THE DOCTRINE OF *UTI POSSIDETIS*

That decision set the scene in Africa for the rest of the century and, probably, for all time. Its effects are manifest in any subsequent examination of African boundaries. Although the resolution probably has no binding effect under international law, the principle embodied in it recognises one of the basic tenets of international law – namely that *frontiers do not 'lapse' when de-colonisation or cessation takes place*. The resolution has provided the basis for a rule of regional customary international law binding upon states which have unilaterally declared their acceptance of the principle of the *status quo* as at the time of Independence.

That principle is generally referred to by the Latin tag *'uti possidetis juris'* or simply *'uti possidetis'*. Interestingly, Africa was in fact borrowing from the experience of South America when its states adopted this resolution. *Uti possidetis* was a Latin American idea by which the administrative boundaries of the old Spanish empire in South America were deemed to constitute the boundaries for the newly independent successor states. The theory behind it was that gaps in sovereignty over territory which might lead to border conflict and intervention by third-party states should not arise.

From a legal point of view, the effect has been to throw every African state back to its colonial roots or those of its neighbours whenever a dispute has arisen. No determination of an African boundary can take place without examination of its historic root of title. That is why Professor Ian Brownlie's monumental work *African Boundaries* is an indispensable starting point for any African boundary investigation; it details the source of each boundary. It would be a fascinating exercise to go through the book to analyse the potential areas of border dispute and examine their historical roots. Instead, I shall look briefly at how the doctrine of *uti possidetis* has played out in practice and how other principles have come into play in cases of uncertainty.

The doctrine has, for example, had the effect of preventing the emergence of a series of secessionist states; examples are Nigeria (the Biafran conflict in 1967), the Sudan (a process started in 1983 with the Islamisation of the economy and laws) and the former Belgian Congo. The doctrine has, however, been subjected to severe strains in the Horn of Africa.

The principle of *uti possidetis* was the subject of discussion by a Chamber of the International Court of Justice (ICJ) in the case of *Burkina Faso* v. *The Republic of*

Mali. The special agreement in that case actually specified that the settlement of the dispute should be based upon respect for the principle of the 'intangibility of frontiers inherited from colonization'; the Chamber stated that the principle has the effect of freezing the territorial title existing at the moment of independence to produce what the Chamber described as a 'photograph of the territory' at the critical date.

The Chamber went on to say that the principle of *uti possidetis* had developed into a general concept of contemporary customary international law which was unaffected by the emergence of the right of peoples to self-determination enshrined in such instruments as the 1960 UN Colonial Declaration, the 1966 International Covenant on Human Rights, the 1970 Declaration on Principles of International Law and, indeed, the UN Charter itself.

The clash between the principle of self-determination and *uti possidetis* is seen most clearly in the case of Somalia which was one of the two countries (Morocco was the other) which refused to accept the 1964 Cairo Resolution. Somalia claims parts of Ethiopia and Kenya on the basis that Somali tribes populate regions of both those countries, but these claims have received very little support from the international community.

Generally speaking, where there is a colonial treaty in existence, the line of delimitation established by that treaty is definitive for the establishment of the boundary. In cases of uncertainty, the notion of *effectivités* or effective control comes into play. These *effectivités* may be both colonial and post-colonial. The existence of *effectivités* has particular relevance in establishing whether or not there has been acquiescence by one state in the control over territory administered by another. The exercise of such control and its effects is an area frequently visited by the ICJ.

If neither *uti possidetis* nor *effectivités* provide guidelines, the Court has recourse to equity *infra legem* – equity in accordance with the law. The form which equity takes will depend on the circumstances of the particular case.

The other African country which did not accept the Cairo Resolution was Morocco. Morocco has made extensive claims to parts of Mauritania, the Western Sahara and Algeria, based on the fact that these territories historically belonged to the old Moroccan Empire. Like the Somali claims, they are essentially political claims and have no basis in law. The Court in the *Western Sahara* case in 1975 accepted that there were historical legal ties between the tribes in that area and both Morocco and Mauritania. However, the Court declared that these ties were not of such a strong and binding nature as to override the right of the inhabitants of the colony to self-determination and independence. Twenty-four years on, the United Nations is still trying to organise a plebiscite for the inhabitants of the Western Sahara, effectively to determine whether their future is to be independent of Morocco.

However, whilst the Cairo Resolution has been remarkably successful in allaying boundary conflicts, it could not be, and never was, a panacea for all African boundaries. Where problems existed before de-colonisation, they continued to exist after independence and still required resolution by the states concerned. Boundaries that were inadequately described in treaty instruments and boundaries where no – or no effective – demarcation had taken place remained possible sources of future problems.

Add to this economic and topographical changes and it will be clear why some of those potential problems have become major sources of dispute. The discovery of oil and the feasibility of extracting it all around the coast of West Africa and now, increasingly, of East Africa, has made the question of maritime delimitation a priority. The pressure for delimitation has been increased by the UN Convention on the Law of the Sea (UNCLOS) coming into force in November 1994. Thirty-four African coastal states have ratified UNCLOS but the process of maritime delimitation has been a slow one. The real pressure for delimitation is economic, as the oil companies increasingly exert influence on coastal states to take control of what is, for many states, the promise of previously undreamed-of riches. This economic pressure is bound to have considerable political implications and may lead to further strife as competing regimes seek to establish sovereignty over lucrative oil wells situated in sensitive boundary areas.

Topographical changes are perhaps less frequent, but may also end up in court. The changes may be natural or artificial – for example, where dams are built. In the *Botswana/Namibia* case there is a dispute over an island situated in the middle of a river. Uncertainty arises over the interpretation of the Anglo–German Berlin Treaty of 1890, it being unclear, one hundred years later, on which side of a disputed island the main channel of the Chobe river lies.

The *Nigeria/Cameroon* case, currently before the ICJ, presents a classic instance of a border which has the three elements of inherited uncertainties from the colonial era, being affected by topographical change, and being subject to economic pressures. The land boundary has been the subject of delimitation by colonial instruments but still awaits adequate demarcation in many areas. The terrain is very difficult (Figure 5) and leads to problems on the ground (Figure 6). The drying up of Lake Chad has transformed a huge lake – formerly the third largest in Africa – into an area with some fishing and many settlements (Figure 7). The seaward part of the boundary runs through one of the richest hydrocarbon regions off the coast of Africa.

The stresses caused on this boundary are most evident in the southern Bakassi peninsula area near Calabar (Figure 8) where we have the unfortunate spectacle of large numbers of troops deployed by both Nigeria and Cameroon keeping a wary eye on one another, with sporadic outbreaks of fighting – although, fortunately, neither side has indulged in full-scale warfare.

In other regions, ways of resolving boundary issues are not so stressful. Malawi and Zambia have a dispute which goes back to pre-colonial history. Malawi's claim arises out of the extent of the pre-colonial Maravi Empire. This is a claim which rejects the *uti possidetis* doctrine, but it is not clear how actively it is being pursued.

Disputes over the boundary in Lake Nyasa between Tanzania and Malawi arose from the same Anglo–German Berlin Treaty of 1890 as the *Botswana/Namibia* case. The treaty defined the relevant boundary as running along the eastern shore of the lake; Tanzania claimed a median line boundary. Evidence of German colonial activity in Tanganyika extending into the lake was supported by certain official British sources between the world wars, indicating a median line boundary. This dispute, which appears to challenge the accepted principles of *uti possidetis*, continues to rumble on, although there are periodic rumours of settlement.

Zambia has recently announced the setting up of a Joint Boundary Commission to work on its border with the Democratic Republic of the Congo.

Further north is the Halaib Region to the north of the 22nd Parallel between Egypt and Sudan, which has been the subject of dispute since Sudan's independence in 1956. This dispute is based on the question of the effect of a 1902 decree which placed the Halaib area, which was on the Egyptian side of the political border by virtue of an 1899 Anglo–Egyptian Agreement, under Sudanese administration (Figure 9). The dispute was exacerbated by the fact that this is a boundary which runs into the Red Sea where not only is the fishing rich, but there is also the promise of oil. In March 1998, however, the countries indicated a more peaceful means of settling this dispute, with a joint statement by their presidents stating that they 'had agreed to turn Halaib into a region of consolidation of popular ties between the two countries instead of a source of dispute'.

Enclaves are classic examples of boundary problems leading to stress, or worse. The oil-rich Cabinda enclave became part of Angola following indepen-dence from Portugal in 1975 and has been the scene of near-continuous conflict ever since. On the other hand, the dispute between Morocco and Spain concerning Spanish enclaves in North Africa at Ceuta and Melilla has been largely peaceful.

I have mentioned the *Burkina Faso/Mali*, *Nigeria/Cameroon* and *Botswana/ Namibia* cases. A fourth land-boundary dispute which has been before the ICJ in this last decade is that between Libya and Chad. This case turned on the interpretation of the 1955 Franco–Libyan Treaty of Friendship and Good Neighbourliness, and in particular on whether that Treaty resulted in a boundary; only if it had not would the ICJ have needed to consider the case on the basis of the rights and title of the inhabitants, including the pre-colonial situation. The ICJ held that the Treaty held good even though it had been concluded for a period of only 20 years and *effectivités* were irrelevant.

Maritime boundaries have also been the subject of dispute resolution before the ICJ. *Libya/Tunisia*, *Libya/Malta* and *Guinea Bissau/Senegal* have all been adjudicated upon, although only the first two led to ICJ judgments. In fact, if one looks at the docket of the ICJ since the Second World War, one sees that no fewer than six of the cases decided by the Court or still pending arise out of African boundary disputes. This is out of a total of some 15 boundary cases which the ICJ has considered in the past 50 or so years, and out of 10 such cases since 1982.

Boundary disputes traditionally arise out of historic tensions. Historic tensions in Africa came to be characterised by colonial activity. The first part of the new order imposed on Africa to reduce those tensions was the adoption of the Cairo Resolution in 1964. I would submit, however, that the second aspect of the new order has been the steady stream of cases referred to the ICJ. Much of the modern jurisprudence on international boundaries arises out of these African cases. Whilst it is regrettable, of course, that there should be disputes over boundaries, it is nevertheless a fact of life, whether it is between domestic neighbours or states. The encouraging development of the latter part of this century has been the readiness of African states to refer these issues to third-party adjudication. Of the 60 or so states which have signed up to the optional jurisdiction of the ICJ, 17 are African.

States bringing themselves within the jurisdiction of the ICJ or UNCLOS or submitting to international arbitration are demonstrating their commitment to the rule of law and a world order fashioned not by the sword, but by the jurist's pen. Thus, whilst the Secretary-General is right to express dismay at many aspects of life in Africa today, he may possibly take some small comfort from the encouraging way forward being shown by those African nations who have embraced international, peaceful resolution of their disputes. Is it too much to hope that growing trust in such organisations as the ICJ, conventions such as UNCLOS and cooperation with other UN organs such as the Office of the High Commissioner for Refugees, will lead increasingly to a respect for the values embodied in the Universal Declaration of Human Rights adopted by the UN in 1948?

African states have not shown much enthusiasm for the Commission of Mediation, Conciliation and Arbitration also set up in 1964 for the peaceful settlement of African disputes, preferring ad-hoc mediation efforts. The OAU itself has achieved a measure of success. It set up an *ad hoc* commission of African states to settle issues arising out of the 1963 Algeria/Morocco boundary dispute, and attempted to mediate in the Ethiopia/Somalia conflict. Whilst that commission failed to resolve the dispute, it did reaffirm the principle of *uti possidetis*.

The Commission has been activated to help resolve the current Ethiopia/Eritrea dispute. Facilitators – Rwanda and the United States – have been appointed to help to try to defuse the situation. They came up with Four-Point Proposals which were clearly designed to steer the parties down the *uti possidetis* route.[1]

A further encouraging development is the enthusiasm shown by African nations for the setting up of an International Criminal Court (ICC), the Statute of which was adopted in Rome on 18 June 1998. One of the forerunners of the ICC was the establishment by Resolution 955 of the Security Council in 1994 of an International Tribunal for Rwanda with the power to prosecute those responsible for serious violations of international humanitarian law committed on Rwandan territory in 1994.

These are all hopeful pointers. The tensions caused by history can be alleviated. President Clinton was right to find hope in his 1998 tour of African nations. That hope has expressed itself, and will hopefully continue to express itself, in the mature resolution of boundary and other issues between African states by means other than the use of force.

NOTE

1   Sadly, since this paper was presented, all-out warfare has broken out between Eritrea and Ethiopia with much loss of life.

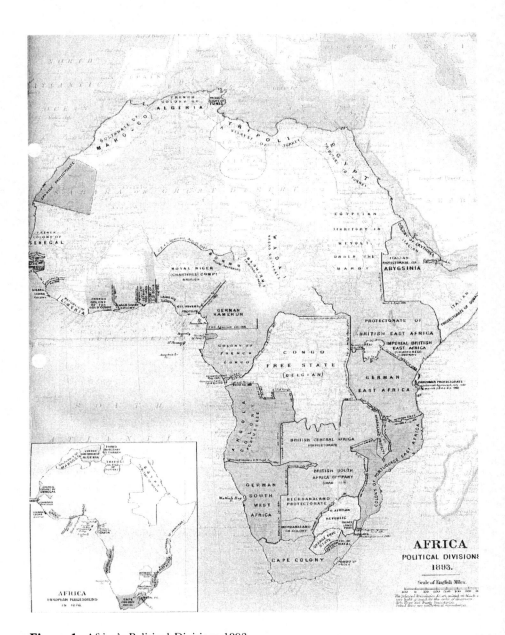

Figure 1: Africa's Political Divisions 1893

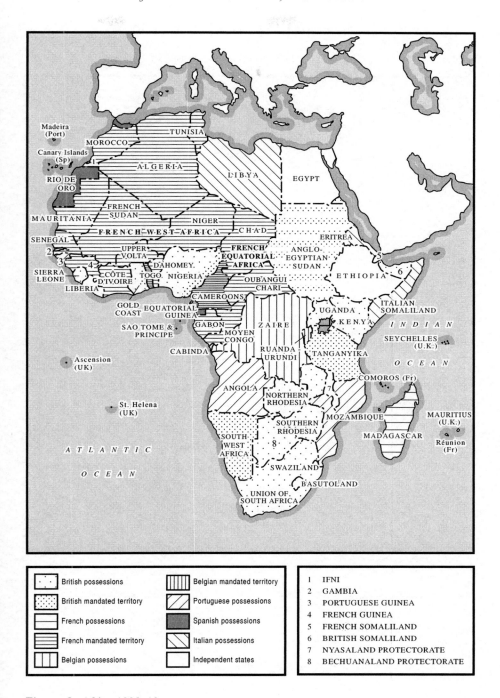

Figure 2: Africa 1926–46

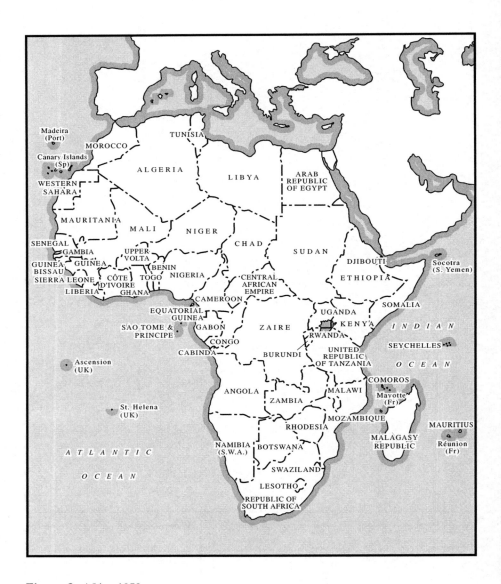

Figure 3: Africa 1978

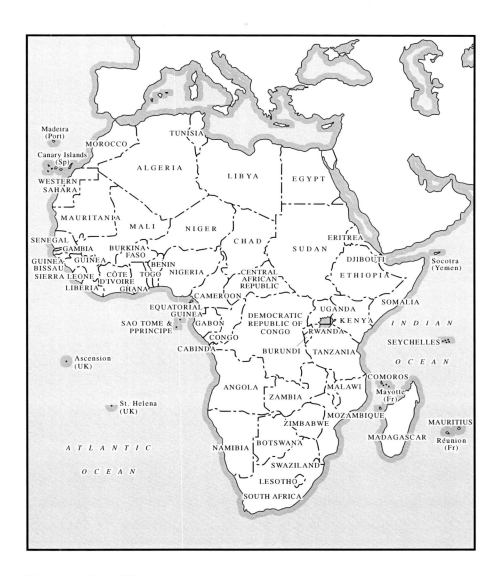

Figure 4: Africa 2000

Figure 5: The Cameroon–Nigeria boundary

Figure 6: Hills south of Lip, Taraba State, looking south-east towards Mount Kombon

Figure 7: Drying fish at Darak, Lake Chad

Figure 8: River estuaries near Calabar

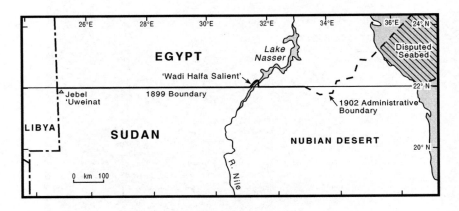

Figure 9: The Egypt–Sudan boundary

12
Designing Boundaries for a Continent: The Geopolitics of an African Renaissance

Richard A. Griggs

The term 'African Renaissance' is more than a catch-phrase about economic upliftment on a poor continent. It stands for a grand geo-strategy: a new spatial design for Africa that challenges the existing geopolitical order including old models of state sovereignty, state boundaries, national identity and, most particularly, northern hegemony. It also challenges the theory that globalisation will lead to cultural homogenisation, global government and global civil society (Mlinar, 1992; Hannerz, 1990; Lipschutz, 1992); it might instead suggest new kinds of divisions and conflicts between regional blocs or even whole 'civilisations' (Huntington, 1996; Marden, 1997).

The idea of an African Renaissance was first raised in an address in April 1994 by President Nelson Mandela to the Organization of African Unity (OAU) summit in Tunis. The first indication that it was more than rhetoric came in a speech by Deputy-President Thabo Mbeki to the United States Corporate Council on Africa (Barber, 1997). He opened his talk with the line: 'The African Renaissance is upon us.' Soon afterwards, numerous speeches, papers, editorials, articles and commentaries stressed African renewal through a new political economy of regional integration and cross-border initiatives. In July President Mandela described the renaissance in clear geopolitical terms:

> the creation of a new world order that involved the reconstruction of countries through regional economic associations capable of successfully competing in the global economy. (Seale, 1997.)

Within Southern Africa, foreign policy is already driven by the discourse of an African Renaissance. For example, this vision has been included in the strategic documents of South Africa's ruling party, the African National Congress (ANC):

> [The] African Renaissance is being advanced as the main pillar of our international policy not only relating to Africa, but in all our international relations globally. The concept of an African Renaissance provides a powerful vision not only for the African continent but for the development of a just and equitable world order. It is for this very reason that an African Renaissance poses a threat to the strategy of globalising capitalism. In fact, globalisation contradicts the very agenda of the Renaissance ... [Since] it is inevitable that an African Renaissance and transformation of international relations will necessarily entail the transformation of neocolonial relations, it is important to realise that the responses of major powers to such an initiative might not be positive. (ANC, 1998.)

Borderlands Under Stress (M.A. Pratt and J.A. Brown (eds), ISBN 90-411-9790-7).
© Kluwer Law International, 2000.

There are clear indications that South Africa intended to take a lead role in promoting the African Renaissance, but other Southern African leaders have sought to play this role too. In an address to a special ministerial session of the OAU in September 1998 Zimbabwe's President Robert Mugabe referred to it as 'a rebirth and renewal that is reshaping not only African societies but also African relations with the rest of the world' (Africa News Online, 1997). President Mugabe is attempting to wrest regional influence, wealth and power from South Africa. He has been encouraging Zimbabwean banks and mining enterprises to assume what was expected to be South Africa's role in the Democratic Republic of Congo (DRC). Such competition suggests that the 'renaissance' is being perceived in strategic, economic and geographic terms.

The idea of a 'rebirth and renewal' raises the question of what is 'new' about an African Renaissance, since these spatial plans have been part of agreements and movements that are decades old. The social construction of pan-Africanism dates to the period of independence. The idea of achieving African unity through regional organisations like the Southern African Development Community, or SADC (pronounced 'Sadec' and used as a proper noun without an article), dates back to the Lagos Plan of Action that was adopted by the OAU in April 1980.

What is new is *not* African unification based on the starting blocks of African regionalism, but the location, strategy and tactics for that achievement. First, the African Renaissance is being launched from SADC where 12 out of 14 member states have democratically-elected governments (Swaziland and the DRC are the exceptions). Secondly, it is being based on market-led approaches and not the old order of state-controlled economic development. The very term 'African Renaissance' has proved a useful marketing tool in both organising an increased share of global trade and stimulating Africans to seek greater control over the continent's human and material wealth. The once debatable wisdom of a pan-African agenda is now taken for granted, owing to the widely perceived need to create economies of scale to compete in a rapidly globalising and capitalist world.

Claiming a greater share of global power and wealth for Africa is geopolitics in its most classic sense. Nearly all the elements of an African Renaissance raise issues of territoriality and shared space. The three most important spatial corollaries for Southern Africa include:

- creating a regional trading bloc with enough economic clout to compete in a globalising economy dominated by 'northern' interests
- overcoming the colonial inheritance of poorly-designed boundaries by enhancing cross-boundary cooperation and infrastructure (e.g. establishing transport corridors and spatial development initiatives)
- expanded participation in south–south political and economic alliances to counter northern hegemony in spatial planning processes.

The intention of this paper is to examine the probable impact of this geo-strategic discourse on the political spaces of Southern Africa. A geopolitical analysis can help to:

- clarify the spatial objectives sought by powerful geopolitical actors, both north and south
- identify probable areas of conflict and accommodation between them
- assess the relative power of Africans to define and construct the spaces required for an African Renaissance in the face of a globalisation process dominated by northern states.

NORTH AND SOUTH PERSPECTIVES REGARDING THE AFRICAN RENAISSANCE

The basic model of uneven global development remains both a practical and popular explanatory tool for understanding the regional impact of globalisation processes (Slater, 1997). Figure 1 points to disparities in political and economic power that help produce these geopolitical divisions on a massive scale. The seven richest and most powerful countries in the world, the G7, are located in the northern sphere. Located here is about 25 per cent of the world's population but more than 75 per cent of all global trade. The poorest eight countries, the P8, are concentrated in the southern sphere where debt, poverty and hunger are concentrated. There you find the members of the Non-Aligned Movement (NAM), who base their political and economic strategies on the accepted wisdom that the older industrialised nations dominate the global state system. Individual African countries like South Africa have also modelled their foreign policies on these assumptions (ANC, 1998; Parliament of the Republic of South Africa, 1995).

The north–south division is the most potent area of contention in the shaping of the African space economy. There is no doubt that any African Renaissance will be a product of both northern and southern role-players. The very term 'renaissance' was generated in centres of northern power. The starting block for remodelling Africa's political spaces is a political map drawn largely in Europe. Most of the projects operated by Africa's regional organisations are funded by the north. In southern Africa 90 per cent of the project money for southern African development comes from northern countries and only ten per cent from member states!

The complete intertwining of north and south in the construction of Africa's political and economic spaces means that the spatial aspects of the African Renaissance must be understood in terms of the points of convergence and divergence between northern and southern visions. By first analysing those broad objectives, we can take a better look at the probable areas of conflict and accommodation, leading to some tentative predictions regarding spatial outcomes.

The African Renaissance as a northern geo-strategy

Since the time of the European Renaissance there has been a huge demand by those in the north to control the profits, real or potential, from Africa's geological wealth, energy wealth, land wealth, bio-diversity, human labour and marine resources. In the colonial era the north's chosen geo-strategy was territorial occupation and annexation based on the highly organised and technically proficient use of force (McNeill, 1982; Boahen, 1971). In the post-independence era the north exerted its domination through financial institutions, multinational companies and technological superiority. The Cold War years generated some interventions in Africa for strategic reasons but the post-Cold War years have returned us to a northern motive in Africa that is not particularly new: profit.

Today wealthy northern countries have saturated markets and seek expansion through foreign sales, investment opportunities and access to cheap raw materials. Naturally, traders, companies and corporations seek out those parts of the globe which offer the highest returns and neglect areas offering a low return. Africa sits on the far perimeter of the world economy, attracting less than five per cent of global trade. This condition is unlikely to change very soon. A Merrill Lynch Gallup Survey (Galli) in May 1998 found that:

- only three per cent of US fund managers favoured southern Africa as an emerging market
- the Japanese do not favour the area at all (nought per cent)
- only British fund managers expressed reasonable interest (16 per cent).
- South Africa's own fund managers prefer investing nearly 2:1 in Europe over southern Africa (26 per cent v. 42 per cent).

Africa's peripheral position in the world economy presents a major challenge to northern governments which are taking a longer geopolitical view than banks, corporations, speculators and short-term investors. Governments have an interest in building the infrastructure and political relations that keep economies going. Even though investor confidence in Africa is low, it is common knowledge that Africa is a continent of vast potential wealth. This keeps wealthy northern powers such as the G7 members involved in African diplomacy, nudging government leaders toward political and economic agreements that open up and secure markets for northern business.

A survey conducted by a World Bank affiliate identified the top obstacles to foreign investment in Africa. The study, based on 4,000 entrepreneurs in 69 countries, reported that high inflation, crime, corruption, inadequate supply of infrastructure, high taxes, political instability, and stringent regulations on investment, currency and labour practices prevented both higher trade flows and investment (International Finance Corporation, 1998). The results, specified by five African regions, showed that the biggest obstacles to investment in Southern Africa were inflation, corruption, stringent labour and tax regulations, high taxes, crime and theft.

These surveys and numerous other studies (e.g. Spira, 1998) reveal the analysis upon which northern policy toward Africa is based. Basically, higher levels of investment are blocked by the structure of African governments themselves. They are cut off from private capital markets and real competition because red tape and protectionism raise investor risk levels, excessive public spending fuels inflation, and corruption both undermines the delivery of infrastructure and creates instability. It is this northern portrait of mismanaged and corrupt economies that shapes the north's geopolitical strategies in Africa. It is premised on the idea that Africa's failure to benefit from the world economy is due to its own interference with the marketplace.

The north uses its control of powerful financial organisations and capital to operate two main levers to pry African governments out of the marketplace and open the way for unfettered international trade. First, it uses the gentle persuasion of development finance. There are many examples of this, including the US government's African Growth and Opportunity Act which rewards African states that liberalise, privatise and democratise. 'Opportunities' include business partnerships, debt relief, loan guarantees and access to US markets. The persuasive influence of northern capital is also revealed in the structure of the African Development Bank; it is 40 per cent owned and managed by northern capital with decisions being taken by a 66.6 per cent majority (Dludlu, 1998).

Secondly, northern control of capital can be coercive. This does not exclude the use of raw force such as the financial assistance that the French state oil company ELF provided to Angolan troops in the 1997 overthrow of the Congo's Lissouba regime (Misser, 1998). More commonly, its control is exercised through the north's international banking institutions, the International Monetary Fund (IMF) and the World Bank. These Bretton Woods twins can force indebted states to cut spending and hence the size of government. For instance, Zimbabwe was coerced into cutting its spending levels by a punitive freezing of IMF aid from 1994 until its compliance in 1998 (Hartnack, 1998). On a wider scale, some 32 African countries seeking debt relief must comply for six years with more than 100 conditions of fiscally prudent management before qualifying for aid.

IMF-managed countries are restructured toward northern ideals: industry is privatised, public spending cut and markets are opened to foreign investors. These 'structural adjustment programmes' can bring the books to balance and result in higher economic growth rates. One example is Uganda, which has followed the IMF-led structural adjustment programme to realise growth rates of between seven and eight per cent a year. While these programmes are appealing in terms of gross national product, they typically raise unemployment levels, reduce medical care, eliminate food subsidies and incur other social costs that can lead to civil unrest (e.g. in Kenya and Zambia). Clearly, the G7 members believe these programmes work to their own benefit, as they are now seeking an amendment to the IMF constitution stating that financial liberal-isation is the organisation's central purpose.

A far stronger vehicle for liberalising the African space economy is yet to come. The constitution for a rules-based global economy is being worked out by the Organisation for Economic Cooperation and Development (OECD) which represents the world's 29 wealthiest countries. Upon completion, this will give the World Trade Organization (WTO) the power to compel all 132 member countries to completely liberalise the flow of trade, investment, labour and finance capital. A significant global power shift is occurring in which the private sector – and especially multinationals – are strongly influencing policy. This means opening up all southern economies to northern investors on equal terms. Laws regulating the entry, behaviour and operations of foreign companies will be eliminated and there will be strong punitive measures for non-compliance. To southern complaints that this is tantamount to re-colonisation, the north replies that it is the best way for developing countries to attract much-needed foreign investment.

Popular culture in the north also exerts an influence on the African Renaissance through commercial marketing, the entertainment industry and its internationally subscribed news media. In the north's popular press, economic liberalisation is usually equated with democratic liberation. There are zealous media descriptions reminiscent of the nineteenth-century missionary discourse aimed at civilising Africa – except now the mission is to bring Africa into line with northern economies and globalisation processes. Africa is being 'freed' from the socialist tyranny of the past and is entering a new era much like that already experienced in the more advanced north. The tenor of popular northern discourse on the African Renaissance is well illustrated in this *Time Magazine* description:

> What's new is that the enduring example of Nelson Mandela has heartened all Africans with a fresh vision of leadership, how men of their own kind can be admired, respected, even emulated. For so long the victim of historical circumstance, Africa is finally a beneficiary. The end of the cold war freed countries from 30-odd years of disastrous involvement in the superpowers' proxy conflicts. Old ideologies crumbled taking with them the failed socialist methods of Marx and opening the way to capitalist reforms. The demise of apartheid gave the continent a huge psychological – and economic and political – boost. A generation of African leaders who grew up to despise the exploitation of postcolonial dictators and kleptocrats has begun to supplant them. (McGeary & Michaels, 1998.)

Altogether, northern views on the African Renaissance, whether expressed by investors, institutions of international finance, the G7, the OECD or even popular culture, are relatively uniform: Africa has structured its own unequal relations. However unfair the past might have been, outdated African ideologies and economic mismanagement in a globally competitive world have driven out investment and opportunity. The northern vision of a new Africa refers to a new leadership capable of embracing a neo-liberal ideology that will open borders to a relatively unregulated global economy in which northern and southern traders compete on equal terms.

Interestingly, northern-based discourse on an African Renaissance usually focuses on Africa's 'evolution' toward modernisation. This camouflages a vital factor influencing this interpretation: the enormous profits that northern companies could derive from economic liberalisation. In 1997 the IMF put

$500 million into African economies while taking out $1.1 billion in repayments, excluding interest (DeSarkar, 1998). This profit of $600 million is a tiny fraction of what liberalising African economies means for the north. Open African borders could mean billions of dollars in dividends for the north. This would include consultancy fees on privatisation, interest fees on loans, payments for northern technology, better access to cheap raw resources, new sources of energy, unfettered investment opportunities and the profits that accrue from unequal currencies, economies and terms of trade.

Geopolitically, the shape of this 'Northern Renaissance' can be reduced to two basic spatial formations: increased levels of regional organisation and borders open to trade between north and south along *laissez faire* lines. Regional organisation offers many advantages for the north: it helps open borders, lowers the costs of transacting business, eliminates tariffs, pools local resources to provide needed infrastructure and provides for speedier negotiations and agreements (one multilateral agreement v. negotiating many bilateral agreements). Opening borders to a relatively unregulated trading environment increases the profits for competitive northern companies that hold a winning hand in terms of information management, capital and know-how.

The African Renaissance as a southern African geo-strategy

Within Africa, the discourse on an African Renaissance suggests very different motives and objectives than in the north. African governments are seeking to overcome a peripheral if not subservient position in the global pecking order. There are widespread perceptions that centuries of northern hegemony forced Africa into unequal relations of trade, providing cheap labour and raw resources for the industrialising north where power, capital and information came to be concentrated. This process began with slavery and proceeded through several stages of colonialism to reach this late stage where most African economies are controlled if not managed by northern-run and -staffed institutions like the World Bank, the IMF and the WTO.

Unlike the leaders of the Cold War past, the new leadership fully acknowledges the geopolitical realities of northern hegemony under the Pax Americana. This is not a rejection of past leadership, as the popular northern view suggests, but the *realpolitik* of a new era in the long-term African struggle to liberate itself from a history of northern oppression, of which late neocolonialism is an accepted part. Many Africans still believe that the north has a moral obligation to help rectify the disastrous effects of slavery, colonisation, neocolonialism and superpower rivalry on the continent.

An example of this distinction between southern and northern views is the campaign by Southern African leaders to have their debts cancelled by the G7 countries so that this region can fully enter the global economy (for many states it exceeds 20 per cent of GNP). The heads of state for SADC argue that Africa's high debt ($122 billion) is an historic legacy of colonial relations that is stalling the necessary economic and democratic reforms (Dow Jones, 1998; Fine, 1998).

'Write off our debts and then see our ability to reform,' argued Zambian leader Frank Chiluba (Fine, 1998). The G7 rejected this bid and referred the leaders to the IMF's Highly Indebted Poor Country initiative (HIPC), with its numerous conditions for debt relief. Namibian President Sam Nujoma responded,

> The G7 are defending their own interests. Namibia is not prepared to forget the legacy of colonialism ... what is demanded of the international community is genuine investment. (*Natal Witness*, 1998.)

Few African leaders, 'new' or 'old', appear to accept the neoclassical ideology that economic liberalisation is inherently beneficial. Numerous foreign investments in Africa have not been seen as 'genuine' or beneficial. Africans have seen the repressive measures that have accompanied some foreign investment, such as the extrajudicial executions of Ogoni nation leaders to secure silence over the lucrative relationship between the Nigerian state elite and Shell Oil. Many believe that northern-owned industries in Africa offer little local employment and yet repatriate the profits made on African soil. Capital surges in and out of their economies from northern speculators have prompted the collapse of currencies, fuelled inflation and wiped out jobs.

For many Africans, the Global Agreement on Tariffs and Trade (GATT) and the new WTO threaten to fix north–south relations in a form of 'collective colonisation' (Abdul-Raheem, 1997). Many fear that if rich northern countries continue to set the rules for globalisation, there will be few if any mechanisms with which African countries can control economic activities on the continent. This will escalate the transfer of wealth out of Africa, increase debt, deepen poverty, create unemployment and further erode African cultures. Even United Nations Development Programme figures show that Africa stands to lose up to six billion rand a year from trade liberalisation (Machipisa, 1998).

It is indicative of this north–south schism that only two African leaders attended the fiftieth anniversary party of GATT in Geneva in May 1998. Nearly all African leaders deliberately boycotted the event to send the message that this was a party for rich northern states. President Nelson Mandela carried the message from Africa to the northern ministers and heads of state in attendance:

> Fifty years ago, when the founders of GATT evoked the link between trade, growth, and a better life, few could have foreseen such poverty, homelessness, and unemployment as the world now knows. (The Mercury, 1998.)

Altogether, today's leaders in southern Africa accept that globalisation is not a choice. In an information age of global connectivity, a retreat would only leave them outstripped by more dynamic regions. Thus it owes more to *realpolitik* and less to an embracing of neo-liberal philosophy that Africans play by the rules of a northern-directed power game while working on strategies to keep Africa in African hands.

POINTS OF CONFLICT AND ACCOMMODATION

Interestingly, the ambiguous term 'African Renaissance' offers something to northern paymasters while building strength within Africa. Despite two diametrically opposed objectives (claiming more of Africa for Africans v. claiming more of Africa for the north), there are some common points of geo-strategy. For instance, repaying debt, developing infrastructure to attract investment, privatising industry, establishing fiscal rectitude and pooling resources through strong regional economies could prepare Africans to engage meaningfully in global trade.

This convergence of strategies does not mean that the objectives of African leaders or their rendition of an African Renaissance are the same as those of their northern counterparts. For instance, regionalisation serves African interests by building the economies of scale to resist northern hegemony while it is establishing a global power base of south–south alliances. Only from such a broader base of global power can Africans hope to restructure the space economy of Africa in ways that serve Africans. This includes finding a way to influence the rules of global trade (i.e. taxes on buying and selling foreign exchange, regulation of finance, and debt cancellation).

Examined below are the three main spatial dimensions of the African Renaissance from an African perspective:

- strengthening regional levels of authority
- cross-border spatial development initiatives
- south–south cooperation.

The prospects of success or failure for each will be assessed in terms of the opportunities and constraints generated by the conflict between northern and southern role-players in the Southern African region.

Strengthening regional levels of authority

Regionalisation is the lynchpin of the African Renaissance since it helps negate the spatial impact of the European partitioning of the continent at the 1884-85 Berlin Conference. Many African leaders, like former Tanzanian president Julius Nyerere, see the central problem of the colonial legacy as spatial: 'arbitrarily drawn borders resulting in little states that make little sense and which if left on their own cannot develop at all' (O'Grady, 1997). As Figure 2 illustrates, half of the 14 SADC countries are landlocked, while exclaves, enclaves, prorupt territories and other boundary irregularities impact on southern African development. Theoretically, the creation of regional trading communities pools political and economic resources, eliminating the need for potentially destabilising boundary changes.

Can regional integration provide the basis for an African Renaissance? With a coordinated plan for sharing resources across boundaries, southern Africa has the energy, resources and workforce to become an economic giant. Figure 3 illustrates

SADC and the dates on which the 14 member states were admitted. With the admission of Namibia, South Africa, the DRC, Seychelles and Mauritius in the 1990s, SADC has doubled its territory to put into place one of the wealthiest organisations in the world in terms of resources. This includes the world's richest fisheries, vast hydroelectric potential, huge timber reserves and strategically situated ports mid-way between east and west. The mineral wealth is legendary: 99 per cent of the world's chrome reserves, 85 per cent of its platinum, 70 per cent of its tantalite and 68 per cent of its cobalt, not to mention at least 50 per cent of the world's vanadium, diamonds and gold (Ramano, 1998).

The 14 member states are also a potentially large market, comprising nearly 200 million people. The bigger market could attract larger capital flows and build a cooperative basis for industrial development. A strategic spin-off of industrialisation would be less dependency on the First World and the construction of the middle class vital to sustaining democracy (Mbaku, 1997).

The biggest obstacle SADC has faced is the slow pace of economic integration and development. This relates to both southern and northern factors. First, regionalisation has been impeded by the colonially induced trap of exchanging raw materials for First World manufacture (Mbaku, 1997). Until South Africa's admission in 1994, this left most member states too much in debt and too hungry for foreign currencies to kick-start regional economies. Breaking out of the trap requires negotiating development aid, debt relief and genuine investment from the same northern countries that have derived long-term benefits from exploiting Africa's resources, especially cheap raw materials. Furthermore, the proxy wars of the Cold War accompanied by apartheid-era occupations, wars and bombings left a very weak SADC at the time of South Africa's first democratic elections.

When South Africa joined SADC, analysts both north and south agreed that this country had the infrastructure and political leadership to become the engine of regional economic development. However, the Southern African Development Coordination Conference's (SADCC) launching of 'Front-Line States' against apartheid has created an organisational culture in which political agendas overshadow economic ones. Most decisions are arrived at through long and difficult negotiations. For instance, many political sensitivities have surrounded South Africa's role since it can derive as much as 60 times the trade benefit as some of its smaller partners. In consequence, any kind of independent sovereignty for the organisation that might lead to South African hegemony has been avoided. The result is an organisation run by heads of state lacking any independent system by which to coordinate their activities. Decisions negotiated between SADC leaders often turn into long and time-costly political wrangles, such as the three-year-long spat between Presidents Nelson Mandela and Robert Mugabe over who should head the component on conflict resolution (the so-called Organ for Politics, Defence and Security)!

Rather than being opposed to the successful regional integration of SADC, the north is impatient with its slow pace. In July 1998 the United States made further progress a condition of its 'general system of preferences' in trade; only those countries that have signed the SADC free-trade protocol qualify (Barber, 1998). More generally, there is near-global consensus on the desire to quicken the speed of African regionalisation to include the United Nations Economic Commission for Africa, the World Bank, the African Development Bank, the European Union and the OAU.

The convergence of interests on regionalisation is marred by distinctions between northern and southern geo-strategies. First, the top priority for the World Bank in southern Africa is to facilitate a large role for private-sector decision-making (Simon, 1997). This disappoints African states seeking to direct the economic upliftment of the poor. Secondly, SADC wants to achieve a common tariff to external markets until a globally competitive level of regional integration has been achieved (Gibb, 1997). The north pushes for more immediate liberalisation. Since SADC seeks external funding for regional projects, it is likely to compromise its policies and plans to whatever degree is sufficient for attracting northern investors.

Given the relative convergence of northern and southern interests in constructing a regionally-based space economy, it is in this arena that southern African states have fallen short of completing the tasks set for themselves. Certainly some of this failure is related to the hardships of the colonial past, but the bulk of the problem is having to negotiate conflict within SADC. Eight protocols have been drafted since 1994, covering issues of crime, mining, education, energy, shared water, transport and communication, liberalisation of trade, and immunities and privileges. As of June 1998 only the last had been ratified and only Botswana had ratified them all. Only three members (Mauritius, Tanzania and Botswana) had ratified the most far-reaching of these – liberalisation of trade. The Maseru Protocol was drafted in August 1996 with the intention of dismantling all tariffs within six months.

SADC's seemingly interminable political negotiations do not mean that there has been no progress. World Bank figures for 1996–1997 show that southern Africa is one of the fastest-growing regional economies in the world, expanding at a rate of five to six per cent a year (Seale, 1998). The 1998 World Development indicators also show that between 1965 and 1996 the world's fastest-growing economy was SADC-member Botswana (Leshilo, 1998) – although one must temper this with the understanding that the starting point was a tiny economic base. At the time of writing, SADC accounts for no more than one per cent of global trade. Perhaps geopolitical advances provide a more realistic picture. SADC has:

- negotiated sensitivities surrounding South Africa
- piloted its way through rapid geographic expansion
- moved away from Marxist economic models
- made significant headway in establishing the Spatial Development Initiatives (examined in the next section).

These are the geographic foundations for a regional community that could very well open the gateways to faster internal and global trade.

Altogether, southern Africa's advancement toward an African Renaissance through regional organisation ultimately rests on the pace and structure of regional integration, an area over which members can exercise considerable control. Can SADC hurdle its political obstacles fast enough to catch up with other regions, and do so in a manner that empowers the poor? On the one hand, the slow pace of change keeps foreign investors occupied elsewhere; on the other, large-scale poverty, unemployment and high rates of illiteracy are a melting pot for potential instability, as exemplified by coup attempts (Zambia), war (the DRC, Angola) and civil unrest (Lesotho, Zimbabwe). Security concerns should keep southern leaders scrambling for ways to empower a directorate to fast-track regional plans and establish a parliament that can both legislate and adjudicate disputes. On this score, the Achilles heel of the African Renaissance is a basic unwillingness to sacrifice state sovereignty for the sake of the spatial integration process.

Spatial development initiatives

Figure 4 illustrates the cross-border Spatial Development Initiatives (SDIs) that cut across central and southern African states. SDIs use roads or rail to link major nodes of potential investment such as ports, parks, tourist facilities, mining areas and major industrial developments. The largest project of this kind upgrades the Maputo Harbour and links it to South Africa's industrial heartland, saving 150km on the comparative journey from the port of Durban. This both cuts costs for South African mining and industry and helps to rehabilitate Mozambique's infrastructure and industry, long shattered by civil war. A total of 184 different projects are involved on both sides of the border, including an aluminium smelter, iron ore works, tourism projects, casinos and agricultural developments.

These spatial developments are the clearest geographic indicator that a renaissance is underway. First, these are cross-boundary projects managed by joint authority (e.g. the Maputo Corridor Company). This includes cooperation in speeding up customs and managing border posts. The result is more open southern African borders, an outcome sought by both north and south.

Secondly, these corridors are largely financed by private capital. Bids, commissions and concessions were used to attract investors to the Maputo Corridor, based on the real-market value of these projects. For instance, the cross-border toll road is privately financed by trans-African concessions and will be operated for 45 years before reverting to government ownership. Owing to this strategy, this project was awarded the highest rating ever in project finance worldwide for its ability to meet the debts incurred (Hlophe, 1998). In some of these projects, public–private partnership has been fostered by the World Bank – another clear indication of convergent north–south interests.

Finally, these corridors involve increased economic interaction between provinces and towns on both sides of the international border, leading to integration in real geographic terms while overcoming the legacy of arbitrary colonial boundaries.

Of all the spatial issues, the development corridors are the strongest areas of mutual north–south interest. The World Bank estimates that approximately $170 billion is required to upgrade the transport infrastructure in Southern Africa (far more than the governments can afford). In this effort it has located private-sector finance and supported these projects with preliminary studies (*Mail and Guardian*, 1997). However, it has not dominated these projects. Much of the finance is from local investment banks, the Development Bank of Southern Africa, consortiums of corporate investors and Black empowerment groups.

The major point of contention in these schemes is not north v. south or even south v. south – it is the poor and disadvantaged v. the private investors; the small entrepreneurs v. big business. It is too early to foretell the degree to which the poor will have their lives upgraded and empowered. Fruit sellers, small businesses, taxis, tourist lodges and small truckers have all complained about the effects of the corridor. The siting of the toll roads has sometimes separated local communities from their schools and shopping centres. Small haulers complain about the high costs of tolls. There was almost no participation by small business in the development and planning of the Maputo Corridor. In many cases, the only benefit that some affected communities can derive is by purchasing shares in the project (Hammond, 1998).

Strengthening south–south political and economic alliances

Figure 5 shows SADC's emergent south–south alliances linking four continents and three oceans across the entire breadth of the southern hemisphere. In addition to other African states, a rim of countries surrounding the Indian Ocean are forging trading ties, a South Atlantic alliance is budding with the Mercosur states, and ties to the economic giants of the developing world like China, Malaysia and India are rapidly becoming established. All these areas are rich in strategic resources, offer complementarities in the production process and represent large, unrealised markets. Through trade, shared technology and diplomatic agreements these southern countries are also taking deliberate steps to escape the geopolitical pressures of northern hegemony.

Could a southern trade bloc succeed in its mission? Long-term geopolitics could be in its favour, as it is a programme that the north can delay but not eliminate. Furthermore, while the north dominates industry and information on a global scale, the vast majority of natural resources including fisheries, minerals, forests and energy are in the south. Just between South Africa and the Mercosur states lies the potential to monopolise 80 per cent of the world's trade in hake. Argentina and Zimbabwe could tie up 30 per cent of the beef market (Mills, 1998). With large enough markets in the south, the Southern African states could catapult to political and economic power through the strategic control of minerals. These alliances also include linkages with some of the world's top oil producers such as Saudi Arabia, Libya, Iran and Angola.

Although both SADC and the Mercosur states have a strong interest in expanding trade, and even established a commission to pursue this, tangible southward shifts in capital will be very slow to effect. Both regions are emergent economies in global terms, still on the rebound from authoritarian regimes, and have restricted policy options because of debt to northern banking institutions and unequal terms of trade. Currently Mercosur's trade with SADC countries is about one per cent of its total volume (Mills, 1998).

The 15 Indian Ocean rim states (Figure 5) constitute another very youthful pillar of south–south trade, but one with huge potential. The region includes some 1.5 billion people and is centred on the three industrialised countries of South Africa, India and Australia. A major study was completed in May 1998 by Britain's Elsevier Reed group that endorses the formation of this regional bloc. They argued that the economic outlook for South Africa's participation is so promising that 25 per cent of its total trade might lie within the IOR block within a few short years (Robertson, 1998).

The alliances with China and India include formal signed agreements that tie SADC to two of the world's largest economies. Economics and demographics suggest that China, already the third most powerful economy, will overtake the US to become the world's biggest global trader soon after the turn of the millennium – China has already planned 30 new industrial development projects in South Africa – and India could take second position before the middle of the next century (Sapa, 1998).

The geopolitics of south–south alliances came into sharpest relief with the renewed vigour that South Africa put into the Non-Aligned Movement (113 southern states are members). As the new president of the organisation, Nelson Mandela engaged in some shuttle diplomacy to set the agenda for the meeting in September 1998 which focused on 'Global Apartheid'. The final statements fell far short of any particular agenda. Furthermore, South Africa was sidelined by the 'old guard' of African leaders because of its ambition to lead the renaissance. The outbreak of war in the Congo also cast a black shadow over the discussions.

The biggest and most hopeful opportunity for positioning southern Africa as the engine of an African Renaissance is in the arena of south–south relations, since it counterbalances northern control of spatial development processes. Such alliances also pose the greatest dangers. Southern Africa's long-term strategic interests in creating south–south alliances are at odds with the north's own long-term geo-strategy: to simultaneously increase north–south flows of trade and maintain a superior status in international commerce. There are many examples of such conflict:

- Malawi's diplomatic contacts with Libya have met with US and British anger.
- South Africa's strong relations with Cuba and rumoured secret arms sales with Cuba, Libya, Syria and Iran have all led to diplomatic rows with the US.
- South Africa has also upset the American defence industry by procuring arms contracts with Saudi Arabia.

- The DRC has awarded major development contracts to China while both Europeans and Americans were scrambling for them.

Too many spats could raise the geopolitical pressure for northern role-players to return to the subversive use of force in African affairs, as France did in the 1997 handling of Congo–Brazzaville.

PROBABLE SPATIAL OUTCOMES

Continued northern control of trade could mean that the African Renaissance will have a stronger impact ideologically and philosophically across continents where elites mix, while the extent of extra-continental trade far outpaces the growth of intra-continental trade. Under the Pax Americana we are likely to see Africa pay homage to northern powers while building the regional loyalties for a project of African empowerment that will take many decades to manifest. Given the tremendous potential force of south–south alliances, this system may gradually change – and the entire focus of the global economy with it – to a world focused on China and India. But however likely, this will be decades in the making.

Thus, the spatiality of an African Renaissance must be tempered by some hard African realities related to prospects for the rural poor. There is an acute urban/rural split within Africa that may be accentuated as whole regions will not benefit from globalisation. Some 80 per cent of the southern African population resides in rural areas where, on average, the nearest telephone is 50km away (Holman, 1998). All of Africa has access to just two per cent of the world's telephone lines – less than New York City or Tokyo (*Finance Africa*, 1997); on the other hand, African cities conduct more telephone traffic per subscriber than the US or Japan (*Finance Africa*, 1997). This suggests that urban elites will plug into the global network of relations at a much faster rate than poor rural people. While African elites are connected to cyberspace in the cities, rural areas will remain far removed from such technology owing to far more immediate priorities – health, sanitation, water and electrification.

Another factor that helps to confine the real renaissance to the urban centres is the low levels of education. Many rural residents cannot even read or write. This means that there is a woefully poor supply of adequately trained workers. Although this is being addressed well in some countries like Tanzania, the educational dimension of the renaissance is a trans-generational project. The pattern of an urban, educated elite dominating the African space economy will continue for an appreciable time.

As globalisation accentuates Africa's rural/urban divide, it will shape a geography of inequality both within the cities and between cities and their rural hinterland. City populations will swell with rural immigrants who cannot compete with the intensified agriculture resulting from globalised trade in agriculture. Since new employment at a decent wage will be in service and information industries will require high levels of education, the dislocated rural immigrants are likely to become an alienated population ('underclass') dependent on charity or crime. Cities themselves will become increasingly fortified, with a proliferation of 'security villages' in the suburbs.

Integrating many disadvantaged economies may not be sufficient to produce quality industrial goods at globally competitive prices. Combined with poor education and a decline in the value of unskilled labour, African workers will gain very little from an open labour market. Many skilled workers will be attracted to jobs outside Southern Africa. This combination of factors will not allow the majority of SADC states to move rapidly from a dependence on exporting raw material exports to the highly skilled production of industrial products; it will certainly prevent them from dominating global markets any time soon (Mbaku, 1997).

Another scenario is that wars and instability will mar the region and prevent any sizeable cross-border cooperation. War and instability in Angola and the DRC have already split SADC members into opposition alliances. This dampens the prospects of linking central Africa's vast oil, gas, petroleum and mineral deposits to South Africa's refining and distribution capacity. Angola has already mortgaged its petroleum profits to fight UNITA and war in the Congo effectively bars southern Africa's access to its massive hydroelectric potential. Further instability may force South Africa to jettison the notion of an African Renaissance in favour of another social construction that enables it to take individual advantage of new south–south relations or even old north–south relations. This would see a new concentration on strengthening South Africa's borders against immigrants, refugees and illegal goods – a total unravelling of SADC.

War and violence is the quickest and surest way to terminate the African Renaissance. Central, southern and east African leaders may already be too badly divided to reconcile themselves to a properly organised SADC region. Devastation caused by war is reducing the infrastructure for development. In the meantime, investors are backing away from notions of a renaissance and returning to the more conservative view of Africa as a 'basket case' of conflict and corruption. Concerns ranging from refugees to troops crossing borders could lead to the development of increased levels of security along interstate boundaries – a return to the Westphalian system of closed, hard-line borders rather than the open, free-trade zone promised by the renaissance advocates.

Changing this bleak outlook on southern Africa's space economy will take more than discourse. It will require a rapid restructuring of the geopolitical relations between north and south and a formal SADC body that speeds up integration while moving the regional organisation away from clashes based on personalities and power politics. The potential for Africans to invent a new spatial design for Africa is hampered by many geopolitical factors. A positive outlook on southern Africa's space economy will require a new kind of geopolitics that involves:

- a tempering of the widespread ideology that trade liberalisation is tantamount to liberation and enriches all countries that take advantage of it
- the inclusion of developing and developed countries as equal partners in drafting regulations on international trade and finance; such regulations should include designs to reduce the capital surges and speculative practices that have devalued African currencies, raised interest rates and depressed emergent economies
- increased north–south dialogue based on respect, sensitivity and an historic sense of moral responsibility
- SADC leaders promoting a real regional parliament beyond the consultative forum emanating from the 1996 Windhoek protocol
- a restructured and democratised United Nations that brings countries both north and south into a transparent and inclusive process of global decision-making.

There are indications that all these factors are under debate, but none have been implemented. Until they are, the 'renaissance' ideal of side-stepping the legacy of poorly drawn colonial boundaries with open borders and free trade is unlikely to succeed, and the Westphalian system of 'hard' boundaries that attempt to enforce a system of sovereign states will persist, despite any rhetoric about an African renaissance.

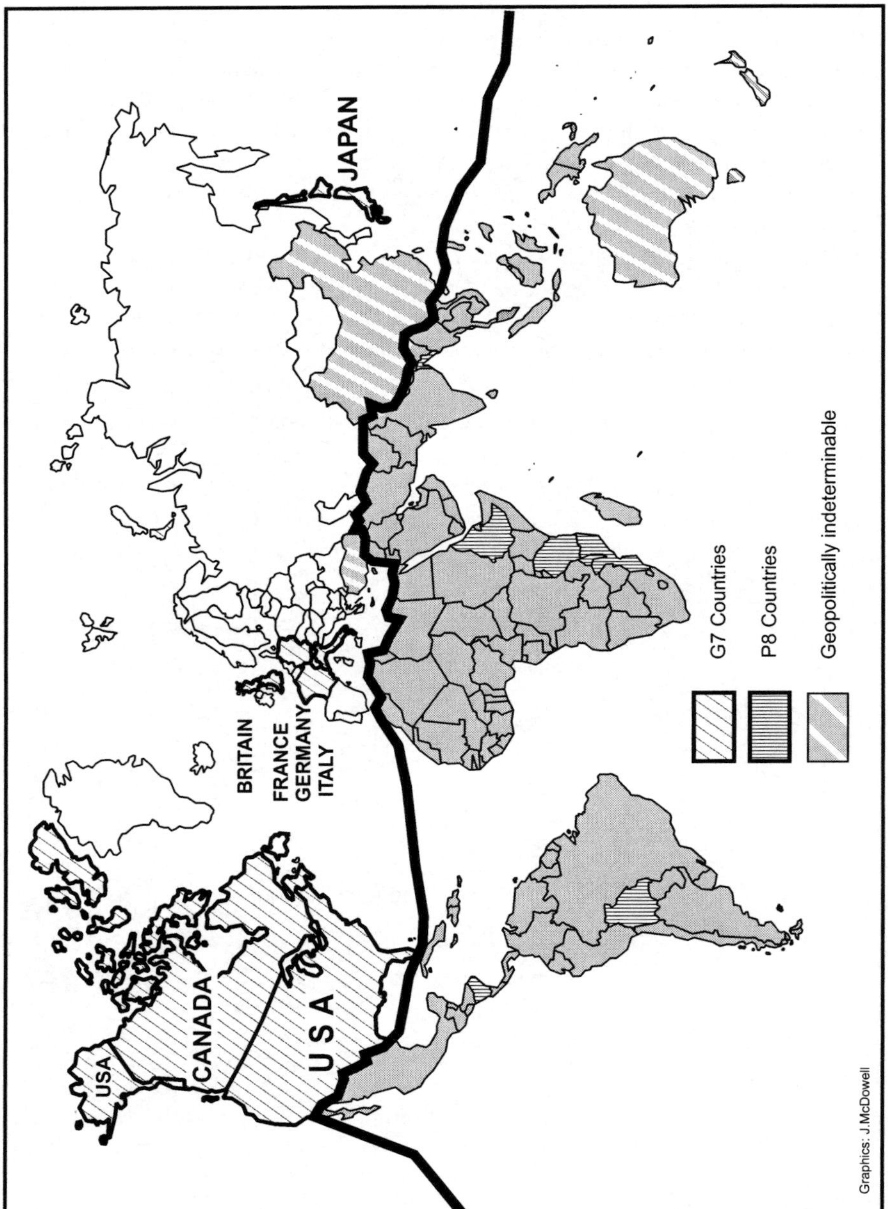

G7 Countries

P8 Countries

Geopolitically indeterminable

JAPAN

BRITAIN
FRANCE
GERMANY
ITALY

USA

CANADA

U S A

Graphics: J.McDowell

Figure 1: Northern hegemony in a North/South world

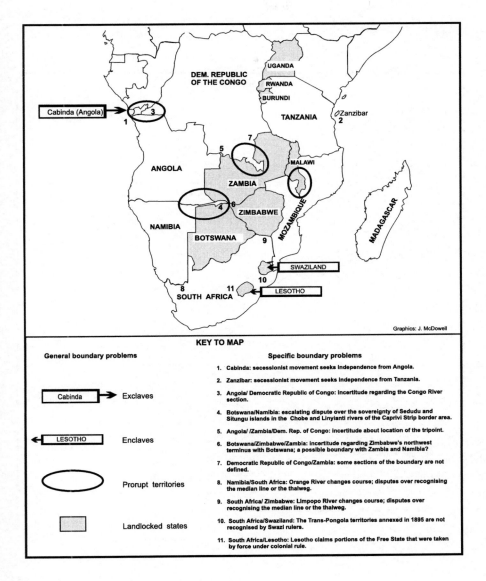

Figure 2: Boundary problems in the SADC area

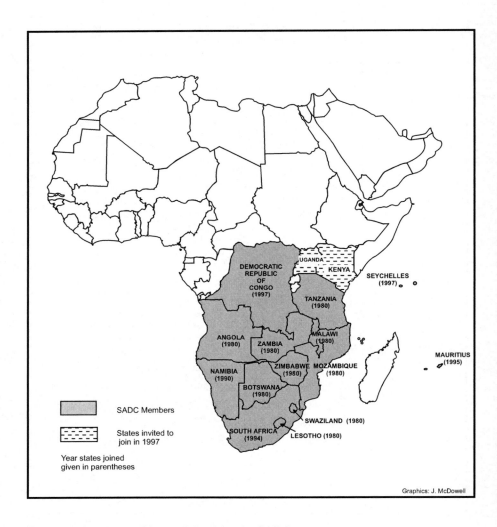

Figure 3: Southern Africa as defined by the SADC

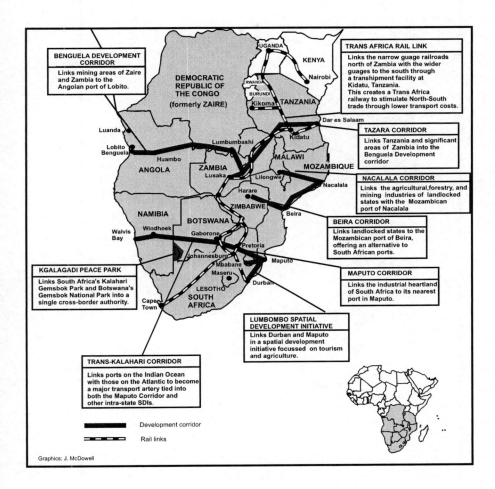

Figure 4: Spatial development initiatives in southern Africa

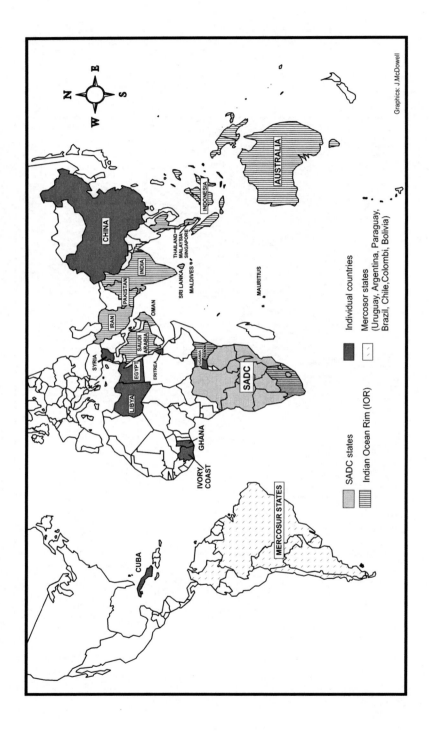

Figure 5: Emerging south–south political and economic alliances

REFERENCES

Abdul-Raheem, T. (1997) 'Is Africa being recolonised?', *Southern African Political Economy Monthly*, Vol. 10 (8), 15 June: 5–7.

Africa News Online (1997) 'Mugabe Says "Renaissance" Taking Place Across Africa', http://www.africanews.org/atlarge/stories/19970925.

ANC (African National Congress) (1998) 'Developing a strategic perspective on South African Foreign Policy', Discussion Paper, December.

Barber, S. (1997) 'Taking a leading role on the African stage', *Sunday Times*, 27 April: 16.

Barber, S. (1998) 'New US trading protocol for SADC', *Business Day*, 3 July: 2.

Boahen, A. A. (1971) *African Perspectives on Colonialism*, Baltimore: John Hopkins University Press.

Chomsky, N. (1997) 'The tyranny of globalisation', *Mail and Guardian*, 13 June: 24–25.

DeSarkar, D. (1998) 'Call to cancel Africa's debt', *Sunday Tribune*, 17 May: 18.

Dludlu, J. (1998) 'African countries fight to keep control of continental bank', *Business Day*, 2 June: 9.

Dow Jones (1998) 'Chiluba pursues debt relief', *Business Day*, 19 May: 5.

Electronic Mail and Guardian (1997) 'A closer World Bank look at Southern Africa', http://www.mg.co.za.mg/news, 1 October.

Finance Africa (1997) 'Telecommunications in Africa', November–December: 36–37.

Fine, A. (1998) 'Region's window of opportunity opens', *Business Day*, 21 May: 17.

Galli, P. (1998) 'SA falls off the radar screens of investors in emerging markets', *Sunday Independent Business News*, 14 July: 5.

Gibb, R. (1997) 'Regional Integration in Post-Apartheid South Africa: The Case of Renegotiating the Southern African Customs Union', *Journal of Southern African Studies* 23 (1): 67–86.

Griggs, R. (1997) 'The Boundaries of an African Renaissance', *Boundary and Security Bulletin* 5 (2), Spring: 64–68.

Hammond, S. (1998) *The Sunday Independent Reconstruct*, 14 June: 1.

Hannerz U. (1990) 'Cosmopolitans and locals in world culture', *Theory, Culture, and Society* 7 (2): 237–252.

Hartnack, M. (1998) 'IMF carrot needs some more stick', *Business Day*, 4 June: 9.

Hirst, P. (1997) 'The Global Economy – Myths and Realities', *International Affairs* 73 (3): 409–425.

Hlophe, N. (1998) 'Top rating for toll road', *Mercury Business Report*, 8 June: 1.

Holman, M. (1998) 'Satellite halo lets Africa dial the world', *Sunday Times Business Times*, 19 April: 11.

Huntington, S. (1996) *The Clash of Civilizations and the Remaking of the World Order*, New York: Simon and Schuster.

International Finance Corporation (1998) 'Blows to Trade Flows', *Business in Africa*, Vol. 6 (3), June: 15–17.

Lamont, J. (1998) 'Pleas for debt relief rebuffed', *Mercury Business Report*, 19 May: 19.

Leshilo, T. (1998) 'Botswana the world's fastest growth economy', *Mercury Business Report*, 17 April: 5.

Lipschutz, R. (1992) 'Reconstructing world politics: the emergence of global civil society', *Millennium* 21 (3): 389–421.

Machipisa, L. (1998) 'Little to smile about', *Sowetan*, 26 May: 10.

Marden, P. (1997) 'Geographies of dissent: globalisation, identity and the nation', *Political Geography* 16 (1): 37–64.

Mbaku, J. M. (1997) 'Africa in the Post-Cold War Era: Three Strategies for Survival', *Journal of Asian and African Studies* 32 (3, 4): 222–244.

McGeary, J. and Michaels, M. (1998) 'Africa Rising', *Time Magazine*, 151 (13): 38-48.

McNeill, W. (1982) *The Pursuit of Power*, University of Chicago Press.

Mills, G. (1998) 'The SADC has to learn from Mercosur', *Business Day*, 2 June: 9.

Misser, F. (1998) 'Lissouba sues French Oil Company', *New African*, April: 33.

Mlinar, Z. (1992) *Globalisation and Territorial Identities*, Aldershot: Avebury.

Natal Witness (1998) 'Row over Africa's Debt', 19 May: 1.

Ngidi, T. (1998) 'Professor Kwesi Kwaa Prah, leading academic, activist, gun-runner, and Pan-Africanist, gives his views on Thabo Mbeki's "African renaissance"', *Sunday Tribune*, 31 May: 26.

O'Grady, K. (1997) 'Africa facing a hard slog into a bright future says Nyerere', *Business Day*, 17 October: 14.

Ohmae, K. (1990) *The Borderless World*, London: Collins.

Ohmae, K. (1995) *The End of the Nation-State: The Rise of Regional Economies*, London: Harper-Collins.

Parliament of the Republic of South Africa (1995) *Report of the Portfolio Committee on Foreign Affairs*, 10 May.

Ramano, M. (1998) 'The new African revolution: from state to private sector ownership', *World Trade and Investment*, January: 8.

Robertson, D. (1998) 'Indian Ocean countries largely isolated from major trading blocs', *Sunday Times Business Times*, 3 May: 7.

Sachs, J. (1998) 'International Economics: Unlocking the Mysteries of Globalisation', *Foreign Policy* 110: 97–111.

Sapa (1998) 'Chinese Private Sector Earmarks 30 New Projects in SA', http://www.anc.org.za/ancdocs/briefing/nw1990407/23.html

Sassen, S. (1996) *Losing Control? Sovereignty in an Age of Globalisation*, New York: Columbia University Press.

Seale, T. (1997) 'Mandela's ode to a rising Africa', *Daily News*, 16 July: 12.

Seale, T. (1998) '"African renaissance" takes off', *Daily News*, 20 March: 12.

Shapiro, M. J. & Alker, H. R. (1996) *Challenging Boundaries: Global Flows and Territorial Identities*, Minneapolis: University of Minneapolis Press.

Simon, B. (1997) 'World Bank makes regional integration a priority', *Business Day*, 1 October: 3.

Slater, D. (1997) 'Geopolitical imaginations across the north–south divide: issues of difference, development and power', *Political Geography* 16 (8): 631–653.

Spira, J. (1998) 'Foreigners look east rather than south to invest', *Cape Times*, 19 April.

The Mercury (1998), 'Mandela, Castro slam rich states', *The Mercury*, 20 May: 2.

13
Frontiers, Identity and Security in Europe:
An Agenda for Research[1]

Malcolm Anderson, Didier Bigo and Eberhard Bort

INTRODUCTION

Since the fall of the Berlin Wall, frontiers have reappeared in the political and academic discourse on Europe. New international frontiers have been created and others have fundamentally changed their function, particularly in the case of the former Iron Curtain. At the same time, the rhetoric about a borderless Europe (i.e. the European Union) has been, at least partly, translated into reality, since the implementation in March 1995 of the 1985 and 1990 Schengen Agreements.

Yet open borders are not solely seen as a positive development; they are also accompanied by anxiety and even fear. Will open borders be an invitation for criminals to cross freely and for illegal immigrants to move easily between one European country and another? According to the Schengen process, the abolition of border controls at the internal frontiers must be matched by a standardised strengthening of controls at the external frontiers of 'Schengen-land'. Does that mean that the eastern frontier of the European Union (EU), opened in 1989–90 from the east, is subsequently experiencing a degree of closure from the west? How does that affect attempts at developing institutionalised cross-border cooperation along that frontier?

All the eastern neighbours of the EU have applied for membership. Five of these applicant states (Poland, the Czech Republic, Hungary, Slovenia and Estonia) began negotiations for accession in 1998. Most of the erstwhile Iron Curtain that forms the current eastern frontier of the EU (the exception being that part of the Iron Curtain which ran through the middle of Germany) is destined to become an internal EU boundary in the first decade of the new millennium.

Part of the accession process is the demand by EU member states and by the EU itself that the applicant states police their eastern frontier efficiently. Schengen standards, in other words, are being exported eastwards in order to secure the future eastern frontier of the EU.

The main issues at stake are immigration and crime which are being made, with or without good reason, into a single, general problem. Against the backdrop of an economic divide which is even deeper at the southern frontier of the EU than along its eastern borders and which is replicated at the future eastern frontier of the EU, organised crime, both in smuggling of illegal goods

Borderlands Under Stress (M.A. Pratt and J.A. Brown (eds), ISBN 90-411-9790-7).
© Kluwer Law International, 2000.

and illegal persons, is perceived as a threat to Western societies. Economic divides are seen as hampering cooperation, particularly police and border-guard cooperation; in many areas where fragile neighbouring regimes, like the Ukraine, cannot even pay their frontier guards, corruption blurs the boundaries between the so-called forces of law and order and the lawbreakers.

It is anticipated that minority problems (e.g. 600,000 Hungarians live in Slovakia, 2.7 million in Romania)[2] may be exacerbated by the new dividing Schengen frontiers if, for example, Hungary is accepted into the EU but its neighbours are denied membership. As the wars in the Balkans – from Croatia and Bosnia–Hercegovina to Kosovo and Albania – have demonstrated, this could in turn produce further migratory pressure.

The result is an intricate, sometimes unclear or even contradictory picture of the conflicting functions of frontiers – especially the external frontiers and the anticipated future frontiers of the EU – with states torn between enhanced cooperation and integration (requiring open frontiers) and the perceived need for strict controls (requiring limits to this openness). This confusion produces a political discourse which highlights the issue of migration and the need for harmonised and strict identity controls and police cooperation at the borders, in border zones, and far beyond national frontiers – a need for what has been called a return to spatial approaches to security and control.

This paper will look at the research agenda required to analyse this situation. A geopolitical tour of some of the critical parts of the EU's external frontier and its hinterland serves as an introduction to the field of research on frontiers, security and identity.

THE SOUTHERN FRONTIER

While migration from the east is seen as putting pressure particularly on the German frontiers, migration from the south is mainly aimed at France. It is estimated that there are already more than two million immigrants from North Africa in the EU – 70 per cent of them in France. Most of them are legal immigrants. The *Front National* may allege that there are 1.5 million illegals living in France, but this figure seems wildly exaggerated. There is a partial amnesty in France, and 143,000 illegals (known as '*sans papiers*') have applied for regularisation. There is a consensus that perhaps the same number again have not come forward for residence papers. It would be reasonable to estimate from this that there are a maximum of 300,000 illegals in France. The migratory potential of North Africa is difficult to quantify but, again referring to the analysis of the secret services, if only every fifth of the currently unemployed young men between 20 and 30 years of age should decide to emigrate from North Africa, this would add up to another million immigrants in the EU. There is, therefore, strong migratory pressure from the south and a determination by the EU member states, apparently backed by public opinion, to resist this by all practical means.

The disparities in what are sometimes referred to as the three Ds – demography, development and democracy – between the northern and southern shores of the Mediterranean make cooperation in the fields of immigration and crime control much more difficult. The dynamic demographic growth on the southern shore, which contrasts with demographic stagnation or decline on the northern, the huge disparity in all the indicators of economic prosperity between south and north, and the lack of freedom and democracy and sometimes repressive nature of the regimes on the southern shore combine to make the Mediterranean 'Europe's Rio Grande' (King, 1998).

Tighter immigration controls – identified with the Schengen system but not restricted to it (*vide* the United Kingdom which remains outside because the Schengen controls are not considered sufficiently clear) – have brought about a situation of uncertainty and sometimes provoked resentment in the countries of emigration with long connections with European countries. The free movement between France and the Maghreb states has long disappeared, but the French drive since 1974 to restrict immigration, combined with Schengen, inevitably placed tighter controls on movement between these states, despite the large resident population of North African origin in France. The French aim, proclaimed in 1993 by Interior Minister Charles Pasqua, of zero immigration proved to be impractical. France has continued to naturalise about 100,000 foreigners a year; people have been admitted to the country legally for reasons of family re-groupment, asylum and study and skill shortages; in addition, many people have found their way to France illegally. In 1998 even Pasqua was forced to admit that frontier controls were not effective against people determined to enter the country, and he advocated, in a change of position which many found surprising, that most of those without legal residence should have their position regularised. The objective of a hermetically sealed frontier is, as Pasqua admitted, an impractical one.

Fairly tight controls on immigration into the EU are, however, politically inevitable, given the anti-immigrant feeling in public opinion, particularly in the more northern European countries. Such feeling is also developing in the southern countries. In Italy, in particular, the rise of violent crime in the north is blamed on immigrants (Borngässer, 1999a&b). The situation is unlikely to change in the foreseeable future, although tight immigration control may not be in the economic interests of the EU states, because of the unsatisfied demand for labour in certain sectors, and may complicate relationships across the Mediterranean.

The 1985 and 1990 Schengen agreements which came into force in 1995 were designed to cope with the effects of dismantling identity checks at frontiers between member states by strengthening and harmonising checks at the external frontier. Since free movement of persons also implies the free movement of criminals, persons wanted for serious criminal offences, persons in need of protection and general *personae non grata* were reported through the Schengen Information System, available on-line in all the member states and at the major ports of entry to the EU. There are probably now about 45,000 on-line access points and about 14 million records.[3] A rapid-response system (the Sirène offices) was put in place in member states to act in case of any transfrontier criminal threat, or in case additional information was required about persons or about the legality of a request.

This system inevitably had an effect on the neighbouring states of the EU and even on distant states which had privileged relationships with members of the EU (e.g. Latin America with the Iberian states). The Schengen agreements established a visa policy common to all Schengen states, with the result that millions who were previously free to enter Europe freely now required a visa. A further administrative burden for academics and business people from the 120 or so countries requiring visas is caused by the fact that a single visa is required for entry into every Schengen country except the UK and Ireland; a separate visa is required for entry into these states. Cooperation in the field of law enforcement, with the exclusion of the often rudimentary exchange of information through Interpol, exists on a bilateral basis between member and non-member states of the EU, but there is a new system of closer cooperation between the member states in this domain, reinforced by a new, non-operational European police office, Europol, in The Hague.

At a meeting of the ministers of the interior of all 12 Schengen states in Berlin in December 1998, visa harmonisation was declared a top priority. The following aims were agreed:

- to reduce the 'grey list' of countries, whose citizens required visas for some Schengen states but not for others; because of the lack of restriction between the Schengen states, it was easy for such citizens to enter visa-requiring countries via visa-free countries
- to support a 'black list' of countries whose citizens required a visa to enter any Schengen state
- to support a 'white list' of countries whose citizens were free to enter any Schengen state without a visa.

At the same meeting, the ministers decided that control of persons would remain in place at Greece's frontiers, since Greece had not passed the efficiency test of the Schengen inspection group.[4]

THE EASTERN FRONTIER

When Austria and Italy implemented Schengen (between 1 October 1997 and 1 April 1998), the former Iron Curtain, opened from the east in 1989, became the external Schengen frontier of the EU. This was seen as a threat to cross-border relations in the neighbouring states to the east. The trial run of Schengen external frontier controls at the Italian–Slovene border in October 1997 caused considerable disruption (Richter-Malabotta, 1998). Yet by April 1998 the expected barrier has not materialised – at least, not to the extent expected (Gasperlin, 1997). The Slovenian border authorities had taken the Schengen threat seriously and persuaded their own government to adopt the Schengen criteria (of identity and customs checks) at their Croatian frontier, and convinced the Italian, Austrian and EU authorities that Slovenia had – practically – implemented Schengen, without being part of it, at its external, non-EU frontiers. This made it possible for border controls with Italy and Austria to remain relatively flexible, even after Schengen had become fully operational on 1 April 1998.

However, this does not obscure the unease which is being felt beyond the EU's external frontier about the Schengen process. From Poland to Slovenia, there is concern at having to implement Schengen norms that were agreed in negotiations in which these countries had no right to participate.[5] Slovenia may have been successful in saving its partially-open frontiers with Italy and Austria, but there has been a price. As a crossing from Bratislava to Vienna will demonstrate, Slovakia has not been as successful – or, perhaps, has not tried as hard to implement Schengen-type frontier controls at its eastern frontier. Long queues are also reported from the Austro-Hungarian borders (Frank, 1999). Hungary, the Czech Republic, Poland and Estonia – those states with whom negotiations for EU accession started in March 1998 – are under increasing pressure to police their eastern frontiers efficiently. This seems to have resulted in far-reaching changes in border controls, particularly in Poland but also in the Czech Republic and Hungary.

These changes have not been without implication; for example, the closure of the Hungarian–Romanian frontier has gravely affected the large Hungarian minority in Romania. The economic price of these measures is heavy. In east Poland, more than 1,000 local traders rallied against the 'economic catastrophe' caused by tighter border controls. Incomes in eastern border towns have dropped dramatically and unemployment has risen. There has been a sharp fall in trading, not only in the border areas but also at Warsaw's economically important 'Russian bazaar', where trading has fallen by about 30 per cent since the introduction of the new aliens' law and the new visa regime (according to Poland's Market Economy Research Institute, the 1997 turnover of the Warsaw bazaar was in the region of GB£350 million). In the border area of Bialystok alone, 50,000 jobs are dependent on local cross-border trade (Schmidtendorf, 1998). So far, Poland has not followed the demand by EU spokesmen to introduce visa requirements analogous to those of the EU, because the limited restrictions already introduced have affected sales to visitors from Russia and Belarus (and Germany); the informal export trade is estimated to earn Poland GB£5.9bn a year (Traynor, 1998).

But there are also problems of policing, because Poland's eastern neighbours cannot, or will not, cooperate. 'Chaos and corruption' was the recent verdict of the *Süddeutsche Zeitung* regarding the situation at the frontiers between Poland and Kaliningrad in the north, and Lithuania, Belarus and the Ukraine. This verdict applied not necessarily to all control points, but specifically to the large 'green border' – 407km with Belarus and 526km with the Ukraine (*Süddeutsche Zeitung*, 1998b). While in Belarus the army still exercises a measure of control over the border, the Ukrainians are totally deficient in their policing of the border; when Ukrainian frontier guards ceased to receive their salaries in 1997, they were wont to recoup the money by assisting illegal migrants to cross the frontier. However, corruption is reported to be widespread on both sides of the Polish–Ukrainian border (*Süddeutsche Zeitung*, 1998c; Urban, 1998).

As frontiers are only controllable if there is cooperation between the two sides, Poland attempts a delicate balancing act: stabilising and effectively controlling the borders – since 1991, more than 80,000 illegal immigrants have been arrested at the Ukrainian border alone (Kazmierczak & Schmidtendorf, 1999) – but simultaneously avoiding total closure towards the east. On a visit to Bonn in November 1997, Poland's Foreign Secretary, Bronislaw Geremek, stressed that: 'Poland, too, does not want barriers at its eastern frontiers.'[6] The Polish Minister for Europe, Ryszard Carnecki, drew the image of a tightly controlled border which could, at the same time, function as a bridge to the large markets of Russia, Belarus and the Ukraine. Stabilising the states which have emerged from the rubble of the Soviet Union, he stated, must be in both Poland's and the West's interest (*Süddeutsche Zeitung*, 1998d).

Marek Bienkowski, in charge of the Polish border guards, announced the building of 15 new border crossings on the eastern frontier by 2001, along with an increase in the number of border guards and the installation, aided by EU PHARE money, of electronic passport-reading equipment at border check-points.[7] Poland introduced a new aliens law at the beginning of 1998 which led to protests from Russia; several border crossings were blocked by Russians and Belarus withdrew its ambassador from Warsaw. But there is also protest from Polish traders who depend on cross-border traffic. Ukrainians and Lithuanians must now prove that they have sufficient means to sustain themselves in Poland. Russians and Belarussians must have Polish invitations or pre-paid hotel-vouchers before they are allowed to cross into Poland (Traynor, 1998).

Clearly, the Schengen agreements cast a shadow beyond the borders of the current EU. The EU Commissioner in charge of the Single Market, Mario Monti, told the Polish government that Poland's chances of joining the EU depended to a great extent on how well it could police its borders. The strengthening of Poland's eastern frontier is seen – particularly in Germany – as an attempt to erect the first serious obstacle to illegal immigration and illegal trade from east to west. To be more effective in doing this, Poland aspires to become a member of the EU and of the Schengen accord, with access to the Schengen Information System (SIS) at Strasbourg.

The Saxon Minister for the Interior supported the wish of applicant states in east and central European countries to participate in the SIS and maintained that a full link to the Strasbourg-based computer system could be established by mid-1999 (*Statewatch*, 1997). Yet the SIS computer cannot cope with the Scandinavian enlargement of Schengen, let alone extension to the east. The system needs to be redesigned and equipped; the new, revamped system is not expected until around 2003.

In January 1998 the Czech Republic listed 12 countries – including the

Ukraine, Russia and Belarus – for which it would introduce visa requirements. However, by the end of that year it had not acted upon this intention. Immediately after the opening of the border, the Czech Republic started a programme of renovating and enlarging border-crossings along the 810km frontier with Germany; this has led to Rozvadov/Waidhaus now functioning as a motorway crossing.

The number of illegal immigrants arrested at the Czech–German border reached 43,000 in 1993, but by 1995 had declined to 19,000, nearly the same level as in 1991. Initially, the new international frontier between the Czech Republic and Slovakia (established at the beginning of 1993) was credited with this reduction; it was claimed that the new border acted as a filter for the Czech–German frontier (Bort, 1996). However, there seems to be reluctance on both sides of that new frontier to introduce rigorous measures – hardly anybody in the area can envisage the Czech–Slovak border as a future external frontier of the EU (Brod, 1998) – and since 1996 the number of illegal immigrants has risen again. The Department of Migration in Prague now puts the temporary decline in arrests down to the drastic tightening of the German asylum laws in 1993; in 1997 there were 29,339 arrests and in 1998 the total was 32,859.[8] Among those arrested were illegal immigrants from further east and from Turkey. However, since the beginning of the Kosovo crisis, the bulk of the immigrants have been ethnic Albanians from Kosovo, via what the Czech police call a 'human-smuggling pipeline running through the former Czechoslovakia' (Connolly, 1998). Kosovo Albanians and other refugees from the former Yugoslavia are, in most cases, bound for Germany, where 'colonies' of their compatriots already exist. Germany is the destination of 72.2 per cent of the illegal immigrants, and 60 per cent of them cross into Saxony. Mostly, they try to cross in groups, paying up to GB£5,000 for the services of organised human smugglers. Between January and September 1998 more than 650 'Schleuser' (criminal human traffickers) were arrested at this border.[9] To get a better perspective on these figures, they must be viewed against the backdrop of no less than 210 million legal crossings of the Czech frontiers in 1997.

Cooperation between the border authorities in Germany, Poland and the Czech Republic seems better developed – regular meetings, comparing notes, frequent communications, common training and exchanges – than further south. For example, at the Austrian–Slovak crossing of Berg/Bratislava communication between the two sides is rare and often has to be conducted indirectly via Vienna and Bratislava. Long queues have been reported at the Austro–Hungarian border (historically one of the most symbolic of European frontiers) since Schengen was fully implemented by Austria on 1 April 1998; they have been attributed to the Austrian border police, a new police force with a 'martial outlook' (Frank, 1999).

Using European PHARE money,[10] Hungary has undertaken to open three new border-crossings on its Romanian border, two on its Ukrainian border and one on the Slovene border, and to upgrade Rajika on the Slovak border as a motorway crossing. As mentioned earlier, if Hungary joins the EU (and

Schengen, which was integrated into the *acquis communautaire* by the 1997 Amsterdam Treaty on European Union) a sizeable Hungarian minority in Slovakia and Romania will be left stranded. And while Slovakia, with its new government after Meciar, might rejoin the 'fast-track route' to EU membership (Gillespie, 1999b), there is little hope that Romania will do likewise. It is also noteworthy that not all the refugees from ex-Yugoslavia are heading west; by the autumn of 1998, more than 300,000 ethnic Hungarians had fled Serbia and moved across the border into Hungary (Long, 1998).

Estonia, the fifth applicant state likely to be an early entrant to the EU, is also in a difficult position. Like the other candidates for EU membership, Estonia is under pressure to strengthen its border controls and bring them in line with Schengen procedures. However, this could create difficulties if it is not synchronised with Latvia and Lithuania. Moreover, Estonia is on extremely bad terms with Russia, mainly, the Russians argue, because of the precarious status of the Russian third of the Estonian population, who are discriminated against in terms of language, minority and citizenship rights. This Russian concern is shared by the EU and the Council of Europe. Estonians counter that Russia has unilaterally fortified the border, contrary to international practice (borders are traditionally demarcated in consultation with neighbours). This border was formerly a purely administrative border between two Soviet republics, and was the result of an imperial transfer of territory after the Second World War, when Stalin forced a large strip of eastern Estonia to be ceded to Russia. Even after the fall of communism, Russia has insisted on maintaining this borderline and, in compliance with the EU conditions for accession – i.e. no claims are to be made to foreign territory – Estonia has relented. However, Russia continues to refuse to sign the negotiated settlement; according to Estonia, she is attempting to keep all her options open.

It is a highly 'unnatural' and martial border (leading, in one case, straight through the middle of an Estonian house), characterised by watchtowers, barbed wire and a no-man's land. For some commentators it is reminiscent of the Iron Curtain. The situation is further exacerbated by the fact that the Russian border region of Pskov has returned an ultra-nationalist from Zhirinovsky's LDPR party as regional governor; this party calls for the restoration of the Soviet-era borders.

Russia is still determined to block any move by the Baltic states to become members of NATO and has instead proposed a 'Pact of Regional Security and Stability'. However, by October 1997 only Lithuania had signed a border treaty with Russia.

All the Baltic states are regarded as highly permeable transit countries for illegal immigrants. But in view of EU enlargement, potential legal labour migration within an enlarged EU has also caused concern, particularly among Conservative politicians in Germany who see huge problems if EU enlargement towards the east does not go hand in hand with a very long transition period before the introduction of free movement of people. They argue that 340,000 to 680,000 additional work migrants a year would put pressure on the ailing labour markets of western Europe. The Christian Democrats have therefore demanded that freedom of movement only become operational by 2015 at the earliest (Lambeck, 1998). The Bavarian government orchestrated these fears by stating that they expected another two million ethnic Germans from the former Soviet Union to exercise their right to come to Germany (Schmitt, 1999). The debate about changes in citizenship laws proposed by the new German 'red-green' government, and particularly the proposal of dual citizenship (*The Scotsman*, 1998), have given rise to highly speculative figures concerning a potentially massive influx of relatives of foreigners with dual citizenship into Germany, especially from Turkey.[11] Politicians of the Bavarian CSU have come up with a figure of up to 600,000 additional immigrants. Yet, as Klaus Barwig has shown, this is a 'horror scenario' without any foundation; he calculates a realistic number as being closer to 4,000![12]

But this is not just a phenomenon of the German right. People in the Austrian borderlands, for example, appear to be more than a little reluctant to welcome Hungary into the EU:

> Many Austrians actively oppose it, especially those living in border regions such as Burgenland, in the belief that free labour migration will endanger their jobs and an increased flow of refugees put pressure on already stretched Austrian capacity to receive the 500,000 or so people they have absorbed in recent years. (Gillespie, 1999a.)

Yet, all these figures, and the fears based on them, seem to ignore the fact that, in Germany for instance, the data for 1997 indicates that more foreigners left the country than entered it; 615,000 new arrivals were outnumbered by 637,000 who left (*Die Welt*, 1998). They also seem to ignore the fact that the 'wave' of labour migration predicted when Spain and Portugal joined the EU did not materialise.[13]

A final paradox is that policing internal as well as external frontiers has resulted in the creation of border zones – sometimes referred to as a return of the *limes* (Foucher, 1998) – in which random checks are allowed.[14] In April 1997 the Austrian Secretary of State in the Ministry of the Interior revealed that with the implementation of Schengen in October 1997 a 30km-wide 'security veil' would be installed along the German border, with a significantly increased police presence, and that German police could pursue criminals into Austria, unlimited by space and time (Pándi, 1998). Dr Horst Eisel, Assistant Director for Frontiers at the German Ministry of Internal Affairs, has put it thus:

> The spatial approach clearly ought to take precedence over the purely linear approach to geographic boundaries. The latter is no longer appropriate for today's challenges, because individual and collective security begins beyond our borders and continues well on this side of them.[15]

A survey conducted at the University of Hamburg found that new surveillance technologies are detaching the concept of 'border' from its erstwhile geographical connotation, and broadening it into a concept of thresholds, gateways and hurdles, accompanied and made possible by a switch from traditional criminological towards social instruments of surveillance (e.g. biometrical identifiers) and control (Nogala *et al*, 1998).

CROSS-BORDER COOPERATION

Cross-border regionalism has flourished over the past two decades, beginning in the heartlands along the western border of Germany and taking a new step in the 1990s when – in response to the opening of the Iron Curtain – Euro-regions were set up from the Finno–Russian border down to Austria, Slovakia, Hungary and Slovenia (Bort, 1998).

Peripheral borderlands are one of the legacies of the nation-state, particularly along the east–west divide (*vide* the German '*Zonenrandgebiet*'). In the borderlands of Europe the new rhetoric about the lasting importance of the nation-state is viewed with scepticism. Regionalism, and in particular cross-border regionalism, has been seen not only as a challenge to traditional notions of state sovereignty (Bort, 1997), but also as a tool to develop formerly peripheral regions. Wherever possible, Euro-regions are based on common cultural and historical experience; but they are primarily a pragmatic economic enterprise for economic development, funded by the EU's Interreg[16] and PHARE programmes. The Czech Republic, for example, received 340 million ECU through PHARE between 1995 and 1999 (Neuss *et al*, 1998).

The establishment of cross-border cooperation seems to show that a translation of practical concerns from west to east is well underway. The frequently expressed need for cross-border cooperation (environment, infrastructure, tourism and security) is reflected in certain regional reform concepts which devolve planning authority and decision-making processes to the regions. The regional context may also be more conducive to solving the problems of national minorities and even provide regional solutions for international problems. Regionalisation and 'integrated borderlands' (Martinez, 1994), rather than a nineteenth-century model of the nation-state, could offer a more tranquil future for non-homogenous states with large ethnic minorities within their borders.

Cross-border regionalism seemed to develop, for example, in the German–Czech borderlands despite the fraught negotiations between Germany and the Czech Republic concerning the property of, and compensation for, the Sudeten Germans. The accord of January 1997 took nearly a year (and changes in government on both sides) to be fully implemented, but it is generally seen as opening up new opportunities for intensified cross-border cooperation (Schmitt, 1997).

There are, however, reasons for being cautious about a simple transfer of western models to the eastern borderlands. Different centre–periphery relations ought to be considered. Jutta Seidel of the State Chancellery of the Free State of Saxony, speaking about her experience in organising transfrontier cooperation between Saxony and Poland, and Saxony and the Czech Republic, emphasised the initial difficulties which had to be overcome and which resulted from administrative centralisation in the Czech and Polish Republics. According to Frau Seidel, it took years to create trust and a willingness in Warsaw and Prague to allow their western border regions a degree of planning autonomy which would allow them to negotiate directly with their German counterparts.[17]

The potential for conflict between centre and periphery may be exacerbated by the major differences between the situations in the west and the east. While in the west, especially along the German frontier, states with roughly similar wage levels and costs of living started collaborating across their borders after the Second World War, the eastern frontier of the EU became, under the conditions of the Cold War, a profound economic frontier (Langer, 1996; Krämer, 1997). If problems of extreme economic inequality have caused anxieties among the countries bordering the EU to the east about economic and political subordination (Anderson, 1996), are other regions within Poland, the Czech Republic and other central and eastern European countries not confronted by a similar question: why should the regions bordering the EU be privileged by cross-border incentives? In other words, is the newly emerging – perhaps common – identity of the transfrontier regions a forerunner for integrating the whole of the states concerned into the EU, or does it reinforce the considerable disparities between east and west, town and country, within the applicant states? Does it cause resentment against these apparently privileged regions and, by challenging state centralism, threaten the integrity of the state itself (Dauderstädt, 1996)?

On aggregate, cross-border cooperation is undoubtedly deemed to be a positive force, enhancing communication and collaboration, and thus adding to stability and, by implication, to control.[18] In the borderlands, any functional change of frontiers is felt immediately, whether it has been the implementation of Schengen or a consequence of EU accession. Institutionalised cross-border cooperation is a laboratory for these European concepts (Jung, 1998; Bort, 1997b).

The implementation of Schengen and the accession process of central European states to the EU, highlighted by the establishment of these Euro-regions which, in order to function effectively, require a high permeability of borders – the border as bridge, as communicative channel rather than barrier – add up to a confusing, sometimes even contradictory and ambiguous picture of a frontier with elements of both openness and closure (Anderson, 1998).

SECURITISATION

Adding to the complexity described above is the fact that the subject of migration control has become intricately linked with the subject of crime and security and the process of 'securitisation' (Bigo, 1999). This institution of a security continuum which combines the control of frontiers and immigration with the fight against crime, is not a natural response to changes in criminality; it is simply a proactive mixing of crime and immigration issues. In the notorious strategy paper concerning the Geneva Convention, which the Austrian government formulated during Austria's presidency of the EU (and which was withdrawn following severe criticism), the refugee issue was categorised under 'illegal migration' and migration policies were explicitly linked with policies against organised crime (Prantl, 1998).

The images of reinforced borders and a fortress mentality are often invoked when Schengen is criticised, but they are not conceivable as practical solutions for internal security needs. It is undeniable that the security of individuals has become de-territorialised (Bigo, 1999). Internal security now implies collaboration with foreign countries and is thus linked to foreign policy, and the 1980s and 1990s marked the beginning of a public debate on policing which combined the issues of urban insecurity and the need to halt the immigration of unskilled workers (Anderson *et al*, 1995; Sheptycki, 1995 & 1996).

Immigration, not always distinguishing between legal and illegal, has thus become a dominant theme in public debate across Europe. The past few years have seen a barrage of alarming – or, perhaps, more alarmist rather than alarming – news about millions of people waiting to cross the frontiers of Europe, some legally, most of them illegally. In August 1998 it was reported that the secret services (no clearer specification was given) were warning that there was sustained migratory pressure on the EU from the east and from the south (Scherer, 1998). Figures were named: two and a half to three million potential migrants from Russia, Belarus and the Ukraine were intending to emigrate via the Baltic states to Scandinavia; in Kiev alone, 200,000 migrants were reported to be waiting for human traffickers to smuggle them to western Europe; 500,000 migrants were ready to go in Poland; in Turkey, the ultimate aim of up to one million illegal residents is to reach the West. A recent survey published in January 1999 and conducted in all the major sender countries by the European Observatory for Migrations contradicts these prognostications, suggesting that the propensity to emigrate is high, but that the potential immigrants want to go to the US, Canada, Australia and New Zealand rather than to Germany, France or the UK.

What is apparent is that people in Europe seem to harbour an unfocused, general anxiety that frontiers no longer provide the protection they once did. Organised cross-border crime, the trafficking of drugs and other smuggled goods, and organised human trafficking seem to indicate that frontier controls are no longer as effective as they once were. This anxiety may be abating as populations become more accustomed to the absence of frontier controls at the internal frontiers, an absence which is widely welcomed in frontier regions. In general, the French – normally very sensitive to these matters – seem to have adopted a reasonably relaxed attitude about open frontiers, and those living in the frontier regions seem very pleased with the new situation. Law-enforcement agencies seem to have adapted to the new situation without undue difficulty. The nature of frontiers is perceived as changing. New information technology for surveillance and identity control is widely seen as a key factor in securing efficient frontier controls.

The quest for – and the intertwining of – internal and external security, and its potential conflict with the maxim of free movement for EU citizens within the EU, as laid down in the Maastricht and Amsterdam treaties, have to be examined in relation to the means that are employed, especially at the frontiers, for checking identity, and the reasoning behind surveillance. Issues that are raised include democratic control and social cohesion, security and liberty, the process of re-fashioning political obligation (citizen–state), and diplomatic relations between the EU and its neighbours.

FRONTIER CONTROL AND FREE MOVEMENT

Research is needed on the techniques and methods used to monitor who crosses the internal and external frontiers of the EU, and those who reside in this area, and the effects of these controls on the processes of inclusion and exclusion. There are many wide-ranging questions to be asked on these topics.

The Maastricht Treaty and the Schengen agreements appear to promote inclusion by conferring on the citizens of the 15 EU member states the right to move freely within the EU area and, by introducing European citizenship rights, to work more easily in other countries and to participate, within certain limits, in political life. Although these principles are accepted, there are significant variations in practice, according to the implementation of national legislation and/or the local practices of agencies responsible for control. Significant variations may be seen according to the type of frontier crossed (airports, seaports, land borders), the type of person who crosses the frontier (national citizens, citizens of member states and citizens of third countries), where the controls are carried out (at the frontier, within the state territory, in consulates), and the circumstances – war, political violence or international crisis of peace (Gulf War, special anti-terrorist measures such as UK anti-terrorist legislation and Vigipirate in France).

One of the main objectives of research into the connection between frontier and identity controls is to understand how the free movement of people within the European space can be fully effected whilst the practices of control of identity at the frontiers and on national territory vary markedly from one country to another and remain un-harmonised. This is a matter of mapping the effects of convergence criteria to discover the actual control practices and not merely looking at the harmonisation of public policy statements and legal rules. Variations in practices concerning who is controlled and who crosses frontiers uncontrolled, or who travels without identity checks within a state's territory, are a reflection of the images which agencies of control have of citizens and non-citizens, images which do not necessarily coincide with the legal status of these individuals. What, then, are the sentiments of exclusion felt by those who are citizens but who are frequently subject to controls for other reasons? What is the link between frequency of controls and feelings of being placed in a separate category of persons. Do these controls have negative effects on national and European social cohesion? Conversely, does the absence of frontier controls encourage better integration of EU citizens? How are the specific forms of control (e.g. entry formalities, visas) applied to non-EU citizens resident in the European space experienced by them and to what extent are they effective?

It is evident that the practice of controlling identity checks has an effect on the process of integration and exclusion in EU countries, even if it is only one of a number of factors. Until now, no one has attempted to carry out a systematic study of these matters by asking the following empirical questions:

- Who is controlled? On what legal basis, and on what practical criteria? Among the persons crossing the frontier, how are nationals distinguished from other EU citizens or from third- country nationals? How are some individuals controlled and others allowed to pass unchecked? Have the Schengen agreements changed these controls in a major way?
- Who controls? Which agencies are charged with checking entry documents and with identity controls in the national territory of each European country? Is there a privatisation of certain forms of control?
- Where are controls located? If the frontier remains a significant location for controls, Europeanisation has opened the possibility of shifting controls to frontier zones, or so-called high-risk areas or areas with a high proportion of foreign residents. Are these possibilities far removed from the original concept of a free-movement area? The increasing number of joint police stations on the internal frontiers and closer transfrontier police cooperation at the local level has changed the pre-existing situation. Controls are often more mobile than static – are they more efficient now than previously?
- How are the controls carried out? What knowledge, what technologies (e.g. legal, computer, electronic) are deployed? Which agents are charged with administering controls, and according to what criteria? Are the personnel sufficient in numbers and how are crisis situations dealt with? Is there a transfer of knowledge and technology between security agencies in Europe, and what part do European meetings play in this transfer? What are the legal and technological means of protecting civil liberties in the face of national, SIS, Interpol and Europol databases, taking into account information-sharing and the human links between these databases, and also taking into account potential links between the aforementioned databases and those of health and education services, social security administrations and/or banks?
- Why are certain groups controlled more than others? How is an image of 'risk groups' constructed? How are the identities constituted which are imposed or assumed by the groups who feel themselves the main targets of controls?

For each of these questions, national policies at the governmental level and also at the level of the services or administrations involved will have to be evaluated, taking into account outcomes, the convergence criteria adopted and the contradictions to be resolved.

FRONTIERS, SECURITY AND IDENTITY

The themes of frontiers, of security (both internal and external) and of identities is the subject of a large number of studies concerned with history, sociology, political science and international relations.[19] But little work has been done which investigates the interaction between these fields, nor has there been much general analysis. For example, the theme of identities has been much explored in research on exclusion, but often from a very philosophical or social-interactionist perspective. The perceptions of 'otherness', the relations of 'otherness', hardship and discrimination and other matters are frequently discussed in this literature but, paradoxically, controls of identity and the production of identity documents (e.g. national identity cards, passports) have been little examined (Kershen, 1998). There have been few field studies observing control at frontiers or in those urban areas thought by governments to be at risk – still fewer have been conducted since the implementation of the Schengen agreements.

This field of enquiry is fundamental to an understanding of the changes taking place in Europe which affect social identity and the emergence of a European consciousness, and/or encourage the exclusion of non-EU populations and those citizens who closely resemble non-EU citizens in appearance and attitudes. Structural change is very quickly modifying allegiance to the nation-states and these changes extend far beyond the collective psychology and shared knowledge to which the inclusion/exclusion relationship is often too quickly reduced. The questions we are raising from a political science perspective concern the relationship (producing effects both of inclusion and exclusion) between the production of identities, control of identities and surveillance of certain social groups, and the emergence of new cleavages between EU citizens and persons of non-EU origin.

Many studies have shown that immigrants and certain minorities are justifiably the main targets of controls.[20] The focus on immigrants is seen in the converging observations of immigrant communities, the introduction of particular legal categories, the establishment of statistical correlations between crime and immigrants, drugs and immigrants and un- or under-employment and immigrants, and immigrants subverting the welfare state and the rule of law. But it has been too hastily assumed that criteria categorising immigrant groups and citizens are clear and easily applied by the agencies of control. This is not the case. From this starting point, the focus will be on the effects on immigrants and minority groups of the extension of control procedures at frontiers, in public places and by social, educational and health administrations. These controls could touch on the interests of all citizens if even a part of the rhetorical demands of various politicians are implemented in the name of the search for security and the fight against clandestine immigration.

The quest for internal and external security will have to be examined in relation to what it involves, especially at the frontiers, for the procedures of control and the reasoning behind surveillance (Bigo, 1996). The contrast between the creation of a free-movement area and the tendency towards closure of frontiers will have to be analysed, especially as expressed in specific forms of surveillance. The economic dimension of the flow of persons often restricts the implementation of policies reinforcing security. Beliefs in a climate of insecurity (produced by international disorder, internal difficulties and risks of urban disorder) have the same tendency because the compensatory measures implemented are often considered insufficient. In manipulating notions of frontiers and citizenship, civil servants in charge of implementing free movement often undoubtedly have the impression of treating difficult but resolvable technical and organisational questions. But in considering these matters, they are touching on forms of legitimisation, and of symbolic power relating to the political obligation of citizens to the nation-states. They call into question relations of authority, obedience and, to some extent, the allocation of resources between citizens and governments.

On the basis of these observations we propose, as a working hypothesis, that the control of identity documents goes far beyond matters to do with the management of organisations. It is crucial in the process of re-articulation of political obligation, and a central theme in diplomatic relations between states within the EU and between the EU and its neighbours. If we are experiencing a certain 'de-territorialisation' of controls and some transnationalisation of the controlling bureaucracies charged with analysing and anticipating the flows of people, we are also witnessing a new security/liberty equilibrium, mainly at the European level. The resulting issues of democratic control and social cohesion are largely unexplored. This observation leads to the second main objective of our study: an assessment of the changes in the methods of identity control, including an analysis of the democratic basis of these controls and the accountability of those who administer them.

A COMPARATIVE APPROACH

There is a tendency, because of the absence of a comparative approach, to impute blame to Europeanisation and to free movement for encouraging racism and the phenomenon of exclusion. In doing so, the effects of European integration are confused with the more general phenomena of transnationalisation and globalisation.[21] A comparative study of NAFTA and the Schengen area would provide the means by which to identify the specific effects of Europeanisation on social cohesion and migration, as well as on security policies.

The context of NAFTA and the EU are, of course, very different in terms of institutional framework, public policy, relations between the partners, the scale of the migratory movements across frontiers, and the nature of the frontiers. Nonetheless, some of the problems relating to the control of frontiers and identity are similar. The strategies of American agencies can be usefully compared with various national strategies in Europe. The public language of US federal and state governments can also be compared to the positions adopted by the European Commission and Parliament, and to certain national governments in Europe. The dynamics of inclusion and exclusion and the language used to describe clandestine immigration are also comparable. The crucial benefit of the comparison is that NAFTA rejects the principle of free movement, which is at the heart of the European project, but has relatively similar controls at frontiers and on identities. We therefore have a variable which facilitates a better identification of the uniqueness and real impact of European integration.

AN AGENDA FOR RESEARCH

Finally, six general questions seem to be of outstanding structural importance for a programme of research in this area:

- Which agencies in each country of the EU are charged with identity and frontier controls? These may be found either within public administration or in the private sector (e.g. the passing on of passport control to airline companies). The various administrative agencies may have different terms of reference and legal powers (e.g. police, *gendarmerie*, customs, immigration offices). Controls of identity at the frontier are relatively well-defined but to an increasing extent the fight against clandestine immigrants and a certain public rhetoric suggest extending controlling powers to other agencies (e.g. social security, health, educational institutions). What is the situation in each country? A survey based on direct observation has not yet been carried out, although some documentary sources provide a certain amount of comparative information about which agencies and which legal criteria are involved in control of identity. Comparison with the US–Mexican frontier will undoubtedly help to identify tendencies in coordination between agencies, and in the public language concerning the risks to welfare services posed by clandestine immigrants.
- Which agencies issue identity documents for travel outside and inside countries? Does the absence of the obligation in some countries to carry national identity documents make any difference? Are the citizens of these countries less controlled than others, or are they controlled by other means? British, Nordic and US experiences will be compared with that of countries in which identity cards are obligatory and individuals are frequently asked to show them.
- What are the relationships between the agencies charged with frontier controls, those whose responsibility is control of identity, and those which have more general responsibilities in the field of internal security. How are

the relationships between police, customs, intelligence services and armed forces articulated? How is coordination effected at the national level, at the European level between governments, and at the local transfrontier level between agencies in different countries? The relationships between control of identity, the pro-active strategies of the police, the surveillance of high-risk groups, and military and political intelligence need to be closely studied.

- What is the relationship between the practices of agencies and public policy in the area of repression of clandestine immigration? Is public policy largely symbolic or are agencies given legal powers, adequate personnel and budgets to implement effectively the search for illegal immigrants? What are the national policies concerning transborder flows of people and how do they match Schengen and the European arrangements? The separation of Schengen from EU membership, if countries outside the EU join Schengen, will be considered. What kind of controls could then exist? Would the arrangement of buildings at airports have to be changed again? Comparison with the situation at the US–Mexican frontier will illustrate the scale of transfrontier movement and the methods of control envisaged by the governments.

- Has the European framework resulted in convergence of the practices of the various agencies involved in this field? What are the connections between the different agencies and administrations through informal meetings, Schengen agreements, the Third Pillar, etc? Do governments feel bound by declarations and actions agreed under the Third Pillar? Without the establishment of a European judicial space, is further cooperation possible? What will be the boundary between the First and the Third Pillars after Amsterdam, and will the rationale of controls of frontiers be changed?

- Finally, what would be the impact of putting in place new kinds of frontiers in Europe, frontiers that distinguished clearly between EU citizens and non-Europeans? How would it affect the way they experience their identity on a daily basis, and their allegiances (especially individuals from former colonial territories who had previously enjoyed the right of free movement)?

A 'FUZZY LOGIC'

Migration control may well be a myth (Bigo, 1998) but its connections and associations with the issue of security, problems of citizenship and control of frontiers, particularly in the sensitive field of identity controls, makes it a timely and necessary target for inquiry, particularly – but not exclusively – in relation to the external borderlands of the EU which, with all the ambiguities referred to earlier, are perceived as being under migratory stress.

In a recent article, *The Economist* referred to the different time zones *and* the different economic zones at the Estonian–Russian border (*The Economist*, 1998).

Not only do people on either side of this border live in different actual time zones, but (and they share this experience with many other border regions in east–central Europe) they also live, figuratively speaking, in different time zones – i.e. in different phases of development. And what is true for central Europe might well have implications for the Mediterranean, if at least the moderate goals formulated at the Barcelona Conference of November 1995 are to be translated into reality.

It might help to start with Michel Foucher's notion of borders being 'time inscribed into space or, more appropriately, time written in territories' (Foucher, 1998) – i.e. temporary, functional arrangements – and that in a central Europe which embarked on fundamental changes in 1989–90, 'a "fuzzy logic", less rational but allowing historical transition to take place' (Foucher, 1999) may be a necessary condition with which we have to live for the foreseeable future.

NOTES

1 The research agenda in this paper is based on a proposal submitted to the European Commission's TSER programme. The project, if accepted, will be conducted jointly by FNSP CERI, France (Bigo, Crowley, Tsoukala, Ceyhan, Brousse), University of Edinburgh (ISSI), UK (Anderson, Bort, Cullen, Sheptycki, Raab, Huysmans, Walker), NED Madrid, Spain (Reinares, Jabardo, Miranda, Jimenez, Llamazares), University of Augsburg, Germany (Waldmann, Schmid, Guggemos, Lenz), University of Gent, Belgium (Can Outrive, Ponsaers, Klinckhamers), University of Klagenfurt, Austria (Langer, Vendrey), University of Panteion, Greece (Papastamou, Lekkas, Koskinas) University of Joensuu, Finland (Hayrynen).

2 Paul Gillespie uses the figure of 2.7 million for Romania (Gillespie, 1999a); Romanian sources, citing the census of 1992, speak of 1.62 million Hungarians living in Romania. Jürgen Nowak also gives the estimated figure of 570,000 Hungarians in Slovakia, according to the census of 1991 (Nowak, 1994). Alasdair Stewart gives the Hungarian minority in Romania as 'numbering some 2m' (Stewart, 1992). See also Schöpflin (1993) and Dunay (1997) who both tend towards the unofficial figure of two million.

3 Evidence to the House of Lords, Select Committee on European Communities Sub-Committee F, 9 January 1999.

4 Greece started to participate in the Schengen procedures on 1 December 1997. See *Süddeutsche Zeitung*, 1998a.

5 A point emphasised by Jazek Sayusz-Wolski in a lecture for the Europa Institute in Edinburgh on 30 April 1998.

6 Quoted in *Süddeutsche Zeitung*, 1997.

7 The EU is supporting the modernisation of Polish frontier surveillance technology with nearly GB£30 million. See Schmidtendorf (1998).

8 Information received from Milos Mrkvica, Head of the Migration Group in the Directorate of the Alien and Border Police Service, Prague.

9 Figures supplied by Dr Milos Mrkvica, interviewed by E. Bort, Prague, 24 September 1998. See also Fietz (1998).

10 The Phare Programme is the European Union's initiative which provides grant finance to support its partner countries in Central and Eastern Europe through the process of economic transformation and strengthening of democracy to the stage where they are ready to assume the obligations of membership of the European Union.

11 For the background, see Klusmeyer (1993).

12 Klaus Barmer, a migration expert of the Catholic Academy of Stuttgart-Hohenheim, quoted in Prantl, 1999.

13 Kneissl (1998). It is perhaps worth mentioning that Paris became the second largest Portuguese city before labour mobility was possible because the French did not use drastic measures to remove any undocumented Portuguese.

14 Generally speaking, Schengen envisages a 20km border zone, but in reality the whole of Bavaria, for example, is now defined as a 'border zone'.

15 Quoted in Molle, 1996.

16 The Interreg Community Initiative, which was adopted for the first time in 1990, was intended to prepare border areas for a community without frontiers. The central aim of the Interreg II programmes is to develop cross-border co-operation and help areas on the Union's internal as well as external borders to overcome their specific problems arising from their comparatively isolated position *vis-à-vis* other national economies and the Union as a whole.

17 Jutta Seidel, in conversation with Malcolm Anderson and Eberhard Bort, Edinburgh, 13 May 1996.

18 Particularly in an external and comparative perspective, as in Asiwaju (1996).

19 See, for example, Malchus (1975); Barth (1969); Strassoldo (1970); Tägil (1977); Strassoldo & Delli Zotti (1982); Anderson (1983); Cohen (1986); Day (1987); Prescott (1987); Foucher (1990); Donnan & Wilson (1994); Raich (1995); Anderson (1996b); O'Dowd & Wilson (1996); Éger & Langer (1996); Ganster *et al* (1997); Krämer (1997); Brunn & Schmitt-Egner (1998); Neuss *et al* (1998); Anderson & Bort (1998).

20 See, for instance, the two special numbers of *Cultures et Conflits* (1996 & 1997).

21 Fear of globalisation seems most acute in France, where the French way of managing the economy and French culture are widely thought to be at stake. The most striking symptom of this anxiety was that V. Forrester's *L'Horreur Economique* remained on the bestseller list for several months in 1997–98.

REFERENCES

Anderson, M. & Bort, E. (eds.) (1996) *Boundaries and Identities: The Eastern Frontier of the European Union*, Edinburgh: ISSI: 61–62.

Anderson, M. & Bort, E. (eds.) (1997) *Schengen and EU Enlargement: Security and Cooperation at the Eastern Frontier of the European Union*, Edinburgh: ISSI.

Anderson, M. & Bort, E. (eds.) (1998) *The Frontiers of Europe*, London: Pinter.

Anderson, M. (1996) *Frontiers: Territory and State Formation in the Modern World*, Cambridge: Polity.

Anderson, M. (1998) 'Transfrontier Cooperation – History and Theory' in Brunn, G. & Schmitt-Egner, P. (eds.) *Grenzüberschreitende Zusammenarbeit in Europa: Theorie–Empirie–Praxis*, Baden-Baden: Nomos: 78–97.

Anderson, M. (ed.) (1983) *Frontier Regions in Western Europe*, London: Frank Cass.

Anderson, M., den Boer, M., Cullen, P., Gilmore, W., Raab, C. & Walker, N. (1995) *Policing the European Union: Theory, Law and Practice*, Oxford: Clarendon Press.

Asiwaju, A. (1996) 'Public Policy for Overcoming Marginalization: Borderlands in Africa, North America and Western Europe' in Nolutshungu, S. (ed.) *Margins of Insecurity: Minorities and International Security*, Rochester, NY: Rochester University Press: 251–83; especially 272–78.

Barth, F. (ed.) (1969) *Ethnic Groups and Boundaries*, London: Allen and Unwin.

Bigo, D. (1996) *Polices en réseaux: l'expérience européenne*, Paris: Presses de Science Po.

Bigo, D. (1998) 'Frontiers and Security in the European Union: The Illusion of Migration Control' in Anderson, M. & Bort, E. (eds.) *The Frontiers of Europe*, London: Pinter: 148–64.

Bigo, D. (1999) 'The Landscape of Police Cooperation' in Bort, E. & Keat, R. (eds.) *The Boundaries of Understanding*, Edinburgh: ISSI.

Borngässer, R. (1999a) 'Wieder fliehen Tausende übers Meer', *Die Welt*, 26 January.

Bort, E. (1996) 'Coping with a New Situation' in Anderson, M. & Bort, E. (eds.) *Boundaries and Identities: The Eastern Frontier of the European Union*, Edinburgh: ISSI: 61–62.

Bort, E. (1997a) 'Crossing the EU Frontier: Eastern Enlargement of the EU, Cross-Border Regionalism and State Sovereignty' in *Interregiones* 6: 20–31.

Bort, E. (1997b) 'Boundaries and Identities: Cross-Border Cooperation and the Eastern Frontier of the European Union' in Svob-Dokic, N. (ed.) *The Cultural Identity of Central Europe*, Zagreb: Culturelink/Institute for International Relations: 133–44.

Bort, E. (1998) '*Mitteleuropa*: The Difficult Frontier' in Anderson, M. & Bort, E. (eds.) *The Frontiers of Europe*, London: Pinter: 91–108.

Brod, P. (1998) 'Ideal für illegalen Transit', *Süddeutsche Zeitung*, 31 October.

Brunn, G. & Schmitt-Egner, P. (eds.), *Grenzüberschreitende Zusammenarbeit in Europa–Theorie–Empirie–Praxis*, Baden-Baden: Nomos, 1998.

Cohen, A. P. (ed.) (1986) *Symbolising Boundaries*, Manchester: Manchester University Press.

Connolly, K. (1998) 'Hundreds held in border logjam', *The Guardian*, 9 October.

Cultures et Conflits (1996) 'Circuler, Enfermer, Eloigner', No. 23, Autumn.

Cultures et Conflits (1997) 'Contrôles: Frontières-Identité', No. 26/7, Summer–Autumn.

Dauderstädt, M. (1996), 'Ostmitteleuropas Demokratien im Spannungsfeld von Transformation und Integration' in *Integration* 4/96, October: 208–223.

Day, A. J. (ed.) (1987) *Border and Territorial Disputes*, (2nd edn.), London: Keesings Reference Publications.

Die Welt (1998) 'Immer mehr Ausländer verlassen Deutschland', 31 July.

Donnan, H. & Wilson, T. (eds.) (1994) *Border Approaches*, Lanham, MD: University Press of America.

Dunay, P. (1997) 'Hungarian–Romanian Relations: A Changed Paradigm?', *Chaillot Papers*, No. 26, Paris: Institute for Security Studies of WEU, June: 6.

Éger, G. & Langer, J. (eds.) (1996) *Border, Region and Ethnicity in Central Europe*, Klagenfurt: Norea: 49–67.

Fietz, M. (1998) 'Warum Tschechien in seine Grenzen investieren muß', *Die Welt*, 20 October.

Forrester, V. (1996) *L'Horreur Economique*, Paris: Fayard

Foucher, M. (1990) *Fronts et Frontières, un tour du monde géopolitique*, Paris: Fayard.

Foucher, M. (1998) 'The Geopolitics of European Frontiers' in Anderson, M. & Bort, E. (eds.) *The Frontiers of Europe*, London: Pinter: 235–50.

Foucher, M. (1999) 'Europe and its Long-lasting Variable Geography' in Bort, E. & Keat, R. (eds.) *The Boundaries of Understanding*, Edinburgh: ISSI: 163-69.

Frank, M. (1999) 'Da gerät Europa an seine Grenzen', *Süddeutsche Zeitung*, 5 January.

Ganster, P., Sweedler, A., Scott, J. & Eberwein, W-D. (eds.) (1997) *Borders and Border Regions in Europe and North America*, San Diego: San Diego State University Press.

Gasperlin, M. (1997) 'Schengen needs Modification: A Slovenian Perspective' in Anderson, M. & Bort, E. (eds.) *Schengen and EU Enlargement: Security and Cooperation at the Eastern Frontier of the European Union*, Edinburgh: ISSI: 102–103.

Gillespie, P. (1999a) 'Hungary presses reluctant EU for accession date', *The Irish Times*, 16 January.

Gillespie, P. (1999b) 'Not much success as Czechs find fruits of democracy sour', *The Irish Times*, 9 January.

Jung, W. (1998) 'Grenzverkehr', *Süddeutsche Zeitung*, 11 November.

Kazmierczak, M. & Schmidtendorf, H. (1999) 'Polen wirbt im Westen für die Ukraine', *Die Welt*, 2 January.

Kershen, A. J. (1998) (ed.) *A Question of Identity*, Aldershot: Ashgate.

King, R. (1998) 'The Mediterranean: Europe's Rio Grande' in Anderson, M. & Bort, E. (eds.) *The Frontiers of Europe*, London: Pinter: 109–34.

Klusmeyer, D. B. (1993) 'Aliens, Immigrants, and Citizens: The Politics of Inclusion in the Federal Republic of Germany' in *Daedalus*, 122, 3: 81–114.

Kneissl, K. (1998) 'Die Grenze im Kopf wird lange bleiben', *Die Welt*, 24 October.

Krämer, R. (1997) *Grenzen der Europäischen Union*, Potsdam: Brandenburgische Landeszentrale für Politische Bildung: particularly 68–88.

Krämer, R. (1997) *Grenzen der Europäischen Union*, Potsdam: Brandenburgische Landeszentrale für Politische Bildung.

Lambeck, M. S. (1998) 'Union sieht Gefahren bei Ost-Erweiterung', *Die Welt*, 8 July.

Langer, J. (1996) 'The Meanings of the Border in Central Europe' in Éger, G. & Langer, J. (eds.) *Border, Region and Ethnicity in Central Europe*, Klagenfurt: Norea: 49–67.

Long, A. (1998) 'NATO membership point of no return for Hungary', *The Irish Times*, 7 October.

Martinez, O. J. (1994) 'The Dynamics of Border Integration: New Approaches to Border Analysis' in Schofield, C. H. (ed.) *Global Boundaries*, London: Routledge: 1–15.

Molle, P. (1996) *External Borders Pilot Project: Placement Report*, Strasbourg: Centre des Etudes Européennes: 6.

Neuss, B., Jurczek, P. & Hilz, W. (eds.) (1998) *Grenzübergreifende Kooperation im östlichen Mitteleuropa*, Tübingen: Europäisches Zentrum für Föderalismus-Forschung.

Nogala, D., Sack, F. & Lindenberg, M. (1998) *Social Control Technologies: Aspekte und Konsequenzen des Technikeinsatzes bei Instanzen strafrechtlicher Sozialkontrolle im nationalen und internationalen Kontext*, Hamburg: Aufbau- und Kontaktstudium Kriminologie der Universität Hamburg: 450.

Nowak, J. (1994) *Europas Krisenherde*, Reinbek bei Hamburg: Rowohlt: 133, 135.

O'Dowd, L. & Wilson, M. (eds.) (1996) *Borders, Nations, States*, Aldershot: Avebury.

Pándi, C. (1998) 'Bayerische Polizei bekommt in Österreich mehr Kompetenzen' in *Neue Kronen Zeitung*, 17 April.

Prantl, H. (1998) 'Europa verschließt sich Flüchtlingen', *Süddeutsche Zeitung*, 3 September.

Prantl, H. (1999) 'Wieviel Nachzug?', *Süddeutsche Zeitung*, 22 January.

Prescott, J. R. V. (1987) *Political Frontiers and Boundaries*, London: Allen and Unwin.

Raich, S. (1995) *Grenzüberschreitende und interregionale Zusammenarbeit in einem 'Europa der Regionen'*, Baden-Baden: Nomos.

Richter-Malabotta, M. (1998) 'Some Aspects of Regional and Transfrontier Cooperation in a Changing Europe' in Anderson, M. & Bort, E. (eds.) *Schengen and the Southern Frontier of the European Union*, Edinburgh: ISSI: 41–72 (especially 65–67).

Scherer, P. (1998) 'Geheimdienste schlagen Alarm', *Die Welt*, 21 August.

Schmidtendorf, H. (1998) 'Polens Marsch in die EU verärgert die Nachbarn', *Die Welt*, 17 February.

Schmitt, P. (1997) 'Neue Chancen für "Euregio Egrensis"', in *Süddeutsche Zeitung*, 27 January.

Schmitt, P. (1999) 'Noch zwei Millionen "Rußlanddeutsche"', *Süddeutsche Zeitung*, 9 January.

Schöpflin, G. (1993) 'Hungary and its Neighbours', *Chaillot Paper*, No. 7, Paris: Institute for Security Studies of WEU, May: 37.

Sheptycki, J. (1995) 'Transnational Policing and the Makings of a Postmodern State', *British Journal of Criminology*, Vol. 35, No. 4, Autumn: 613–35.

Sheptycki, J. (1996) 'Law Enforcement, Justice and Democracy in the Transnational Arena: Reflections on the War on Drugs', *International Journal of the Sociology of Law*, 24: 61–75.

Statewatch (1997) November/December: 9.

Stewart, A. (1992) *Migrants, Minorities and Security in Europe (Conflict Studies 252)*, London: Research Institute for the Study of Conflict and Terrorism: 8.

Strassoldo, R. & Delli Zotti, G. (eds.) (1982) *Cooperation and Conflict in Border Regions*, Milan: Angeli.

Strassoldo, R. (1970) *From Barrier to Junction: Towards a Sociological Theory of Borders*, Gorizia: ISIG.

Süddeutsche Zeitung (1997) 'Kohl sagt Polen Unterstützung zu', 20 November.

Süddeutsche Zeitung (1998a) 'Personenkontrollen bei Griechenland-Reisen bleiben', 17 December.

Süddeutsche Zeitung (1998b) 'Deutsch–Polnische Hausaufgaben', 20 August.

Süddeutsche Zeitung (1998c) 'Ostgrenze der EU sichern', 20 August.

Süddeutsche Zeitung (1998d) 'Deutsche profitieren von Polens Beitritt', 9 April.

Tägil, S. (1977) *Studying Boundary Conflicts*, Stockholm: Scandinavian University Books.

The Economist (1998) 'Good fences', 19 December.

The Scotsman (1998) 'New German coalition agrees to modernise citizenship law', 15 October.

The Scotsman (1999) 'Italy's Northern League in anti-immigrant rally', 18 January.

Traynor, I. (1998) 'Fortress Europe shuts window to the east', *The Guardian*, 9 February.

Urban, T. (1998) 'Nach Westen isoliert', *Süddeutsche Zeitung*, 18 September.

von Malchus, V. (1975) *Partnerschaft an europäischen Grenzen*, Bonn: Europa Union.

14
Boundaries to Communication: Borders in the Baltic Sea Region

Dennis Zalamans

INTRODUCTION

Everyone makes a number of decisions about limits, levels and boundaries on a daily basis. Sometimes such decisions occur spontaneously without deeper thought; sometimes they occur consciously with an expected result. The Swedish language has a common word – *gräns* – to cover the general concept of 'that which separates things', while the English language uses several different words. In a geographical context, 'boundary' is the word that is often used, but the American term 'border' is also quite common, although there are some differences between the two. One might define a border as being a soft and more psychological concept than a boundary, which is normally fixed and more physical. Common to both borders and boundaries is the fact that they are, to some extent, regulated by laws or decrees, while other concepts of division and separation depend more upon personal beliefs or interpretations.

An interesting issue to study in this context is the relation between people, nations and states. These three words have different meanings in different languages and much of this difference derives from political traditions. A group of people of similar ethnic background will create a nationality. To belong to a certain nationality a number of requirements must be fulfilled. These requirements normally differ from nation to nation, but language and identity are two basic components. There are various definitions of 'nation', and Harald Runblom has, with help from Sven Tägil, summarised the notion as:

> a group of people that associate with a nation-state. They might have established a state, consider themselves to be a group that bears up an existing state or they might have the aim to found one. It does not matter whether their ambitions are realistic or not. (Runblom, 1995.)

The difference between a nation and a nation-state can be found in the legal and political power of the regime in a specific territory (Lundén, 1997).

The first part of this paper deals with a number of general topics related to the Baltic Sea region. The countries in the region, especially those along the eastern coast, have undergone dramatic changes in several areas of society over the last ten years. Both physical and mental boundaries have shifted due to economic, political and social changes. After the collapse of the Soviet Union,

Borderlands Under Stress (M.A. Pratt and J.A. Brown (eds), ISBN 90-411-9790-7).
© Kluwer Law International, 2000.

the discussion concerning differences between east and west has reopened; it seems as though a general boundary between the two is necessary for some people. But such delimitation is no longer possible. The boundary is not fixed and, even if it were, it would follow neither the points of the compass nor state borders (Gustavsson, 1997). However, there are general patterns to be found and perhaps the most interesting is the paradox that countries from the west are heading towards a more open political structure in connection with the expansion of the European Union (EU), whilst many countries in the former Soviet Union and their dependencies are developing in the opposite way in their enthusiasm to be independent, and are nationalising states (Brubaker, 1996).

The second part of this paper presents a summary from a recent fieldcourse which focused on the remarkable situation of a twin-town situated on the border between Estonia and Latvia, namely Valga/Valka, and some of the problems it faces. Valga is the Estonian part of the town and Valka the Latvian part. During the Soviet period the town was united and considered as one. Even though the border between the Soviet Republic of Estonia and the Soviet Republic of Latvia ran through the middle of it, at that time the border had no real function. In 1991 both Estonia and Latvia regained their independence – an event which few would have considered possible even just a few days before it occurred. Neither Estonia nor Latvia was prepared for the new situation and, after the initial joy, freedom meant a great struggle to rebuild the two states – a struggle which is still going on. Independence completely changed the situation in Valga/Valka. Instead of there being a soft, almost invisible border running through it, the state border between Estonia and Latvia was raised again. The new border reinforced the boundary between the two countries, both mentally and physically. For the inhabitants of Valga/Valka the new situation is confusing and normal life is considerably affected.

PART I: THE BALTIC SEA REGION

Today the terms 'northern Europe' and 'the Baltic Sea region' do not mean what they used to mean. From the end of the Second World War until recently the terms referred to West Germany and the Nordic countries; since the fall of the iron curtain and the break of the Soviet Union, mental maps have changed dramatically (Lundqvist & Persson, 1995; O'Loughlin, 1993). Today the Baltic Sea region consists of at least nine countries: Sweden, Finland, Russia, Estonia, Latvia, Lithuania, Poland, Germany and Denmark. Sometimes Norway, Belorussia and other countries are included in the community since the area has no precise geographical definition. In other words, the boundary differs according to the aim or purpose of the classification (Westin, 1995).

To be defined as a region, at least two criteria have to be fulfilled: there must be some kind of spatial unity, and formal or functional unity. Regarding the spatial aspect, the connecting link for the region in this context is of course the

Baltic Sea, which simultaneously divides and unites. The formal/functional aspect is not as easy to define, but during the last decade significant efforts have been made by the countries around the sea to re-establish historical ties – for example, the Hanseatic League and sea-transport nodes – and to create new forums for collaboration at different levels of society. Many of these efforts have resulted in the exchange of information, personal networks and concrete programmes in various fields – the twinning programme between municipalities in different countries is one example.

According to several experts, the Baltic Sea region is one of the most heterogeneous areas in the world. The region has significant economic and social differences and, even more significantly, a variety of cultures and languages. The countries of the region also have varied histories. Some of them have been occupied almost throughout history, while others have been either occupiers or, at least, independent for most of the time. Between the World Wars, the Baltic Sea region was rather homogenous, with similar political systems and standards of infrastructure and tangible assets. With the Soviet annexation of the Baltic states and its domination of Poland and East Germany after the end of the Second World War, the differences between east and west were strengthened again – differences that prevail even though all the countries around the Baltic Sea have now been independent for a number of years.

East and west

The differences between countries on the eastern and western sides of the Baltic Sea are very apparent in many areas of society. Sixty years ago, at the end of the 1930s, living standards and levels of infrastructure were almost equal on both sides, but fifty years of Soviet domination have had a marked effect on the countries along the eastern shore. Many people are concerned about the differences between east and west, or eastern divergences from western standards, and for that reason the two are often compared. To make things comprehensible, people look for a fixed borderline, but such a line is impossible to set. The truth is that there are a several boundaries in the Baltic Sea region; the aim of this paper is to define and discuss some of them, with a special focus on the states of its eastern rim.

Over the last ten years the physical appearance of the much of the eastern side of the Baltic has changed considerably. New countries and cities have formed or re-formed, and many streets, parks and buildings have been renamed. In major cities the core areas have been given a facelift and many new restaurants, shops and small enterprises have been established. In general one can say that life in these cities is no longer different from life in similar cities in the west. More interesting, however, is what is going on in people's imaginations. Geographers often approach this with the help of mental maps. How do people from the east and west of the region look at themselves, their neighbours and their surroundings?

Political boundaries

In a political sense, Europe in the last decade has been characterised by two basically unrelated processes. On the one hand is the collapse of the Soviet Union and the liberation of eastern Europe; on the other, the efforts for a further union in western Europe. One might view these as parallel but paradoxical processes. While strong nationalistic forces strive for further independence and national democracy in eastern Europe, many regimes in western Europe are planning for closer ties which may mean reduced independence and the elimination of some democratic rules (Zalamans, 1994).

It is very difficult to foresee the situation in ten years' time, especially when almost all of the countries in eastern Europe have applied for membership in both the European Union (EU) and the North Atlantic Treaty Organisation (NATO). Hungary, Poland and the Czech Republic have already acceded to NATO , and even traditionally neutral countries like Sweden and Finland are discussing the possibility of future membership.

In the Baltic states, possible membership in NATO is a controversial question. Russia has pronounced that it will not accept membership in NATO for the Baltic states. In a bid to reduce the tension and to allow some collaboration, NATO has established an alliance called Partnership for Peace. Russia, as well as Sweden, is a part of this alliance.

Regarding applications to the EU, five countries from eastern Europe have been accepted for the first round: Estonia, Poland, the Czech Republic, Slovenia and Hungary. One of the main issues is whether Estonia should enter the EU if Latvia and Lithuania are left out. Sweden supports Estonia's application, for security and moral reasons. Finland also supports Estonia's application, even if Estonia is the only Baltic state to be accepted in the first instance, since this would influence Russia's attitude. There is also contention over Poland which, according to several experts, would represent a major problem for the EU given its size and its large number of farmers (Wahlbäck, 1997).

Another interesting issue is the differences between the people living around the Baltic Sea. One wonders if the main difference is political values. Has communism changed or obliterated older solidarity and cultural ties, or is it the case that the cultures found in the eastern countries today are traditional, genuine – and different from each other? In the former eastern bloc maintaining a sense of cultural identity was often the only hope people had of survival. However, whilst the consciousness of their own cultures was strong, neither culture nor language was able to develop in contact with the rest of the world (Taube, 1997). In Estonia and the rest of eastern Europe the theory of a 'total society' was seen as the only valid one, and there was no belief in the existence of independent civil societies. The incidents at the end of the 1980s, during the so-called singing revolution, definitely show the opposite. Thanks to the introduction of more open politics in the former republics of the Soviet Union during the period of *perestroika* from 1985 onwards, political decision-making began to change, becoming more bottom-up than top-down (Lagerspetz, 1997).

Russia's current relationship with its Baltic neighbours is complicated. In the case of Lithuania the problems have been relatively simple, and a comprehensive boundary agreement was signed in October 1997. An agreement based on cartographic delineation was reached with Latvia in 1998, and the situation in this area looks relatively bright, although there are still significant problems related to the large Russian population in Latvia (about 700,000). The situation with Estonia is uncertain regarding both boundaries and other issues (*The Baltic Times*, 1997). Both Estonia and Latvia claim that the period between 1940 and 1991 should be seen as an historical parenthesis, and they refer back to earlier laws, land areas, and so on. The Lithuanian situation differs somewhat because some parts of today's Lithuania – including the capital, Vilnius – did not belong to Lithuania during the interwar period. Lithuania thus gained in territory through the Soviet annexation, while Estonia and Latvia lost.

Geography has to do with specificity of place. Political geography is concerned with the way in which each area resolves to govern itself. In eastern Europe there are major problems related to how each country handles the differences of orientation resulting from nationalism in their state structures, and how they make policy depending on local circumstances.

Linguistic boundaries

In the Baltic Sea region at least 25 different languages are spoken. All of them originate from two language groups that have been in contact with each other since prehistoric times: Uralic and Indo-European. Finnish, Estonian and Sami are Uralic languages, while the Indo-European languages are further divided into the Baltic, Germanic and Slavic language groups. In total there are four different language groups in the region (Gustavsson, 1995):

- Finnish–Ugrian (Finnish and Estonian)
- Germanic (German, Danish and Swedish)
- Baltic (Latvian and Lithuanian)
- Slavic (Russian and Polish).

In Estonia, Estonian is the dominant and only official language, even though more than 30 per cent of the population has Russian as its mother tongue. However, the Finnish and Estonian languages are closely related. During the Soviet era Estonians in the northern part of Estonia could listen to Finnish radio and watch Finnish television, with the result that many Estonians in northern Estonia speak and understand Finnish. There is a kind of big-brother/little-brother relationship between the two neighbours, with Estonians generally keener to learn Finnish than vice versa. Until the Second World War Swedish was also a minority language in Estonia. Both Finnish and Swedish are the official languages of Finland, although Swedish is the minority language.

In northern Germany, Denmark and Sweden, German, Danish and Swedish are the dominant and only official languages of their respective countries. The southern part of Sweden belonged to Denmark until the seventeenth century, and the Swedish still spoken in the south was formerly a Danish dialect (Olsson, 1978 & 1979). Danish and Swedish are closer to each other than Danish and German. Swedish and German have some similarities, but they are not mutually comprehensible.

Latvian and Lithuanian are the only official languages of their respective countries. However, in Latvia more than 40 per cent of the population has Russian or another Slavic languages as its mother tongue. In Lithuania not more than about 15 per cent of the population is non-Lithuanian, which means that the state faces limited language and other ethnically-related problems. Latvian and Lithuanian are normally considered the oldest languages in Europe, but even though they belong to the same language group, their speakers have severe difficulty understanding each other.

In Poland and Russia, Polish and Russian are the only official languages of their respective countries. Russian- and Polish-speaking people can understand each other to some extent. The Polish language was the object of Russian oppression for more than a century, especially at the end of the nineteenth and beginning of the twentieth centuries. In Belorussia the language is Belorussian, a language very closely related to Russian; there are people who claim that Belorussian is merely a Russian dialect.

Among the great number of minority languages in the region, the Sami language is of particular interest. Cultural and linguistic boundaries do not always follow state boundaries, and the Sami language is an excellent example. 30,000 people in four countries – Sweden, Norway, Finland and Russia – speak the Sami language (Gustavsson, 1995). In Sweden and Norway the Sami people are considered the only autochthonous minority, and they are therefore in possession of ancient rights dating from before the rise of the state. According to the Sami population, Swedes, Norwegians and Finns are all immigrants to Sapmi, the land of the Sami people. Within the Sami population there are great linguistic differences. The Sami language can be divided into three major groups, and in each group many dialects can be found. When a Sami from the north of Sweden meets a Sami from the southern part of the Sami area, they usually have to speak Swedish in order to communicate (Beach, 1989). The Sami language is important to the distinctive character of the Sami population, and it is regarded as being one of three criteria in defining a Sami. The other two are self-identification and Sami origin. The written language evolved during the fifteenth century, and literature is an important cultural expression. Nonetheless, the verbal tradition is very strong and the 'jojk-singing' is both an exciting and unique feature of Sami culture (Beach, 1989).

It has been said that language is an instrument for identity and communication, and the latter has a lot to do with individual languages. Almost all communication assumes that the persons communicating can understand each other from a linguistic point of view. From a historical perspective, different languages have dominated the Baltic Sea region. German, Danish and Swedish have all been dominant languages in the area, as well as Russian. After the Second World War English became the most commonly spoken language in the west, while Russian dominated in the east. In Estonia, Latvia and Lithuania Russian was forcibly imposed as the official language and seen as a metaphor of superior power. For this reason Russian can never be the common language in the Baltic Sea region, even though the majority of people in the region speak it. English is the only possible common language, because of its neutrality.

Religious boundaries

Several different forms of Christian belief are represented in the region, principally Catholic, Protestant and Orthodox. Perhaps the most important barrier between east and west is the cultural boundary – i.e. the boundary between Catholic and Orthodox beliefs (Gustavsson, 1997). This boundary can be roughly drawn between the Baltic states and Poland on one side and Russia, Belorussia and Ukraine on the other side (Tegborg, 1997). Another religious boundary can be seen, although less clearly, between Protestant and Catholic beliefs. Broadly speaking, this boundary runs in a mainly north-south direction, with the northern part of Germany, the Nordic countries, Estonia and a part of Latvia on one side, and Lithuania, Poland, Germany, part of Latvia, and the rest of central Europe on the other side. There are some basic differences between Orthodox believers and the others. The most important is probably that Protestants and Catholics strive towards growth and development, while progress is unimportant for Orthodox believers, who instead strive for harmony (Tegborg, 1997).

Before the Second World War, Judaism was strongly represented in the Baltic Sea region. At the beginning of this century, about 90 per cent of all Jews in the world lived in this area. At this time Vilnius used to be called 'little Jerusalem'; about 40 per cent of its population was Jewish, and the city contained a large number of synagogues. Today only a fragment of this population remains in Vilnius and in other parts of eastern Europe.

Over the centuries the power and standing of different religions has changed dramatically in the Baltic Sea region. A general consciousness of religion and pilgrimage led to the spread of Christianity during the Middle Ages. Some years later, new thoughts and ideas were developed which formed Protestant belief and Lutheran theory. Along the shores of the Baltic Sea, Catholics and Protestants have always been dominant, but from Constantinople the Orthodox belief was spread northwards towards the central parts of Europe.

There are people, especially Roman Catholics, who believe that religion made the strongest contribution to the end of communism. In Lithuania and Poland, religion has been very important in the liberation process.

Economic boundaries

In all the countries around the Baltic Sea, regardless of political system, there is a great orientation towards a market economy. There is a strong orientation to the west in a broad perspective, but it is mainly for geopolitical and not geo-economic reasons (Bunkse, 1994). All the countries along the eastern shore, with the exception of problem-ridden Russia, show tremendous improvement during the last couple of years, especially at the macro level. Estonia and Poland have been most successful.

In all western countries there are developed welfare systems with strong mechanisms for controlling authorities and private individuals. These functions are more or less absent in eastern countries, with the result that a few people have, usually through dubious activities, managed to build up enormous fortunes in a very short space of time. There is always a risk when the same people have both financial and political power, which is often the case. A number of foreign companies have taken advantage of the situation as well. At the same time, segregation in society has increased, as have levels of poverty.

The economic situation in the Baltic Sea region can be defined as unequal. Russia and Poland are great powers, at least on a regional level, on the basis of the size of their territory and population. With the exception of Finland, the countries along the eastern shore have lower living standards and their currencies are worth less in real terms. The Baltic states need to develop production and transit services between east and west in order to link with markets in the Nordic countries and the rest of Europe (Hanson, 1994).

One phenomenon in Poland and other countries in eastern Europe is that their western parts show more initiative and business orientation than other parts of the countries. Low salaries and advanced technical skills are positive factors, while old patterns and a lack of organisation and market activities are negative factors. The most difficult challenge is perhaps to change attitudes from passive observation to independent and responsible action (Illeris, 1994).

A country's productivity is the only sure way of judging its competitive strength. Lack of production is a problem in Russia, Latvia and Lithuania, while Estonia and Poland are performing better. In the Soviet era the average number of employees in a normal factory, or *kolchos*, was around a thousand. Many of these units are still owned by the state and most of them are too big for modern production. Because of their size local authorities have difficulty finding buyers. Even though many countries in the east wish to retain ownership of these units, this is not possible for several reasons, and foreign investors are therefore invited in. However, since owners of multinational companies usually have their head offices abroad, there is a greater risk of shutdowns in the future (Malmberg, 1993).

It is noteworthy that while the world in general regards the Baltic states as a single region, they view themselves as three separate countries and put a lot of effort into developing their own distinctive profiles. Symbolic of this are the enormous customs stations which have been built on their borders. There is collaboration in a few fields, such as tourism, but not to the extent one would expect. There are also a number of general agreements between the states, but little has come of them.

Ethnic and social boundaries

National identity is the leitmotiv for modern politics, and geography and history are basic components of national identity (Lowenthal, 1994). In early France national identity was based on a simple principle: everything that belonged to the King was considered French (Claval, 1994). Today things are more complicated.

The ethnic debate in the area, especially in the Baltic states, is at present a burning and sometimes inflamed question. To a great degree, the discussion revolves around what is meant by national identity. According to the definition of the Sami identity, language, self-identification and origin are necessary. These or similar attributes seem most valid or, at least, are most applied. There are other definitions; some experts prefer to say that national identity depends on sentiment, similarity and idealism (Roth, 1997).

In the same context Roger Brubaker talks about mis-identity, and prefers to reconceptualise nationalism and national identity and to separate these ideas from those of nations, nationhood and nationness (Brubaker, 1996). Moreover, Brubaker discusses the terms 'national minorities', 'nationalising states' and 'external homelands'. His definition of a national minority does not differ from that of others, but his definition of a nationalising state seems to be a new concept. A nationalising state can be described either as a nation-state with a dynamic political stance, or as an unrealised nation-state. A homeland is an external national homeland for ethnic nationals or co-nationals who live outside the territory – for example, Russia for Russian minorities living abroad.

In the Baltic Sea region the concept of an external homeland is a serious problem for the Baltic states, especially Estonia and Latvia. During the interwar period Estonia and Latvia had two of the most liberal systems for minorities in Europe (Brunkse, 1994). Although subject to increasing criticism (see below) their systems can be said to have remained liberal today, at least in comparison with countries such as Germany (Wahlbäck, 1997). In Estonia about 35 per cent of the population are non-Estonians; in Latvia, more than 40 per cent are non-Latvians. Both Estonia and Latvia distinguish between minorities who have lived in the country for generations, and post-war immigrants; the ratio is approximately 20/80.

After independence in 1991 both Estonia and Latvia reinstated their earlier citizenship laws from the interwar period. Latvia, with 700,000 inhabitants without Latvian citizenship out of a population of 2.5 million, has been most criticised so far. The main reason for the criticism is the citizenship law, which is based on a so-called 'window-model'. This model allows only a few inhabitants of a certain age to apply for citizenship during a certain period (e.g. a calendar year). The authorities have chosen to start with the youngest and thereafter go upwards in age. During 1996 some 33,000 youngsters between 16 and 20 years of age were able to apply, but less than 600 did so. This figure is really remarkable, and the question is whether the authorities consider this result to be a success or a failure. Most probably there is no single explanation for the result, but some of the arguments put forward are: the unimportance of the issue; ethnic reasons; military duties; and splits in families (even though the splits are only administrative).

Two comprehensive surveys in Estonia show that non-Estonians are seriously concerned by the ethnic nationalism of Estonians, and therefore many of them hesitate over whether or not to apply for Estonian citizenship if the opportunity arises. On the other hand, most of them would like to live and work in Estonia in the future (Attiat, 1996). Some professions are closed to non-citizens – e.g. police, firemen and pharmacists – and they have no voting rights in parliamentary elections.

A great deal of international support is given to ease communications between different ethnic groups in the Baltic countries. In Estonia a group of researchers in cooperation with the United Nations Development Programme (UNDP) has presented the results from a research project aiming to reduce the friction associated with assimilation and prevent the segregation of a number of linguistic minorities, towards a society with one official language. The study *Ethnic Reidentification in Ukraine* (Rapawy, 1997) has examined how people in Ukraine look upon their nationality. It shows that some people make a distinction between passport citizenship and ethnic nationality or community, depending on what is most convenient at that moment. Some inhabitants who in the past called themselves Russians, now prefer to call themselves Ukrainians.

The social boundary between east and west is very clear regarding material values. The living standard in all the eastern European countries is less developed, especially in the countryside. Sixty years ago the situation was different, as the relationship between Estonia and Finland demonstrates. In 1938 Estonia and Finland had almost the same standard of living; in 1988 standard of living in Finland was five times higher than in Estonia. When it comes to more sentimental and non-material values, the situation is more difficult to estimate.

PART II: THE TWIN-TOWN OF VALGA/VALKA

Between 7 and 16 May 1998, students and leaders from the (human) geography departments at Stockholm, Tartu and Riga Universities participated in a fieldcourse in Estonia and Latvia. The aim of the trip was to study the twin-town of Valga/Valka, situated on the border between Estonia and Latvia. In many ways Valga/Valka is just like any other small or medium-sized town – with the exception that Valga is situated in Estonia and Valka in Latvia.

History

Valga/Valka was first mentioned in 1286, at which time the town was already divided between two counties. The importance of the town grew, and Valga/Valka became an important trade and transport centre between Tartu and Pskov in the east and Riga on the Baltic shore in the west. In 1889 when the railway between Pskov and Riga was opened, with a connection to Tartu, large engineering and locomotive workshops were located in Valga/Valka, and the town became an important railway centre. In the decade between 1883 and 1893 the population more than doubled to approximately 11,000.

In 1920, when Estonia and Latvia became independent states, Valga/Valka was divided into two cities. The boundary between them was delimited on the basis of ethnic principles, like the rest of the boundary between Estonia and Latvia. Since time immemorial Estonians and Latvians had inhabited different parts of the town even though there was no fixed boundary. After the Second World War and annexation to the Soviet Union in 1945, the town of Valga/Valka was once more united, at least in the practical sense, even though Valga was situated in the Estonian Soviet Republic and Valka in the Latvian Soviet Republic. During this period the Estonian and Latvian populations maintained their housing patterns and, in general, kept to their respective sides of the city. For the Slavic population, mainly represented by ethnic Russians, who moved to Valga/Valka in larger numbers during the Soviet era, there were no such limitations, and they spread out all over the twin-town.

Since 1991 Valga and Valka have been divided again. Valga, the bigger of the two towns with approximately 17,000 inhabitants, seems to be a little ahead of Valka, which has fewer than 8,000 inhabitants. Cooperation between the two towns is very poor. One reason is that relations between states are normally managed by governments and not by regional or local authorities. The new independence brought the inhabitants of Valga/Valka a lot of difficulties, some of which are outlined below.

Crossing the boundary

The boundary between the two states serves at least three general functions. First, it separates two different administrative systems. Neither side considers the principles of the other when making decisions related to national laws and regulations. Secondly, it acts as a physical language barrier. Estonian and Latvian are two completely different languages, and the language many people have in common, Russian, is both restrictive and unpopular among both Estonians and Latvians. Thirdly, the boundary prohibits or restrains the movement of some of the inhabitants of both sides. In Valga/Valka non-citizens and inhabitants with other citizenship – mainly Russians – are particularly affected.

Reasons for crossing a border are sometimes described in terms of 'push and pull' factors. In Valga/Valka the most common reason to cross the border seems to be to visit relatives and friends. The inhabitants of Valga/Valka can be placed in three groups: Estonians, Latvians and others. Amongst the first two groups, the need to cross the border for this reason are low, at least among ethnic Estonians and Latvians. The third group – i.e. non-citizens and citizens of other countries – has a greater need to cross the border; but this group is also the one which is restricted. Another factor is the wider choice of shopping and dining in Valga, where prices often are lower. Studies and work are two other factors, although the latter is relatively unimportant since few inhabitants on one side of the border take work on the other side.

Other reasons for crossing the border are cultural events, leisure, sport and religion. Common cultural events seldom take place nowadays. During the Soviet era there was greater integration and cultural events were not regarded as 'national' events. When it comes to leisure and sporting activities, the lakes in southeast Estonia seem to attract Latvian fishermen and a new sports arena is currently under construction in Valga, which might in future attract inhabitants from Valka. With regard to religion, Valka has no Russian Orthodox church or Catholic cathedral, both of which are on offer in Valga, which provides a clear reason for crossing the border; meanwhile, several Orthodox and Catholic graveyards dating from the Soviet era are located in Valka.

The maximum number of permissible border-crossings for non-citizens with alien passports is 90 a year. For those with specific needs, such as schoolchildren, special permits have been authorised. About 300 special permits are granted every year – a serious restriction considering that there is a large group of inhabitants who need to cross the border on a regular basis. Far more people are now applying for permits. While people with Estonian and Latvian passports can cross the border just by showing their passports, non-citizens require a stamp in their passports. These passports have about 25 pages for stamps, which means that they have to be renewed at least twice a year if the holder makes 90 crossings. In addition to the stamp, Russian citizens also need a visa in order to cross the border.

There are three official border points in Valga/Valka. Between the three points and just outside the towns a special 'green line' runs along the border. Border guards patrol the green line 24 hours a day. At the moment patrols on the Estonian side are more active than on the Latvian side, due to a Latvian lack of money, and while the Estonian guards have a professional training, the majority of the Latvian guards are doing their compulsory military service. There is no direct cooperation between the two sets of guards, the main reason being a lack of resources and differences in laws. On a few occasions criminals have taken advantage of this poor cooperation and slipped over the border at an unguarded spot. The average delay for a car crossing the border is about half an hour, but on market days or special occasions it can be much longer.

There appear to be three sets of people who cross the border illegally: those who do not have the legal right to cross the border; those who have the legal right to cross the border but, for convenience, cross the border illegally; and those who are smuggling. Those who cross the border illegally receive a warning the first time, and are fined the second time. Those who smuggle, or who cross the border illegally several times, risk being sent to jail.

Physical planning and dependence

During the Soviet era Valga/Valka was one city in terms of planning and development of infrastructure. During the first years of independence the situation has been the complete opposite; in other words, there has been no cooperation at all. The hypothesis of this paper is that Valga/Valka has a lot to gain from cooperation, not least regarding physical planning. Both money and the environment can be saved by shared infrastructure, and future goals such as developed tourism will be easier to reach through collaboration. The factors that will contribute to cooperation are self-governance in each municipality, the position of the municipality in a national setting, financial and personal resources, and attitudes and the willingness to cooperate.

With regard to self-governance, Valga and Valka are very different. Estonia is much more decentralised than Latvia; the municipality is the only administrative level, with the state acting as a controller/distributor. According to the 1995 law of planning and construction all municipalities in Estonia are expected to have their own master plan. Valga's master plan is still being drawn up but the authorities of Valga hope that it will be ready before the end of 1999. The situation in Latvia is a little unclear, but the real power lies with the counties rather than the municipalities. There is no law in Latvia similar to the Estonian law of planning and construction, just a government decree dating from 1994 which does not say anything about the planning process, and several of whose paragraphs contradict one another. This situation has recently led to the initiation of a planning process in Valka County.

The financial situation is quite tense in Valga, and even worse in Valka. In Valka lack of money affects the most essential needs. In both Valga and Valka counties there is an expectation of a future merger between some of the municipalities which has led to a kind of 'wait and see' mentality.

In 1995 the ESTLA project was established. ESTLA is a joint project between the twin-town Haparanda/Tornio, situated on the border between Sweden and Finland, and Valga/Valka. The aim of ESTLA, which is financed by the EU, is to strengthen the ties and to share experiences between the twin-towns. For Valga/Valka the project should be seen as a good start for the future, with Haparanda/Tornio setting a good example of twin-town cooperation.

In the former Soviet Union there is great suspicion of the terms 'cooperation' and 'collaboration'; the meaning of these words under the Soviet system was very different to what it is today. Valga/Valka is no exception and, on top of this, the state border serves as another barrier. There are no physical or environmental obstacles but, on other hand, there are no connections either. It is very much a question of attitudes. Estonians often see Latvians as people from the backwoods, while Latvians often believe that Estonians ride on their high horses; in other words, the relationship between Estonians and Latvians can be described as normal but with minor tension. At the local government level most of the difficulties are due to differences in political systems.

In both Valga and Valka it is said that physical planning is a political high priority. One of the most important things to be developed is an openness on the part of the public. During the Soviet era all planning was secret. Now the two towns face many similar problems but do not cooperate at all. For example, both towns have had problems with the quality of their drinking water and have therefore both recently constructed their own sewage-treatment plants. The size of each plant is big enough to serve both towns, and both sides express a wish to supply clean water to the other – which of course is now impossible. A similar development has occurred in healthcare, with the building of two hospitals.

Citizenship and nationality

The situation between different ethnic groups in Valga/Valka appears to be calm and without great problems. Indeed, 'no problems' is the most common response when local people are asked about the ethnic situation. Nevertheless, the boundary between Estonia and Latvia is indisputable in the twin-town, and the borderline is obvious. With respect to nationalism, the boundary can be viewed in two ways. First, it defines the physical territory or the place where each nation belongs. Secondly, it is a cultural barrier or a mental definition for the people belonging to each nation. Even if a person has citizenship in the country where they live, there is no guarantee that they will be looked upon as a 'real citizen' by other citizens; the definition of nationality is much more than just citizenship.

The language barrier in Valga/Valka appears to be a major problem. Estonian, Latvian and Russian are three completely different languages belonging to three different language groups. In Estonia Estonian is the only official language, and the same is true in Latvia of Latvian. It appears that Estonians are more unwilling to speak Russian than Latvians, partly because of their greater linguistic difficulties with the language. Even though all Estonians and Latvians over the age of 20 speak Russian more or less fluently, it is seldom used in conversation. During the Soviet era both Estonian and Latvian were included in primary schools, but on each side of the border the teaching of the language of the other side was seen as a 'joke'. Today it is essential to have a good knowledge of the language, history and constitution to become an Estonian or a Latvian citizen. For many reasons, a large part of the population in Valga (about 40 per cent) and Valka (about 25 per cent) do not have, respectively, Estonian or Latvian citizenship.

Street names have a strong but sometimes hidden power when used by political regimes. In contrast to monuments, street names often engender low tension: citizens will be reminded every day, but without dramatic gestures. In Valga/Valka, several streets have had the same name for a long period of time, but those names with a specific Russian or communist meaning have been changed, often to names with a territorial meaning.

The actual boundary between Estonia and Latvia was based on ethnic and linguistic divisions in 1918–1920, and was devised with the help of an English officer. During independence between the World Wars, the boundary in Valga/Valka was quite porous. During the Soviet era it was just an administrative border, with hardly any real function. Today the boundary is very definite, probably due to a desire on the part of the authorities of both Estonia and Latvia to strengthen the definition of their respective states. In Valga/Valka the common centre has become a periphery since both sides are turning towards their capitals. It is surprising that the 'Russian' communities on either side have little or no contact with each other on an official level, while it seems that they are the ones who pass the boundary most frequently on private business.

Media – national, regional and local

The media situation in the Baltic countries is rather heterogeneous, but what all media have in common is how different they are in both content and expression to what they were in the Soviet era. Back then all media were controlled in one way or another, especially the news. The censoring organisation worked irrationally and the media never knew in advance what news would be accepted. The initial period after independence was characterised as being quite chaotic for all media, because suddenly they were supposed to give information about everything. This led to a situation whereby a lot of rumours and 'half truths' were published in the press. After some time the influence of the international media helped to create a general consciousness and a better quality of published news. Ethical and moral regulations can be found in all the Baltic countries today, but they are not as strong as they are, for example, in the Nordic countries.

The Estonian media of today are quite impressive. There are four Estonian television channels, about ten radio channels, and three major newspapers that cover all Estonia. All operate in the Estonian language, except two radio stations which broadcast in Russian. In smaller towns and in the countryside one can find local media as well, which cover only the nearby region. With regard to international news, the media focus on Russia and the EU, with special attention to Finland and Sweden. Published news about Latvia and Lithuania is quite rare, and when it occurs it is often related to Estonian interests. The Latvian media are largely similar to those in Estonia, with the difference that Latvia seems to have a greater supply of media in Russian.

In Valga/Valka, the media situation is surprisingly similar to the general situation in Estonia and Latvia. Even though Valga/Valka is a twin-town situated on the border, the news is clearly divided into Estonian news on one side and Latvian news on the other. In Valga there is one local newspaper, *Valgamaaline*, and two local radio stations, Radio Valga and Radio Ruut, all in the Estonian language. Once a month a shorter summary of *Valgamaaline* is published in Russian, and the radio stations also occasionally broadcast in Russian as well. In Valka, there are two local newspapers, *Ziemellatvija* and *Tava Balss*, and a local television station that broadcasts twice a week, all in Latvian.

The conclusion drawn from the interviews about the media situation in Estonia and Latvia in general, and in Valga/Valka in particular, is that each country has little or no interest in the other. This is shown not only in the lack of information about the neighbouring country, but also in the attitudes of the people who were interviewed. The student who investigated the media situation was very active during the fieldcourse and conducted several interviews in

Tallinn, Valga/Valka and Riga. On a national scale it seems as though Estonia considers itself to belong to the Nordic countries, while Latvia is more confused about its situation and its allies. For Estonia, its geographical location and the similarity of its language to Finnish are important factors, especially when the language difficulty between Estonia and Latvia is seen as the major problem between the two countries.

Education

The structure of the education systems in Estonia and Latvia is similar. In both countries children begin school at the age of seven and a majority of the pupils proceed to gymnasia (upper secondary schools). One difference which emerged during interviews in three schools/gymnasia is that the Estonian schools seem to have changed their school literature to a larger extent than is the case in Latvian schools. Another difference seems to be that a low standard of teachers' education is a problem in Valga but not in Valka. There are a few pupils, 10–20 from each school, who cross the border every day to attend school on the other side, but all of them have Estonian or Latvian passports which give them no trouble at the border. The fact that no non-citizens cross the border for education purposes gives rise to the question: is it due to problems with crossing the border or just to a lack of interest in other educational opportunities?

In Valga there are five schools. Three of them are comprehensive schools; two of them include both comprehensive schools and gymnasia. In the town of Valka there are seven schools, of which two are gymnasia. There are both Estonian- and Russian-speaking schools in Valga, and Latvian- and Russian-speaking schools/gymnasia in Valka. Contact with schools across the state border is rare between Estonian- and Latvian-speaking schools and, surprisingly, non-existent between Russian-speaking schools. On the other hand, contact between Estonian/Russian and Latvian/Russian schools on each side are quite frequent.

According to the interviews, educational reform seems to be more developed in Estonia than in Latvia, at least when comparing Estonian- and Latvian-speaking schools/gymnasia. With regard to Russian-speaking schools/gymnasia, it appears to be the other way round. Estonian and Latvian pupils cross the border for education purely for linguistic reasons. The reason why Russian-speaking pupils with Estonian or Latvian citizenship cross the border from Valga to Valka is unclear, but one explanation may be that while the Russian-speaking school in Valga is situated outside the town, the one in Valka is situated within the town, giving some pupils from Valga a shorter distance to travel.

An interesting point is that there are far more pupils of Russian nationality in Estonian schools/gymnasia than there are in Latvian schools/gymnasia. In some classes in Valka, pupils with Russian as their mother tongue are in the majority. The fieldcourse student involved in this issue could find no explanation for this, but she did notice a difference in the attitude of the two principals she interviewed: in Estonia educators believe that pupils with Russian as their mother tongue have severe difficulties in managing their studies, while this reaction was not noticed at all in Latvia.

In both Valga and Valka, schools within the town have a better reputation than those outside. The major reason for this is the quality of the teachers, but the availability of resources in general is also significant. There is also a wider choice of subjects in the town schools. The result is that large numbers of pupils from the countryside travel into town for schooling every day.

Finally, it is noteworthy that all the schools/gymnasia interviewed during the fieldcourse have links with 'adopted' schools/gymnasia in Nordic countries, and teachers and pupils from Valga and Valka visit these schools. It is remarkable that the Russian-speaking schools/gymnasia that were interviewed have had no contact at all with schools/gymnasia in Russia.

Healthcare

During the Soviet era healthcare was shared in Valga/Valka. Patients could get treatment at the closest hospital or nursing home irrespective of their nationality, and in emergencies patients were treated wherever they happened to be at that moment. When specialist treatment was required they were sent to the specialist clinic that was geographically – rather than ethnically – closest.

Today healthcare is strictly connected to the country in which the patient lives. In emergencies initial treatment can be given over the border if necessary, but sometimes emergency patients are taken to the border by ambulance for onward transportation to hospital on their own side. Cooperation between the healthcare sectors in Valga and Valka is almost non-existent. It only occurs in two circumstances: first, when emergency cases have to be treated on 'the wrong side', which happens a couple of times a month and is paid for by the 'home' side; secondly, when special strata treatment has to be given to Valga patients, which happens ten to fifteen times a month. The hospital in Valka has special x-ray equipment for strata treatment, which is used by Estonian patients as well and is, of course, paid for by Valga; the alternative is to send these patients to Tartu, about 90 kilometres away.

In Valka there is one hospital with 114 beds; in Valga there is another hospital with 137 beds. The hospital in Valka was first built in 1965 and then extended in 1987. At that time, when the town was united, the intention was that it would handle patients from both Valka and Valga. Today it is too large, leading to severe problem for an already-stressed economy. To Nordic eyes at least, the hospital appears to be old-fashioned and poor, worn but clean. In 1987 Valga had only two smaller hospitals, a military hospital and a hospital for staff working on the railroad, but these are now closed. Instead, Valga recently opened its own hospital, a brand new construction with equipment of Nordic standard.

Savieniba

Savieniba is the name of the northern part of a street located in Valka in Latvia. The street is unique because it is inhabited mainly by Estonians, and their situation has several times been discussed at government level by both countries, so far without a solution. The street and its houses were established during the Soviet era, between 1950 and 1980, as an extension of the Estonian street Pohja, which means that no agreement exists from the first period of independence. All those who moved to Savieniba were aware that there was an old boundary in the area but they could not have imagined that the importance of the boundary would resurface so soon.

In Valga/Valka there are only three border stations where people are allowed to cross. Two of them are situated in the town and can only be used by locals; the third is international and situated outside the town. The people living on Savieniba have to choose one of these stations by which to cross the border, which means a lot of inconvenience. The authorities in Valga/Valka have agreed to the granting of a special permit allowing those with permanent addresses on Savieniba to cross the border on the street itself. However, several inhabitants live on Savieniba in practice, but their permanent addresses are elsewhere on the Estonian side, and they are therefore ineligible for the special permit. These Estonian citizens prefer to have an Estonian address for several reasons, but mainly to ease insurance and labour issues. On rare occasions, arrests have occurred on the Latvian side when people have tried to cross the border in the street illegally.

At the time of the field study there were 35 people living on Savieniba in nine houses; one house owned by a Latvian is empty due to sickness. Of the 35, 26 were Estonian citizens, seven were Latvian citizens and two were so-called non-citizens. Of the group of seven Latvians, two are of Estonian origin and have taken Latvian citizenship to make life easier, although they still consider themselves to be of Estonian nationality. The two non-citizens, of Russian origin, also consider themselves to be Estonians although they have lived in Valka all their lives. The average age of the 35 residents is relatively high, and no schoolchildren belong to the group.

The main reason that inhabitants of Savieniba cross the border is to work; most of the Estonians have their place of work on the Estonian side. It is perhaps ironic that the Latvian residents, who have no need to cross any border, are currently unemployed. Other major reasons for crossing the border are to visit friends and relatives, and to shop. The Estonians also receive their mail on the Estonian side of the border, a procedure that was also practised during the Soviet era.

Other problems that the Estonians living on Savieniba face relate to electricity, telephones, road maintenance and emergency healthcare. Electricity is supplied by the Estonian side as it always has been, but the Latvian authorities want to change over to a Latvian supply. Electricity is much cheaper in Estonia than in Latvia, so the Savieniba residents do not want any change. The telephone system is Latvian. This has led to all of the Estonian residents choosing not to have a telephone at all, since calls to the Estonian side are considered to be international calls and are therefore very expensive. This lack of telephones is a real handicap. Road maintenance is conspicuous by its absence. Neither

Estonian nor Latvian authorities maintain the road. The Estonian side says it is too complicated and expensive, while the Latvian side does not seem to have a good excuse. With regard to healthcare, if any of the Estonian residents of Savieniba need emergency treatment from their hospital, which is situated in Valga, it might be difficult to cross the border quickly enough; the same issue arises in the case of a doctor from Valga needing to make house-calls in Valka. Clearly, this situation is far from satisfactory.

Ownership of land is another uncertain issue. It is not clear who owns the land and the houses in Savieniba. The juridical right to the land belongs to a Latvian citizen, simply because the land belonged to him or his family during the first period of independence. However, he has not shown much interest in the land so far, and in fact left Valka a long time ago. Supposing that this owner wished to sell his land, another problem would arise: according to Latvian law, a foreigner is not allowed to own land within two kilometres of the Latvian border. This means that the Estonian residents of Savieniba will never be able to own the land where they live, just their houses. Some of the Estonian residents have, with reluctance, thought of selling their houses and moving to Valga, but this area is on the periphery of Valka and it seems that no Latvians wish to move to what is considered a 'problem area'.

The territory of Savieniba, just 2.6 acres, seems to be a hard nut to crack and because of its complexity no single solution can be recommended. The deputy mayor of Valga has been bold enough to suggest two possible solutions. The first is that Latvia offers the territory of Savieniba to Estonia, in payment of the 'debt' of about 20 acres which Latvia has owed Estonia since the demarcation of the new boundary in 1995. The deputy mayor admits, however, that this solution is unlikely to come about. The second solution is that a border station be put up on Savieniba. This solution is perhaps more likely and should ease the situation for the inhabitants, but the question is whether it would be a genuine improvement.

Finally it should be mentioned that there are at least two committees with both Estonian and Latvian participants working on boundary issues between the countries. One committee deals with general issues, while the other concentrates on the Valga/Valka situation in particular. Because boundary issues pertain to the state, both committees have been set up at government rather than municipal level, and both have taken up the issue of Savieniba.

BIBLIOGRAPHY

Part I: The Baltic Sea region

Attiat F. O. *et al* (1996) 'Ethnic Anxiety: A Case Study of Resident Aliens', *Journal of Baltic Studies*, Vol. XXVII, No. 1: 21–46.
Beach, H. & Runblom, H. (red) (1989) *Det mångkulturella Sverige*, Uppsala: 339–351.
Brubaker, R. (1996) *Nationalism Reframed*, Cambridge: Cambridge University Press.

Bunkse, E. V. (1994) 'Baltic peoples, Baltic culture and Europe', *Geojournal*, Vol. 33, No. 1: 5–7, 15–17.

Claval, P. (1994) 'From Michelet to Braudel: Personality, Identity and Organization of France' in Hooson, D.(ed.) *Geography and National Identity*, Oxford: 39.

Gustavsson, S. *et al* (1995) *The Multicultural Baltic Region, Part 2, Peoples of the Baltics*, booklet No. 4, Uppsala: 5–11.

Gustavsson, S. (1997) Lecture: 'The multilingual Baltic Region', Uppsala, 25 September.

Hanson, A. (1994) Lecture: 'Baltikums ekonomiska framtid', Stockholm, 16 February.

Hooson, D. (ed.) *Geography and National Identity*, Oxford.

Illeris, S. (1994) *Essays on Regional Development in Europe*.

Lagerspetz, M. (1997) 'Sociala problem och Estlands sjungande revolution', *Nordisk Öst-forum*, No. 1.

Lowenthal, D. (1994) 'European and English Landscapes as National Symbols' in Hooson, D. (ed.) *Geography and National Identity*, Oxford.

Lundén, T. (1997) 'Makten över marken. En politisk geografi', *Studentlitteratur*, Lund: 18.

Lundqvist, L. & Persson, L. O. (1995) *Baltic Regions and Baltic Links. From a North European to a Baltic Region perspective*, NordREFO.

Malmberg, B. (1993) *Problems of Time-Space Coordination – A Key to the Understanding of Multiplant Farms*, Uppsala.

Ohlsson, S. Ö. (1978) *Skånes språkliga försvenskning 1*, Lund.

Ohlsson, S. Ö. (1979) *Skånes språkliga försvenskning 2*, Lund.

O'Loughlin, J. & van der Wusten, H. (1993) *The New Political Geography of Eastern Europe*, London: Belhaven Press: 1–8.

Porter, M. E. (1990) *The Competitive Advantage of Nations*.

Roth, H-I. (1997) Lecture: 'National identities', Uppsala, 20 October.

Rapawy, S. (1997) *Ethnic Reidentification in Ukraine*, Washington, DC: International Programs Center, Population Division, U.S. Bureau of the Census.

Runblom H. (1995) 'Majoritet och minoritet i Östersjöområdet', *Natur och Kultur*, Stockholm: 82–84.

Taube, C. (1997) Lecture: 'Citizenship in the Baltic States', Uppsala, 14 October.

Tegborg, L. (1997) Lecture: 'The religious diversity in the Baltic Region', Uppsala, 30 September.

The Baltic Times (1997) 'Crossing the line with Russia', Vol. 2, No. 77, 18–24 September.

Wahlbäck, K. (1997) Lecture: 'Swedish politics towards the Baltic Region', Uppsala, 2 October.

Westin, C. (1995) *Meeting Place Baltic. Peoples of the Baltic*, Booklet No. 1, Uppsala: The Baltic University: 6.

Zalamans, D. (1994) 'Lettlands geografi', Rapport för Baltiska institutionen vid Stockholms universitet.

Part II: The twin-town of Valga/Valka

Black, J. (1997) *Maps and Politics*, London: Reaktion Books.

Deutsch, K. (1953) *Nationalism and Social Communication*, Mass, Cambridge.

Kant, E. (1932) *Valga: Geografaaline ja majanduse ülevade*, Tartu.

Lundén, T. (1973) *Individens rumsliga beteende i ett gränsområde*, Stockholm.

Lundén, T. (1993) 'Språkens landskap i Europa', *Studentlitteratur*, Lund.

Lundén, T. (1997) 'Makten över marken. En politisk geografi', *Studentlitteratur*, Lund.

Lundén, T & Zalamans, D. (1998) 'Valga/Valka – delad stad', *Geografiska notiser* 1/98.

Nousiainen, R., Piliste, I. & Udre, D. (1997) 'ESTLA Project 9604 BA 006', ESTLA Interim report.

Törnqvist, G. (1996) *Sverige i nätverkens Europa*, Malmö: Liber-Hermods.

Waack, C. (1996) 'Divided Border Cities in the Baltic States', Conference paper from Wisal, Poland.

Fieldcourse reports

Mõttus, L. & Säfström, T. (1997) *Gränsöverskridande mellan Valga och Valka*, Stockholm.

Eklund, H. & Kloth, M. (1997) *Fysisk planering och gränsregionalt samarbete i Valga/Valka*, Stockholm.

Bylund, J. (1997) *Nationalismens infrastruktur*, Stockholm.

Jägerholm, A. (1997) 'Media in the Baltic States', Draft version.

Holmström, C. (1997) *Skolor i gränsstaden Valga/Valka*, Stockholm.

Båvner, E. (1997) *Sjukvård i gränsland – exemplet Valga/Valga*, Södertörn.

Forsström, N. (1997) Fallet Savieniba – en gränstvist, Stockholm.

15
Territorial Claims in the North Caucasus

Anna Matveeva

The end of Russian military intervention in Chechnya in August 1996 did not bring peace into the North Caucasus. Moreover, it exacerbated the existing boundary disputes in the region, such as territorial claims over the administrative border between Chechnya and Dagestan, and those between North Ossetia and Ingushetia which have already led to the violent conflict of 1992. The international borders between the Russian Federation on the one hand, and Georgia and Azerbaijan on the other, have witnessed ongoing disputes and numerous violations of the border regime which have contributed to the already hostile relations between the countries. The tensions are significant not only in the light of the existing border regime, but also because of the worrying implications for the viability of the Ossetian and Lezgin communities split between, respectively, North and South Ossetia, and Dagestan and Azerbaijan. However, the most significant problem is the present 'unsatisfactory compromise' in the situation of Chechnya, the present policy of 'containment' of the republic and the *de facto* reinforced militarisation of the area.

This paper will examine the current territorial claims in the North Caucasus and the policies adopted to pursue these claims. Three kinds of disputes will be assessed:

- territorial claims between constituent parts of the Russian Federation, namely the North Ossetian/Ingush conflict and the claims pursued by the Cossacks in the southern Russian *krais*
- the situation of the divided peoples, namely Ossetians and Lezgins, and the cross-border dynamics between the Russian Federation and the states to the south
- the security situation around Chechnya; arguably, the present Chechen assertiveness can be regarded as the defining element in the North Caucasian boundary disputes.

It will conclude with some reflections on future options and potential risks, and their broader implications for the stability of the region.

TERRITORIAL CLAIMS BETWEEN PARTS OF THE RUSSIAN FEDERATION

There are at least 20 actual or potential disputes in the North Caucasian region

Borderlands Under Stress (M.A. Pratt and J.A. Brown (eds), ISBN 90-411-9790-7).
© Kluwer Law International, 2000.

(Tsutsiev & Dzugaev, 1997). This paper highlights only those which display distinct leanings towards further escalation.

North Ossetian/Ingush conflict

The North Ossetian/Ingush conflict, the only incident of large-scale inter-communal violence within the Russian Federation, erupted in 1992 over the issue of jurisdiction over Prigorodnyi *rayon*. The *rayon*, historically Ingush territory, was populated by the Cossacks between the 1820s and 1920s, at which point the Cossacks were deported and the Ingush brought back. The Ingush were deported in 1943, together with other North Caucasian peoples, and Prigorodnyi was allocated to North Ossetia. After the deportees returned in 1957, Prigorodnyi remained a part of North Ossetia.[1] The Ingush made every effort to return to the territories they considered to be their historical homeland, but faced problems obtaining *propiska* (residence permits).[2] The Soviet system, however, exercised some affirmative action programmes for the Ingush.[3]

The Ingush justify their present claim to Prigorodnyi *rayon* by the resolution of the USSR Supreme Soviet adopted in November 1989 and by Articles 3 and 6 on territorial rehabilitation of the Law on the Deported Peoples adopted in April 1991.[4]

The period between November 1991 and October 1992 saw increased armament on both sides.[5] The conflict started in October 1992 when, as a result of mounting tensions, the North Ossetian OMON (special police task force) killed three Ingush and Ingush self-defence units advanced towards Vladikav-kaz, the capital of North Ossetia.[6] In a few days Russian federal troops interfered on the North Ossetian side and, supported by the National Guards and North Ossetian OMON, drove the Ingush out of the republic.[7] This event created fears in Chechnya that this was the beginning of a Russian advance to take over the rebellious republic. However, the federal troops stopped on the administrative border of the Ingush *rayons*.[8]

Since then tensions have remained but major violence has been avoided. The situation was aggravated[9] when the Ingush president, Ruslan Aushev, appealed in July 1997 to the Russian leadership to introduce direct presidential rule in the territory of Prigorodnyi. The protest meetings in North Ossetia called for a re-creation of the self-defence units, and the then President, Akhsarbek Galazov, threatened that North Ossetia would break away from Moscow rule. A number of terrorist acts took place. The tension was exacerbated by the statements of the Chechen leaders that if the North Ossetian leadership could not bring peace to the republic, Chechnya was willing to dispatch an armed unit to restore Constitutional order.[10]

Since then official relations have improved. The signing took place on 15 October 1997 of the Programme of Joint Actions by the State Bodies of the Russian Federation, Republic of North Ossetia-Alania and Republic of Ingushetia to facilitate the return of displaced persons (DPs) and improve the psychological atmosphere. The programme envisages repatriation to all places of settlement, including Vladikavkaz, not only to the villages of Prigorodnyi *rayon*. The legal relationship has been established by the Treaty Regulating Relations and Cooperation between Republic of North Ossetia-Alania and Republic of Ingushetia, signed in September 1997. The Ossetian side has abolished one law and three pieces of legislature which obstructed the repatriation, on the recommendation of the representative of the President of the Russian Federation in North Ossetia/Ingushetia (the federal body set up in order to facilitate the resolution of conflict). At the same time, the Constitution of Ingushetia still contains Article 11, which insists on 'the return of the territory which Ingushetia was illegally deprived of'. The article contradicts federal legislation and the Ossetian side has a right to appeal to the Federal Constitutional Court to abolish it. However, the existence of such a provision equally serves the interests of those Ossetian nationalists who want to paint the image of an Ingush aggressor.

Alexandr Dzasokhov's election to the presidency in January 1998 was welcomed by the Ingush side, not least because he was not associated with the conflict. A dialogue between Dzasokhov and Aushev was established. Dzasokhov made efforts to put some political weight behind the repatriation programme and the Ossetian side began to pursue initiatives to improve the psychological atmosphere for the first time.[11] However, when the repatriation programme shifted from being a political slogan into imminent reality, the fragility of the dialogue between the leaderships became apparent. Popular resistance on the Ossetian side intensified, while the Ingush grew increasingly impatient. This led to a wave of kidnappings and killings and a general deterioration in the security situation, as well as a break down in elite communication throughout the summer of 1998.[12]

The Ingush appear to be the net losers in the conflict, and the essence of their present campaign is *de facto* restoration of the status quo – i.e. the return to the areas of original settlement as of 1992. At present, the main obstacles to repatriation are as follows:

- Ethnic tensions at the popular level are still acute and the degree of ethnic resentment between communities has not diminished; the dialogue between political elites is yet to transform itself into grassroots support. The slogans of 'impossibility of mutual co-existence with the Ingush' on the Ossetian side and 'reconstruction of the territorial integrity of Ingushetia within the 1944 borders' on the Ingush side remain highly popular.[13]
- Both sides are dissatisfied with the pace of the DPs' return.[14] The Agreement on Measures on DPs Return was signed by the North Ossetian and Ingush leaders in March 1993 in Kislovodsk, but the Ingush side largely blames the Galazov leadership for lack of commitment to its implementation.[15]
- There is a proliferation of armaments in the conflict zone.[16]
- There are many refugees from South Ossetia, 9,000 of whom live in the original Ingush houses in Prigorodnyi.[17]

- There is no credible security guarantee for the Ingush, who doubt the capacity of the North Ossetian police forces to protect them effectively.

The Cossacks

The last major redrawing of borders of the Soviet period took place in the North Caucasus in 1957–58 when the Russian (formerly Cossack) agricultural *rayons* were transferred to the ethnic republics in order to provide them with wheat-growing capabilities (the mountain peoples primarily grew maize and did not grow wheat) and to ensure their further Russification by supplementing them with sizeable Russian communities.[18] Thus, North Ossetia gained Mozdok *rayon*; Kabardino-Balkaria gained Prokhladnenskii and Maiskii *rayons*; Checheno-Ingushetia gained Naurskii, Schelkovskii and Nadterechnyi *rayons*; and Dagestan gained Tarumovskii and Kyzlyar *rayons*. The North Caucasian ethnic republics border on the predominantly Russian Krasnodar and Stavropol *krais* which were deprived of these territories in favour of the republics.

At present Stavropol *krai* shares a common border with four out of six North Caucasian republics, and the former Cossack *rayons* of Chechnya and Karachaevo-Cherkessia more than once considered the possibility of joining the *krai*. Stavropol *krai* has one of the largest intakes of DPs into its territory; the number of immigrants grows by 1.5 per cent each year and every twelfth migrant in the Russian Federation (RF) is registered in the *krai* (McFaul & Petrov, 1998). Given the immigration pressure, the *krai* legislature adopted a law, On the Status of a Resident of Stavropol *krai*, in August 1995 stating that resident status (actually more like 'citizen' status), bringing with it the entitlement to buy real estate and land, can be acquired only after seven years' temporary residence in the *krai*. High tariffs for temporary registration were also introduced. In April 1996 the federal Constitutional Court ruled against the law, but the *krai* deputies refused to give up and adopted the Immigration Code, unique in the country, which has been applied since February 1997. Resentment of North Caucasians in the *krai* was exacerbated by the terrorist acts in Mineral'nye Vody in 1993–94, hostage-taking in Budennovsk in 1995, the overspill of crime from neighbouring Chechnya, and immigration pressure. Relations between the population and the authorities of Stavropol *krai* on the one hand, and its North Caucasian neighbours (especially Chechens and Dagestanis) on the other, remain extremely tense.[19]

After the Budennovsk raid the necessity to protect the border areas became a priority for the *krai* authorities, and the Cossacks, whose influence is stronger in the southern, borderland areas of the *krai*, acquired some support from the administration. Petr Fedosov, the Stavropol Cossacks *ataman* (leader), was co-opted as a member of Stavropol government. The Cossacks campaign for the right to create self-defence units and carry arms, as well as for the return to Stavropol *krai* of the Shelkovskii and Naurskii *rayons* of Chechnya, where Russians still live. In December 1997 they blocked the railways and airport in Mineral'nye Vody in order to attract attention to their demands.[20] The bill they drafted regarding the return of the *rayons* was to be considered by the Russian State Duma.

The Cossack movement is supervised at the federal level by the Main Directorate of the Cossack Hosts under the RF president. In 1996–97 the federal authorities introduced the incorporation of Cossack organisations into State *Reestr* (registration), which meant the transformation of the Cossack groups from public organisations into state structures with state financial support and tax benefits.[21] The reaction to that measure was not straightforward. On the one hand the Cossacks regarded the registration as an acknowledgement of their role as a stronghold of federal authority in the North Caucasus. On the other hand, internal feuds were exacerbated and the movement split into loyalists and oppositionists because, in order to become registered, the rules and nominations of the *atamans* had to be approved by the regional or republican authorities, and the state authorities normally had the upper hand. Moreover, the Cossacks from all the North Caucasus had to integrate into Terskoye and Kubanskoye Hosts, but the objectives of the Cossack organisations from the ethnic republics were sometimes different from that of Stavropol and Krasnodar *krais*.[22]

The rise of the Cossack movement in Stavropol *krai* and the possible tacit support for it by the Stavropol *krai* authorities present a concern to the North Caucasian leaderships.[23] The combination of large migration, closeness to Chechnya and threat of terrorism makes the Stavropol Cossacks more radical than the others.[24] At the same time, the Cossack movement, internally split and lacking decisive leadership, does not present a credible force capable of military or political undertakings. However, if the crime wave from Chechnya does not stop, the Cossack movement may gain some muscle in a few years' time, if led by Russian DPs from Chechnya. The *krai* is also an arena of nationalist organisations such as Derzhava or the Russian Patriotic Movement of Stavropolie; lately the *Russkie Vityazi* (Russian Warriors), a loose offshoot of the Russian National Unity (RNE, better known as *barkashovtsy*) stepped up its activities.[25] Amidst increasing controversy, RNE held its regional conference in Stavropol in September 1998. The following objectives are attributed to nationalist movements in the *krai*:

- the return to Krasnodar and Stavropol *krais* of the Russian-populated *rayons* allocated to the republics in 1957
- the abolition of North Caucasian republics and creation of non-ethnic *guberniyas* (provinces) headed by *atamans*.

THE DIVIDED PEOPLES

Ossetians and relations with Georgia

The cross-border dynamic is determined by the uneasy relations between Russia and Georgia, the main issues being Russia's role in conflicts in Abkhazia and South Ossetia, dispute over the Soviet military inheritance, Russian military presence in Georgia and competition over the Caspian pipeline route. After Eduard Shevardnadze regained power, Georgia initially agreed to the stationing of Russian border guards on the Georgian/Turkish border which had been jointly policed by Russian and Georgian troops, as a result of which the Russian/ Georgian border in the North Caucasus remained open and controls were minimal. However, with the general deterioration of interstate relations and the rise in the smuggling of spirits, the regime was tightened and customs points introduced. In 1998 an agreement was finally reached to move Russian border guards to the Russian/Georgian border. With the subsequent division of former Soviet border-troops' property, formal demarcation of the border has begun.

The tensions on the Russian/Georgian border have aggravated the relations between the two states several times since independence. The dispute on the Georgian Military Highway at Upper Lars over control of supplies of spirits into Russia in December 1997 resulted in the Russian decision to move the border post into Georgian territory. This was followed by another downturn in interstate relations and reinforced Tbilisi's decision to withhold ratification of military agreements with Moscow and to demand once more the withdrawal of Russian border troops from Georgian territory. The clash was exacerbated in June 1998 when Russian border troops resisted a five-hour assault by unknown gunmen from the Ingush side, and in August there were almost daily attacks by groups coming from the northern side of the border.

Another issue is the unresolved conflict involving ethnic Ossetians which erupted in 1991–92 between the Georgian central government and the breakaway republic of South Ossetia. During the conflict the North Ossetian authorities adopted a cautious stance. The republican Supreme Soviet did not pass a decision on unification, although the South Ossetian leadership issued appeals on a number of occasions.[26] In 1992 North Ossetia refused passage through its territory to volunteers of the nationalist Russian Legion and a detachment of Confederation of Mountain Peoples of the Caucasus (KNK) who were going to fight in South Ossetia.

In six years the conflict has reached the stagnation stage, and the possibility of resumption of hostilities seems unlikely. The South Ossetian leadership claims that it would settle for an equal status to the one negotiated with Abkhazia. The present obstacles to resolution seem to be as follows:

- the absence of credible security guarantees for the Ossetians
- the fact that the Georgian authorities assist only those who have a proven record of being forcefully deprived of residence rights and property
- and primarily, the fact that many Ossetians regard their economic prospects as being better in North Ossetia.

The unresolved status of South Ossetia remains a burden to the North, and there is widespread pessimism as to this burden ever being relieved. South Ossetia is *de facto* being gradually incorporated into the economic and social space of the Russian Federation, with transport and energy supplies coming from the North. An agreement for the economic rehabilitation of South Ossetia between Russia and Georgia is discussed but money remains a problem. Although the Georgian government is taking steps to enable repatriation,[27] most of the people involved are not willing to return. Many made money controlling the wholesale cross-border trade and presently occupy lucrative positions in the new market economy. Moreover, some benefited by acquiring the property of the Ingush who fled violence. Meanwhile, emigration from South Ossetia continues.[28]

The relative progress made in resolution of the conflict was facilitated by the fact that the Georgian President, Eduard Shevardnadze, is not associated with the conflict which largely took place under ex-President Gamsakhurdia's regime. The election of Alexandr Dzasokhov and his positive dialogue with the Georgian President also brought some encouragement to the process. However, while economic prospects for the South Ossetians are better in the North, the status quo is likely to persist.

Lezgins and relations with Azerbaijan[29]

Lezgins live on both sides of the river Samur in southern Dagestan (250,000) and in northern Azerbaijan (177,000). They have been divided since 1860, but only after the break-up of the USSR, when the border with Azerbaijan became international rather than merely administrative, did the Lezgins find themselves in the position of a truly divided people.

The Lezgin issue is caught up in the tense relationship between Russia and Azerbaijan, which is characterised by disagreement over a number of important issues, such as the legal status of the Caspian Sea, Russian military bases in Azerbaijan and the conflict in Nagorno-Karabakh. Azerbaijan, unlike Dagestan, does not acknowledge that the division of the Lezgins by the international border presents a problem, as such acceptance might imply giving in to some Armenian demands over Nagorno-Karabakh. There is an implicit tension around the Lezgin issue in Azerbaijan, although there are no discriminatory policies against them. However, the Lezgins' campaign for national-cultural autonomy is vehemently rejected by the Azerbaijani authorities who drew the lesson from the Nagorno-Karabakh experience that autonomy is the quickest road to conflict and secession.

Azerbaijan's reluctance to join the Commonwealth of Independent states (CIS) in 1992–93 and rejection of Moscow's bid for Russian border guards to have a role in policing the Azerbaijani–Iranian border led to a gradual tightening of the regime. The situation was further aggravated by the war in Chechnya. The border with Azerbaijan was closed by Russia in December 1994, and controls and customs were introduced. The official reason was to secure the border against the penetration of weapons and foreign mercenaries into Chechnya, but the occasion was also used to score a point against Azerbaijan.[30] establishment of border controls came as a shock for the local population. In April 1996, under pressure from the Dagestani government, the regime was relaxed and local residents, mainly Lezgins, were allowed to cross the border freely. After signing the Khasavyurt Accords in August 1996 the Russian government finally decided to open the border and allowed larger number of local conscripts to serve in the border troops, but tensions remain over the issue of whether a five-kilometre 'alienation zone' will ultimately be established.[30] The tactics adopted by the Lezgins was to lobby the People's Assembly to put the issue on the political agenda and force the government to raise it with Moscow. From 1996 the Dagestani authorities took a more proactive approach, exchanging official visits with Azerbaijan, signing a Treaty on Friendship and Cooperation and supporting efforts at economic cooperation and border delimitation. Relations between the leaderships remain extremely good.

Ethnic tensions between Lezgins and Azeris began in 1992 but reached a peak in mid-1994, the time of heavy losses on the Karabakh front. In May that year violent clashes occurred in Derbent, and in June in the Gussary region of Azerbaijan. In Dagestan in 1991, the Lezgin national movement Sadval called for the creation of an independent Lezgistan. The Dagestani authorities, although sympathetic to the fate of the divided people, never supported this claim and it was officially rejected in April 1996 at the sixth congress of Sadval. The fear of assimilation by Turkic nationalist policies[31] and the perception of a threat to the Lezgins' viability as a distinct community remain powerful. Lezgin radical organisations and activists in Dagestan claimed that the Lezgins' very survival is under threat. The activists are mainly members of the intelligentsia, with little grassroots support and no cooperation from the Dagestani authorities, and in this sense their direct influence over political developments is minimal. However, as extremely vocal individuals they can damage Dagestani–Azerbaijani relations and put a cloud of suspicion over Lezgins in general. Lately some Lezgins changed their orientation towards Azerbaijan, while others spoke about the creation of an autonomous Lezgin district within RF, but independent of Dagestan. The possible explanation is twofold: anticipation of an oil boom in Azerbaijan and a desperate attempt to attract the Dagestani authorities' attention which currently diverted to Chechnya.

Sadval in Dagestan pursues a more realistic course, calling for the establishment of a customs union between Russia and Azerbaijan, the creation of the Samur free economic zone in southern Dagestan and northern Azerbaijan, and the introduction of dual citizenship for Lezgins in Russia and Azerbaijan – the only point on which the Dagestani government distances itself from Sadval's agenda.

In September–October 1997 a number of 'sports camps' attributed to the Lezgins appeared in Magaramkent *rayon* (Dagestan). The trainees had been well equipped and were obviously undergoing military training, but nobody possessed firearms and the authorities had no legal right to arrest them (one person was eventually arrested and two escaped). The Azerbaijani authorities became alarmed and moved 5,000 heavy armed troops to the border, and Dagestan appealed to the federal government to move the 136 Buinaksk Brigade and border troops there.[32] Meanwhile, villagers resorted to street protests alleging that the trainees were involved in the murder of a local businessperson.[33] After the intervention of the republican authorities the camps seem to have disappeared.

The situation is further complicated by various criminal activities. With the disruption of official economic ties as a result of the war in Chechnya, many illegal opportunities were opened up, including arms- and drugs-trafficking, and the Russian–Azerbaijani as well as the Russian–Georgian border rapidly emerged as zones of international cross-border crime.

IMPACT OF INSTABILITY IN CHECHNYA ON THE NORTH CAUCASUS

At present the conflict in Chechnya has been transformed from a national into a regional security problem. Many local observers in the Caucasus claim that there is a link between the aggravation of the North Ossetian–Ingush tensions, as well as the situation on the Russian/Georgian border, and the Chechen attempts to finally break away from Russia. The effects of the unresolved situation around Chechnya are felt across the North Caucasus, but primarily in Dagestan. Although Dagestan remained relatively calm during the fighting in Chechnya, the post-war situation has brought about new dangers and the most serious potential for conflict lies in the tensions between Dagestan and Chechnya.

Chechens are one of the indigenous ethnic groups in Dagestan, numbering some 90,000. Before the Russian military intervention the attitude of the local Chechens and Dagestanis as a whole towards Dudayev's regime was largely negative, and his independence bid was regarded as unrealistic. This negative attitude changed, especially after the storming of Grozny in 1994, which sent shock waves across the Caucasus. Soon after the war started there were significant public protests in Dagestan, with demands for the Dagestani authorities to condemn the Russian invasion. Although sympathising with the Chechen predicament and disapproving of the military operation, the authorities in Dagestan maintained strict neutrality between the Russian federal government and the Chechens.

When the war ended, the Dagestani authorities began to fear that if Chechnya gained independence from Russia, it would have a dramatic impact on Dagestan. This fear has been exacerbated by post-war developments. Russian troops have been withdrawn from Chechnya into Dagestan, and the border is no longer properly guarded, allowing criminal gangs from Chechnya, and others who are armed, to enter Dagestan. Subsequent developments have shown that the internal turmoil in Chechnya, with blood feuds and the struggle for power-forging alliances and enmities across the North Caucasus, is becoming more destabilising for Dagestan than the straightforward conflict between Chechnya and Russian federal power.

The current factors of instability are as follows: violence in border areas and territorial claims pursued by the Chechen leaders; a military link between Islamic radicals in Chechnya and in Dagestan; tensions among the local Chechen population; the militarisation of Dagestan; and developments in the transportation sector resulting from Moscow's intention to build alternative communications.

Official relations between Djohar (capital of Chechnya, formerly Grozny) and Makhachkala (capital of Dagestan) are at a low point, although the Dagestani authorities tried to initiate dialogue. The People's Assembly of Dagestan established interparliamentary relations with the Chechen parliament in January 1998. The main obstacle in official relations is the Chechen leadership's reluctance to sign a Treaty on Friendship and Cooperation, drafted by the Dagestani side in November 1996 in order to provide a framework for practical measures. The Dagestani leader, Magomedali Magomedov, failed to sign the treaty in February 1998 during his visit to Djohar, as the Chechen leadership argued that, while Chechnya is an independent state, Dagestan is a subject of the Russian Federation and therefore could sign a bilateral agreement only with an individual district of Chechnya, not with the Chechen government. This, however, did not prevent Chechnya from signing friendship and cooperation treaties with Stavropol *krai*, Tatarstan and Bashkorstan. The Dagestani position is that the republic has already signed similar treaties with Azerbaijan and Kazakhstan, both independent states.

The stance adopted by the Dagestani leadership towards the Chechen authorities is one of apprehension of provoking any hostile reaction.[34] Presumably, this cautious stance can be justified by their fear of undermining the positions of Aslan Maskhadov and his relatively moderate supporters, potentially making way for more radical forces. Another, probably more plausible explanation is that Dagestan suffers its own political and social turmoil. The leadership, therefore, fears that any violation of the status quo may completely jeopardise internal stability. It chooses to play a balancing act to mitigate the existing tensions rather than adopt a more proactive policy.

For a long time the Dagestani leadership did not respond publicly to any claims to its territory coming from the other side of the border, however widely publicised. Meanwhile, the idea of unification between Chechnya and parts (or all) of Dagestan has gained momentum in Chechnya. The Islamic Nation movement, founded in Djohar in August 1997 at a congress of Chechen and other North Caucasian delegates, declared as its proclaimed goal the creation of an Imamate, a state formation which would incorporate all the lands unified by Imam Shamil, the leader of the great Caucasian war against the Russians in the nineteenth century. The Foreign Minister of Chechnya, Movladi Udugov, who chairs the movement, pointed out that the territories of Dagestan populated by ethnic Chechens should join the first independent state in the North Caucasus. Nadirshah Khachilaev, the Chairman of the Union of Muslims of Russia and a Lak from Makhachkala, expressed his support for the concept of an independent Dagestan (*RFE/RL Newsline*, 1997). The other religious figure campaigning for unification on Islamic grounds was Ahmad Akhtaev, who founded the All Union Islamic Renaissance Party in 1990.[35]

According to the Islamic Nation unionists, the movement does not aspire to annex the 'historical' Chechen lands, but would rather promote the notion of Chechnya joining Dagestan in a single Islamic state. It calls for the restoration of Dagestan to its 'historical borders'. This is a convenient formula to avoid any formal accusation of pursuing territorial claims on Dagestani territory. As articulated by Movladi Udugov, 'our aim is to prevent the splitting of the Chechens and the peoples of Dagestan on the grounds of ethnicity, to preclude Chechnya from being isolated from Dagestan' (Rotar, 1998a). In the view of some Chechen strategists, such a unified Chechen–Dagestani state formation would enjoy increased economic viability, enhanced by the access to the Caspian Sea, and therefore might have more chance of gaining recognition in the long term. The practical way to achieve this was articulated by Movladi Udugov at a Round Table with Dagestani authorities in December 1997 in Novolak *rayon*, when he expressed the view that Dagestan is a Russian colony and the revival of the peoples of Caucasus is impossible without decolonisation. The Chechen proposals were:

- to create the Congress of Peoples of Chechnya and Dagestan[36]
- to establish joint patrolling of the border and create a Caucasian *Interpol*
- to adhere to *Shari'a* laws in mutual relations, and try criminals from both sides according to the *Shari'a* justice system
- to promote ties between the republics and exchange information.

Despite Dagestani officials' opposition, the Congress did take place, in Djohar on 26 April, headed by Shamil Basaev, the then acting Prime Minister of Chechnya, who declared unification of Dagestan and Chechnya in one free state the ultimate goal of the new organisation.[37] Dagestan was not represented by any officials or by the influential informal leaders. The Dagestani authorities responded with a joint declaration protesting against the Congress and its resolutions, signed by everyone influential in the republic.[38] Nevertheless, in June the Chechen leadership initiated the Congress military forces manoeuvres, which took place in the border areas of Chechnya and Dagestan and were attended by senior Chechen politicians.

The present unification attempt is officially based on religious unity. However, the Dagestani authorities firmly believe that the Chechen leadership is far more interested in access to the Caspian Sea and oil transit than in commitment to the common faith. The Dagestani leadership is convinced that, having failed to attract the Dagestani elite to the idea of separation from Russia, the next step of the Chechen leadership will be to undermine the integrity of Dagestan from within.

The likely allies for the unification option are Dagestani Chechens, or *Chechentsy-Akkintsy*, who live in lowland Dagestan on the border with Chechnya. In 1944 they suffered deportation to Central Asia along with other Chechens and since their return they have aspired to resettlement in their historical areas in Novolak and Khasavyurt *rayons* and to restore Aukhov *rayon* (despite the fact that Aukhov *rayon* existed as an administrative unit for only four months before the Chechen deportation). These territories, however, are occupied by Laks and Avars who were forcibly resettled there from the mountains. The tensions centre around the disputed villages of Leninaul and Kalininaul and over the question of where the Laks and Avars would go, once persuaded to move from the villages, and where the resources would come from to facilitate such an undertaking.[39]

These disputes, however, have been recently overshadowed by the suspect loyalty of the *Chechentsy-Akkintsy* in the eyes of the Dagestani authorities. This fear was articulated by the then Security Council Secretary, Magomed Tolboev, who said: 'Grozny has created a bridgehead in the Khasavyurt *rayon* for seizing all of Dagestan. The local Chechens have been assigned the role of the fifth column.' (Rotar, 1998c.) There are indeed certain indications which give rise to various speculations. Basyr Dadaev, the leader of the *Chechentsy-Akkintsy*, frequently asserted that, from the point of view of Chechen historiography, this whole region is 'the traditional land of the Vainakhs'. In the present circumstances the Dagestani government has little incentive to facilitate any resettlement, assuming that, should the Chechens acquire the land and settlement rights, there would be no obstacle to them joining independent Chechnya.[40] The Dagestani Chechens campaigning for the resettlement blocked the roads in the area for three weeks in August 1998, while the Dagestani authorities blamed Moscow for its failure to allocate funds to facilitate the move (Maksakov, 1998). At times local tensions have led to situations in which Chechen fighters making raids from Chechnya have been resisted by Avars alone. In the view of local authorities in the Avar areas, the most acute inter-ethnic tensions in Dagestan lie between the Chechens and Avars.[41] Local Chechens are already excluded from serving in police forces in the border areas. The Khasavyurt branch of *Tenglik*, the Kumyk national movement, declared that in the case of an escalation of violence between the Chechens and Avars, the Kumyks would remain neutral and support neither side.

As a result, the position of moderate Dagestani Chechens, who would prefer to be disassociated from the developments in Chechnya, has worsened. There is a threat that if abductions and looting from across the border cannot be stopped, the Dagestani Chechens will become hostages to spontaneous violence from other Dagestani groups. The precedent took place as a result of Raduyev's raid on Kyzlyar in January 1996, when Dagestani Chechens were threatened by local Avars.[42]

The other, more formidable ally is represented by the forces of radical Islam. The Islamic radicals in the North Caucasus call themselves Salafiyun ('following the path of our forebears') or 'Muslims of Jamaat'; the authorities prefer to call them Wahhabis. 'Wahhabism' is a term used loosely by post-Soviet officials to designate any type of Muslim radicalism, often completely unrelated to the Wahhabi sect in Saudi Arabia.[43] Their form of Islam is close to the literal Koran and they follow its prescriptions to the letter; they do not smoke, drink or shave their beards, and they reject state authority, especially in the restriction of arms possession. It is believed that the first radicals in the region appeared as a result of *haj* (Kisriev, 1997a). Another view is that they already existed in Dagestan in the early 1980s, but the KGB at that time was more effective in suppressing them.[44]

The link with Islamic radicals in Chechnya was established during the war.

The Jordan-born field commander Emir Khattab organised an armed unit based on Wahhabi affiliation in which many Dagestanis served. The Dagestani radicals who fought in the war in Chechnya returned home with a determination to built an Islamic state. During 1997 the military and organisational support from Chechnya to Dagestani radical Muslims became more manifest, and it is widely believed that financial assistance came from the Arab countries.[45] The Central Front of Liberation of Caucasus and Dagestan claimed responsibility for the armed raid on the Russian 136 Brigade in December 1997 and distributed leaflets to this end. A number of Islamic radicals have been trained in camps in Chechnya under the supervision of Wahhabi military instructors; it is believed that at least four camps are operational (Rotar, 1998b). Although this training is open to anybody, only Islamic radicals have taken up the opportunity. One of their spiritual leaders, Kizilvyurt mullah Bagauddin Mohammed, publicly claimed that 'Dagestan can stay within Russia only if the latter becomes an Islamic state' (*Nezavisimaya Gazeta*, 1998b).

It is ultimately difficult to establish who is a so-called Wahhabi in Chechnya and who is not. Emir Khattab identifies himself as such, whilst Salman Raduyev vehemently distances himself from Wahhabism; it is also known that the two men are worst enemies. Movladi Udugov, the leader of the Islamic Nation, abstains from public identification with the Wahhabis but is widely believed to be one. Despite dubious religious credentials, Salman Raduyev and the leadership of the Fighting Squads of Jamaat of Dagestan established relations with the December 1997 signing of the Treaty on Military Mutual Assistance. This document claims that the Islamic Jamaat of Dagestan and the Djohar's Army of Raduyev represent forces which fight for a unified Islamic state in the Caucasus and for independence from Russia (*Nezavisimaya Gazeta*, 1998c). The initiative for signing the agreement perhaps lies with the willingness of Dagestani groups seeking separation from Russia to forge alliances with anybody who has military capacity to offer. Another organisation, the Sword of Islam, took responsibility for the explosion of an electric-energy distribution station in the disputed Novolak *rayon*, a Dagestani Chechen area, in March 1998, calling on Laks to leave the Chechen homeland. In May 1998 Dagestani police officers sent to disarm the Karamakhi Islamists were rapidly encircled by them, and 50 people were held hostage. The tension reached its peak in August when three villages in Buinaksk *rayon* announced the creation of a separate Islamic territory in which Dagestani (and Russian) laws were not applicable, and their willingness to defend it by force. Radical Chechen commanders, including Shamil Basaev, offered their military support.

The policy responses formed by the Dagestani authorities combined punitive and propaganda measures.[46] Before the alliance with the Chechens became public, the Dagestani authorities made efforts to incorporate Islamic radicals into the mainstream debate, arranging television debates between them and traditionalists in May 1997.[47] When the radicals claimed responsibility for violence, a few young men from Karamakhi were arrested, on the grounds that they were suspected of participating in the Buinaksk raid; they were soon released. In December 1997 the People's Assembly (Dagestani legislature) voted on the Law on the Freedom of Religious Confession. The Law, which was adopted in accordance with Russian Federal Law, makes it very difficult for radicals to register their congregations, build mosques, publish papers and import religious texts from abroad. The Dagestani authorities also claimed external interference and accused Muslim fundamentalist groups from Kuwait and Saudi Arabia of instigating *jihad* (holy war) in Dagestan. However, even if these accusations have some truth in them, there is apparently no evidence which would enable the authorities to launch official protests at the Arab governments.[48]

In the eyes of the Dagestani authorities, 'Wahhabism, although not possessing a wide social base and not being popular among majority of Muslim population of the republic, still represents a real and serious threat in reinforcing religious extremism.'[49] In reaction to the proclamation of an 'Islamic territory', the Dagestani authorities threatened forceful measures, and strong-worded statements have been issued. However, after the assassination of Saidmuhamed-haji Abubakarov, Mufti of Dagestan and an outspoken critic of Wahhabism, the Dagestani leadership resorted to negotiations. Perhaps the reason behind the compromise was that, if the radicals felt themselves to be physically threatened, they were likely to turn for support to the armed groups from Chechnya and then the authorities would have to deal with the symptoms rather than the root causes of the problem.

The rise of Wahhabism in the North Caucasus can be explained by the fact that the social ground for a radical movement has already been prepared.[50] It should not be surprising that social and economic discontent is being expressed in Islamic terms and that a more purified and rigorous doctrine gains momentum. For impoverished, disillusioned populations in the mountains, the burden of traditional Islam, deeply imbedded in demanding Caucasian traditions, has become unbearable. Moreover, Sufi Islam, widespread in North Caucasus, with its escapist, inward-looking approach, does not provide answers to the acute problems of today, such as social justice and political change. Islamic radicalism is a reaction of the desperate rural populations and disaffected youth in the cities to the moral delay and lawlessness of the present order, of those who resent the present injustice and seek a way out. It also crosses ethnic and clan divisions in society more effectively than traditional Islam. The official Islamic clergy in the North Caucasus often failed to become credible agents of civil society which could serve as intermediaries between the authorities and the population, conveying the popular mood and speaking from a broader humanistic platform. Instead, they have been too pliant towards leadership and lacked an independent political stance.

Policy responses

The Dagestani (and Russian) leadership is in the process of finding an adequate response to the challenges coming from Chechnya. In October 1997 the administrative regime on the border between Chechnya and Dagestan was tightened and the border was temporarily closed. Another measure adopted in November 1997 was to dig a trench along the low-lying sector of the border. Although the trench is designed to be a physical barrier against the looting of cattle and hijacking of cars, it is also a step towards the creation of border installations. The Dagestani Deputy Interior Minister, Magomed Omarov, complained that effective border protection is undermined by the absence of a legal foundation for enforcing it: the border is *de facto* an international frontier, but has the status of an administrative one and can be protected only by local police forces and Interior Ministry troops (Tesemnikova & Torin, 1998).

In these circumstances the Dagestani authorities resort to measures they can undertake locally, and aspire to create self-defence forces or, more plausibly, to incorporate the private armed units which already exist into some form of order. Such initiatives were fostered by the fact that the Russian federal armed units, brought from various Russian regions to the republic and stationed there, not only failed to perform their duties, but also increasingly became targets of terrorist attacks by the Chechens. The raid against the Russian brigade in Dagestan in December 1997 was the worst incident because it exposed the involvement of Dagestanis as well as Chechens. The same brigade was fired at in February 1998. In May 1998 a column of Russian border-guard troops was fired at in Dagestan. Apparently Moscow can guarantee the security neither of the civilians in the border areas nor of the representatives of its own protective forces.

In November 1997 the Dagestani Security Council adopted a decision to create self-defence units from the local population in the areas bordering Chechnya. The realisation of such a proposal would in reality mean that the administration heads might become local fiefs with micro-armies of their own. Gaji Makhachev, the leader of the Imam Shamil Avar National Front, claimed at the session of the People's Assembly that in the aftermath of the Buinaksk raid on the Russian brigade, the Chechen and Dagestani terrorists were chased by an armed detachment of the Shamil National Front – the only force capable of opposing terrorism.[51] Such developments caused a sensation of unease among other ethnic groups, and fears that the self-defence units would enable Avar armed formations to operate independently of Makhachkala. Violence in Makhachkala in May 1998 demonstrated that the Laks also have armed units, led by the Khachilaev brothers.

Belated Russian opposition to the creation of self-defence detachments came in January 1998. A number of alternative measures were initiated by the federal authorities.[52] The Russian federal government created a headquarters in Makhachkala in order to coordinate the activities of all federal power structures in the republic. In emergency situations, the Russian Interior Ministry would assume responsibility over the headquarters and the actions of all federal bodies. Moreover, a detachment from Novorossiisk Paratroopers Division was assigned to Botlikh (a highland *rayon* on the Chechen border) to strengthen the frontier. However, popular faith in the ability of the federal troops to protect Dagestanis is on the decline. Political and economic crises in Moscow mean that federal politicians' attention is regularly diverted from the North Caucasus, and the centre has neither the resources nor sufficient interest to protect the Dagestani/Chechen border effectively. In November 1998 the Russian Interior Ministry announced that police units drawn from outside the republic were to be withdrawn and no further outside units would be allocated, while security would be maintained exclusively by the local police force.

At present the formation of *de facto* local units seems unstoppable. The process of legislating the informal armed structures which have started to emerge since the radical economic and political changes, and of servicing the new ethnic elites, is going ahead in Dagestan and probably in other republics. The new armed structures in *rayons* increase the local administrations' control over the situation in the villages and towns they govern (Kisriev, 1997b). The danger is that such detachments could turn into rogue armed groups, composed along ethnic lines and operating independently of republican authorities, which might come into conflict with one another. It may be recalled that internal destabilisation in Chechnya prior to Russian military intervention also started with the formation of armed groupings.

The prospects for Dagestan joining Chechnya in a unification drive are bleak. The Chechen unification drive tends to overlook the danger presented by the multi-ethnic composition of Dagestan.[53] Even if some groups decide to side with the Chechens in an attempt to break away, other groups might declare themselves autonomies within the Russian Federation.[54] Moreover, the Chechen pro-independence drive is not shared either by the elite or by large segments of the population of Dagestan. Separatism is not on the political agenda, and those advocating the creation of an Islamic state and separation from Russia are in a tiny minority. As articulated by M-S. Gusaev, the Dagestani Minister for Nationalities:

> Some political forces in Chechnya are under an illusion that an anti-Russia oriented person can come to power in Dagestan. Equally futile illusions are being cherished by some federal politicians who search for pro-Russia oriented leaders in Chechnya. Moscow, Grozny and Makhachkala have to come to terms with the real situation. (*Nezavisimaya Gazeta*, 1998d.)

The potential danger, however, lies in another direction. The continuous instability in Chechnya exacerbates internal problems and tensions within Dagestan. Domestic political fragmentation makes Dagestan exceptionally vulnerable to penetration by external political interests. According to the Chairman of the Council of Muftis of Russia, Ravil Gainutdinov, the present situation in Dagestan mirrors that of Chechnya before the war (*Argumenty I Fakty*, 1998). The negative impact may be felt in the following areas:

- the weakness of civil authority and its inability to adopt a clear policy and effectively protect the population
- the possible violation of inter-ethnic peace between Dagestani Chechens

and other ethnic groups, which might endanger inter-ethnic stability in more general terms

- the rise in violent crime and terrorism; as more and more people acquire arms, disputes are increasingly settled by force
- intra-confessional tensions between radicals and traditionalists; Islamic extremism, once emerged, tends rather to reject than seek incorporation into the existing order.

Other republics

The establishment of Chechnya as an independent state would present a future problem for Ingushetia because of the potential border dispute and possible sympathies towards Chechens on the part of the population led by the Islamic clergy.[55] For North Ossetia the effects of Chechnya, apart from the crime overspill, derive from the fact that it is a stronghold of Russian military presence in the region and federal troops serve as targets of attacks. In Karachaevo-Cherkessia and Kabardino-Balkaria the main concern is that the mountain ski-resorts are empty, as holiday-makers will not venture into unstable territory (*Nal'chik*, 1998).

FUTURE OPTIONS AND POTENTIAL RISKS

The process of border contention is ongoing and the trends are far from clear, especially in the light of the uncertain future of a Russian Federation stricken by political and economic crisis. There are a number of options for the future, by no means exclusive, but overlapping, which could shape the course of events.

Preservation of the status quo

This option might be the most attractive for Moscow's politicians, but it is likely to prove unsustainable in future. First, there are sufficient groups and powerful individuals in the Caucasus who are deeply unsatisfied with the present situation. For the Chechen leadership the 'obscure compromise' with Russia's authorities which looked like success in 1996 could easily turn into a pyrrhic victory. Unfulfilled economic promises and rampant crime, as well as widespread militarisation and flourishing warlordism in the republic, make the legitimate leadership a hostage to the existing situation rather than a governing body. In such circumstances the activities of the Chechen 'rogue armies' could easily be directed externally, rather than contribute to an already volatile internal situation. Moreover, a unified Chechen and Dagestani territory would have a better chance of survival as a rebellious state formation.

There are also other actors opting for change. Although the official Ingush leadership has agreed to abstain from further attempts to retake Prigorodnyi *rayon* by force, more radical groups exist which are prepared to wait until the balance of power changes in their favour, with possible help from their Chechen neighbours. The radical Russian groups in the border areas, while witnessing the plight of ethnic Russians in Chechnya, increasing Russian emigration from the North Caucasus and anticipating the possibility of Russia's complete withdrawal from the region, are gaining weapons and becoming better organised.

The final reason why the status quo is unlikely to survive is the depressing economic situation and an increasing need for subsidies from the federal centre. Meanwhile, in the present economic crisis, the centre's capacity for subsidising borderland populations has diminished. As a result, deepening poverty and widening social polarisation prepares the ground for radical action.

Chechnya gains independence

There are two main obstacles to this solution: the principle of territorial integrity which is crucial for any state, and the establishment of formal borders. The former is of greater concern to the political establishment in Moscow than to ordinary Russians, but the public would still not readily countenance Russia being deprived of any of its territory by force. On the other hand, the recent economic collapse and political crisis have made both the elite and the population at large concentrate more on Russia's immediate survival needs than the plight of an impoverished territory on the country's periphery.

The other issue is the establishment of formal borders and border installations, for which reinforced security provisions would be required. Moreover, in the first instance borders with Ingushetia must be formally delimited, and two Russian-populated *rayons* in the lowland areas of Chechnya would become a real bone of contention. Any formal borders established would probably be unpopular and heavily contested by various criminal groups. Whether the federal centre in Russia, as well as the leaderships in the North Caucasian republics, are capable of creating a new kind of border-guard service which is committed to its duty and not corrupt, is highly doubtful under the present circumstances.

Chechnya, in turn, anticipates a hostile Russian policy and actively seeks new cross-border links. Likewise, relations with Georgia and Azerbaijan become important. The leadership in Azerbaijan might even cherish dreams of using Chechens to resolve their conflict with the Armenians over Nagorno-Karabakh.

At the same time, there is also increasing apprehension about the fact that Chechnya is engaged in an Islamic state construction, and such a state might emerge as the vanguard of radical Islam in the Caucasus.

Pan-Caucasian confederation

Secessionist politicians in the Caucasus, most importantly the Abkhaz and the Chechens, pursue the idea that the Caucasus, like, for instance, Europe, is a unique and interrelated organism with a strong regional identity and sufficient interdependence. Therefore, the Caucasus should follow the European Union model and create a confederation based on economic cooperation and cultural ties, while the states and sub-state groups would join such a confederation as equals. This would resolve the seemingly insoluble contradictions between the principles of self-determination and territorial integrity, and the issue of sovereignty would wither away.

Such an option, however, has significant drawbacks. Georgia and Azerbaijan have acquired their independence only recently, giving them the opportunity to create states of their own for the first time in modern history. They have invested heavily in state-building projects. Any suggestion that they should be deprived of their independence at this stage is hardly compelling. Officially, Russia broadly adheres to the same view. Moreover, advocates of a confederation have to face the fact that tensions and opposition between various Caucasian groups are acute, and competition, rather than cooperation, is the present mood. Finally, it would be extremely difficult for the confederation to create a mechanism for making and enforcing unpopular decisions.

Russia's withdrawal from the Caucasus

A trend towards a strategic retreat from the Caucasus is apparent in current Russian policy in the North Caucasus, despite the assurances of Moscow's politicians to the contrary. The landmarks on this road include the acquisition of *de facto* self-governing powers by the North Caucasian leaderships, the Russian military defeat in Chechnya, the increasing ineffectiveness and vulnerability of Russian military and police troops in the area, and the end of federal capacity for allocating subsidies. Diminishing numbers of ethnic Russians, a deteriorating economy, the lack of significant natural reserves and a virtually unmanageable criminal situation might make policy-makers in Moscow admit publicly what is being discussed privately: namely that Russia is paying dearly for territorial integrity and a share of access to the Caspian Sea.

Apart from the territorial integrity principle, any Russian initiative to 'shake off its weakest parts' would falter in the face of the weakness of the pro-independence movement in the North Caucasus, since only Chechnya and a tiny minority in Dagestan are genuinely in favour of independence. However critical people might be of Moscow's policies, the predominant mood of the area's population is that it would be better to remain within the Russian Federation. Nevertheless, if the current Russian crisis continues and the reshaping of the Federation's geopolitical order becomes imminent, in the resulting chaos the North Caucasus would be the most likely area to find itself economically and politically detached from Russia.

NOTES

1 Tensions simmered throughout the post-war period and a protest demonstration took place in October 1981 in Vladikavkaz demanding the expulsion of the Ingush. In response to that, the USSR Council of Ministers adopted a resolution in March 1982 limiting the registration rights of the Ingush in Prigorodnyi.
2 By 1992 the Ingush officially constituted five per cent of the republic's population.

3 Interview with Vladimir Mamsurov, member of North Ossetian parliament, April 1998.

4 The Ingush deputies to the USSR Supreme Soviet were among those who heavily lobbied for this law. The North Ossetian deputies, including Alexandr Dzasokhov, as it was later revealed, seldom attended the sitting of the Supreme Soviet and failed to take part in the debate.

5 North Ossetia was a major site of defence enterprises.

6 Felix Corley, however, argues, that the North Ossetians moved first (Corley, 1994: 401).

7 The 1992 violence claimed 583 lives, 350 of them Ingush, 192 Ossetian; 261 are still missing (208 of whom are Ingush). Data of the Operational Department of the Office of Presidential Representative in North Ossetia/Ingushetia, cited by Dzadziev.

8 By that time the Ingush and the Chechens agreed to split the dual-nationality republic of Checheno-Ingushetia in order to create units of their own. The formal border, however, was never established.

9 Twenty-nine people were killed as a result of inter-ethnic tensions in 1997 (Dzadziev, 1997b).

10 During summer 1997 senior Chechen politicians, including President Maskhadov, Vice-President Vakha Arsanov and Vice-Premier Movladi Udugov, made assertive statements (quoted by Dzadziev, 1997a: 39).

11 Under Galazov it was only the presidential representative's office which undertook such steps. Author's interview with Victor Soloviev, adviser to the Presidential Representative in the Zone of the North Ossetian/Ingush Conflict, April 1998.

12 Whether a new government would show enough political will to change radical attitudes and provide real security guarantees for the returning Ingush remains to be seen. In June 1998 Aushev openly accused Dzasokhov of siding with the nationalists.

13 The returnees normally live in segregated communities. In Chermen, for instance, where the Ingush have returned, the two parts of the village do not communicate with each other.

14 The Ingush consider it slow, while the Ossetians consider it too rapid.

15 In the aftermath of violence in 1992, 40,300 Ingush left Prigorodnyi, only 31,000 of whom had proper residence permits. Between August 1994 and December 1997, 11,691 Ingush officially returned; in reality, only about 6,530 live permanently in Prigorodnyi.

16 In 1997 the RF Rapid Reaction Regiment of the Interior Ministry discovered 460 light weapons held by the population in the conflict zone. Source: Office of the Presidential Representative, *Deyatel'nost Polnomochnogo Predstavitelya Presidenta RF v RSO-A i RI* (Activities of Plenipotentiary Representative of the RF President in North Ossetia/Ingushetia), No. 1 (Vladikavkaz/Nazran, 1998).

17 In December 1997 there were 37,700 refugees in North Ossetia, including 28,100 from Georgia. Data from the *North Ossetian Migration Service*, cited by Dzadziev.

18 There is a widespread belief that the former Cossack *rayons* were allocated to the North Caucasian republics in order to compensate the deported peoples for the lands they lost. This is not the case; the republics gained territories irrespective of whether they had deported peoples or not.

19 In April 1998 25,000 ethnic Chechens lived in *krai*, according to Alexandr Chernogorov, governor of the *krai*.

20 This action was also a protest against the court ruling which found one Cossack guilty of possession of firearms.

21 On the federal policy towards Cossacks, see Andreev (1997).

22 See, for instance, Khoperskaya (1997): 38–40. The same process is taking place in Krasnodar *krai* (*NG-Regiony*, 1998). Stavropol Cossacks became a part of Terskoya Host, which meant that the rich and powerful *krai* organisations had to be supervised by what was regarded as an unauthorised leadership from Vladikavkaz.

23 The Ministry of Nationalities of Dagestan recommended that the Dagestani leader Magomedali Magomedov pay a visit to Stavropol to reduce tensions and support the Dagestani diaspora.

24 Atamans Churekov and Shevtsov are regarded as the more radical ones.

25 The persistent rumours are that they benefit from the arms acquired from the federal troops withdrawn from Chechnya into Stavropol *krai*.

26 At the popular level, many South Ossetians were originally against ethnic Russians in North Ossetia, whom they regarded as 'guests' on historical Ossetian lands.

27 For instance, during the land privatisation certain lands were reserved for Ossetians who fled from these territories.

28 According to Ludwig Chibirov, the president of South Ossetia, 50,000 live in the republic, 35,000 of them Ossetian and 12,000 Georgian.

29 For more detail see Matveeva & McCartney (1997).

30 During the war in Chechnya, arms shipments regularly came across the Azerbaijani–Russian border en route to the Chechen resistance forces. There has been speculation that the Chechen resistance enjoyed the tacit support of Baku. The Chechen government's decision to name a street in the capital after Heidar Aliev, and Maskhadov's symbolic gift of a pistol, may be seen as an indirect confirmation of this (*James Town Foundation Monitor*, 1998).

31 Its establishment was postponed because of the protests of the local population, but the decision is still in force.

32 The plight of Kurds in Turkey is often cited.

33 *Sadval* leader Ruslan Ashuraliev vigorously denied any involvement.

34 Interview with Musa Efendi Velimuradov, head of the Magaramkent administration, October 1997. It was widely believed that the trainees were getting 500 roubles ($84) per month. Various speculations involving Armenian, Russian and Chechen security structures were discussed in the republic, including Berezovskii's mission and attempts to intimidate Azerbaijan.

35 The Dagestani authorities raised their voice only once during Magomedov's visit to Djohar, protesting against the kidnapping of Yusuf Khibirov, Deputy Minister for Agriculture, in summer 1997.

36 Akhtaev died in March 1998.

37 The Congress was to have legislative powers and included 36 members, 13 from each side. Only three of these were representatives of the authorities; the others were representatives of public movements. Dagestan argued against this proposal. This initiative mirrors the creation of the Chechen National Congress in 1991, which proclaimed itself the only legitimate authority in Chechnya and became a vehicle of separation from Moscow rule.

38 Basaev was proclaimed Emir of the joint-state formation. In July 1998 Basaev resigned as Prime Minister to be appointed the deputy Commander-In-Chief, a position he left at the end of August 1998.

39 Apart from the official authorities, the declaration was signed by the leaders of two Kumyk, Lak, Avar, Nogai, Lezgin and Tabassaran national movements, the Spiritual Board of the Muslims of Dagestan, local branches of Russia's Democratic

Choice, the Communist Party, Russia is our Home, and others (*Nezavisimaya Gazeta*, 1998a). The Union of Muslims was the only sizeable organisation which sent its representative to the Congress.

40 The Laks agreed to move to the lands near Makhachkala but the Kumyks declared them their historical homeland. Moreover, climatic conditions there are very unfavourable.

41 The fact that the majority of Dagestani Chechens voted in the presidential elections in Chechnya in January 1997 came as an unwelcome surprise for the authorities.

42 Author's interview with Zalumkhan Sadulaev, head of administration of Charodinskii *rayon*, September 1997.

43 Plans to take local Chechens hostage and exchange them for Dagestani prisoners were articulated by the local Avar informal armed groupings, and only the involvement of federal troops shifted the focus away from such an option (Kisriev, 1996).

44 Wahhabism is a religious movement in Sunni Islam which emerged in Arabia in the mid-eighteenth century. It was founded by Mohammed Abd-al-Wahhab and was named after him. Wahhabis insist on strict monotheism and reject the cult of local saints, as well as the authority of elders.

45 Author's interview with Gussein Abuyev (Makhachkala), ex-KGB officer at that time involved in dealing with the Wahhabi issue, April 1998. Abuyev mentioned that 66 people were identified and detained for questioning in 1983, including Bagauddin; they went underground during the Soviet times and became active again during *perestroika*.

46 Interview with Gussein Abuyev, April 1998. Various reasons for Arab assistance, apart from religious fanaticism, are cited, such as an attempt to destabilise the Caspian Sea basin so that oil from the Middle East would not face competition.

47 The propaganda followed the familiar Soviet pattern. Local observers, however, regard it as 'preaching to the converted' in the sense that it does not reach the target constituency. Interview with Enver Kisriev, Senior Research Fellow, Dagestani Research Centre, Russian Academy of Sciences, April 1998.

48 The authorities are very apprehensive of the Wahhabi propaganda effort. The Dagestani Procurator's office initiated criminal changes against Magomed Tagaev, the author of *Our struggle, or Imam's Army of Rebellion*, a book being distributed in Dagestan by the radical Islamists. Although few people saw the book itself, a parallel was immediately drawn with the period during the early stages of conflict in Nagorno-Karabakh, when Zorii Balayan's book, *Ochag* [*Fireside*], provoked tensions.

49 Publications, however, claim, that such evidence exists (Polyakova, 1998).

50 Information of the Ministry of Nationalities of Dagestan.

51 Unlike in Dagestan and Chechnya, in Karachaevo-Cherkessia the Wahhabis did not make themselves public. However, there is reason to believe that fundamentalism has some ground there (Polyakova, 1998). Wahhabis exist in Kabardino-Balkaria, and are gaining influence among young people. President Kokov attributed the 1997 explosions to the Wahhabis, but no evidence was produced.

52 The clashes started in Kazbek *rayon* and resulted in the Chechen side capturing seven Dagestani policemen who did not have enough arms to defend themselves. However, the Avar fighters lent armaments to the police force and together managed to fight back. This was the first public acknowledgement that the national movements possessed combat-ready armed units.

53 They ordered an additional 1,000 policemen to put the border under additional

guard. Such measures had been implemented before, and failed to alter the situation much.

54 There are 34 ethnic groups in Dagestan which number slightly over two million.

55 The attempts of the Dagestani authorities to persuade the Chechen leadership that the idea of separation from Moscow is not popular in Dagestan does not get a sympathetic hearing. Instead, it makes the Chechen side believe that the process of unification might take a longer period of up to one and a half years rather than several months, as originally planned. Author's interview with Magomed Salikh Gusaev, Minister of Nationalities of Dagestan, April 1998.

56 In addition, some Chechens in the border area might want to stay in the economically more prosperous Ingushetia.

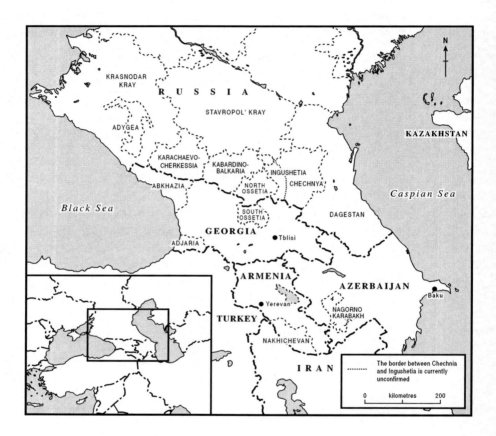

Figure 1 The Transcaucasus Region

BIBLIOGRAPHY

Andreev, V. (1997) 'The Cossacks: a Tribute to History or a Real Political Force in Contemporary Russia?', *Prism*, Vol. III, No. 9, 16 May & 13 June.

Argumenty I Fakty (1998), Interview with Ravil Gainutdinov, 15 April.

Corley, F. (1994) 'The Ingush-Ossetian Conflict', *Jane's Intelligence Review*, September: 401.

Dzadziev, A. (1997a) 'Novyi Vitok Napryazhennosti v Zone Ossetino-Ingushskogo Konflikta' in *Bulletin of the Ethnological Monitoring and Early Warning of Conflicts Network*, No. 5 (16) December, IEA and CMG: 39.

Dzadziev, A. (unpublished manuscript, 1997b) 'Ossetino-Ingushskii Konflikt: Sovremennoye Sostoyani'e' ['Ossetian/Ingush Conflict: Present Situation'], material submitted to *Bulletin*, Summer–Autumn: 1–2.

JamesTown Foundation Monitor (1998), Vol. IV, No. 90, 11 May.

Khoperskaya, L. & Kharchenko, V. (1997) 'Kazachye Dvizheniye v Respublikakh Severnogo Kavkaza', *Bulletin*, No. 2 (13), May: 38–40.

Kisriev, E. (1996) 'Kyzlyarsko-Pervomayiskie Sobytiya v Dagestane' ['Events in Kyzlyar and Pervomayskoie in Dagestan), *Research Papers in Applied and Urgent Ethnic Studies*, Moscow: Institute of Ethnology and Anthropology.

Kisriev, E. (1997a) 'Clash of Faith', *War Report*, No. 52, June–July: 16.

Kisriev, E. (1997b) 'Dagestan: Legalization of the Military Formations', *Bulletin*, No. 5 (16), December: 27.

Maksakov, I. (1998) 'Ocherednyie Volneniya Chechentsev Dagestana', *Nezavisimaya Gazeta*, 8 August.

Matiev, T. (1998) 'Pravda Pobezhdaet ne Tol'ko v Skazkakh', *Ingushetia*, 31 March.

Matveeva, A. & McCartney, C. (1997) *The Lezgins: A Situation Assessment Report*, London: International Alert.

Nal'chik (1998), Interview with Khasan Dumanov, April.

Nezavisimaya Gazeta (1998a) 'Dagestantsy Serdyatsya na Sosedei', 19 May.

Nezavisimaya Gazeta (1998b) 'Organizatory Terakta v Buinakske Obeshayut Prodolzhit' Voinu', 29 January.

Nezavisimaya Gazeta (1998c) 'Raduev Otmetilsya v Buinakske', 3 February.

Nezavisimaya Gazeta (1998d) 'Dagestan Ostanetsya Edinoi Nedelimoi Respu-blikoi v Sostave Rossii', Interview with M-S. Gusaev, 12 May.

NG-Regiony (1998) 'Kak Kondratenko Kazakov Obidel', No. 2 (5), February.

McFaul, M. & Petrov, N. (1998), 'Social and Political Portraits of the Regions' ['Sotsial'no-Politicheskiye Portrety Regionov'], *Political Almanac of Russia*, Vol. 2, Moscow: Moscow Carnegie Center, Vol. 2: 404.

Polyakova, A. (1998) 'Wahhabism v Importnoi Upakovke', NG-Stsenarii, No. 5: 7.

RFE/RL Newsline (1997) 'Chechnya Repeats Territorial Claims on Dagestan', Vol. 1, No. 182, part 1, 18 December.

Rotar, I. (1998a) 'Nezavisimyi Dagestan Zhiznenno Vazhen dlya Chechnyi', Nezavisimaya Gazeta, 12 February.

Rotar, I. (1998b) 'Chast' Musulman Gotova k Gazavatu', Nezavisimaya Gazeta, 27 January.

Rotar, I. (1998c) 'Dagestan on the Brink of War: Moscow and Grozny Fight for Influence in the Republic' in *Prism, James Town Foundation Monitor*, Vol. 3, No. 17, Part 2, February.

Tesemnikova, E. & Torin, V. (1998) 'Buinaksk Zhivet v Osade', Nezavisimaya Gazeta, 5 February.

Tsutsiev, A. & Dzugaev, L. (1997) *Severnyi Kavkaz: Istoriya I Granitsy, 1780–1995*, Centre of Ethno-Political Studies of North Ossetian 'Reforma' Foundation.

16

In Search of 'Normal Conditions': Reassessing the Functions of UNFICYP's Buffer Zone in Cyprus

Peter Hocknell

INTRODUCTION

'Alternative' approaches to territorial management in border areas have traditionally centred on the formalised delimitation and maintenance of various 'zones' which, in effect, temporarily suspend sovereignty in a newly-bounded territory. It is suggested in this paper that the efficacy of such zones would appear to be dependent crucially upon the temporal and spatial scales along which they are evaluated, given that the effectiveness of boundary management as a whole is increasingly being determined by multi-dimensional functions – not just short-term military and 'national' (read: 'state') security concerns, but also other, longer-term priorities – that operate at national, regional and local scales. International boundaries, as Newman and Paasi recently reiterated, may have a differential impact at different scales of analysis (Newman & Paasi, 1998: 197).

When considering the primary functions of international boundaries, although classifications invariably interlink in practice, it is possible to broadly distinguish legal/political from socio-economic functions. Ever since the Treaty of Westphalia in 1648, international boundaries have primarily performed a security role, and this has commonly reduced boundaries to the function of containerisation, with border-related problems centred on territorial disputes and violations of 'sovereign space' (Taylor, 1994). Conceptions of regions contiguous to a boundary correspondingly remained rooted in a tradition preoccupied with peripherality and under-development (Brown, 1997). Boggs's seminal work on international boundaries illustrated a more general view, that boundaries could not promote trade or human intercourse; he suggested that boundaries simply functioned as 'institutionalised *buffer zones*'.[1] Contemporary research on border regions and border landscapes, however, offers conflicting evidence and exposes a static perception of boundary functions employed within traditional international relations and localisation theory. Most vividly, the combination of a so-called 'Europe of regions' and a 'Europe without borders' has highlighted the increasing importance of 'networks', 'connectivity' and 'interoperability' in transboundary European relations (Ratti & Reichman, 1993). Even in cases where political divisions retain their primacy in dictating inter-state relations, common cultural landscapes at the local level have begun to create transborder regions (Bufon, 1994). Indeed, Cappellin has suggested,

Borderlands Under Stress (M.A. Pratt and J.A. Brown (eds), ISBN 90-411-9790-7).
© Kluwer Law International, 2000.

and is supported by Duchavek's work in North America, that transboundary cooperation may reduce core-periphery disparities by encouraging the integration of peripheral regions into the wider political system.[2]

When reconsidering traditional 'alternative' approaches to territorial management, therefore, this new 'borderlands turn' – both across academic disciplines and in practice – begs a number of questions. How effective have such arrangements been, on the one hand, in reducing tension and, on the other, in encouraging inter-group cooperation? While formalised 'zones' invariably serve as symbols of the international community's immediate concerns, what other purposes have they served in practice? This need to re-examine alternative approaches to territorial management has been highlighted elsewhere. Blake examined various attempts at politico-territorial arrangements in which state sovereignty was shared in some form, and three border alternatives, employed at various times and in various localities during this century, stood out (Blake, 1992, 1993, 1994). Although distinct, clear parallels are evident. First, neutral zones have generally been established in disputed territories (e.g. Gibraltar (UK) and Spain since the mid-eighteenth century) or agreements made between potential conflicting states to jointly administer a zone (e.g. between Kuwait and Saudi Arabia from 1923 to 1965). Second, demilitarised zones (DMZs) are usually established as a necessary post-conflict measure (e.g. the 1949 Armistice Agreements which established DMZs between Israel and Syria). Although they were most popular immediately after the Second World War, they remain a salient means of border management today. In April 1991, for example, a DMZ was created along the Iraq–Kuwait boundary with the establishment of the United Nations Iraq-Kuwait Observer Mission (UNIKOM). One of the most celebrated DMZs, in essence a 14km-wide boundary established between North and South Korea in 1953, continues to act as a container for over 3,300 square km of territory (Hocknell, 1996: 68).

Third, buffer zones are also invariably demilitarised but appear to differ from DMZs in their function. As geopolitics has taught us, so-called 'buffer states' have a history of being constructed where there is a desire to reduce the possibility of contact between two powerful states (Prescott, 1965: 46). Blake has argued that '[b]uffer zones are [...] generally temporary phenomena, with less permanence than neutral zones or demilitarised zones' – for example, the creation of a buffer zone to facilitate the disengagement of Israeli and Egyptian forces after the Second Sinai Agreement of September 1975 (Blake, 1993: 39). Nevertheless, as illustrated by the UN Disengagement Observer Force (UNDOF) in the Golan Heights (whose operations, coincidentally in parallel with the United Nations Peacekeeping Force in Cyprus (UNFICYP), have been undertaken largely within a buffer zone since the summer of 1974), it is critical to recognise that the international community must be prepared to remain in place for an extended period of time (Carnegie Commission, 1997: 65).

Other alternative territorial arrangements could be considered given that, as White has recently noted, today's UN and other multinational military personnel increasingly have the basic core function of a 'buffer force', supervising an established cease-fire between the parties (White, 1997: 263). In post-Dayton Bosnia and Hercegovina, an ambiguously termed 'Zone of Separation' was eventually set up around what was the agreed cease-fire line but which now largely constitutes the 'Inter-Entity Boundary Line'. The zone, which is all but demilitarised, extends for up to 2km on either side of this line in open terrain, yet was narrower than 1km in parts of Sarajevo.[3]

For the rest of this paper, however, analysis will focus on the Cyprus case. In this study, it is argued that the *de facto* border in Cyprus provides both a timely and topical case for reconsidering the effectiveness of such alternative approaches to territorial management in contested border areas – timely if only because July 1999 marked the 25th anniversary of the Turkish military intervention in Cyprus and the establishment of the United Nations Buffer Zone (UNBZ), and topical because, as observers have been keen to highlight in the post-Cold War period, there remain many lessons to be learned by critically examining this, the longest-standing UN peacekeeping mission and, in turn, one of the most durable examples of a traditional territorial management alternative (Grundy-Warr, 1994a; Evriviades & Bourantonis, 1994).

THE UNFICYP BUFFER ZONE

Given the regular six-monthly renewal of UNFICYP's mandate over the past 34 years, it would appear that the roles of both UNFICYP and the buffer zone it administers have been accepted by all parties concerned. On the contrary, the disputants' contested view of UNFICYP's mandate, and the UN's more general role on the island, is a growing feature of studies on the Cyprus conflict.[4] Indeed, to more fully understand the meaning of the mandate from 1974, one must briefly re-examine its origin. On 4 March 1964, directly following intercommunal clashes at the end of 1963, UN Security Council Resolution 186 recommended, *inter alia*:

> that the function of the Force [UNFICYP] should be in the interest of preserving international peace and security, to use its best efforts to *prevent a recurrence of fighting* and, as necessary, to contribute to the *maintenance and restoration of law and order* and a *return to normal conditions*.[5]

This mandate, it should not be forgotten, was only timetabled for a three-month period.

Unsurprisingly, given its ambiguous use of language, each of the involved sides interpreted the mandate differently.[6] In the view of the Greek Cypriot community, although UNFICYP was to operate as a neutral, this did not mean it would treat everyone equally; rather, Greek Cypriots believed that UNFICYP's role was to assist them in the elimination of the separatist movement and, in so doing, return Turkish Cypriot territorial enclaves to 'government' control. By contrast, the Turkish Cypriot side greeted UNFICYP as protectors and, more importantly, understood a 'return to normal conditions' to mean a restoration of the equal status of the two Cypriot communities according to the 1960 Constitution of Independence, if not according to geographical equality (UN, 1985: 274). The UN rejected both of these interpretations. The mandate, while recognising one side as the legitimate government, was to be informally interpreted such that UNFICYP could maintain an 'uneasy equilibrium'.[7] As for the 'return to normal conditions', this was seen to necessitate providing assistance in ameliorating administrative, economic, social and judicial problems arising from the communal divisions.[8] For both communities and for the UN, therefore – if for completely different reasons – a 'return to normal conditions' was seen spatially to redress the island-wide political circumstances. This was to prove significant when, after the creation of the buffer zone in 1974, this part of the mandate was re-centred necessarily onto *borderland* activities.

In spite of its contested meaning, this mandate was to remain intact throughout the rest of the 1960s, and then, crucially, beyond the events of summer 1974 – which were to once again radically alter the political geography of the island – given the lack of vocal consensus within the Security Council, where it was seen as preferable not to provide a new mandate for UNFICYP (Fetherston, 1994: 56). Instead, the geography of UNFICYP's mandate was reconfigured such that it should administer nearly 300 square km of buffer zone, delimited by the cease-fire lines of the Greek Cypriot National Guard and the Turkish Forces. Indeed, in the light of their spatial redeployment, UNFICYP personnel became almost entirely confined to the UNBZ (Figure 1). In turn, this territory became their central focus after the population transfers in 1975 and, from this point on, UNFICYP became more of a 'buffer force' (Grundy-Warr, 1994a: 72). With this in mind, the rest of this paper is divided into two main sections which reconsider what are commonly understood to be the main functions of the UNBZ (as dictated by UNFICYP's mandate): on the one hand the management of the military and territorial status quo and, on the other, the facilitation of a return to so-called 'normal conditions'.[9]

MANAGING THE MILITARY AND TERRITORIAL *STATUS QUO*

When evaluating the UNBZ's effectiveness in managing the military and territorial status quo, three sub-divisions are practical: maintenance of the delineation of cease-fire lines, control of border crossings, and prevention of a recurrence of fighting through the maintenance and restoration of law and order (as carried over from the 1964–74 period).

Maintaining the cease-fire lines

The scale of the Turkish military intervention in 1974 dictated that UNFICYP was downgraded to the wholly ineffective role of bystander.[10] Yet it was soon to return to the forefront as facilitator of an informal cease-fire agreement and, accordingly, UNFICYP was positioned between the opposing forces (Figure 2). Significantly, however, it appears that no formal agreement on the delimitation of the cease-fire lines (CFLs) was ever negotiated in 1974, nor has been since. In this respect, UNFICYP has been at pains to keep the status quo, preserving what is commonly referred to (in notably state-centric terms) as the territorial 'integrity' of the buffer zone. Troop deployment or training exercises within 1km of either side of the UNBZ without prior notification are considered to be cease-fire violations, as are breaches of maritime security lines on the coast and overflights by military or civilian aircraft.

As this suggests, micro-scale 'violations' of the UNBZ can escalate to dangerous proportions if not properly handled (Szulc, 1993). Hundreds of such incidents occur each year, particularly in areas where the CFLs are in close proximity – while the UNBZ runs from east to west for approximately 180km, it varies in width from 7km near Athienou to only 3m in Nicosia's old walled city. By 1978 the CFLs had begun to stabilise, but UNFICYP was able to provide either side with only a trace of their respective lines.[11] Even then, Turkish Forces initially declined to review their CFL, while negotiations with the Greek Cypriot National Guard were ongoing.[12] Accordingly, by late 1980 UNFICYP still found itself with the unenviable task of operating without any agreement with either protagonist as to the delineation of the lines. In practice, UNFICYP (as one UN secretary-general put it) supervised 'by loose mutual consent, two unmarked, constantly disputed cease-fire lines', and on a self-confessedly *ad hoc* basis.[13]

It is not surprising, therefore, that the belief in a strong military presence along the UNBZ has survived even UNFICYP's most recent soul-searching financial review, in 1993, when infantry units were still preferred over military observers to maintain effective control of the UNBZ (Kostakos, 1994: 65). UNFICYP itself, however, is the first to recognise its limited resources. Following the violent clashes at Dherinia in 1996 – which brought about the worst period of intercommunal killings for 22 years – the UN, along with UK and US diplomats, sprang to reintroduce a proposal for indirect dialogue between the commanders of the opposing forces that would seek to extend an 'unmanning agreement' of May 1989 to all areas along the UNBZ, especially where opposing forces are in close proximity along the 'green line' of Nicosia. The presence of soldiers only metres apart inevitably invites confrontation and has resulted in numerous shooting fatalities – and the present agreement covers 24 military observation posts in certain parts of the 'green line' in central Nicosia alone.[14] Immediately after the unmanning of positions was implemented in May 1989, the number of UNBZ incidents in Nicosia fell to the lowest level since 1974.[15] However, since 1989, and even since the 1996 proposal, there has been no extension of this initial agreement.

Conflict prevention

Supplementary to their maintenance of the military status quo, UNFICYP must also preserve the 'integrity' of the UNBZ from unauthorised entry by civilians.

accidents, fires, thefts, and rubbish and sewage disposal are only secondary concerns to that of crowd control, a role which has proven vital if often unrealised. The force has no mandate to impose peace, insisting instead on the principle that deadly force must not be used by either side, except in clear situations of self-defence. UNFICYP maintains that whenever civilians cross the other side's CFL in a 'nonbelligerent manner', they and their belongings should be returned without delay.[16] While UNFICYP has lost 168 personnel since its establishment, only a minute percentage of the deaths have occurred within or along the buffer zone.[17] Nevertheless, over the last 10 years there has been a visible increase in civilian demonstrations along and invariably within the UNBZ, originating largely in the (Greek Cypriot) south.

Perhaps not coincidentally, this has developed in parallel with the reduction in UNFICYP's troop strength – most dramatically in 1993, following Boutros-Ghali's financial reassessment, when UNFICYP was reduced in size by 44 per cent, such that its strength temporarily dipped below 1,000 (*The Blue Beret*, October 1996: 5). Even now, UNFICYP totals just over 1,200 military observers, police and infantry,[18] and its limited resource power and mandate was vividly illustrated at Dherinia in August 1996. At any one time during the increased state of alert, it had 80 per cent of all personnel on duty and, even then, the Greek Cypriot government and press questioned the degree of force used in preventing the violent Turkish Cypriot counter-protests (*The Blue Beret*, October 1996: 5). Rauf Denktash, president of the Turkish Cypriot's internationally-unrecognised state, pointed out that UNFICYP (along with the Greek Cypriot police and troops) proved incapable of protecting the UNBZ, thus repeating the Turkish military's long-held belief that it is the Turkish Forces, rather than UNFICYP, that makes the difference to security along their 'border'.[19]

Border-crossing control

Since the creation of the UNBZ, up to three places have developed where the two main Cypriot communities can formally cross, either north or south. Only one – the Ledra Palace Hotel checkpoint in central Nicosia – provides anything resembling an 'open' border-crossing point, however. Here, diplomats and tourists must pass through three separate halts – Greek Cypriot, UN, and Turkish Cypriot – in order to cross from one side to the other. There is little encouragement to travel south-to-north and, given that the Greek Cypriot government has declared all seaports and airports in the northern territory 'prohibited ports of entry and exit', non-Cypriots are not allowed to enter the south from the north. Through an agreement with UNFICYP, however, Greek Cypriot police allow Turkish Cypriots (but not Turkish 'settlers') to cross south for humanitarian purposes.[20]

As for the northern authorities, Greeks and Armenians are specifically prevented from crossing to the north. While all other crossings through Ledra Palace are encouraged, administrative hurdles have developed. In April 1988 the Turkish Cypriot authorities required certain categories of Greek Cypriots and foreign nationals to present their passports for stamping.[21] Both the Greek Cypriot government and the UN secretary-general immediately recognised this as a move to establish crossing-point procedures synonymous with an international border, and thus called on Denktash to restore the status quo. Even more recently, during April 1998, the Turkish Cypriot authorities imposed new regulations and fees for entry and exit from the north.[22] For the first time in the history of the UNBZ, a GB£15 'visa' fee for Greek Cypriots and Maronites crossing north was established, along with a GB£4 tax for all peoples crossing the checkpoint southwards.[23] While tourists were still encouraged to cross north, therefore, other visitors were effectively controlled.

Overall, in traditional security terms, UNFICYP's buffer zone has proven something of a palliative. While Alan James has noted the prophylactic effect of having a buffer zone which, by definition, is a threat to neither side,[24] it must be recognised that UNFICYP has further institutionalised the conflict through its institutionalisation of *de facto* territorial partition.[25] But these arguments have been rightly tempered by those who have noted that cease-fire maintenance remains an essential prerequisite to any meaningful negotiations (Grundy-Warr, 1994a: 72). The belief in maintaining a buffer zone to manage 'space' in the territorial sense (i.e. national responses at the island-wide scale) has thus far been vindicated by the low number of killings and the general maintenance of the military status quo.

IN SEARCH OF 'NORMAL CONDITIONS'

As previously indicated, it is now customary for commentators to criticise UNFICYP's consolidation of an 'abnormal' status quo and inhibiting of the long-term need for a new and viable 'political order' (Stegenga, 1968: 186). While to some extent complementing this line of argument, the rest of this paper will focus away from the traditional, state-centred national scale, towards the sub-national or so-called 'borderland' scale, in an attempt to counter what appears to be a general ambivalence over the role of the UNBZ. Is the UNBZ simply a means of territorial management *per se*, or is it also a mechanism for facilitating intercommunal rapprochement and ultimately conflict resolution? It is posited, in other words, that more significant questions remain over the continued use of the buffer zone to manage contested space in terms of other social, economic and psychological concerns, most notably local responses at the borderland scale.

After 1974, UNFICYP had to continue encouraging a return to what was ambiguously described as 'normal conditions', UNFICYP's promotion of which was now centred on a new 'borderland'. Yet, just as there is no agreement between UNFICYP and the opposing forces on the delimitation of the UNBZ, nor is there any formal agreement on the use and control of the zone. While the other two functions of UNFICYP, as declared in their original mandate –

maintaining the cease-fire, and restoring law and order – are relatively self-explanatory, it is in the 'return to normal conditions' that UNFICYP's mandate has been most broadly interpreted since 1974 (Fetherston, 1994: 52). Instead of altering the mandate, the Security Council adopted a number of resolutions which required the Force to perform only certain additional functions.[26] 'Good offices' were still made available for negotiating over public services, particularly water and electricity crossing the UNBZ (Hocknell, 1998; 1999a), and a humanitarian element to encourage the resumption of 'normal' civilian activity was institutionalised with the establishment of a special Humanitarian and Economics Branch at UNFICYP HQ on 22 July 1974 (Zacarias, 1996: 50).

In principle, peace-building became more developed at the 'micro-level', as UNFICYP quickly realised that it was not in the interest of either side to turn the UNBZ into a 'waste land' or a 'barren, depopulated zone'.[27] In the restoration of economic activity, UNFICYP therefore encouraged '*ad hoc* measures designed to save lives, minimise suffering and, to the *extent possible*, restore civilian activities'.[28] The 'extent possible', it can be assumed, was largely determined by the degree to which the 'return to normal conditions' (the second sub-mandate) was dependent on maintaining the cease-fire and restoring law and order (the first sub-mandate). Soon after UNFICYP's establishment in 1964, UN secretary-general U Thant considered the relationship as sequential, the first preceding the second (Fetherston, 1994: 53). Clearly, U Thant's view provokes two concerns: has this approach largely predetermined the primacy of the military/security function of the UNBZ over and above its integrationist function; moreover, and just as importantly, which time period was 'normal conditions' referring to – the 1960–1963 'Cyprus', which was itself unstable and increasingly 'abnormal', or the 1963–1974 'Cyprus'?

Access and utilisation

Above all, there remain questions over access to and utilisation of the zone itself. UNFICYP is positioned between the opposing forces and, since 1986, an all-weather patrol track has run along the whole length of the UNBZ, facilitating UNFICYP surveillance, the re-supply of observation posts (OPs), and rapid reaction to any incidents (Figure 2) (James, 1990: 232–3). Within the UNBZ itself, five villages remained populated, designated 'civilian use areas' and manned by local civilian police.[29] The 8,000 inhabitants are almost entirely Greek Cypriots, except in Pyla, a mixed village that includes over 350 Turkish Cypriots.[30]

Within this territorial regime, access to and development of the buffer zone have been extremely convoluted since 1974; indeed, the best way to illustrate this is through an examination of agricultural practices in the zone. UNFICYP has never failed to point out that the buffer zone contains some of the most valuable agricultural land in Cyprus. Indeed, it has been estimated that at the time of its establishment, the UNBZ, while only taking up three per cent of the land area, accounted for nearly 10 per cent of cultivated agricultural land on the whole island (Grundy-Warr, 1987: 75). UNFICYP chose to allow farming and other economic activities with two crucial provisos: primarily, cultivation should not be a threat to the legitimate security interests of either side, and, secondarily, proof of ownership or rightful employment was needed before access was permitted. From 1974 farming permits were issued ad-hoc at various stages along the UNBZ. By mid-1975, however, Turkish Forces were reported to be placing new restrictions on the farming, grazing and harvesting activities of Greek Cypriots in areas where such activities had previously been permitted;[31] indeed, many Greek Cypriots were being arrested in the zone.[32] UNFICYP was forced to develop an innovative system of escorting farmers, shepherds and others working in areas of confrontation: a Farming Security Line (FSL) was established to administer these largely agricultural economic activities, its delimitation dependent upon the two principal guidelines of security and ownership (Figure 2).[33]

The first major test case for these new regulations occurred at Avlona, an abandoned Greek Cypriot village 21km west of Nicosia, which after 1974 had become bounded by Turkish Forces not only to its south, but also to its west, at Morphou, where the citrus plantations fed by Cyprus's most important groundwater aquifer and dam lay (Figure 3). From the autumn of 1974 Greek Cypriot farmers were able, under UNFICYP escort, to farm their land in this area within 500m of the Turkish Forces' CFL; indeed, this practice had been formalised within a year by an agreement with the local Turkish command.[34] By the spring of 1976, however, there were moves to repopulate Avlona by Turkish Cypriots, whose authorities had sought UNFICYP's agreement to a 200m-wide strip of land forward of their CFLs to be made available to the new village inhabitants. The implications of this issue were eventually discussed amongst officials of the UN and Turkish and Cypriot communities. It became clear that the Turkish Cypriot side objected to what it perceived as an inequitable division of land within the buffer zone, proposing instead the use of 'grid line 90 Northing' as the 'approximate boundary' for farming.[35] This line, however, would have necessitated the transfer to Turkish Cypriots of land previously cultivated by Greek Cypriots, and behind the lines previously agreed upon in 1975. Furthermore, the Turkish Cypriot side proposed the formation of an ad-hoc committee to review all existing practices between the CFLs.[36]

The implications of this proposal, not only for the local communities' economy but also for the precedent being set for future transboundary issues, spilt over into localised violence in September 1976, as Turkish Cypriots attempted to work the contested land.[37] Even the UN secretary-general himself became involved in high-level discussions as the crisis escalated. While compromise proposals were eventually drawn up, the Greek Cypriot authorities continued to reject, on principle, any transfer of Greek Cypriot-owned land to Turkish Cypriot farmers, which they saw to be disturbing the status quo within the buffer zone.[38]

By mid-1977 there were over 100 different locations along the length of the UNBZ where informal, 'local agreements' had been made with the Turkish

Forces to allow limited Greek Cypriot farming.[39] From then, however, expansion was slow, such that there were only 160 locations recorded by May 1979.[40] General activity steadily increased during the following years, and agricultural practices re-emerged to the extent that, by 1993, the UN secretary-general reported that over 1,500 landowners farmed in the UNBZ – indeed, farming had been extended 'almost to the limit of land available'.[41] Clearly, however, the limit of land available was determined by several factors, many of which were to all intents and purposes far from 'normal'. There was, for example, an outstanding problem with mines. During the construction of defensive positions in August 1974, neither side complied with international procedures for marking minefields.[42] Although UNFICYP undertook to record those known, the problem has failed to be resolved, with neither side assisting in confirming its scale. According to recent UN estimates, there are still 38 minefields and booby-trapped areas inside the buffer zone, and a further 73 located within 500m of it.[43] An estimated 16,000 mines are contained in these areas.

Yet the greatest remaining problem was that of delimiting the FSLs, to the extent that UNFICYP was forced to begin demarcating these during 1982.[44] By 1988, however, concern was expressed by the Turkish Forces over the close proximity to their CFL of some Greek Cypriot farming activities.[45] In October of that year, UNFICYP was able to formulate a general agreement with the Commander of Turkish Forces such that, while the current farming situation would be 'frozen', no new farming up to 200m from the Turkish Forces' CFL would be authorised by UNFICYP, and any new farming in the 200–400m bracket from the Turkish Forces' CFL would be discussed with the Turkish Forces Command level to assess security implications. While UNFICYP continues to state explicitly that this intra-boundary 'no-go' area is established purely for 'security reasons', and in no way constitutes any extension of Turkish Cypriot 'sovereignty', it unquestionably represented another *de facto* appropriation of territory.[46]

A 'liminal state'

Clearly, access and utilisation of the buffer zone have proven problematic. The development of the zone as a region of post-conflict rapprochement or 'transborder collaboration' (as advocates of the 'Europe of regions' might phrase it) has become even more stunted over time. Perhaps the best way of illustrating this observation is by drawing on a metaphor employed by Wilson in his 1993 anthropological examination of 'liminality' in the Irish border region. Wilson suggests that 'liminality' is a metaphor for both the situation in which people at the border live, and for the conditions which travellers who cross the border experience. This liminal state is

> temporary, necessary, and polluting.... a paradoxical condition of permanent transition.... At the risk of taking this metaphor too far, ... international borders and border zones are liminal states (i.e. transitional conditions of culture and

community) between the ordered, structured, and unpolluted 'conditions' of nation and state. Frontiers are expected to be different and uncomfortable. (Wilson, 1994: 104.)

This metaphor aptly captures the abnormal conditions of the UNBZ where, in principle, UNFICYP seeks to recreate a semblance of normality.

In Cyprus, in 1976, the UN secretary-general had observed that 'in the area between the lines, the status quo ... is maintained, without prejudice to an eventual political settlement concerning the disposition of the area'.[47] The present, in other words, is represented as being transitory and with a(n as yet undefined) time limit. While this approach is understandable in terms of maintaining diplomatic neutrality, it has of course held repercussions for those who live or work in, or indeed cross, the UNBZ. Indeed, this would appear to be the case for the three main interested parties. As gatekeepers to this area, UNFICYP's time in the zone is a brief one, as dictated by what is commonly a six-month tour of duty. In turn, its decision-making powers are similarly limited. UNBZ-related incidents are dealt with by UNFICYP through a liaison system which starts with the ground-troops, and then moves to the sectoral headquarters, with UNFICYP HQ as the last stop (Fetherston, 1994: 51). As a consequence of this low-level liaison with opposing forces and borderlanders, great responsibility is placed on ground-troops, particularly considering the cumulative number of 'small' incidents that are resolved at the first port-of-call each and every day. In military terms, as Fursdon observed,

> Through briefing and experience on the job, the UN soldier soon gets to know *the pattern of normal activity* authorised in his [*sic*] area. He learns, for instance, the type and level of farming work authorised in his part of the buffer zone, and its associated movement; the normal military routine of the soldiers of the two sides manning positions in his area.... He will memorise the look of their dug-in defensive positions. (Fursdon, 1990: 15.)

On one hand, given the overall duration of UNFICYP's operation on the island, it has developed a more detailed understanding of local and human space than any other interested party on the island, and relative to many other UN missions worldwide (Grundy-Warr, 1994b: 183). However, given the condition of 'permanent transition' of each and every peacekeeper, the subsequent lack of continuity can translate only into sub-optimal decision-making. Moreover, these 'normalities' are of a predominantly military nature and – contrary to what UNFICYP's mandate implies – fail to offer sufficient evidence of a return to any sense of non-militarised normality.

The two other interested parties are naturally those who wish to make use of the buffer zone – the two Cypriot communities. In practice, this has been predominantly Greek Cypriot landowners who, in periods of relative peace, have been encouraged to apply for permits. Conversely, incidents in certain areas have brought about a sudden drop in applications to farm. The violent clashes at Dherinia in August 1996, for example, had widespread repercussions. The disrupted lives of one Greek Cypriot couple illustrate quite graphically the transitory nature of borderlanders in the buffer zone. Farming just a mile outside Dherinia, about half of their land fell within what became the UNBZ, which they sought to continue using because of the soil quality and access to a highly productive private water borehole. In turn, they had to visit a one-roomed house each day to water their greenhouse. A relationship built up with UNFICYP's patrol whereby the couple, because of the regularity of their visits, were informally excused from bringing and showing their permits each day. At times, therefore, working in the UNBZ was much like farming elsewhere in the south. However, following the reduction in UNFICYP's patrols after the 1993 financial review, and the subsequent violence of August 1996, the couple increasingly operated in an environment of fear and insecurity. Neither of them now stayed overnight in their house as they once had the option of doing, especially after rumours that Turkish Forces were reconnoitring their area after dark. A certain uneasiness pertained to farming with 'alien' soldiers looking on, as one UNFICYP peacekeeper ironically put it.[48]

Such vignettes, as Krishna has declared elsewhere, 'serve to acquaint us with a part of the world we have pulverized in our minds into a space dominated by "the border"' (Krishna, 1996: 209). The sense of transition one experiences when one consciously ceases to map the UNBZ as abstract space, and begins to recognise it as a real place, is significant in that it has parallels with Greek Cypriot farmers' own sense of transition in actively breaking down the 'walls' in Cyprus and reuniting the island. And the converse is largely true with Turkish Cypriot borderlanders. Although, from 1982, UNFICYP reported a slight upturn in the area farmed by Turkish Cypriots north of the FSL, land north of the FSL has been largely utilised as scrub or for the rough grazing of goats.[49] Two main factors contributed to the apparent Turkish Cypriot disinterest in utilising this space. One of these was the presence of 3km-deep Turkish military zones north of the UNBZ which discouraged (both physically and psychologically) Turkish Cypriots from utilising buffer zone land. In addition, and perhaps more significantly, while the Turkish Cypriots had access to more cultivable land relative to their counterparts as a whole, they had previously owned little of the land which now fell within the buffer zone. This was clearly evident in the two most rural sectors of the UNBZ. By early 1997, in UNFICYP's Sector 1, west of Nicosia, where over 5,000 plots of land were allowed to be worked, out of 1,118 permits only five were held by Turkish Cypriots.[50] The area to the east of Nicosia (Sector 4) was solely Greek Cypriot-farmed, save for 10 Turkish Cypriots farming 'Haliland' on the Pyla-Pergamos plateau.[51]

CONCLUSIONS

In terms of evaluating the efficacy of UNFICYP's quarter-century-old buffer zone, the overall level of violence and territorial 'violations' has been contained and, ultimately, an inter-NATO war has thus far been prevented (Maynard, 1994: 111). This is vitally important given that, as the events of August 1996 fully illustrated, there are occasional dramatic failures in containing violence.[52] The UNBZ technically remains in a cease-fire situation, northern Cyprus (as Boutros-Ghali was always keen to highlight) is regarded as one of the most densely-militarised areas in the world, and an arms build-up continues island-wide. Yet, as has been argued more generally, UNFICYP's 'good fences make good neighbours' approach has in fact prevented inter-communal association (Ryan, 1995).

UNFICYP's role in the 'micro-diplomacy' that has become part of the everyday life in and along the UNBZ cannot be underestimated. In handling resource management issues, while respecting innocent civilian activity and the exercise of property rights, it has successfully adopted a damage-limitation approach.[53] Nonetheless, resources within the UNBZ have effectively been quarantined; the benefits to be gained from this action have been confined to certain sections of the border region and, in turn, to certain issue areas dictated by security concerns. By definition, this boundary management will always be sub-optimal because UNFICYP is in essence generating its own powers of inclusion and exclusion.

This paper has demonstrated that narrowing the geographical focus from the 'all-island' to the borderland scale facilitates an examination of issues from more of a 'bottom-up' perspective which takes into account how borderlanders are involved in and affected by the management of the buffer zone. UNFICYP's mandate has reaffirmed the primacy of military and security over socio-economic and psychological concerns in the border region and the limited involvement of borderlanders in the main decision-making. It must be noted, however, that border residents have never been merely passive victims of structures and decisions imposed from above. Some have responded to marginalisation by turning the border into an economic resource through smuggling and, more recently in the south, the accessing of grant-economies (Hocknell, 1998). Even so, such strategies have not proven antidotes to the overall socio-economic disadvantages in the buffer zone and in areas of close proximity.

The UN's involvement in this case, as in others (e.g. Lebanon, Golan Heights), has given further credence to those at pains to distinguish between peace*making* and peace*keeping* activities. It is evident that the successive renewal of UNFICYP's mandate to manage a buffer zone must be more seriously questioned. Perhaps more precisely, however, it is necessary to recognise that the functions of this buffer zone have been defined by the guiding principles of UNFICYP's mandate, and not those principles that now guide new boundary narratives on borderlands. While the UN's overall peacemaking potential has been undermined further by the disputants and related parties, the successful management of the status quo contrasts starkly with the problematic management of other boundary functions, and would strongly suggest the need to reconsider the buffer zone's viability and desirability as a model for anything but a temporary territorial management alternative.

NOTES

1 Boggs (1940: 11, emphasis added), as noted in Herzog (1991c: 588). Prescott (1965: 76) later conceded that 'the only function of a boundary is to mark the limits of authority or ownership'.

2 Cappellin (1992); Duchavek (1986a; 1986b). This work is synonymous with other studies on globalisation, which emphasise the reconfiguring of what is understood to be domestic and foreign policy both between contiguous border regions, and with distant centres of economic and political power.

3 Indeed, mirroring UNFICYP's mandate, the Bosnian, Croatian and Serbian parties to the Dayton Agreement were generally obliged 'to recreate as quickly as possible *normal conditions of life* in Bosnia and Hercegovina' (Annex 1A, Article 1, para. 1, emphasis added).

4 See, for example, Grundy-Warr (1994a: 76–78); Richmond (1998) and Ker-Lindsay & Richmond (1999).

5 UNSC Resn. 186 (1964), 4 March, para. 5 (emphasis added).

6 For a fuller breakdown of positions than provided here, see Grundy-Warr (1994a) and Ker-Lindsay & Richmond (1999).

7 *UN S*/5950, para. 220, cited in Grundy-Warr (1994a: 77).

8 *UN S*/6102, para. 24.

9 This paper concentrates less on what generalisations, if any, can be drawn from the Cyprus case, and more on the empirical details that enrich this borderland. More extensive treatment of conceptual and theoretical implications of the Cyprus case can be found in Hocknell (1996; 1998).

10 A major exception was UNFICYP's protection of Nicosia International Airport (see Henn, 1994).

11 *UN S*/12723, para. 21.

12 *UN S*/12946, para. 25.

13 *UN S*/14275, Annex, para. 4.

14 *UN S*/20663, para. 14.

15 *UN S*/21010, para. 10.

16 *UN S*/1998/488, para. 16.

17 *UN Secretary General Statement at Opening of Cyprus Talks, Troutbeck, New York, 9 July 1997*, reproduced in *The Blue Beret*, Vol. 34, No. 3, July 1997.

18 UNFICYP also has a civilian complement of 335, of whom 295 are locally recruited, with the rest coming from the international community.

19 Post-1993 and the reduction in personnel, UNFICYP has increasingly found itself hearing but not observing shooting incidents, to the extent that while it continues to protest such incidents to both sides, there is little scope for carrying out investigations. For illustrations of this growing occurrence, see *UN S*/1996/1016 and *UN S*/1998/488.

20 *The Cyprus Mail*, 17/4/92.

21 *UN S*/19927, para. 26. It also became compulsory for other Greek Cypriots wishing to cross to the north to complete formal entry forms.

22 *UN S*/20310, para. 17.

23 While Greek Cypriots were allowed a GB£10 payment per month for multiple visits, Maronites were granted a reduction of GB£30 per year for multiple visits for the whole family (*UN S*/1998/488, para. 21).

24 James (1990: 235). Maynard (1994: 109) went so far as to suggest that the absence of

a clear geographic dividing line pre-1974 prevented UNFICYP from fulfilling its peacekeeping mandate.

25 See Hocknell (1999b) for a more extensive treatment of this process.

26 See UNSC Resns. 353, 354, 355, 359 and 361 (1974).

27 *UN S*/12253, para. 71; *UN S*/12723, para. 68.

28 *The Blue Helmets* (1990: 295), cited in Fetherston (1994: 52), emphasis added.

29 These are, from east to west: Troulli, Athienou, Pyla, Mammari, and Dhenia. In addition, the village of Strovilia which falls within the British Dhekelia Sovereign Base Area is adjacent to the UNBZ. There are officially two other 'civilian use areas' at Paphos Gate, on Nicosia's Venetian wall, and the Dhali-Lymbia road.

30 *UN S*/411, para. 3.

31 *UN S*/11717, para. 18.

32 *UN S*/11717, para. 27.

33 *UN S*/11900, para. 21.

34 *UN S*/12253, para. 21.

35 This, according to UK-drawn Military Survey maps used by UNFICYP, was approximately 3509° latitude.

36 *UN S*/12253, para. 27.

37 *UN S*/12253, para. 24.

38 By 1977 UNFICYP was forced to propose a *modus vivendi* for the tending of two large, poorly irrigated citrus orchards (*UN S*/12342, para. 19).

39 *UN S*/12253, para. 20; *UN S*/12342, para. 19.

40 *UN S*/13369, para. 25.

41 *UN S*/26777, para. 18.

42 *UN S*/11568, para. 29–30.

43 *UN S*/1998/488, para. 12. The Turkish Forces have subsequently indicated their readiness to negotiate the minefield issue immediately following an extension of the unmanning agreement.

44 *UN S*/15812, para. 33.

45 *UN S*/20310, para. 21.

46 *Interview*, UNFICYP Senior Humanitarian Branch Officer, UNPA, 26 November 1996.

47 *UN S*/12253, para. 19.

48 *Pers. Comm.*, UNFICYP Humanitarian Assistant, Sector 4 (AUSCON), 15 February 1997.

49 *UN S*/15149, para. 31.

50 *Pers. Comm.*, UNFICYP First Humanitarian Office Assistant, Sector 1 (ARGCON), 18 January 1997.

51 'Haliland' remains officially the property of the Republic of Cyprus. UNFICYP handled it on the premise that no additional buildings were allowed, only farming and flock-grazing activities. (*Interview* with UNFICYP Humanitarian Assistant, Sector 4 (AUSCON), September 1997.)

52 Diehl (1993: 55), cited in Maynard (1994: 110).

53 Grundy-Warr (1994b: 181). See Grundy-Warr (1994a, b) for an introduction to this informal 'micro' and 'macro' peacekeeping division.

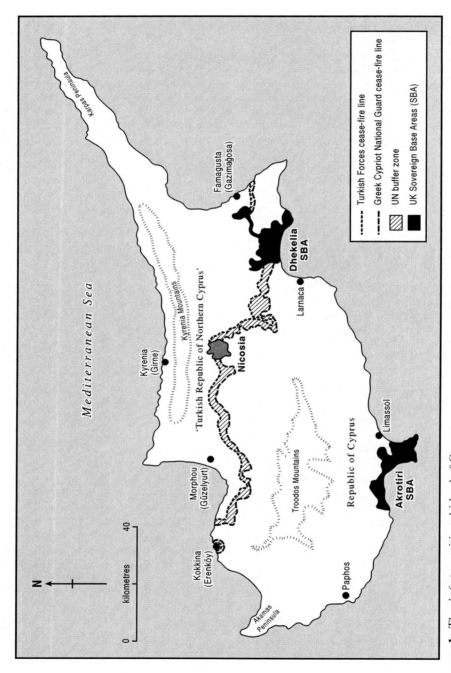

Figure 1: The *de facto* partitioned island of Cyprus

Copyright: Hocknell (1998)

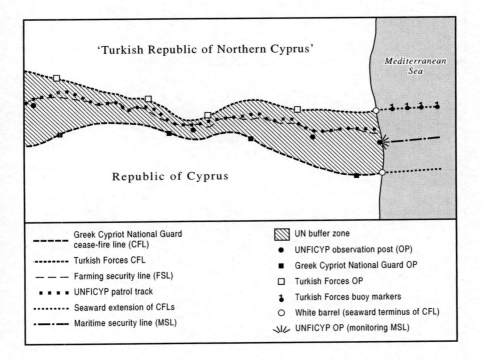

Figure 2: Diagrammatic representation of the management of the UNBZ

Copyright: Hocknell (1998)

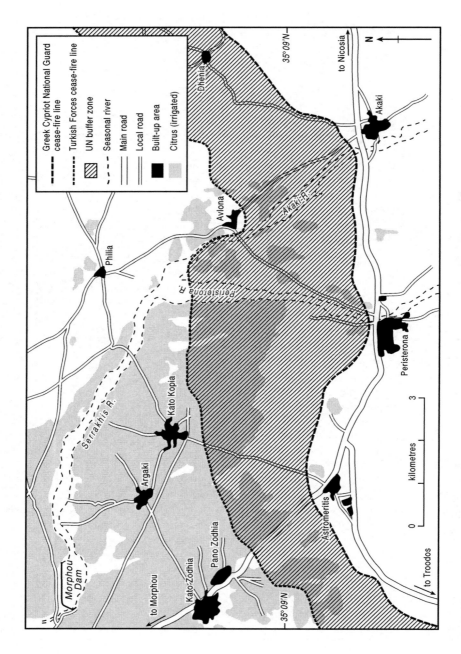

Figure 3 Avlona and the UNBZ

BIBLIOGRAPHY

Aristotelous, A. (1995) *Greece, Turkey and Cyprus: The Military Balance – Arms Doctrines and Disarmaments, 1995-96*, Cyprus Centre for Strategic Studies: Nicosia (south).

Blake, G. H. (1992) 'Territorial alternatives', *Boundary Bulletin*, No. 3, January: 9–12.

Blake, G. H. (1993) 'Transfrontier collaboration: a worldwide survey', in Westing, A. H. (ed.) *Transfrontier Reserves for Peace and Nature: A Contribution to Human Security*, UNEP: Nairobi: 35–48.

Blake, G. H. (1994) 'International transboundary collaborative ventures', in Gallusser, W. A. (ed.) *Political Boundaries and Coexistence*, IGU Symposium, Peter Lang: Basle: 359–371.

The Blue Beret, UNFICYP: Nicosia.

Boggs, S. (1940) *International Boundaries: A Study of Boundary Functions and Problems*, Columbia University Press: New York.

Boutros-Ghali, B. (1992) *An Agenda for Peace: Preventive Diplomacy, Peacemaking and Peacekeeping*, UN Department of Public Information: New York.

Brown, C. (1997) 'On the edge: a new approach to understanding border regions', *Regions: The Newsletter of the Regional Studies Association*, No. 207, February: vi–viii.

Bufon, M. (1994) 'Local aspects of transborder cooperation: a case study in the Italo-Slovene border landscape', in Gallusser, W. A. (ed.) *Political Boundaries and Coexistence*, IGU Symposium, Peter Lang: Basle: 19–29.

Cappellin, R. (1992) 'Theories of local endogenous development and international cooperation', in Tykkylainen, M. (ed.) *Development Issues and Strategies in the New Europe*, Avebury: Aldershot: 1–19.

Carnegie Commission (1997) Preventing Deadly Conflict: Final Report, The Carnegie Commission on Preventing Deadly Conflict: Washington, DC.

Coufoudakis, V. (1976) 'United Nations peacekeeping and peacemaking and the Cyprus question', *Western Political Quarterly*, Vol. 29, No. 3: 457–473.

Diehl, P. (1993) *International Peacekeeping*, The John Hopkins University Press: Baltimore.

Duchavek, I. (1986a) 'International competence of subnational governments: borderlands and beyond', in Martínez, O. J. (ed.) *Across Boundaries: Transborder Interaction in Comparative Perspective*, Texas Western Press: Austin, Texas: 11–27.

Duchavek, I. (1986b) *The Territorial Dimension of Politics: Within, Between and Across Nations*, Westview Press: Boulder.

Evriviades, M. & Bourantonis, D. (1994) 'Peacekeeping and peacemaking: some lessons from Cyprus', *International Peacekeeping*, No. 1, Vol. 4, Winter: 394–412.

Fetherston, A. B. (1994) *Towards a Theory of United Nations Peacekeeping*, St Martin's Press: New York.

Fursdon, E. (1990) 'UN peacekeeping in Cyprus', *Conflict Studies*, 232, June: 11–18.

Grundy-Warr, C. (1987) 'Political division and peacekeeping in Cyprus', in Blake, G. H. & Schofield, R. N. (eds.) *Boundaries and State Territory in the Middle East and North Africa*, Middle East and North African Studies Press: Cambridge: 70–83.

Grundy-Warr, C. (1994a) 'Peacekeeping lessons from divided Cyprus', in *Eurasia, World Boundaries*, Vol. 3, Routledge: London: 71–88.

Grundy-Warr, C. (1994b) 'Towards a political geography of United Nations peacekeeping: some considerations', *Geojournal*, Vol. 34, No. 2, October: 177–190.

Henn, F. (1994) 'The Nicosia Airport incident of 1974: a peacekeeping gamble', *International Peacekeeping*, Vol. 1, No. 1, Spring: 80–98.

Herzog, L. A. (1991c) 'International boundary cities: the debate on transfrontier planning in two border regions', *Natural Resource Journal*, Vol. 31, Winter: 587–608.

Hocknell, P. R. (1996) 'Partitioned state, divided resources: North/South Korea and cases for comparison', *Boundary and Security Bulletin*, Vol. 4, No. 2, Summer: 65–71.

Hocknell, P. R. (1998) 'Post-partition Management of Transboundary Resources: The Case of Cyprus', unpublished Ph.D. thesis, University of Durham, Durham.

Hocknell, P. R. (1999a) 'Cooperation, coexistence or conflict?: rethinking transboundary resource management in Nicosia', *Journal of Mediterranean Studies* (in press).

Hocknell, P. R. (1999b) 'Buffer zone, nekri zoni or siniri?: the institutionalisation of territorial partition in Cyprus', *Boundary and Territory Briefing*, Vol. 3 (forthcoming).

James, A. (1990) *Peacekeeping in International Politics*, St Martin's Press: New York.

Joseph, J.S. (1985) *Cyprus: Ethnic Conflict and International Concern*, American University Studies, Peter Lang: Berne.

Ker-Lindsay, J. & Richmond, O. P. (1999) *Promoting Peace and Development: Reviewing Five Decades of United Nations Involvement in Cyprus*, MacMillan: London (forthcoming).

Kostakos, G. (1994) 'UN peace-keeping missions in the Mediterranean region', in Gillespie, R. (ed.) *Mediterranean Politics*, Vol. 1, Pinter Publishers: London: 58–81.

Krishna, S. (1996) 'Cartographic anxiety: mapping the body politic in India', in Shapiro, M. J. & Alker, H. R. (eds.) *Challenging Boundaries: Global Flows, Territorial Identities*, Borderlines Vol. 2, University of Minnesota Press: Minneapolis and London: 193–214.

Maynard, W. K. (1994) 'The Peace Operations Schema: Rationalising United Nations Peacekeeping in the Post-Cold War Milieu', unpublished Ph.D., Department of Political Science, University of Alabama.

McDonald, R. (1993) 'Cyprus: a peacekeeping paradigm', *The World Today*, October: 182–184.

Newman, D. & Paasi, A. (1998) 'Fences and neighbours in the postmodern world: boundary narratives in political geography', *Progress in Human Geography*, Vol. 22, No. 2: 186–207.

Patrick, R. (1976) *Political Geography and the Cyprus Conflict, 1963–1971*, University of Waterloo Press: Ontario.

Prescott, J. R. V. (1965) *The Geography of Frontiers and Boundaries*, Hutchinson: London.

Ratti, R. & Reichmann, S. (eds.) (1993) *Theory and Practice of Transborder Cooperation*, Helbing and Lichtenhahn Verlag AG: Basel.

Richmond, O. P. (1998) *Mediating in Cyprus: The Cypriot Communities and the United Nations*, Frank Cass: London.

Ryan, S. (1995) *Ethnic Conflict and International Relations*, (2nd edn.), Dartmouth: Aldershot.

Stegenga, J. (1968) *The United Nations Force in Cyprus*, Ohio State University Press: Columbia.

Szulc, T. (1993) 'A time of reckoning', *National Geographic*, Vol. 184, No. 1, July: 104–130.

Taylor, P.J. (1994) 'The state as container: territoriality in the modern world-system', *Progress in Human Geography*, Vol. 18, No. 2: 151–162.

UN S/5579– (1964–), Report of the Secretary General on the United Nations Operation in Cyprus, six-monthly reports, Security Council, Official Records Quarterly Supplements, UN: New York.

UN (1985) *The Blue Helmets: A Review of United Nations Peacekeeping*, (2nd edn.), UN Department of Public Information: New York.

UN (1996) *The Blue Helmets: A Review of United Nations Peacekeeping*, (3rd edn.), UN Department of Public Information: New York.

Wilson, T. (1994) 'Symbolic dimensions to the Irish border', in Donnan, H. & Wilson, T. (eds.) *Border Approaches: Anthropological Perspectives on Frontiers*, University of Press America, Inc: London.

White, N. D. (1997) *Keeping the Peace: The United Nations and the Maintenance of International Peace and Security*, Manchester University Press: Manchester and New York.

Zacarias, A. (1996) *The United Nations and International Peacekeeping*, I. B. Taurus Publishers: London and New York.

17
The Israeli–Jordanian Peace Boundary

Moshe Brawer

INTRODUCTION

One of the main outcomes of the 1994 Israeli–Jordanian Peace Treaty has been the relief of the stress which prevailed continuously for 45 years over the issue of the common borderlands of both countries. The Treaty also resulted in the first, in the countries' long history, exactly delimited and demarcated boundary between the territories east and west of the Jordan Valley.

The new boundary between Israel and Jordan is largely based on a line delimited in 1922 by a British decree (Order in Council) designed to separate politically Jordan (then known as Transjordan) from Palestine, both at that time under British sovereignty. Following the First World War both countries formed one entity administered by Britain under a League of Nations Mandate. In 1922 Jordan (Transjordan) was separated from Palestine to become the autonomous Arab Hashimite Emirate which, however, remained under British control until 1946. The decree delimiting the boundary between both countries reads as follows:

> A line drawn from a point two miles west of Aqaba in the Gulf of Aqaba up the centre of the Wadi Araba, the Dead Sea and the river Jordan to the junction of the latter with the river Yarmuk, thence up the centre of the river Yarmuk to the Syrian Frontier. (*Official Gazette*, 1922.)

Physically, this boundary consisted of three main parts:

1. the section along the centre of the rivers Yarmuk and Jordan (115km, although due to the many tortuous meanders of these rivers it actually extended over 213km)
2. the section along the centre of the Dead Sea (80km)
3. the section along the Arava Valley (Wadi Araba) (181km).

Over the long history of the Holy Land, much of the region through which this line runs – i.e. the Jordan Rift Valley – has been a buffer zone between the lands to the east and west, due to its extreme aridity and unproductive soils. Most of it was either unpopulated or roamed by small groups of nomads.

Borderlands Under Stress (M.A. Pratt and J.A. Brown (eds), ISBN 90-411-9790-7).
© Kluwer Law International, 2000.

THE YARMUK–JORDAN SECTION

The Yarmuk is the main tributary of the river Jordan. Before its diversion for irrigation purposes, its annual average discharge nearly doubled that of the river Jordan. It follows a tortuous course through a deep, narrow valley. According to the abovementioned delimitation, the boundary between Palestine and Transjordan followed this river for 18km. The Jordan, from its confluence with the Yarmuk to the Dead Sea, meanders very extensively through the deep soft marl which covers its floodplain (Figure 1). Before it lost most of its natural flow, its main course underwent frequent changes, especially during winter floods (Schattner, 1962). The Transjordan–Palestinian boundary therefore shifted with it, thereby transferring small areas of land from one side of the boundary to the other, in both directions (Figure 2). This fact was ignored until a comparatively conspicuous change in the position of the main bed of the river took place in 1927, transferring an area of approximately 200 acres from the western (Palestinian) to the eastern (Transjordanian) bank. However, in view of the fact that this was only an administrative border between two lands under British sovereignty, the British authorities ruled that the boundary would continue to follow the main course of the Jordan no matter what changes occurred in the position of its bed.[1]

The banks of the river were, at that time, uninhabited. Legal traffic across the Jordan was mainly confined to two bridges (Allenby and Damia), although the river did not form an obstacle to much uncontrolled crossing, especially from east to west.

THE DEAD SEA SECTION

Large parts of the shore line of the Dead Sea are bordered by high cliffs. Where these retreat, there are narrow, almost flat, coastal strips extensively dissected by the mouths of numerous wadis which drain the neighbouring highlands into the Dead Sea. These flat strips are densely covered by coarse gravel. Until the recent construction of modern roads, access to the shores of the Dead Sea was extremely difficult and it was impossible to traverse the shoreline, even on foot. The shore and the lands surrounding the sea were desolate and uninhabited except for a few very small, isolated oases.

At the time of the delimitation of the 1922 boundary, the sea and its surroundings were a formidable barrier between Palestine and Transjordan. It was only with the development of its mineral resources and its potential for health resorts (mainly since the middle of the twentieth century) that the Dead Sea 'came to life' and the position of the boundary which divided it became significant.

THE ARAVA VALLEY (WADI ARABA) SECTION

The expression 'centre of Wadi Araba' in the 1922 delimitation was interpreted by the British Palestine administration to mean 'a line connecting the lowest points' (the 'Thalweg', as it was termed) along the desert-like, uninhabited valley between the southern shores of the Dead Sea and the Gulf of Aqaba.[2] What was believed to be this line was then provisionally demarcated on the only maps of this region available at that time. These maps were inaccurate.[3]

Dissatisfied with the inaccuracy of the boundary line in the Arava Valley, as presented in the official maps of the British administration, the director of the Survey Department repeatedly requested financial grants in order to demarcate this section of the Palestine boundary properly.[4] The requests were rejected on the grounds that the demarcation would serve no useful purpose as the region was only frequented by small numbers of Bedouin. This attitude was maintained even after it became obvious that the line, as marked on official maps, did not concur with the actual 'line of lowest points', nor with any other reasonable interpretation of 'the centre of Wadi Araba' as defined in the 1922 delimitation. A letter dated 29 September 1930 was sent from the War Office in London to the British High Commissioner of Palestine requesting a map on which to mark the accurate position of the boundary between Palestine and Transjordan in the Wadi Araba. The map provided was accompanied by letters from the High Commissioner and the director of the Palestine Survey Department stating that the line given on the map did not represent the accurate position of the boundary.[5]

It was only in 1946, after Transjordan gained its independence to become the kingdom of Jordan, that the budget for the demarcation of the boundary in the Arava Valley was approved.[6] However, only 4km from the shores of the Gulf of Aqaba northwards had been demarcated by the time the British government decided to give up the administration of Palestine in 1947, at which point the demarcation project was abandoned. Thus, by the time the newly established State of Israel took over Palestine's part of the Arava Valley, the official maps of the former British administration continued to be used and the real position of the boundary remained to be determined.

CROSS-BOUNDARY CONCESSIONS

Two developments during the early years of the British administration had a significant impact on the newly delimited boundary between Palestine and Transjordan. These figured prominently during the making of the Israeli–Jordanian peace boundary (1994).

The first was a concession granted in 1921 to the Palestine Electric Corporation (a Jewish company) to exploit the waters near the confluence of the rivers Jordan and Yarmuk for a hydroelectric power station. The operation of this power station involved the local diversion of both rivers, to be achieved by the building of three dams and the acquisition, by the Palestine Electric Corporation, of Jordanian lands. The power station, its facilities and the quarters of its employees (mainly Palestinian Jews) were built on Jordanian territory. It started operating in 1928, supplying electricity only to Palestine and effectively forming a Palestinian (Jewish) enclave on the Jordanian side of the boundary. However, the output of this power station was small. With the rapid growth of the population and electricity consumption in Palestine, thermal power stations were later built on the Mediterranean coast, and the hydroelectric power station on the river Jordan lost much of its economic importance.

The second development was a concession granted in 1929 to the Palestine Potash Company (a British–Jewish concern) for the exclusive exploitation of the mineral resources of the Dead Sea. It started operating in 1931 and exported potash mainly to Britain. All the company's plants were built on the Palestinian side of the sea, but the works at the southern end of the sea depended on water supplied by springs in Jordan (Luke, 1930).

Both these concessions were granted by the British government with the approval of the Emir Abdullah, then head of the autonomous authorities of Transjordan. The plants established under these concessions operated fully until the Palestine War in 1948, when they were totally destroyed.

BORDERLANDS UNDER STRESS

Before the Israeli–Jordanian Peace Treaty (1994), the borderlands between these countries were constantly under stress and occasionally under high tension following violent border incidents. This situation applied to the sections of the borderlands along the Arava Valley, the southern half of the Dead Sea and the northern part of the rivers Jordan and Yarmuk after the 1948–49 Palestine War, and to the northern part of the Dead Sea and the southern part of the Jordan Valley after the 1967 war. On the Israeli side, electric fences and partly mined, heavily guarded security zones extended along the rivers Yarmuk and Jordan, parts of the western shores of the Dead Sea and the Arava Valley. The Jordanian side of the border was also fortified and heavily guarded with extensive closed-security areas. The floodplain through which the Jordan meanders thereby became a 'no-man's land' into which only military patrols ventured. With the exception of two strictly controlled crossing points, on bridges on the river Jordan, the area formed a barrier which totally separated the two countries.

Israeli forces occupied and held a small area southeast of the Jordan–Yarmuk confluence (most of the area of the former enclave of the Palestine Electric Corporation) and parts of the Arava Valley, east of what was believed during the period of the British administration to be the boundary between the countries. The fact that the location of the boundary line in the Arava Valley had never been properly established, added to the security requirements of the region (there were attacks on traffic on the main road to Eilat), provided Israel with the excuse to extend control over substantial areas in this valley which Jordan considered its own territory. This made it possible for Israeli settlers in the Arava Valley to cultivate land and drill wells in these areas.

While much development work was carried out on the Israeli side, the Jordanian side of the valley remained desolate, with only military posts and activities, throughout the period during which the borderlands of the Arava Valley were under stress.

CHANGES IN PHYSICAL CONDITIONS AND POPULATION

Before discussing the boundary-making of the 1994 Israeli–Jordanian Peace Treaty, it is necessary to briefly portray the extensive geographical changes, both physical and human, which have taken place over much of this frontier during the last four to five decades.

The River Jordan

The section of the river Jordan along which the boundary between the countries ran, has lost many of its natural characteristics. As a result of the diversion of more than 80 per cent of its normal discharge by Israel (through the National Water Carrier from Lake Tiberias) and by Jordan (through the Ghor Canal from the Yarmuk), the previously frequent shifts in the position of the river became rare and very small in extent. Except during short spells of heavy winter floods, the Jordan now carries little water and many of its meanders and oxbows have dried up. Air-photographs of the river taken over the 20 years from 1974 to 1994 clearly indicate hardly any changes in the position of its main bed. This is a radical change from its behaviour before the 1960s.[7]

The borderland along this section of the river has become more populated than ever before. The Jordanian side is now irrigated by the Ghor Canal and other recently developed water resources. It now supports a large rural population and is the country's most productive agricultural region. The Israeli side is inhabited by numerous Jewish agricultural settlements, mostly established since 1967, which produce early crops of vegetables and fruit on irrigated land. The state of stress which prevailed here restricted the development of land, especially close to the banks of the river, which, with the proper techniques and irrigation, could have become very productive. The natural and cultural landscape of this part of the borderlands in the 1990s is very different from what it was when the 1922 boundary was delimited.[8]

The Dead Sea

The Dead Sea has undergone extensive transformations over the last 30 years as a result of the diversion of the waters of the rivers Jordan and Yarmuk, some of their tributaries and a few small streams which used to drain into the sea. In the early 1920s when the boundary drawn through its centre divided it between Palestine and Transjordan, its surface was 392m below sea level and its area was 1,040 square kilometres (sq km). By 1994 its surface had fallen to approximately 410m below sea level and its natural area had shrunk to approximately 700 sq km. The southern basin of the sea and the strait connecting it with the northern basin have dried up completely. The former southern basin (254 sq km) has been turned by the Israeli (west) and the Jordanian (east) potash companies into evaporation ponds filled with water pumped from the northern basin. A secret agreement on the division of the southern basin of the sea between the Israeli company (which began its operation in 1952) and the Jordanian company (ditto 1978) was in operation long before the conclusion of the peace treaty between both countries, although a dam built by the Israeli Potash Company along the former southern basin gives Israel a somewhat larger share of this basin than that left to the Jordanian company (Figure 3).

Further, the shrinking of the northern basin of the sea has not been symmetrical. Here, the sea along the western (Israeli) shore is comparatively shallow while the sea along the eastern (Jordanian) shore is much deeper. With the large fall in the level of the sea (18m) the shore line on the Israeli side gradually moved inward while it remained almost unchanged on the Jordanian side. Thus the centre of the sea is now closer to the Jordanian coast than it was in 1922.[9]

The coasts of the Dead Sea are now much more populated than they were during the period of the British administration. Several settlements, including spas with many large, modern hotels, have sprung up on the Israeli side of the sea. The warm, almost rainless winter, the high mineral content of the seawater and hot springs and the health resort facilities attract tourists from many countries. The Arab population on the Jordanian side has also increased very considerably and a tourist resort is being developed on the Jordanian coast. Every part of the coast is now accessible by good roads. The Dead Sea is no longer a region of desolation with the sole function of acting as a barrier between two countries.

The Arava Valley

The desert-like, uninhabited Arava Valley of the British administration is now equipped with two busy, modern ports and tourist resorts: Aqaba, Jordan's only outlet to the sea, and Eilat, Israel's outlet to the Red Sea and Indian Ocean. Each has an international airport. Twenty-one settlements and farms on the Israeli side and three on the Jordanian side of the valley have sprung up since the 1950s. These depend largely on irrigated agriculture exploiting the very hot and dry climate and the groundwater made available by recent geological research. The indifference of the British administration to the position of the provisional boundary line has been replaced by a careful examination of the respective interests which each side seeks to protect in what it claims as its share of the valley.

Detailed maps produced using advanced techniques after the valley was carefully surveyed, exposed the gross inaccuracies of the maps on which the boundary was provisionally delimited in 1922.[10] It became apparent that over much of its length, the boundary line did not follow the valley's lowest points. The beds of the sporadic streams which drain much of the valley shift widely within their respective floodplains. Further, the valley has three small endoreic basins[11], each with its own lowest points. The southern part of the valley is drained by at least two parallel outlets to the Gulf of Aqaba, with almost identical low points. The boundary line originally drawn on maps since 1922 actually allocated approximately two-thirds of the area of the valley to Jordan and only about one-third to Palestine.

Geological surveys also established the presence of groundwater resources, mainly in the eastern part of the valley. However, it is estimated that these potential resources would only suffice to irrigate a small part of the valley.[12] It is, therefore, unlikely to maintain a much larger population than the existing one (urban 100,000, rural 2,800); the population of Eilat is already mainly supplied by a desalination plant.

THE PEACE BOUNDARY ALONG THE RIVER JORDAN[13]

An understanding reached at the outset of the peace negotiations between Israel and Jordan established that the boundary between the countries, as delimited by Britain in 1922, would form the basis for an agreed new boundary. Where necessary, the 1922 delimitation would be redefined or adapted to the prevailing realities in the areas which it crossed. The actual meaning of the wording of the delimitation decree would be open to discussion and negotiation.

It was agreed that the northern section of the boundary, along the rivers Yarmuk and Jordan, would remain unchanged. It would follow the 'centre' of the rivers, concurring with the British delimitation. Unlike the practice of the British administration, according to which the boundary followed the centre of the river no matter what shifts occurred in its course, in future every such change (unlikely under the present conditions) would be subject to review by representatives of both countries. The river would not be allowed to create territorial gains or losses for its riparian states. Agreement was also reached regarding cooperation in the maximum exploitation of the waters of both rivers by building dams and reservoirs for the storage of floodwaters. The small area (approximately 2,000 acres) southeast of the Jordan–Yarmuk confluence occupied by Israel reverted to Jordanian sovereignty but nearby Israeli settlements would be allowed free access and continued use of the area for agricultural purposes (plantations). In fact, this area has become a clearly demarcated Israeli economic enclave on Jordanian territory.

SHARING THE DEAD SEA

With regard to the Dead Sea, there were two possibilities: either the boundary would follow a median line based on the present extent and shape of the sea, as stated in the 1922 delimitation; or the new peace boundary would remain as it was before the extensive fall in the level of the sea. As already mentioned, a median line drawn at present would allot Jordan a smaller part of the sea than it was given in 1922.

It was finally agreed that in the northern basin (which is actually what is left of the sea) the boundary would basically follow the line which appeared on the maps of the British administration – i.e. the median line before the great fall in the level of the sea. This means that Jordan got more than half the northern basin in its present dimensions. This dividing line will continue to be adhered to in future, even if the level of the sea continues to fall and its area shrinks further, in which case Jordan's comparative share in the actual water body of this basin is likely to grow.

In the now dry southern basin, the new boundary follows the dividing line between the areas actually held or in use by the Israeli and the Jordanian potash companies. It concurs with the partition of this basin previously agreed between the potash companies, which gave Israel a greater share of its area.

This compromise division of the Dead Sea was accepted by both sides as being fair. In addition, there are prospects for cooperation in the production and export of the Dead Sea's minerals.

THE DIVISION OF THE ARAVA VALLEY

The Arava Valley was the most contested area in the boundary negotiations of the peace treaty. It was first suggested that the *status quo ante*, namely the boundary as delimited on the maps of the British administration, be revived, as this was also, formally, the boundary line of the 1949 armistice agreement between Israel and Jordan. It was also argued that this line had been marked, since 1949, on most Israeli official maps. In practice, however, it never functioned as a border line. The Bedouins who resided in this valley (about 600 in the mid-1940s) were either not acquainted with the position of the boundary or they ignored it. Similarly, the occasional patrols of the Palestine Police who were almost the sole representatives of the administration in the Arava Valley, moved about and took action irrespective of the boundary. It appears from some of their reports that they most probably did not take the trouble to acquaint themselves with its exact position (Buller, 1931). From 1949 the same applied to the Israeli security forces, who had been much more conspicuous and dominant in the valley than the Jordanians. As already mentioned, they controlled areas and held positions well to the east of the abovementioned provisional line. The Israelis consistently objected to a return to the provisional undemarcated boundary of the British administration especially since, officially, the British themselves considered it erroneous.

Differences arose between the Israeli and Jordanian negotiators as to the actual meaning of the wording of the 1922 decree delimiting the boundary. The first argument concerned the meaning of 'Wadi Araba'. Did this 'geographical term' apply to the rift valley between the Dead Sea and the Gulf of Aqaba or to the bed of a short, small, sporadic stream in the southwestern corner of the valley? The short wadi runs into the sea within the municipal boundaries of Eilat, actually over 2km west of the point defined by the British administration as the starting point of the boundary between the countries. Ultimately it was agreed that 'Wadi Araba' applied to the rift valley. This followed the presentation of ample convincing evidence that this was what 'Wadi Araba' meant to prominent Arab (medieval and more recent) and European geographers and historians.

Another disputed interpretation concerned the term 'centre'. Was it a line connecting the lowest points along the valley or a median line dividing the valley 'geometrically' (Figure 4)? As mentioned, a detailed geographical and geological study of the valley and its accurate mapping revealed that the provisional boundary did not match the line of lowest points. Further, the lowest points had shifted considerably since 1922 and are not a stable feature; they often change position as a result of heavy flood flows. Some of the lowest points in the southern part of the valley are on its eastern side, well away from the provisional boundary. In winter, the drainage system of the valley carries a few short, sporadic flows of largely varying force and discharge. These cause frequent shifts in the actual beds of the wadis within their respective floodplains. Thus the assumption that by choosing the line of lowest points (the 'Thalweg') the boundary would be attached to a stable natural physical feature was erroneous.

On the other hand, acceptance of the claim that 'centre' actually meant a median line dividing the valley, longitudinally, into two almost equal parts would have presented the extremely difficult task of determining, scientifically or practically, the eastern and western limits of the valley. The geological faults and rock formations which flank the valley have complicated characteristics. They do not present continuous, sufficiently homogeneous features to determine the limits of the valley. The same applies to the geomorphological attributes of the valley, which is flanked on its eastern side by much wider and higher alluvial fans than those on its western side. Even what is considered as the nearly-flat bottom of the valley has a varied relief. It rises gradually from about −390m at the former southern end of the Dead Sea to nearly 200m about 100km further south, and then descends to sea level at the Gulf of Aqaba. It is extensively dissected by the many wadis which come down from the bordering highlands and by outliers of these highlands. Therefore, a median line could only ever be an agreed arbitrary line which could not hope to cut the valley into two equal longitudinal parts.

The compromise boundary agreed upon was based on a recognition of the new realities in the Arava Valley – mainly the existence of new Israeli settlements and their agricultural lands, and Jordanian development projects and territorial interests. The peace boundary is a new interpretation and implementation of the 1922 delimitation which had never been properly installed. It is understood that, in deviating from the provisional boundary delimited by the British administration to meet new realities, no side will make substantial territorial gains – i.e. Jordan will continue to hold more than half the valley.

The short section of the boundary (approximately 4km) near the shore of the Gulf of Aqaba, demarcated by the British administration in 1946, was accepted by both sides. For the next 12km the peace boundary follows the former provisional British line. The area of Aqaba airport on the eastern side, and land utilised by Israeli concerns on the western side, made it impossible to introduce any 'improvements' to this section of the border. However, this section has been opened to much cross-boundary cooperation. Aqaba airport is already used by passengers destined for Eilat and should, in future, become the main airport for both cities. There is lively traffic of tourists and local inhabitants between Aqaba and Eilat. Further north for about 150km the boundary is a tortuous line which, except for very short sections, does not follow any physical feature (e.g. wadis). It conspicuously evinces adaptation to contemporary realities in the valley (Figure 5). Where it bulges eastwards, it clearly circumvents lands cultivated by Israeli farms. However, along most of its length the peace boundary runs through the western part of the valley, not along its approximate 'centre'. Only in the extreme north, approaching what was the southern coast of the Dead Sea and the surrounding swamps, does the boundary run for about 10km along the centre of the deep and wide floodplain of the Wadi Jeib (Nahal Haarava), a prominent physical feature which was also followed by the provisional British border.

Only at one point, about half-way along the valley at the village of Tsofar, did Israeli plantation extend deep into the eastern part of the valley (Figure 6). This territory was handed back to Jordan. However, under the peace agreement these lands (approximately 800 hectares) and the wells used to water them were leased by the Jordanian government to the farmers of Tsofar for a period of 25 years, with free access and permission to transfer the crops to Israel. This is effectively the second Israeli economic enclave on Jordanian territory created by the peace boundary.

The position of the maritime boundary along the northern part of the Gulf of Aqaba was determined a few months after the signing of the peace treaty. It is almost a median line (the Gulf here is 6–7km wide) extending southwards for approximately 6km from the starting point of the land boundary to a point opposite the Egyptian–Israeli boundary in the Gulf.

The boundary agreement provided for the likelihood that the West Bank, or at least most of it, will be ceded in the future to a Palestinian authority, in which case a large part of the line of delimitation will become a boundary between Jordan and Arab Palestine. This will be subject to the acceptance of this line by the Palestinians. The boundary between Jordan and the West Bank, according to the Israel–Jordan peace agreement, conforms with that of the former British administration.

DELIMITATION AND DEMARCATION

The boundary, along its entire length, was delimited on an up-to-date series of 1:20,000 orthophotos of the frontier zone, which forms an appendix to the peace treaty. The demarcation of the boundary along the Arava Valley took place during 1995 and included minor local rectifications to meet surface conditions. For the first time in the long and eventful history of the Bible Lands, a clearly defined and demarcated boundary between the countries east and west of the Jordan Rift Valley has come into existence. It is perhaps worth noting that geographers on both sides actively participated in the negotiations on the delimitation of the peace boundary, a new phenomenon in the Middle East for handling territorial and boundary issues. Several new border crossing positions, for passengers and goods, have come into operation since the implementation of the peace treaty. The stress along the Israeli–Jordanian borderlands has been greatly relieved by the establishment of the peace boundary but has not entirely disappeared. Strict security measures are still in force, especially on the Israeli side, along the river Jordan and several other parts of the boundary, in view of occasional infiltrations by members of hostile organisations. Practically, therefore, the electric, high-security fences and the closed military areas along the boundary continue to function.

Little change has taken place in the Israeli–Jordanian borderlands over the four years since the implementation of the peace treaty, with two conspicuous exceptions: the extreme south and the extreme north of the frontier. In the south, close contacts and cooperation have developed between Aqaba and Eilat, especially where tourism is concerned. There is much traffic between these towns and, as mentioned, Aqaba airport is already used by flights to Eilat. A new bridge (Sheikh Hussein bridge) over the river Jordan in the north, built by common effort, has become an important artery of communication between Israel and Jordan, much used for tourism and trade. Small cultivable areas along both banks of the river Jordan have been made accessible to 'reliable' farmers. Israeli allocations of water, in compliance with the peace treaty, have brought some relief to water shortages in the northern part of the Jordanian borderland. The extreme sensitivity of both sides to intrusions of aircraft into their respective borderlands faded away after each opened air space to the other's civilian flights.

It is too early to survey changes in the landscape and the pattern of activities in the borderlands along the peace boundary. Developments are slow and largely depend on the mood of the population, which is strongly influenced by progress in Arab–Israeli relations and by various local and regional events. The fate of the negotiations between Israel and the Palestinian Authority is bound to have a far-reaching impact on the future character of the Israeli–Jordanian borderlands.

NOTES

1 Correspondence between the Colonial Office, London, and the High Commissioner, Jerusalem, 29 September 1930, 31 October 1930, PRO–CO /733/142/802 1284 44559.

2 Government of Palestine, Statement of the Legal Adviser, 12 July 1923. Palestine Survey Archives, Israel National Archives.

3 British military maps of the Sinai Peninsula (1:125,000), which include the Arava Valley, hastily prepared on the eve of the First World War.

4 Letter dated 4 July 1923 from the director of the Palestine Survey Department to the Chief Secretary (the second highest authority in the administration) concerning the inaccuracy of the boundary line in the Wadi Araba and making requests for the demarcation of the line. Memorandum on the Palestine–TransJordan boundary in the Wadi Araba submitted by the director of the Palestine Survey Department, 15 June 1931, requesting that the boundary be demarcated. Palestine Survey Archives, Israel National Archives.

5 Letter from the War Office, London, to the High Commissioner, Jerusalem, dated 29 September 1930, and replies dated 24 October 1930 and 31 October 1930. Palestine Survey Archives, Israel National Archives.

6 Report of the demarcation of the 4 km section of the Palestine–TransJordan frontier from the Gulf of Aqaba to the centre of Wadi Araba, 5 May 1946. Palestine Survey Archives, Israel National Archives.

7 A comparison of air-photographs of the Lower Jordan Valley taken in the 1940s and 1950s with those taken in the 1980s clearly indicates the nature of these changes.

8 Comparing air-photographs of the region taken during the First World War (1917, 1918) and during the 1930s with recent air-photographs. Also recent annual reports of the Ministries of Agriculture of both countries.

9 Comparing maps and air-photographs of the Dead Sea from the 1930s with those of the 1990s (Brawer, 1988).

10 Both Israel and Jordan carried out detailed surveys and mapping of their respective parts of the Arava Valley. Israeli military maps of the Arava Valley (1:50,000), largely based on photogrammetric surveys, became available in the late 1950s. The Israeli Geological Institute produced a series of geological maps which covered those parts of the valley which were under Israeli control. Geological surveys and maps of the Jordanian side of the valley were prepared by teams of foreign geologists (mainly Austrians).

11 An endoreic river basin is a river basin that does not drain into the ocean.

12 Lectures on the hydrology of the Arava Valley given in 1996 by J. Kolton, an Israeli geologist and hydrologist with the Department of Geography, Tel Aviv University.

13 The Peace Treaty between The State of Israel and the Hashemite Kingdom of Jordan (November 1994), including the map album of orthophotos, 1:20,000 and 1:50,000, of the entire length of the boundary and the borderlands. This album is part of the Peace Treaty.

Figure 1: A typical section of the floodplain through which the river Jordan meanders. The plain is flanked by a zone of badlands – i.e. regions characterised by soft rock that have been eroded into often fantastical sculptures and steep, furrowed hills.

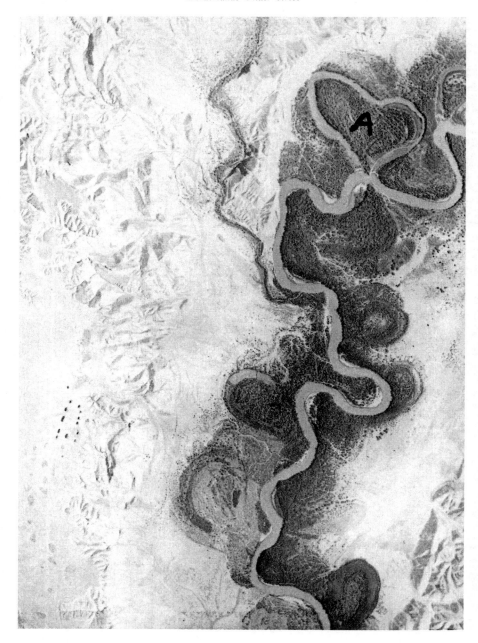

Figure 2: Changes in the main course of the Lower Jordan during 1920–1940, with numerous cut-off meanders. Area A was Transjordanian territory transferred to Palestine when the meander enclosing it was cut off.

Figure 3: The former southern basin of the Dead Sea, now taken up by the evaporation ponds of the potash companies. The boundary between Israel and Jordan runs along the eastern side of the dam (built by the Israeli company) which divides the basin. On the Israeli side the ponds extend beyond the former area of the sea. On the opposite side is the Jordanian village of Safi, with its irrigated lands.

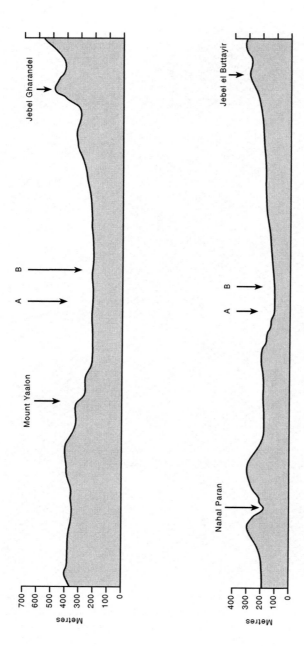

Figure 4: Cross-sections of the Arava Valley (1:100,000): the upper one of a narrow part of the valley (width approximately 8km) near the settlement of Yahel; the other of a wider part of the valley (14km) 90km north of Eilat. A = the position of the provisional boundary of the former British administration. B = the approximate 'geometrical' centre of the valley (based on geological structural features). The distance between A and B is 1,200 m and 1,000 m, respectively.

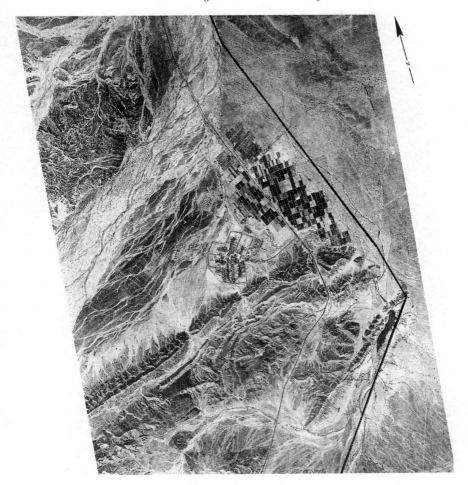

Figure 5: The new boundary running east of the Israeli settlement of Paran and its agricultural lands and then east of Wadi Jerafi (Nahal Paran). The British provisional boundary ran further west inside this wadi.

Figure 6: The Israeli settlement of Tsofar (110km north of Eilat) and its cultivated lands. Under the peace agreement area A was ceded back to Jordan but leased to Israel for 25 years so that the farmers of Tsofar could continue to utilise it.

BIBLIOGRAPHY

Brawer, M. (1988) *Israel's Boundaries*, (Hebrew), Tel Aviv: Yavneh Publishing House: 172–173.

Buller, Major R. S. Y. (Transjordan Frontier Force) (1931) Maps and notes of Wadi Araba (March) Palestine Survey archives, Israel National Archives.

Luke, H. C. (1930) *The Handbook of Palestine and Transjordan*, London: Macmillan: 338, 363.

Official Gazette (1922) Government of Palestine, Special Issue, 1 September.

Schattner, I. (1962) *The Lower Jordan Valley*, Jerusalem: Magnes Press: 56–84.

18
The Eastern Hills of India:
An Emerging Frontier

T. Lanusosang and R. C. Sharma

As in other parts of the world, many border regions of South Asia have taken on the frontier-like characteristics of the American 'wild west' – that is, they have become unsettled areas where the normal laws and ethos of the nation-state do not apply. As a consequence, integration and coexistence between neighbouring states are put to a severe test, raising questions about the relationship between sovereignty and territory. The Indian borderlands of Punjab and Jammu and Kashmir, and the states of Nagaland, Manipur and Mizoram are examples of regions facing such critical situations. The problems arising are likely to increase if proper territorial management and confidence-building measures are not initiated soon. Broadly speaking, the core–periphery relationships in these areas are under severe stress and a serious geopolitical evaluation is urgently needed.

GEOGRAPHICAL MILIEU

Northeast India, which is connected with the rest of India by a 20 km strip of land near Siliguri called the 'Chicken Neck', occupies a vast territory, with a total geographical area of 22,500 square km and a total population of 31.5 million (1991). It has a 4,200 km long international boundary with Bhutan, China, Myanmar and Bangladesh. The northeast, especially the Eastern Hills, is both on the periphery of India and at the junction between Southeast and East Asia. The Eastern Hills, incorporating the states of Nagaland, Manipur and Mizoram, cover 60,000 square km (40 per cent of the northeast region) and have a population of 3.73 million (10 per cent of the total population of the northeast region). Most of the population is tribal and predominantly Christian.

With the exception of the dominant Brahmaputra Valley and the Imphal Valley, the northeast region abounds with hills and mountains, the Patkai Hills being the backbone of the Eastern Hills. These areas are highly inaccessible, partly due to geography but mostly due to man's inertia in developing essential infrastructure. This inertia is historical; Roy Burman observes that 'the backwardness of the northeast region is the legacy of the colonial rulers, who after ruling for a prolonged period did not make much productive investment' (Burman, 1984). Even after 50 years of independence, the situation has not

Borderlands Under Stress (M.A. Pratt and J.A. Brown (eds), ISBN 90-411-9790-7).
© Kluwer Law International, 2000.

changed much. The colonial mechanism has persisted and much of the wealth from these areas has been siphoned out.

The region is a melting pot for socio-cultural phenomena from Tibet, Myanmar and the Gangetic Plains, and lately from Nepal and Bangladesh. The immigration of workers, herdsmen and businessmen from outside the region has kept population growth high in comparison to the national average. The highest decennial growth may be observed in Nagaland (56.86 per cent) and Mizoram (28.86 per cent) (1991 figures). These are predominantly rural areas with urban centres occurring at intervening distances of 30 km to 65 km. Urban population growth was also high between 1981 and 1991: 160 per cent in Mizoram, 75 per cent in Nagaland and 35 per cent in Manipur. This is indicative of massive shifts of population from the surrounding areas. The undocumented and disguised infiltration of migrants and refugees is indeed quite significant. A large number of immigrants from Bangladesh – in the region of 7.5 million – have crept into the region. Noteworthy numbers of Nepalis have also immigrated and found work in animal husbandry and agriculture. In addition, large number of Chakma refugees and Muslim repatriates from Myanmar have settled in these hilly states.

The region has abundant natural resources but growth has stagnated due to inadequate infrastructure, difficult access, the apathy and corrupt practices of development agencies and long-term insecurity in the region. The region's industrial base is weak with a pronounced imbalance, both spatial and sectoral. The bulk of industrial activity is in the form of small-scale and cottage industries, but there are also sugar mills in Manipur and paper and pulp plants in Nagaland and Mizoram. The economy is dominated by the primary sector, with a strong tertiary sector; the secondary sector is rather poor, fragile and incoherent. The primary wealth of these hills, namely the resources of the forest, has been greatly misappropriated and badly exploited by traditional shifting cultivation and merciless commercial exploitation. The young, educated portions of the population rarely find immediate employment, and are often attracted to the activities of regional insurgent groups.

The economy is further weakened by the complex ethnic character of the population. Mizoram is almost uni-ethnic – the Mizos account for 81.3 per cent of the state population – but Manipur and Nagaland are multi-ethnic in character. The physical contours defining the watershed basins in Nagaland, and partially in Manipur, set the limits for the various ethnic groups in these states. Ethnic groups tend to remain confined and isolated in their basins, thus preserving their ethnic characteristics. This has caused enormous difficulties in the process of integration both within these hills and with the rest of the country.

COLONIALISM, PERIPHERALITY AND LACK OF INTEGRATION

Both history and geography are responsible for the state of affairs in the Indian northeast and the Eastern Hills. Geographically, the adversities of its terrain have always made this region remote. Historically, although British imperialism integrated much of the rest of India, it did little to change the administrative set-up of this part of the country. The overall development of the region was concentrated in Assam, which retained its supremacy in terms of economic development until recently. Although a part of Assam, these nation-states remained independent, self-sufficient, fragmented and undefined. In addition, during the colonial period the hills witnessed rebellion and political resistance (Mackenzie, 1989); the Nagas strongly resisted joining the Union of India, as did other tribal groups from the states of Mizoram, Manipur and Tripura. The legacy of British imperialism and its apathetic attitude towards this region have continued into the post-independence era. The geographical remoteness, a legacy of unconcern and lack of integrative systems, and the introduction of an inner-line permit system have all contributed towards isolation and the more or less independent status of these hills. They remain peripheral. The lack of economic development and political integration along with an unrealistic perception on the part of the government of India has resulted in gross neglect and inaccessibility, and consequent secessionist movements and demands.

POLITICAL AND INSURGENT MOVEMENTS

The long-drawn-out neglect of the region, particularly the peripheral Eastern Hills, along with its ethnic identities, which are alien to the Aryan polity of mainland India, and its history and geography, can be seen as the bedrock for the development of ambivalent socio-political contours. Most of the insurgent groups which have a special niche in the northeast region are different from those existing elsewhere. Their aim, which has been threatening the process of integration and unity in the country, is political emancipation and the establishment of a separate homeland – in other words, a sort of sub-nationalism within the broader frame of country-level nationalism. These groups existed throughout the period of British rule. The Naga Club, formed under the auspices of the British in 1918, provided the initial base for the Naga National Council (NNC) which spearheaded the earliest movement for the independence of the Naga territory, including those Naga-inhabited areas in Arunachal Pradesh, Assam, Manipur (India) and Myanmar. It was not until after independence from Britain, however, that the movement became really active. Under the leadership of A. Z. Phizo, the NNC declared independence for Naga territory in August 1947 and continued the struggle against Indian occupation of their land. In 1961 the state of Nagaland was established, and in 1964 a cease-fire agreement was signed. But the ensuing peace was a mirage and did not prevail for long. The Naga underground movement resumed its activities against the Indian government and resorted to military confrontations. In 1975 the Shillong Accord was signed between the government of India and the Naga underground movement. This constituted a challenge to the leadership of A. Z. Phizo and resulted in the creation of the National Socialist Council of Nagaland

(NSCN), which later split into two groups – NSCN(I-M) (Isak-Muivah) and NSCN(K) (Khaplang). The NSCN tried to internationalise the Naga issue as well as trying to establish a firm base in the region by forging links with other insurgent groups such as the People's Liberation Army (PLA), the People's Revolutionary Party of Kangliepak (PREPAK), the Bodo Security Force (BSF) and the United Liberation Front of Assam (ULFA). NSCN(I-M) has tactical links with the Liberation Tigers of Tamil Eelam (LTTE) group in Sri Lanka and has extended its activities throughout the northeast region. Unity among the different Naga groups has been forged through the common goal of freedom and self-determination.

Other areas of the northeast region are also affected by such activity. There is an insurgent movement in Tripura, which is adjacent to Bangladesh, directed against the non-tribal peoples and especially the Bengali immigrants from Bangladesh, which is spearheaded by Tripura Upajati Yuva Samiti (TUYS) and the National Liberation Front of Tripura (NLFT). The ULFA emerged in 1979 and was also against the foreign-national immigrants from Bangladesh; later it resorted to guerrilla tactics and fought for separation from India. Some other significant movements include the Bodo/Boro Security Force of Assam and the Kuki National Army (KNA). Mizoram went through a period of political turmoil in the early 1960s. Under the leadership of Laldenga, the Mizo National Famine Front (MNFF) was formed to withstand the famine. In 1962 this movement transformed into the Mizo National Front (MNF) which moved for separation from India, resulting in bloody encounters with the Indian Army. Peace and tranquillity were restored with the signing of the Mizo Accord in 1968. The only states in the northeast region free from such movements have been Meghalaya and Arunachal Pradesh.

On account of the existence of such movements, there is a high degree of suspicion between the northeast region and central government of India. On one side central-government policies are seen as attempts at enslavement; on the other, the northeast is seen as a 'renegade region'. The result is that attempts to establish confidence-building measures become entangled in mistrust. In addition, outside agencies are at work trying to destabilise India; it is said that every insurgent movement has strong links with these agencies and has established bases in Myanmar, Thailand and some of the South Asian countries.

MIGRANTS, ILLEGAL TRADE AND EXTORTION

The Eastern Hills are currently generating unprecedented waves of migrants and refugees, due in part to the disturbed situation in Nagaland and Manipur but mostly to external factors. Business communities are fleeing the insecurity of life, threat to property and high taxation caused by the insurgents. Taxation is imposed at between 10 and 30 per cent of income; bribery is rife, and practically the norm in the towns of Nagaland and Manipur. An army presence in towns like Mokokchung (Nagaland) does not necessarily offer security. Mizoram appears to be relatively safe, but here too frequent army checks and hold-ups by insurgents effectively impose a curfew on the local population.

The situation in Manipur is particularly problematic, not because of army–insurgent confrontations but because of in-fighting. During the 1970s and 1980s Imphal, Manipur's capital town, was a booming business centre with a rich cultural ethos; now it has become the worst affected town and the townsfolk live in daily fear. Conflict amongst and between the hillsmen and plainsmen has worsened over the years. The army, in theory the custodian of peace, order and security, is often a symbol of terror, suppression, nepotism and reckless killing. Added to this is a rampant illegal cross-border trade not only of merchandise but of arms and ammunition. The border town of Moreh may be seen as a representative centre of this cross-border activity; one may come across everything there, including foreign products not only from Japan, Korea, Taiwan, Singapore and China but reportedly from Europe and the USA. Other centres of such activity are growing along the Nagaland–Myanmar and Mizoram–Bangladesh–Myanmar borders.

Thailand and the Myanmar area are at the hub of an illicit drugs and narcotics network which extends through points like Moreh into the Eastern Hills and thence to Pakistan and on to the western world. In Afghanistan drug peddling is rampant and maintained by strong, wealthy mafias who are supported by insurgents, politicians and the army, working together to harvest the illegal riches. The local administration in the Indian northeast is often part of this framework. The political elite in the Eastern Hills not only promote insurgency but act as the nexus. The Myanmar and Bangladesh borders provide the transit point for this drug trafficking. Checks are practically impossible because of the inaccessibility of the terrain – hills and meandering, shifting river channels. The army and the Border Security Force (BSF), which has limited resources and personnel to man the border outposts find it extremely difficult to cope with the apparent collusion between the locals, the smugglers and the illegal migrants.

QUESTIONS OF PEACE, ORDER AND DEVELOPMENT

The combination of extortion, drug trafficking, uncontrolled immigration, ineffective administration, crime, insecurity, unstable social ethos and inter-ference from external agencies over the border have turned the eastern borderlands into an entity beyond any effective control. Local administration in Nagaland and Manipur is in a shambles and officials are often involved in a variety of nefarious activities. Mizoram alone is currently enjoying the semblance of peace and development.

Who is to blame? When and how could peace come to the Eastern Hills? These are difficult questions and any answers require a balanced view that takes into account both the framework of the Indian Constitution and the vision and ambitions of the people of the troubled areas; isolated views provide no solutions.

Total independence and self-determination are not in keeping with the Indian constitution or Indian sovereignty. However, the democratic framework of India lends support to the perception, ambitions and decisions of the people, and needs to be applied with sincerity and honesty. The last three or four decades have seen much use of force, especially the brute force of the army, but this has not been able to provide the region with a permanent solution or a sense of security. Peace requires the application of honest confidence-building measures. It requires a different type of administration, one which can generate confidence among individuals and parties. The frontier-like character of the hills demands non-routine government systems to be put in place to achieve dialogue and understanding between the relative parties. The political elite must act in the role of negotiator and confidence-builder. An early solution is required for the Eastern Hills; delay only serves to make the area more unmanageable.

REFERENCES

Acharyya, N. N. (1987) *A Brief History of Assam*, New Delhi.

Achaya, A. S. (1994) 'Insurgency in Nagaland', *The Administrator, Special Issue on North-East*, Vol. XXXIX.

Alemchiba, M. (1970) *A Brief Historical Account of Nagaland*, Jurhat.

Bhuyan, B. C. (1989) *Political Development of North-East*, New Delhi.

Burman, R. (1984) 'Issues in North-East: An Appraisal' in Abbi, B. L. (ed.) *North East Region, Problems and Prospects of Development*, Chandigarh.

Das, A. K. (1982) *Assam's Agony*, New Delhi.

Datta, B. (1994), *North-East as I see it*, New Delhi.

Gangmumei, K. (1984) 'Insurgency in Manipur Valley' in Abbi, B. L. (ed.) *North East Region, Problems and Prospects of Development*, Chandigarh.

Gordow, P. M. (1971) 'Ceasefire politics in Nagaland', *Asian Survey*, Vol. II.

Harin, G. (1988) 'North-East: Roots of Separatism', *Mainstream*, January.

Longkumar, L. (1996) 'Core–periphery Relationship in North-East India with a Focus on Nagaland', unpublished Ph.D. Thesis, Jawaharlal Nehru University, New Delhi.

Mackenzie, A. (1989) *The North-East Frontier of India*, Delhi: 537–586.

Maxwell, N. (1978) 'India and the Nagas', *Third World Unity*, Vol. 5.

Milton, I. (1983) *National Unity: The South Asian Experience*, New Delhi.

Nag, S. (1990) *Roots of Ethnic Conflicts: Nationality Question in North East India*, New Delhi.

North Eastern Council (1994) *North-Eastern Region at a Glance*, Shillong.

Pakem, B. (1990) *Nationality, Ethnicity and Cultural Identity in North-East India*, New Delhi.

Reid, R. (1983) *History of Frontier Areas Bordering on Assam*, Delhi.

Saikia, P. D. & Borah, D. (1992) *Constraints of Economic Development in N.E.N.F. India*, New Delhi.

Sarin, V. I. K. (1985) *India's North-East in Flames*, New Delhi.

Sengupta, S. (1994) *Tribes of North-East India: Biological and Cultural Perspective*, New Delhi.

Talukdar, A. C. (1984) 'Problems and Prospect of National Integration in North-East India' in Abbi, B. L. (ed.) *North East Region, Problems and Prospects of Development*, Chandigarh.

19

After Amado Carrillo Fuentes:
New Trends in the Drug War on the
US–Mexico Border

Jose Z. Garcia

INTRODUCTION

In the six months following the death of leading drug-trafficker Amado Carrillo Fuentes, from July 1997 to February 1998, a violent turf war was waged in Ciudad Juárez (hereafter referred to simply as Juárez) and other places along the US–Mexico border for control of the largest drug cartel in Mexico – possibly the largest in the western hemisphere.[1] Newspapers in Juárez reported over 70 violent deaths, often in public places, of people believed to be members of rival factions trying to secure control over the drug traffic in the region.[2] For unknown reasons, the level of cartel-related violent deaths dropped sharply after 19 February 1998. No clear-cut replacement for Amado appears to have surfaced, although drugs continue to flow relatively unimpeded across the border in the region, and people monitoring drug organisations cautioned that violence might be renewed.

The violent character of the war, and the revelations about the full range of operations of the Carrillo empire, elicited a public reaction on both sides of the border that influenced the political campaigns for governor of the state of Chihuahua and mayor of Juárez in July 1997, sparked renewed debate over the efficacy of the anti-drug war, and raised the profile of crime in the region as tourism to Juarez declined sharply.

As these events were unfolding, the US and Mexican governments were stepping up formal measures in a common cause against the cartels. This paper describes these events and attempts to place them within the context of recent changes in drug-related US–Mexico relations.

PART I: CHANGES IN THE TRANS-BORDER FLOW OF DRUGS AFTER 1996

In 1996 new actors stepped in to replace the key leaders of the Cali cartel who had been arrested, had surrendered or had died. Colombian organisations continued to export and distribute cocaine, but Mexican organisations expanded their operations into the US market in various ways, establishing

Borderlands Under Stress (M.A. Pratt and J.A. Brown (eds), ISBN 90-411-9790-7).
© Kluwer Law International, 2000.

motorcycle gangs as major suppliers of methamphetamines, increasing production of heroin and marijuana, transporting cocaine through Mexico, and deepening their involvement in US domestic cocaine distribution.

According to Drug Enforcement Administration (DEA) reports (DEA, 1996), high-speed boats, freighters and fishing vessels enter Mexico through the Yucatan Peninsula and the west coast. Small aircraft drop bales of cocaine into southern Mexico or land on small airstrips. Once in Mexico, cocaine is moved overland or by air to staging posts in northern Mexico. From northern Mexico shipments are broken down into smaller loads for smuggling across the border in automobiles or trucks or, for the smallest packages, on foot. Typical shipments consist of 20–50 kg hidden in concealed compartments, under floors and in gas tanks of automobiles, pickups and vans, and in larger quantities in trucks commingling cocaine with perishable items such as frozen fish and vegetables. In addition, some cocaine is introduced by 'mules' who cross at ports of entry or across the desert, although this system of transportation is more frequently used for heroin and marijuana. At crossing points traffickers use high-powered video recorders, radios and telephones equipped with counter-surveillance equipment, and sometimes resort to violence. Once in the US the drugs are stored in residences or commercial warehouses for future distribution. Proceeds of sales are collected from cities and towns all over the country and consolidated in New York, Miami, Houston and Los Angeles, for shipment back to the country of origin. At the retail level, distribution is controlled by street gangs, often ethnic in origin.

Four major cartels in Mexico control drug smuggling on the US border. The most violent, known as the Arellano Felix Organisation, operates out of Tijuana, Mexico, and transports drugs into southern California, from the coast to Mexicali. One of the brothers involved, Francisco, is in prison, while Benjamin and Ramon continue to do business. The organisation is believed to be responsible for the assassination of a number of Tijuana law-enforcement officials. Another cartel, believed to be working in association with the Arellano Felix brothers, is known to be headed by Miguel Caro-Quintero and operates in Sonora, below Arizona, smuggling drugs into Arizona and weapons into Mexico. A third was headed by Juan Garcia Abrego, based in Matamoros, Tamaulipas. Garcia Abrego was arrested in January 1996 in Monterrey, expelled to Houston, and tried and convicted for trafficking and laundering. Much of his organisation was taken over by the growing power of a fourth cartel, Juarez. The Juarez cartel, controlled by Amado Carrillo Fuentes until his death in 1997, is described below.

Other drug organisations exist or have existed, such as the still-active Sinaloa cartel, the Herrera Corral clan which specialises in heroin in Durango, and the Amezcua organisation which traffics in methamphetamines across the US–Mexico border. A cartel operating in Ojinaga was broken in 1989 (Pappa, 1992), the Guadalajara cartel has been crippled, and the Garcia Abrego organisation, while still operating, is now largely under the control of the Juarez cartel. It appears to be relatively difficult to establish the connections necessary to secure a cocaine pipeline from Colombia, a factor which reduces the potential number of cocaine cartels, and the organisational skills needed to sustain large drug operations similarly restricts participation. The difficult combination of organisational capability, Colombian connections and access to cross-border smuggling networks – all necessary for an integrated, large-scale operation that can buy cocaine at wholesale prices and deliver it to US-based buyers – encourages successful operators to secure what amounts to monopolistic control of the drug market in specific regions close to the border.

The organisational structure of the cartels in Mexico appears to have evolved since the 1980s, when an increase in trafficking began. The Guadalajara cartel started with an alliance between Rafael Caro-Quintero, Miguel Felix-Gallardo and four others to ship heroin and marijuana into the US, but eventually it began working with Colombian mafias to traffic in cocaine (Shannon, 1988). A loose consortium of smuggling groups operates through fluid divisions of territory, with shifting alliances as some organisations grow and others wane. Cartel heads are the top decision-makers, in charge of relatively well-defined territorial regions. They negotiate with the relevant government officials, negotiate the purchase of drugs from abroad or in Mexico, meet with distributors from the US to arrange shipments, and supervise all movement of drugs through their territory, including shipments made through other cartel families. Below the cartel heads is a second level of trafficker loosely identified by function – for example, international transportation and warehousing, reception of drugs from Colombia, security, and money-laundering. It is at this level that the decisions made by the cartel head are implemented. At another level, near the US–Mexico border are associates with a knowledge of specific local environments and who may move drugs for other independent traffickers when given permission to do so. Finally, at the bottom of the hierarchy are small operators who can be relied on to recruit and transport and store drugs in specific locations. At every level the actors may be directly involved in trafficking activities of their own, but pay the head for the various kinds of services he may provide, including protection, warehousing and the supply of drugs (DEA, 1996).

The Juarez cartel and the death of Amado Carrillo Fuentes

Amado Carrillo Fuentes died on 4 July 1997 on a hospital operating-table in Mexico City, apparently undergoing plastic surgery to alter his appearance. The exact cause of death is somewhat unclear, as is whether or not it was deliberate; there were reports that Carrillo's blood contained a lethal combination of an anaesthetic, Dormicum, cocaine and other medicinal substances. The bodies of two of the doctors involved in the operation were discovered on 2 November 1997 in oil drums mixed with cement and dirt on the Mexico City–Acapulco highway. Preliminary tests indicated that the victims were tortured for a prolonged period, beaten, burned and then strangled with cables. A third doctor is now living under protection in the US.

Carrillo, who died aged 41, was the major drug trafficker in Mexico, shipping four times more cocaine to the US than any other single source in the world, and amassing a fortune estimated at over 25 billion dollars (Barnet, 1997a). He had extensive experience as a trafficker in Guadalajara and then in Ojinaga, where he helped the Pablo Acosta organisation before its collapse in 1989. His ability to corner a large proportion of the market to the US appears to have rested on:

- his connections with Colombian suppliers, which enabled him to pioneer the use of 727 jet airliners to transport the product directly to secret airfields in northern Mexico rather than relying on intermediaries
- his ability to connect with local 'runners' on the US–Mexico border, controlled by smugglers with several generations of experience
- his success in bribing government officials, such as former General Gutierrez Rebollo, commander of the 5th Military Region in Guadalajara
- his skill in negotiating tricky operational agreements with potentially rival drug organisations such as the Herrera Corral group in Durango.

After his death it was unclear whether control of the cartel would transfer to his brother Vicente, 34, who was overseeing operations in Juarez, or to other capos in the Juarez organisation. Two other cartels – one run by Caro-Quintero, which had been smuggling drugs across the Arizona–Sonora border since 1985, and the other an amphetamine ring operating in the Sonora region run by Jesus Amezcua Contreras – were not considered strong enough to make a take-over bid. But a potential rival drug organisation was headed by the Arellano Felix brothers from Tijuana, who controlled most of the drug trafficking between Tijuana and Mexicali and who are considered ruthless enough to have attempted a take-over. Within the Juarez organisation, Juan Jose Esparragoza Moreno, 'El Azul', was a potential leader. Like Carrillo, El Azul was from Sinaloa; he knew Carrillo well and was wanted in connection with the assassination of presidential candidate Colosio. Although his name was not mentioned at the time, Rafael Munoz Talavera, a former capo in the pre-Amado days of the Juarez cartel, had been released from jail just a few months earlier; he had been imprisoned in connection with the largest single cocaine transaction in US history, a 21 ton deal that had been busted at Sylmar, California. Munoz's close friend, Rafael Guardado, who belonged to one of the three major families controlling the Juarez operation, was killed by Amado in one of several successful moves he had made as part of his bid to take over the Juarez cartel in 1993. He had been the owner of a popular restaurant, the Florida, in Juarez, and maintained an extremely low profile.

The Juarez cartel turf war of 1997–98

Within days of Carrillo's death, Juarez was the scene of a number of high-profile murders of people suspected of working for the Juarez cartel. On 19 July Juan Eugenio ('El Genio') Rosales Ortiz, a suspected mid-level trafficker, was gunned down in front of his home. He was the fifth person to be killed after 4 July. On 3 August six people were killed at the Max Fim restaurant across the street from the bullring, just after the bullfights ended; three men with AK-47s fired on a small group of customers including Alfonso Corral Olaguez, 36, owner of the restaurant and nephew of the leader of the Herrera Corral drug clan in Durango, an organisation believed to support the activities of the Juarez cartel. Olaguez was later identified as the person in charge of local operations for Amado at the time of his death. On 17 August seven people were kidnapped in various locations in Juarez. One man's body was later found lying face-down in the street. Seven others were kidnapped from a hamburger stand, the Space Burger, including the owner and two customers; the kidnapping victims were discovered in the trunks of abandoned automobiles, hands tied behind their backs, with ice-pick wounds and plastic bags over their heads (Barnet, 1997b).

Over the next four months more and more dead bodies were discovered in car trunks, and local-newspaper reporters came up with a new name for the victims: *encajuelados* ('trunked'). On 22 August Ricardo Prado Reyna, a lawyer for the Max Fim restaurant, was wounded during a high-speed chase in downtown Juarez at 6pm on Friday evening. He was alleged to have been laundering 1.4 million dollars per month in cash transactions at Juarez money exchanges. On 23 August four doctors were found strangled to death after they left a hospital to attend to a wounded man in his home. The hospital, the Guernika, was later closed down by the government for being a front for the Juarez cartel. The police later received anonymous information revealing that the doctors had tried to help one of Prado Reyna's assassins, who was apparently wounded in the attack. On 13 October Prado Reyna's law partner, Sergio Roldan Ramos, was killed in broad daylight in downtown Juarez. According to DEA reports, Roldan had at one time worked for Rafael Aguilar Guardado, founder of the Juarez cartel.

On 31 August four people were killed leaving Geronimo's bar across the street from Max Fim's. Ballistics tests indicated that the bullets were fired from the same AK-47 weapons used in the Max Fim murders on 3 August. Maria Lopez, killed in the attack, was believed to have been affiliated with the Juarez cartel. On 4 September a 27-year old man on parole after two cocaine convictions was killed by gunfire on the interstate highway in El Paso.

Financial scope of the Juarez cartel

In the weeks following Carrillo's death Mexican federal authorities seized over 60 properties belonging to Carrillo (Barnet, 1997c). On the US side, agents arrested 89 people allegedly connected to the Carrillo organisation, including nine people in El Paso. Five of those arrested in El Paso were members of the Pedro Guerrero family, alleged to be members of the Carrillo organisation. They were said to own small houses on El Paso's west side, where they would store drugs shipped from Juarez. The Guerrero family was alleged to have moved drugs to the New York city market, previously dominated by Colombian cartels. Their properties were seized, along with five million dollars, and they were charged with possession, distribution, conspiracy and money-laundering.

In other US operations, agents seized over 11 tons of cocaine, six tons of marijuana and 18.5 million dollars in cash. The cartel was discovered to have operations in El Paso, Tyler, San Diego, Chicago, Albuquerque, Tucson, Battle Creek, Jersey City and New York. As a result of these raids, the DEA estimated that Mexican drug lords had expanded their operations sufficient to account for one-third of the cocaine distributed in the US, in a market long monopolised by Colombians. Carrillo's operation flew cocaine from Colombia to secret airfields, mostly near Juarez. Drugs were then trucked into El Paso where they were transferred to rented semi-trailer trucks owned by a corporation in Battle Creek, Michigan. These, in turn, were transported to New Jersey where they were stored in warehouses large enough to hide the trucks, which would download and return to Juarez. According to an anonymous source quoted in a Juarez newspaper (*El Norte*, 1 November 1997) the Amado Carrillo and other cartels had been stealing refined Pemex petroleum near the US–Mexico border and converting it to jet fuel for their extensive fleet of 727s and DC9s which transported cocaine from Colombia.

In the wake of the power struggle following Carrillo's death, authorities in Juarez began to focus on the financial underpinnings of Carrillo's operation. Federal police seized 10 properties, including two hospitals, alleged to be owned by a group of investors working for the cartel. On 29 October a fleet of 21 armoured vehicles was confiscated from a warehouse owned by the family of Amado Carrillo. Silvano Corral, director of the Guernika hospital, was accused of complicity involving a consortium of properties acting as a front for the cartel. He was a cousin of Alfonso Corral, killed in the Max Fim attack on 3 August. He was also believed to be one of the key money-launderers, along with Prado Reyna, for the Carrillo cartel. Manuel de Jesus Bitar Tafich, a real-estate developer in Juarez, was arrested in Mexico City, accused of being the primary mover of the cartel's financial operations; the DEA asked the Mexican authorities to freeze his accounts. Bitar was part-owner of the Guernika hospital, which was seized along with nine other properties.

The financial authorities in Mexico City found 18 bank accounts, in Banamex, Bancomer, Serfin and Banpais, used to launder 17 million dollars. Drug dealer Jose Jesus Echegollen Barrueta allegedly used these banks to transfer funds from the US. A report by George Harkin of the Finance Administration Office of the DEA said Mexican corporations controlled by Mexican drug traffickers owned a number of banks in Central America. Harkin explained that Mexican cartels had become more cautious in using Mexican banks because the government was enforcing new regulations against money-laundering operations. According to another newspaper report, the Juarez cartel employed an 'army' of money-launderers, some of whom made constant trips to Central and South America, especially Cuba, Peru, Chile and Brazil (*Frontera Norte/Sur*, 1997a). In March 1998 the Mexican authorities revealed that the Juarez cartel had become the first criminal organisation to purchase a bank directly. According to sources, the cartel purchased the bank in 1995–96 for around 10 million dollars, and were using it to launder money. The chief executives of the Grupo Financiero Anahuac were the leader of the National Electrician's Union and an industrialist, both said to be connected to the son of Amado Carrillo, Luis Vicente Carrillo.

The war continued into the autumn of 1997. On Saturday 15 November a 33-year old man was shot to death while dining at the Kinsui Teppan sushi bar in the tourist zone in Juarez (*Frontera Norte/Sur*, 1997b). On 2 December two tortured bodies were found in an abandoned Ford Explorer van in downtown Juarez. On 4 December the owner of a Juarez money exchange was found dead and tortured. He was reported to have been involved in money-laundering. Between 26 and 30 December, seven Juarez residents were kidnapped, executed and found *encajuelados*. Five had been tortured and strangled, repeating a pattern found in 19 homicides in previous months. Police agents noted that these last murders were similar in style to the killing of alleged drug-trafficker Fernando Cueva Cordoba and four doctors who worked for the Guernika and San Rafael hospitals in August. All in all, police claimed that there had been 60 executions in Juarez from 4 July to the end of 1997, all attributable to criminal organisations, and accounting for nearly one-quarter of the 260 reported homicides (*Frontera Norte/Sur*, 1998a).

On 11 January 1998 another victim was found dead and tortured. On 18 January the leader of an El Paso auto-theft gang known as Los Bimbos was found *encajuelado* in Juarez. The El Paso police said the victim, Jorge Garcia Larralde, 25, had died of torture and strangulation. On 25 January the bodies of a man and a woman were found stuffed inside two barrels of lime about 10 miles south of the US–Mexico crossing at Sta. Teresa, just outside Juarez. On 28 January a municipal police officer and an El Paso man were killed in what the police believed to be related shootings.

On 3 February the state attorney general named four people he said were involved in some of the killings, including Arturo Hernandez, known as 'El Chaqui', who was suspected of being responsible for the strangulation of the four doctors in August 1997 and of five other people in December 1997. The other named alleged assassins were said to be connected to the Max Fim and Geronimo's killings (Barnet, 1998a).

After 19 February 1998 the killings stopped for a period, for reasons that are unclear. But by then the authorities had learned enough to issue warrants for the arrest of 65 people believed to be associated with the Juarez cartel. Also in February, US and Mexican government officials announced the creation of a bilateral anti-drug force, to be centred in three Mexican border cities. The Juarez unit included 150 Mexican soldiers, 80 agents from the Special Prosecutor for Crimes Against Health (FEADS), and 20 anti-narcotic agents from the US DEA.

On 15 June 1998 the bodies of two men were found *encajuelados*, the 15th and 16th drug-related murders of the year, according to police. One had performed as a musician in bars, and the other did legal work for the police's Office of Internal Investigations.

PART II: RECENT DRUG-RELATED POLICY SHIFTS IN MEXICO AND THE US, AND THE BILATERAL RELATIONSHIP

The 3,200km border between Mexico and the US has 39 crossings and 24 ports of entry. Over 250 million people, 75 million cars and 3.5 million automobiles entered the US from Mexico in 1996. In addition, official sources estimate that four million illegal crossings into the US occur each year. The volume of trade between Mexico and the US has increased from 59 billion dollars to almost 130 billion dollars in 1996. Over the last six years the volume of inbound commercial traffic into the US has nearly doubled, and the number of rail cars entering increased from 184,000 to over 285,000 (ONDCP, 1997). By any measurement, control over drug penetration into the US over the border from Mexico is a major challenge.

Failure in US–Mexico anti-drug cooperation until 1996

The speed with which the US acted in order to imprison members of the leaderless Carrillo organisation was a testament to the growing cooperation between Mexico and the US, and to changes in the respective drug strategies of each country. Until quite recently US policy was based primarily on:

- taking unilateral action to discourage the production of coca leaves, poppies and marijuana in their countries of origin
- prohibiting the entry of such supplies from abroad
- intercepting trafficking operations inside the US
- deterring overall drug trafficking through the application of strong penalties for conviction and the forfeiture of property used in drug deals.

On the Mexican side, as early as 1995 government policy enlisted the support of the armed forces. Cooperation with the US actually deteriorated between the early and mid-1990s, when the Mexican government stopped accepting most forms of US counter-narcotics assistance. The falling price of drugs in the US, steady supply lines and relatively stable hardcore addiction patterns led to a more comprehensive approach in 1996, one which more strongly emphasised reducing demand, increasing interagency cooperation, and cooperating more closely with the US government.

Efforts taken by the Mexican government

Persistent rumours to the effect that the brother of Mexican President Salinas was involved in protecting drug trafficking, and revelations that General Jesus Gutierrez Rebollo, head of the national anti-drug agency, was an associate of Amado Carrillo Fuentes, appear to have convinced Mexican strategic-policy-makers that corruption associated with drug trafficking constituted a serious security threat, in that it imperilled the sovereignty of the nation. Since that time the government of Mexico has raised the drug war to a high priority. In 1996 the Attorney General fired 1,200 federal police for corruption or 'unsuitability'. A new anti-drug agency, the Special Prosecutor for Crimes Against Health (FEADS), was created in mid-1997, replacing an older agency. The law-enforcement screening process (vetting) for agents now includes polygraph testing and background security checks. The federal prosecutor's office (PGR) has also been thoroughly reorganised, with a stronger vetting process, improved recruitment and longer training periods. Drug testing is required for PGR officials, and PGR officials implicated in the theft of cocaine seizures have been prosecuted. In September 1997, while the turf war was raging in Juarez, 18 PGR officers were arrested for allegedly smuggling drugs in a PGR aeroplane.

Several legal measures have been taken to facilitate the enforcement of drug laws in Mexico.[3] In November 1996 an Organized Crime Law was passed, enabling greater use of plea bargaining and easier use of informant and co-defendant statements, creating witness-protection programs, and giving greater legal access to electronic surveillance. In addition, the Organized Crime Law provided for the forfeiture of assets related to illegal drug activities. It was under this law that the Mexican authorities seized 60 properties belonging to Carrillo. The US promised to cooperate with Mexico in the sharing of forfeited property, which is to be used solely for combating drug trafficking. Money-laundering laws were passed in 1996 and revised in 1997, making money-laundering a crime, rather than simply a tax offence. As in the US, under Mexican law banks and other financial institutions must report currency transactions over 10,000 dollars and keep better records of customer accounts. Some of the people associated with the Juarez cartel are being prosecuted under these new statutes. The US Treasury, State and Justice Departments have worked with Mexican officials to develop anti-laundering laws, and have offered training for investigators. The Mexican Treasury Department has established a Financial Intelligence Unit. Finally, in 1996 the Mexican government reversed its long-standing refusal to extradite Mexican citizens to the US, although this is still a highly sensitive issue and wholesale extradition is not expected.

The most important evidence of the Mexican national resolve to target cartels for destruction has been the mobilisation of the armed forces, especially along the US–Mexico border, where they have essentially merged with the federal police in investigations. Interdiction efforts have been increased and light, mobile special forces units (GAFE) have been deployed. Military garrisons (15 of 20 are along the US–Mexico border) have been expanded from 30–35 troops to 60–80 troops, and instead of static assignments they now go on patrol (*Revista del Ejercito y Fuerza Aerea Mexicancos*, 1996). Three new cavalry units have been assigned to the border. The border mission of the armed forces has recently been restructured to focus on illegal activities. Under Article 29, section 4 of the constitution the armed forces are permitted to search people for weapons, a provision that enables them to play an active role in interdiction. Military commanders are rotated every 18 months and appear to be extremely reluctant to intermingle socially with any sectors of the population.

Changes in US strategy

US policy has changed as well. Until quite recently it was based on unilateral action to stop supply. With respect to regions that produced or shipped drugs to the US, the approach was to demand that action be taken in return for small amounts of technical assistance. In Bolivia and Peru funds were made available to compensate peasants for not growing coca leaves. The stick used was certification, a technique that gained some prominence during the 1980s when the US Congress used certification both as a leverage against the Reagan administration and against governments or military organisations receiving aid. The failure of this policy led to the evolution of a more comprehensive approach that stresses the domestic goals of demand reduction, crime reduction and health treatment for addiction, as well as the interdiction of drugs at entry points and the breaking up of drug organisations and cartels inside the US and abroad.

At present, interdiction operations appear to have evolved into rather complex interagency initiatives.[4] Joint interagency task forces in Key West, Alameda and Panama coordinate interdiction in transit zones to the US. There is a Customs Department Domestic Air Interdiction Coordinating Center in Riverside, California, which monitors air traffic approaching the US. The Office of National Drug Control Policy (ONDCP) has designated 25 areas inside the US as high-intensity drug-trafficking areas (HIDTA), and helped coordinate counter-narcotic activities among various local, state and national entities.

On the US–Mexico border Customs continues to be the primary means of drug interdiction at crossing points, although border-patrol stations inland sometimes make sizeable seizures of drugs that have slipped through Customs inspection stations or have been transported between ports of entry. The DEA maintains EPIC, an intelligence-gathering agency with clients at local, state and national levels of drug enforcement. In addition, Operation Alliance, operated by the Treasury and Justice Departments and located in El Paso, coordinates the activities of the law-enforcement agencies in HIDTAs and Joint Task Force Six.

Joint Task Force Six (JTF6) is the only element in the US military with operational responsibilities in drug enforcement. Located at Ft. Bliss, near El Paso, Texas, JTF6 considers itself a force multiplier in the interdiction effort, providing all kinds of assistance to law-enforcement units throughout the US. Local law-enforcement agencies apply for assistance to Operation Alliance, which then enlists the efforts of voluntary military units across the country.

Strengthened US–Mexico cooperation

After 1996 a series of cooperative agreements were initiated between the governments of the US and Mexico to strengthen bilateral relations on the drug front. Through a memorandum of understanding signed in 1996, Bilateral Border Task Forces have been formed to coordinate the efforts of the Mexican federal police and the US DEA. One hundred and four new DEA agents were stationed in El Paso in late 1998, and several more were stationed in Juarez to work with federal police. Also in 1996 a US–Mexico High Level Contact Group was established to provide cabinet-level access for coordinating drug policy and developing a Joint US–Mexico Drug Strategy. A Senior Law Enforcement Plenary Group at the deputy attorney general level of both countries meets several times a year to discuss operational strategies related primarily to drug enforcement. Technical and consultative working groups meet several times a year to exchange information, plan coordinated strategies and share information.

In May 1997 President Clinton visited Mexico to sign the Joint Declaration of the US–Mexico Alliance Against Drugs, outlining 16 mutually agreed counter-drug goals focusing on better cooperation, information sharing, and coordination of efforts. The US is cooperating with the Mexican government in several training assignments for Border Task Force and Organized Crime Unit officers, sponsored by the FBI, Treasury, DEA and other agencies. In 1997 40 Mexican officials from 11 agencies took courses in the investigation of firearms trafficking. The Internal Revenue Service has helped Mexico draw up its asset-forfeiture and laundering laws. Similarly, DEA and FBI agents in Mexico have attended training courses with counterparts. The US Department of Defense has helped in the training of rapid-reaction units for counter-drug operations; initially 300, and in 1997 1,500 Mexican military personnel were trained in a variety of courses. Coastguard and Navy nation-to-nation contacts have also been established at the operational level for drug interdiction efforts. On the US–Mexico border a Border Liaison Mechanism was created in 1993 to improve local communications between law-enforcement officers in a number of border cities.

While these and other cooperative measures have yet to be evaluated for their overall effectiveness, they nevertheless reverse a long-standing pattern of isolation between US and Mexican military forces, and provide further evidence of Mexican resolve to cooperate with the US in counter-drug operations.

Evaluation of the anti-drug effort

The death of Amado Carrillo Fuentes, the ensuing violent battles between internal rival factions for control of the organisation and the subsequent revelations about the financial pillars of the Amado regime – all served to highlight the need for a combined US–Mexican force to fight the so-called war on drugs in the border area. The failure of both the US and the Mexican authorities to understand the true scale of the activities of the Juarez cartel – scale of volume introduced into the US, scale of distributional efforts in the US, scale of financial operations – pointed to the overall weakness of the efforts by both nations to gain some modicum of control over the activities of drug cartels.

Drug flows into the US, as measured by narcotics seizures by Customs officials at ports of entry – the main source of entry for cocaine and a major source of entry for heroin and marijuana – indicated that in the troubled period following Carrillo's death, drug organisations were able to continue supplying drugs into the US at about the same rate as before. Twenty-six per cent of drug seizures made in the El Paso sector in the fiscal year 1997 were made during the most violent months of the drug war, July, August and September – exactly the proportion one would expect in any normal year.

However, the rapidity and effectiveness with which both US and Mexican authorities moved to shut down the major financial enterprises serving the cartel pointed out the growing priority given to drug-cartel control by the Mexican government and the greater level of cooperation between the two countries. US drug czar Barry McCaffrey has indicated that he intends to target the Juarez and Tijuana cartels, strongly suggesting that he believes the Mexican government is similarly committed to bringing them down. That major figures within the Juarez cartel are maintaining an extremely low profile, and the fact that no single leader appears to have emerged to lead the cartel suggests that cartel leaders have been impressed with current bi-national efforts against them. Whether cartel organisations can adapt to the changing security conditions remains to be seen.

Strategic considerations

In the long run, cooperation between the US and Mexico on the drug front depends on the mutuality of interests perceived by the leadership of both national governments. For the US government the threat posed by drug trafficking is the supply of illegal drugs available to its citizens and the pattern of social ills that accompanies drug addiction: health costs, higher crime rates, the increasing addiction of children, and the general social malaise seen in communities affected by high rates of addiction. A secondary perceived threat is against the integrity and legitimacy of law-enforcement officials vulnerable to the corruption implied by large-scale drug trafficking. In short, in the US the major threat is against society at large.[5]

In Mexico the threat pyramid is reversed. The major threat to Mexico is 'colombianization': the corruption of the institutions of law enforcement at all levels, including the armed forces, and thereby the threat to the sovereignty and legitimacy of an already precarious state which is undergoing rapid change toward a more open and pluralistic political system. The secondary threat as perceived in Mexico is the primary one in the US: the social cost of drug addiction. While 34 per cent of the US population has used illegal drugs at one time or another, in Mexico the corresponding figure is less than 4 per cent. It is the growing power of the cartels, not drug trafficking itself, that is the major threat to Mexico, whilst it is the market share delivered by the cartels to the US ghetto that makes them an attractive target for US anti-drug officials.

Thus, while there are important differences in the perceived threats to each country, for the foreseeable future it appears that a high degree of cooperation is likely between the two governments in order to dismantle the cartels.

However, there is another asymmetry which complicates common coordination between the two countries. In Mexico for many decades a major subtheme in the discourse of US–Mexico relations was precisely the issue of maintaining sovereignty in the face of the Goliath to the north. Mexican policy pointedly prohibited foreigners from owning corporations or land; the government steadfastly refused to participate in US AID programmes during the heyday of the 1960s and 1970s; and Mexico maintained an international policy strongly independent of the US, particularly in hemispheric affairs, throughout the Cold War. In fact, evidence suggests that the Mexican government often used the sovereignty card to harness public opinion. Mexican public perception of US foreign policy toward Latin America is highly sceptical, at best, and Mexico is not alone in Latin America in this assessment. This has made it difficult for the Mexican government, already struggling to legitimise neo-liberal policies that abandoned the rhetoric of several decades of economic and trade policy, to cooperate with the US in drug-related matters. Mexican society, as in most areas of Latin America, views the drug issue as a peculiarly US problem, brought about by the demand in ghettos which is generated in part by highly sedimented inequality systems toward certain minority groups, including blacks and Hispanics. The Mexican government has thus been in the position of sorting out the balance between two perceived threats to sovereignty: the traditional one which views the US as a threat, and the newer one which sees the cartels as a greater threat.

In the US, on the other hand, the epidemic of ills associated with drugs is only one of several perceived threats to society, and the motivating force in the anti-drug campaign is not so much the government as it is powerful interest groups reflecting public opinion. Immigration is another such issue. But the immigration policy, since it is directed principally against illegal immigration from Mexico, coincides with the drug issue in ways that complicate cooperation between US and Mexican officials on the US–Mexico border itself.

The US federal government's emphasis on drug enforcement has expanded the duties of migration officers to include drug interdiction. The Border Patrol, Immigration and Naturalization Service and Customs all have important missions in the drug war, and the priority given to these has led to large increases in their budgets. But while the national agenda may stress drug interdiction as a primary goal, local agendas often focus as much attention on immigration from Mexico, or conflate Mexican immigration and drugs, reinforcing negative stereotypes about Mexicans and exacerbating tensions in the relationship between Mexican Americans and Mexicans; evidence suggests that Mexican Americans have tended to adopt a relatively conservative attitude toward Mexican migration to the US.

What is especially noticeable in drug policy as it is practised at the US–Mexico border is the lack of serious interface between the US and Mexican sides. While intergovernmental cooperation at the local level is stressed in the HIDTA programme, the presence and requirements of JTF6, the El Paso Intelligence Center and Operation Alliance, there is little encouragement to make frequent, sustained and serious contact with Mexican counterparts. When asked, US officials uniformly cite fears that Mexican law enforcement may be too thoroughly corrupted to be trusted. These fears, while completely plausible given the evidence that is emerging about official vulnerability to threats, extortion and outright corruption, nevertheless contrast sharply with emerging cooperation at national levels.

CONCLUSIONS

It is still unclear whether the increased priority given by the Mexican government to dismantling cartel activity, combined with the more comprehensive measures taken by the US government and the greater cooperation between the two countries, will have a significant effect on the volume of illegal drug trafficking along the US–Mexico border. Nor is it certain that dismantling the border cartels, given the multiplicity of potential targets for drug penetration outside the border region, would significantly diminish supplies of illegal drugs to the US. These caveats aside, it seems likely that the Mexican government will intensify its efforts to destroy the Juarez, Tijuana and Sonora cartels, and that the US government will cooperate towards this end. It also seems likely that the Mexican government, should it make this a strong priority, has the means at its disposal to accomplish this goal. Thus, for the short term it seems likely the US and Mexico have a common, if not identical, interest in targeting the cartels. Differences in the strategic origins of anti-drug efforts along the US–Mexico border, however, suggest there may be dissimilar goals and, therefore, limits to long-term cooperation in drug-enforcement activities.

NOTES

1   Various writings issued by the Office of National Drug Control Policy (http:// whitehousedrugpolicy.gov) over 1998 have stressed this. By any measurement, illicit drug consumption in the US, while still significant, is on the decline, as are most forms of crime. In 1995 US citizens spent about 57 billion dollars on drugs, significantly down from the 91 billion dollars spent in 1988. The numbers of users of cocaine, marijuana and heroin are down from a high of 2.7 per cent of adults to 0.7 per cent in 1994, although marijuana and LSD consumption has risen among high-school students and the number of frequent users has stabilised at 0.3 per cent. That reduction in usage is not a product of better enforcement is suggested by the fact that the price of cocaine, marijuana and other drugs has remained stable for over a decade, with a slight tendency to decline. US New and World Report (1996) reported that although about one-third of the cocaine produced in the world is seized by enforcement agents, the supply to the US continues to outstrip demand by 60–100 tons out of a total estimated entry of about 350 tons per year. But despite significant decreases in consumption in most illicit drug categories, resources devoted to the so-called 'war on drugs' continue to rise. Total drug enforcement budgets under the Federal Drug Control Program grew from about three billion dollars in 1986 to over 17 billion dollars in 1999. State and local governments spent approximately the same

amount, at a total bill of 34 billion dollars. In 1996, 9.9 per cent of all arrests made in the US were for the sale, manufacture or possession of illicit drugs, up from 7.4 per cent in 1987. By 1996 the proportion of narcotics cases had risen to one in four, up from one in 11 in 1983. Prison sentences for drug-related offences have tended to increase sharply. The war on drugs is popular. According to Mathea Falco (1996) citing a 1995 study, 85 per cent of the US public place 'stopping the flow of drugs' at the top of their list of priorities. Other studies (*Public Perspective*, 1995). indicate that public opinion is strongly (over 60 per cent) in support of using US military forces in combatting the flow of illegal drugs into the US. Lower priority for military intervention is given to countering foreign aggression, stopping a civil war abroad or restoring law and order within a foreign county (40 per cent).

2   Much of the material that follows, dealing with the aftermath of the death of Amado Carrillo Fuentes in Juarez, was obtained from the archives of *Frontera Norte/Sur*, a monthly electronic newsletter dealing with the US–Mexico border in the Paso del Norte (El Paso–Juarez) region. Most of the material in this excellent source of data was written by Jeff Barnet, who digested information from the *Diario de Juarez* and *El Norte*, both Juárez newspapers, from the *El Paso Times*, and occasionally from other sources cited in the text. A chronology summarised drug-related events each month for several months.

3   Most of this information was summarised from ONDCP (1997) and from US State Department (1998).

4   Much of the material that follows in the next few paragraphs is summarised from DEA (1996), US State Department (1998) and various reports from the ONDCP Website. All material is readily available in Web format.

5   This section uses the language adopted in Buzan, Waever & de Wilde (1997).

REFERENCES

Barnet, J. (1997a) 'Top Drug Lord Reported Dead: Juarez Cartel Changes Hands', *Frontera Norte/Sur*, http://nmsu.edu~frontera, 1 August: 1.

Barnet, J. (1997b) 'Narco-Guerra: Juarez in Crisis?'; 'Six Killed in Massacre–Motive Unknown'; 'Seven Disappear August 17 – One Killed'; 'Lawyer Wounded, Doctors Strangled: Investigators Find Weak Link in Cases', *Frontera Norte/Sur*, http://nmsu.edu~frontera, September.

Barnet, J. (1997c) 'Police Reveal Cartel's Financial Deals'; 'Chronology', *Frontera Norte/Sur*, http://nmsu.edu~frontera, October.

Barnet, J. (1998a) 'State Officials Name Murder Suspect'; 'Sources Say Munoz, Carrillo at War', *Frontera Norte/Sur*, http://nmsu.edu~frontera, March.

Buzan, B., Waever, O. & de Wilde, J. (1997) *Security: A New Framework of Analysis*, Lynne Reiner Publishers.

El Norte

El Paso Times

Diario de Juarez

Falco, M. (1996) Foreign Policy, Spring: 120–33.

Frontera Norte/Sur (1997a), quoting *El Norte*, http://nmsu.edu~frontera, 7 October.

Frontera Norte/Sur (1997b), http://nmsu.edu~frontera, 1 December.

Frontera Norte/Sur (1998a) 'Police Say Kidnappings, Executions Related to Internal Drug War', http://nmsu.edu~frontera, January.

ONDCP (Office of National Drug Control Policy) (1997) 'US–Mexico Counterdrug Cooperation', Introduction, http://www.whitehousedrugpolicy.gov: 1.

Pappa, T. C. (1992) *Drug Lord*.

Public Perspective (1995) April–May: 44–47.

Revista del Ejercito y Fuerza Aerea Mexicancos (1996) 'El Esfuerzo de Mexico en la Lucha Contra el Narcotrafico', July: 12.

Shannon, E. (1988) *Desperados*.

DEA (Drug Enforcement Administration) (1996) *The NNICC Report 1996*, available in electronic format at http://www,usdoj.gov/dea/pubs/intel/nnic97.htm#COCAINE.

US New and World Report (1996) 4 November: 41.

US State Department (1998) 'International Narcotics Control Strategy Report, 1997', resealed by the Bureau for International Narcotics and Law Enforcement Affairs, March 1998; section on Mexico, available on http://state.gov/www/global/na. . .997_narc_report/camex97_part2.html.

PART III

Islands, Sovereignty and Maritime Jurisdiction

20

Is it Either Necessary or Possible to Clarify the Provision on Rocks of Article 121(3) of the Law of the Sea Convention?

Alex G. Oude Elferink

INTRODUCTION

Article 121(3) of the Law of the Sea Convention (hereinafter LOS Convention)[1] provides that '[r]ocks which cannot sustain human habitation or economic life of their own shall have no exclusive economic zone or continental shelf'. This article has the potential to significantly limit the extent of coastal state maritime zones, especially in the case of isolated insular features. Furthermore, this provision has had an impact on the delimitation of maritime zones between neighbouring states. Article 121(3) appears to have been regularly invoked as an argument to deny an island any weight in establishing a maritime boundary.

An assessment of the impact of Article 121(3) of the LOS Convention on the extent of maritime zones is seriously hampered by the fact that it has raised a number of complex issues of interpretation. These include: what size leads to the classification of an island as a rock, and what qualifies as 'human habitation', 'economic life' or 'of their own'? These questions have attracted significant scholarly attention, providing thoughtful consideration of the intricacies involved. Although this has made it possible to limit the range of interpretations of the terms of Article 121(3) to some extent, the literature generally acknowledges the impossibility of an authoritative interpretation on the basis of existing materials. One recent discussion of the rocks provision in fact concludes that it is evident that only state practice and the case law are capable of undertaking the task of clarifying Article 121(3).[2]

These considerations indicate that a further attempt to clarify the provisions of Article 121(3) cannot lead to more detailed conclusions than those reached by other authors. On the other hand, the submission that state practice and the case law are capable of providing a clarification of this article has hardly been addressed. This paper proposes to undertake this task, looking at the different contexts in which states and other actors will have to interpret or apply Article 121(3). The nature of the processes involved to a large extent defines the possibilities of clarification of Article 121(3). For instance, a court having to deal with the interpretation of Article 121(3) can be expected to approach this matter differently from a state which has to consider its relevance for the definition of its maritime zones.[3]

Borderlands Under Stress (M.A. Pratt and J.A. Brown (eds), ISBN 90-411-9790-7).
© Kluwer Law International, 2000.

Although this paper does not venture another attempt at interpreting the provisions of Article 121(3), it starts with an overview of the questions raised by the different elements of the article. This provides a background for understanding the issues and makes it possible to assess the potential significance of various processes for its clarification. After this overview, the paper assesses the role of national legislation, decisions of national and international courts, the Commission on the Limits of the Continental Shelf (CLCS), and the community interest in the Area and the high seas in the clarification of Article 121(3). The conclusion evaluates the contribution of these different processes and discusses the need and possibilities for additional efforts to clarify Article 121(3).

THE UNCERTAINTIES CONCERNING THE CONTENTS OF ARTICLE 121(3)

The discussions on what was to become Article 121(3) at the third United Nations Conference on the Law of the Sea (UNCLOS III) indicate that one relevant consideration in establishing what is a rock, was the size of the island concerned.[4] Although widely varying figures have been suggested in this respect,[5] it has to be assumed that islands above a certain size never qualify as rocks, even if they meet the other criteria mentioned in Article 121(3).[6] It seems doubtful that one specific size can be established under which each island becomes a rock, as this also depends on an application of the other elements of Article 121(3) to each specific case.

To qualify as a rock, it is not necessary that an island be a rock in the geological sense. Article 121(3) can be equally applicable to, for instance, an island consisting of sand.[7] The terms 'cannot sustain', 'human habitation', 'economic life' and 'of their own' leave significant scope for different interpretations.[8] The reference to 'or' between 'human habitation' and 'economic life' has been interpreted both as being conjunctive[9] and disjunctive.[10]

The significance of Article 121(3) is limited by the existence of the LOS Convention provisions on archipelagic and straight baselines. These provisions do not in any way limit the establishment of baselines to specific categories of islands.[11] Islands which might qualify as a rock under Article 121(3) can be included in a system of baselines and as such be used to establish the outer limit of the exclusive economic zone (EEZ) and continental shelf.[12]

A final preliminary question is whether Article 121(3) has become a part of customary international law.[13] Legal doctrine is divided on this issue,[14] but an analysis of state practice suggests that the article has not acquired customary law status. State practice attributes an EEZ and continental shelf to almost all insular features.[15] The indeterminate nature of Article 121(3) possibly contributes to the fact that only in exceptional circumstances has a state limited itself in extending its EEZ and continental shelf from islands.

NATIONAL LEGISLATION

Practice of individual states concerning Article 121(3) mostly consists of national legislation establishing the outer limits of maritime zones. Two types of legislation on outer limits can be distinguished:

- legislation which only provides that the outer limit of the continental shelf or EEZ is measured from the baselines of the territorial sea
- legislation which defines an outer limit by reference to geographical coordinates.

In the former case, legislation implicitly seems to attribute an EEZ or continental shelf to all islands, as rocks in the sense of Article 121(3) also form part of the baseline.[16] The fact that in many cases existing baseline legislation is used would seem to limit the possibility that Article 121(3) has been taken into consideration, as this legislation is not necessarily reviewed in establishing an EEZ or continental shelf.

Although a review of legislation suggests that states generally do not take into consideration Article 121(3) in establishing the limit of the EEZ and continental shelf,[17] some caution is required. Some legislation in the first category mentioned contains generally-worded exemption clauses,[18] and for some states Article 121(3) may not be relevant.

An exceptional example of legislation which qualifies the extent of the EEZ or continental shelf is the Mexican Federal Act, which provides that islands have a continental shelf and EEZ but 'rocks which cannot sustain human habitation or economic life of their own' do not.[19] A map of the Mexican EEZ published by the Secretary of the Foreign Ministry in June 1976 reportedly took into account all Mexican islands except for the Alijos.[20]

The recent redefinition of the United Kingdom fishery zone off Rockall shows that Article 121(3) can have an impact on national legislation. Rockall, which is almost 200 nautical miles (nm) from the Scottish coast and measures only 624 square metres (sq m), has been considered one of the most notable examples of a rock within the meaning of Article 121(3).[21] Denmark, Iceland and Ireland had protested the use of Rockall as a basepoint for the British fishery zone established in 1977.[22] The UK decision on the rollback of the fishery zone limit, which was taken in connection with its accession to the LOS Convention, indicated that it was considered that 'Rockall is not a valid base point for such limits under Article 121(3)'.[23] One important conclusion to be drawn from this step upon ratification of the LOS Convention is that the UK apparently considers that practice of the parties to the Convention cannot be taken to have led to an interpretation of Article 121(3) which would exclude Rockall from its scope of application.

It seems possible that national legislation in the future can contribute more to the clarification of Article 121(3) than has been the case until now. States becoming a party to the LOS Convention may take a step like the UK did in respect of Rockall.[24] Also, some states are still in the process of defining their position concerning their baselines, which may result in modifications.[25]

The extent of potential conflict of national legislation with Article 121(3) may be further clarified by the obligations of states parties to the LOS Convention to provide information on the limits of their maritime zones.[26] Under Articles 75 and 84 of the Convention coastal states shall indicate the outer limit lines of the EEZ and the continental shelf on charts of a scale or scales adequate for ascertaining their position. Where appropriate, lists of geographical coordinates of points, specifying the geodetic datum, may be substituted for such lines.[27] The coastal state shall give due publicity to these charts or lists and shall deposit copies thereof with the Secretary General of the United Nations, and in the case of the continental shelf also with the Secretary General of the International Sea-Bed Authority (ISA).[28] As an evaluation of the status of insular features depends on their possible use as basepoints for straight or archipelagic baselines, it is also relevant that states parties to the Convention have similar obligations in these cases.[29]

The articles of the Convention on charts and lists do not indicate a time limit within which parties have to make a first deposition of the required information and few states have taken action in this respect.[30] The absence of a time limit does not, however, imply that the inaction of a coastal state is without consequences. Depending on the further circumstances of a case, non-compliance with the obligation to give due publicity to the limits of maritime zones may make these unopposable against other states.[31]

DECISIONS OF NATIONAL COURTS

The conformity of baselines and outer limits of maritime zones with the provisions of the LOS Convention can become the subject of litigation before national courts. A 1996 Judgment of the Supreme Court of Norway provides an interesting example of the role national courts may play in the clarification of Article 121(3).[32] One of the arguments of the appellants was that the baseline from which the outer limit of the fishery zone of Svalbard was measured was not in accordance with international law on three counts. One of these was that Abel Island, on which a basepoint was located, was an uninhabitable rock within the meaning of Article 121(3) of the LOS Convention. The Court held that Abel Island, which measures 13.2 square kilometres (sq km) in area, was too large to be a rock within the meaning of Article 121(3), and found support for this in state practice. Moreover, the Court held that Abel Island also did not meet the requirement of Article 121(3) that it should not sustain human habitation or an economic life of its own. The island would be able to support a significant polar bear hunt, were such hunting not prohibited for conservation reasons.[33] Two other recent national cases concerning issues related to baselines also indicate the potential of this form of state practice for the clarification of Article 121(3).[34]

THE DELIMITATION OF THE EEZ AND THE CONTINENTAL SHELF BETWEEN NEIGHBOURING STATES

Some bilateral delimitation agreements suggest they give partial weight to potential rocks in the sense of Article 121(3) in the delimitation of the continental shelf or the EEZ, implying that the feature concerned is not a rock. Recent examples concern two Finnish delimitation agreements with, respectively, Estonia and Sweden, involving the Finnish islets of Bogskär, and the delimitation between Denmark (Greenland) and Iceland involving the latter's Kolbeinsey.[35] Another case is formed by the delimitation agreements of the Netherlands, France and the United States with Venezuela, giving full weight to the Venezuelan islet of Aves.[36]

Bogskär consists of two islets measuring approximately 3,700 sq m and 1,110 sq m, which are some 340 m apart, and some smaller islets and rocks. The total area of Bogskär is approximately 5,000 sq m. Bogskär lies 62 nm, 16.4 nm and 22.6 nm from the Estonian, Finnish and Swedish coasts respectively.[37] On one of the islets stands a lighthouse, on which the Finnish Frontier Guard has installed surveillance equipment. Kolbeinsey, which measures a few hundred square metres and has a maximum altitude of six metres, lies approximately 55 nm to the north of the coast of Iceland.[38]

In the cases of Bogskär and Kolbeinsey, the states involved disagreed over whether these islets could be used as basepoints for the establishment of a 200 nm zone.[39] However, they did agree that the boundary line should in principle be an equidistance line. The solution which was eventually adopted in the three delimitation agreements was a division of the area between the equidistance lines giving full weight to the islets and those giving no weight to the islets. This treatment might suggest that it was recognised that the islets were valid basepoints which were accorded a limited effect in the establishment of the boundary line. However, closer consideration indicates that this is not the case. As far as can be established, the boundary lines were the result of a compromise between the states involved, and there was no discussion of the legal merits of the arguments concerning the islets.[40]

Aves, which is situated centrally in the eastern Caribbean, lies some 435 km from the nearest Venezuelan territory and some 200 km from the Northern Lesser Antilles. The islet measures about 585 m in length and, at its narrowest point, 30 m in width. The delimitation treaties of Venezuela with France, the Netherlands and the United States seem to accord Aves an EEZ and continental shelf as there are areas on the Venezuelan side of the boundary which are within only 200 nm of the coasts of Aves and these other states.

Antigua and Barbuda, St Kitts and Nevis, and St Vincent and the Grenadines have made objections regarding these three agreements. These protests note that, as recognised in customary international law and reflected in the LOS Convention, rocks which cannot sustain human habitation or economic life of their own shall have no EEZ or continental shelf. It is indicated that the three agreements appear to grant Aves an EEZ and continental shelf, and that

Antigua and Barbuda, St Kitts and Nevis, and St Vincent and the Grenadines have not acquiesced in them.[41] It seems that France, the Netherlands and the United States thus far have not reacted to the protests.[42]

According no weight to an island, as was for instance the case with Rockall in the continental shelf delimitation between Ireland and the UK,[43] does not in itself provide conclusive evidence that an island is considered to fall under the definition of Article 121(3). Giving no weight to Rockall could also be considered to be in conformity with maritime delimitation law if Rockall was entitled to its own EEZ and continental shelf.

The above cases suggest that most bilateral delimitation agreements cannot contribute to a clarification of the contents of Article 121(3). It is to be expected that, in most cases, states will refrain from classifying an island as falling under Article 121(3) if a compromise can be reached without doing so. Agreements which seem to recognise that the islands concerned have an EEZ, such as the treaties concerning Aves and Kolbeinsey, might be considered to provide some indication concerning the interpretation of the article. However, in these cases there are a number of other considerations which caution against such an approach. The agreements concerning Aves refrain from explicitly recognising the entitlement of the islet to extended maritime zones. Furthermore, the delimitations effected suggest that the states involved reached agreement without direct recourse to the material rules of maritime delimitation law.[44] Similar considerations apply in the case involving Kolbeinsey.[45]

THE CASE LAW

Taking into account the eminent role of the International Court of Justice (ICJ) and arbitral tribunals in the definition of the law applicable to the delimitation of maritime boundaries, a similar contribution to the clarification of Article 121(3) might be considered a possibility. However, due to a number of circumstances the ICJ or a tribunal may not always address the issue of Article 121(3), even if it is raised by one of the parties to the proceedings.

The cases concerning maritime delimitation which have been decided until now have not assessed Article 121(3) in any detail. The status of Article 121 was addressed in the *Jan Mayen* conciliation.[46] Interestingly, the Conciliation Commission found that Article 121 of the then Draft Convention reflected 'the present status of international law on this subject'.[47] The Commission did not indicate how it reached this conclusion.[48] On the basis of a brief description of Jan Mayen, the Commission concluded that it had to be considered an island entitled to an EEZ and a continental shelf.[49] Taking into account the size of Jan Mayen, which is some 373 sq km, this conclusion does not seem particularly relevant in most cases in which interpretation of Article 121(3) is required.

The abovementioned Icelandic islet of Kolbeinsey figured in the *Jan Mayen* conciliation and the *Jan Mayen* case. Its treatment in both instances provides examples of how certain issues can be circumvented in an adjudication. In the

Jan Mayen conciliation the Commission recommended a continental shelf boundary following the Icelandic 200 nm outer limit which was, in part, measured from Kolbeinsey. The Commission did not define this line in an unequivocal manner, but only noted the agreement between Iceland and Norway to give the former a full 200 nm economic zone in relation to Jan Mayen.[50]

In the *Jan Mayen* case the ICJ, in establishing the relevant area for the delimitation, adopted as the southern limit the limit of the 200 nm zone claimed by Iceland, which in part was influenced by the presence of Kolbeinsey. Denmark had requested the Court to limit its decision in this way, a position which was accepted by Norway.[51]

These examples suggest that a court has ample opportunity to avoid discussion of the significance of Article 121(3) in cases involving the delimitation or outer limits of the EEZ and continental shelf.[52] Whether it is possible to leave certain questions unanswered depends to a certain extent on the formulation of the questions submitted to the courts.[53]

A first possibility is to refrain from discussing the status of the island involved, and to proceed directly to a delimitation. Such an approach is possible in all cases in which the island is part of a larger delimitation, and is not the only basepoint from which parts of the overlapping claims result.

If an island which might fall under the definition of Article 121(3) is the only basepoint of one state which results in an overlap with the EEZ or continental shelf of another state, it is still possible to avoid discussion of its status. In the *Jan Mayen* conciliation this was accomplished by referring to the boundary as coinciding with the outer limit of the Icelandic 200 nm zone. If a boundary is established by a straight line, the definition of the terminal point of the boundary can be avoided by referring to the boundary as continuing along a specific bearing until the outer limit of the maritime zones of the states involved is reached.[54]

If a boundary has to be established between a mainland coast and an island or between two islands, one of which might be considered a rock in the sense of Article 121(3), avoiding the issue of its classification becomes difficult. However, even in this case such an approach remains possible in certain instances. For instance, if there is a limited extent of overlap between the EEZ and continental shelf of the parties, a court could rule that, taking into account the disparity in coastal lengths, an equitable delimitation results in attributing the larger coast a maritime area which coincides with its 200 nm outer limit.

One final way of avoiding discussion of the status of an island under Article 121(3) is what has been referred to as contextualisation. In this strategy, a judge looks at the issues of a case from the perspective of opposability of the parties' claims *vis-à-vis* each other, instead of looking at them in terms of general rules.[55] An example of this approach in the case law on maritime boundary delimitation is the treatment of Eddystone Rocks in the *Anglo-French Continental Shelf* arbitration. France and the UK disagreed over whether Eddystone Rocks was an island or a low-tide elevation. In deciding on this issue the Court of

Arbitration did not express itself on this particular point, but limited itself to noting that France had accepted Eddystone Rocks as a relevant basepoint during earlier negotiations.[56]

These considerations indicate that there is ample opportunity for refraining from an interpretation of Article 121(3). However, the article might in certain instances be difficult to circumvent. This concerns cases where a ruling on whether an island falls under the definition of Article 121(3) provides the only possibility of resolving a dispute. Such disputes might concern the outer limits of the EEZ and continental shelf which in principle have *erga omnes* validity.

However, even if such cases arise, clarification of Article 121(3) will probably take place only gradually. The article contains a number of elements which raise considerable interpretative uncertainties, and a case does not necessarily have to address all of these issues at the same time. Moreover, a judge may only appraise whether the requirements of the article are met in general terms, without elaborating on each of them or indicating the minimum threshold for each element.[57]

THE COMMISSION ON THE LIMITS OF THE CONTINENTAL SHELF

The CLCS, which has been set up in accordance with Article 76(8) and Annex II of the LOS Convention, is to make recommendations to states on matters related to the outer limit of their continental shelf where it extends beyond 200 nm from their coasts.[58] In this procedure the CLCS may be confronted with submissions which use as a baseline an island which other states may consider to be a rock in the sense of Article 121(3). As Article 76(8) provides that the limits of the continental shelf established by a coastal state on the basis of the recommendations of the CLCS shall be final and binding, it would seem pertinent that some evaluation of the baselines as submitted by the coastal state take place. The CLCS itself will apparently not carry out this task.[59] This is reflected in the Rules of Procedure of the CLCS, which indicate that, in the case of land and maritime disputes (which might involve a dispute concerning Article 121), the Commission will refrain from considering the submissions of any of the states involved unless these states reach an agreement on joint or separate submissions.[60] This may imply that in certain instances states will have to address the issue of Article 121(3) in connection with the extension of their continental shelf beyond 200 nm. This may induce states to take up certain issues which otherwise would not have been addressed for the time being.

Interestingly, a draft of the Scientific and Technical Guidelines of the Commission seems to make explicit reference to the need to take Article 121(3) into consideration in certain instances. However, the exact implications of this provision are not clear (e.g. how it relates to the fact that the CLCS in principle is not charged with assessing the validity of baselines), and the guidelines are subject to further discussion.

THE COMMUNITY INTEREST IN THE AREA AND THE HIGH SEAS

The classification of an island as a rock in the sense of Article 121(3) can have significant consequences on the extent of the high seas and the Area. In this case it is not another coastal state which is adversely affected but the community of states as a whole. The protection of this community interest will depend mostly on the actions of the interested states. Attributing this role to the ISA in respect of the Area could have been an option. All rights in the resources of the Area are vested in humankind, on whose behalf the ISA shall act.[61] However, the LOS Convention defines the Area negatively as the sea-bed and ocean floor and its subsoil beyond the limits of national jurisdiction. The definition of these limits is the responsibility of the coastal state.[62]

Interested states are likely to begin action against a coastal state's claim which infringes on the high seas or Area with informal consultations or diplomatic protests. Such steps may contribute to some clarification of Article 121(3), as states may indicate the grounds for protesting a claim and the coastal state for upholding it. However, if no further steps are taken, these arguments are not subject to legal evaluation. States can submit a dispute over the applicability of Article 121(3) to third-party settlement, if such procedures are applicable between them, or, if this is not the case, they can reach a compromise to do so.[63] In the case of third-party settlement the considerations set out above apply.

CONCLUSIONS

The interpretation of Article 121(3) in the first instance has to be addressed by individual states establishing the outer limits of their continental shelf and EEZ. However, the above analysis indicates that this practice does little to clarify Article 121(3). One exception seems to be the British practice with respect to Rockall.

At a next stage, the interpretation of Article 121(3) can become an issue either in disputes over the outer limit of the EEZ and the continental shelf, or in the delimitation of these zones between neighbouring states. Although entitlement to and delimitation of maritime zones are closely related, in the case of Article 121(3) these issues seem to have different implications. This is explained by the actors involved and the questions requiring solution.

A review of state practice and the case law indicates that in the delimitation of maritime boundaries between states, in most cases either it is not necessary to resolve or it is possible to circumvent the question of whether or not a particular island is a rock in the sense of Article 121(3). As the delimitation involving Kolbeinsey indicates, states may even choose not to address this issue if the island concerned is the only feature resulting in an overlap of EEZs and the continental shelf. This suggests that for most delimitations of maritime boundaries the clarification of Article 121(3) is not a matter of great urgency. This is mostly explained by the contents of the rules of international law applicable to the delimitation of maritime boundaries, which allow for sufficient flexibility to achieve an equitable result without ruling on the applicability of Article 121(3).[64]

The establishment of outer limits from a potential rock which do not result in an overlap with the maritime zones of neighbouring states, generally does seem to require a ruling on the applicability of Article 121(3) in case of conflict. However, in this case the actors involved seem to impede a resolution of the dispute involving an authoritative interpretation of Article 121(3). An outer limit of the EEZ or the continental shelf encroaching upon the extent of the high seas or the Area places the coastal state's interest against the much more diffuse interest of the community of states.[65] This community interest can only be expressed through the actions of individual states. The interest of these other states is of another nature than that of the coastal state. By using a potential rock to establish the outer limits of its EEZ and continental shelf the coastal state *inter alia* secures exclusive access to the resources of the area involved. States protesting such a claim do not stand to gain similar benefits, as a rollback of a claim would open the area to all states. This suggests that states may not always be willing to litigate such a dispute (if this is an option) due to the resources this requires, and may limit themselves to, for instance, diplomatic protests.[66]

Whether the judiciary can address the interpretation of Article 121(3) depends first on the questions being submitted by the parties to a conflict. In any case, it seems safe to assume that interpretation by the judiciary will be an incremental process, as courts will limit themselves to addressing only the issues needed to resolve the case before them. To some extent it may also be difficult to transpose the results of the application of Article 121(3) to a specific island to other islands.

The CLCS is not set to play any role in the clarification of Article 121(3), although the process related to the definition of the continental shelf beyond 200 nm may contribute to bringing certain disputes over the status of islands under Article 121(3) into the open.

These considerations indicate that it is likely that state practice will provide most incidents of relevance to Article 121(3). Taking into consideration the nature of most of this practice, it does not seem likely that it will contribute much to the clarification of this article. Protests do not seem to go beyond rephrasing the contents of Article 121(3). More results might be expected of cases before national courts on, for instance, the enforcement of fisheries legislation in areas within 200 nm from a potential rock. Whether a court can actually evaluate the legality of national legislation establishing the outer limits of maritime zones against the requirements of international law depends on the legal system of the state concerned.

One final question to be addressed is whether there is a need to clarify Article 121(3) by other means than the ones outlined above and whether this would be acceptable to the interested states. One option would be the clarification of the article at a diplomatic conference through the elaboration of a more detailed text.[67] However, the experience with Article 121(3) at UNCLOS III suggests the futility of such an approach.

Another option is the adoption of alternative procedures for the assessment of claims concerning the application of Article 121(3). The present analysis suggests that this does not seem to be required for cases involving the delimitation of maritime boundaries between states. However, it might be an option in cases involving a coastal state claim infringing on the high seas and the Area. It has been suggested that the ISA, as a representative of the international community in respect of the Area, should have a role in its definition.[68] Although this might seem an attractive suggestion, it is not likely to be acceptable to all states concerned. During UNCLOS III broad margin states persistently rejected a large measure of international control over the definition of the limits of their continental shelf. As a compromise, the procedure under Article 76 involving the CLCS was devised. It seems highly unlikely that this compromise enshrined in the LOS Convention will be overhauled.[69] Opponents of giving a more significant role to the ISA can argue that the community interest is already protected by the CLCS.[70] For the 200 nm zone, the idea of international control was never taken up at UNCLOS III, except through the provision obliging coastal states to submit information on such limits to the Secretary General of the United Nations.

A less ambitious but more realistic approach than giving the ISA a formal role in this matter might be the convening of a meeting of experts under the aegis of the Division of Ocean Affairs and the Law of the Sea (DOALOS) of the United Nations Secretariat. Such a meeting could result in the adoption of a report containing guidelines on the interpretation of Article 121(3).[71]

In conclusion, it appears that state practice, and possibly the international judiciary, will continue to be the main source for establishing the more precise meaning of Article 121(3). In all likelihood this implies that some uncertainties are to persist, although it can be expected that state practice will address this issue in more detail and more often than in the past. As most practice concerning islands is now generated by states parties to the LOS Convention, it is moreover of greater relevance for the interpretation of Article 121(3).

NOTES

1   United Nations Convention on the Law of the Sea of 10 December 1982 (*International Legal Materials* 21, 1982: 1261).

2   Kolb, 1994: 908; see also Kusuma-Atmadja *et al*, 1997; Kwiatkowska & Soons, 1990: 176; Van Dyke *et al*, 1988: 439. The observation of Kolb is applicable to any rule of international law. However, in most other instances the uncertainty surrounding a rule does not concern its constitutive elements to the same extent.

3   The significance of specific instances of state practice or judicial decisions for the interpretation of a rule of international law can vary greatly. For instance, national

legislation which is not enforced has little probative value. A discussion of this issue is beyond the scope of this paper.

4 See Nandan & Rosenne, 1995. The discussion on Article 121 at UNCLOS III suggests that proposals to limit the extent of maritime zones served two distinct purposes. One was to deny small islands any entitlement to an EEZ and continental shelf, the other to deny islands such zones in the delimitation with neighbouring states.

5 Brown, 1992: 38, points to two definitions of rocks, one of Hodgson, defining a rock as having an area of less than 0.001 square miles. Another definition of rocks is given by the International Hydrographic Bureau, which defines them as being less than one sq km in size.

6 See also Kolb, 1994: 904; some doubt in this respect is expressed by Kwiatkowska & Soons, 1990: 167; see also *infra* note 49.

7 See Kolb, 1994: 904–905; Kwiatkowska & Soons, 1990: 151–153; Van Dyke *et al*, 1988: 435. *Contra* Prescott, 1998: 74.

8 See e.g. Brown, 1992: 38–39; Kolb, 1994: 899–908; Kwiatkowska & Soons, 1990: 153–173; Lucchini & Vlckel, 1990; Van Dyke *et al*, 1988: 433–439.

9 See e.g. Kolb, 1994: 906.

10 See e.g. Kwiatkowska & Soons, 1990: 163–165.

11 See Articles 7 and 47 of the LOS Convention.

12 See also Kolb, 1994: 899; Kwiatkowska & Soons, 1990: 147–148; Nandan & Rosenne, 1995: 338.

13 Increased ratification of the LOS Convention is bound to diminish the relevance of this question. States with a particular interest in Article 121(3) which have not yet become a party to the Convention include Colombia, Nicaragua, the United States and Venezuela. The United States seems to take the position that any insular feature which can generate a territorial sea can also generate an EEZ (see Van Dyke *et al* (1988): 430–432).

14 See Kwiatkowska & Soons, 1990: 174–175; Charney, 1995: 733; Symmons, 1998: 83.

15 See also United Nations Division for Ocean Affairs and the Law of the Sea, 1994: 14.

16 For an overview of national legislation on this issue see e.g. United Nations Division for Ocean Affairs and the Law of the Sea, 1992b.

17 A number of states have established a continental shelf and/or EEZ off islands which might be considered to be rocks (see e.g. Kwiatkowska & Soons, 1990: 177; Van Dyke *et al*,1988: 444–463 and 487–488).

18 For instance, legislation of Japan establishes that provisions of treaties apply when they provide otherwise than the legislation concerned (Law on the Exclusive Economic Zone and the Continental Shelf (Law No. 74 of 1996) (*Law of the Sea Bulletin* No. 35: 94–96), Article 4). Under the Danish Act No. 411 of 22 May 1996 on Exclusive Economic Zones, the Minister for Foreign Affairs may determine that the Act does not apply to waters covered by special circumstances (*Law of the Sea Bulletin* No. 33: 32, Article 1(2)). Admittedly, this latter provision was reportedly included in connection with the dispute with Poland over the weight to be accorded to the Danish island of Bornholm in a maritime delimitation. Bornholm is in any case not a rock in the sense of Article 121(3).

19 Federal Act relating to the Sea of 8 January 1986, Article 51 (United Nations Division for Ocean Affairs and the Law of the Sea, 1986: 193, at 194) and Article 63 (United Nations Division for Ocean Affairs and the Law of the Sea, 1989b: 172 at 174).

20 See Symmons, 1979: 125–126; see also van Overbeek, 1989: 262. It seems that the

Mexican baselines are under review at the present time. Information on the outer limits of Mexico's EEZ may be submitted to the United Nations some time in 1999.

21 See e.g. Anderson, 1997: 778; Churchill, 1997a: 114. It seems that the UK also did not take into account Shag Rocks and Black Rock in establishing a 200 nm limit off South Georgia in 1993. Although this is not apparent from the relevant legislation (Proclamation (Maritime Zone) No. 1 of 1993 (*Law of the Sea Bulletin*, No. 24: 47–48); The South Georgia and South Sandwich Islands (Territorial Sea) Order 1989 (Statutory Instrument 1989 No. 1995 and Explanatory Note)), the chart depicting this outer limit reportedly reflects this treatment of the islands (see also Churchill, 1997b: 473–474).

22 See Churchill, 1997a: 114; Symmons, 1988: 81.

23 Statement by the Foreign and Commonwealth Secretary, cited in Anderson, 1997: 778. The limit of the fishery zone was redefined accordingly through the Fishery Limits Order 1997 (Statutory Instrument 1997 No. 1750 of 22 July 1997).

24 *Cf.* Churchill, 1998: 273.

25 *Cf.* Churchill, 1997b: 465–466.

26 See also Churchill & Lowe, 1988.

27 LOS Convention, Articles 75(1) and 84(1); see also Article 76(9).

28 *Ibid.*, Articles 75(2) and 84(2); see also UN Doc A/52/487 of 20 October 1997, paras. 82–85.

29 See *ibid.*, Articles 16 and 47 (see also *supra*).

30 As of 30 September 1997 Argentina, China, Costa Rica, Cyprus, Finland, Germany, Italy, Jamaica, Japan, Myanmar, Norway and Romania had complied with the obligation to deposit charts and/or lists of geographical coordinates relating to their maritime zones (UN Doc A/52/487 of 20 October 1997, para. 83).

31 *Cf.* Fisheries Case (*United Kingdom* v. *Norway*), Judgment of 18 December 1951 (Reports of Judgments, Advisory Opinions and Orders; The International Court of Justice, *ICJ Reports*, 1951: 116 at 139).

32 Judgment of 7 May 1996, *Public Prosecutor* v. *Haraldsson et al.* The account given here is based on the more extensive discussion of this case in Churchill, 1996.

33 *Ibid.*: 579. The Court did not examine whether Article 121(3) was actually applicable. The Convention itself was not applicable and it has been doubted whether Article 121(3) represents customary international law (*ibid.*; see also *supra*).

34 *United States of America, Plaintiff* v. *State of Alaska*, US Supreme Court, Decision of 19 June 1997; *Public Prosecutor* v. *Van Beers et al*, Court of Appeal (The Hague, The Netherlands), Decision of 15 November 1996 (not published). For further references to decisions of national courts concerning baselines not directly related to Article 121(3) see e.g. Brownlie, 1993: 190, n. 56; 192, nn. 68–69.

35 Agreement between the Government of the Republic of Finland and the Government of the Kingdom of Sweden concerning the Delimitation in the Åland Sea and the Northern Part of the Baltic Sea of the Finnish Continental Shelf and Fishing Zone and the Swedish Economic Zone of 2 June 1994 (Charney & Alexander, 1998: 2553); Agreement between the Republic of Finland and the Republic of Estonia on the Boundary of the Maritime Zones in the Gulf of Finland and the Northern Baltic Sea of 18 October 1996 (12 *International Journal of Marine and Coastal Law* (1997): 375); Agreement between the Government of the Kingdom of Denmark along with the Local Government of Greenland on one hand and the Government of the Republic of Iceland on the other hand on the Delimitation of the Continental Shelf and the

Fishery Zone in the Area between Greenland and Iceland of 11 November 1997 (13 *International Journal of Marine and Coastal Law*, 1998: 613). In none of these cases were both states involved a party to the LOS Convention at the time the bilateral agreements were concluded.

36 Maritime Boundary Treaty between the United States of America and the Republic of Venezuela of 28 March 1978 (United Nations Division for Ocean Affairs and the Law of the Sea, 1987: 126); Boundary Delimitation Treaty between the Republic of Venezuela and the Kingdom of the Netherlands of 31 March 1978 (*ibid.*: 139); Delimitation Treaty between the Government of the French Republic and the Government of the Republic of Venezuela of 17 July 1980 (*ibid.*: 132).

37 Finland seems to have argued that Bogskär might be included in its system of straight baselines (for the implications of such inclusion see further *supra*). For the legal aspects of the delimitation involving Bogskär see further Oude Elferink, 1996: 546–548.

38 Maritime Delimitation in the Area between Greenland and Jan Mayen (Denmark/Norway) (hereinafter *Jan Mayen* case); Memorial Submitted by the Government of the Kingdom of Denmark, Vol. I: 8, para. 15.

39 The position of Estonia in this respect is not known. The Soviet Union, which had conducted negotiations with Finland over this delimitation had rejected any weight for Bogskär, referring to Article 121(3) of the LOS Convention.

40 The explanatory memorandum of the Danish Foreign Ministry in respect of the delimitation agreement between Denmark and Iceland notes that in the establishment of the boundary line particular attention was given to good neighbourly relations (Beslutningsforslag nr. B 2, Folketinget 1997–98 (2. samling) of 26 March 1998: 7).

41 These protests have been reproduced in LOS/SP/1, LOS/SP/2 and LOS/SP/3.

42 A full discussion of all aspects of this issue is beyond the scope of this paper. Formally, the agreements do not bind the protesting states. Moreover, the agreements do not explicitly recognise that Aves generates a full EEZ and continental shelf. On the other hand, the agreements appear to give considerable political support to Venezuela's position concerning Aves. The three delimitation agreements seem to give too much weight to Aves if viewed solely from the perspective of the material rules of maritime delimitation law, especially because of the great disparity in coastal lengths.

43 Agreement between the Republic of Ireland and the United Kingdom of Great Britain and Northern Ireland concerning the Delimitation of Areas of the Continental Shelf between the Two Countries of 7 November 1988 (United Nations Division for Ocean Affairs and the Law of the Sea, 1992a: 6). The fact that no weight was accorded to Rockall is mentioned in Charney & Alexander, 1993: 1770.

44 See *supra* note 38.

45 See further Oude Elferink, 1998: 609.

46 Continental Shelf Area between Jan Mayen and Iceland (Jan Mayen Continental Shelf), Report and Recommendations to the Governments of Iceland and Norway of the Conciliation Commission of 19–20 May 1981 (62 *International Law Reports*: 108; 20 *International Legal Materials*, 1981: 797).

47 62 *International Law Reports*: 114. Legal doctrine has judged this finding of the Commission differently (see Kwiatkowska & Soons, 1990: 174–175).

48 Describing its task, the Commission had pointed out that it had thoroughly examined state practice and court decisions in order to ascertain possible guidelines for the

practicable and equitable solution of the questions concerned (62 *International Law Reports*: 125).

49 62 *International Law Reports*: 114. In the *Jan Mayen* case the ICJ did not address this issue. Denmark had not objected to these entitlements of Jan Mayen, concurring with the view of the Commission in the *Jan Mayen* conciliation (see *Jan Mayen* case, Reply submitted by the Government of the Kingdom of Denmark, Vol. I: 121, para. 328). It has been suggested that Article 121(3) may have been an unstated factor in the ICJ's decision-making process in the *Jan Mayen* case (Kwiatkowska, 1997: 106–107).

50 See 62 *International Law Reports*: 126. In its Rejoinder in the *Jan Mayen* case Norway stated that: '[t]here is no express agreement or specific understanding between Norway and Iceland providing for recognition by Norway of Kolbeinsey as an Icelandic basepoint. Nor has there been any formal unilateral determination by Norway on the issue. The relevant Agreements between Norway and Iceland imply that, in the absence of any further specification, and of any particular statement of reservation on the part of Norway, the delimitations as between the economic zones and between the appurtenant parts of the continental shelf of the Parties must be determined on the basis of such basepoints and baselines as may from time to time be applied by Iceland in conformity with international law.' (*Jan Mayen* case, Rejoinder Submitted by the Government of the Kingdom of Norway: 10, para. 25.)

51 *ICJ Reports*, 1993: 47, para. 18.

52 Such an approach can be explained by the fact that a court is required to resolve a specific dispute and not to clarify the law in the abstract. Leaving unaddressed certain controversial issues which are not essential to resolving a dispute may facilitate agreement within the court.

53 However, a court has a certain liberty in this respect. See e.g. Case concerning the Continental Shelf (Libyan Arab Jamahiriya/Malta), Judgment of 3 June 1985 (*ICJ Reports*, 1985: 13, at 22–28, paras. 18–23).

54 *Cf.* Guinea/Guinea-Bissau Maritime Delimitation *Maritime Delimitation* arbitration, Decision of 14 February 1985 (*International Boundary Cases, The Continental Shelf*, 1992, Vol. II: 1301 at 1356, para. 130); Colson, 1993: 61.

55 See further Koskenniemi, 1991: 32–34.

56 Arbitration between the United Kingdom and France on the Delimitation of the Continental Shelf, Decision of 30 June 1977 (United Nations Reports of International Arbitral Awards (UNRIAA), Vol. XVIII: 3, paras. 139–143). In this context it is worth noting that the court emphasised that: 'it is not concerned in these proceedings to decide the general question of the legal status of Eddystone Rocks as an island or of its entitlement to a territorial sea of its own. [...] [T]he Court is here concerned with the Eddystone Rocks only in the particular context of the delimitation of the continental shelf by a median line in the Channel as between the Parties now before the Court' (*Ibid.*, para. 139).

57 *Cf. Jan Mayen* conciliation referred to *supra*.

58 On the CLCS see further Karagiannis, 1994; Nandan & Rosenne, 1993: 882 and 1003–1018.

59 A study prepared by the Division for Ocean Affairs and the Law of the Sea of the United Nations Office of Legal Affairs, undertaken with a representative group of experts, notes that the LOS Convention 'assigns to the Commission no responsibility relating to the determination of baselines by the coastal State' (SPLOS/CLCS/INF/1 of 10 June 1996, para. 42).

60 CLCS/3/Rev.1 of 14 May 1998, Annex I. CLCS/3/Rev.1 contains the Rules of

Procedure of the CLCS. Submissions in case of maritime disputes are addressed in Rule 44 and Annex I to the Rules. The Commission has adopted its Rules of Procedure and reached consensus on the Annex, but it was decided that the Annex would be adopted by the Commission only after it had been considered by the Meeting of Parties of the LOS Convention (see SPLOS/28 of 15 May 1998, paras. 1–2). The result of this Meeting was that states parties might make written comments on this issue. These comments will be considered by the CLCS before giving its final approval to Annex I (see SPLOS/31 of 4 June 1998, para. 45).

61 LOS Convention, Article 137(2).

62 See *ibid.*, Articles 1(1)(1) and 134. This absence of a role for the ISA is confirmed by the fact that the Convention does not give it rights to the Area as such, but charges it to organise and control activities in the Area, particularly in respect of its resources (see *ibid.*, Articles 137 and 157; see also Mahmoudi, 1987: 77). The ISA might play a limited role in the activities of the CLCS with respect to the continental shelf beyond 200 nm. However, this only concerns the exchange of scientific and technical information (LOS Convention, Annex II, Article 3(2)), excluding baseline considerations (see also *infra*).

63 Under the LOS Convention disputes over the location of the baselines and outer limits of maritime zones are subject to the dispute settlement mechanisms of its Part XV.

64 See also Kwiatkowska & Soons, 1990: 181.

65 See also Kolb, 1994: 897.

66 The *Fisheries Jurisdiction* cases of 1974 (Fisheries Jurisdiction Case (*United Kingdom* v. *Iceland*; *Federal Republic of Germany* v. *Iceland*), Judgment of 25 July 1974 (*ICJ Reports*, 1974: 3) indicate that there may be instances in which states with an interest in the high seas may go to great lengths to protect these interests. In this case the UK and the Federal Republic had a vested interest in the area concerned, which would be gravely damaged if the Icelandic claim were recognised.

67 See Articles 312 and 313 of the LOS Convention for the rules applicable to its amendment.

68 Reisman & Westerman, 1992; see also Karagiannis, 1994: 192.

69 See however, McDorman, 1995: 173, who suggests that the ISA is likely to become an active player in all discussions related to ocean issues that affect the extent of the Area.

70 *Cf.* Case concerning the Delimitation of the Maritime Areas between Canada and France, Decision of 10 June 1992 (31 *International Legal Materials*, 1992: 1149 at 1172, paras. 78–79; Karagiannis, 1994: 164).

71 The feasibility of this approach is illustrated by a similar project on the probably equally controversial issue of baselines (see United Nations Division for Ocean Affairs and the Law of the Sea, 1989a).

BIBLIOGRAPHY

Anderson, D. H. (1997) 'British Accession to the UN Convention on the Law of the Sea', 46 *International and Comparative Law Quarterly*: 761–786.

Brown, E. D. (1992) *Sea-Bed Energy and Minerals: The International Legal Regime; Volume 1 The Continental Shelf*, Dordrecht: Martinus Nijhoff Publishers.

Brownlie, I. (1993) *Principles of International Law* (4th edn.), London: Clarendon Press.

Charney, J. I. & Alexander, L. M. (eds.) (1993) *International Maritime Boundaries*, Vol. I, Dordrecht: Martinus Nijhoff Publishers.

Charney, J. I. & Alexander, L. M. (eds.) (1993) *International Maritime Boundaries*, Vol. II, Dordrecht: Martinus Nijhoff Publishers.

Charney, J. I. & Alexander, L. M. (eds.) (1998) *International Maritime Boundaries*, Vol. III, The Hague: Martinus Nijhoff Publishers.

Charney, J. I. (1995) 'Central and East Asian Maritime Boundaries and the Law of the Sea', 89 *American Journal of International Law*: 724-749.

Churchill, R. R. & Lowe, A. V. (1988) *The Law of the Sea*, Manchester: 44–45.

Churchill, R. R. (1996) 'Norway; Supreme Court Judgment on Law of the Sea Issues', 11 *International Journal of Marine and Coastal Law*: 576–580.

Churchill, R. R. (1997a) 'United Kingdom's Decision to Defer Accession to the UN Convention on the Law of the Sea: A Convincing Move?', 12 *International Journal of Marine and Coastal Law*: 110–121.

Churchill, R. R. (1997b) 'Falkland Islands – Maritime Jurisdiction and Co-operative Arrangements with Argentina', 46 *International and Comparative Law Quarterly*: 463–477.

Churchill, R. R. (1998) 'United Kingdom; Accession to the UN Convention on the Law of the Sea', 13 *International Journal of Marine and Coastal Law*: 263–273.

Colson, D. A. (1993) 'The Legal Regime of Maritime Boundary Agreements' in Charney, J. I. & Alexander, L. M. (eds.) (1993) *International Maritime Boundaries*, Vol. I, Dordrecht: Martinus Nijhoff Publishers: 41–73.

International Boundary Cases, The Continental Shelf (1992) Vol. II, Cambridge.

Karagiannis, S. (1994) 'Observations sur la Commission des Limites du Plateau Continental', 8 *Espaces et Ressources Maritimes*: 163–194.

Kolb, R. (1994) 'L'Interprétation de l'Article 121, Paragraphe 3, de la Convention de Montego Bay sur le Droit de la Mer: Les "Rochers qui ne se Prêtent pas à l'Habitation Humaine ou à une Vie Economique Propre..."', 40 *Annuaire Français de Droit International*: 876–909.

Koskenniemi, M. (1991) 'Theory: Implications for the Practitioner' in *Theory and International Law: An Introduction*, London: The British Institute of International and Comparative Law: 1–45.

Kusuma-Atmadja, M., Mensah, T. A. & Oxman, B. H. (eds.) (1997) *Sustainable Development and Preservation of the Oceans: The Challenges of UNCLOS and Agenda 21*, Honolulu: The Law of the Sea Institute: 665.

Kwiatkowska, B. & Soons, A. H. A. (1990) 'Entitlement to Maritime Areas of Rocks which Cannot Sustain Human Habitation or Economic Life of Their Own', 21 *Netherlands Yearbook of International Law*: 139–181.

Kwiatkowska, B. (1997) 'Equitable Maritime Boundary Delimitation as Exemplified in the Work of the International Court of Justice during the Presidency of Sir Robert Yewdall Jennings and Beyond', 28 *Ocean Development and International Law*: 91–145.

Lucchini, L. & Vlckel, M. (1990) *Droit de la Mer; Tome 1*, Paris: Pedone: 337–339.

Mahmoudi, S. (1987) *The Law of Deep Sea-Bed Mining*, Stockholm: Almqvist and Wiksell International.

McDorman, T. (1995) 'The Entry into Force of the 1982 LOS Convention and the Article 76 Outer Continental Shelf Regime', *International Journal of Marine and Coastal Law* 10: 165–187.

Nandan, S. N. & Rosenne, S. (1995) *United Nations Convention on the Law of the Sea 1982; A Commentary*, Vol. III, The Hague: Martinus Nijhoff Publishers: 321–339.

Nandan, S. N. & Rosenne, S. (eds.) (1993) *United Nations Convention on the Law of the Sea 1982; A Commentary; Volume II*, Dordrecht: Martinus Nijhoff Publishers.

Oude Elferink, A. (1996) 'The Law and Politics of the Maritime Boundary Delimitations of the Russian Federation: Part 1', 11 *International Journal of Marine and Coastal Law*: 533–569.

Oude Elferink, A. (1998) 'Denmark/Iceland/Norway; Bilateral Agreements on the Delimitation of the Continental Shelf and Fishery Zones', 13 *International Journal of Marine and Coastal Law*: 607–616.

Prescott, V. (1998) 'The Uncertainties of Middleton and Elizabeth Reefs', 6(1) *Boundary and Security Bulletin*: 72–77.

Reisman, W. M. & Westerman, G. S. (1992) *Straight Baselines in International Maritime Boundary Delimitation*, New York: St. Martin's Press: 209–211.

Symmons, C. R. (1979) *The Maritime Zones of Islands in International Law*, The Hague: Martinus Nijhoff Publishers.

Symmons, C. R. (1998) 'Ireland and the Rockall Dispute: An Analysis of Recent Developments', 6(1) *Boundary and Security Bulletin*: 78–93.

United Nations Division for Ocean Affairs and the Law of the Sea (1986) *The Law of the Sea; National Legislation on the Exclusive Economic Zone, the Economic Zone and the Exclusive Fishery Zone*, New York: United Nations.

United Nations Division for Ocean Affairs and the Law of the Sea (1987) *The Law of the Sea; Maritime Boundary Agreements (1970–1984)*: New York: United Nations.

United Nations Division for Ocean Affairs and the Law of the Sea (1989a) *The Law of the Sea; Baselines: an Examination of the Relevant Provisions of the United Nations Convention on the Law of the Sea*, New York: United Nations.

United Nations Division for Ocean Affairs and the Law of the Sea (1989b) *The Law of the Sea; National Legislation on the Continental Shelf*, New York: United Nations.

United Nations Division for Ocean Affairs and the Law of the Sea (1992a) *The Law of the Sea; Maritime Boundary Agreements (1985–1991)*, New York: United Nations.

United Nations Division for Ocean Affairs and the Law of the Sea (1992b) *The Law of the Sea; National Claims to Maritime Jurisdiction*, New York: United Nations.

United Nations Division for Ocean Affairs and the Law of the Sea (1994) *The Law of the Sea; Practice of States at the Time of Entry into Force of the United Nations Convention on the Law of the Sea*, New York: United Nations.

Van Dyke, J. M., Morgan, J. R. & Gurish, J. (1988) 'The Exclusive Economic Zone of the Northwestern Hawaiian Islands: When Do Uninhabited Islands Generate an EEZ?', 25 *San Diego Law Review*: 425–494.

van Overbeek, W. (1989) 'Article 121(3) LOSC in Mexican State Practice in the Pacific', 4 *International Journal of Estuarine and Coastal Law*: 252–267.

21
Effect of the Diaoyu/Senkaku Islands Dispute on Maritime Delimitation

Daniel J. Dzurek

The sovereignty dispute between Japan and China (including Taiwan) over the Diaoyu/Senkaku islands[1] at the eastern edge of the East China Sea involves 500-year-old claims, fisheries and potential offshore oil development. The countries appear to be treating the dispute differently, depending on which resource is in question. They have made modest progress in handling fishing near the islets, but have not advanced in permitting offshore oil exploration.

Sovereignty over the islets could affect 71,140 square kilometres (sq km) of surrounding continental shelf/exclusive economic zone (EEZ).[2] On 24 June 1998 a flotilla of five boats, manned by protesters from Hong Kong and Taiwan, challenged 50 Japanese Maritime Safety Agency (MSA) ships near the islands. The protesters were unable get closer than six km to one of the islets. During the ensuing chase, the Hong Kong vessel, named the 'Diaoyutai', sank; 25 passengers abandoned it without injury. Chinese protesters claimed that the vessel had been rammed by an MSA patrol boat. Japan reiterated that it was sovereign of the islands, denied any collision, and suggested that the boat had been scuttled. A People's Republic of China (PRC) foreign ministry spokesman said that the boat had been struck by a Japanese vessel, repeated China's sovereignty claim, and said that 'the Japanese side would be held responsible for the consequences' (Kyodo, 24 & 25 June 1998; Xinhua, 25 June 1998). Since Hong Kong is now completely controlled by Beijing, this recent challenge to Japanese control appears to bear the PRC's approval. The incident promises another round of protests and counterclaims over flyspecks that may or may not have any extended jurisdictional effect.

GEOGRAPHY

There are five small volcanic islands and three rocky outcroppings in the Diaoyu/Senkaku group. They have a total land area of some seven sq km. Most of the islets are clustered around the largest island, Diaoyu/Uotsuri, which covers roughly eight hectares and lies 170 km northeast of Taiwan and 410 km west of Okinawa. Huangwei Yu/Kobi-sho and Chiwei Yu/Akao-sho, two outlying islets, are respectively located 31 km and 108 km from Diaoyu/Uotsuri island (see Figure 1). None of the islets is inhabited. All the features lie within the

Borderlands Under Stress (M.A. Pratt and J.A. Brown (eds), ISBN 90-411-9790-7).
© Kluwer Law International, 2000.

200 metre (m) isobath, at the edge of the Asian geologic continental shelf. The Okinawa Trough, which is 2,270 m deep, lies seaward of the Diaoyu/Senkaku islands, separating them from the nearest undisputed Japanese islands.

PROGRESS ON FISHERIES

During May and June of 1996 the PRC and Japan ratified the 1982 UN Convention on the Law of the Sea and adopted legislation claiming EEZ jurisdiction out to a maximum of 200 nautical miles (nm) (370 km) from their respective baselines. The countries also delimited straight baselines (US Department of State, 1998; Dzurek, 1996).

Against this background, the island dispute became more salient. In 1996 members of the extremist Japan Youth Association landed on one of the disputed islets, built a solar-powered, aluminium lighthouse five metres high, and requested that the Japanese MSA designate it an official navigational signal. Eight years earlier, the group had set up a similar structure on the western shore of Diaoyu/Uotsuri island to reinforce Japan's sovereignty claim (*Sankei Shimbun*, 1996). Taiwanese and Hong Kong Chinese responded to the 1996 landing with demonstrations and flotillas of boats, which were intercepted by Japanese MSA vessels. One Hong Kong activist died near the islands on 26 September 1996 when he attempted to swim from the protest boats to an islet. On 7 October protesters briefly landed on Diaoyu/Uotsuri island and raised the PRC and Republic of China (ROC) flags, which were later removed by the Japanese. Diplomatic protests were lodged. Japan claimed that it could not act against the lighthouse because it was built on private land, but Foreign Minister Ikeda met with his Chinese counterpart and told him that Japan had no plans to recognise the lighthouse. Chinese Premier Li warned Japan about provoking China but all the concerned governments began to caution protesters and call for calm (Kyodo, 26 September 1996; *Washington Post*, 1996b). 'Private' negotiations between Tokyo and Taipei to permit Taiwanese fishermen to fish outside the 12 nm territorial sea of the disputed islands failed to progress, but the sides agreed to meet again (*Chung-kuo Shih-pao*, 1996).

There was progress on regulating fishing during 1997. The PRC and Japan resumed working-level (deputy foreign minister) discussions. During March 1997 Foreign Minister Ikeda visited Beijing, where he agreed to defer formal delimitation of an EEZ boundary, which had foundered on the island disputes, consented to setting interim fishing limits, and promised to restrain Japanese ultra-nationalists from causing trouble in the islands (Kyodo, 29 March 1997; *Tokyo Shimbun*, 1997). On 6 May a Japanese Diet member briefly visited Diaoyu/Uotsuri island. Prime Minister Hashimoto called the action regrettable. The PRC and ROC foreign ministries complained. The MSA dispatched patrol boats to intercept a planned Chinese protest flotilla but the government on Taiwan pressed the protesters to abandon the attempt.[3] On 26 May, the day when Taiwan released a white paper on the

Diaoyu/Senkaku dispute, Japan's MSA deployed 60 ships to prevent Chinese protesters from landing on the islets, and detained two Hong Kong activists. Nonetheless, the MSA permitted three members of the extremist Japan Youth Association to land on the islets on 13 June, despite calls by the private owners of the island to stop the group from trespassing. However, the 20 June talks between Beijing and Tokyo remained on schedule, and the ROC foreign ministry announced that the third round of fisheries negotiations with Japan would be held later that year.[4]

In July 1997 President Li Teng-hui announced that Japan had agreed to permit Taiwanese boats to exercise traditional fishing rights in waters near the disputed islands. He explained that the traditional rights referred to a triangular zone between Taiwan, the Diaoyu islands and Yona island, which was delimited in a 1930s accord. Three days later a Japanese spokesman denied that an accord had been reached and said that negotiators had refrained from defining the 'traditional fishing grounds' until a formal accord could be agreed (Kyodo, 7 July 1997; *Chung-Kuo Shih-Pao*, 1997).

During Premier Li Peng's visit to Tokyo on 11 November 1997 the countries signed a provisional fisheries agreement for the East China Sea. China and Japan agreed jointly to manage the area between 30°40'N and 27°N that lies beyond 52 nm (96 km) from their respective shores (Figure 2). They agreed to set fishing quotas within the zone and maintain current fishing south of 27°N in the vicinity of the disputed Diaoyu/Senkaku islands (Kyodo, 3 September & 11 November 1997; NHK General Television Network, 1997). The reported zone limits correspond roughly to the latitudes of tripoints with South Korea in the north and with Taiwan in the south. However, the zone extends about 110 km into the area potentially affected by an equidistant line that gives full effect to the Diaoyu/Senkaku islands. The fisheries boundary implicitly recognises Taiwanese jurisdiction in the southern East China Sea but it seems to ignore the disputed islands. However, Taiwan stated that it would not 'accept the fisheries accord sealed between Tokyo and Beijing that might infringe upon its sovereignty or damage the rights of its fishermen' (Taiwan Central News Agency WWW, 12 November 1997). In apparently discounting the Diaoyu/Senkaku islands, the PRC and Japan may have followed the lead of the United Kingdom, which revised its extended fisheries zone to disregard Rockall during July of that year (IBRU, 1997).

OFFSHORE OIL

Despite progress in addressing fishing issues near the islands, the claimants have made no headway in resolving offshore oil exploration issues. Chinese survey vessels continue to probe the nearby areas. Japan periodically renews its sovereignty claim (Kyodo, 28 April & 24 June 1998; *Sankei Shimbun*, 1998). In early June 1998 the PRC began exploiting the Pinghu oil field from a newly established rig in the central East China Sea. Although the rig is on China's side of a hypothetical median line, it shows that the quest for offshore deposits is reaching farther from shore. Without settled boundaries, the potential for conflict will increase near the islets.

Oil had intensified the Diaoyu/Senkaku islands dispute in 1970, following a 1968 United Nations Economic Commission for Asia and the Far East report suggesting petroleum deposits under the East China Sea. The law of the sea at that time emphasised natural prolongation in determining continental shelf jurisdiction. Ownership of the Diaoyu/Senkaku islands would permit Japan to bridge the Okinawa Trough and have secure basepoints from which to claim mainland shelf area. When Taiwan and Japan began offshore leasing, their island sovereignty dispute and related overlapping claims became obvious. In September 1970 protesters planted the Taiwanese flag on one of the disputed islets. The 1971 Japan–US Ryukyu Islands Reversion Agreement triggered protests by the PRC (Lee, 1987; Li, 1975: 143–47).

HISTORY OF THE CLAIMS

Japan alleges that it discovered the Senkaku islands and incorporated them in 1895, when they were *terra nullius* (unclaimed). It maintains that the incorporation met with no Chinese protest. (The two countries were at war at the time.) Tokyo says the islets were always treated as part of Okinawa and not transferred under the Treaty of Shimonoseki, as China claims. Japan cites development activities in the islands by its nationals from 1897 until the Second World War, and American administration under Article 3 of the 1951 Japanese Peace Treaty signed in San Francisco (hereafter referred to as the San Francisco Treaty). It views the 1971 Ryukyu reversion agreement with the United States as validating its sovereignty (Okuhara, 1971; Ragland, 1973; Prescott, 1992: 31–32).

The PRC and ROC claim that the Chinese discovered the islands in 1372 and subsequently used them as navigational aids. The islands were incorporated into China's maritime defences in 1556. They also cite usage by Taiwanese fishermen and an 1893 imperial edict of the Dowager Empress that awarded Diaoyu Dao, Huangwei Yu, and Chi(wei) Yu to a Chinese pharmacist who had gathered rare medical herbs on the islands. China contends that the islets were transferred to Japan by the Treaty of Shimonoseki, which ended the 1894–95 Sino–Japanese War, and that they should have been returned after the Second World War, under the provisions of the 1943 Cairo Declaration, 1945 Potsdam Proclamation, and Article 2 of the San Francisco Treaty.[5]

None of the claimants disputes the fact that Japan exercised control of the Diaoyu/Senkaku islands from 1895 until the Second World War. They differ on whether the islets were free for the taking in 1895, how Japan obtained control in that year, whether the islands were traditionally associated with Taiwan or Okinawa, and the implications of various peace treaties and the 1971 Ryukyu reversion agreement.

In 1971 Japan and the US signed an agreement returning the Ryukyu (Okinawa) and Daito islands to Japanese administration. All of the disputed Diaoyu/Senkaku islands are within the polygon delimiting the returned islands, the coordinates of which were listed in the Agreed Minutes that were appended to the 1971 agreement.[6] Diaoyu/Uotsuri island is 33 km within the western limit of the polygon. During Senate ratification of the agreement, the US specified that the agreement did not affect the determination of sovereignty over disputed islands (US Senate, 1971). The US government continues to take no position on the sovereignty of the Diaoyu/Senkaku islands.

It is clear that the US administered the Diaoyu/Senkaku islands with the Okinawan islands under Article 3 of the San Francisco Treaty and transferred the islets to Japanese administration in the 1971 agreement. However, these provisions were not predicated on the transfer of sovereignty. It was in Article 2, not Article 3, of the 1951 San Francisco Treaty that Japan renounced rights to various areas, including Formosa (Taiwan). The reversion agreement cited Article 3. Therefore, the US action restored the Diaoyu/Senkaku islands to the administrative status they held before the war.[7] Although the US agreement with Japan cannot be viewed as changing the true sovereignty of the disputed islets, the American inclusion of the islets in a geographic definition of the Ryukyu islands clearly supports Japan's contention that these were associated with Okinawa (Li, 1975: 151).

Other documents which might be relevant lack detail that would clarify the islets' status. The 1895 Treaty of Shimonoseki mentioned the 'Island of Formosa together with all Islands appertaining or belonging to the said Island of Formosa'. The 1951 San Francisco Treaty included a renunciation of all Japanese rights, title and claim to 'Formosa and the Pescadores' in Article 2. However, neither the ROC nor the PRC took part in the San Francisco conference and neither signed the treaty. The 1952 Treaty of Peace between the Republic of China and Japan cited Article 2 of the 1951 San Francisco Treaty and reiterated that 'Japan has renounced all right, title and claim to Taiwan (Formosa) and Penghu (the Pescadores) as well as the Spratly Islands and the Paracel Islands'. It also recognised that 'all treaties, conventions and agreements concluded before December 9, 1941, between China and Japan have become null and void as a consequence of the war'. The 1972 Joint Communique between the PRC and Japan mentioned that Japan 'adheres to its stand of complying with Article 8 of the Potsdam Proclamation'. The 1978 Treaty of Peace and Friendship between the PRC and Japan merely confirms the Joint Communique. Perhaps it is understandable that the Diaoyu/Senkaku islands were not separately cited in early documents. They are minuscule and have never been inhabited; they had little value until offshore oil exploration began in the 1970s. But one might have expected the issue to be addressed in agreements from that period.

US DEFENSE COMMITMENTS IN THE DIAOYU/SENKAKU DISPUTE

The Japan–US security pact clearly applies to the Senkaku/Diaoyu islands. The US defense pact with Japan is crafted to cover areas *administered* by Japan. No doubt, this was a clever American attempt to exclude the Northern Territories/ Kuril islands from the agreement because they are administered by Russia. It also excludes Liancourt Rocks (Tokdo/Takeshima), which are claimed by Japan but controlled by the Republic of Korea. Although the US takes no position on the question of sovereignty over the Diaoyu/Senkaku islands, it returned those islands to Japanese administration in the 1971 Ryukyu reversion agreement. Thus, the disputed islands fall within the area covered by the defense pact. However, the pact only obligates the US to 'act to meet the common danger in accordance with its constitutional provisions and processes' and to report to the UN Security Council in the event of a threat. America is not committed automatically to 'defend the islands in case of emergency', as foreign ministry official Masaki Orita told the Committee on Foreign Affairs of the Japanese House of Councillors in 1996 (*Tokyo Shimbun*, 1996). However, the question has never been explicitly addressed. Is the US obligated to aid Japanese forces on or near the disputed islands if they are attacked by forces from mainland China or Taiwan?

Confusion about where US defense commitments apply could lead to serious miscalculations by countries claiming disputed Asian islands. Japan could become unwarrantedly provocative if it believed that it had American backing. The other claimants could underestimate a US response. There are times in international relations when ambiguity serves the interests of peace and security. This is not the case with mutual defense treaties. The peoples of America and Japan deserve clarity about what and where they are pledged to defend.

PROGNOSIS

After the initial rush for offshore oil, the claimants to the Diaoyu/Senkaku islands reached a *modus vivendi* which shelved the sovereignty issue until recently. There have been occasional flare-ups, such as when the PRC listed the islands in its 1992 territorial sea law, but the sides have foregone some provocative opportunities. Japan did not include the islands in its straight baseline claim. In the recently promulgated EEZ legislation of the PRC and Japan they did not delimit the zones' outer limits and they coupled the new laws with calls for negotiating boundaries in overlapping areas. The June 1998 fishing agreements may reduce tensions in that sector but the incident with the protest vessels during the same month indicates that the sovereignty issue will continue to fester and may inhibit full exploitation of offshore resources, especially oil.

International law gives ambiguous guidance on many unanswered questions about the Diaoyu/Senkaku islands dispute. How does one resolve questions of intertemporal law? Can claims of sovereignty based in fourteenth century Asia be judged by norms developed in Europe centuries later? What is the nature of discovery and occupation for uninhabited islands? What is the critical date when the dispute crystallised? Were the Diaoyu/Senkaku islands part of Taiwan or of Okinawa before 1895? How does one interpret ambiguous treaties? Finally, how will the disputed islands affect maritime jurisdiction? Even if ownership of the islets is settled, is that sovereign entitled to claim an EEZ or continental shelf from islands that have never been inhabited and seem to have no economic life? The 1982 UN Convention on the Law of the Sea would appear to say no but several countries claim extended jurisdiction from such features.[8]

The sovereignty issue seems nearly insoluble, in part because it is linked to the status of Taiwan which claims the islets and is nearest to them. The most practical approach to easing offshore resource use in the East China Sea may be to discount the jurisdictional effect of the disputed islands. In their recent interim fisheries agreement the PRC and Japan appear to be doing just that. If the trend of ignoring small islets continues in maritime delimitation, the Diaoyu/Senkaku islands dispute and many others may be diffused. Ultimately, the legal niceties are less important that the political will and motives of the claimants. If they really want the oil and fish, they will find some way to reach an accommodation.

NOTES

1   Japan calls the islands Sento Shosho or Senkaku Retto. The People's Republic of China terms them the Diaoyu Tai, and the Republic of China renders the same Chinese characters (meaning 'platform where one fishes with a hook') in a different romanisation system as Tiao Yu T'ai.

2   Measured by the author as constructed on US NIMA nautical chart 94016, 2nd edn. (23 September 1995), scale 1:1,000,000. The estimated uncertainty is 68 sq km.

3   AFP, 28 April & 13 May 1997; AP, 6 May 1998; Reuters, 6 May 1998; Xinhua, 6 May 1998.

4   AFP, 26 May 1997; AP, 13 June 1997; Kyodo, 10 June 1997; Taiwan Central News Agency WWW, 26 & 27 May 1997; Reuters, 26 May 1997.

5   Xinhua, 18 October 1996; Tao Cheng, 1973–74; Li, 1975; *Zongguo Tongxun She*, 1996; *Wen Wei Po*, 1996.

6   'The territories defined in paragraph 2 of Article I [of the Reversion Agreement] are the territories under the administration of the United States of America under Article 3 of the Treaty of Peace with Japan, and are, as designated under Civil Administration Proclamation Number 27 of December 25, 1953, all of those islands, islets, atolls and rocks situated in an area bounded by the straight lines connecting the following coordinates in the listed order.' The Minutes continue with a table listing the following points: (28°N, 124°40'E), (24°N, 122°E), (24°N, 133°E), (27°N, 131°50'E), (27°N, 128°18'E), (28°N, 128°18'E) and (28°N, 124°40'E), as found in *UN Treaties and Other International Agreements* (1972).

7   See Marcelo G. Kohen, 'Is the Notion of Territorial Sovereignty Obsolete?' elsewhere in this volume for a discussion of the transfer of control versus the transfer of sovereignty.

8   See Alex Oude Elferink, 'Is it Either Necessary or Possible to Clarify the Provision on Rocks of Article 121(3) of the Law of the Sea Convention?' elsewhere in this volume for a detailed discussion of the island versus rock issue.

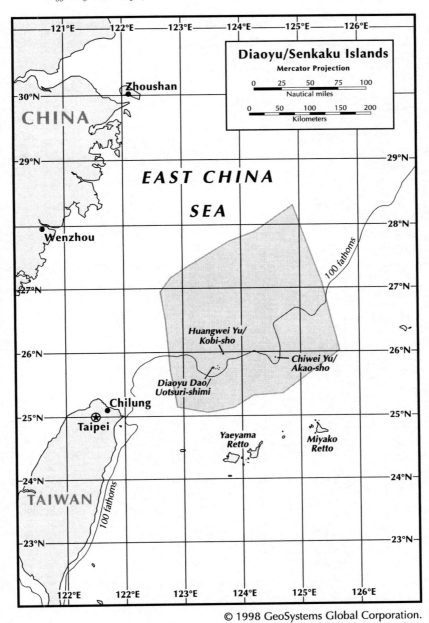

© 1998 GeoSystems Global Corporation.

Figure 1: The location of the Diaoyu/Senkaku islands and the area over which they give rise to maritime jurisdiction.

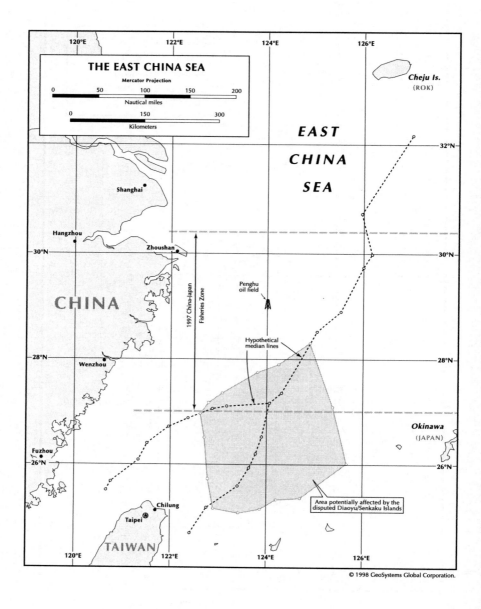

Figure 2: The 1997 China–Japan joint fishing zone and hypothetical median lines in the east China Sea.

BIBLIOGRAPHY

AFP (Agence France Presse) news service.

AP (Associated Press) news service.

Cheng, T. (1973–74) 'The Sino-Japanese Dispute Over the Tiao-yu-tai (Senkaku) Islands and the Law of Territorial Acquisition', *Virginia Journal of International Law* 14: 248–60.

China and Japan, Treaty of Shimonoseki. Peace Treaty between the Emperor of Japan and the Emperor of China. Shimonoseki, 17 April 1895. Israel, F. L. (ed.) (1967) *Major Peace Treaties of Modern History*, New York: Chelsea House, Vol. 2: 1101–07.

China, People's Republic of, and Japan. Joint Communique between the People's Republic of China and Japan. Peking, 29 September 1972. Israel, F. L. (ed.) (1980) *Major Peace Treaties of Modern History*, New York: Chelsea House, Vol. 5: 373–378.

China, Republic of, and Japan. Treaty of Peace between the Republic of China and Japan. Signed at Taipei, on 28 April 1952. *United Nations Treaty Series* 138 (1952): 38–48.

Chung-Kuo Shih-Pao (1996) (Taipei), 'Special Dispatch', 6 October: 2, translated in *Daily Report: China* (1996) 10 October.

Chung-Kuo Shih-Pao (1997) (Taipei) 5 July: 4, translated in US Foreign Broadcast Information Service (FBIS), FBIS-CHI-97-190.

Dzurek, D. J. (1996) 'The People's Republic of China Straight Baseline Claim', *IBRU Boundary and Security Bulletin* 4 (Summer): 77–89.

IBRU (1997) *Boundary and Security Bulletin* Vol. 5 No. 3: 52–54.

Japan and United States. Agreement between the United States of America and Japan Concerning the Ryukyu Islands and the Diato Islands. *United States Treaties and Other International Agreements* (1972), Washington, DC: Government Printing Office, Vol. 23, Part 1: 447–81 [TIAS 7314].

Japan and United States. Treaty of Mutual Cooperation and Security. *United States Treaties and Other International Agreements* (1960), Washington, DC: Government Printing Office, Vol. 11, Part 2: 1632–35 [TIAS 4509].

Japan. Japanese Peace Treaty. San Francisco, 8 September 1951. Israel, F. L. (1980) (ed.) *Major Peace Treaties of Modern History*, New York: Chelsea House, Vol. 4: 2641–56.

Kyodo (Tokyo) news service.

Lee, W. (1987) 'Troubles under the Water: Sino–Japanese Conflict of Sovereignty on the Continental Shelf in the East China Sea', *Ocean Development and International Law* 18: 586.

Li, V. H. (1975) 'China and Off-Shore Oil: The Tiao-yü Tai Dispute', *Stanford Journal of International Studies* 10 (Spring).

NHK General Television Network (1997) (Tokyo) broadcast 3 September, translated in FBIS-EAS-97-246.

Okuhara, T. (1971) 'The Territorial Sovereignty over the Senkaku Islands and

Problems on the Surrounding Continental Shelf', *Japanese Annual of International Law* 15: 97–102.

Prescott, J. R. V. (1992) 'Maritime Jurisdiction' in Morgan, J. & Valencia, M. J. (eds.) *Atlas for Marine Policy in East Asian Seas*, Berkeley: University of California Press: 25–35.

Ragland, T. R. (1973) 'A Harbinger: The Senkaku Islands', *San Diego Law Review* 10 (May): 668–69.

Reuters news service.

Sankei Shimbun (1996) Tokyo, 17 July: 1, translated in FBIS (1996) *Daily Report: East Asia*, 19 July.

Sankei Shimbun (1998) Tokyo, 17 June: 1, translated in FBIS-EAS-98-175.

Taiwan Central News Agency WWW.

Tao Cheng, 1973–74.

Tokyo Shimbun (1996) 13 December.

Tokyo Shimbun (1997) 16 March: 2, translated in FBIS-EAS-97-076.

UN Treaties and Other International Agreements (1972) Vol. 23, Part 1: 475.

US Department of State (1998), Bureau of Oceans and International Environmental and Scientific Affairs. *Straight Baseline and Territorial Sea Claims: Japan*, Limits in the Seas No. 120. Washington, DC: US Department of State.

US Senate (1971) *Hearings on the Okinawa Reversion Treaty before the Senate Committee on Foreign Relations*. 92nd Congress, 1st Session.

Washington Post (1996a) 'Protester Dies in Defense of Disputed Asian Islands', 27 September: A32.

Washington Post (1996b) 'Premier of China Joins Fray', 1 October: A15.

Wen Wei Po (1996) (Hong Kong) 'China Will Never Yield an Inch of Territory', 12 September: A2, translated in FBIS *China* (1996) 16 September.

Xinhua news service.

Zongguo Tongxun She (1996) (Hong Kong) broadcast, 'Japan Cannot Claim Sovereignty over Diaoyu Islands by Citing the "Preemption" Principle', 12 September, translated in FBIS *Daily Report: China* (1996) 17 September.

22
The Spratly Dispute and Southeast Asian Security: Towards a Pluralist Regional Order?

Liselotte Odgaard

> The large area north-westward of the recommended track ... is known to abound with dangers. No systematic surveys have been carried out and the existence of unchartered patches of coral and shoals is likely; the positions of the charted banks and shoals cannot be relied upon. Vessels are warned not to attempt to pass through this area.
>
> (B[ritish] A[dmiralty] 967, November 1985,
> quoted in Hancox & Prescott, 1995: 43)

The British Admiralty's description of 'Dangerous Ground', a term often applied to the Spratlys, points out the uncertainty surrounding the physical geography of the area. This uncertainty as to what may lie in wait also surrounds the dispute between the People's Republic of China (PRC), the Republic of China (ROC),[1] Vietnam, the Philippines, Malaysia and Brunei over this collection of ragged features and its adjacent maritime space. The contending states seem to be oscillating between a strategy of occupation and negotiation. This pattern of behaviour enhances the unpredictability and insecurity characterising the regional environment in Southeast Asia at present. However, the intractability of the dispute also urges the states to come up with alternative instruments in order to prevent the dispute from producing threats towards their own survival. This combination of insecurity and innovation displayed in the Spratly dispute reflects the central issues of security and order which the region's states are facing towards the end of the millennium.

This paper argues that the Spratly dispute brings together the power-political foreign policy tradition of the PRC and the practice of interstate dialogue and cooperation developed in maritime Southeast Asia.[2] Through the meeting between these two practices, a framework for a new security order is unfolding. The germs of this order emerge out of the complex disagreement over sovereignty and boundaries in the Spratly dispute.

In the post-Cold War era, the PRC is trying to establish itself as a Southeast Asian power. With the end of the Cold War, many of the distortions in the PRC's relations with the Southeast Asian region have been removed. The PRC-backed communist insurgency, the 'overseas Chinese problem', the abnormal relations between the PRC and Indonesia, and the Cold War between the PRC and

Borderlands Under Stress (M.A. Pratt and J.A. Brown (eds), ISBN 90-411-9790-7).
© Kluwer Law International, 2000.

Vietnam are largely historical issues (Wah, 1993: 16). These barriers to a closer relationship between the PRC and Southeast Asia have been replaced by a gradual rapprochement, as witnessed by the PRC's participation in the Cambodian conflict-resolution process, its contribution to the International Monetary Fund (IMF) bail-out of Thailand and Indonesia, and the interests the two parties share in resisting western human-rights pressures. However, the PRC has also emerged as an increasing security concern for Southeast Asia as it proceeds with its plans to build a blue-water navy and changes its security focus from a north-bound continental perspective into a south-bound maritime perspective.

The change in Southeast Asia's strategic environment, which the PRC's advancement into the region produces, leads to a confrontation between the power-political tradition of the PRC and the tradition of interstate dialogue and cooperation which has developed in maritime Southeast Asia within the Association of Southeast Asian Nations (ASEAN), and is now spreading in continental Southeast Asia through the expansion of ASEAN. The power-political foreign policy tradition of the PRC may be summed up as the tendency to use military, economic and diplomatic capabilities to enhance the individual state's relative power *vis-à-vis* other states – for example, by giving priority to national defence rather than international security cooperation, by concentrating on bilateral interstate relations rather than multilateral conference diplomacy, and by conducting foreign policy according to national conceptions of justice rather than internationally-agreed rules. In contrast, the ASEAN tradition of dialogue and cooperation may be summed up as the tendency to restrain the use of force to protect the interests of a collectivity of states, to establish inclusive, integrative organisations designed to solve common problems, and to form common conceptions of justice as the basis of their foreign policies. The Spratly dispute reflects and affects the evolving patterns of state interaction which this clash of security practices produces by virtue of its role as an arena for the display and testing of their viability as a basis of Southeast Asian order in the post-Cold War era. Through this process, a third pluralist alternative is emerging which combines a structure of power balancing based on deterrence with a practice of limited interstate dialogue and cooperation to contain crises. This pluralist order allows the states to retain individual identities while also developing a sense of common destiny (Almonte, 1997–98: 90).

This paper comprises three sections. The first section looks at the strategic issues arising from the policy of effective occupation in the Spratlys. It is argued that the military tension produced by the competition for control of the Spratlys points to the need for a structure of power balancing which constrains power projection in the region. The second section looks at the diplomatic issues arising from the need for interstate cooperation to develop the resources in the area. It is argued that the differing views on the desirability of institutionalised interstate dialogue have resulted in the establishment of an informal dialogue. The most important result of this process has been recognition of actual differences of opinion concerning the dispute. The third section looks at the issues of justice which arise from the rudimentary political framework that currently characterises the relationship between the PRC and Southeast Asia. It is argued that the contradictory conceptions of international justice which come to the fore in the states' advancement of their individual claims highlight the need for the establishment of a code of conduct which defines a common conception of justice to which all states in the region have given their positive consent.

THE POLICY OF EFFECTIVE OCCUPATION AND REGIONAL GOVERNANCE

The Spratly islands constitute largely uninhabitable territory. Therefore, it is not immediately obvious why so many states consider possession of these features an important asset. Apart from the possible use of the islands as bases in a forward defence structure, it is not so much the territory itself as control of its surrounding maritime space which makes the Spratlys a potentially valuable asset. One alleged benefit is the influence on the sealanes to the west of the Spratlys which may follow from possession of the islands. These sealanes link the Indian and Pacific Oceans and form vital lines of communication and transport (Smith Jr, 1994: 276). Moreover, the sea contains large resources of fish (McManus, 1994), and unknown quantities of oil, gas and mineral deposits are located on and under the seabed (Valencia, 1985: 78–89; Salameh, 1995–96).

How is control of the Spratlys and the surrounding maritime space obtained? Jurisdiction over maritime space is regulated by the United Nations Convention on the Law of the Sea (UNCLOS). However, UNCLOS operates on the premise that a particular state has undisputed title over the territory from which the maritime zone is claimed (Smith & Thomas, 1997: 9). This leaves us with the question of how territorial sovereignty is obtained. Sovereignty over territory means the right to exercise therein, to the exclusion of any other state, the functions of a state (*The Island of Palmas* case, 1928). Sovereignty does not give any moral directions as to which state's freedom is to be preferred (Koskenniemi, 1990: 18). Territorial sovereignty therefore merely requires that the state continuously demonstrates the ability to administer the territory. This definition has invited the claimant states in the Spratly dispute to embark on a policy of effective occupation.

An omission which paved the way for the competition to effectively occupy the islands in the post-war years was the failure to settle the sovereignty issue over the Spratlys subsequent to the Japanese troop withdrawal in 1945 after six years of occupation (Samuels, 1982: 63–66, 77–81). Until the early 1970s, claims to the Spratlys were mainly presented as official statements and declarations, apart from the ROC's occupation of Itu Aba from 1945 to 1950, and again from 1956 onwards. In 1971 the Philippines began an official policy of effective occupation, and the Republic of Vietnam sent troops into the Spratlys in 1973. Malaysia joined the scramble in 1983 with its occupation of Swallow Reef, and the PRC occupied features from 1988. Brunei is the only claimant state not to have occupied any features in the Spratlys.

The policy of armed occupation undertaken in the course of the 1970s and 1980s portended the possibility of military confrontation. The most serious incidence occurred in 1988, when the PRC and Vietnam fought a brief naval battle which demonstrated the former's military superiority (Chang Pao-Min, 1990: 25–29). Since then, low-intensity confrontation in the form of arrest and detention of fishermen and the occasional opening of fire have become recurring features of the Spratly dispute. The PRC's acquisition of Philippine-claimed Mischief Reef in 1995 represented a new turning-point in the competition for occupation because the action indicated that maritime Southeast Asia was no longer insulated from Chinese power projection. The Philippines returned the provocation in 1997, when it landed civilians and military personnel on Scarborough Reef (*The Economist*, 1997). Such actions set a dangerous precedent, for whereas Southeast Asian skirmishes may be restrained by the practice of non-use of force, no such practice of self-restraint has yet been worked out between the PRC and Southeast Asia.

The course of the Spratly dispute from official statements to militarised occupation and later instances of military confrontation can be interpreted as a very slow escalation of the dispute over the years from diplomatic confrontation to a situation where the use of force between the claimant states cannot be ruled out. Confrontation between the states of Southeast Asia has mainly occurred in the form of arrest and detention of fishers. Consequently, these contenders have maintained hostile incidents at a low level of intensity. This behaviour is in line with the traditional focus of maritime Southeast Asia on internal consolidation rather than the protection of external frontiers. Intra-regional strife was effectively circumscribed by the establishment of ASEAN in 1967, through which a policy of non-interference in the domestic affairs of neighbouring states was developed (Frost, 1990). This practice has ensured that disputes among the member states do not spill over into military conflict. Consequently, there is no tradition of using force for the purposes of dispute settlement.

While all of continental Southeast Asia has begun to embrace the ASEAN doctrine of non-interference, the PRC does not complement its entrance into Southeast Asia with subscription to the region's security arrangements. The direct challenges to the territorial possessions of other states which the PRC has posed in the Spratlys may therefore be interpreted as a continuation of the PRC's willingness to use force to settle intractable disputes in the post-war era. For example, it fought border skirmishes with India in 1962 and with the Soviet Union in 1969, and Vietnam lost the Paracels in the northwestern part of the South China Sea to the PRC in 1974. The nationalist rhetoric which surrounds the PRC's policy on the Spratlys leaves the impression that the PRC is determined to defend by the use of force these islands which it sees as yet another national gate to be protected against hostile enemies (*Daily Report China*, 1994).

The PRC's willingness to use force to protect its external borders may not be founded so much in expansionary dreams as it is in the pre- and post-communist Chinese preoccupation with safeguarding the nation's territorial integrity in the face of recurring threats of foreign invasion. However, such defensive motives do not alter the fact that the PRC's and Southeast Asia's first lines of defence overlap in the Spratlys. In the face of the PRC's traditional willingness to use force to settle disputes, the Southeast Asian states take the view that the prospect of large-scale violence in the area cannot be ruled out (*The Jakarta Post*, 1995).

The unpredictability which surrounds the PRC's intentions points to the need for the establishment of a governance structure which restricts power projection. A governance structure implies that the powers deliberately contrive the balance of power and restrict the use of war, with a view to maintaining regional stability and peace. The governance structure which is taking shape in Southeast Asia in the post-Cold War era combines deterrence with a policy of reassurance.

Deterrence is directed at the intentions of opponents: if the forces of the deterrer are estimated to prevent the opponent from achieving gains through aggression, the opponent will refrain from attack (Snyder, 1961). The United States (US) is one of the central pillars in the emerging Southeast Asian deterrence structure, since it has maintained its military presence in the area. However, there are strict limits to the military guarantees the US extends to Southeast Asia. The US is attempting to become a regional book-end power, meaning that it is only prepared to intervene insofar as global peace and stability and US national interests are threatened by regional developments. Thus, the US is willing to act as a military balancer but is not prepared to become entangled in local conflicts such as the Spratly dispute. The US reaction to the PRC's occupation of Philippine-claimed Mischief Reef illustrates this policy. The US administration stated that freedom of passage was a fundamental interest of the US (Shelly, 1995), but it refrained from giving the Philippines military assistance. So long as freedom of navigation and overflight is maintained in the South China Sea, the US is unlikely to interfere directly in the Spratly dispute (Lord, 1996).

However, because the primary object of US regional military balancing is the PRC, the US does look to the PRC's Spratly policy as an indication of its possible bid for regional hegemony. The PRC's gradual move forward into the area, combined with a military modernisation programme which may support a forward military presence in the Spratlys, are worrying developments. Although the PRC at present does not have the resources to project a major conventional force beyond its territory, its acquisitions in the 1990s of fighter aircraft, submarines, destroyers and satellite technology indicate that it is slowly but steadily advancing towards its goal of becoming a major maritime power (*The Military Balance 1997/98*, 1997; *Far Eastern Economic Review*, 1998b; Snyder, 1996–7: 149–150).

As a response to the PRC's gradual move into the South China Sea, the US and the small and medium powers of Southeast Asia are drawing closer together. For example, Malaysia, Indonesia and Singapore allow access to the US navy and airforce, the Philippines, Brunei and Thailand have offered the US increased military cooperation, the bilateral defence agreements between the US and the Philippines and Thailand have been maintained, and Vietnam and the US have discussed the establishment of defence cooperation (Dibb, 1997;

Freeman, 1997; Dobson & Fravel, 1997: 262–263; Findlay, 1994: 131). In addition, the countries have embarked on modernisation of their navies and airforces. These efforts have come to a temporary standstill because of the economic crisis in the region, a situation which makes the states more dependent on defence cooperation with the US (*Far Eastern Economic Review*, 1998a).

The pattern of military collaboration and weapons acquisitions indicates that a structure of deterrence is emerging in Southeast Asia. The US forward military presence is central to this structure as it shields the local powers from direct confrontation with each other. However, currently the strategic situation is imbalanced to the disadvantage of the PRC, a fact which threatens to isolate it. In view of the PRC's historical preoccupation with threats of foreign occupation, this is a dangerous development. To guard against this tendency there is a need to supplement the structure of deterrence with a policy of reassurance between the regional powers. The US has taken steps towards a rapprochement with the PRC under the heading of the doctrine of preventive defence, which implies regular discussions on strategic thinking and defence (Perry, 1996). The PRC acknowledges the need for the establishment of a constructive strategic partnership between itself and the US and has agreed to high-level exchange between the military structures of the two states. The emerging collaboration between the US and the PRC has been strengthened by the much warmer relationship produced by the state visits of PRC President Jiang Zemin and US President Clinton in 1997 and 1998 (*Beijing Review*, 1998; *South China Morning Post*, 1997). The policy of reassurance arising from the tendency of the two great powers to put aside their differences may promote a level of confidence between them sufficient to rule out their use of force towards each other.

Between the PRC and the small and medium powers of Southeast Asia a similar need for a policy of reassurance has been recognised (Joint Statement, 1997). In 1995 the PRC and ASEAN established a political consultative system at the vice-ministerial level, in 1996 the PRC became a full dialogue partner of the ASEAN, and in 1997 the China–ASEAN Joint Cooperation Committee was set up. In view of the power differential between ASEAN and the PRC, what may be hoped for with these steps towards a consultative relationship is the establishment of Chinese primacy, which implies that the use of force or the threat of force is ruled out and, as a general rule, the independence, equality and sovereignty of the lesser powers is respected (Bull, 1977: 214–215).

As yet the policies of reassurance are in their early stages. Therefore, it remains to be seen whether a governance structure which controls power projection will be established in Southeast Asia. Insofar as such a structure emerges, it is likely to be rudimentary. The ideological and political differences between the US and the PRC, and the military and economic power differentials between the PRC and Southeast Asia are too great to allow for any structure resembling a concert or a condominium. Instead, a structure of deterrence combined with regular consultation to prevent military power projection from threatening regional stability and peace is likely to develop. While such a structure may prevent the outbreak of war, it does not ensure the development of institutionalised mechanisms which promote state cooperation on issues where it is needed to contain crises.

THE PROBLEM OF RESOURCE DEVELOPMENT AND INTERSTATE DIALOGUE

Constraints on the use of force may prevent the outbreak of violent conflict over the Spratly dispute. However, such measures cannot ensure that the states may begin to develop the resources of the area. The inability of the states to reconcile their conflicting claims indicates that a model of cooperation which is based on the pooling of their resources might be the most feasible way to allow for resource utilisation without infringement of the alleged rights of the other claimants.

Insofar as the states choose to use UNCLOS despite the fact that it does not in principle apply due to the unresolved territorial dispute, provisions are available for interstate cooperation over the exercise of rights. Article 122 states that a semi-enclosed sea 'means a gulf, basin or sea surrounded by two or more States and connected to another sea or the ocean by a narrow outlet or consisting entirely or primarily of the territorial seas and exclusive economic zones of two or more coastal states' (United Nations, 1983: 39). It has been questioned whether the South China Sea may be termed a semi-enclosed sea, since the northern approaches arguably do not fit the requirement of a narrow outlet (Cordner, 1994: 71). Nevertheless, other authors seem to agree that the geographical features of the South China Sea justify calling it a semi-enclosed sea (Haller-Trost, 1990: 77; Valencia, 1995: 64; Djalal, 1997: 278). As such, it is covered by Article 123, which requires that the bordering states of a semi-enclosed sea 'should co-operate with each other in the exercise of their rights and in the performance of their duties under this Convention' (United Nations, 1983: 39). The provisions of UNCLOS suggest that cooperation is the most feasible way forward if the non-conflictual exercise of rights is to be brought about.

The idea of joint development appears to have attracted the most attention as a way of realising interstate cooperation concerning resource development (Valencia, 1995: 50–67). It implies that the claimant states shelve the sovereignty issue and cooperate on the joint development of resources in the disputed area. There are precedents for the application of such a model in Southeast Asia. For example, Malaysia has concluded agreements with Thailand as well as Vietnam on joint petroleum development, and Indonesia has signed an agreement with Australia on joint development in the Timor Gap (Townsend-Gault, 1997: 303–304). One attraction of the model appears to be that it allows states to postpone the resolution of sovereignty issues, the main bone of contention in the Spratly dispute. However, the application of the model requires a level of mutual confidence sufficient to ensure that neither party will reclaim its decision-making authority at a later date. At present, this precondition is not fulfilled.

The PRC has demanded recognition of its sovereignty over the South China Sea in principle, in return for its acceptance of a model of joint development (*Beijing Review*, 1992). This demand may be seen in the light of the PRC's history as a great power which has not been recognised as such on a par with the US and the Soviet Union. The PRC was not in the past able to exploit its preponderance in relation to its surroundings to the same extent as were the two primary powers of the Cold War. Consequently, it did not feel obliged to protect any state interests except its own. The PRC's foreign policy became an almost prototypical example of *realpolitik*: no eternal allies or perpetual enemies exist; only national interests are permanent (Chang, 1993: 158). With the disappearance of Soviet power projection, the PRC eyes a chance to enhance its political status. The status of a great power implies special rights as well as obligations. The PRC applies this concept to the South China Sea with its demand that the neighbour states must recognise its special rights in the area, even if it refrains from taking advantage of these rights in practice. Only then is the PRC prepared to make concessions by sharing the resources of the area with the other claimant states.

The PRC's demand for recognition of its special rights is not acceptable to the lesser powers involved in the dispute. It is recognised that the PRC is a great power and, therefore, a sustainable solution to the Spratly dispute cannot be found without its participation (Baginda, 1998). However, these states are not prepared to recognise Chinese sovereignty in principle, since such a concession would signal the reintroduction of discriminatory practices on a par with those exercised by western powers in the nineteenth and early twentieth centuries (Gong, 1984) or by the traditional Chinese empire (Fairbank, 1968). The small and medium powers of Southeast Asia demand recognition of their equal rights and obligations as states. If they cannot obtain recognition of their equal rights as states, they will not risk entering into a joint development agreement with the PRC.

The inability of the claimant states in the Spratly dispute to agree on a joint settlement makes it difficult to undertake resource development. Fishing fleets operate in the area but pay the price of recurring incidents of arrest and detention of fishermen and boats. The commercial value of the hydrocarbon resources in the Spratly area is uncertain. Furthermore, exploration requires a longer-term physical presence and the participation of foreign companies due to the cost and complexity involved. With an unsettled dispute adding to the difficulties, very little exploration has actually taken place (Snyder, 1996–7: 144–147). Only the Philippines, the PRC and Vietnam have attempted drilling in the area (Valencia, 1997: 52–53). To remove the obstacle to resource exploration and exploitation which the states' inability to cooperate represents, the need for an organisational framework through which interstate confidence may be brought about has been recognised.

An organisational framework here means the institutionalisation of interstate cooperation by means of diplomacy. The one which concerns the Spratly dispute is the result of a compromise between the practices of state interaction employed by the PRC and the ASEAN states.

A primary characteristic of the PRC's practice of state interaction is independence. This priority stems from the widely accepted belief within the country that foreign exploitation and influences have been the principal causes of the nation's poverty, social ills, demoralisation and loss of greatness. This attitude was pertinent in the PRC's foreign policy during the Cold War, when it alternated between support for the US and the Soviet Union without giving either of them a firm alliance commitment, apart from a brief interlude with the Soviet Union in the 1950s (Tow, 1994: 115–157).

The PRC's preference for an independent foreign policy includes a reluctance to make any long-term commitments which involve other states. In the dialogue on the South China Sea disputes, this has meant that the PRC is opposed to a formalised, multilateral dialogue. The PRC resists raising the dialogue to that level because it does not trust that its viewpoints and interests will be taken into account in an international environment from which it appears to be increasingly isolated. The PRC is not willing to risk entanglement in negotiations in which it expects to find itself in a minority position.

To break the barrier created by the PRC's resistance towards formal multilateral negotiations and establish an interstate dialogue, the Workshops on Managing Potential Conflicts in the South China Sea were initiated. The workshops were convened from 1990, and PRC participation began with the second workshop in 1991. They are informal gatherings which bring together researchers and government officials in their private capacities. The workshops take up a wide range of issues, such as legal matters and marine environmental protection. The aim is to establish a practice of cooperation which includes the PRC (Djalal, 1997: 276–277).

The concept of an informal dialogue has been criticised. As long as the level of informality is maintained, the workshops function as a forum for the exchange of viewpoints and discussion of ideas on how cooperation is brought about, but the states remain exempt from making binding commitments. Substantial negotiations require that the issue is brought up at the formal level, since only states can enter into authoritative agreements (Hamzah, 1998).

On the other hand, formal discussions do not necessarily indicate an improved dialogue. When officialdom takes over, great care must be taken to get the words right (Baginda, 1998). Therefore, formality requires that the parties have clarified their points of view to an extent sufficient to enable them to negotiate at a substantial level. The imprecision which surrounds exactly what cooperation in the Spratly area entails, and the continuation of border skirmishes in the seas indicate that the states have not yet developed a level of trust which would allow them to begin negotiations that will necessarily involve compromises on national interests.

The workshop process is not merely constrained by the PRC. The ASEAN practice, which may be described as non-confrontational and process-oriented, has likewise made its imprint on the discussions. The focus is on extensive consultation and consensus-building aiming at compromise. If a compromise cannot be reached, it is deferred to a later time (Caballero-Anthony, 1998: 57–60; Almonte, 1997–98: 81). This practice indicates that the positive aspects of a relationship are developed, whereas the negative aspects are not dwelled upon; instead, the parties move on to issues where some measure of common ground may be found. The ASEAN practice of state interaction is therefore reflected in the workshop process on the South China Sea. Most conspicuously, the conflicting sovereignty claims which lie at the heart of the Spratly dispute are presented, and then the debate stops. There is no discussion; the parties simply agree to disagree and then move on to the next issue. The danger of this approach is that issues of contention are left unanswered (Baginda, 1998). And when such conflictual issues give rise to serious foreign policy problems, no mechanisms for conflict resolution have been put in place. Thus, the situation may be allowed to deteriorate.

Nevertheless, the workshops have broken new ground in the relationship between the participating states, in that different points of view have been brought out into the open. In view of the fact that the workshops represent a beginning rather than an ending in the process of dispute resolution, it may be said that the most important outcome of the workshop process so far has been the will to recognise actual differences of opinion rather than ignore them. This ensures that the cooperative projects which the states might agree to put into practice are not based on false premises of unity.

So far cooperative initiatives are in the very early stages. Technical working groups have been established in areas such as marine scientific research and resource assessment and ways of development. Potential opportunities for cooperation on non-controversial issues have been addressed. For example, hydrographic data and information exchange have been discussed and a biodiversity training course has been held. However, in the main, the cooperative initiatives and proposals still await implementation.[3] The initiatives mentioned above indicate that the dialogue is centred less on the highly controversial security issues and more on the less contentious technical issues. This shift in focus is founded on the expectation that constructive interaction in the long run is a more effective way of preventing conflict than directly confronting the divisive issues of sovereignty and boundary delimitation. Whether this approach will prove fruitful remains to be seen.

However, one underlying condition needs to be fulfilled if a common practice of state interaction is to be developed which ensures regional peace and stability and allows for unrestrained development of the area's resources. The states must agree sufficiently on what constitutes international justice, so that they are able to define mutual limits of acceptable behaviour. The following section addresses the conceptions of justice applied by the PRC and Southeast Asia in the region.

THE PROBLEM OF INTERNATIONAL LAW AND A REGIONAL CODE OF CONDUCT

The protracted Spratly dispute has given rise to criticism of international law for not being able to provide solutions to disputes concerning uninhabited islands or rocks within unilaterally declared maritime zones (Haller-Trost, 1990: 78). Such criticism seems to miss the target. States are responsible for acting in accordance with international law (Manning, 1975: 106–108) but international law cannot be better than the political framework from which it derives its authority. In the relationship between the PRC and Southeast Asia, the political framework is rather weak. Consequently, instead of applying international law with the intention of finding a settlement which is acceptable to all, the states use whatever provisions they can find to promote their individual claims. Hence, the PRC (and the ROC) and Vietnam mainly use arguments of historic rights of discovery, effective occupation and recognition as justification for their claim to all of the Spratlys; the Philippines puts forward a host of arguments, including discovery, historical title, national security, indispensable need and abandonment; and Malaysia and Brunei use the continental shelf provision of the Law of the Sea. Moreover, the PRC, the ROC, Vietnam and the Philippines have incorporated the Spratlys into their provincial administrative systems (Haller-Trost, 1990; Roque Jr, 1997). By elevating their claims to national territory by law, the states indicate that they do not intend to compromise on their claims.

The individual justifications which the states continue to put forward in the Spratly dispute imply that they do not recognise their responsibility towards the general interests of the region. International law is not applied for the purpose of finding a solution which is acceptable to all, but is solely used to advance the individual interests of the claimant states. The fact that the social obligations of the region's states towards each other have been left undefined means that there is no joint commitment to apply international law with the intention of finding a settlement which is acceptable to all. To bring about such a commitment, there is a need for a regional code of conduct which stipulates the limits of acceptable behaviour. Such a set of overall guidelines would mean that the states had given their positive consent to a common definition of justice in their relations with one another, which they are obliged to follow in cases where their national interests can only be pursued at the cost of the common good of the region. The ASEAN states have recognised the need for a code of conduct. Their experience of the South China Sea disputes as a source of unpredictability and insecurity in their immediate environment has prompted them to recommend all parties concerned to establish a code of international conduct over the South China Sea (*ASEAN Declaration on the South China Sea*, 1992).

A code of conduct is a formal mechanism for conflict management. As such, it is not likely to be established until the states have worked out a practice of state interaction which is sufficiently stable that it may be elevated to the level of recognised principles. However, fragments of what may in future develop into a code of conduct have emerged. The 1997 Joint Statement of the Meeting of Heads of State/Government of the Member States of ASEAN and the President of the People's Republic of China suggests what such a future code of right and wrong conduct may consist of. Here the heads of state stated that the most fundamental norms guiding their relations would be respect for each other's independence, sovereignty and territorial integrity, and the principle of non-interference in the internal affairs of other states (*Joint Statement*, 1997).

The principle which both the PRC and the ASEAN states stress as the core element guiding their relations may be summarised as absolute sovereignty. There is nothing particularly new or sophisticated about this idea. Moreover, this principle has contributed to undermining regional peace and stability by inviting the states to undertake occupation before negotiation. Nevertheless, it has proven a valuable instrument for securing the survival of the fragile states which characterise the region.

Absolute sovereignty implies that no authority exists above the state which may oblige it to act in specific ways without its consent (Hinsley, 1986: 226). This principle formed the basis of both Chinese and Southeast Asian foreign policy during the Cold War. However, whereas the PRC has traditionally stressed the aspect which concerns the right to exercise freedom of action, Southeast Asia has stressed the obligation to respect the right of neighbouring states to do the same. The mutual commitment to both the right of independence and the obligation of non-interference is a tentative step towards mutual acceptance that both sides must be prepared to accommodate each other's conceptions of international justice.

Two central implications for the relationship between the PRC and the ASEAN states follow from this guideline. First, by confirming their mutual respect for each other's absolute sovereignty, they oblige each other not to encroach upon the individual state's right to control its internal affairs and be externally independent, whatever pending disagreements they may have. Thus, as a general rule the states are allowed to look after their national interests provided they do not pose a threat to the security of other states.[4] Secondly, the mutual commitment to absolute sovereignty implies that cooperation is not intended to be an all-encompassing feature of state interaction. Instead, cooperation is confined to specific issues where the alternative may be the prospect of violent conflict. The states may choose to enter into cooperative projects, such as joint development, which means that in practice they may have to shelve sovereignty issues. However, such arrangements are likely to be the exception to the fundamental rule that the states retain the right to be left alone.

Thus, the code of conduct which may be established will not represent a complete break with the old practices of state interaction adhered to by the PRC and Southeast Asia. Rather, it is likely to express the respect for the other parties' independence and integrity which is a precondition for establishing joint action between states who share no tradition of cooperation.

CONCLUSION: IS A PLURALIST REGIONAL ORDER EMERGING IN SOUTHEAST ASIA?

Initially this paper posed the question: is a pluralist regional order emerging concurrently with the PRC's positioning of itself as a Southeast Asian power?

Insofar as we take a pluralist order to mean that each state retains its own identity but the states also have a sense of common destiny, the answer is yes. In working out this order, the PRC and Southeast Asia bring to bear different practices of state interaction. The PRC's practice may be summed up as: willingness to use force in extreme situations of external threats towards its borders; reluctance to form any long-term commitment to other states which would constrain its ability to pursue its national interests; and adherence to the principle of absolute sovereignty which gives it the right to abstain from submission to any external authority. The ASEAN practice of state interaction may be summarised as: abstention from the use of force; commitment to consultation and consensus-building to develop interstate tolerance and compromise; and adherence to the principle of absolute sovereignty which obliges the states to respect each other's internal political authority and external independence.

The meeting of these two practices of state interaction in the Spratly dispute has produced an environment of unpredictability and insecurity, but also a realisation of the need to reconcile the different practices in the interest of regional peace and stability. The uncertainty surrounding the PRC's willingness to use force has resulted in the emergence of a structure of deterrence combined with a policy of reassurance which is to prevent violent conflict. The differing views on the desirability of institutionalised interstate dialogue have resulted in the establishment of an informal dialogue which allows for clarification of differences of opinion and initiation of cooperation in areas where some common ground can be found. The prevalence of the attitude that 'anything goes' when it comes to the application of international law has promoted the realisation that a common conception of justice is needed which is based on the recognition that absolute sovereignty is about both the right to exercise freedom of action and the obligation to respect the right of other states to do the same.

NOTES

1 The main concern of this paper is the relationship between the PRC and Southeast Asia. The ROC's behaviour and claims in the Spratly dispute will be left out of the discussion.

2 A term of convenience which also includes Thailand.

3 'Workshop and Technical Working Group Statements', 1992–1996; 'Project Activities', 1993–1997.

4 Internally, the ASEAN states have recently relaxed their strict interpretation of the principle of non-interference in the affairs of other states. For example, the Thai government has commented on Myanmar's internal politics. However, there are no signs that such tendencies have been brought to bear on the relationship between the PRC and the ASEAN states.

BIBLIOGRAPHY

Almonte, J. T. (1997–98), 'Ensuring Security the "ASEAN Way"', *Survival* 39 (4), Winter: 80–92.

ASEAN Declaration on the South China Sea (1992), Manila, Philippines, 22 July, http://www.asean.or.id/politics/pol_agr5.htm

Baginda, A. R. A. (1998), Executive Director, Malaysian Strategic Research Centre, interview 20 February.

Beijing Review (1992) 30 March–5 April.

Beijing Review (1998) 26 January–1 February, 2–15 February.

Bull, H. (1977) *The Anarchical Society: A Study of Order in World Politics*, London: MacMillan.

Caballero-Anthony, M. (1998) 'Mechanisms of Dispute Settlement: The ASEAN Experience', *Contemporary Southeast Asia* 20 (1), April: 38–66.

Chang, P. H. (1993) 'Beijing's Policy Toward Korea and PRC-ROK Normalization of Relations' in Lee, M. & Mansbach, R. W. (eds.) *The Changing Order in Northeast Asia and the Korean Peninsula*, Seoul: The Institute for Far Eastern Studies, Kyungnam University: 155–172.

Cordner, L. G. (1994) 'The Spratly Islands Dispute and the Law of the Sea', *Ocean Development and International Law*, Vol. 25: 61–74.

Daily Report China (1994) FBIS-CHI-94-119, 21 June: 9–11.

Dibb, P. (1997) 'Defence Force Modernization in Asia: Towards 2000 and Beyond', *Contemporary Southeast Asia* 18 (4), March: 347–360.

Djalal, H. (1997) 'Territorial disputes at sea: Situation, possibilities, prognosis' in Hassan, M. J. & Sheikh Raffie, A. (eds.) *Bringing Peace to the Pacific*, Papers presented at the Tenth Asia-Pacific Roundtable Kuala Lumpur, 5–8 June 1996, Kuala Lumpur: ISIS Malaysia: 275–286.

Dobson, W. J. & Fravel, M. T. (1997) 'Red Herring Hegemon: China in the South China Sea', *Current History* 96 (64), September: 258–263.

Fairbank, J. K. (1968) (ed.) *The Chinese World Order: Traditional China's Foreign Relations*, Cambridge, Mass.: Harvard University Press.

Far Eastern Economic Review (1998a) 5 February.

Far Eastern Economic Review (1998b) 30 April.

Findlay, T. (1994) 'South-East Asia and the new Asia-Pacific security dialogue', *SIPRI Yearbook 1994*, Stockholm: Stockholm International Peace Research Institute: 13–52.

Freeman, C. W., Jr. (1997) 'Trends in military technology and the Asia-Pacific region', *Asia-Pacific Review* 4 (2), Fall/Winter: 25–38.

Frost, F. (1990) 'Introduction: ASEAN since 1967 – Origins, Evolution and Recent Developments' in Broinowski, A. (ed.) *ASEAN into the 1990s*, London: MacMillan: 1–31.

Gong, G. W. (1984) *The Standard of 'Civilization' in International Society*, Oxford: Clarendon Press.

Haller-Trost, R. (1990) 'The Spratly Islands: A Study on the Limitations of

International Law', *Occasional Paper No. 14*, Canterbury, Kent: The Centre of South-East Asian Studies.

Hamzah, B. A. (1998) Director, Maritime Institute of Malaysia, Kuala Lumpur, interview 24 February.

Hancox, D. & Prescott, V. (1995) 'A Geographical Description of the Spratly Islands and an Account of Hydrographic Surveys Amongst Those Islands', *Maritime Briefing* 1 (6), Durham: International Boundaries Research Unit.

Hinsley, F. H. (1986), *Sovereignty*, (2nd edn.), Cambridge: Cambridge University Press.

Joint Statement (1997): Joint Statement of the Meeting of Heads of State/ Government of the Member States of ASEAN and the President of the People's Republic of China, 'ASEAN-China Cooperation Towards the 21st Century', 16 December, http://www.asean.or.id/summit/subml.htm.

Koskenniemi, M. (1990) 'The Politics of International Law', *European Journal of International Law* 1 (1/2): 1–32.

Lord, W. (1996) 'Southeast Asia Regional Security Issues: Opportunities for Peace, Stability, and Prosperity', Statement before the House International Relations Committee, Asia and Pacific Subcommittee, by the Assistant Secretary of State for East Asian and Pacific Affairs, May 30, http: // www.state.gov/www/regions/eap/960530.html.

Manning, C. A. W. (1975) *The Nature of International Society* (2nd edn.), London: MacMillan.

McManus, J. W. (1994) 'The Spratly Islands: A Marine Park?', *Ambio* 23 (3), May: 181–186.

Pao-Min, C. (1990) 'A New Scramble for the South China Sea Islands', *Contemporary Southeast Asia* 12 (1), June: 20–39.

Perry, W. J. (1996) 'Remarks as Prepared for Delivery by William J. Perry, Secretary of Defense, John F. Kennedy School of Government, Harvard University', Ref. No.: 278–96, 13 May, http://www.defenselink.mil/news/ May96/b051396_bt278-96.html.

'Project Activities', 1993–1997, http://www.law.ubc.ca/centres/scsweb/meet- ings.html#1997.

Roque Jr, H. H. L. (1997) 'China's Claim to the Spratlys Islands under International Law', *Journal of Energy and Natural Resources Law* 15 (3), August: 189–211.

Salameh, M. G. (1995–96) 'China, Oil and the Risk of Regional Conflict', *Survival* 37 (4), Winter, 133–146.

Samuels, M. S. (1982) *Contest for the South China Sea*, New York: Methuen.

Shelly, C. (1995) 'Spratlys and the South China Sea', *Position of the U.S. Department of State*, 10 May.

Smith Jr, E. D. (1994) 'China's Aspirations in the Spratly Islands', *Contemporary Southeast Asia*, 16 (3), December: 274–294.

Smith, R. W. & Bradford, T. (1997) 'Island Disputes and the Law of the Sea: An Examination of Sovereignty and Delimitation Disputes', Paper prepared for Korea Maritime University, Maritime Boundary Issues and Islands

Disputes in East Asian Region, An International Workshop Jointly Hosted by Centre for Social Science Research, Korea Maritime University, Korea Institute of Maritime Strategy, and Korea Society of the Law of the Sea, In Corporation with SEAPOL, SLOC-Korea and Ministry of Maritime Affairs and Fishery, Sorabol Hotel, Pusan, Korea, 4 August.

Snyder, C. (1996–97) 'The implications of hydrocarbon development in the South China Sea', *International Journal*, LII (1), Winter: 142–158.Snyder, G. H. (1961) *Deterrence and Defence: Toward a Theory of National Security*, Princeton: Princeton University Press.

South China Morning Post (1997) 23 October.

The Economist (1997) 24 May.

The Island of Palmas Case (1928) 22 *American Journal of International Law*.

The Jakarta Post (1995) 6 April.

The Military Balance 1997/98 (1997) London: The International Institute of Strategic Studies: 167, 170, 176–178.

Tow, W. T. (1994) 'China and the International Strategic System' in Robinson, T. W. & Shambaugh, D. (eds.) *Chinese Foreign Policy: Theory and Practice*, Oxford: Clarendon Press: 115–157.

Townsend-Gault, I. (1997) 'Jurisdictional disputes at sea: Progress and prognosis' in Hassan, M. J. & Sheikh Raffie, A. (eds.) *Bringing Peace to the Pacific*, Papers presented at the Tenth Asia-Pacific Roundtable Kuala Lumpur, 5–8 June 1996, Kuala Lumpur: ISIS Malaysia: 287–317.

United Nations (1983) *The Law of the Sea: Official Text of the United Nations Convention on the Law of the Sea with Annexes and Index*, New York: United Nations.

Valencia, M. J. (1985) *Southeast Asian Seas: Oil under Troubled Waters: Hydro-Carbon Potential, Jurisdictional Issues, and International Relations*, Singapore: Oxford University Press.

Valencia, M. J. (1995) 'China and the South China Sea Disputes', *Adelphi Paper 298*, Oxford: Oxford University Press.

Valencia, M. J. (1997) 'Troubled Waters', *The Bulletin of the Atomic Scientists*, 53 (1): 49–54.

Wah, C. K. (1993) 'Regional Perceptions of China and Japan' in Jeshurun, C. (ed.) *China, India, Japan and the Security of Southeast Asia*, Singapore: Institute of Southeast Asian Studies: 3–25.

'Workshop and Technical Working Group Statements', 1992–1996, http://www.law.ubc.ca/centres/scsweb/statement.html

Index

444